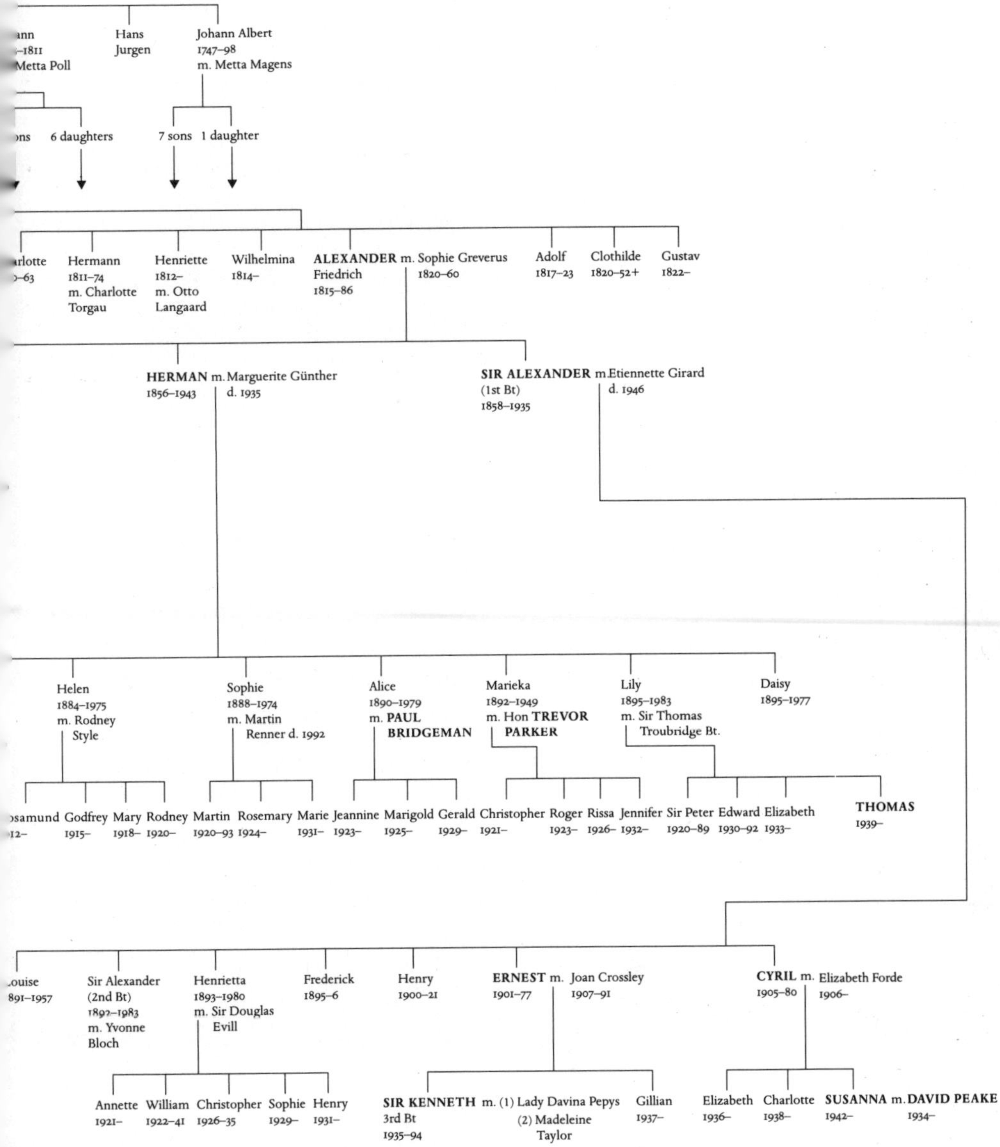

…ann
…–1811
m. Metta Poll

Hans
Jurgen

Johann Albert
1747–98
m. Metta Magens

…ons

6 daughters

7 sons

1 daughter

…arlotte
…–63

Hermann
1811–74
m. Charlotte
Torgau

Henriette
1812–
m. Otto
Langaard

Wilhelmina
1814–

ALEXANDER m. Sophie Greverus
Friedrich
1815–86
1820–60

Adolf
1817–23

Clothilde
1820–52+

Gustav
1822–

HERMAN m. Marguerite Günther
1856–1943
d. 1935

SIR ALEXANDER m. Etiennette Girard
(1st Bt)
1858–1935
d. 1946

Helen
1884–1975
m. Rodney
Style

Sophie
1888–1974
m. Martin
Renner d. 1992

Alice
1890–1979
m. **PAUL**
BRIDGEMAN

Marieka
1892–1949
m. Hon **TREVOR**
PARKER

Lily
1895–1983
m. Sir Thomas
Troubridge Bt.

Daisy
1895–1977

…osamund
…12–

Godfrey
1915–

Mary
1918–

Rodney
1920–

Martin
1920–93

Rosemary
1924–

Marie
1931–

Jeannine
1923–

Marigold
1925–

Gerald
1929–

Christopher
1921–

Roger
1923–

Rissa
1926–

Jennifer
1932–

Sir Peter
1920–89

Edward
1930–92

Elizabeth
1933–

THOMAS
1939–

…ouise
…891–1957

Sir Alexander
(2nd Bt)
1892–1983
m. Yvonne
Bloch

Henrietta
1893–1980
m. Sir Douglas
Evill

Frederick
1895–6

Henry
1900–21

ERNEST m. Joan Crossley
1901–77
1907–91

CYRIL m. Elizabeth Forde
1905–80
1906–

Annette
1921–

William
1922–41

Christopher
1926–35

Sophie
1929–

Henry
1931–

SIR KENNETH m. (1) Lady Davina Pepys
3rd Bt
1935–94
(2) Madeleine
Taylor

Gillian
1937–

Elizabeth
1936–

Charlotte
1938–

SUSANNA m. **DAVID PEAKE**
1942–
1934–

Kleinwort Benson

Kleinwort Benson

THE HISTORY OF TWO FAMILIES
IN BANKING

Jehanne Wake

OXFORD UNIVERSITY PRESS
1997

Oxford University Press, Walton Street, Oxford OX2 6DP
Oxford New York
Athens Auckland Bangkok Bogota Bombay
Buenos Aires Calcutta Cape Town Dar es Salaam
Delhi Florence Hong Kong Istanbul Karachi
Kuala Lumpur Madras Madrid Melbourne
Mexico City Nairobi Paris Singapore
Taipei Tokyo Toronto
and associated companies in
Berlin Ibadan

Oxford is a trade mark of Oxford University Press

Published in the United States
by Oxford University Press Inc., New York

British Library Cataloguing in Publication Data
Data available

Library of Congress Cataloging in Publication Data
Wake, Jehanne.
Kleinwort, Benson : The history of two families in banking / Jehanne Wake.
p. cm.
Includes bibliographical references.
ISBN 0–19–828299–0
1. Bankers—Europe—Biography. 2. Merchants—Europe—Biography.
3. Kleinwort family. 4. Germany—Genealogy. 5. Benson family.
6. Great Britain—Genealogy. 7. Merchant banks—Europe—History.
8. Kleinwort Benson Lonsdale (Firm) I. Title.
HG1552.A1W25 1997
332.1′092′24—dc20 [B] 96–22240

3 5 7 9 10 8 6 4 2

Printed in Great Britain
on acid-free paper by
The Bath Press, Bath

For William, Katie, and David
and for David and Elizabeth

AUTHOR'S NOTE, AND ACKNOWLEDGEMENTS

THIS book is by no means the usual corporate history. It is first and foremost a history of the Kleinwort and Benson families and throughout I have endeavoured to show both how family connections and interests led to the development of the Kleinwort and Benson businesses and how they survived through so many vicissitudes and changing circumstances. Inevitably, in a story that begins in the thirteenth century and ends in the last decade of the twentieth century, it is also something of a hybrid in that it is really five books in one volume: a history of the Kleinwort family and of the Benson family, a history of the Kleinwort business, and of the Benson business, and a history of the Kleinwort Benson Group. And, whilst I can claim complete editorial independence over the first two and a half parts of the book, the last chapter and the postscript have had to reflect the realities of banking confidentiality and the ever-changing perspectives on recent events.

My first acknowledgement is to the Kleinwort Benson Group which has given me such whole-hearted support throughout the long gestation of this book; the courtesy and co-operation of its directors and staff have been exemplary. I should particularly like to thank Lord Rockley and Simon Robertson, who have been most supportive; Charles Anson, who has now taken up another appointment; Peter Churchill-Coleman and the Corporate Affairs Department—especially Deborah Lowe, whose help, often on a daily basis, has been invaluable, Michael Purton, who located papers for me in the KB archives, and Eddie Nutt, who helped me contact KB pensioners. My heartfelt thanks also go to the many KB pensioners who talked and wrote to me, and to those at KB who submitted to interviews.

My greatest debt is to David Peake and David Benson. They not only lent me papers and photographs and directed me to people who knew the families and businesses of the bank, but they also entered into frank discussions about every aspect of the history and read innumerable drafts of the book with unflagging interest; no author could have hoped for more trust or received more unfailing help and understanding.

For her wise counsel, forthright comments, and tremendous generosity I am forever indebted to Elizabeth Benson, without whom this book would have taken even longer to finish. I am also deeply grateful to Susanna Peake for guiding me through the Kleinwort family, welcoming my visits, and allowing me to use her papers and photographs.

The contribution of other members of the extended Kleinwort and Benson families cannot be overstated; for their help and many kindnesses, not least unearthing family memorabilia and allowing me to use so much of it, I should like to thank Mr Henry Andreae, Mr Mark Andreae, Mr Peter Andreae, the late Mr John Andreae, Lady Ashe, Dr Angela Brown, Mrs Annette Donger, Mrs Charlotte Heber-Percy, Mr Joachim Kleinwort, the late Mrs Joan Kleinwort, Colonel Alexander Martin, Dr Gerald Martin, the late Mr Martin Renner, Sir Godfrey Style, Mr Tom Troubridge, Mrs Marguerite White; Mr Jeremy Benson, Mr Michael Benson, Ms Rosemary Benson, Mr James Cropper, Mrs Elaine Drake, the Reverend Christopher Drummond, Mrs Nancy Gardner-Brown, the late Mrs Lucy Hoare, Sir Benedict Hoskyns Bt., Lady Molly Howick, Mrs Nancy Morse, Mr and Mrs Peregrine Pollen, Lady Tomkins, Lady Turner, and Mr Roger Turner. I also remember with gratitude the late Mr Nicholas Benson, who introduced me to Benson history and portraiture; the late Sir Kenneth Kleinwort, who talked to me at length about the family firm; and especially the late Mr Peter Wake, whose perceptive comments and entertaining recollections brought the past to life in a most enjoyable way.

I would like to thank all those who took the time to read and comment upon the manuscript, in part or in whole: Mr Peter Andreae, Sir Norman Biggs, Mr David Clementi, Mr Peter Ellis, Mr Michael Hawkes, Mr David Hinshaw, Sir Martin Jacomb, Mr Robert Jeens, Mr William Legge-Bourke, Mrs Betty Macpherson, Mr Brian Manning, Mr Ronny Medlicott, Mr Bobby Nicolle, Mr David Robertson, Mr Simon Robertson, Sr Jaime Carvajal, and Mr Charles Sebag-Montefiore. I owe an especial debt to the following readers, both were most generous in sharing their knowledge of the firms and families: Sr Pepe Mayorga, who also lent me his extensive notes, and Mr Bobby Henderson, whose advice and suggestions have been of immeasurable benefit.

The list of relations, friends, and colleagues who have been prodigal of their time and hospitality, allowed me to use unpublished papers in their care, and talked or written to me in connection with this book is incredibly long. To them and to all mentioned below I am extremely grateful: the late Mr Herman Abs; Mr Jonathan Agnew; Mr Archie Andrews; the late Hon. Luke Asquith; Mr Bill Baldock; Mr Tim Barker; Mr John Barrett; Sir Frederick Bennett; Mr Robert Benson; Mr John Brew; Miss Marigold Bridgeman; Mr Bobby Brooks; Mr Mark Burch; Mr Dominic Cadbury; the late Mr Andrew Caldecott; Lord Chandos; Dr Sydney Chapman; Mr Malcolm Chase; Mr Herbert Cherrill; Sir William Clarke; Mr Robert Clifford; Mr Cyril Colbach; the late Miss Eileen Coutts; the late Mr Alastair Craig; Mr Clive Crook; Mr Michael Devas; Mr William Drake; Mr George Duthie; Mr Jack Ernest; Mr Nicholas Fitzherbert; Mr Edward Fitzsimmons; Mrs Margaret Fogg; the late Sir Alistair Frame; Mr John Gillum;

the late Mr Tom Girtin; Mr William Glazebrook; Mr Dermot Gleeson; Mr David Glynne; Mr John Glynne; Mr Peter Green; Mrs Grenyer; Mr and Mrs William Harris; Mr Frank Hislop; Mr Ben Hoare; Mr Richard Hoare; Mr George Howard; Mr Basil Irwin; Mr F. James; the late Mr Gerald Jamieson; Mr David Kenyon-Jones; Lady Kleinwort; Mr Frank Künzel; Dr Adolf Ladiges; the late Mr Victor Lewis; Lord Limerick; Mr Norman Lonsdale; Mr James Lonsdale; Mr Christopher Loyd; Mrs Audrey Mackenzie-Smith; Mr John Maclean; Mrs Mary Maclean; Mr Colin Maltby; Mr Sydney Mason; Mr Martin Mays-Smith; Mrs Ann Meikle; Mrs Milroy; the late Mr Victor Montagu; Mr Christopher Moorsom; Mr Bill Mundy; Sir Arthur Norman; Mrs Lucie Nottingham; the late Mr Ricard Ohrstrom; the late Mr Denys Oppé; Dr John Orbell; Mrs Joan Osiakowski; Mr Christopher Palmer; Mr Anthony Passmore; Mr George Pinto; Mr Stuart Pixley; Sir Adam Ridley; Dr Robert Rosenfeld; Mr Edmund de Rothschild; Mr Lionel de Rothschild; Mr Brian Rowntree; the late Sir Francis Sandilands; Dr K. Schikorski; Mrs Patricia Shepherd; Mr and Mrs Peter Spanoghe; Lord Tenby; the late Mr Gerald Thompson; Mrs Bridget Trump; the late Mr Stephen Unwin; Mr David Wake-Walker; Captain Ronnie Wallace; Mrs Betty Whyman; Mr Philip Ziegler.

For permission to reproduce copyright material and documents in their care I thank the Trustees of the Armitt Library; Baring Brothers & Co./ING; the Bank of England; the Trustees of the British Library; Cambridge University Library; Close Brothers Ltd.; Guildhall Library; Hambros Bank; the Controller of Her Majesty's Stationery Office for material in the Public Record Office; the Honourable Society of the Inner Temple; Lace Mawer; Liverpool City Libraries; the Maritime Museum Archives; the National Library of Scotland; the New York Historical Society; the New York Public Library; Price Waterhouse; Rathbone Brothers & Co. Ltd.; the Rigsarkhivet, Copenhagen; N. M. Rothschild & Sons; Schwerin State Archives; Staatsarchiv Hamburg; the University of Durham; University Library, Hamburg; and University Library, Liverpool.

As always, I am grateful to the many librarians and archivists who have helped me, particularly the staff of the Guildhall Library, the London Library and the Royal Commission of Manuscripts.

I should also like to thank Ivon Asquith, Tony Morris, and Anne Gelling of Oxford University Press for bringing the book to fruition, and Sylvia Jaffrey for her skilful copy-editing. I am especially grateful to David Kynaston, without whose editing prowess and informed help much in this book would have been different.

I would like to acknowledge the contributions of Fiona Calnan and Martin McMyler, who compiled the financial data, and Michelle Amey, who kindly typed it; Charles Sebag-Montefiore, who very generously provided the appendix on Robert Benson as a collector; and Robin Brockway, who provided designs for the dust-jacket.

Several people have helped with the research. I am especially indebted to Dr Dorothea MacEwan, who undertook all the German research on my behalf and whose mastery of German palaeography was invaluable. I am also grateful to Dr Andrew Duncan, who examined public documents and investigated a number of collections of private papers on my behalf with professional skill and tact. I would also like to thank Dr Paul Hopkins, who shared his encyclopedic knowledge of historical Scottish business records with me.

This book could never have been written without the generous help of friends and family. I am immensely grateful to Annabel Buchan, Jeannie Hodgson, Isla Maclean, Henrietta Benson, Sarah Evans-Lombe, and Kate Benson for secretarial and research assistance at various stages of the project; to Patrick Benson for informed advice on the dust-jacket; to John Challis, who took many of the photographs; to Harriet Wynne Finch, who helped to compile family trees, and with Emily Lane-Fox for picture research; and emphatically to Mary Wynne Finch who brought good sense and good humour to deciphering the source notes and so much else besides.

Most of all I wish to thank my children, who accepted with great patience my disappearances to the City, and my husband William Wake, who gave me more help than anyone else and whose continued support has been vital to this book.

J.W.

March 1996

CONTENTS

LIST OF ILLUSTRATIONS

Note: names in capitals denote involvement in Kleinworts, Bensons, or their constituent businesses.

A NOTE ON THE TEXT

I HAVE used the generic terms 'Kleinworts' and 'Bensons' throughout the text to refer to the two firms of Kleinwort, Sons & Co. and Robert Benson & Co., and I have omitted the apostrophe except where the context calls for the possessive.

Where figures in square brackets follow an amount of money, they indicate the approximate equivalent value in 1995.

PART ONE

Merchants on the Move 1250–1886

1 Early Kleinworts and Bensons

THE Kleinwort name first became associated with banking in 1786 when Hinrich Kleinwort went into partnership with Otto Paul Müller and opened an office in Altona, which was then in Holstein. The Kleinworts were enterprising folk—a combination of ambition and good fortune had enabled them to improve their situation over the preceding centuries. They were not native Altonans, their history unfolding from the north of what is now Germany, a fertile but often inhospitable flat country ravaged by the icy winds that sweep down from Siberia. Over the centuries it has been much trampled by the manœuvres of marauding armies fighting in the recurrent dynastic wars that have scoured Western Europe. There was little stability for its occupants when even the unimportant small villages bordering the south bank of the River Elbe were rent by occasional spasms of warfare. In consequence there occurred a steady migration across the broad waters of the Elbe to what was perceived as a safer harbour on the other side.

According to family legend and surviving documents, the Kleinworts emerged from Saxony where, early in the fifteenth century, the first Kleinworts of whom we have a direct view decided to exchange that 'cold, colourless country' for 'the luxuriant pastures and meadows' of the duchy of Holstein by means of the nearest ferry across the Elbe. Despite its bleakness and the frequent ravages of war, Holstein was a 'northern Arcadia' renowned for its dairy produce, cattle, and horses, and formed with its neighbour Schleswig a bridgehead between Germany and Scandinavia. By moving there, the Kleinworts automatically became Danish citizens.[1]

Although Danish by association, the people of Holstein were geographically remote from Denmark. Bounded by the North Sea on the west and the Baltic Sea on the north-east, the only link between Holstein and its administrative overlords in Copenhagen was by sailing-ship. Hence the south-eastern corner of Holstein which bordered the River Elbe looked to Hamburg for communication and trade rather than to Copenhagen, so that when the Kleinworts moved to Holstein they had no need to abandon their Germanic heritage. They settled in the village of Wedel, a natural destination since it was the site of one of the ferries operating across the Elbe and, consequently, a place of importance and prosperity. In 1592, for example, the income of the Wedel and the neighbouring Blankensee ferries, which in that year alone transported 23,000 oxen across the Elbe, provided one-sixth of the total income of the duchy of Holstein.

The Kleinworts of the sixteenth and early seventeenth centuries were the Holstein equivalent of English yeomanry, freeholders who owned their own farmland and could enter into contracts to purchase and sell land and to trade. They were thus a cut above the general medieval peasantry. The first known Kleinwort ancestor was Johann Albert Kleinwort who, in 1613, was the *Deichgraf* of Wedel, the official responsible for keeping the dykes and dams in good repair to prevent flooding of the flat, lush farmland bordering the river. It was an honorary position but one that carried great weight in the community and was usually held by a man of stature and wealth. His date of death is unknown—largely because few records survived the vicissitudes of war, plague, and fire—and nothing is known about his family until the birth of his grandson Johann Kleinwort in 1650. It was this Johann who, in 1692, married Anna Holtmann whose family owned the Wedel ferry service and were commensurately rich.

The Holtmanns had also owned the farmstead licensed to function as an inn that was conveniently near the ferry. The inn was the hub of the village. It stood on the crossroads of the high road, which ran from east to west, and of the drovers' path, which ran from north to south, and provided shelter both for the drovers who came to the Wedel cattle market and for the many passengers waiting to cross on the ferry. As such it was a lucrative business that greatly swelled the coffers of the Holtmann family. The seventeenth century, however, was particularly scarred for the peoples of Holstein, Denmark, and the Germanic states by the Thirty Years War, in which Catholic Europe was pitted against Protestant Europe. The War devastated both the cattle markets and the transport business across the Elbe, bringing general destruction of towns and trade in its wake. The inn at Wedel burned down and by the time it was rebuilt as a farmhouse it no longer belonged to the Holtmanns.

On 17 December 1710 Johann bought it back into the family to augment his small farm and the two houses he already owned. He then proceeded to link the farm once again to his father-in-law's profitable ferry business, renting out the pasture lands surrounding the farmstead as an overnight stop for cattle awaiting shipment across the Elbe or on their journey to market. In this way he had amassed considerable wealth by 1712, the year he died from the plague then devouring Northern Europe. His widow Anna took charge of the farms and the business until their only surviving son Johann, born in 1699, had attained his majority.

Three years later, in 1723, Johann Kleinwort married Anna Ladiges, who came from a local family long resident in Wedel and whose descendants continue to live there to the present day. She bore him twelve children, of whom only three sons and two daughters survived. Little is known of them save that when a great fire scorched through the countryside in 1731 and burnt down the thatched farmstead, Johann received compensation of 16 *Reichstalers* [*Rt.*] from the Danish Crown. This enabled him to purchase two trees with which to build a larger house, parts of which still stand in the market town of Wedel.

His second but eldest surviving son Joachim Hinrich Kleinwort was not destined to live in this enlarged house for long. Born in 1727, Joachim was blessed at his baptism by a rich godfather, Joachim Litzau, who has retained his obscurity. His death was, however, an event of great significance for Joachim since he inherited the Litzau estate in Altona, a generous gift that significantly increased the fortunes of the Kleinwort family overnight.

Although when he moved to Altona, a growing new city at the mouth of the Elbe, Joachim was still in Holstein and subject to Danish laws and sovereignty, little else remained the same. His godfather had left him not only the Rosenhof estate but also a successful business with which to sustain it. The word *hof* signifies a building that is both a dwelling and a business and, in the case of the Rosenhof, the buildings incorporated a brewery. In the Danish/Germanic environment of the eighteenth century a brewer was a man of considerable stature and wealth, who held an important position in the town. As perhaps the most profitable business to own it was strictly licensed by the King of Denmark. The Rosenhof thus supported with ease Joachim, his wife Anna Groth, a widow from Wedel whom he had married in 1752, and their seven children as well as his younger brother Johann with his family of eleven. Moreover, all these children continued to use the Rosenhof as a family base in adulthood, returning to live there throughout their married lives, so that it remained almost a Kleinwort commune. Only an extremely profitable enterprise could provide so well for so many. It was also sturdily built, surviving until the Second World War; now only the walls of the estate exist in what has become a rather run-down part of Hamburg.[2]

In moving to Altona, Joachim also exchanged the life of a small, if thriving, village for that of the second largest city in Denmark. Altona was a mere fishing hamlet on the road from Hamburg to Denmark when, in 1640, the Danish king recognized its potential as a trading competitor to Hamburg and captured it. He had not only protected and encouraged its commercial development but also granted it the then rare right of freedom of religious worship. This attracted many Portuguese, Jewish, and Dutch merchants, at a time when less enlightened rulers persecuted or expelled such people from their territories. Built on a gentle undulating hill, shelving down to the broad waters of the Elbe,

Altona was so close to Hamburg that only an avenue of linden trees, a fence, and a creek separated the two; indeed, with reference to its neighbour, the town is not inappropriately named, for Altona originates from the German *allzu-nah*, meaning 'all too near'. From a commercial point of view, though, such proximity carried great advantages for trade. Altona merchants enjoyed freedom of taxes on the export and import of specific goods and low taxes on the export of goods to neighbouring countries. This attracted business, especially as Hamburg goods could be exported tax-free via Altona.

The Rosenhof was situated at the north-east corner of this old-fashioned, picturesque city of 'much apparent life and bustle', a city with an extensive maritime trade, flourishing manufacturing industries and fine villas and mansions in which to house its successful merchants. Altona was also home to a strong cultural and foreign community: sons of prominent European and British citizens learning the intricacies of northern mercantilism, consular gentlemen representing their countries' interests, literary exiles and visitors such as the Wordsworths who came to pay homage to Friedrich Klopstock (whom Coleridge regarded as 'the venerable father of German poetry'), and society ladies whose salons in country houses overlooking the Elbe were much sought after in the summer.[3]

It was into this milieu that Hinrich Kleinwort, Joachim's youngest son, had been born in 1762. While his two elder brothers Johann Hinrich (1753–97) and Joachim Hinrich (1757–1820) had continued the family business at the Rosenhof, where Joachim Hinrich also opened a distillery, Hinrich had determined to make his way in the world as a merchant, the first Kleinwort to do so. Moreover, it was through him that the Kleinwort name first became associated with banking. Kleinwort & Müller, the firm he and Otto Müller started in 1786, specialized in the English trade.

A British influence pervaded Altona and nearby Hamburg, and was especially evident in the popularity of English fashions among German and Danish youth. Coleridge declared that 'to be an Englishman is in Germany to be an Angel—they almost worship you'. The mercantile community was no doubt swayed by other considerations when they chose their British trading partners. In Hinrich's case, since Müller had experience of the English trade which was immensely profitable at this time, it was a natural area of operation for Kleinwort & Müller, and one in which Hinrich was now well placed to participate. A rise in wheat prices had led to an increase in productivity in Holstein where, unable to dispose of the surplus in Denmark, farmers looked to Altona merchants who found new markets in England, demand growing there under stimulus of industrialization. Thus the volume of grain exported from Altona to England, which had increased in order to supply British troops during the

American War of Independence that had ended three years previously, continued after the peace. One merchant kinsman of Hinrich's sent his Baltic ships laden with grain six times a year to England. They returned equally laden with colonial produce such as tea, coffee, and sugar as well as British cloth, stoneware, and tin; crockery was also in great demand.[4]

With trade booming in Altona, Hinrich decided to open a counting-house in Hamburg, since a presence there was considered vital for any merchant involved in foreign trade in the eighteenth century. This Hanseatic city possessed the best natural harbour on the German North Sea coast, her position on the Elbe provided an internal avenue of trade second only to the Rhine, and a neutral stance during the various wars between the sea powers had bestowed a beneficial position of monopoly. Her foreign trade was immense, with only about 160 of the 2,000 ships that used the port owned by residents, the rest coming from abroad.

Hamburg was at that time the centre for the export of grain, Silesian linen, and Bohemian glass from the eastern part of the country. Hinrich was able to act for such manufacturers who dealt solely through commission agents in the belief that there was less risk in depending upon reliable local agents than in establishing their own connections abroad. Hinrich could also act as a distributor of coffee and sugar from the colonies to Russia and Scandinavia, for Hamburg was an important centre for the Baltic trade, long the mainstay of the Hanseatic ports.[5]

Its chief attraction for Hinrich, however, was as the centre for the English and Colonial trade, in which his firm continued to participate. He was now in closer proximity to the large British mercantile community that had become established there through the long trading association between Hamburg and Britain—an association dating from the war between England and Spain during which British merchants were invited to form the Hamburg Company, created in 1567. In conjunction with the English trade, Hinrich also maintained American connections. He acted as agent for the firm of Martin Eggers & Co. in Pennsylvania whose bills were traded in Hamburg. The Eggers, too, came from Altona and were related through marriage to the Anglo-German house of Schröders, future City rivals of Kleinworts; by the mid-nineteenth century H. H. Eggers & Co. would become the leading importers of coffee in Hamburg. Unfortunately the nature of Hinrich's business with Martin Eggers is lost to posterity, as is the identity of any other of his American correspondents.[6]

The dearth of surviving records in Germany makes it impossible to chart Kleinwort & Müller's business. We do know that by 1792 extra premises were required in Hamburg at Catherinenstrasse. The firm clearly conducted an extensive trading business since it possessed an account with the Hamburg

Bank, a facility strictly confined to substantial companies that traded regularly and in large amounts. The nature of the business none the less remains a mystery, just as Hinrich himself remains something of a mystery to his descendants. Stories that he attended university and travelled to North America, that he lost everything in the Napoleonic Wars and died penniless in Hamburg, leaving only his youngest son capable of restoring the family fortunes, are the strands woven by the generations into family legend—but, with the exception of a few threads of truth, are for the most part at variance with the dates and facts of his life.

In 1792 he had married Catherine Elizabeth Lohmann, who died thirteen years later at the age of 34. She had borne him ten children, of whom seven survived, and when she died the youngest was barely ten months old. Until 1800 they had lived at the Rosenhof but in May of that year Hinrich had moved his family out of Holstein and eastwards to the Satow district in the duchy of Mecklenburg. He was following a path already familiar in English society whereby merchants, having made substantial fortunes, set themselves up as country gentlemen by obtaining a seat in the country. Hinrich had purchased the seigneurial or *Rittergüter* estate of Gerdeshagen. Such a move was much less common in Germany than in England. In Germany the landowner of such an estate was usually a ruling prince or a nobleman; landed proprietors of mercantile origins from families grown rich in the towns did exist, but their numbers were kept comparatively small by the restrictions placed upon their purchase of old feudal estates. In the eastern Germanic states especially, it was quite rare to be able to find an estate out of the hands of the local nobility. Control was easily retained because any *Rittergut* had to swear to the *Lehneid*, an oath of fealty, as vassal to the dukes of Mecklenburg—as Hinrich did in September 1800—as well as gain the permission of the Court for the purchase.

The Gerdeshagen estate was an extensive one of over 1,500 acres which included the dependent estate of Charlottenthal as well as Gerdeshagen itself. The everyday life of Hinrich and his family was not very different from that of the English squirearchy living a simple patriarchal existence in peace and comparative comfort on their estates. In Germany such a man 'took no more notice of the great world than was necessary . . . allowed himself an occasional carousel, bred his foals, sold his wool, and disputed with his parson. If he was not too strict he maintained tolerably good relations with his subjects'.[7]

As *Rittergut*, Hinrich employed some 200 people at Gerdeshagen alone, where the family lived surrounded by the usual trappings of a completely self-sufficient eighteenth-century country estate: it included the five large agricultural cottages that housed the peasants who had lived and worked on the estate all their lives and never travelled farther from it than Satow, the nearest market town; the brewhouse, distillery, and malthouse where beer was brewed; the windmill, the bakery, and the brickworks. In the adjoining massive barns every kind of food required by the Kleinworts was stored and prepared. There was also an administrator's house with separate stables, as such an estate could not be run successfully without skill and knowledge.

Yet unlike the eighteenth-century English squire in his mansion, the German *Rittergut* did not hold a lofty sway over his domain, as a Silesian *Rittergut* explained:

These fortunate folk lived simply but contentedly in houses that were for the most part quite unpretentious even though always dignified with the name of 'Schlosser', houses which, however lovely the country might be, were not constructed to afford the aesthetic delight of a distant prospect, but to allow the family to see from their windows what was going on in their stables and barns . . . The ambition of the men was to be sound farmers, and the pride of the ladies was a reputation for good housekeeping.

Hinrich differed from these *Rittergüter*, who led humdrum lives and were often isolated from the outside world. This was as much from necessity as from inclination. Roads in Germany were notoriously bad; the nearest main road was usually 'an ill-defined cart track' and a journey of 25 miles took 12 hours of discomfort on a good road, but 37 hours on a poor one. The roads in Mecklenburg and the north-east in general were very bad and full of 'ruts which swallowed the carriage up to the axle and piles of mud which stood, ground up by the action of the wheels, like walls'. Most Germans, not surprisingly, preferred to stay put.[8]

Hinrich, however, was foremost a man of commerce and, unlike other *Rittergüter*, he needed to keep abreast of world events and to have easy access to the nearest large town and especially to Hamburg. It would have been impossible for him to commute from Gerdeshagen, so the likelihood is that he left his family at home while he worked in Hamburg and later in Lübeck. And indeed, from papers concerning a boundary dispute between Gerdeshagen and the neighbouring estate of Mieckenhagen, it emerges that Hinrich was absent for long periods.

The year that he purchased Gerdeshagen was also the year he went into business on his own at 8 Brauerknectsgraben in Hamburg. The seven-year partnership of Kleinwort & Müller had suddenly been dissolved in the previous year. The reasons for the liquidation of Kleinwort & Müller in 1799 are now unverifiable. While Müller may have wished to retire or withdraw his share of the capital, it is more likely that the firm was caught in the Hamburg Crisis of 1799. Hamburg had maintained its traditional neutrality for as long as possible during the decade of European warfare stemming from the French Revolution in 1789. Although Hamburg merchants had been officially proscribed from trading freely since the outbreak of the first French war in 1791 their businesses had not been unduly affected; indeed, many firms (including Kleinwort & Müller) had continued to prosper from the boom in their colonial trade with Britain.

In 1795 the French conquest of Hamburg's trading rival, Amsterdam, meant that Hamburg became busier than ever as the emporium of middle Europe. By 1799 France's impatience with the Anglo-Hamburg trade axis spilled over into a French embargo of Hamburg vessels that, at first, brought trade to a standstill. Coincidentally shipments of colonial merchandise arrived in Northern Europe, leaving Hamburg merchants with large stocks at a time when Hamburg banks were withdrawing lines of credit after the Bank of England had refused to guarantee the finance of international trade during wartime. Kleinwort & Müller may have been amongst the 150 firms or more that failed during the ensuing commercial crisis.

If reversal there was, Hinrich must have possessed or retained sufficient assets to survive it, since he continued the business under his own name, though at a new address. Unfortunately the progress of this first Kleinwort banker can only be glimpsed through petitions to the Danish Court and the skeletal entries in the commercial almanacs of the day. Hinrich is described as 'a merchant in banking', so he probably continued to act as a commission agent advancing credits and arranging the necessary loans and payments for merchants and manufacturers engaged in the growing import and export business. Imports from England alone had risen from £2.4m. in 1793 to £12m. by 1800 and there was also the considerable trade in goods with France, Spain, and Portugal.[9]

Trade flourished during the period of peace that followed the Treaty of Amiens (1802) between Britain and France, but it was disrupted in 1803 by the recurrence of hostilities. Napoleon's victorious march through middle Europe, defeating the Austrians at Austerlitz in 1805 and the Prussians at Jena in 1806, did not end with victory over Britain: the planned invasion foundered at Trafalgar. In retaliation French troops occupied Hamburg in the autumn of 1806 and Napoleon imposed a Continental blockade against all trade with Britain, which led to a period of great hardship for the people of Hamburg.

Although Hamburg refused to be browbeaten and remained, through the black market, the 'great clearing-house' for British funds and goods *en route* to Europe, commercial life became distinctly dangerous and the costs prohibitive for reputable merchants such as Hinrich. They had to resort to bribes to secure the passage of their goods. This illicit trade became so regularized that the risk of breaking the French cordon was calculated exactly and added to the price of goods. Safe passage was by no means secured, however, since the only open coastal route via Heligoland, a nearby island off the North German coast, not only cost much more but was also no guarantee of evading the French cordon. The British agent reported that by 1810 goods to the value of £4m. lay stranded at Heligoland awaiting shipment, which spelt ruin for those merchants whose funds were thus irretrievably tied up for the duration of the war.

Hinrich and his colleagues also had all their goods of British origin seized and any profits earned in such trade forfeited by the occupying French military government. The years 1813–14 proved especially bad ones. In 1813 the French had confiscated the reserves of the Hamburg Bank so that Hinrich lost his deposits and any other funds channelled through the bank. Furthermore, although Mecklenburg had been a French ally so that the family had been able to live relatively peacefully at Gerdeshagen for the past few years, in March 1813 the Duke of Mecklenburg became the first German ruler to desert the French alliance and declare for their enemies, Russia, Austria, and Prussia. This meant that Mecklenburg became a war-zone and the Kleinworts at Gerdeshagen suffered from the shortages, pillage, and occupation which tend to accompany the fortunes of war.

As the conditions of occupation hardened in Hamburg, Hinrich decided to centre his affairs in Lübeck on the Baltic coast so as to evade the worst of French attention—but trade also became severely disrupted there. Like Hamburg, Lübeck was a free port with an illustrious past. As chief of the Hanseatic League, trade boomed there in the thirteenth century when 'she held in her hands the sceptre of European commerce' and the treasures of Asia and Africa passed through the port. The herring industry later provided the ballast of her trade with Europe and Russia. By the time Hinrich had an office there, Lübeck was a town in decline though still serving as a centre for the exchange of raw materials from the Russian Baltic coast with Western European industrial goods. Her manufacturing industries were sugar refining, leather, gunpowder, and tobacco, and Hinrich may well have acted as a commission agent for some of these concerns during wartime. His credentials in Lübeck had no doubt been considerably improved by his marriage in 1809 to Wilhelmina Maria Dorothea Sophia von Hövell, who was descended on both sides of her family from patrician stock, the prefix 'von' signifying that the Hövells and Lutzows were *Adliger*, which placed them on that rung of the nobility below barons and counts.

The first mayor of Lübeck had been a von Hövell and he was followed by successive generations with such consistency that the mayoralty became almost a family preserve. In the same way, von Hövell then followed von Hövell as state councillors at the Danish Court. Wilhelmina's father, Gotthard von

Hövell, was also a man of substance since he held the position of *Landrat* in Mecklenburg and Court of Appeal assessor in the neighbouring duchy of Lauenburg. Despite such an illustrious lineage, Wilhelmine's own circumstances were limited: by the age of 13 she had lost both her parents to consumption. She married Hinrich when she was 26 and bore him eight children. The youngest two, Clothilde and Gustav, were born in Lübeck because by then Hinrich had sold Gerdeshagen.[10]

The reason for the sale remains unknown; possibly, along with many of his fellow countrymen, Hinrich's business was ruined by the perilous conditions prevailing in northern Germany during the Napoleonic Wars, followed after 1815 by years of famine and plague. In the new conditions of peace, internal markets were limited and German goods could not compete with English ones. If Hinrich had funds tied up in ships either as shares in ownership or in freight seized in transit, then he may well have lost large sums (as did his second cousin Hinrich Dultz) and have had no alternative but to sell up and leave Gerdeshagen.[11]

The family belief, however, is that Hinrich had gambled away his considerable fortune and was forced to sell off his only remaining asset, namely Gerdeshagen. Hinrich was indeed a gambler. In a case heard by the Danish courts in 1786, he had appealed against the sentence imposed for having 'contravened the law by playing a game of chance'. It seems the authorities discovered this unlawful behaviour when one of the players not unnaturally tried to recover his winnings. Furthermore, 'because of proven unlawfulness Kleinwort and Breide were further condemned to eight days and three days arrest respectively with water and bread'. This did not dampen Hinrich's gambling ardour unduly, for the Register of Fines shows him still gambling eighteen years later. This does not prove, however, that he incurred such heavy debts that he had to sell Gerdeshagen; nor does it show that as a result of gambling he had to move to Hamburg where he died penniless. Whatever the reason, and it may have been simply the desire to settle his growing family nearer his work or provide for his elder sons, he was able to buy another property and start up a new business partnership.[12]

The contract of sale dated 16 December 1819 shows that Hinrich moved to Lübeck after selling Gerdeshagen to another Altona merchant for *Rt.* 66,000. He therefore made a loss of *Rt.* 14,000 on the property, no doubt reflecting the state of the market after the wars. *Rt.* 66,000 was no small sum and proved ample enough for the purchase of a small estate in Altona. He paid about 8,000 marks for the house, outbuildings, garden, and paddocks. It was here that he settled with his family and, in 1823, he had sufficient capital to form the firm of Hinrich Kleinwort & Borchert of Altona.

Once again, this is at variance with later familial accounts of his career, which have him eking out a miserable, penniless existence in Hamburg, supported by his children who are reduced to seeking work as nursery nurses. Such accounts ignore the Rosenhof connection and the fact that Hinrich did not have to rely solely upon his business for funds. When his father had died in 1783 he had inherited, in accordance with prevailing law, an equal one-sixth share of the Rosenhof estate. This had been ably administered by his rich guardian uncle, Johann Albert, who himself had inherited the Wedel property and was worth well over 185,000 marks. Moreover, even if Hinrich had lost everything, the Kleinwort family was rich enough to support an erring nephew or younger brother and his large family at the Rosenhof; there was no need for them to slum it in Hamburg. As it was, Hinrich lived with his family next door to the Rosenhof, where he died on 29 September 1831. Six months previously he had obtained an apprenticeship for Alexander Friedrich, his second son by Wilhelmina von Hövell. It was this son who would introduce the Kleinwort name into the heart of banking in the City of London.[13]

The year that Hinrich had formed the first Kleinwort trading firm in Altona proved equally significant in the annals of the Benson family. During the autumn of 1786, Robert Benson and his wife, 'beloved Sally', received a family visitor at their house at Stricklandgate in Kendal. Sally's only brother, William Rathbone IV, came to stay at an auspicious moment in his brother-in-law's career, because Robert's long partnership agreement with his brother George Benson jnr. was due to end in that very year; Robert therefore had some crucial decisions to make. Both he and George jnr. had built up a prosperous business but, as the younger by seventeen years, Robert would always be the junior member of the partnership. Furthermore, both of them had sons and adequate capital with access to even larger resources. Now, if ever, was surely the time for the brothers to strike out independently. Through the influence of John Wakefield and, more recently, of his marriage with its attendant new connections, Robert was in a position to contemplate a change of course and, if necessary, a change of residence.

William, however, pre-empted any such decision-making process. He arrived armed not just with family news but also with an important proposition, namely that he and Robert should form a 'connection' or business partnership in Liverpool. 'From the time it became probable that thy connection with thy Brother would dissolve,' he stated, 'I have been uniformly possessed with an affectionate wish, unmixed with any reference to my own interests, that if no other opening presented which would be viewed with encouragement, the situation of my business might be such as to [induce thee to join me].'[14]

William was by then a partner in his father's firm of William Rathbone & Co., but his father was an ailing man of 60 and William felt it expedient to share the responsibilities of running an expanding business with a man of his own age, temperament, and beliefs. Naturally he looked to the network of Quaker kin to fulfil such requirements, all of which Robert satisfied. Moreover, Robert was by far the most obvious candidate in terms of the three interconnected mainstays of Quaker life—religion, family, and business.

After an evening of lengthy discussion, William wrote from Liverpool on 23 September: 'I have thought of our Connection with frequent & serious attention . . . & I have carried the idea with me into the Counting House & endeavoured to suppose the connection really existing & to see & feel its various attendants & consequences.' Such imaginings were obviously pleasing since, he continued, 'I will add that the uniform impression in these different situations hath been such as to make me regard it with peace and satisfaction'; and, with an eye to future profits, he claimed 'to feel a comfortable hope that it will be productive of some valuable advantages both as aiding our endeavours to make a suitable provision for the wants of our situation, & as furnishing that kind & that degree of employment which will best accord with our own wishes & with those of our connections'.

The wishes of the two most important 'of our connections' had yet to be determined. And, no matter how advanced the two brothers-in-law might be with their future plans, these two vital connections had to be consulted before Robert returned to Liverpool from a business trip. They were, in fact, William's father and father-in-law. As William put it, '& if the influence of my Fathers (I feel tempted to say of our Fathers for they are almost such) should have the tendency which I expect, it will not only enable us to determine on this important subject but also give an additional degree of hope in the propriety of our views'.[15]

William's father-in-law, Richard Reynolds, was a man of great position in that eighteenth-century world. He had married into a family of famous ironmasters, the Darbys of Coalbrookdale in Shropshire, whose invention of smelting iron with pit-coal transformed the metal and engineering industries of Great Britain—identified by many as the starting-point in the development of the Industrial Revolution—and had become head of the firm in 1763. As a staunch Quaker, Reynolds had the furnaces stopped for a few hours every Sunday regardless of the damage caused to the manufacturing process, and also refused to profit from increased prices during wartime.

Despite such unorthodox business practices, the works prospered under his management. He pioneered the idea of using cast iron for the laying of rails and for water- and later gas-pipes. Such inventions produced enormous profits;

and when, in 1789, he retired, an extremely rich man, he began to put into practice his belief that it is the duty of every man to give away as much as possible of a fortune during his lifetime. His daughter, Hannah Mary Reynolds, had married William Rathbone in 1785. The two families were part of that close-knit Quaker world which attended meetings at Kendal and were already connected by marriage. Thus it was only natural that, before embarking on such an important course of action, the younger Rathbone and Benson should wish to consult the great old man of their family.[16]

'Father Reynolds' had no objection to William's choice of partnership, William informing Robert on 17 November that 'his sentiments of thy character are as favourable as thou wouldst wish'. His views on partnerships in general were not so glowing, 'yet in that proposed for us he thinks some solid advantages may be reasonably expected'. This opinion was more than echoed by their other important connection, William's father and Robert's father-in-law, William Rathbone III. He urged them to go ahead in the belief that such a step would 'secure comfort and a desirable degree of independence' for the Bensons and their offspring.[17]

By the time that Robert knew him, William Rathbone III was 'a very typical Quaker merchant of the eighteenth century', according to his nephew Dr John Rutter. He was 'not a man of brilliant talents . . . but all he said and did was directed by a judgement singularly upright'. Considered 'very diligent and active' in business, he nevertheless demonstrated that, in keeping with other Quakers, his management of business was never wholly bound by mercantile self-interest. Because of their refusal to treat business and wealth as an end in itself, based on the tenets of the Quaker creed of equality and an irreproachable integrity towards everything and everyone, Quaker businessmen seemed to possess an almost dispassionate approach to life. In William Rathbone III's case, his nephew recalls how 'the concerns of business disturbed him not; and when at the close of day he sat down with his family, there was such calmness, such composure in his aspect and demeanour', despite the fluctuating conditions of trade or volatility of prices.

A friend of William Roscoe and part of his literary circle known as the 'Liverpool Saints', William Rathbone III joined them in promoting the Society for the Abolition of the Slave Trade formed in 1787. Thomas Clarkson, who like Wilberforce was a leading abolitionist, noted that Rathbone 'would not allow any article to be sold for the use of a slave-ship, and he always refused those who applied to him for materials for such purpose'. It had not always been so, for the foundation of the Rathbone fortune and business was built on the Africa slave trade.

William Rathbone III's father, another William Rathbone, had become in turn a timber merchant, a general commission merchant, and, eventually, a shipowner. Like most Liverpool merchants of the period he was inevitably a supplier, if not builder, of ships. His firm owned or hired five or six small ships which traded chiefly with the West Indies, the Southern States of America or 'Plantations', and the Baltic. They carried cargoes of mahogany from the West Indies, cargoes of West Indian produce and salt from Liverpool to the Baltic in return for timber from Norway and Sweden, and earthenware and linen to Philadelphia returning with tobacco and grain.

Nevertheless it was difficult to remain in business without supplying materials for the African trade and, even after the Quaker injunction of 1763 forbade Friends to engage in such activities, the Rathbones continued in this line of business. Twenty years later records show the firm supplying timber for the third voyage of the *Preston*, a ship engaged in the Africa slave trade and owned by Thomas and William Earle, who were prominent in the slave trade and close friends of the Rathbones. This was the last piece of business connected with the slave trade, however, for when, in the mid-1780s, William Rathbone III was approached to take a share in an African ship and was tempted by the high offer, his son William dissuaded him on religious grounds and shortly afterwards he, too, became a keen abolitionist. No doubt the diversification of their business not only enriched them but also enabled them to withdraw from serving the slave trade without seriously damaging the family interests.[18]

It was William Rathbone IV, Robert's brother-in-law, who was responsible for this diversification and, more importantly, for the specialization of trade with America. This was an area upon which Robert also wished to concentrate, and it proved to be the highly profitable mainstay of the operations of the firm Rathbone & Benson that the two men formed in 1786. In removing his family and business interests to Liverpool, Robert was emulating his father George, who had forsaken hearth and heritage in order to improve his family's prospects. It had been a great wrench for George Benson, since Westmorland had sustained the family for over five centuries.

The Bensons emerged from the shadows of the medieval world two centuries earlier than the Kleinworts, though they, too, were a family whose horizons stretched far beyond the confines of their original birthplace. And, like the Kleinworts, the Bensons drew resilient strength from their roots in thriving rural communities and Nonconformist faith. The family were yeoman farmers who surfaced in the thirteenth century in the north-western corner of England. Possibly of Viking stock, arriving with a Norse invasion similar to that which planted Bjornsons in the Whitby area and founded the Yorkshire line of Bensons, they are more certainly connected with the Benedictine foundations of Furness and Conishead as native 'Benedict-sons', tenants of the Benedictine Priory at Furness on the coast of Lancashire.

In 1300 they moved eastwards in search of water-power to process their wool, taking the route to Conishead used by the Furness Priory monks. Travelling from the shores of Morecambe Bay across the treacherous sands, up Tilberthwaite, they descended into the secluded Little Langdale valley at the heart of the Lake District in Westmorland. The late Mr John Benson believes these first Bensons accompanied the monks into the valley as far as the wooden or stang bridge placed across a stream of the river Brathay, where they broke their journey; some decided to settle at what became the Benson estate of Stangend, others travelled on to Grasmere.

Early on in their history, the Bensons demonstrated an aptitude for identifying profitable new ventures. In the first instance, they built the fulling mills used by local weavers to shrink and compress their cloth. Apart from abundant water-power for their mills the Bensons also found cheap, barren, rocky ground that was worthless for agriculture, but which could be utilized as tenter fields where cloth could be stretched and dried. By the fifteenth century almost every stream in the district capable of turning a mill was used by Bensons, who had a great influence on the woollen industry around Grasmere and deployed their increased prosperity to purchase valuable freeholds.[19]

They were undoubtedly at the height of their wealth and influence in the Lake District during the sixteenth century. Three brothers had formed the first Benson partnership in 1506 to enclose fell-land in Langdale; thirty years later another three brothers, Thomas, Michael, and Robert, formed the second Benson business when they seized the opportunity presented by the dissolution of the monasteries to purchase ecclesiastical lands in order to expand their mill operation.[20]

Thus, by the time the first mention is made of Nicholas Benson of Skelwith, the first direct ancestor of the Bensons of Stangend, the Benson clan possessed both money and land, and was allied by marriage with other prominent Lake District yeomanry families. They rose on the great wave of the woollen trade to become substantial wool merchants or, to use the medieval vernacular, clothiers. The middle years of the sixteenth century were, however, a paradoxical time. Real wages halved and many agricultural workers and smallholders were dispossessed through the increasing practice of enclosure. On the other side of what one historian has called 'the great divide', the growth of world trade and the effects of the plunder of the Church at the Reformation, and ensuing transfer of ownership of land, resulted in a massive redistribution of wealth—so that the nation as a whole was richer but the poor were much poorer. A document of 1591 suggested that these economic changes 'made of yeomen and artificers gentlemen, and of gentlemen knights, and so forth upwards; and of the poorest sort stark beggars'.

In keeping with the upwardly mobile Tudor times, by 1546 the Bensons had entered the ranks of gentlefolk, possessing the right to carry a coat of arms. Whilst 'the great divide' of those Tudor years affected all working folk, the Bensons, as substantial clothiers, escaped much of the hardship of their fellow men and flourished, as 'those who were fortunately placed on trade routes to London or a port, the skilful and the lucky, could prosper by production for the market'.[21]

Unfortunately they were not to enjoy the fruits of prosperity for long. In 1577, the year when Nicholas Benson of Skelwith married Isabel Holme of Oxenfell, plague struck the valleys. This first outbreak lasted a year and it raged worst in the Langdale area, where the ferocity of the disease was such that, when people sickened and died, they were sometimes left until the walls of their cottages fell in ruins upon them. Survivors were unable to cope and, later, fields and dwellings associated with the plague were shunned as poisoned, haunted places.

Nicholas Benson survived but kept only two of his four children. Twenty years later the plague struck again, sounding the death knell to the people and already languishing wool trade of the Langdale valleys. The Benson clan, which peopled so much of this area, shrank and almost died out with the demise of the cloth trade. Only the hardier, more skilful and successful clung on. Of these, it was left to Nicholas Benson's eldest great-grandson, George (1636–1712), to revive the Benson fortunes. He was deemed by his peers to be 'a remarkable character' and he grew up during a remarkable period in the history of his country. These decades were probably among the most terrible which the country has ever endured, with people experiencing extreme poverty and hardship. On top of the series of disastrous harvests of the 1640s came the disruption caused by the Civil War. George Benson grew up during that war, a time of revolution when Throne, Parliament, and privileges were abolished or reformed, when 'the old world . . . is running up like parchment in the fire'.[22]

The defeat of the Royalist armies in the pro-Royalist North, together with a lack of clergy, left a greater spiritual void in the north of the country than in the traditionally Puritan centres of the south and east, so that radical ideas were more easily disseminated by the itinerant clothiers, merchants, craftsmen, and the crowds of 'masterless men', those victims of enclosure and agricultural depression. The result was that sects such as the Levellers and Quakers sprang up offering new political and religious solutions to the problems besetting people everywhere. The middle years of the seventeenth century saw the rise of the 'mechanick preachers', laymen such as Bunyan and Fox whose interpretation of the Bible supported these solutions and whose message was carried at a gallop through the countryside by posses of ordinary folk. On George Benson's weekly trips from Stangend to sell cloth at Kendal and Hawkshead markets, a brew of strange ideas flowed around him in the market-place in a heady mixture of fervour and excitement for change. So, by the time Fox and other Quakers came to Westmorland, George was eager to join the ranks of Seekers who believed that God's Holy Spirit would lead them to know the right course to follow in all circumstances and that religion should not be separated from their daily activities but lived out through them. George was converted at a meeting in the Langdale valley a few years after the death of his father in 1663.

The later image of Quakers as steady, quiet people, plain-clothed and plain-spoken, would be unrecognizable to their seventeenth-century forebears. When George became a Quaker he became a revolutionary who had joined the 'Roundheaded rogues', a term then used to describe political radicals. Quakers were deemed radical because they believed that all are equal in the sight of God and they called for an end to the superstition and dogma promulgated by other forms of religion, especially the established hierarchical religion headed by the monarch.

Once George started preaching the word through neighbouring counties and 'appeared in the Ministry', he was considered 'a sower of sedition, or a subverter of the laws, a turner of the world upside down, a pestilent fellow'. He automatically became an opponent of the Established Church and all it stood for in those days as the buttress of the existing social order. Charles I had declared that 'religion is the only firm foundation of all power'; with his execution and the breakdown of ecclesiastical authority, people were free from prosecution for 'sin', free to assemble and to choose their own preachers. The old order was indeed turned upside-down by such men as George Benson who, in common with all radicals, preached against priests and against the payment of tithes.[23]

The Bensons were Parliamentary in their sympathies during the Civil Wars and, at the Restoration, when king and ejected vicar alike again came into office, they refused to pay the tithes due on their properties. Such refusals warranted huge fines or imprisonment because the attack on tithes undermined the whole concept of a state church; if parishioners could not be legally compelled to pay them, there would be no livings for the clergy to occupy and no fees for the gentry to collect. At the proceedings against the Bensons at Ambleside in 1663 only the four most prominent and wealthy were cited, including George's father Thomas and his kinsman Robert Braithwaite of Baisbrowne, who owed fourteen years of arrears of £129 18*s*. *od*.: a substantial sum that gives some idea of the wealth of the Benson circle at this period. In 1666 George himself was taken from a Quaker meeting and imprisoned for refusing to pay tithes.[24]

He could also be imprisoned or fined for the Quaker use of 'Thee' and 'Thou' in discourse and the refusal to remove a hat in the presence of authority and social superiors on the grounds that all men are equal. These seemingly innocent eccentricities were understood by seventeenth-century authority as gestures of social protest and revolt. Nor was he safe from persecution in his own home. Whenever a meeting of the Quakers' Society of Friends was held at Stangend, the farm would be watched and a report sent to the authorities, who then would imprison those taking part. A Quaker journal describes George as 'being often exposed to various kinds of suffering both by reason of keeping meetings at his house, and in other respects relating to . . . the ancient testimony of truth, which faithful friends at that time were liable unto: all which he bore with much patience and courage'.[25]

Even after the Restoration, when the Toleration Act finally allowed freedom of worship, Quakers continued to suffer imprisonment and if fines could not be met then a craftsman's tools would instead be taken away or vandalized: 'And when they had made spoil of a poor weaver's goods, they brake his loom in pieces with the work in it, the only means he had to get bread for himself, his sick wife and a young child.' The effect of such continuous persecution was to bind the Quaker brotherhood ever more tightly in 'their joyous fellowship'.[26]

George was 64 at the beginning of the eighteenth century and the change in his outlook mirrored that of the Quaker movement which, after the joyous fellowship of his youth and the persecution of his middle age, had become the 'quiet in the land'. Quakers applied themselves to improving their livelihoods, consolidating their businesses, and leaving the ministry and proselytizing to a small band of Friends. Although 'a faithful Minister', George now remained with his family at Stangend rather than on the road promoting Quakerism.

He had married Margaret Braithwaite, daughter and heiress of a neighbouring family long resident at Colthouse near Hawkshead. The Braithwaites, like the Bensons, were originally of Viking stock and had settled at Furness, moving from there to the Hawkshead Valley where they were the most numerous clan between 1568 and 1704. They mirrored the Bensons: originally smallholders and farmers, they too had risen on the back of the woollen trade and had intermarried with other rich north-country trading families. In common with the family into which the Kleinworts married, they had a further substantial source of income in the ferry which for centuries had crossed Lake Windermere to link the market towns of Hawkshead and Kendal. Just as in Holstein, the right of ferriage in Westmorland was a prized and jealously guarded privilege, which in the seventeenth and eighteenth centuries belonged to the Braithwaites.

George Benson and Margaret Braithwaite were thus already part of a large cousinhood before their marriage. They had five children of whom only two lived to maturity. Their youngest daughter Dorothy married Anthony Wilson, a waller by trade who by 1728 was in a position to build High Wray House, which is still owned by the family. In contrast, little is known of George's eldest surviving son, John Benson (1668–1737), who settled at Bridge End, another farm in the neighbouring valley of Tilberthwaite. In his will he left Stangend to his eldest surviving son, another George. It is this George who took the decision that was to redirect the course of his family's life.[27]

In 1729 he too married into the Braithwaite family, to whom he was already related through his grandmother, Margaret Braithwaite. His wife, Abigail, was the daughter of William Braithwaite of Elterwater Hall. There seems to have been some opposition to their marriage. Perhaps the Braithwaites, though kinsmen and fellow Quakers, felt George's prospects at Stangend were not sufficient for their daughter. George himself lamented the difficulties facing their union. In a letter written shortly before their marriage he reassured Abigail 'that she will love him well enough in time, and that if she will only hold on his side, he will make bloody work with his enemies' and thereby secure their future.[28]

George jnr. was already a determined but realistic man. Abigail brought to the marriage a dowry of £100 and a fervent adherence to the Society of Friends, in whose cause she travelled widely, preaching at meetings throughout the north of England. She bore him eight children and, in 1750, after the birth of Robert, their youngest child and sixth son, George took the decision to uproot his family from the low-lying, whitewashed farmhouse at Stangend and dispatch them beyond the confines of the secluded valley of Little Langdale, the gleaming lake of Grasmere, and the desolate mountain solitude of Oxenfell.[29]

He realized that the days of the smallholding were numbered especially if they were in 'a very solitary place'. Daniel Defoe described the landscape as 'eminent only for being the wildest, most barren and frightful of any that I have passed over in England'. The acreage was unyielding and George's third son, William, could recall 'the dangers and hardships' that his father underwent in tending sheep 'in the mountain districts about Stangend, more particularly in winter, and when the precipices were concealed by drifting snow'. George had six sons to provide for, which would require capital expenditure. His profits, however, were not increasing and he needed to use capital to augment his holdings in order to compete with the growing tendency of other farmers to consolidate acreage for greater profit.[30]

As Quakers, none of the Bensons could go to university nor could they enter the professions. Their refusal to take oaths barred Quakers from politics, the practice of law, or service as Justices of the Peace; the Army and Navy were also closed to them as they were pacifists, so they either owned land and farmed or entered industry and became merchants. Through the family's strong Quaker ties, George was aware of the opportunities opening up in the commercial world owing to the increasing importance of trade in the economic life of the nation. He therefore decided to sell Stangend and, with the proceeds, go into trade with his eldest son.

Trade had become the national occupation and the cause of Britain's increasing wealth and power. The expansion of trade with settlements in America, Africa, and Asia, and especially the re-export of colonial goods, was spectacular, while in no other country could money be borrowed so cheaply or so easily—the rate of interest in 1749 was 3 per cent. No longer was it considered an ungentlemanly occupation since the sons of country gentlemen went into trade, the East India Company, and the law, whilst the self-made men of the eighteenth century were too numerous to ignore; 'in short trade in England makes gentlemen, and has peopled this nation with gentlemen'.[31]

In order to secure places for his sons in this exciting, opportunistic world, George moved to Hawkshead, thereby following a national trend especially for Quakers who were flocking into the towns owing to the lure of the large and rapid profits frequently made in trade, compared with the generally small and slow returns from agriculture. George, however, was not just following a national trend. He had identified a gap in the market. Although a developing market town and parish with a textile industry and a rich merchant and county population, Hawkshead contained no linen draper's business. George would have been aware of the prosperity since many of these merchants were fellow Quakers. The cordwainer Clement Satterthwaite, for example, left estate valued in 1740 at £1,629, a considerable sum in those days.[32]

George had already placed his elder sons on the first rung of the ladder of commercial life by using the Quaker network to secure apprenticeships for them. On their fourteenth birthdays they were sent off to David Kendall, a Yorkshire heckler (a comber of flax and hemp) and linen weaver. Each of their indentures was purchased for £10, 'for which the Master undertook to teach [that apprentice] his business, to chastise and correct him in due manner, and to allow him two weeks schooling in the year'.[33]

For eight years George prospered as a linen draper, until his death in 1758, when the inventory of his goods and moneys was valued at £737. After leaving

Abigail the house and outbuildings, the interest on her dowry with the remainder in trust and £50 for the upkeep of their children, he left the residue of his estate to be divided equally amongst his surviving children whose numbers were halved by consumption at the time of their mother Abigail's death in 1761.[34]

The four surviving sons decided to move away from such sad memories. William, 'an honest, quiet, good man' founded the Ulverston branch of the family. He established a flax and grocer's business with Thomas who died from consumption in 1766. Young George jnr., now the head of the family, sold the Hawkshead business and moved to Kendal, where he had the undoubted advantage of the Quaker network and good maternal connections. George Braithwaite had a firm of shearman-dyers (a wealthy élite of cloth finishers and dyers) and a dry saltery and could keep an avuncular eye on his young nephews. Taking his 12-year-old brother Robert with him as an apprentice, George jnr. proceeded to start a grocery business.[35]

Grocers in the eighteenth century were general wholesale dealers in commodities and raw materials. George jnr. needed a shop and warehouses, as he acted both as a supplier to other grocers in surrounding towns and hamlets and as an importer. Kendal was a grand junction where fourteen routes converged, allowing the passage of no fewer than nineteen pack-horse teams each week before 1777. It acted as the entrepôt of a huge trading network for the textile industry and warehousing, drawing in materials from surrounding areas and sending out saleable goods to the towns. The Benson brothers supplied writing paper, pins, twine, and rope as well as soap, whale oil, candles, Fuller's earth, potashes, and salt. Ledgers of two Kendal firms—the dyers Isaac Braithwaite & Son and the hosiers and linsey manufacturers Thomas Crewdson & Son—confirm the Bensons as wholesalers of a variety of raw materials used by local manufacturers. Expansion in their business usually took the form of ownership of a warehouse in the nearest port, followed by a share in a vessel that had brought sugar and spices from the West Indies, and the Bensons' expectation would be to follow this line of progression in due course.

After he had completed his education at the Friends School near Hawkshead and then at the one in Kendal, Robert had become apprenticed to George jnr. in 1765. This was the usual introduction to a mercantile career for a young man. Although his indenture does not survive it was doubtless of the same ilk as those of his brothers and his cousin, John Wilson, who was apprenticed to his father Isaac. Close family ties were not allowed to alleviate the conditions of apprenticeship in any way; Robert would have been required 'to dwell and continue with and serve' his brother for seven years. He would learn to keep accounts and write business letters while performing routine tasks around the store and warehouse. He was neither to commit fornication nor matrimony, nor frequent taverns or alehouses, or such places of idleness, nor play at cards, dice, or any other unlawful games. In return George jnr. would instruct him in his trade and provide him with 'good wholesome and sufficient meat, drink, washing and apparel suitable to his degree and business'.

Having survived this somewhat puritanical but quite normal regime, Robert used his inheritance as capital in a partnership in the family business of 'George & Robert Benson, Grocers' in 1772. The partnership agreement extended for fourteen years and excluded either partner from engaging in any other trade or business 'or separate advantage'. In the early years of their partnership, Robert made many journeys to visit suppliers and customers throughout the north-east and west. Goods would be consigned to him and he was trusted to dispose of them at the best price. He thereby became acquainted with distant markets and merchants, learning about trading methods, and earning the commissions that he needed to save in order to accumulate capital.[36]

His brother had already accumulated capital sufficient to be able to marry into the most prominent Quaker family in Kendal, namely the Wakefields. George's bride, Deborah, was the daughter of the third Roger Wakefield and Mary Wilson. The Wakefields originally combined the business of shearman-dyer with lending money at interest, which implied an ability to amass substantial sums surplus to requirements. They prospered and Deborah's father owned a dyeing business, houses on the west side of Stricklandgate in Kendal, and a frizzing mill.

Deborah's engagement to George Benson jnr. appears to have elicited a note of caution. 'Patience & Perseverance accomplish things', their mutual cousin Isaac Wilson observed. It seems that their marriage had been 'long held in suspense', probably until George's business was judged sufficiently prosperous to allow it. In a letter to his wife on 30 January 1769 Isaac Wilson declares his cousin George jnr. to be 'a steady valuable man' and that the marriage would be successful since 'I have no fear of their being happy in each other'. George jnr.'s future bride evidently had a will of her own, which trait she no doubt inherited from her mother, a formidable woman. Mary Wakefield had carried on the sizeable family business under her own name after the death of Deborah's father in 1756. By the time of Deborah and George jnr.'s marriage she had taken her eldest son, John, into partnership.[37]

John Wakefield, an outstanding entrepreneur, was to play a significant part in young Robert Benson's career. In tune with the increasing diversification of Kendal's industries, he expanded the business to include a brewery, cotton mills, and a gunpowder mill, the latter to meet increased demand, especially from Africa where it was one of the commodities exchanged for slaves. As

Wakefield's businesses expanded, so their bills of exchange began to circulate more widely, and by 1788 he was successful enough to start his own bank, possessing the obligatory capital of £10,000 and adequate diversification of business interests. It was a huge advantage to the Benson brothers to have such a dynamic and successful brother-in-law, one whose shipping interests in Liverpool would prove influential in the future career of young Robert Benson.[38]

Whilst in partnership with his brother, Robert had begun some diversification of his own by expanding into the linen drapery trade, his father's business in Hawkshead. This did not mean he stood behind a counter and sold yards of cloth to customers. Rather, Robert acted in the capacity of a merchant, purchasing materials such as Kendal cottons and calicoes and forwarding them to Manchester and London for printing, or straight to Liverpool for export to America and the West Indies. Surviving ledgers show his cousin Isaac Wilson also exported 'cottons' from Liverpool to the West Indies, and both men used one of the fleet of five ships that John Wakefield operated from Liverpool to carry Kendal cloth to the West Indies and sugar from Jamaica back to Liverpool.

This profitable business was severely disrupted, however, by the American War of Independence, which broke out in 1775. Trade with Ireland and the Baltic soon took the place of that with the Americas. The Bensons had substantial customers in Newcastle, then the main north-eastern port for the Baltic trade, and Robert concentrated upon the export of salt and the import of wood and hemp at Liverpool. This city proved more attractive than ever when, in 1781, he decided to marry Sarah 'Sally' Rathbone, the eldest daughter of William Rathbone III.

Their marriage, which was to last for twenty-one years, was happy and based on a deep mutual attachment. His frequent absences on business trips to the north-east were marked by loving letters home in which he would reiterate his 'tenderest affection' for her and confess how 'my weary mind bends towards thee, my tenderly beloved Wife, and leans upon thy Bosom, and extracts consolation from the mutual tenderness of our Affections'.[39]

In keeping with the prevailing system of arranged marriages, Quaker marriages were not usually undertaken for reasons of love and attachment alone. Property and business were of far greater importance in forming alliances, especially since business amongst Quakers was such a family affair. Unfortunately records of the Benson firm have not survived. For George jnr. to have been deemed an acceptable husband by the Wakefields and Robert by the Rathbones, they must have been eminently respectable and of the utmost integrity, as well as having amassed considerable capital and been successful merchants. Through their marriages the House of Benson not only prospered but broadened its horizons, as Robert now took his place amidst what was possibly the most influential and wealthiest group in the business life of the country.[40]

When Robert and William started Rathbone & Benson in 1786, they already had much in common. Both were moral, upright, intelligent men who greatly liked and respected each other and whose drive and business acumen were always tempered by their strong Quaker beliefs. They had dealt with each other earlier, when Robert was in business in Kendal. William had offered him a consignment of sultanas and raisins to sell to a third party, though stipulating, in Quaker fashion, 'Please to tell them however that I would not have them trust to the quality or condition from my description but [to] appoint a friend to inspect both'. Such fair practices were always a feature of Rathbone & Benson's way of doing business and were inculcated into their business philosophy.[41]

In terms of temperament, however, the two partners were very different. Robert was a kind, softly spoken, contemplative man, given to moments of self-doubt and self-examination: 'I see many little matters relative to myself that I could now wish had been otherwise'; yet he was also a man of good spirits, secure in his family and confident in the future, a man whose advice was sought and who commanded the respect of his peers. Although he could write to his wife 'tho I see many faults and flaws in my heart and many inadvertencies in my intercourse with the world', he always remained at heart optimistic.[42]

In contrast William was impulsive, 'quick to rouse, passionate and outspoken'. Having made up his mind, he acted immediately, regardless of the cost to himself. When he decided that his education was incomplete, he studied French, Latin, and history far into the night after a long day's work in the office. The only way to stay awake was to adopt a position of great discomfort so, by covering his head with a wet towel and pursuing his studies in a kneeling position, he kept going, but in those days of spartan living conditions the cost to his health must have been severe. His unrestrained espousal of radical causes and political ideas, such as opposition to the slave trade and the war in France, made him so unpopular in Liverpool, especially with his well-to-do neighbours, that an attending doctor asked leave to pay his visits after nightfall, explaining that it would injure his practice for his carriage to be seen standing at William's door.

He led a far more public life than his brother-in-law and, at the height of the abolitionist movement, there is more than one story of his having ridden straight into a hostile, seething, swirling mob and persuading them to disperse quietly. Whereas William was the doer of the partnership, Robert was the supporter and adviser who used his persuasive skills and balanced, dispassionate arguments to dissuade William from some impulsive act which might be to the detriment of Rathbone & Benson's operations. Robert was far more like his father-in-law than his brother-in-law in his approach to life and business.[43]

By the time of his father-in-law's death in 1789, Robert had settled into the business and social life of Liverpool. Compared with the relatively small market town of Kendal, Liverpool was even then a bustling, noisy port city, where the clamour and clatter of warehouses and wharves, with their constant traffic of men and horse-drawn vehicles, was unceasing. It was also an exceedingly dangerous place in which to live and work: dangerous from a general lack of sanitation—its streets 'tortuous and narrow, with pavements in the middle, skirted by mud or dirt' and obstructed by piles of refuse locally known as 'corporation beds' (from the tradition that the local nobs and townsmen, returning from the hospitality of the Town Hall or a nearby inn, often subsided into them, there to spend the night)—and dangerous from the raucous uncontrolled crowds who roamed the streets, many of whom 'were plunged in the deepest vice, ignorance and brutality'.

The population was rapidly increasing from some 41,000 in 1785, mainly due to immigration from Ireland after the famine of 1782, to over 74,000 in 1800. When fleets were in port, the place teemed with sailors flush with prize-money to dispense in the numerous brothels and taverns, while press-gangs scouring the streets for future crewmen often resorted to violence to intimidate and capture any member of the public who took their fancy. The only men who reputedly escaped their ferocious clutches were the crews of the slaving ships—they were too depraved even for the press-gangs. 'Scarcely a town by the margin of the ocean would', one resident recalled, '[have] more salt in its people than the men of Liverpool . . . so barbarous were they in their amusements, bull-baiting, and cock and dog fighting, and pugilistic encounters.' Yet, he added, what could be expected when the city's prosperity was mainly derived from the slave-trading and privateering which produced 'the three-bottle and punch-drinking man' as the rule of the table?[44]

No wonder that merchants, however successful and well-to-do, deemed it necessary to live either over their counting-houses or as near to them as possible in order to protect their property. Of course, this conviction was strengthened by the universal belief that the making of money was a full-time occupation that necessitated the constant presence of partners and easy access to the centres of business, which in the case of Liverpool usually meant the docks.

Rathbone & Benson's counting-house was at 20 Cornhill, close to Salthouse Dock. William's grandson recalled that he 'was born at Cornhill, a piece of land between the Salthouse Dock and the river [now the site of Albert Dock warehouses]. There my grandfather and father in turn had possessed a large warehouse, an office and their dwelling-place.' So William lived in the nearest street to it, Liver Street, before moving to Cornhill after his father's death, whilst Robert settled a few hundred yards away in York Street. This facilitated the constant shuttling back and forth between their offices in Cornhill and the Exchange and meant that after all the letters had been written and shipping and customs forms completed, which often took until well into the night, the journey home was as short as possible to avoid the dangers lurking in the streets.[45]

Rathbone & Benson grew out of somewhat inauspicious beginnings. In 1784 the first consignment of American cotton was landed in England. The importer was William. Customs House officials in Liverpool immediately seized it as contraband, since the existing navigation laws decreed that imported goods must be carried in British ships and this consignment arrived on an American ship. They declared that, anyway, 'no cotton was grown in America'! William eventually managed to obtain its release but only to discover that the cotton was of a different quality and type than usual, so it took some time to find a purchaser. This did not deter him unduly and Rathbone & Benson's American cotton business soon prospered to the extent that according to William's grandson the firm sometimes had 'as many as twenty or twenty-five ships consigned to it in dock at the same time'.[46]

The early years of Rathbone & Benson's existence were boom years for business in Liverpool, by far the most important port in Britain and carrying twice the tonnage of London. Liverpool's historian, Baines, observed that the only time that the port's wealth did not increase in the eighteenth century was during the first American War. After the peace of 1783 Liverpool had eagerly taken up her customary mercantile mantle. *Williamson's Advertiser* reported in 1783:

> The Mercantile World is in a hurry and bustle unknown at any former time. The merchants are endeavouring to outstrip each other in the race of traffic. European goods, and particularly the produce of England, being greatly wanted in the ports of America, the destination of many of the vessels now in the river [Mersey] is altered from the West India Islands to the American ports, where it is expected the cargoes will sell at an immense profit.

William had immediately chartered a ship to carry textiles, crockery, and hardware to New York and Philadelphia, and this was the first transaction after the peace. Rathbone & Benson continued in this line of business and expanded the shipbuilding side of their operations to meet the increased demand.[47]

Robert still maintained his Kendal connections—John Wakefield mentions on 9 April 1790 his use of Rathbone & Benson ships to convey bales of cottons to Philadelphia. Such voyages, if successful, were immensely profitable: a net return of double if not treble the original outlay of capital was the normal profit. Within a partnership, it was usual for the partners to take shares equal to one-third or one-half of the total owning and operating costs of a vessel, thereby spreading the risk. It seems that on average the gains on a voyage were equal to about one-third of the value of the ship. Rathbone & Benson's partnership records have not survived, but the fact that they had twenty to twenty-five ships loading or unloading at any one time gives some idea of the scope of their operations and the extent of the profits available to the two partners. John Gladstone, a partner in Corrie & Gladstone, then one of their smaller competitors, had £5,000 capital in his firm which yielded £1,300 in 1795; he had an investment of £4,547 as shares in seven ships; and his net worth was just under £16,000 [£576,000]. As a partner in the leading American firm in Liverpool, Robert's capital and profits would have been considerably higher.[48]

After a decade of peace and increased prosperity, it looked as if the whole operation of Rathbone & Benson would be threatened by the outbreak of yet another war. Pitt, alarmed by the progress of the French Revolution, declared war on France on 11 February 1793 and forthwith a deputation of Liverpool merchants, including Robert and William, demanded 'the protection necessary to be afforded to the shipping of the port'—with the result that most of the trade of firms such as Rathbone & Benson was carried on in tolerable safety under the protection of British ships of war. The immediate effect of war was to create a nationwide panic in which hundreds of commercial houses failed and three-quarters of country banks stopped payment. Although Liverpool's banks stopped payment, in the event only one failed. Dr James Currie noted on 16 March 1793 that 'the first merchant in Liverpool has failed, and many others must follow. Private credit is entirely at a stand.' Merchants, choosing to disregard the upheaval across the Channel, had speculated widely in the African and West Indian trades based on a continuation of peace. They had forecast wrongly and had to pay the price. William and Robert, among 112 merchants, petitioned the Common Council of Liverpool to issue promissory notes to a limit of £300,000 against due security, which ultimately revived trade.[49]

Unlike some of their competitors, Rathbone & Benson were not badly caught out and the crisis of 1793 did not involve them in any losses, mainly as a result of their membership of the international Quaker network. Friends kept up a constant correspondence with their brethren abroad, which was widely circulated by the recipients amongst fellow members of their meeting-houses; while ministering Friends maintained strong links through combining religious visits with trading voyages. And since there were Quaker merchants in most of the ports with which Rathbone & Benson had commercial dealings, it was inevitable that the intelligence they received through their correspondents and their travelling Friends included details of the current political situation along with reports of prices and news of the recent monthly meeting. Thus, news from their French Friends had prepared Rathbone & Benson for the outbreak of war with France so that they conducted their business accordingly—with extreme caution.

Moreover, Quakers had to consider the state of their businesses in the context of their faith, an effective influence upon their commercial behaviour. Every Sunday at the meeting-house, Robert and William would be examined about being 'careful to live within the Bounds of their Circumstances, and to avoid launching into Trade or Business beyond their ability to manage'. The observation of the Quaker founder, George Fox, that 'when people came to have experience of Friends' honesty and faithfulness, and found that their yea was yea and their nay was nay; that they kept to a word in their dealings, and that they would not cozen and cheat them', customers flocked to do business with them, still held true.[50]

This was certainly the case with Rathbone & Benson who, far from seeing their business disrupted, actually did well out of the war. Their shipbuilding business expanded to become the second largest on Merseyside, employing over eighty shipwrights and apprentices. The wartime convoy system created a huge demand for their shipping and also ensured the continuation of their foreign trading operations, the antithesis of conditions facing Hinrich Kleinwort across the North Sea.

During the French war, Rathbone & Benson continued to nurture their large American trade with the aid of printed circulars which advised potential customers of commodity prices and prospects in the markets. In 1795, one American Quaker house netted in this way was Alsop & Hicks of New York, active in the shipping and commission business. They ordered salt from Rathbone & Benson, and crockery, advising that their customers preferred the low-priced blue, white, and cream-coloured pots. From such small beginnings, a larger trade soon emerged.

It had been given a welcome boost by the defeat of the French Navy in the West Indies in 1794, which opened up further prospects of commerce for Liverpool. The main risk of this Atlantic trade was ensuring payment because credits of 12–18 months were standard; indeed 2–3 years could elapse before a firm such as Rathbone & Benson could recoup their investment. Much depended upon the choice of agent or correspondent. Once again, belonging to the Society of Friends was a great advantage in forming business connections. Whilst other American merchants failed, Alsop & Hicks as good Quakers exercised prudence and caution. They made payments to Rathbone & Benson through the firm Samuel P. Lord Junior ('no house in America is safer', said Hicks, reporting it as worth £20,000 in real estate alone) and remained sound, valued correspondents.[51]

Despite the excellent state of their business, the war years were not without difficulty for Robert and William. Both partners were part of a group of Radicals whom their enemies named the 'Liverpool Jacobins' as they promulgated policies hostile to the Liverpool establishment—calling for free trade and the abolition of both the monopoly of town government, which openly promoted the slave trade, and the trading monopoly of the East India Company. They were also denounced by the majority of Liverpudlians over their public opposition to war with France, the partners arguing that the weapon of blockade against the French would interfere with American shipping and damage Anglo-American relations. Their personal safety was under great threat from the violence of the increasingly desperate forays of the notorious press-gangs. 'It was no uncommon circumstance in those days for persons to be unaccountably missing, men in really respectable positions in life, who would after a year or two suddenly turn up, having been impressed and sent to a foreign station,' recalled one nonagenarian resident.[52]

With the safety of his family and clerks a continual anxiety, Robert's own health was a further source of worry. After a series of debilitating attacks of gout in 1797, he decided to relinquish control of the day-to-day business, leaving William in sole control as senior partner, with the help of their junior partner James Cropper, in what was effectively a holding operation until such times as his health improved. Robert planned to continue to act as a consultant and to manage his own investments.

Events conspired against him. First of all, James Cropper decided to leave the partnership in order to set up on his own in 1799. His partner was Robert's nephew, Thomas, son of George jnr. Under Robert's patronage, he and James Cropper formed the firm of Cropper, Benson. It was not the best time to start up a new business; the winter of 1799–1800 was notable for commercial distress in both Germany and Britain. As firms failed in the Hamburg crisis, so Liverpool merchants faced ruin as the prices of sugar and other colonial produce plummeted.

The uncertainty of trading conditions did little to improve Robert's health. Although Sally Benson could write to their son, Robert Rathbone Benson, in February 1800: 'Thy dear Father has had his health generally well this Winter, but sometimes is toil'd in attending to his little business, it having lain heavier upon him since Cousin Thomas left him,' by the next month it was apparent to all of them that in the grip of consumption he could never regain his old strength. On 23 March he signed a deed to dissolve the partnership of Rathbone & Benson, thereby enabling William to take on all remaining profits or losses and, if necessary, to enter into new partnership agreements. This was the official position; unofficially, Robert retained shares in ships and other family investments but was free to interest himself in outside business.[53]

Then at the end of the year he became 'very poorly' and had a paralysing stroke on 31 December 1800. 'One arm rendered useless, and one side of his face perceptibly altered. Very affecting was this account to us all,' confided Hannah Rathbone to her diary, 'and deeply my soul sympathised with my dear afflicted sister.' That he remained in a weak and failing state of health was evident when his eldest brother and former partner, George jnr., died in May 1801. As Sally Benson told her son, 'this circumstance has very deeply affected thy Father, indeed my dear Robt, I was almost afraid for a few days it would have prov'd too much for his weak frame to bear; not being in a state of health to attend his Funeral render'd it still a greater tryal'. As she feared, he suffered another stroke after attending the weekly Meeting on 3 October 1802, William staying all night with him. Finally on 1 November, Hannah Rathbone recorded in her diary: 'During the day it became evident his release drew nigh. And about eight o'clock our dear and excellent Brother was quietly released from his sufferings. It was the death of the righteous!'[54]

2 Benson Merchants on the Move

THE peace treaty signed at Amiens in March 1802 after nine years of war had provided Hinrich Kleinwort and Robert Benson with a brief respite from the anxiety of wartime trading. Robert's concerns had centred upon the future of his son Robert Rathbone Benson (to be known as Robert R.). As the time had approached for him to leave school, 'I unavoidably became very concerned about his introduction to the knowledge of business, as well as about the line of business to which I should introduce him,' Robert had confided to an American friend, Matthias Maris. 'After much deliberation nothing appeared so peaceful, as the business I had myself so long laboured in and was so fully acquainted with'. The difficulty lay in choosing the right firm to provide his son with an apprenticeship that would lead to an eventual partnership.

He had deemed three possibilities worthy of consideration but had ruled out the first, his own former firm of Rathbone & Benson, for the good reason that William's two elder sons, contemporaries of Robert R.'s, were being groomed to succeed their father. In the meantime William had taken on two other partners, William Hughes and William Duncan. Of the second possibility, namely to start up his own house where his son could serve an apprenticeship, Robert astutely judged that 'the apprehension of opening myself at my time of life to the cares and toils of a trade that might possibly be extensive, alone and without any to divide those cares and toils with me, seemed to forbid it'; whilst to retain his son with him 'without full and active employment seemed to be big with danger to him'.

After much deliberation he had decided that the third possibility, to join Cropper & Benson, afforded by far the best long-term prospects for his son. 'Thou will possibly have been a little surprised at my again entering into the American business,' he had informed Matthias Maris. 'I am Thou knowest fully and very intimately acquainted with both my partners, and have been so from their early years.' James Cropper, the man who had started Cropper & Benson, had been a special protégé of Robert's when he had served his apprenticeship with Rathbone & Benson in the early 1790s.[1]

James Cropper had entered Rathbone & Benson through his uncle Jonathan Binns, who was a fellow 'Liverpool Jacobin' and active in promoting many of the causes Robert held dear. James's father, Thomas Cropper, farmed at Winstanley, near Wigan, and supplied Rathbone & Benson with barley and malt. Robert had done much to encourage his protégé, who, despite being described as a 'tall, country lad', early on displayed a sure grasp of mathematical calculation. Robert had absolute confidence in his abilities. 'I care nothing as to the price that or any other Article ought to obtain with you,' he wrote on one occasion to James Cropper, 'and leave it wholly to your judgement,' which proved well-founded on Robert's part. James Cropper's rise through Rathbone & Benson was so meteoric that, at the extremely young age of 22, he became a partner.

In 1797, when Robert had been forced through continued ill-health to retire, James Cropper had left Rathbone & Benson to launch his own business as an importer of American grain and flour, to some extent in competition with Rathbone & Benson. As he later told his sons, 'You can be very very little aware of the care, the anxiety and the exertion' involved in such a momentous step. Although James Cropper emphasized the difficulties—'when I commenced . . . I knew not one individual in the World to whom I could look for business and I had a very small capital to begin with'—he was not strictly accurate. He had contacts with the foremost American houses through Rathbone & Benson and he maintained close relations with his former partners, William and Robert.[2]

Indeed, Robert had suggested that James Cropper went into partnership with his nephew Thomas Benson so as to increase the capital base, spread the risks and, hopefully, decrease 'the anxiety and the exertion'. Robert, in fact, had sponsored Thomas and, with an eye to the future, contributed part of Thomas's share in the new firm—Cropper, Benson—which had commenced business on 1 September 1799. Unfortunately, Thomas had become ill with consumption and had outlived his father, George jnr., by only a matter of months. Robert and Sally Benson had been at Kendal where they 'staid till the close of his pilgrimage . . . which was very painful indeed'. He was, Robert revealed to a friend, 'an amiable youth, as thou knowest, and we were bound to him, and he to us, by strong ties, having become like a Son of our own'. Thomas was only 23 when he died and his death had left an unexpected vacancy in the Cropper, Benson partnership. This had been filled by his brother, William. As a result of his father's death, William had been able to add his inheritance to Thomas's share in Cropper, Benson. However, since William was only 25 years old, Robert had wanted to ensure a place for his son Robert R. in Cropper, Benson because he believed it would go from strength to strength as a business. It was for this reason that he had bought a share of the company, which in recognition had become Benson, Cropper & Benson, of No. 1 Graving Dock by Salthouse Dock gates, active in the American trade.

As with all partnership articles, the agreement was dissolvent on the death of any of the parties. With this in mind, Robert had expressed a wish in his will that in the interests of Robert R. 'such a partnership should be continued for the benefit of my family until my son attain the age of twenty-one years and afterwards given up' to him. In order to expedite this, Robert had authorized his trustees to allow his share to remain in Benson, Cropper & Benson, with the profits being paid to Sally Benson until Robert R. became 21. Since Robert R. was only 17 when his father died, his mother became a sleeping partner in the business which dropped the first Benson and reverted to its original title of Cropper, Benson & Co.[3]

Before he could join Cropper, Benson, however, Robert R. had to serve an apprenticeship. He had done well at Mr Sandon's Quaker School in Reading, shown 'dilligence in learning' which had naturally pleased his proud parents. Although it would have been 'an *infinite* blessing' to have had 'a Father to take thee by the hand & introduce thee into the World', Robert R. had to start his career without the benefit of paternal guidance; instead he relied upon William Rathbone, who became the most formative influence on his early life.[4]

In 1803, Robert R. joined his Uncle Rathbone's firm of Rathbone, Hughes & Duncan to serve a two-year apprenticeship. It was, in effect, joining the family firm, as the Bensons and Rathbones continued to live in each others' pockets. For instance, William, stepping off the London to Liverpool mail coach at dawn, knew he would find a bed at the Benson house in Thurlow Street. When he arrived, he slept in his nephew Robert R.'s bed, which his son, little Benson, was sharing. In turn, because Robert R.'s eldest Rathbone cousin, Willie, was delicate from birth and needed country air, William had purchased a farmhouse called Greenbank, and this became a second home for all the Bensons.[5]

After attending Sunday meeting the family would congregate on the double verandah to greet the young apprentices and clerks from the counting-house. William kept open house every Sunday for all the young men in the office. There would be up to fifteen of them to dinner and tea which included Robert R. and his Rutter cousin, Henry Chorley, who was an apprentice at Cropper & Benson. As family, they would also stay for the night.

The best of Liverpool's society frequented the parlours and copious library at Greenbank where Robert R. heard literary works read aloud by friends of his father and uncle, such as William Roscoe and Robert Owen. The American naturalist John James Audubon described a summer's day there in his journal: 'I have been drawing for Mrs Rathbone, and after dinner we went through the Jardin potager. How charming is Greenbank and the true hospitality of these English friends.'[6]

The charming Greenbank days must have been a welcome respite after a long, dreary week in the counting-house. However willing to learn, the life of an apprentice was one of sheer drudgery. It was no different for Robert R. despite his connections; indeed the greater expectations for his success probably meant a heavier workload. Henry Chorley hated it and declared that 'a clerk in a Liverpool merchant's office, when we were young, was expected to be a mere machine—neither a gentleman by birth nor a man of education, still less a man of individual propensities. It was a terrible subjection', if not 'a slavery ill-compensated for by any indulgence or hope of advancement'.

In the days before the telegraph or any machine capable of reproduction existed, everything was done by hand. Robert R.'s long day was passed in transcribing the details of the day's market in each commodity of interest to the firm. As prices changed so the lists would be rewritten, ten to twenty times in a day. The particulars of the cargoes of each ship arriving and departing were also taken down and copies made by hand. Days would be taken up with writing out the corrected copies of trade circulars distributed to numerous clients, whilst the recopying of letters addressed at the last moment to the American cotton ports to be delivered by a departing ship was never a light task and could last until 2 a.m. This was frequently the case on weekly post days.

Then there were the ledgers and invoices to be tallied. 'When I have a bad dream, now that I am old,' Henry Chorley recalled, 'I see ledgers which will not be balanced, figures wrongly set down, and wake in the midst of such shame and self-disrespect.' The two skills demanded of any mercantile apprentice were numeracy and legible handwriting. As far as Robert R.'s handwriting was concerned, much as in the case of his contemporary Alexander Friedrich Kleinwort, it is not clear how he was ever able to pass muster.[7]

Robert R.'s time at the firm was cut short by the death of his cousin William Benson, who had inherited the Benson consumptive tendency and, in 1805, followed his brother Thomas and Robert R.'s sister, Rachel, to an early grave. Fearful for the health of her three remaining children (Robert R., Margaret, and Abigail), Sally decided to move away from the dock area to the leafy, open spaces of Lodge Lane. Robert R., however, continued to base himself at Salthouse Dock, usually sleeping either at the counting-house or with the Croppers at Duke Street, because he had at last assumed his place in the partnership of Cropper, Benson.

All Robert R.'s early business experience was gained under conditions of war. The commerce of Europe was lost to its Continental ports and concentrated in British ports such as Liverpool, but Napoleon was determined to invade England and, by May 1803, France and Britain were again at war. Although Liverpool immersed herself in a frenzy of patriotic preparation Robert R. and his cousins refrained from joining the fray: as Quakers they were morally opposed to war and forbidden to fight, even for their country.

They nevertheless had their own battles to keep the business afloat. Trading conditions were much more testing during this second French war and both Cropper, Benson and Rathbones (as Rathbone, Hughes & Duncan was commonly called) were sorely tried at times to maintain profitability. Robert R.'s first full year at Cropper, Benson was a year of crisis. The erection of the Continental and British Blockade resulted in a war of commercial extermination that also destroyed the trade of neutral countries such as America. While Britain claimed the right to search neutral ships for enemy goods, France simply seized them in retaliation. The effect upon such American houses in Liverpool as Cropper, Benson and Rathbones is clear from a letter William wrote in December 1806: 'Our own situation cannot be otherwise than a subject of considerable anxiety . . . The present stock of Cotton is large & our expected supplies are also large; & if there be none or but a very limited sale, the pressure must be very heavy.' It was already taking its toll on other merchant houses. In 1807 alone, Liverpool lost nearly a quarter of its entire trade. West Indian traders might be delighted by the exclusion of American ships carrying rival cargoes of sugar and cotton from the French, Spanish, and Portuguese American colonies to Europe but, after America retaliated by imposing its own embargo, traders such as Cropper, Benson saw their business being destroyed.[8]

As the waters of American trade froze against their ships, Cropper, Benson sought warmer waters elsewhere for their vessels. Robert R. and James Cropper succeeded because they possessed those attributes of any successful merchant, namely courage, flexibility, and resourcefulness in discovering new markets; the closing of one order book was but a prelude to the opening of another.

As Napoleon tried to close the Baltic and Scandinavian ports, Cropper, Benson sent ships to Archangel through the Arctic seas. Only the most daring of merchants undertook such risky business, but it was immensely profitable. Cropper, Benson bought fine white sugar from Cuba at 30 shillings, a 'very low price owing to their having no America trade', and shipped it over to Archangel using Russian-built vessels manned by Prussian and Russian sailors. If the ship managed to avoid the blockades and docked safely, Cropper, Benson were assured of a good profit because demand in Archangel was high. 'There is *no* fear of a market in Russia for fine white Sugars for Archangel alone takes off *two thousand tons*,' reported Thomas Cropper, younger brother of James and now a partner, in 1807. Cropper, Benson's ship then returned to Liverpool laden with hemp and tallow. And when the Portuguese royal family fled to

Brazil to escape Napoleon, thereby opening the Brazilian trade to Britain, Cropper, Benson sent ships to Pernambuco for supplies of Brazilian cotton. Their enterprise in finding alternative markets under exceedingly difficult trading conditions paid off handsomely. An entry in James Cropper's letterbook reports that in 1807 receipts 'for the last four months considerably exceeded £1,000 per day on an average'.[9]

In the charter or purchase of vessels, Cropper, Benson frequently took half-shares with Rathbones and relations between the two houses remained very close. Then in 1809 William fell seriously ill, suffering 'great pain, faintness, and difficulty of breathing, yet through it all having business interviews, writing letters, or dictating', for he had remained the mainstay of the firm. Robert R. came most evenings to take his turn in sitting up with his uncle and business mentor. William spoke of his approaching death as a 'serious matter, but nothing dismal' and of his coffin as 'only a packing-case'. Robert R. was with him when he died on 11 February 1809. His net estate was nearly £110,000, equivalent to over £3m. today.

William's sons Willie and Richard Rathbone were ready to assume their heritage, but the existing older partners Hughes and Duncan did not relish sharing the business on an equal footing with two young inexperienced men. The family turned to the senior partner of Cropper, Benson for help in resolving the quarrel. 'James Cropper came to meet W.H. and W.D.—a painful meeting,' Hannah Rathbone noted in her diary on 1 March 1809. The outcome was that the Rathbone brothers set up on their own account as commission merchants though at the time it seemed as if their firm would not survive. They were so inexperienced that James Cropper sent his head clerk to coach them. He also recommended them to Cropper, Benson's American clients in such favourable terms that even Robert R. had to remonstrate with him: on the strength of such strongly worded letters, the Americans would surely believe that Cropper, Benson were about to relinquish their business to Rathbone Brothers![10]

Although America had withdrawn her trade embargo against Britain in the hope of stimulating the repeal of the Orders in Council, the British Government persisted in enforcing them to the detriment of Anglo-American relations. By 1812, more than a thousand American vessels had been seized and impounded in English ports. Finally, after withstanding four years of vociferous opposition, Lord Castlereagh announced the suspension of the hated orders on 18 June 1812. He was too late. News that President Madison had declared war on Britain arrived on 20 June, three weeks before Castlereagh's suspension announcement could reach America by boat. The war was disastrous for Liverpool in general and its American houses in particular.

Like other houses specializing in the American trade, Cropper, Benson suffered loss of trade and loss of ships; that the effects were far less serious than they might otherwise have been was due to their strategy of diversification. Having weathered ten years of the French wars, they were in a stronger position to withstand the hardships of this latest war. It was not an easy task. The funds and commissions owed on their sales of American produce in Europe were not forthcoming during wartime; credit to their American clients remained extended for the next two years. In the general economic depression which ensued, it was impossible for Cropper, Benson to recoup their losses by selling American produce at high prices on the home market.

Added to this was the huge increase in premiums of insurance on cargoes and the uncertainty that a vessel would escape capture by American privateers. Liverpool privateers had put their faith in the Admiralty to protect their shipping and discovered, to their cost, that the King's cruisers were never where they were most wanted. So, although British power was superior in every way, including numerically, the Americans did by far the most damage. Cropper, Benson suffered the loss of one of their ships, the *Eliza Ann*, whilst on the Liverpool–Baltimore run. 'The *Eliza Ann* will make over £2,000 out,' Thomas Cropper had informed Robert R. on 22 July 1813. Captured by the celebrated privateer brig *Yankee*, she was sent into Boston, causing Cropper, Benson to lose their £2,000. The fact that Cropper, Benson paid a tax for protection of their ships, in the form of convoy duty, served only to increase their anger at the Admiralty's evident powerlessness to provide adequate protection.[11]

Fortunately, Cropper, Benson were more successful on other fronts. In addition to shipping Cuban sugars to Russia, they did a fair business in importing Cuban coffee for clients in Scotland. Thomas Cropper opened up a connection with the Leith firm of Dudgeon, Dixon & Co. whereby they shipped colonial produce to Sweden. While the Cropper brothers were pursuing new business and visiting correspondents in Scotland, Robert R. held the fort in Liverpool. His dealings, or lack of them, did not always meet with the approval of his elder partners. Their Prussian agent, Mr Becker, had sent them a large supply of hemp which proved difficult to move. 'I wish you could pull off Beckers Hemp as there are several anxious sellers in L'pool,' Thomas Cropper urged Robert R. on 25 July 1813. 'You must go after the buyers or you will not be able to sell.' Accounts arrived from St Petersburg that shipping was very scarce, so that freight rates on hemp had risen to £10 per ton and were expected to rise further. Robert R. presumably used this information to persuade buyers to act immediately before costs rose, for the next Cropper letter congratulates him on getting good business from sales of hemp.[12]

Robert R. had been less attentive of business affairs than usual because he had lately married and set up house at 19 Seel Street, near the docks. His bride, Mary Dockray, came from an old Lancashire Quaker family, long part of the Benson circle. It was in 1665 that Thomas Dockray and George Benson of Stangend were taken from a Hawkshead meeting and sent to prison for refusing the oath. More importantly for Cropper, Benson, Mary brought a generous dowry and excellent connections. Her father, David Dockray (1732–1807), had amassed a considerable fortune as a 'West India' merchant with interests in a brewery and an iron smelting works. Her mother, Esther Dillworth, was the daughter of William Dillworth, an eminent Quaker banker who took for his second wife John Wakefield and Deborah Benson's mother. Through Mary Dockray, Robert R. became doubly connected to two of the most solid country banks, the Kendal and the Craven; though in 1816 he preferred to borrow £3,000 from her marriage settlement trust rather than from either bank when he decided to increase his capital share in Cropper, Benson, who had extended their business to include India.[13]

The East India Company had managed to retain its trading monopoly to India and China despite the long-standing campaigns of merchants such as the Bensons and their circle to bring about the freedom of trade to the East. William had been active in the unsuccessful campaign of 1792, a casualty of the French wars. Robert R. held the same views as his father and uncle and supported free trade. As far as he was concerned the case for ending the monopoly of the East India Company and removing its political patronage was clear: Liverpool should have the same rights of access to this trade as the Port of London.

The Charter of the East India Company was due for renewal in 1813 so, in the spring of 1812, eighty Liverpool merchants prepared their campaign. Robert R. and James Cropper represented Cropper, Benson at the meetings organized to compose the petition for application to Parliament to open up the trade to all ports. A deputation from Liverpool joined those from other parts of the country to assail Parliament. This application was successful with regard to India but the East India Company retained its monopoly of the China trade for another twenty-one years. This meant, for example, that no private ship unlicensed by the East India Company could import tea or silk.

Yet restrictions on the trade to India still existed; ships had to be at least 350 tons burthen and could not carry Indian goods directly to Continental ports. Nevertheless, Cropper, Benson were amongst the first firms to obtain a licence to ship to Bombay, Calcutta, and Madras. The fluctuations in the supply of American cotton caused by the American War of 1812 led them to seek a source elsewhere and India seemed the best alternative. Although slower off the mark than John Gladstone, whose ship the *Kingsmill* sailed in May 1814, their ship the *Bengal*—410 tons, newly built on the Clyde, and jointly owned with Rathbones—

sailed for Calcutta shortly afterwards. Given wartime conditions, there was an understandable fear of attack from privateers and the French. As a staunch Quaker house, Cropper, Benson could not allow their ship to be armed. They did, however, resort to installing wooden cannons at the portholes in order to scare off the enemy. This ploy proved successful and the *Bengal* returned safely with a cargo of Indian cotton for spinning in Lancashire. On her second outward journey the *Bengal* was laden with Lancashire printed cottons to sell in India.[14]

Although involved in Indian affairs as a partner holding a personal share in the *Bengal*, Robert R. was far more concerned in the active management of the firm's American trade. With the Treaty of Ghent, which brought the Anglo-American war to an end on Christmas Eve 1814, and the final cessation of hostilities in the French war, the Atlantic Ocean was once more open and safe for trade. Unfortunately the advent of peace heralded a post-war slump as a great wave of ruin flooded the country. During 1815–16 alone, 240 banks suspended payments or became bankrupt.

Thomas Cropper, who had gone to Nice to convalesce, urged caution upon his young partner Robert R. in managing the American side during such difficult trading conditions: 'I see the Cotton Market has had a serious tumble since I left home. The Americans must have been losing a great deal of money by their shipments of Flour, Cotton & in fact almost everything,' he wrote, '& in my opinion our old & well established system of Caution will be as much or more than ever necessary.' Robert R. was feeling unusually discouraged and even fleetingly contemplated giving up the cares and responsibilities of his position. Thomas Cropper put it down to overwork—he was 'so deeply engaged in the concerns of so extensive a business'—but before he could take a holiday, Robert R. became engrossed in an exciting development on his side of the firm's operations.[15]

Through his eldest Dockray brother-in-law, Robert R. had come to know the Thompson brothers, Quakers who were engaged in the woollen trade in Yorkshire. Jeremiah Thompson had settled in New York in order to organize the sales of the woollens manufactured by the family firm at home. He had gained first-hand experience of the frustrations encountered by 'regular' trading firms such as Cropper, Benson when the departure date of ships was delayed for days or even weeks in the hope of attracting more cargo or passengers to achieve full capacity. Robert R.'s nephew described how he had once posted thirty letters on thirty consecutive days in the letter box of a single ship that was waiting to sail for Bombay, but was detained day after day for a month—in this case by contrary winds. It could just as easily have been delayed by a half-empty hold.[16]

In the autumn of 1817, Jeremiah Thompson had the brilliant idea of starting a shuttle service between New York and Liverpool in partnership with Cropper, Benson and Rathbones. They introduced the principle of 'line' or 'berth' service with ships sailing on schedule between the two ports. Their first four square riggers 'will positively sail, full or not full from Liverpool on the 1st and from New York on the 5th of every month, throughout the year', they announced in the *Liverpool Mercury* of 5 December 1817. The *Courier*, burthen 380 tons, inaugurated the line when she sailed from Liverpool on 1 January 1818. Her crossings averaged 40 days westwards and 23 days eastwards.

This completely changed the pattern of ocean trading and increased the American trade of Liverpool, which became the undisputed terminus on the English side for the machine-made textiles of Lancashire and Yorkshire and the pottery and hardwares of the Midlands. Cropper, Benson's participation in Thompson's Black Ball Line of copper-bottomed sailing packets placed them in an unrivalled position in the league table of American houses in Liverpool and earned huge profits for the partners.

Although there was the risk of sailing only half-full with the loss of extra freight earnings, this situation rarely transpired because the removal of the uncertainty of departure dates attracted increased custom from shippers and passengers. Cropper, Benson and Rathbones naturally used these ships to transport their own goods and the line was a success from the start.

In the event of adverse winds, they employed a steam boat to tow their vessel out of the Mersey to sea to ensure it kept to schedule. They were also quick to seize the initiative by using similar methods of operation on other occasions. When they received information of a bad harvest they immediately chartered the first available boat, in this case a Liverpool pilot-boat, to take the news out to their correspondents in New York and request extra cargoes of wheat to be sent to meet the expected increased demand. A westerly gale in the Mersey had prevented the movement of ships for days, so they employed a little Mersey ferry-boat to tow the pilot-boat out to sea. When this vessel returned home from New York, she found that the westerly winds still prevailed and all the other vessels were still waiting to leave harbour![17]

The successes on the American side of the business were not reflected on the Indian side. Although Cropper, Benson had hoped the East would provide an alternative yield of cotton, it had soon become apparent that East Indian cotton did not compare in either quality or price with American. The eastward crossings of Black Ball Line ships conveyed ever larger quantities of superior quality American cotton—brought from the southern states to New York by Jeremiah Thompson—into Liverpool for Cropper, Benson. They took a gloomy view of Indian cotton: 'it was pretty certain we shall get litle from India in 1823', since India had not responded to high prices as America had done. Furthermore, they did not have the benefit of a shuttle service of packets to Calcutta and Bombay. The long distances and increased shipping risks were not conducive to their style of operation. 'I think you have your Ships too much of a heap, too many Eggs in one Basket,' Thomas Cropper, shortly before his death in May 1819, had warned Robert R. 'It does not appear to me the proper plan to have every ship in port together.'

Yet there seemed little Robert R. could do about it, given that he had to collect a full complement of freight for the much larger vessels licensed to trade with India. Most East Indiamen were over 1,000 tons whereas the average tonnage on the American run was 200–300 tons, so that it was no easy task to find the extra cargo at short notice. It was certainly difficult to make profits on Indian voyages. In 1820 and 1821 the rival firm of Gladstones had deficits on four Indian voyages totalling £22,000. Cropper, Benson avoided such losses through turning to the importation of spices, silk, rice, coffee, indigo, and sugar.[18]

It was, indeed, the issue of East Indian sugar which predominated over any other for the partners during the early 1820s. Sugar became the mainstay of their Indian business; and, as Quakers, it was the vehicle by which they united their opposition to two powerful forces—slavery and trade monopolies. In 1818 they had been founder members of the Liverpool East India Association, chaired by John Gladstone, father of the great statesman. As the bulk cargo of their trade, they had a special interest in removing the existing differential of 10 shillings between East Indian and West Indian sugar. However, the powerful West Indian lobby was working to increase this duty, not to remove it. Open warfare broke out between the two organizations and, more damagingly for Cropper, Benson, between John Gladstone and James Cropper.

In 1823 James Cropper published a letter entitled 'The Impolicy of Slavery'. His former colleague and rival trader John Gladstone replied for the West Indian lobby, under the signature of 'Mercator'. Their correspondence became increasingly acrimonious as Gladstone found his position as former East Indian Association campaigner for the equalization of sugar duties irreconcilable with his position as a substantial slave owner and exporter of West Indian sugar. He refused to keep the debate to the economic interests; instead he queried Cropper's motives as 'the most considerable importer of East India sugar into this port' not to mention his 'slave-owning connections in the United States, who consign their cotton, the produce of the labour of slaves, to his house in Liverpool for sale'.

Although Cropper had declared his interests right from the start, this was a criticism which all Quaker abolitionist merchants were well aware of and one which caused them much anguish as they tried to reconcile their beliefs and principles with the interests of business. Cropper wrote to his son-in-law, Joseph Sturge:

It is a very difficult thing to keep from touching in any shape slave produce, whether sugar or cotton. We have nearly one million of persons employed in this country in the manufacture of cotton which is the produce of slave labour, and some of our best and warmest friends are engaged in this business. Should we propose that such should shut up their works and turn off their workmen? . . . I am engaged in ships, must they refuse to carry it [slave produce] whilst their sails and cordage are made from hemp and flax, the produce of Russian slaves?

It was a conundrum every Quaker merchant faced; few were able to resolve it satisfactorily. An earlier generation had no hesitation in placing conscience above trading interest; subsequent ones were guided less by moral principles but felt greater guilt and doubt in consequence.[19]

The campaigns over slavery, East Indian sugar and the monopoly of the East India Co. in China continued over many years. This meant that James Cropper's interests were increasingly focused elsewhere, to the detriment of Cropper, Benson. The burden of management increasingly fell upon Robert R. as senior partner *de facto*, Hugh Mure, a former clerk who had taken the place of Thomas Cropper on his death in 1819, and James Cropper's young sons, John and Edward.

Trade in the early 1820s was buoyant, especially in American cotton, and in 1823 Cropper, Benson formed what their New Orleans agent Vincent Nolte termed 'the Quaker Confederation' to speculate on the rising price of cotton. They believed that consumption was overtaking production, thereby inevitably increasing the price.

The membership of this loose confederation illustrates the international scope of Cropper, Benson's contacts and their position in the cotton trade. They brought in Rathbones; Isaac Cooke of Cooke & Comer, the most prestigious firm of cotton brokers in Liverpool; Daniel Willinck, the Dutch Consul in Liverpool who was supported by Barings and by Hopes of Amsterdam, leading bankers in Holland; Hottinguer & Cie of Paris and Le Havre; Jeremiah and Francis Thompson of New York; and Vincent Nolte in New Orleans.

The year 1824 saw the Quaker Confederation at the height of its speculative activities. Edward Cropper described one day's trading in November of that year when the price of cotton rose as each vessel successively docked: 'the accounts brought by each succeeding vessel continued the advance till it had reached 1¼ from the lowest point—there was then a slackness and the market gave way ½'. Cropper, Benson timed it nicely to purchase 400 bags of cotton before the price rose again, when 'there then came on a very active speculative demand' and they sold a total of 2,153 bales of which 650 bales of Orleans cotton,

882 of Uplands (Georgia and South Carolina cotton), plus a further 100 Uplands were bought 'on spec'.[20]

In addition to their activities in cotton, Cropper, Benson were one of the largest importers of East Indian sugar, and had speculated in corn for many years. They imported grain from America, Ireland, and the Baltic for the home market. Much, however, depended upon expectations of the domestic harvest and in good harvest years they lost money. It was vital in this line of business to have a good agricultural spy network to supply information on crop development. In a letter to Robert R. from Head Office, David Hodgson relayed the latest reports from the crop front. These could prove somewhat contradictory as when 'Henry keeps up the report of frit [a fly destructive of wheat and grass shoots] in his district and he was got into Warwickshire, but George who was last at Downham takes no notice of anything of the kind and as he advances he thinks the wheat improving.' Meanwhile from their man Self in Lynn, Norfolk, 'we have had alarming accounts common to all . . . Self made a real Examination and found the barley exceedingly grown but the wheat very little so'. Elsewhere, another agent declared wheat 'very much grown', although one Ellis reported from Leicester that 'sound wheat is out of the question there'.

How Cropper, Benson evaluated these reports in terms of crop trading is not clear, but their use of crop investigators came in for criticism. In his book *Rural Rides* William Cobbett abhors agricultural spying, complaining that teams of gaugers enter people's property without permission and proceed to cut out a square yard or so of their crop for sampling. As a former farmer, Cobbett naturally resented Liverpool merchants and bankers such as Cropper, Benson who prospered from their business whilst half the farmers were bankrupt. Evaluation of crops was not all, for the vagaries of the weather had also to be taken into account, so that dealing activity must have proved an extremely risky business. 'Everything further is in the weather,' Hodgson admitted on 7 September 1821, 'and it was uncommonly wet and warm from the afternoon of yesterday till this morning and is now close with a lowering barometer'. On the strength of this, they purchased 7,000 bushels of 'excellent Dansey wheat', with results unknown.[21]

The early 1820s were, however, profitable ones for them. In 1824 a summary of the state of their finances revealed a capital of £60,000 with £10,000 due for goods sold and £9,000 with their bankers, Brown, Janson & Co. of London. Their acceptances for two months over Christmas and the New Year were £26,000 and £23,000 respectively. Although their rivals, Gladstones, had in 1820 a capital of £150,000, part of that included mortgages and advances held on West Indian plantation property. Cropper, Benson's capital base, including neither property assets nor personal fortune, was considered eminently respectable, indeed enviable, for a Liverpool house and entirely in keeping with their position as that City's premier American house.[22]

Secure in their pre-eminent position, Cropper, Benson debated whether to expand their premises. Before they could do so, the speculative market was undermined by Dennistoun, Mackie & Co. a small Scottish merchant house which in 1825 imported 5,000 bales below the market price and destroyed the Quaker Confederation by bursting the bubble of high prices. This caused a collapse in the market and, subsequently, the bankruptcy of Nolte, Willinck, several small Liverpool houses, and, most disastrously of all, Jeremiah Thompson. The Black Ball Line had to be sold and Cropper, Benson lost one of its most profitable operations.

Besides losing the profits generated by a booming market, Cropper, Benson suffered from holding large stocks of cotton and from being major creditors to Nolte. Moreover the fate of Cropper, Benson's Quaker Confederation had mirrored a national trend. The benign trading climate of the previous few years had become submerged in a speculative mania which engulfed banks and companies. By the summer of 1825 the exchanges became unfavourable, the Bank of England 'became stiff about discounting and further drew in its issues', the discount houses followed suit, and London bankers refused to help their country correspondents. By the end of 1825 'Great Britain and Ireland was [*sic*] in one scene of confusion, dismay and bankruptcy'.

Although many of the northern banks withstood the strong runs on them, they could not do so indefinitely. On 10 February 1826 a Crewdson cousin of the Bensons recorded in his diary: 'Heard of the stoppage of Dilworth and Co.' and that afternoon there was a run in Kendal on another family bank, Wilson, Crewdson & Co. It survived as did Messrs John Wakefield & Sons, for many preferred a 'Jackie Wakefield' note to one of the Bank of England. The outlook none the less remained dismal, John Gladstone gloomily declaring in August 1826, 'in all my experience for above forty years as a man of business, I never could look forward with less satisfaction and more dread', and the crisis claimed another family business, Dockray & Co. As overseer of the family funds, Robert R. was involved in trying to ascertain the liabilities and decide whether the family should bail out his brother-in-law David Dockray's manufacturing business.[23]

It was, however, only too easy to give offence: 'it appears to me, thou hast looked with too scrutinizing an eye on our side of the question', John Dockray argued. The Bensons did their best but Abigail Dockray had expected the sale of her husband's business and property to yield a large enough sum to settle outstanding debts and still 'have placed them in affluence', Hannah Dockray explained, 'and that it is not so is a heavy grievance to them'. Robert R., nevertheless, went out of his way to help Abigail, secretly purchasing the neighbouring industrial estate of Chapel Fields, investing the rentals to provide an income, and leaving the whole property to her and her children in his will. His son Robert jnr. and nephew Robert Dockray only discovered the source of this generous gift thirty years later. The death in 1827 of Sally Benson, that 'sweet spirited woman', removed a strong conciliatory force from the family counsels. Robert R. lost not only a 'dear and honoured mother' as he told Elizabeth Fry, but also a confidante and wise counsel in business matters.[24]

These years were also witness to a commercial development of the utmost importance to the Benson business, namely the creation of the railways. The Bensons would derive much of their prosperity from this new industry, in whose promotion Robert R. was centrally involved. Liverpool was linked with its most profitable trading hinterlands by a canal system that by 1824 was not only insufficient for the volume of traffic but also uneconomic. The Bridgewater Canal, the most important for Liverpool's merchants, carried goods at 12*s*. 6*d*. per ton, but it could profitably have charged 5*s*. Yet the owner's agent, 'one of the great commercial toughs of the day', refused to diminish the huge profits, averaging at least £50,000 per annum, by reducing the carriage rates.

Robert R. wanted to abolish this monopoly and it was primarily as a member of the canal resistance movement that he, James Cropper, and John Moss, a banker heading the movement, promoted the idea of a railway link between Liverpool and Manchester. Robert R. became a member of the committee formed in May 1824 to prepare a bill and fight the landed canal interest. 'We cannot conceal from ourselves that the opposition will be tremendous,' the Secretary, G. Pritt, admitted. On 11 February 1825 the Liverpool and Manchester Railway Company Bill was introduced in Parliament, supported by William Huskisson, MP for Liverpool and Secretary of the Board of Trade. 'We congratulate you on the committal of your Railway Bill and on the distinguished support it seemed to meet with in the House,' a business colleague wrote to Robert R. The congratulations came too soon, for the Bill was lost in committee, the landowning dukes having ensured its demise. 'This devil of a railway is strangled at last,' the diarist Creevey jubilantly recorded, having denounced 'the loco-motive Monster . . . navigated by a tail of Smoke and Sulphur'.

He, also, spoke too soon; for after a new survey of the route, the Bill was reintroduced. Although the chief danger remained in the Lords—'What chance can we, a few Liverpool merchants, have against Lord Derby?' wailed John Moss—it passed both Houses, receiving royal assent in May 1826. As one of the largest canal owners Lord Stafford's purchase of 1,000 shares in the Liverpool and Manchester Railway Company was crucial to its early development and weakened the landed opposition, who started to receive large sums for selling the ownership of passage rights over their estates. Even before the railway was opened in 1829, an event marred by the death of Huskisson who was run over by the train, its directors, who included Robert R. and James Cropper, were exploring larger ventures to take the railway to Birmingham and into the heart of the canal zone.

The Liverpool–Manchester railway was a source of great profit to them. Two years after its opening, James Cropper noted that the weekly revenue from passengers was £3,600 and from goods £1,000: 'I think there is a probability that the gross earnings of the first three months of this quarter will be at least £52,000 & next I think will be £39,000.' He calculated that 'if the expenses are same as last half year say £35,000 it would leave £56,000 nett on a dividend of £7 per share'. Thus from this source alone, he and Robert R. would each receive an income of about £2,800 per annum [£113,000]. Understandably, much of their time was now taken up with railway development generally and Robert R., in particular, began to deal through his stockbrokers in all the new railway shares, including Continental ones such as Belgian Railways and the Paris and Rouen Railway Co.[25]

In the main, however, Cropper, Benson's trading interests continued to be devoted to the American trade and the East Indian sugar trade. The firm was considered the first among a small group of accepting houses in Liverpool. These houses, in common with their London counterparts, were merchant firms which specialized in the finance of trade. They operated either as principals, assuming all risks and receiving all profits from the purchase, shipment, and sale of goods on their 'own account' or joint account with other firms—as Cropper, Benson often did with Rathbones, or as agents, arranging the shipment, insurance, and sale of goods for a commission.

Cropper, Benson were not allowed to enjoy a pre-eminent position for long. Larger London houses already had their competitive claws open, ready to snatch the lucrative Liverpool trade by opening branches in that city. London accepting houses were able to charge lower commission rates on acceptances and possessed much larger capital bases. Barings' capital in 1833 was around £750,000, for example, and they charged 1½ per cent on an annual advance of £50,000 for outward consignments to India, with no expectations of receiving orders of produce in return. Cropper, Benson, in contrast, 'would accept against shipments going abroad . . . but they would expect an extension of consignments from India as an inducement'. No doubt Cropper, Benson, with a smaller capital base, did not wish to tie up too great a proportion of their funds, and thus profits, in their Indian business, but their uncharacteristic caution in not placing too many eggs in one basket proved detrimental to retaining a competitive edge.[26]

As it happened, the now middle-aged Robert R. was busily engaged in placing those eggs in a new basket. In 1833 the proponents of free trade had succeeded in ending the East India Company's monopoly of the China trade. In Liverpool, trade with China and Japan was seen as a bonanza, a vast untapped market which would solve the problem of surplus capacity in Lancashire mills. In partial partnership with Timothy Wiggin of the American firm T. Wiggin & Co., Cropper, Benson joined the Far Eastern bandwagon to ship out large cargoes of woollens and cottons to Canton using Jardine Matheson & Co. of Canton as their agents. The trade in textiles never lived up to expectations due to limited local purchasing power. Cropper, Benson's rivals, Gladstones, had also decided to enter the China trade. They found that the best profits were to be made on the triangular run of British goods exported to India, Indian cotton and opium shipped to China, where with the proceeds tea could be purchased in Canton for export to Liverpool. Gladstone, however, like some other merchants, refused to participate in the opium trade and, although the best profits were undoubtedly to be found in this area, Cropper, Benson were of like mind. They would have nothing to do with filling the export gap by transporting opium from India to China, a trade in which their agents, Jardine Matheson, were notably successful.

However, when public sales of tea were introduced into Liverpool in 1834, the market having previously been confined to London, Cropper, Benson began to import China tea. This was profitable from the start, the result of the first sale being 'most brilliant' according to Robert R. He promptly ordered tea of the following year's crop to the value of £12,000–15,000 from Jardines and went on to become their best customer for teas. He also imported silk, but trade with China proved as problematic as early trade with India had been. The Chinese Government did not welcome the sudden barrage of British trade, especially as it involved opium. Palmerston sent out Lord Napier to press for concessions but this only provoked a complete stoppage which, he told Lord Palmerston, could well bring 'the cities of London, Liverpool and Glasgow upon your Lordship's shoulders'. In the conflagrationary climate of the 1830s, years of civil disturbance, workmen's strikes, and demands for Parliamentary reform, such fears were an understatement. Another financial crisis in 1836/7 brought the collapse of T. Wiggin & Co. amongst others. Timothy Wiggin had acted as banker and creditor to Cropper, Benson, so it is unlikely they lost money, though his bankruptcy did disrupt their Far Eastern trade and served to emphasize the hazards of their involvement in it.[27]

Just prior to this, James Cropper had officially retired from the firm. For many years he had taken a back seat in its management, devoting his energies more to the campaign against slavery. He had made up parcels of sugar and coffee and sent them to every MP to show them that slave labour was not essential to their cultivation. Although extremely rich, the Croppers lived simply and the only signs of luxury in their households were used to further their beliefs or social campaigns. Thus the dinner service was specially commissioned, not for the beauty of its design but to remind the family of the evils of the slave trade: each piece depicted a slave in irons surrounded by the mottoes 'Alas my poor brothers' and 'Am I not a man and brother'.

The family believed in sharing their good fortune with their poorer brethren and became a major charitable force in Liverpool. When a begging letter was addressed to 'The most generous man in Liverpool, c/o the General Post Office', it was forwarded without hesitation to John Cropper at Dingle Bank. James had no hesitation in persuading both his sons, John and Edward, that their life work lay in philanthropy rather than in pursuing their careers as partners in Cropper, Benson. This they seemed inclined to accept. There were, however, the three other partners to consider.[28]

At 51 years of age, Robert R. was a successful merchant, the senior partner of one of the top houses in Liverpool, and possessed of a considerable personal fortune. Like James Cropper he was in a position to develop outside interests, but, unlike him, Robert R. had long been plagued by attacks of gout, which took an increasing toll on his health. After a particularly severe attack in the spring of 1836, his elder son was relieved to hear that 'thou was so much better as to have walked the length of the Dining Room on thy crutches—this is a great improvement, more than I had expected to hear of'.[29]

More and more lame, and disposed to pursue other interests, Robert R. was not averse to ending the Cropper, Benson partnership for himself; he would retire quite happily, but only in favour of his elder son, Robert jnr. In fact Robert R. had already transferred part of the Benson capital vested in Cropper, Benson to Robert jnr., perhaps in preparation for his son's entry into the business. Yet with a house the size of Cropper, Benson, it was no simple matter to continue their operations without the capital base of the three Croppers. Either Robert R. would have to inject an extremely large sum of capital or discontinue the wide scope of the business. Since David Hodgson was also in favour of retirement, only Hugh Mure would be left of the original partners to ease Robert jnr. into the firm.

Yet Robert jnr. felt that Hugh Mure could not be relied upon: 'I am not at all surprised to hear that Hugh Mure has behaved shabbily about the *Albion*' (he wanted a larger share of the profits on the vessel), he declared, 'he has not a bit of a Gentleman about him, but this is perhaps speaking rather too strongly.' Robert jnr. thought that Mure wanted 'to slip out of the concern himself', leaving it to the Croppers and Robert jnr. 'to wind it up as they can', when he would pick up the remaining business for himself. Thus, neither of the Bensons was sanguine about continuing a partnership with Mure.[30]

By July 1836, it had been decided to wind up Cropper, Benson. 'It is a great satisfaction to me that the business is so nearly ready to be announced as about to be closed,' Robert jnr. admitted to his father. He expected the initial announcement to be made quickly, yet a month later he found nothing changed. 'The Croppers seem rather dilatory in taking any steps for this purpose,' he complained to his father, 'and I think they ought rather to exert themselves to close the business as soon as they can, and put an end to this unsatisfactory suspense in which we are all kept', especially, he concluded, 'as it is in a great measure themselves who have broken up the connection.' With the impetuous outlook of youth, 22-year-old Robert jnr. expected such matters to be resolved much more quickly than was realistic. Cropper, Benson were still in business, owning thirty-two vessels, none of their clients had been informed, and they were still taking delivery of cargoes from Canton. 'There was a considerable stock of Tea in hand', for example, and Cropper, Benson vessels had continued to ply the seas to India.

Robert R.'s concern was not so much with the actual dismembering of Cropper, Benson, however, as with his son's prospects. He had offered Robert jnr. half his own share in the *Albion* so that they could maintain their shipping interests as a family partnership. Robert jnr. thought this a good idea 'as it will be a mode of investing a part of the money thou transferred to me in Cropper, Benson & Co.'s hands which will be thrown loose when the concern is wound up'. More particularly, as a budding merchant, Robert jnr. recognized that the price seemed low whilst the rate of freight from Bombay of £5 per ton was 'higher than vessels got when I left home'. Nevertheless, Robert R. did not consider shares in a fleet of vessels sufficient to assure his son's future; nor was it an adequate basis for a business. His anxiety grew.[31]

Part of his concern stemmed from feelings of unhappiness and uncertainty about his own future. At this very moment, Robert R. was embroiled in a religious controversy. The tidal wave of early Victorian evangelicalism sweeping through the established Anglican Church and the Methodists, also broke through the traditional quietism of the Quaker Movement, leaving chaos and disunity in its wake. Robert R. was a member of the evangelical wing of Quakerism, supporting Joseph Gurney's belief in placing a greater emphasis on the Scriptures than on the doctrine of the Inner Light—the traditional Quaker belief that God spoke directly to the heart of the believer in the silence of the meeting-house.

So when in 1835 his cousin Isaac Crewdson, a wealthy cotton and silk manufacturer, respected and loved in Manchester for his piety and philanthropy, published *A Beacon to the Society of Friends* attacking the traditional doctrine, Robert R. fully supported him. The book caused a furore. In the ensuing pamphleteer war, Robert R. himself published a collection of articles about Crewdson's book as well as *An Appeal to the Society of Friends* (1836), *Quakerism Examined* (n.d.) and *Correspondence between E. Bates and Others* (1836). Elisha Bates, a strongly evangelical American Quaker minister and close friend of the Benson family, was the prime mover behind the Beaconite campaign to introduce, against traditional Quaker doctrine, the rite of baptism into the Society.

'I have sent thy "Appeals" and 60 "Quakerism Examined" to Moores shop at the corner of Camomile Street and he has made a great pile of them in his window. I hope he will sell them all,' James Foster, a close London friend and fellow evangelical, informed Robert R. at the time of the Yearly Meeting. Their appearance brought matters to a head: 'I never beheld a Meeting in such a state,' wrote one observer. 'Very many were in tears on both sides of the meeting and it was really a most distressing sight.'[32]

In 1836 the resignation of Crewdson and fifty Manchester Quakers sparked off a chain of resignations throughout England. Robert R. was himself under investigation by the elders of the Liverpool meeting, who informed him on 25 October 1836 that 'for a considerable time past' they had 'felt painfully affected with some parts of thy conduct in reference to our Religious Society', notably his decision to publish 'a Work, which we must consider to be intended as an Attack on the principles of the Society'. Without waiting to be disowned by the meeting, Robert R. resigned along with his sister Margaret. The bitterness of the storm in the normally tranquil world of English Quakerism set Friend against Friend and divided families throughout the land.

For Robert R. and his fellow Quakers, resignation from the Society entailed far more than non-attendance at meetings. It was, in Abigail Dockray's words, 'a most painful separation' from a way of life and close-knit circle of family and friends which had influenced and contributed to every facet of their daily lives. A Benson kinsman described the effects in the case of his own father, Joseph Bevan:

> In after life he shrank intensely from any discussion of the Beacon controversy, and we do not wonder when we realise that to him it had involved the sundering of the close ties of religious fellowship with so many dearly loved relatives. Besides uncles, aunts and cousins by the score, three brothers and two sisters . . . had left the Society of Friends, and however much they might strive to prevent it, their paths in life were necessarily more and more widely separated as the years went on.

The Rathbones and the Croppers had also ceased to be Quakers but there remained many of the Bensons' nearest and dearest within the denomination; although the Bensons were no longer strict Quakers, and they enjoyed music and the company of friends and colleagues belonging to other denominations, they nevertheless had continued to observe many of the traditional practices. They still used the old form of 'thee' and 'thou', wore Quaker dress, and did not attend the theatre, even to see a play by Shakespeare, which they would have read with approval in the confines of home.

In business matters, Robert R.'s connections were nearly all derived from the rich merchant seam of Quakers. Cropper, Benson was itself a Quaker house. Even attendance at meetings, especially the Yearly Meeting in London, had provided welcome, informal opportunities to discuss matters of business and cement connections. Perhaps more importantly for Robert R.'s own career, Quakerism had fostered the pursuit of wealth within a steady, solid structure of religious encouragement. Moderate prosperity could progress into great wealth over generations, encouraged by the start in business and opportunity to borrow capital readily offered by fellow members of the Society. It was as if, at the age of 51, Robert R. had been thrown from the nest for the first time in his life.[33]

On 31 January 1838 the long-awaited official announcement of the disbandment of the firm of Cropper, Benson & Co. was published. The business that had enabled Robert R. to consolidate his fortune, providing him with a base of operations, no longer existed.[34]

So it was that a combination of circumstances—the difficult commercial climate, his resignation from the Society of Friends, and the dissolution of the partnership of Cropper, Benson & Co.—led Robert R. and his family to the decision to leave Liverpool. As with their forefather's decision to leave Stangend, it was not easily made. His sister, Margaret Benson, later recalled: 'I have thought much of our change of residence which is what neither of us would have chosen—how long we were before we could resign ourselves to it—and that we were absolutely driven from Liverpool by circumstances over which we had no control.'[35]

Where they should go taxed them severely in the following months. It was decided to maintain a residence in Liverpool, at Lodge Lane, as they wished to be able to return for family and business reasons. Isaac Crewdson and the Manchester Beaconites had decided to form a separate religious organization of their own based in Manchester. Given this and the proximity of the two cities, Robert R. decided to buy the property of Fairfield, then a few miles outside Manchester, and reside there. It seemed an ideal stepping-stone; he would be close to family and friends, could oversee remaining business interests in Liverpool, and worship with the evangelical Friends. In fact after he and his sister were baptized, they joined the great number of ex-Manchester Quakers who 'after wavering about amongst the various sects of Dissenters, finally settled down into sober members of the Evangelical Church of England'.[36]

As Robert R. settled back into a comfortable semi-retirement, the reins of the various Benson business interests were gathered in the hands of his capable elder son. Robert Benson jnr., born in 1814, was a sensitive, earnest young man who, like many an eldest child, had early on learnt to accept responsibility. He was older than his years and, in later life, appeared bowed down by the cares of the world pressing upon his shoulders. He was very close to his brother William who was two years younger, though they were unlike in temperament. William was the confident extrovert whereas Robert jnr. was one who kept his feelings to himself. A clever boy who liked to put matters right, he nevertheless possessed a wistful charm that concealed deep feelings and a need for affection.

Although born and brought up in Liverpool, he was often taken by his mother to stay in the country either with Dockray relations or at his parents' seaside house at Marine Bank, Linacre. He was a delicate little boy and sea-bathing was encouraged. 'We have had delightful weather,' his mother wrote on a June day in 1817, 'a number of large vessels have been passing and at this moment . . . Robert [then aged 3] is gone in a machine with his aunt Margaret, they were bathed yesterday for the first time and all behaved well, but Robt did not like it and . . . as he went out he was saying, "me not pop my head in, only mine little toes", poor fellow'. Despite the terrors of the then new-fangled bathing machine, Robert jnr. had a happy childhood, secure in the warmth and affection of a close-knit family circle.[37]

His mother's frequent travels in the Quaker ministry were sometimes considered excessively long by her family: 'We have now been absent from each other nine weeks and by the time thou proposes to come back it will be almost 3 months', complained her long-suffering husband. Mary's journeys were soon curtailed by a succession of miscarriages before the anxious birth of a long-awaited daughter, Esther Mary, in 1822. Two years later the family's apprehension proved well founded. On a hot summer's day in 1824, poor Mary died in childbirth. A baby son, John, did not long survive her. The bereft Benson children, 10-year-old Robert jnr., 8-year-old William, and 2-year-old Mary, were now mainly brought up by their indomitable grandmother Sally Benson and by Aunt Margaret Benson, their father's youngest and unmarried sister. She was a loving aunt, proud of her two nephews who continued to be educated at home: 'they have a master who comes every morning except Sabbath days for two hours to teach them and they are coming on very nicely. Will [aged 6] began latin grammar this week, with no little pride.'[38]

Within a few years Robert jnr. and William were ready to enter boarding-school and were sent to Grove House at Tottenham, the Quaker equivalent of Eton. Although far from home they were surrounded by many familiar faces, for the majority of their fellow pupils were either kinsmen or the sons of family friends. The Fosters, old family friends and owners of a well-known calico printing works, lived nearby at Bromley Hall in Bow and were happy to act *in loco parentis* to the Benson boys. Sarah Foster was a daughter of Sampson Lloyd, one of the four original partners in Taylors & Lloyds, the first banking firm started in Birmingham and the precursor of Lloyds Bank. The Lloyds had married into the Hanbury, Barclay, Hoare, and Freame families, so that through the Fosters young Robert jnr. had an early introduction and easy access to the world of Quaker bankers in London. Sarah's son-in-law James Foster, who came from the Lake District where his father was a friend of Southey and Wordsworth, was a partner in the stockbroking firm of Foster & Braithwaite, which looked after Benson investments over successive generations.

Since the education of a young gentleman in these pre-Victorian years was not considered complete without undertaking the 'grand tour', arrangements were made for Robert jnr. to set off for the Continent in the spring of 1836. His tour was not conceived solely for educational purposes; it was also a means of introducing him to Cropper, Benson's Continental correspondents and of enabling him to become acquainted with European merchant and banking houses which might prove useful to him in the future. In the interval between leaving Grove House and his travels, he had gained considerable commercial experience in the counting-house of Cropper, Benson in Paradise Street in Liverpool, so that many of the names were already familiar to him.

On his return to Liverpool he maintained his partnerships in various ships and remained active with Jardine Matheson in the China trade. His father, however, fretted that he must use his capital share from Cropper, Benson to invest in some other business. With the family now moving to Manchester, it seemed sensible to look for some concern there. As it so happened, William Worthington, the father of James Worthington, a Rathbone connection, wished to start his son Henry in business and was seeking a more experienced partner.

James Worthington was not only an old schoolfriend of Robert jnr.'s cousin William Rathbone VI, but he was also active in the China trade, where he had set up an agency with the Rathbones. The Rathbone house had experienced such severe setbacks in the American cotton trade that William Rathbone V contemplated leaving it altogether. In 1840 he gloomily noted that 'at present we are living from hand to mouth or rather mouth to hand for it is all going out and little coming in'. When Robert jnr.'s Rathbone cousins had suggested that their firm should switch its attention either to the China trade, as Cropper, Benson had done, or to the profitable cotton-spinning business, their father had vetoed both: 'To small capitals and commerce I fear the time is gone by.' Robert jnr., too, was in the position of having only a small capital to invest in any new venture. He had reckoned, however, without his father's determination that he must be settled in some concern as soon as possible—and what more suitable than the cotton business, so central to Manchester's prominence?[39]

The Worthingtons were prosperous Manchester cotton merchants and neighbours of the Bensons. The two retired fathers had plenty of time to mull over the future prospects of their respective sons. Old Mr Worthington wanted to purchase or build a cotton mill for 19-year-old Henry and was prepared to provide most of the capital. Old Mr Benson jumped at such an opportunity for his son, who in turn could contribute his greater mercantile experience and a share of the property at Fairfield. The two enthusiastic fathers spurred their sons on to form a partnership, Worthington, Benson & Co., in 1837 and to build themselves the Droylesden Mills, which commenced cotton weaving and spinning two years later.

Unfortunately, both sons proved reluctant bridegrooms, neither having much knowledge of the cotton producing business. Although in Manchester at that time the trend was increasingly for merchants rather than manufacturers to run such enterprises, it was nevertheless a challenging if not harrowing experience for these two young men. Robert jnr. was to describe it later as 'a very rash thing to get in . . . at first: and it is fortunate that we have not made more blunders than we have in the arrangement of our mill from ignorance of the trade'.[40]

In May 1840, Margaret Benson reported on the state of affairs at Fairfield to her brother, who, having settled his son at Manchester, was busy elsewhere in search of a suitable alternative residence for the rest of his family. Robert jnr. 'seems to take more hopeful views than he did about business . . . I cannot help hoping that things will do reasonably well in time', she wrote, adding that 'poor Robert has had an anxious and disappointing entrance into life'. It seemed unfair to her that he should have to struggle to establish himself when other members of their family, including her brother, had had much easier career paths to follow. Although Robert jnr. 'certainly seems prudent—particularly in his expenses—and to wish to set out moderately', she could not be blind to the pitfalls surrounding him in such an undertaking.[41]

One of the most obvious was his young partner's complete inexperience and commercial naïvety. Henry Worthington seems to have imagined that no effort was required to run a mill, as Aunt Margaret faithfully reported: 'I quite think that at first his notion was that it was only to put cotton in at one end of the machinery—and it would come out at the other trebled or quadrupled in value—after all expenses had been paid.' Fortunately he was ready to be guided by the more experienced Robert jnr.: 'I should be glad of your directions whether to look out for orders for Twist or Warp, I do not exactly know which pays us best, and whether both are sold at the same price,' is but one example of Worthington's reliance upon him.[42]

It was Robert jnr. who found the customers, arranged delivery, and supervised the bookkeeping. At Cropper, Benson, Robert jnr. had been an importer of American and East Indian cotton which was then sold via cotton brokers to the big spinning firms. As such he had not been concerned when supply was short, since it increased prices. Now he was on the other side of the process and, as a producer of cotton goods, a shortage of supply meant higher prices to be paid by Worthington & Benson. Most spinners seldom had more than a month's supply of cotton in stock, which they sold as yarn to the weaving or finishing manufacturing firms. Worthington & Benson combined both these functions at their mill. So once the yarn was processed into finished cloth, Robert jnr. either sold it through brokers or shipped it on his own account on consignment to India and the Far East in his part-owned ships. Although much more profitable, in those days of slow communication the latter was risky business for a mill-owner. It was safer to sell the cloth through a broker, ensuring a much quicker return on outlay.

Robert jnr. sold the yarn to people he knew of old, such as cousin Isaac Crewdson's brother-in-law William Boulton. 'I hear a good account of the quality of our yarn,' Worthington informed Robert jnr., 'W. Boulton told me that he had sent some of ours and some from another mill abroad, and that the party preferred ours. He gave me an order yesterday for 100 bundles of No. 20 for Lisbon.' While gratifying to receive such news, it was less so to learn that Boulton's business was failing. The Bensons had at least £1,000 tied up in it, not to mention other moneys outstanding from orders. This was a serious blow to a newly established business and Robert jnr.'s father constantly referred to the promised settlement of Boulton's debt to them personally. The only redeeming factor in the sorry affair was the relief felt that Robert jnr. had decided against entering into a proffered partnership with Boulton and his son, Jonathan.[43]

'I do hope dear Robert may shortly be relieved from the pressure of anxiety and discouragement which has been his position ever since he came of age,' Aunt Margaret wished for him in 1842, 'and if the concern should answer in proportion to his outlay of capital—and attention—he will not have to regret the experience the bad times alone could give him.' Robert jnr.'s outlay of capital was the £5,000 which his father had given him, together with his share of his mother's Dockray property. Part of this sum was used to modernize the mill and introduce a new patent throstle. Unfortunately, despite such advances in efficiency of output, hopes of increased profitability were dashed by the dismal economic climate. Trade had been poor generally since 1837, although railway construction had acted as a cushion for parts of the economy. In 1842 the cushion was removed as railway investment slackened, demand slumped as did manufacturing output, and cotton mills began to close in large numbers.[44]

Manchester, the 'cottonopolis' of Britain, immediately felt the effects as, with food prices high, hungry and half-clothed men and women roamed the streets around the cotton factories begging for bread. One soup kitchen had daily to dispense 1,000 gallons of soup to meet demand. Many working people turned from supporting Chartist political action to supporting direct economic action in the form of the 'Plug Strikes'. Cotton operatives raided mills that were still working, such as Worthington & Benson, and pulled out the boiler plugs, thereby enforcing closure. The unrest continued into the next year. 'I hope this unsettlement of your work people will end satisfactorily, either by such a change as will enable you to advance wages; or by their being convinced that it is not reasonable to expect it,' Robert R. wrote from London in November 1843 to his son. He was somewhat tetchy at not having received up-to-date accounts, 'I have no idea how your concern is doing now,' adding, 'from all I hear that it is doing more than pay the change.'[45]

With profits spiralling downwards in the cotton industry, Robert jnr. took on a new 'foreign' venture when he joined his Rathbone cousins to become Liverpool agents for the East India Company. This generated a regular business paid on commission and, more importantly for Robert jnr., it enabled him to remain active in the Indian and China trades. As agent, he supervised the shipping of produce to the Far East and dealt with produce pledged to the Company as security for advances. As an erstwhile merchant he also joined the Rathbones in buying cargoes to fill empty ships and continued the importation of tea and Indian cotton. Thus in many ways, although officially appearing as a smartly turned-out Manchester mill-owner, Robert jnr. unofficially had reverted to wearing his old, well-worn, mercantile cloak.

In this latter capacity he continued the Benson connections with railway development and investment—his real business love. Following on from the first boom in the 1830s, the promoters were now preparing for the second. Robert jnr. took his father's place on the Board of the old Liverpool Manchester Railway Company, which had become the London & North Western Railway

Co. (LNWR); he was soon actively involved in the great issue of whether it should unite with the Grand Junction Railway, of which he was also a director. Such an amalgamation would unite the cotton capital and a great port with the coal-, iron-, and metal-producing areas of the Midlands. The amalgamation went through and in 1846 the Grand Junction became part of the London & North Western Railway Co. By 1845 the climate for railway development had become highly dangerous. The increased number of railway bills before Parliament resulted in political fights over trunk-lines, routes, and amalgamations taking on a fiercer, more cut-throat aspect.

While Robert jnr. was involved in promoting the LNWR Amalgamation Bill, he was also increasing the Benson shareholdings in other railway companies through Foster & Braithwaite. His cousin, young Isaac Braithwaite, had married Louisa Masterman at a time when the Bensons had hopes of an attachment between Robert jnr. and her sister Charlotte; their father John Masterman was a partner in the City house of Masterman, Peters, Mildred, Masterman & Co. This firm was much concerned with railway finance and backed many of the lines in which the Bensons invested, such as the Paris–Rouen–Le Havre line, the London–Southampton line, the Birmingham–Gloucester line, and the Paris–Lyons line. The Bensons now put ever more of their investment portfolio into railways. With new authorized mileage rising from 91 in 1843 to 811 in 1844, and to a staggering 2,883 in 1845, it was a time of great opportunity but, equally, of great risk. The era of 'railway mania' had begun.[46]

'Projectors mapped out undertakings, engineers patronised them, the schemes were advertised and applications inundated the committees.' Hundreds of people subscribed for shares without the means to meet the calls for cash. For the first time stags appeared in large numbers in the market. No deposit was required with share applications, so 'stagging' was easy, costless, and potentially extremely profitable. However, the combination of two events—the doubling of the deposit required from promoters of future railway bills, from 5 per cent to 10 per cent of the proposed capital, and the rise in Bank Rate from 2½ per cent to 3 per cent—produced a setback followed by panic in the market.[47]

Robert jnr. was not a gambler but a long-term investor in railways. He believed in their future profitability and so held on to his railway portfolio to ride out the storm. It was also a relic of his Quaker upbringing that, along with his Rathbone cousins, he could still feel 'well paid if, after working all our waking hours as hard as we could, and knocking about the world, we added £500 a year to the firm's profits'; rather than playing the stock-markets so that 'without any work beyond writing a letter [to sell the shares]' he could pocket £500. Yet the increasingly 'profitable and exciting business' of applying for new shares would prove to be one in which Robert jnr. would become even more involved.[48]

As the boom and panic of 1845 subsided, it became clear that the immediate effects were not wholly destructive. Although many stockbroking firms failed, others such as Foster & Braithwaite recorded a growing income. In addition, the framework of the railway system of Victorian Britain was laid. The promoters and contractors continued to expand the lines and the effect of this railway building was to create a large permanent market in the fixed-interest securities of the major railways such as LNWR, independent of government credit yet virtually as safe as Consols. For the first time the investor seeking safety could find a home for his money in private enterprise. The Bensons' decision to wait until the storm passed, to meet their calls in cash, and hold their stock proved right. From then on, Robert jnr. increased his participation in the railway industry with growing confidence. He had already admitted to his father, 'I have had so many things to think about in Railway matters, that I have not been able to give my attention to anything else'. He was forced to do so, however, by renewed turbulence in the economic climate.[49]

The speculative mania in railways had encompassed other company promotions, as well as trade to India and China. This was accompanied by a potato famine in Ireland, a bad harvest in Britain and a shortage in the American cotton crop, which caused a 75 per cent price rise in 1846. Money was dear, and British purchasers of American cotton were unable to buy at the higher price. Many cotton mills closed, others went on to short-time. The crisis years of the hungry 1840s 'came on afresh with increased severity, and a great many of the old merchant houses and mill-owners came to the ground'. Robert jnr. warned his father, 'I am afraid that the great fall which has taken place in cotton will affect some of our Friends' and 'I fear the Rathbones will not altogether escape some loss', since other Friends were losing £3 a bale of cotton.[50]

Robert jnr. decided, accordingly, that 'it would be well to take every opportunity of reducing' their stake in the business. His heart had never been in cotton mill-owning and ideally he would have liked to get out of it as soon as possible, but only 'if it could be accomplished without loss'. He did not see the point 'of running the risks of business, and incurring the annoyance attended upon the employment of so many operators, merely for the sake of giving [him]self employment if there be no prospect of remuneration'. As he pointed out to his worried father, 'This has been the case ever since I commenced business. And although the times are altered, yet I cannot think that the Cotton Trade can ultimately be looked upon as surer than an investment of capital paying interest of money.' It was certainly a precarious way of earning a living; the cotton trade oscillated between surging prosperity and alarming recession.

Robert jnr. believed he possessed an instinctive understanding of railways and finance that he lacked in cotton. He had never been a 'cotton man' and his years of mill ownership were ones when Manchester merchants and manufacturers were not often free from the fear of commercial collapse lurking behind each temporary revival of trade.[51]

Thus Robert jnr. was being realistic rather than pessimistic about remaining in such a business. He did not, however, expect to be able to extricate himself easily from it. His father remained adamant that the wisest course was to renew the partnership agreement when it expired in 1847. In those days a son did not oppose his father's wishes without forfeiting his support and damaging family, let alone business, relationships. It must have seemed to Robert jnr. that at the age of 32 he was condemned to remain a cotton-spinner for the rest of his life.

Then, in June 1846, the unforeseen occurred. His father died of heart failure after a particularly severe attack of gout. And although Robert jnr. lost a devoted and astute parent and partner, he gained freedom of manœuvre. In his will Robert R. had left a capital sum of between £65,000 [£2.7m.] and £80,000 [£3.6m.]. In Quaker fashion he had divided this considerable fortune equally between his three surviving children. He also showed himself to be a benevolent, understanding parent. In life he may have insisted that Robert jnr. continue in the cotton trade; in death he had instructed his trustees, Margaret Benson, William Rathbone, and John Cropper, to retain the sum of £20,000 for five years after his death specifically to make good any losses in his son's cotton business. This clause enabled Robert jnr. to proceed to extricate himself from Worthington & Benson without diminishing his capital. He had nursed the old Benson interests in Liverpool and now started to discuss forming a partnership there with his father's former partner David Hodgson.[52]

Thus, in possession of capital substantially enlarged by his inheritance and successful investments, he was able to follow his own wishes and complete the journey that the Bensons had started all those years ago when they moved from Stangend. His grandfather had travelled from there to Liverpool; and he, having moved one Benson business to Manchester and retained another smaller one in Liverpool, now migrated to the City of London where, in June 1852, he started the firm of Robert Benson & Co.

3 Alexander F. Kleinwort and the Cuban Connection

ALEXANDER FRIEDRICH KLEINWORT, Hinrich's fourth son, was a year younger than Robert Benson jnr. and, like him, would leave the family home in pursuit of better career opportunities elsewhere. He was born at Gerdeshagen in Mecklenburg at the dawn of peace in that momentous year of 1815, during which Napoleon's second reign, the Hundred Days, had been brought to an end at Waterloo. Alexander was not a Kleinwort name; yet it was a reflection of the times that he should be named after his godfather, Alexander Petit, who had fled France during the Terror which preceded the rise of Napoleon. Petit had joined the swelling ranks of French *émigrés* who had settled in Hamburg and Altona and had established himself as a jeweller. As a Catholic, he had had to obtain the permission of the Danish king before marrying into the staunchly Lutheran Kleinwort family.

The influx of French *émigrés* had done much to make the German bourgeoisie more aware of the finer aspects of life; French clothes, *objets d'art*, and furniture were considered the ultimate in good taste. So it may well have been through Uncle Petit's influence that Alexander Friedrich developed that appreciation of fine clothes which would give him a reputation as a young dandy with a penchant for exotic waistcoats; his marked partiality for yellow trousers led him to be dubbed 'El Canario' in later life.[1]

Alexander Friedrich was 5 years old when Gerdeshagen was sold and 9 when the family returned to Altona. Thus from an early age he was part of the large cousinhood centred upon the Rosenhof. As Hinrich and Wilhelmina's fifth child he also had no lack of companionship at home, with four sisters and three brothers as well as two half-brothers and three half-sisters from his father's first marriage. In later life Alexander Friedrich was seen as a solitary figure without any close family ties, a man who might almost be thought to have turned his back on his family. His children and grandchildren grew up with little idea of their large cousinhood; it was not until his eldest daughter was 20 years old that she even met her Kleinwort relations in Germany. This was despite Alexander Friedrich's large and close family circle, many of whom were also to become partners in his early business activities. In particular he relied upon his eldest half-brother Siegmund, a figure of some importance in the family.

Siegmund was twenty years older than Alexander Friedrich and, as the eldest, was the only brother to attend university, first in the nearby Baltic port of Rostock, then in Heidelberg where he read law, a subject reserved for the best students. This provides an indication of Hinrich's financial position since only a man of considerable means could afford to let his son study law; poorer boys usually had to be content with theology. Siegmund's graduation in 1817 as a jurist automatically placed him amongst the élite of Hamburg and he specialized in commercial and company law, co-founding the *Archive of Commercial Law* and publishing at least seven tracts on issues of legal importance in addition to holding various official positions.[2]

After their father's death, Siegmund assumed the role of head of the family and, being so much older than Alexander Friedrich and his brothers, his position was not disputed. Alexander Friedrich, however, was not above issuing rather peremptory orders to him and registering strong differences of opinion. In fact there seems to have been a streak of resentment underlying his relations with Siegmund, especially after he left home.

Although the Kleinworts were wealthy, Hinrich's estate had to be divided equally amongst his twelve surviving children, after provision had been made for his widow. There was therefore every reason for Hinrich's sons to be placed in apprenticeships in the hope they could augment their relatively small inheritance. And since the family were, above all, men of commerce, be it as brewers or merchants, it was only appropriate that Alexander Friedrich and his brothers should follow the same course. Siegmund, however, as the eldest son, was given the indubitable advantage of a university education, denied to the younger sons and most of their cousins. His position in Hamburg was therefore assured, whereas Alexander Friedrich had to work for one.

Moreover, adding to the potential acrimony, the younger brother's expectations were higher because of his mother's pedigree and connections, which ordinarily would have ensured him an equal if not better social position than Siegmund. Alexander Friedrich's friends were all from the higher echelons of Hamburg society and he shared the outlook of these rich, self-assured young men. What he did not share were their financial resources. This was undoubtedly a bone of contention between him and Siegmund especially as Alexander Friedrich was clearly ambitious from an early age.

Of the other brothers, his half-brother Hinrich is an unknown quantity; his elder brother Hermann became captain and then owner of a ship and was based in Stettin; Adolf, the nearest in age, died aged 6. Thereafter Alexander Friedrich was closest to his youngest brother Gustav, who followed in his mercantile footsteps, undergoing an apprenticeship in the grocery business of a family friend Herr Warnecke, before travelling to America in search of experience and fortune.[3]

It was also through his father's commercial contacts but with the vital financial support of Siegmund that, at the age of 16, Alexander Friedrich was apprenticed to the firm of Anderson & Höber. After his father's death in 1831, Alexander Friedrich looked upon Herr Höber as a substitute paternal figure; it was in the first instance from him, rather than Siegmund, that he sought advice about his career prospects and plans. The well-established, prosperous merchant house that young Alexander Friedrich joined was then engaged in financing the import of colonial goods such as sugar, coffee, and cigars and the export of grain and other German goods—very much the same line ofbusiness as Hinrich had followed. Anderson & Höber was a leading house in the English trade, using Baring Brothers in London and their partners Hope & Co. in Amsterdam as correspondents.

It was an opportune moment to train as a merchant. When Alexander Friedrich first joined Anderson & Höber, the transport of goods was a costly, slow undertaking with, for example, fourteen tolls to be paid on freight being sent along the Elbe from Hamburg to Magdeburg, about 100 miles away, and sixty-three custom frontiers existing between Hamburg and Berlin. He had to learn the extraordinary multiplicity of currencies, weights and measures, and toll charges which formed part of every merchant's commercial language. Whilst the sweeping away of these barriers and tariffs in 1834 rendered such learning obsolete, it dramatically increased trade and prosperity, Hamburg becoming redolent of commerce, and thereby widened the opportunities for Alexander Friedrich to further his career.

He lodged with Siegmund after his mother had gone to live near her married sister in the more northern town of Bützow. She was ambitious for her sons and exerted a certain amount of pressure upon them. 'It seems that no one of our family is getting anywhere,' she observed to Alexander Friedrich on 13 April 1834, 'and were your father still alive he would be disappointed seeing none of his sons fulfilling his expectations.' Although she absolved him from this charge on account of his youth, she continued to remind him of the importance of his apprenticeship and ask about his prospects. Mr Anderson had promised his father that after four years' apprenticeship and if he 'fulfils the hopes put in him', he might be made a commis (a junior clerk). Wilhelmina Kleinwort had no need to worry about her third son for at Easter 1835 he was given his first position as a clerk in the storage and warehouse department. Determined to succeed and rise from this lowly station, he put some of his small capital towards English lessons and laboured to perfect a clear writing hand; both attributes then considered essential for promotion. The latter was an exercise which continued to tax him since, as he admitted to Herr Höber in 1838, 'you know that my handwriting is my weak point'.[4]

Weak it might be, but it did little to lessen his prospects or quench his ambition. Despite Herr Höber's sustained interest in him, Alexander Friedrich knew that with others before him, including Herr Höber's son Adolph, there was little hope of advancement to a partnership in Anderson & Höber. He had no desire to work for others. The Kleinwort tradition was very much centred in proprietorship and the von Hövells countenanced little else. Alexander Friedrich was no exception. He wanted his own business and to assume what he considered to be his rightful position in the world. Everything else in his life was to be sacrificed to this goal—but he needed capital to achieve it.

In the 1830s, according to received opinion, the easiest way to obtain this was to work abroad in the Americas. Unsolicited emigration to the United States had gathered pace in Germany early in the decade, stimulated by an outbreak of cholera, rising prices, revolutions abroad, and disturbances at home, including incidents of anti-Semitism in the usually tolerant Hamburg. The newly independent Brazil had solicited between 7,000 and 10,000 German immigrants by 1830, while the increase in trade between Hamburg and Bremen and the Argentine, the West Indies, and Cuba had created a demand for German-speaking young men.

America was undoubtedly their favoured destination, owing largely to the tremendous influence of Gottfried Duden's *Report on a Journey to the Western States of America*, which found American political, social, economic, and moral conditions better than those of Germany. It created a wave of enthusiasm for America among young, educated Germans, and Alexander Friedrich's circle of friends was no exception. After seven years at Anderson & Höber and armed with letters of recommendation, Alexander Friedrich planned to join some of them in New York. Then he suddenly changed his mind. Two of his closest friends were already working there: Ferdinand Karck had a position with Schmidt & Co. while Ludwig von Bonnighausen was there with Henry Hildgard & Co., before going on to their offices in Rio de Janeiro. So Alexander Friedrich had a clear idea of vacancies from them and, while the fashion continued, there was a glut of Germans seeking positions in New York. More importantly, Anderson & Höber were amply served there both with correspondents and agents to fill their orders. They would not require his services as well. Luckily, this was not the case elsewhere in the southern hemisphere. Alexander Friedrich therefore began to consider other possibilities and, after some serious calculations, he decided to try his luck in the Spanish colony of Cuba.[5]

Two other great friends, Cesar and Adolph Godeffroy, had gone out to Havana in the previous year, 1837. Originally Huguenots, the Godeffroys were a leading Hamburg family, successfully combining commerce with culture. They were shipowners and founded the famous Hamburg–Amerika line as well as the Museum Godeffroy, which also sponsored scientific research in the South Seas. They later planted the German flag in Samoa and Papua New Guinea, where they acted as German consuls and started German colonies. The family business J. C. Godeffroy & Söhne traded first with Spain and then with Central and South American ports. In Havana, Cesar and Adolph imported linen from Silesia and sent sugar and coffee home on their own ships. Alexander Friedrich learnt that merchants in Havana paid high salaries, four to six times higher than in Hamburg. He reckoned that, if he could obtain a position in an office in Havana, he could then start to build up his capital by trading on his own account. He could use the Godeffroy ships to supply Anderson & Höber with goods since, although they had correspondents there, they had no agent. And, he calculated, there was also the prospect of using his friends in New York to form a trading network between Havana, New York, and Hamburg.[6]

Although he may have set his sights higher than most, Alexander Friedrich and his friends were by no means the first ambitious young Germans to seek work in Cuba. Hamburg had strong trading links with Havana, and in 1837–8, for example, sixteen German ships carried goods between Hamburg and Havana. There was also a demand in Cuba for textiles and finished luxury goods, many of which were supplied by Germany. Alexander Friedrich saw great opportunities in Cuba but, with the arrogance of youth, he failed to recognize that many others had similar optimistic visions.

When on 15 June 1838, at the age of 23, he disembarked at Havana from the newly built Godeffroy barque, the *Adolph*, he suffered his first setback. He was met by one of the Godeffroys with the news that there was no vacancy in their office, nor anywhere else in Havana. After enduring a 54-day voyage in the normal discomfort of the times, only to have his prospects immediately dashed, he experienced not surprisingly 'a disagreeable and oppressive sensation' and, as he admitted, 'an attack of despondency trickled for the first time through my limbs'.[7]

An old schoolfriend came to the rescue with the information that there was a vacancy for a copy clerk in his office at H. Rottmann & Co., a small import/export house. Alexander Friedrich must have sailed through the subsequent interview with Herr Rottmann for, as he told Herr Höber, 'after a few moments we came to an agreement. I receive free board and lodgings and a monthly salary of three ounces or *Rt.*178 in our money. You can imagine how happy I was having found such a good position in such a short time.'[8]

His euphoria quickly evaporated. The work 'was not exactly interesting' being composed of interminable copying of invoices and bills and of making duplicates of correspondence. He felt it to be beneath him, and the fact that 'every foreigner arriving here has to start by doing this type of work' did little to ease his irritation. Nor were matters improved by the onset of fever, the bane of most new arrivals' lives; luckily the cure, bloodletting, was successful. Alexander Friedrich intended to avoid further attacks by strict adherence to a regime of bathing twice a week in warm water; an hour's walk at 5 a.m. before the office and one in the evening after office hours; and by abstinence from all wines, spirits, and women. His mother was relieved to read of his unfavourable opinion of local women, joking that she was glad she need not expect him to bring home 'a black beauty' for a daughter-in-law. The self-imposed severity of his way of life was nothing new; in fact he counted himself lucky that he 'had not been used to seeking pleasure in amusements'.

His asceticism was in great contrast to the behaviour of friends such as the Godeffroys; 'the business and private life of both gentlemen is wild', he reported to Herr Höber. Alexander Friedrich might think Havana an 'uneventful, provincial' place where 'every young man who lived merrily in Europe must be unhappy', but others found plenty to amuse and distract them. Above all there was the Tacon opera house, a spacious, well-designed building, easily on a par with Covent Garden both in terms of size and quality of productions. Grisi, Nilsson, and Adelina Patti were among the top artists who regularly appeared there. Boxes were taken by Havana society resplendent in full evening dress festooned with diamonds and 'emeralds the size of small eggs', according to Madame Calderon de la Barca, who noticed that 'even the men were well sprinkled with diamonds and rubies'. Other entertainments included balls and carnivals, receptions for visiting dignitaries, the cockpit and the bullfight, as well as innumerable concerts and theatrical performances. Cuban society was renowned for its gaiety and culture.[9]

Yet Alexander Friedrich avoided all these attractions which, contrary to his stated opinion, were easily comparable with those staged in Europe. As a lowly copying clerk he could not afford such pleasures; nor was he part of the society, including expatriate circles, which frequented them. His resentment at this state of affairs boiled over in a letter to the one brother who would never have found himself in this situation. Siegmund had commented on Alexander Friedrich's dull Cuban life. 'I am very sorry that my letters are not of interest to you,' Alexander Friedrich tartly replied, 'It is true that I have now been practically a year in Havana, but under what conditions. What can I hear of such things as a merchant's clerk in a foreign House? I am not on visiting terms with any educated Spaniards,' adding 'which in any case would not suit me for pecuniary reasons.' As his first year in Cuba drew to a close, Alexander Friedrich was becoming increasingly bitter and depressed. 'My position leaves much to be desired and often puts me in low spirits for weeks,' he confessed, 'my work is repugnant to me and nearly every day I am tempted to throw the whole thing over.' Lonely, poor, and despondent, only one thought kept him from doing so: the desire to become his own master.[10]

Almost from the moment he had settled into the Rottmann counting-house, Alexander Friedrich had single-mindedly set about trading on his own account as part of his strategy to build up capital. In the nineteenth century it was quite acceptable for even the lowliest of clerks in a counting-house to trade for himself under his employer's auspices; such activities brought experience and contacts, not to mention a share in the commissions earned, all of which benefited everyone involved. This would certainly prove to be the case where Alexander Friedrich was concerned, though his first Havana employer might not have accepted his trading activities with such equanimity if he had been aware of the finer details of the operation.

'Wherever I see that I can do something even if it brings me only a small profit, I do not fear any effort or privation to do it,' Alexander Friedrich declared. This would be the guiding principle behind the future accepting house of Kleinwort, Sons & Co. Nor did its founder spare any effort in his early days as a trader in Havana; no deal was considered unworthy of attention, he dealt in anything he could. In effect, the Kleinwort bank was founded on the proceeds of gun-running, shirt and currency smuggling, and cigars.[11]

In partnership with Adolph Höber, the son of his former patron, Alexander Friedrich opened his own trading account with the sale of a dozen red-ribboned purses at $2 each and a dozen condoms also priced at $2 apiece. After his first trade in the latter commodity, he refers to them more guardedly as 'socks' which indeed they resembled, being made of a linen-type textile; the rubber model was not invented until the close of the century. More profitable was the illegal import of guns. In his first letter home Alexander Friedrich had written of his intention 'to sell the shotguns very soon with good profit', openly admitting that he had 'managed to smuggle them into the country by sacrificing a little sum' of $1 in bribes. By September he was able to inform Adolph that he had disposed of one of them for $7.50 and another for $6.50, both excellent prices since 'you cannot count on prices of between $6–7 but you can expect $5–6'. By smuggling them in he had avoided the customs duty of $4. Although pleased that this 'small trial run' had been so successful, he was quick to remind his partner that it had not been achieved without considerable effort on his part 'all the time'. He left nothing to chance and on his only free day he had 'carefully cleaned and oiled the shotguns every single Sunday' in order to obtain the best prices.[12]

The import of fine linen shirts proved even more demanding of his time and energy. He had issued Adolph with precise instructions. The shirts were to be tailored in the latest design out of the finest Bielefeld linen, at a total cost of 90–120 pieces per dozen depending on style, which would yield a minimum 10–20 per cent profit. To avoid the exorbitant customs duty of 30 per cent they were not to appear on the official freight list for, if they did, then Alexander Friedrich would have to bribe the customs officers and they could not be bought off cheaply. When Ferdinand Karck sent him a consignment of pens which by mistake were listed officially, Alexander Friedrich had to pay a bribe of 1 oz. of silver, a third of his annual salary, before he could unload it without paying duty.

So it was imperative that the shirts be sent gradually and surreptitiously with a 'safe' captain, 'a captain you know and whom you promise a decent return under hand'. Alexander Friedrich even supplied the names of such men and their ships, adding 'I know all these masters and they will oblige if you ask them politely—you just have to tell them that I myself will get the goods ashore.' This was the most time-consuming part of the operation. He had to board the ship every evening, remove his coat and shirt, slip on some of the new shirts (he could not wear more than three at a time), replace his own shirt and coat over them, and saunter as nonchalantly as possible down the gangplank to the safety of his lodgings at Herr Rottmann's.

Although he had breezily assured Adolph that there was no danger, the exercise was extremely risky since he had to run the gauntlet of the customs officers, determined to augment their meagre salaries either by collecting the duty plus a little extra for their own pockets from the merchants or by extracting a hefty payment for not doing so from them. There was also the danger to Adolph of incurring Alexander Friedrich's wrath: 'I restrict myself today to making a few remarks which will prove not to be very agreeable to you,' Alexander Friedrich wrote. Adolph had ignored his instructions to purchase the linen and have the shirts made up himself; he had sent out shirts which had obviously been bought from shops; they still bore the shops' labels and, accordingly, were much too expensive.

Alexander Friedrich was furious to discover the first mate on one of his 'safe' ships doing a lucrative trade in shirts of the same quality, selling his for \$3–3½ as opposed to Adolph's \$3–7¼. 'It may be that by sheer luck I can flog them to a stupid person but one cannot be certain and you have to brace yourself for making a loss,' he fumed.

You can imagine how highly embarrassing the whole thing is for me, in the sweat of my brow I smuggle the rubbish on land, I have to [tip] the Captain if I meet him, I have endless difficulties and finally I have to send you an invoice for a sale which made a loss while friends laugh up their sleeve and make 30 to 40% with the same merchandise.

To ensure he was never placed in a similar situation again, Alexander Friedrich took command of any future operation; from this disaster he had learnt not to rely upon others and to organize the fieldwork himself. It was imperative to watch the margins: 'Every schilling which you save me on costs is a rung on the ladder which I climb from nothing to something,' he told Adolph. A month later he instructed Adolph to order three grades of shirts from Bielefeld, but only after discussing cheaper prices with Herr Schnelle, who would direct him about what was a good price.[13]

Alexander Friedrich knew of Schnelle through a new Havana friend, Herr Upmann. They had met through the Godeffroys and at the German Club, when Alexander Friedrich was taken there by richer German friends. Herr Upmann was one of the few European cigar manufacturers in Cuba—he owned the Woodville factory—and a distributor. He came to play an important part in Alexander Friedrich's mercantile career and it was mainly through their joint ventures, in conjunction with his partnership with the Karck brothers, that Alexander Friedrich increased his capital base to the extent of being in a position to form the first Kleinwort banking partnership in London.

Alexander Friedrich was no stranger to the cigar trade. Germans were tremendous smokers and Altona had long been a centre for the traditional craft of cigar-making. In Cuba, a veritable paradise for smokers, even beggars smoked cigars while asking for charity, and theatrical performances were notoriously long in order to allow the audience time to smoke a cigar during each interval. Although sugar was by far the most important cog in the Cuban economic wheel in the late 1830s, tobacco was increasing its market share as demand for cigars and cigarettes grew to the extent of 100 million cigars being imported into Britain alone. The mature tobacco was kept for shipment to Britain in the autumn, leaving the younger tobacco for summer shipment to Germany—the destination of the first Kleinwort cigar trade.[14]

Alexander Friedrich's first consignment of 6,000 Dos Amigos cigars was dispatched to Siegmund on 10 August 1838. He sent three grades, priced to include the currency, freight, town-duty, and 'petty' costs: Regalias at 95 *Pfennig*, Primera at 53 *Pf.*, and Segundo at 30 *Pf.* and 43 *Pf.* Alexander Friedrich suggested that Siegmund ask 120 *Pf.*, 70 *Pf.*, and 60 *Pf.* respectively from his enclosed list of buyers. It was important to purchase the right type of cigars for the market and, as usual, Alexander Friedrich had done his homework thoroughly. He had visited the Hernandez factory, to which Upmann had introduced him in the early morning because later the light became too strong to see the colours of the cigars, and chosen only the light brown / yellow preferred by the Hamburg market over the brown.

From this relatively small beginning Alexander Friedrich's cigar-trading business quickly grew to an average 30,000–40,000 per consignment. He used the Hamburg network of brothers Siegmund and Gustav, cousin Louis Kleinwort, and the Höbers in Hamburg and Ferdinand Karck in New York. Competition for merchandise was fierce but, through Upmann, Alexander Friedrich built up a strong relationship with the manufacturer Domingo Hernandez. Even when Hernandez was overwhelmed with orders, Alexander Friedrich managed to obtain his full half-Primero and half-Segundo quota. Although competition was greater in the American market, Alexander Friedrich's venture with Ferdinand in New York was the most profitable. He generally sent over a minimum order of 40,000 cigars and made nearly 40 per cent on the Regalias and 20 per cent on the Primero and Segundo. Sales there might be slower and more difficult than in Hamburg but, he thought, 'for such profits it is always worth the effort'.[15]

Part of this effort was to ensure that no contact who could be put to use slipped through the Kleinwort mercantile net. As soon as he heard from Ferdinand of their friend Mohring's arrival in Boston he wrote, 'I wanted to drop you a line immediately in order to suggest to you a business trial with me'. The strategy of Alexander Friedrich's trading business is made clear in this letter. He invested his own funds in cigars because he could purchase them, receive them, and arrange their shipment and insurance himself, all in the early hours of the day. Their compact size and lower cargo value were an advantage. Bulkier merchandise would have made dealings too drawn-out for a clerk with limited funds and time. Anyway, as a mere clerk, he could not clear goods through customs; only a long-established merchant could do so. Thus, on all other commodities, Alexander Friedrich had to reimburse Herr Rottmann with half of his earned commission both for the purchase and the sale of goods. Cigars were therefore far easier and more lucrative for him to send to Mohring in Boston, and so he suggested them as the basis for a business in which they would each take a half share of the profits.[16]

Capital, however, remained a problem and, with the increase in cigar transactions, Alexander Friedrich needed a credit facility. It was here that his close friendship with the Karck family proved helpful. Ferdinand had proposed a *contra tercia* deal in cigars to his brother Theodor in Hamburg. To participate, however, Alexander Friedrich would need a loan and it was understood that Theodor would obtain one for him in London where terms were better. Alexander Friedrich felt that an ordinary loan based on the usual conditions of insurance and bill of lading documents would be of little help; what he required was a more flexible credit. 'You know me well enough to be convinced that you would not be taking a risk with regard to me,' he assured Theodor, adding 'if I had more funds, I would not need to make conditions, but if I buy and cannot ship immediately and get the bill of lading signed, I can easily get into difficulties'. It was a problem universally shared by those seeking to make the leap from a small to a larger business, or from 'nothing to something', and the Karcks proved invaluable in solving it for Alexander Friedrich.

Having obtained the credit for him, the plan was to continue with cigars—the safest business in Alexander Friedrich's opinion—and speculate in sugar if prices fell. In the meantime, in exchange for cigars, Alexander Friedrich imported gin from Hamburg, which he sold for 50 per cent profit, and from New York steel pens and small silver coins, which were 'actually contraband which brought us 10 per cent'. Thus, gradually, and by exercising 'thrift, the strictest thrift'—for instance when postage rates were increased he instructed the Hamburg network to hide letters to him in newspapers in order to avoid incurring any charge—he began to climb that ladder from nothing to something. He was making a profit of $83–9 on each cigar trade and on 11 September 1839, just over a year since his arrival, he told Ferdinand that he had managed to save $680 (then £128 [£5,324]).[17]

The improvement in his finances was not echoed by that in his prospects of promotion at Rottmann & Co. As he confided to Herr Höber, 'I cannot help feeling bitter when I see how other young people not as able as myself, favoured by chance, find correspondence and accountancy positions while I with my 25 years have to *copy* sales invoices and bills.' Despite sharing his dreams of getting rich, very few of these young Germans were prepared to live like him in order to save money. Accustomed to Hamburg coffee-house life, they spent their salary as quickly as they received it. 'They are losing their times [*sic*] and health and by the gentlemen-like living they have here get unfit for any European counting-house as well as for any dependent situation in the old world,' he wrote to Ferdinand in June 1839. 'You have no idea of it how these fools are puffing themselves up.' He had no time for most of them and it seemed unfair that they squandered their good fortune while he scrabbled away desperate to find some. He had given up the idea of becoming rich in Cuba because he wanted to return to Europe as a young man. He had decided to be content with making a few thousand dollars. However it was all too clear now that if he was to have a chance of saving even this amount, he must find a better position and he could only do this in a different office.[18]

No sooner had he come to this conclusion than he was offered a position at Drake Brothers & Co. as a copyist in charge of European correspondence in

English and French with a promise of promotion at the first opportunity. Although the work and salary were the same as at Rottmanns, the prospects were far brighter. Drakes was one of the largest and most important merchant houses in Cuba. According to a Barings credit report, the firm was regarded as first-class and enjoyed the best credit. Commensurate with its size was a greater turnover of staff, so Alexander Friedrich reckoned that the promise of promotion was not an idle one. Ever with an eye to the future, he reasoned: 'They have the biggest business in Havana which I can learn about nowhere better than by working as a copyist and this is anyway worth some effort. I will thereby gain skill in writing fast in English and French since judging by the volume of work this position is thought of as the most difficult in Havana.'[19]

This was no understatement. Drakes were the largest shippers of sugar in Cuba. At a time when the island had become the world's largest cane-sugar producer (by 1850 it was producing some 300,000 tons), two-thirds of the sugar exported came from Drakes' warehouses. Part of Alexander Friedrich's work would involve correspondence with London accepting houses such as Barings, Rothschilds, and Frühling & Goschen over the bills of exchange that Drakes drew on them in payment for their shipments of sugar. Thus the position at Drakes would provide Alexander Friedrich with experience of dealing with the foremost accepting houses in the world and with the international sugar and tobacco trade. It would also give him an understanding of trade credit through Drakes' business with the island's sugar-planters to whom the firm extended credit. Alexander Friedrich sensed how important this would be for the furtherance of his career. So, on 1 January 1840, almost eighteen months after his arrival in Cuba, he joined Drakes in their counting-house at No. 7 Officios at the very heart of the labyrinth of narrow lanes comprising the commercial quarter of Havana.

Cuban counting-houses bore little resemblance to their European counterparts. Alexander Friedrich was not seated in a dimly lit, dank cubby-hole of a back office but in a sunlit, spacious marble *palazzo*. Like most buildings in Havana it was of only one storey, but that one storey was over 20 feet high with open rafters and it contained the offices of Drakes. Downstairs the ground floor and central courtyard served as warehouses and were overflowing with merchandise. Richard Dana, the illustrator and yachtsman, was extremely impressed by the offices of the main Havana merchants with their wide, columned, marble entrances and staircases 'almost as stately as that of Stafford House [the Duke of Sutherland's London house in the Mall] the floors of marble, the panels of porcelain tiles, the rails of iron . . . the doors and windows colossal' and shuttered. For in the tropical climate of Cuba buildings were constructed and decorated in marble to provide coolness and shade.

Office dress was also tropical. 'There sits the merchant or banker in white pantaloons and thin shoes, and loose white coat and narrow neck-tie, smoking a succession of cigars, surrounded by tropical luxuries': a contrast to his City of London counterpart in black coat and chimney-pot hat. Several of Alexander Friedrich's letters home contain requests for just such clothes, thin shoes and light-coloured trousers, to be made for him in Hamburg and sent out, thereby saving him the expense of buying them in Havana.

Just a short walk from the calm splendour of the counting-house lay the bustling waterfront where, Sir James Alexander wrote, the 'wharves are crowded with piles of merchandise and barrels of provisions; crowds of half-naked blacks, shouting and singing, were unloading vessels; shipowners and shipmasters were standing in groups, with broad-brimmed Panama hats, and striped linen coats, talking of sugar, coffee, and flour'; while 'the fumes of cigars arose on every side' with 'a pirate or two, or the captain of a slaver walking about, regarding with piercing eye the men who might be fit instruments for their unholy purpose'. Here in the early morning Alexander Friedrich braved the crowds to arrange the shipments of his own consignments of cigars with 'safe' captains.[20]

During his first weeks at Drakes, however, Alexander Friedrich did little business of his own, mainly, he told Theodor Karck who had just joined Schröders in London, because 'I do not know my principals well enough to be able to judge in how far I will be able to engage in large trade for myself. However, I think they will not put obstacles in my path and I intend to use the first opportunity for a joint venture.' After only two weeks there he had 'thank God, every reason to be happy with the change of post'.[21]

Drakes was a family firm, founded by James Drake (1763–1838), the son of an Axminster innkeeper. He was a merchant in Cadiz when regulations restricting Cuban trade with Spanish merchants were relaxed. After obtaining a warrant from Charles IV of Spain in 1792 he settled in Cuba at Cartagena as one of the first foreign merchants shipping tobacco, sugar, and coffee to Europe and importing goods to sell in Cuba and elsewhere in the Caribbean. A shrewd trader, he quickly accumulated a large fortune and in 1800 moved to Havana where he took on an American partner to expand his trade with the United States.

Drake was by now eligible enough to be able to marry into the Cuban aristocracy and he chose well. His wife, Carlotta Núñez del Castillo, was the beautiful niece of the third Marqués de San Felipe y Santiago, a title which incorporated the much higher honour of *grandeza* or Grandee of Spain. The del Castillos were distinguished soldiers and churchmen before they travelled from Spain as colonizers; they owned some of the largest plantations in Cuba and had increased their fortunes through keeping their own commercial establishment to trade in cotton in New Orleans. They were very rich and, through his marriage, James Drake automatically took his place as Don Santiago Drake on the top rung of Creole society with an entrée to the Government circles of the island. He lived in great style both in Havana and on the Saratoga and Jucara sugar plantations which he had bought to increase his social standing as much as his income. After the death of his wife in 1830 he had decided that, with four sons to ensure the succession of his merchant house, he could safely retire to Paris, where he died in 1838.[22]

When Alexander Friedrich started at Drakes in 1840, although the firm was headed by the eldest son, 'Charles Drake does not busy himself much or not at all' with the business. Carlos Drake y del Castillo, Conde de Vega Mar and later Permanent Deputy of the Municipal Council of Havana at the Court of Spain in Madrid, had married a de la Cerda Gand, whose cousin became the Empress Eugénie of France in 1853. He described himself succinctly: 'Born in Havana, of one of the most ancient families in the land, I am proprietor there of a sugar plantation with some 400 slaves'. And although he was also proprietor of Drakes he had no wish to emphasize the mercantile strain of his lineage and be tied to a counting-house. So he shrewdly appointed others to run his business and increase his wealth.

Of the executive quartet, Ulric Zellweger, a Swiss merchant, dealt with the United States and was often away from the counting-house, leaving it in the hands of Charles Respinger and José Morales. 'The two executive principals Rechinger [*sic*] and Morales are both very agreeable people and, as far as I can judge, very competent business men,' Alexander Friedrich wrote. The brilliant, hard-working Morales, an old schoolfriend of Charles Drake, had worked as an employee under Don Santiago but was now the guiding genius behind the firm. Alexander Friedrich worked under him from the beginning and came to know him well. He came to know the fourth partner even better.

James Drake, the second Drake son, had been persuaded to give up his successful business in Matanzas, the second port of Cuba, to join Charles in the family firm in Havana. In effect, James became the family proprietor, leaving Charles to enjoy a sleeping partnership, not that James passed long hours in the counting-house either. A man of wide interests, he opposed Spain's reactionary role in Cuba as well as the slave trade, though he himself owned slaves. He was musical with a fine singing voice and had been the British consular agent in Matanzas. Sir Charles Murray, subsequently a member of Queen Victoria's household, had stayed with him in 1834 and found him to be 'one of the most agreeable and instructive companions whom I had met on the island . . . his mind cultivated and enlarged by travel, as he had resided several years in Germany, and nearly a similar period in England, America and Mexico'.[23]

For the new clerk, however, the Drakes were distant stars in his firmament. His immediate concern was to learn the ropes of 'a difficult position', knowing that 'Time will show whether my hopes for promotion later on will be realised and I only wish that copying will not remain my task for long.'[24]

His hopes were realized sooner than he had anticipated. Barely five months later, in May 1840, he was promoted to chief clerk with a salary of 4 oz. of gold per annum. Morales had recognized the makings of a good counting-house man in Alexander Friedrich; that is to say, as Morales later wrote to a former colleague, a 'hard-working man, from 6 in the morning till 10 at night; correct, prompt at any time, very intelligent', and above all ambitious to succeed in his work. The increased salary was essential to Alexander Friedrich's plan; he needed to save $12,000–15,000 over the next five years in order to be able to return home where he hoped to 'establish himself in one way or another profitably in Hamburg with its many varied businesses' and to marry and support a family. This was what drove him, helping him to withstand not only the teasing of his colleagues that he was a dull dog but also 'the real hardships of want from time to time'. Despite extreme penny-pinching, it remained a pipe-dream. He could only manage to save $75 plus interest a month. A year later in 1841 his savings amounted to the princely sum of $1,800 of which $1,000 was invested with Drakes to yield 9 per cent interest per annum, a higher rate than was customarily offered in British houses.

This represented a complete change in Alexander Friedrich's strategy of trading on his own account so as to amass capital. Partly he no longer had the spare time available as at Rottmanns to see to his own transactions. 'As long as one cannot devote one's attention totally to a business,' he wrote to Herr Höber, 'it is better, I think, to refrain from it completely and this is the reason why I have withdrawn totally from all private business deals.' And partly it was much safer to invest his savings in Drakes for a certain 9 per cent than in a more risky business deal like the import of shirts which might give him a 10 per cent profit yet was far more troublesome to organize.[25]

It was not strictly true that he had withdrawn totally from private business deals. Cigars remained his chief interest but what he now did was to execute his deals (with two exceptions) under the auspices of Drakes. This gave him the usual half-commission as well as the kudos of bringing in new clients from Hamburg, Bremen, and New York, thereby adding to Drakes' own earned commissions; this in turn increased his chances of promotion and with it a higher salary. The exceptions were his ventures with the Karck brothers and Upmann. On 31 October 1841 he invested $400 of his savings in Upmann's cigar company for a return of 12 per cent. Increasingly he saw this business as a means to make money; his intention was to invest more in it whenever funds were available.

1842 proved to be his *annus mirabilis* in Cuba. He started off the year in good spirits after doing his accounts. From his monthly salary of $68—to which he added his agent's fee of $8.40 from the hat manufacturer Herr Dubbes of Altona and $18.80 in interest on his savings, and deducted his paltry monthly expenditure of $8.20—he had managed to increase his savings by $12 to $87 a month. He was able to place a large order for 200 boxes of sugar (1 box = 480 lbs.) from Anderson & Höber in the hands of Drakes and, although Drakes shipped 1,000 boxes that month alone to Hamburg, it was pleasing to be able to contribute to the consignment.[26]

Then, in August, the Drake partnership was dissolved: Charles retired to Madrid leaving a toehold of $100,000 in the business for three more years, a sum Morales considered 'too small to be mentioned', and Charles Respinger also retired to Europe. The new partnership comprised James Drake, Zellweger, Morales, and the third Drake son, the dissolute diplomat Louis. He showed even less interest in the counting-house than his brothers; his death three years later had little effect on the firm except to cause it embarrassment. He had named a young American adventuress in his deathbed will and left $5,000 for the upbringing of their unborn child, an honourable but unheard-of act; a separate letter of instruction was the usual method then employed to take care of such matters.[27]

The partnership changes effectively consolidated executive power in the hands of Morales. As his protégé, Alexander Friedrich immediately benefited. His salary was increased to $1,000 and Morales promised both a further increase as soon as turnover improved and first refusal on any more senior vacancy. Sugar prices were low after a worse than expected harvest and even Drakes had had to reduce expenditure by making three travelling salesmen redundant and removing the gift of free catering from all employees. Alexander Friedrich was the only employee who did not suffer. Morales was as good as his word and shortly afterwards appointed him to the position of second accountant. This was the promotion he had been hoping for, since it freed him from the hated task of copying and bore the huge advantage of providing him with a position 'totally independent from all my colleagues'. He was responsible for the daily stock-taking book and various supplementary books, and all submitted bills had to be checked by him; he also continued to handle all the German correspondence. The promotion spurred him on to save $100 a month and by October his savings amounted to $3,000.[28]

Alexander Friedrich now felt confident enough at Drakes to deal in substantial quantities for his own account. His first large trade was in sugars for his loyal friends Anderson & Höber. It was vital that he executed it successfully. The hazards of international trade and the risks incurred by merchants at that time are well illustrated by the details of this transaction. The order was placed by letter on 10 March 1843 in Hamburg for 400 boxes of white, yellow, and brown sugars depending on availability but stipulating price limits to include all charges. It took roughly eighteen weeks for the order to reach Alexander Friedrich in Cuba and much had changed in the market in the interim. The mails of 1 April were delayed by the weather so that he had no up-to-date instructions regarding price. Moreover prices had already risen, with 'good strong whites' leaping up, and several ships were already fully booked for outward cargo. Using $2,600 of his savings deposited with Drakes plus bills in his name from Upmanns for $1,200 as a guarantee, Alexander Friedrich quietly placed an initial order through Drakes.

By 15 May he had managed to find space in a ship, but only after joining another party in the expensive charter of a *whole* ship, despite rising prices. Six days later he wrote to Peter Dickinson & Co., correspondents of Drakes in London, to confirm the shipment of 200 boxes of whites and 200 of yellows through Drakes for Anderson & Höber, enclosing the bill of lading. The deal was done but he had yet to learn whether it was acceptable to Anderson & Höber. 'I . . . feel confident that you will realise a very fair profit', Alexander Friedrich wrote, 'if your market only maintains the last quotations [of price].' And here, in spite of his successful machinations, lay the rub. The mails arriving on 1 April had been lost and the ship due to arrive on 15 April was late. Alexander Friedrich was understandably concerned about the safe arrival of his cargo; if the ship was lost at sea so would be his savings and he would be engulfed by a tidal wave of at least $8,500 of debt.

Finally on 6 June he received their letters of 24 March and 25 April containing the unwelcome information that the state of the Hamburg market forced them to reduce their limits on sugar prices by half. Alexander Friedrich knew that they would have to accept his shipment but equally he knew that if they were dissatisfied with it they would not place an order his way again. Citing the latest reports of higher prices, he mustered all his powers of persuasion to convince them that he had acted in their best interests. 'The Sugars were purchased very cheap much below the market prices at the time of shipment,' he reminded them, 'and the freight is 7 to 12 per cent below the actual rate for small lots and one of the cheapest which has been accepted for whole cargoes in all this Season.' He concluded with a show of bravado: 'Considering these circumstances I can scarcely regret that your counter-order has come too late and trust that the result may justify my expectation.' It did, and Anderson & Höber placed further orders his way.[29]

Alexander Friedrich continued to deal on his own account in sugars because of the large commissions he could earn. But he remained much happier with cigars, still for him 'the safest business'. He had continued to invest small sums in Upmann's firm and in the autumn he used his by now considerable skills to play the market, help Upmann, consolidate his own semi-proprietorial position, and earn two good commissions in the process. Good-quality tobacco was becoming scarce and accordingly prices were bound to rise. Alexander Friedrich advised Upmann to purchase tobacco worth $10,000 in advance of requirements while prices were reasonably low. Although a small, solid manufacturing firm, Upmann & Co. did not have $10,000 to spare. So Alexander Friedrich approached Drakes for the advance, using the tobacco to be stored in their warehouse as security. He suggested the tobacco be delivered to Upmanns fortnightly in return for payment in cash, with the last bale deliverable in April 1844. As an inducement to Drakes, or rather Morales, since it was he who would make the decision, Alexander Friedrich let slip the fact that he had taken a share in the company for $3,500, the total sum of his savings with Drakes, as a sign of his complete faith in Upmanns.

When Morales agreed to advance the $10,000, however, Alexander Friedrich quickly pointed out the risks he was taking and the interest Drakes would make, thereby justifying his claim to a 2½ per cent commission on the $10,000. In the meantime he had placed an order for tobacco worth $10,000 with Ferdinand Karck in New York at a price lower than the going rate in Cuba and earned himself a further commission on that deal. And, because of keeping the costs low, Upmann was able to sell his cigars competitively for high profits—in which Alexander Friedrich naturally had a share. It was altogether a most satisfactory transaction.[30]

By now Morales was well aware of Alexander Friedrich's mercantile flair. He offered him a firm contract to stay with Drakes until 1 October 1845 as first accountant for a salary of $3,000 per annum. Before the expiry of this contract, however, changes in the partnership had rendered it null and void. Ulric Zellweger retired in the summer of 1845, leaving three partners—James and Francis Drake and Morales. Francis, the fourth and youngest Drake brother, had taken Louis's place in the firm in July 1845. He stayed only a short time, lured away by the stronger attractions of European dancers and actresses; he eventually married a French opera dancer, to the fury of his eminently respectable brother Charles, the newly created Conde de Vega Mar. With the concerns of both Drakes firmly centred away from the counting-house, Morales insisted on the appointment of two managers to help him run the firm. One of them was his protégé.

As a manager, Alexander Friedrich had the power of procuration or signature. He now possessed the authority to sign bills of exchange and cheques, which in the hierarchical world of nineteenth-century business was a mark of immense importance. After only five years, starting from the most lowly level, Alexander Friedrich had climbed almost to the top of the firm. It was an impressive achievement gained by dint of a single-minded, dogged determination, great initiative and unrelenting work. He could now easily save enough to start his own small business in Hamburg. Yet there was an even greater development opening up in his career prospects. In those days the barrier between partners and managers was comparable to the green baize door: usually impassable. Managers very rarely received an offer of partnership. Alexander Friedrich and his fellow manager and friend, Edward Cohen, were the lucky exceptions.

Over the next few years the situation at Drakes played into their hands. There was only one effective partner, Morales. Yet the 1840s had been profitable years for the firm and it had expanded considerably, moving into new offices a few yards from the waterfront and opening three new branches. But it was easier to open new offices than to find reliable men to run them. Morales had found the man at Cardenas untrustworthy: 'Doyle has been making use of our money, and spending freely, and from other information obtained, I hear he begins to be dissipated,' he wrote. 'Consequently [I] cannot think of trusting our business and our money to such a person.' The lack of adequate controls and supervision could also lead to irregularities in the accounts. Edward Cohen was, therefore, made the partner in charge of liaison with the branches in order to control their expenditure.

At head office in Havana, meanwhile, Morales was specifically concerned with the sugar accounts and the American and Spanish business, as well as handling all the general partnership matters, often including petty but time-consuming Drake personal and estate matters. Consequently the extensive European business was somewhat neglected at partnership level. Alexander Friedrich had long nurtured the German business but at a junior level. His rise in the firm coincided with an increased awareness of the opportunities for further expansion in Europe. It was an obvious move to appoint Alexander Friedrich the partner in overall charge of European business, with Cohen overseeing the British end. James Drake did not usually take kindly to suggestions of additional partners who would receive a share of the profits, thereby reducing the disproportionate share the Drake family received. On this occasion, however, he seems to have made no objection to the quiet, diligent, yet gentlemanly Kleinwort and Cohen becoming partners. The promise of increased profits from the European side may have proved an irresistible lure to the somewhat avaricious senior partner.[31]

On 1 November 1848 the partnership was officially restructured on the basis of the following capital contributions:

James Drake	$100,000	25.0%
Francis Drake	$50,000	12.5%
José Morales	$150,000	37.5%
Edward Cohen	$50,000	12.5%
Alexander F. Kleinwort	$50,000	12.5%

Since Alexander Friedrich had only accumulated capital of $4,000 at the end of 1843, how was he able to put $50,000 into the partnership five years later? It is clear from his correspondence ledger that from then up to 1845 he continued to trade on his own account in cigars for increasingly larger orders. His commissions would have doubled from the $200 to the $500 level. Presumably he could add to this the much larger profits reaped from Upmanns, which was becoming a well-known international brand name in cigars. As Upmanns expanded, Alexander Friedrich took a larger 'interest' in the company with commensurately higher rewards. This undoubtedly provided the basis of his capital. His correspondence ledger stops abruptly in 1845 and with it a valuable record of his finances ends. From 1845, though, he was a manager, able to claim not only the higher commission of 5 per cent but also a higher salary linked with Drake profits. His frugal method was always to keep the highest proportion of his salary that he could afford invested in Drakes at 9 per cent, the interest they paid on partners' capital.[32]

And, in the 1840s, Drakes was a most profitable house. It gives some idea of the scale of their operation that in a volatile market, they exported 22,000 boxes (480 lbs. per box) of sugars in an average month in 1843; on the European side (for which Alexander Friedrich would have earned commissions), they dispatched in an average fortnight two vessels to Britain, one to Belgium, and another to Holland carrying a total load of 4,700 boxes; while on the quayside, cargoes amounting to 29,650 boxes were in the process of loading. The firm also flourished on the import side, for they were the largest suppliers to Cuban plantation owners; total sales amounted to $14,505.26 in 1845/6 and by the following year had increased to $25,747.93. In addition, in the absence of banks, Drakes charged handsomely for extending credit to the sugar-planters to finance their crops, equipment, and slave-owning. Large profits were also made in financing the slave trade in which Drakes, like all Cuban merchant houses, were involved. It is therefore not surprising that as a manager with the ear of the executive partner of such a successful house, Alexander Friedrich would have identified and eagerly grasped the many opportunities to make money and increase his capital investment in the firm.

The profits earned by the partners were large by any standards. In 1846 the partnership announced profits of $200,000 [£2m.] after paying $36,000 in interest payments (9 per cent on the $400,000 capital) to the partners. Thus, after

Alexander Friedrich joined the partnership, his penny-pinching days were well and truly over. In 1850, his second year in the partnership, Morales wrote: 'The results of this year's business . . . look brilliant. I think it will exceed $200,000, and at Matanzas about $40,000.' The following year Morales predicted that 'the present House will realise more profit than any previous one . . . we will make it yield something above $250,000'. Thus, in two years, Alexander Friedrich was able to increase his capital by about $60,000.[33]

The customary three-year term of the partnership ended in 1851 when both Francis Drake and Edward Cohen retired from the firm. The new partnership contained Morales and Alexander Friedrich based in Havana and James Drake, who had left Cuba and was comfortably based in a château on the Loire. Distance did not prevent Drake from interfering in the business nor indeed of presenting his partners with a *fait accompli* which enraged them. He suddenly decided to change the name of the House of Drake.

'As Francis Drake withdraws, Santiago changes the firm into that of James Drake & Co., doing just as he pleases, as if we were mere machines,' Morales fumed. Furthermore, Drake wanted to increase his share of the capital, and thus of the profits, to 40 per cent—'without even having signed a letter', as Morales expressed it. For James had lived abroad and done no work in the counting-house for a number of years. Morales, with the largest capital share in the firm, was particularly incensed by James's attempt to force through these changes without consultation. It was after all he who had been running the business, almost single-handedly at times, and any changes to be made should recognize *his* contribution. Morales was more than ready to leave the firm and launch his own business, and he could easily raise the necessary $400,000.

In the ensuing power struggle, a compromise was eventually reached. 'Santiago has assumed a very high tone, particularly as, without us all, he cannot make the machine go', Morales wrote to Henry Coit, an old Drake correspondent. James Drake realized the necessity of keeping the other partners on Drakes' side and so settled for the less contentious name, Drake & Co. But he demanded and reluctantly was given a 40 per cent interest in the firm.[34]

With Morales and Alexander Friedrich still at the helm, Drakes went from strength to strength. In 1852 with profits running at nearly $300,000, Alexander Friedrich embarked on a long-awaited visit to his mother in Germany. His European sojourn produced more business for Drakes and a bride, Sophie Greverus, for himself. His personal wealth continued to increase in line with rising Drake profits, which in 1855 reached $500,000; while a year later they rose to $590,000, more than £5 million today. All this was achieved against a stream of negative comments from James Drake, who had grown more cautious with each partnership. Morales, now backed up by Alexander Friedrich, had always been one to take calculated risks. 'You say we are too ambitious for business and leave no chance for our neighbours,' Morales wrote to a former partner, 'but you don't consider the heavy expenses of the House and that, having credit and a large Capital on which we pay interest, it will not do for us to remain idle. Besides we are here to work, and must keep going and try to make some money.' These words could just as easily have been written by Alexander Friedrich, so well did they express his own business philosophy.[35]

Yet increasingly he now found himself at odds with his former mentor. The partnership had been renewed for another three-year term in 1854 but the growing friction between them made both unhappy and put paid to further collaboration. It was the age-old problem. Morales, for so long the driving force behind Drakes, could not fully accept the younger man as an equal partner. Alexander Friedrich for his part demanded the freedom to act independently as an equal partner in the firm; he had his own ideas about how to manage and where to look for future growth. And he was intolerant of the uncharacteristic restraint and caution with which Morales now greeted his suggestions. Morales, however, thought that Alexander Friedrich had grown 'cocky' and used 'insolent language' to him. He would not tolerate 'such impertinence' from his former clerk who, he thought, owed everything to him.

Relations had broken down between them to the extent that Morales could complain with some justification after Alexander Friedrich had lost his temper with him, that he should 'make use of such brutal language with one that exerts himself & devotes all his time on behalf of the House', but continue with no justification, 'whilst every other partner has made a particular study to work as little as possible!' This was blatantly untrue of Alexander Friedrich who, as Morales well knew, had always been a hard worker. But it was a sign of the discord between them that Morales could have written such words. He believed that the huge profits, from which Alexander Friedrich duly took a 12.5 share, were all due to his management of the sugar account. Alexander Friedrich believed that it was the growth in the European business, in which Morales took little interest but nevertheless interfered with, that swelled the profits. They were at loggerheads and both looked forward to the expiration of what would be Drake & Co.'s final partnership.

Morales had long 'been prepared for changes' and when the time came he was more than ready. He was said to have made close to $3 million, an astronomical figure, during his twenty-five years or more with Drakes, so that he had no difficulty in founding J. M. Morales & Co., which remained one of the most important commercial firms in Havana for a number of years. Alexander Friedrich, of course, had neither the long years of experience and well-earned reputation nor the colossal fortune of Morales behind him. But he, too, had been prepared for changes and planned accordingly. On 1 January 1855 the firm of Kleinwort & Cohen settled into 3 White Hart Court off Lombard Street, just round the corner from Alexander Friedrich's contemporary, Robert Benson jnr. Thus, by the mid-nineteenth century, both the Kleinworts and the Bensons had established their respective businesses in the City of London.[36]

4 Founding Fathers in the City

ALEXANDER FRIEDRICH KLEINWORT and Robert Benson jnr. had much in common, despite their dissimilar backgrounds. They shared the experience of early disappointment. Alexander Friedrich had been denied the education, wealth, and situation in Hamburg fitting to the station that his family's social standing had led him to expect. They both served apprenticeships at firms which, for different reasons, had not led to partnerships. This had been more unlucky in Robert jnr.'s case: as the son of the senior proprietor at Cropper, Benson, a partnership would automatically have been his. Instead he and Alexander Friedrich had had to spend years in what to them were clearly unsatisfactory working milieux, at Worthington & Benson and at Drakes, unable to do exactly as they wanted.

Both men, moreover, were quick to identify opportunities in business and to act upon them. Each by his thirties had demonstrated a proven flair for finance and for setting up deals. Alexander Friedrich had undoubtedly come furthest since he lacked inherited wealth and standing. To compensate, he was far more ambitious, a man driven to achieve his goals by whatever means necessary. Robert jnr. was less single-minded and certainly did not possess the same degree of motivation. Whereas Alexander Friedrich had ruthlessly cut all outside interests and distractions from his life, Robert jnr. had allowed the gentlemanly pursuits of connoisseurship, club membership, and authorship to permeate his. Most importantly they had one ambition in common: to have their own banking businesses. In order to achieve this they required capital and suitable partners. In both cases their marital partnerships led to their business partnerships.

Alexander Friedrich's marriage to Sophie Charlotte Greverus had taken place at the beginning of 1852. Her father and mother were first cousins and on both sides she was descended from a long line of learned, pious clerics. 'So many', a cousin wrote of their ancestors, 'from both Greverus and Kuhlmann dedicated themselves to Theology and exercised their holy office with great devotion and ability.' The earliest ancestor, Gerhard Greverus, was a preacher in Oldenburg from 1636 to 1677 and it took over 150 years before the ecclesiastical chain was broken by Sophie's father, Hermann Diederich Greverus.

He was brought up in the pastor's house at Ganderkersee, a village midway between Bremen and Oldenburg in that north-western corner of Germany which borders the Netherlands. He was the only son out of seven children and four of his sisters died in childhood. His mother, a 'grieving woman', seemed to the growing children 'like a willow bent in the storm beside the powerful strong-willed father'. A clever, good-looking child, Hermann was charming and knew how to get what he wanted.

Although intended for the Church, he had to forgo university education owing to lack of funds. He chose to enter commerce less from inclination than force of circumstances and was duly apprenticed to a Kuhlmann uncle in Bremen. Unfortunately he did not get on with this uncle who 'made his life difficult', and so he suddenly returned home, thereby incurring his father's wrath. After numerous attempts he eventually in 1805 found a trainee position in Liverpool, where he remained throughout his four-year term of clerkship. His letter of application had been so well written that the proprietor could not believe that Hermann, then a boy of 20, was the author of such a forceful letter. His English commercial training would stand him in good stead in his later career but, when he returned home, it did not provide him with immediate employment. By now a handsome, sturdy man with curly brown hair, he whiled away his free time in family visits in the course of which he was captivated by his cousin Friederike Kuhlmann who lived at Varel. A sweet-natured girl with reddish-blonde curls, Friederike possessed the gift of being able to steady Hermann out of his violent changes of mood and the depths of despair into which he plunged in difficult times.

They settled in Amsterdam, where their only child Sophie was born on 26 June 1820, before returning to Germany when Hermann became the agent for the Rhenish-West Indian Company. He also acted for them in Antwerp where his West Indian connections and knowledge of England brought him the offer of the European agency for Drakes. In 1829 Hermann moved his family to London, settling them in Camberwell and opening an office off Lombard Street at 3 White Hart Court. His business was almost entirely confined to trade with Cuba and, as their agent, the Drake account was by far the most important. By 1840 it yielded a commission of £750 a year. Like most astute merchants he also traded on his own account, earning a healthy profit of around £2,000 per annum from sugar and cigar deals with Drakes. As Drakes expanded their European business, chiefly through Alexander Friedrich's efforts, so Hermann's London business grew. When, in 1851, Edward Cohen retired from Drakes and returned to London, Hermann invited him to become a partner in H. Greverus & Co.[1]

Although at first glance this seems a surprising move—after all, Alexander

Friedrich was engaged to Hermann's only child and therefore would be the natural candidate for such an enterprise—there were strong reasons for it. Alexander Friedrich was not really ready to come to London in 1851. He needed to remain in Havana for a few more years in order to increase his capital so that when he did start in business he could be a large if not the principal shareholder.

Furthermore, Edward Cohen was British, knew the City well, and had handled Drake's London business from the Havana end. He now possessed sufficient capital after his three-year term as a partner in Drakes to take a minority shareholding in Hermann's business. Moreover, an injection of capital from a non-family partner would not only spread the risks but also enable Hermann, who at 66 was nearing the age of retirement, to withdraw some of his capital without unduly affecting the family share of the business. Besides which, Edward was not only the eldest son of an old friend and a protégé of Hermann's (in fact it was through him that Edward had been offered a position at Drakes), but he was also a friend and colleague of Alexander Friedrich's. Hermann knew that the two men would work well together after he retired. This indeed was the plan in 1851: Greverus & Cohen would become established in the City; then Hermann would retire as, phoenix-like, Kleinwort & Cohen rose in its place. Sophie being her father's sole heir, the majority of his capital would remain in the new firm after his death, ensuring both a continuation of the business and security for his daughter and her family.

Alexander Friedrich had met Sophie on his visits to her father on Drake business but they had grown closer from 1846. That year his plan of travelling on from London to Germany to see his mother had fallen through when, on his arrival from Havana, he was met at the dockside with the news of her sudden death. In consequence he had stayed longer than originally intended at the comfortable Greverus house in Denmark Hill and there he had ample opportunity to fall in love with 26-year-old Sophie. They did not marry for six years, until Alexander Friedrich could support his wife in the style to which he thought she was accustomed; despite this wait their wedding had to be fixed in an instant in January 1852 during one of his business trips. Now a sleek, prosperous-looking man of 36, he had decided he could afford to marry and there was no time to waste. Sophie had a bare ten days to arrange matters but she was a practical young woman and unflurried by the haste imposed upon her. 'Do not trouble yourself much about *dress*, which I know is often a tiresome thing upon these occasions,' she told one of her bridesmaids, 'my bridesmaids will not be dressed alike, I have no time to be particular'.

She brought to the marriage a multitude of interests which she encouraged Alexander Friedrich to share, prising him out of his somewhat pedestrian mercantile shell into a more cultured ambience, reminiscent of his youth in

Altona and Hamburg. Sophie was a vivacious young woman and an easy conversationalist, attributes that now helped her to withstand the trials of a three-year stay in Cuba. The humid tropical climate did not agree with her as bouts of fever combined with the rigours of childbirth considerably weakened her previously robust constitution. She was more than glad to return to London with Alexander Friedrich in 1855. They settled near to her father who had bought a house for them as a wedding present.[2]

The Glebe was a substantial Victorian house set in park-like grounds on Denmark Hill in the prosperous parish of Camberwell in south London. Although only a four-mile carriage drive from the City, Denmark Hill was still a rural village of meandering country lanes and not yet part of suburban London. The Glebe stood on the crest of a rise commanding a distant view of the newly erected Crystal Palace. It was run by some twelve indoor and six outdoor staff, the usual complement for a relatively well-off family house. By German standards, however, this easily matched the number of staff in some princely households and seemed to Alexander Friedrich's relations proof that he had achieved his ambition to be 'master of his own hearth'. Striding through the grounds after a long day in the City he, too, must have felt that the tremendous effort required to improve his position had not been expended in vain. There was no slackening, however, now that he had his own business to command; indeed, if anything, he directed his energies to work more single-mindedly than ever.[3]

The City in the early 1850s, when Alexander Friedrich and Robert Benson jnr. first worked there, was an exciting place to be. The Great Exhibition of 1851 had symbolized the country's predominant place in the world as, after the hungry 1840s, trade had improved in the home markets and exports greatly expanded, due less to manufacturing better goods than to underselling competitors in all branches of commerce. The City's growing ascendancy as the world's leading financial and commercial centre was reflected in a surge of rebuilding. The medieval street pattern did not easily accommodate such activity being 'a most mysterious and unfathomable labyrinth of lanes and alleys, streets and courts thronged with a bustling multitude'. Merchants and tradesmen, messengers and delivery boys, had to dodge round the myriad of barrow and pavement hawkers all shouting out their wares, as well as the fixed stalls squeezed into the angles made by steps, such as those of St Paul's. Whilst for most it was the street life which showed that 'the city is getting its living', the true heart of the City was to be found in the ill-lit, sepulchral rabbit warrens of City offices containing sloping desks, upon which enormous ledgers were laboriously compiled in copper-plate by the hunched figures of black-coated clerks.

Charlotte Brontë far preferred it to the West End. It seemed 'so much more in earnest; its business, its rush, its roar, are such serious things, sights, and sounds'. Merchants, bankers, and tradesmen no longer lived above their counting-houses and shops or housed their staff there; they drove, took the new omnibus service and in the 1850s 200,000 of them walked daily into the City solely to earn their living. Whereas 'in the eighteenth century it was not considered shabby to live on a fortune in Lombard Street but respectable to live idling on an overdraft in Jermyn Street', as the historian of Glyn, Mills wrote, in the nineteenth century an overt connection with business and trade was deemed socially undesirable. City people had emigrated to the suburbs or moved to the fashionable West End and further west. Alexander Friedrich had chosen the quiet and fresh air of Camberwell whilst Robert jnr., in keeping with his different outlook on life, had settled at the far more fashionable address of 32 Hyde Park Gardens, opposite Hyde Park.[4]

Robert jnr., unlike Alexander Friedrich, had long possessed ample funds with which to marry. Nevertheless he, too, had married into a family whose commercial interests were of considerable benefit and through whom he was to meet his future business partner. His bride Eleanor Moorsom, a pretty young woman of 23, was a talented water-colourist with an interest in history and some decided views. At 17 she found Shakespeare's style admirable but 'hardly proper to be read by young people'. She came of seafaring stock long settled at Robin Hood's Bay near Whitby as mariners and owners of small vessels in the coal and coasting trade.

Her great-grandfather's nickname, 'King Dick' of Airy Hill, reflected the extent of his shipowning empire. His second son achieved an even greater renown as Admiral Sir Robert Moorsom KCB, commanding the *Revenge* at Trafalgar where he 'bore a most distinguished and active part' by successfully attacking a far superior force. He carried the great banner at Nelson's funeral and received rapid promotion to Lord of the Admiralty, and Commander-in-Chief at Chatham. Nor were his skills confined to the quarter-deck. A poet and a water-colourist of merit, he was also a surveyor of note, a talent that he passed on to Eleanor's father, Vice-Admiral Constantine Richard Moorsom, and uncle, Captain William Scarth Moorsom.

Constantine's naval ability was undoubted: the author of *On the Principles of Naval Tactics* (1846), he had devised during his command of the *Fury* at the bombardment of Algiers in 1816 a way of fitting mortars whereby his ship threw double the number of shells than any other in the Fleet; when given command of the *Ariadne*, 'a hopeless failure', he had 'succeeded in making her sail as fast, work as well, and prove as good a sea-boat as could possibly be expected' by the adjustment of her stowage and ballast.

Through his brother William, who became a leading civil engineer, in great demand during the 'mania' years of 1844–5 to survey and lay out most of the major railway systems, Constantine, after leaving the Navy, became secretary of the London and Birmingham Railway Co. This evolved into the London and North-Western Railway (LNWR), of which he duly became chairman and in which the Bensons and the Croppers had long been active.

Joseph Sturge, son-in-law of James Cropper, then asked William Moorsom to survey the country for a proposed railway line between Birmingham and Gloucester. As a result of their railway connections, the Moorsoms, Croppers, and Bensons exchanged visits and when William Moorsom moved to London he took a house next to Robert jnr.'s father in Sussex Square. The friendship was consolidated by Robert jnr.'s brother William being at Trinity College, Cambridge, with Eleanor's brother James, subsequent to sharing chambers with him at the Bar, and by their shared Quaker inheritance.

Eleanor's mother Mary was the eldest daughter of Jacob Maude, a lapsed Quaker landowner and large colliery proprietor in Sunderland, and Ruth Mitchison, whose family were prominent Lake District patrons of Wordsworth, Southey, and Coleridge. The Maudes' only surviving son and heir Colonel William Maude lived at Selaby Hall, near Darlington, which he rented from the Duke of Cleveland. Without children of his own, he had made Eleanor's eldest brother, Con, his heir so they all frequently visited Selaby.[5]

Eleanor and Robert jnr. were married at Edgbaston in 1847 and went to live at Fairfield outside Manchester while he wound up his mill partnership with Henry Worthington. Robert jnr. still had various shipping and commodity interests in Liverpool as well as the investments he had inherited from his father, so it was logical to formalize them by joining John Wakefield Cropper (grandson of James Cropper), David Hodgson (a former partner in Cropper, Benson), and Robert Ferguson (a former senior clerk there) in a partnership based in Liverpool. This did not preclude Robert jnr. from pursuing his own ambition to set up under his own name an office in London, the new centre of railway financing; to be run separately but in conjunction with the Liverpool one. For this purpose he needed a further injection of capital to supplement his own, part of which was now committed to Liverpool.

By this time he was thoroughly immersed in railway finance. His father had sat on the board of the LNWR with Pascoe St Leger Grenfell and had also known his elder brother Charles, likewise much involved in the heady pioneering days of the Liverpool and Manchester Railway. It was, however, through his father-in-law, 'a highly competent though bluff naval officer', that Robert jnr. came to be introduced to George Carr Glyn, the chairman of the LNWR and a partner of Glyn, Mills & Co., who were bankers to the Liverpool–Manchester line.

At that time it was extremely unusual for a London bank of the standing of Glyns to be involved in railway finance. The early railways were provincial undertakings mainly financed by provincial Quakers such as the Bensons and the Croppers. London bankers were noticeably reluctant to raise capital for them, as Disraeli famously pointed out. He found it remarkable that 'the great leaders of the financial world', firms such as Rothschilds and Barings, took no part in it. 'The mighty loan-mongers, on whose fiat the fate of kings and empires sometimes depended, seemed like men who, witnessing some eccentricity of nature, watch it with mixed feelings of curiosity and alarm. Even Lombard Street, which never was more wanted, was inactive.'

The exception was provided by George Glyn, who was by no means the conventional Victorian banker. A prominent Liberal and free trader, he had married Marianne Grenfell. Her brothers Charles and Pascoe had introduced him to the exciting world of the steam engine. As a result, Glyns became known for many years as the Railway Bank, so colossal was the business which came to it through the railways. Whereas in the 1820s Glyns was not a particularly prominent bank, by 1850 'its business was certainly more extended, if not more solid and substantial, than that of any of its competitors'. In 1846, the year that Barclay, Bevan, Tritton & Co. (the precursor of Barclays Bank) passed £107m. through the Clearing House, the largest amount ever for a single bank, Glyns came within a smidgeon with £105m. It was George Glyn's railway business that contributed largely to the increased fortunes of his bank.

When Robert jnr. was casting around for a partner, his father-in-law spoke to George Glyn, who had nine sons. It seemed an obvious choice to follow the Glyn railway and banking connection and as Glyn wished his sixth son, Pascoe, to gain further experience before entering the family bank, on 1 January 1852 Pascoe Glyn joined Robert Benson & Co. Unfortunately, details of the partnership with the amount of capital injected have not survived. Since the firm did not become Benson & Glyn, it is safe to assume that Robert jnr.'s participation was significantly larger than Pascoe Glyn's. Both Robert jnr. and Alexander Friedrich began their City careers as the senior partners of their respective firms, Alexander Friedrich's larger participation being reflected in the name of his firm, Kleinwort & Cohen.[6]

The firm of Kleinwort & Cohen was not, however, destined to become a name to conjure with in the City. In 1858, barely three years after its formation, the partnership was dissolved and remodelled as Drake, Kleinwort & Cohen, known largely and somewhat unfairly as Drakes. In that year the last Drake partnership of James Drake, José Morales, and Alexander Friedrich Kleinwort had not been renewed after it had expired, thereby releasing substantial amounts of capital. Alexander Friedrich quickly took advantage of the situation. James Drake, having acquired a long and illustrious record as a sleeping partner, now regarded business purely as a necessary investment for his capital. The active partners in Kleinwort & Cohen welcomed a further injection of capital. It was a logical progression to marry the two interests.

This time, though, Alexander Friedrich ensured that Drake's share of the profits was not disproportionate but reflected his commercial inactivity. The initial capital of the firm was contributed as follows:

James Drake	£100,000	50%
Alexander F. Kleinwort	£70,000	35%
Edward Cohen	£30,000	15%

The partners would receive an annual interest of 5 per cent on their capital and distribute any additional profits in the ratio of Drake, 40 per cent, Kleinwort, 33 per cent, and Cohen, 27 per cent. As the partnership deed stated that 'the said James Drake de Castillo shall not be compelled to attend to the business of the copartnership more than he thinks fit', the firm was directed by Alexander Friedrich and Edward who, in return, received a salary of £900 and £600 per annum respectively. As the largest active shareholder Alexander Friedrich was undoubtedly the chief executive with Edward very much cast in the supporting role of gentleman banker.[7]

It was none the less a role for which some members of Edward's family did not show quite the right degree of respect, even though they benefited financially. This was not the case on the paternal side. Edward's grandfather Jacob was a Jewish immigrant who became a general merchant in the Whitechapel Road. Edward's father, Edward Cohen also became a merchant but with far greater success. He was of sufficient stature in the City to be appointed a Gold Staff Officer by the Earl Marshal at the Coronation of George IV in 1821. A member of the Scriveners' Company and a Freeman of the City, Edward Cohen had previously been naturalized and become a Christian. This enabled him to marry the daughter of his Islington neighbour Phineas Borrett, a wealthy Aldersgate Street goldsmith and a Freeman of the Goldsmiths' Company. Mary Ann had been married before, to the water-colourist Thomas Girtin who had died in 1802 and by whom she had a son. With her second marriage she brought a strong dose of eccentricity into the Cohen family, inherited by some of her children, though not by Edward. In the words of one descendant, it was probably Mary Ann 'who, with her liking for going around with cherry stones in her shoes, was the genetic source of a certain instability' which Edward's younger brother George certainly manifested.

After their father's death in 1835 the family moved to 3 Rood Lane, later acquired by Kleinwort Sons & Co. and part of the Kleinwort Benson offices today. It was most convenient for the Cohen sons, who were all intended for a City career. George, however, did not prove suitable material. He thoroughly enjoyed poking fun at his banker brother, to whom he was a great trial. George even rented a tobacconist's shop so that every morning, as Edward drove 'in splendour' to the office, he could appear beaming at his shop doorway to wave and call out loudly, above the noise of the horse-drawn traffic, 'Good morning, Brother Edward.' Colouring angrily at the shame of a brother in trade, the merchant banker drove on. It was not long before he paid George a considerable sum, said by the family to be £10,000, to retire from business.

The office to which Edward drove was now located at 7 Mincing Lane, which also housed Rathbone's London office; a Kleinwort and a Benson may well have met on the stair. Here, in the small rented premises, Alexander Friedrich masterminded the astonishing expansion of his business. Whilst the young clerks might bemoan 'the stewing, sweltering existence . . . with the heavy hours, the dry material work and the cold grey eye of Kenilworth' (their name for Kleinwort) fixed upon them, it was only with the imposition of such a regime that Alexander Friedrich was able to mould the firm into one of the City's leading accepting houses.[8]

An inevitable concomitant of his success was the need for more office space. The rented premises in Mincing Lane could not be enlarged so the decision was taken to move. The injection of Drake capital and the firm's growing business gave Alexander Friedrich and Edward the security and confidence to forsake rented accommodation and buy their own building. In 1863 the freeholds of 17–20 Fenchurch Street were purchased for £21,000 and Edward Ellis, a distinguished Victorian architect, was commissioned to design a suitably dignified building. In keeping with the plethora of new office blocks, warehouses, and exchanges, No. 20, as the new building was called, was built of stone in the monumental style of 'commercial Italianate' with the lavish ornamentation so beloved by Victorians. No expense was spared and the cost, a further £21,000, was equally lavish. Like the National Provincial Bank in Bishopsgate, its floor-length windows gleamed between corinthian columns which contained the grand marble pillared banking hall on the ground floor. It consisted of five storeys including a basement, all of which occupied the three former house plots. Alexander Friedrich showed his children round the site when, in the course of development, a Roman bath and a well were unearthed. He took a keen interest in the building and was tremendously proud of this symbol of his firm's solidity. Rothschilds were also engaged in building works at New Court, St Swithin's Lane, but their offices were held on a 100-year lease. Alexander Friedrich apparently told Natty Rothschild that he and Edward had bought

No. 20 outright because they expected their firm to last for far more than 100 years. This it has certainly done and his confidence in its future has paid handsome dividends. No. 20 served as the bank's offices until after the merger with Robert Benson Lonsdale when, in 1969, it was replaced by the present 22-storey tower block, which remains the headquarters of the Kleinwort Benson Group.[9]

Alexander Friedrich's successful strategy was to turn the firm from being a purely mercantile house into a largely banking house by switching from trading in merchandise to financing the trading. At Kleinwort & Cohen he had continued, as at Drakes, to deal in such familiar commodities as Cuban sugars and cigars. By the early days of Drake, Kleinwort & Cohen, with a larger capital base at his disposal, he built the firm into an accepting house. The City's accepting houses provided finance for their customers' trade by means of a negotiable instrument of credit, the Bill of Exchange (basically an IOU), which these houses accepted on behalf of customers and for which they charged a small commission. The usage of bills of exchange, which dates back to before Roman times, enabled merchants to dispense with the physical transfer of coinage and, as their use grew in Britain after the drawing of bills to finance inland trade was legalized in 1697, became the principal method of debt settlement and, by discounting them with a bank, of obtaining bank finance. By the time Alexander Friedrich was establishing his business in the City, the sterling bill had become the main instrument for the settlement of transactions covering the movement of goods between countries, especially as sterling, then freely convertible into gold, was the main currency in which transactions were invoiced internationally. The acceptance of these bills became the principal activity of the City's merchant banks and of Drake, Kleinwort & Cohen.

As this firm's reputation grew, so its services became more and more in demand. Yet although the initial capital base of £200,000 was large by the standards of most nineteenth-century businesses, it was much smaller than that of the leading merchant banks. In 1858 Barings, for instance, had some £600,000, Brown Shipley of Liverpool a capital of over £1m., whilst the market leaders, Rothschilds, possessed upwards of £4m. Within three years, however, Drake, Kleinwort & Cohen had acceptances outstanding of £800,613 and the capital employed in the business had risen to £280,000, a sum which rivalled Hambros, established in the City for over twenty years.

To a considerable extent the firm was benefiting from the favourable expansionist climate. The unilateral adoption of free trade by Britain combined with the recent discovery of gold in California and Australia had heralded an era of prosperity. As an advanced industrial nation with a strong mercantile marine, Britain could supply goods to the gold-producing countries more cheaply than anyone else and, in turn, attract the greatest proportion of the gold supply, which she used in settlement of her imports. In fact the increase in gold stocks in banks abroad led to an expansion of currency and credit everywhere that remained unaffected by the Crimean War, since war expenditure absorbed excess capacity in heavy industry, textiles, and transport. In particular trade with America increased as the new gold stimulated railway building and a rise of imports. It was into this area that Alexander Friedrich directed the firm's operations. To a large extent the spectacular growth in business came from providing acceptances to the United States and Cuba, although Germany came a good third.

Alexander Friedrich had kept up with the important business partner of his Cuban days, Herman Upmann. His firm had expanded into sugars and remained an important recipient of Kleinwort credits. Alexander Friedrich always visited him whenever he went to Germany to find new customers for Drake, Kleinwort & Cohen acceptances. His old contacts in Hamburg and Bremen were naturally part of the client list and his knowledge of their businesses helped him quickly establish the firm as pre-eminent among the London houses providing acceptances there. During the 1860s, German business accounted for some 10 per cent of revenue. From Germany, Alexander Friedrich usually travelled on to St Petersburg and Moscow as part of his expansionist thrust into northern Europe.[10]

While on one of these trips he was urgently summoned home. Sophie had been awaiting the birth of their fifth child and had asked him to postpone his business trip until after her confinement. With his single-minded approach to work he could not allow himself to deviate from the original itinerary. She died on 5 June 1860 before his return. Their baby daughter Charlotte lived only a few days and was buried beside her in Norwood cemetery. The grieving widower sought solace in the City, where he immersed himself in building up the business for his motherless children.[11]

His success is evident from the increase in partners' capital from £280,000 in 1860 to £651,151 in 1865 and from the expansion in the firm's client base; in 1865 there were 600 accounts world-wide, the most important of which were in the United States. Alexander Friedrich had long recognized the potential of the rapidly expanding American economy and in 1860 appointed Simon de Visser, a well-known New York merchant and bill broker, as his agent. By the end of the American Civil War, commission earnings from American business had easily overtaken Cuban revenue, which had formerly provided the single most important source of profits.[12]

At the beginning of 1866 Alexander Friedrich passed three months in the United States visiting old clients and drumming up new business. He journeyed from New York down the eastern seaboard to Charleston and New Orleans, where the Del Castillo family had an office, before going across to Havana to look after some of the remaining Drake interests and renew old contacts. On the return journey he visited customers in Philadelphia and Baltimore before ending again in New York. It was a most successful trip. He had arranged to provide credit facilities for merchants dealing in cotton (especially from the war-torn South, then in the process of reconstruction after the Civil War), in wine, in East India goods, and in Chinese and Japanese fancy goods.

By 1870 the firm under his direction had acquired the coveted description 'first class'. Its capital had risen to £0.91m., much lower than Rothschilds and Barings but larger than Schröders, Hambros, Morgans, and Huths; its acceptances stood at £2.35m., still someway behind Barings with £6.70m. and Schröders with £3.22m. Any pleasure Alexander Friedrich felt at achieving such healthy figures was short-lived. Although the firm's capital increased to £1.07m., the partners needed all the capital they could muster for in that year James Drake retired from the partnership, dying in the following year. His capital account, which had grown from the initial £200,000 to £487,394, had to be transferred to his executor. Alexander Friedrich and Edward informed the Bank of England that the firm would be left with £600,000 and, though the partners' capital continued to increase, it would take twenty-three years for it to stand again at over £1m.—yet their experience was far from unique.

Businesses were exceedingly vulnerable to the hazards of the death or retirement of a partner which immediately affected the capital base. Highly profitable firms could suddenly face extinction solely as a result of unforeseen changes to the partnership. In 1882, for instance, the merchant bank Antony Gibbs had capital of over £800,000 but three years later this had fallen to below £350,000, owing to the death and retirements of some of the partners. Having experienced an unexpected fall in the capital base of his firm, Alexander Friedrich made a plan to limit the impact of Edward's retirement or death, since he was the elder partner. He invested sufficient funds in first-class securities so that when the time came Edward's capital could be paid out without having to touch the working capital of the firm. In the event of his own death, he arranged that his own capital would be paid out over a number of years thereby protecting the stability of the firm for his sons.

After Drake's death the two surviving partners changed the style of the firm to Kleinwort, Cohen & Co., with Alexander Friedrich contributing 70 per cent and Edward 30 per cent of the capital, but dividing the profits by 80 per cent and 20 per cent. Once again this partnership proved short-lived—first because Alexander Friedrich's eldest son, Herman, became a partner with an initial 5 per cent profit participation, which reduced Alexander Friedrich's share to 75 per cent, and secondly because Edward's health began to fail, so that in 1883 he decided to retire. He withdrew his capital of over £200,000 and settled at Brow Head on Lake Windermere, not far from the Benson birthplace at Stangend. It was the end of a 44-year association between the two men and Alexander Friedrich felt it deeply. 'We have worked under the same roof', he wrote on 31 December 1883, 'without one word and as far as I am able to recollect, without one thought of unpleasantness. We part today but only as far as business is concerned. We will I feel sure always continue to be as good friends as we have been since we knew each other.'[13]

Edward's place in the firm was taken by Alexander Friedrich's younger son, Alexander Drake Kleinwort. He and his elder brother Herman each had a capital of £50,000 with a 10 per cent share in the profits, while their father retained 80 per cent. Thus for the first time the firm belonged wholly to the Kleinworts, a fact duly reflected in the change of name at the start of 1884 to Kleinwort Sons & Co. When one of their managers called at the Bank of England to announce the partnership changes, he was told that the house of Kleinwort seemed to have unlimited credit everywhere, a sure sign of its first-class status. After less than thirty years Alexander Friedrich's firm was a force to be reckoned with amongst the leading accepting houses in the City.[14]

Both the Kleinwort and Benson firms were dependent upon American business for much of their growth during the mid-Victorian years. American accounts remained by far the most important and numerous at Kleinworts, while Robert Benson & Co. derived their main business from financing American railways. The California gold discovery had stimulated a further burst of railway building in the 1850s. The United States had for many years offered the bold investor the prospect of spectacular, if risky, profits. The 2,800 miles of line built by 1840 had trebled by 1850 and trebled again by the end of that decade. Even the Civil War did not curb the frenzied onward rush of railway building, in which Americans relied heavily upon European and, in particular, British investors for finance. The British had forgotten the scandalous State defaults of the 1840s when the market in American Rails had been 'absolutely wiped out', and had once more begun to buy American bonds. By 1865, over £100 million of American railway securities were held in Britain.

It was not a market for the novice; even the steely nerved, experienced investor could and did fail. Many of the main lines were corruptly managed, mortgages were piled indiscriminately upon mortgages and the great American 'robber barons', Vanderbilt, Morgan, Gould, Harriman, and Fiske, realized the killings to be made from the railroads with their potential monopoly power. These larger-than-life figures would make them a battleground for their merger, buy-out, and land speculation wars—fiercely fought to the point of near extinction in some cases and sharp political controversy in others—in order to gain control and thereby extend their empires. Inevitably default and bankruptcy were common. None of this, however, seems to have deterred Robert jnr. from becoming heavily involved with the railway that was responsible for the revival of British interest in American Rails in 1852 and, more importantly, for long-standing profits for Bensons.

The Illinois Central Railroad was in many respects a unique undertaking. It was the first of the Midwest land-grant railways, receiving 2.6m. acres in grants of free land by an act of Congress. Most railways were financed by issuing enough stock to cover expenditure; mortgage bonds charged directly on their physical assets such as track, buildings, and engines were a popular choice of finance. In contrast the Illinois used the land grant as its credit base. It was the longest American railroad, with 705 miles of track envisaged, and would require the largest amount of capital of any American project to date. Financing it was a monumental task and bonds were issued, secured by 2m. acres of land, to be repayable as the land was sold, just to meet the immediate $17m. [£160m.] construction costs; 250,000 acres of land had to be reserved merely to guarantee the interest on the bonds.

The promoters, a group of New England financiers, were forced to turn to Britain and the Continent when it became clear that such a huge amount of capital could not be raised entirely in America. Thus the Illinois became dominated by British capital and interests. It was also the first American railway to bypass the Anglo-American houses, such as Peabody and Barings, and retail its bonds direct to the British public—a reflection of the City's mistrust of railways and the fact that the State of Illinois had previously defaulted on its foreign debt payment.

Whilst Barings, Rothschilds, and Hopes looked the other way, a syndicate that included Bensons and was led by Charles Devaux & Co., a smaller merchant bank, underwrote and brought to market a $5m. (£1m.) issue of the construction bonds on extremely favourable terms. The share capital was to be apportioned to bond holders at a rate of five shares for each $1,000 bond, thereby offering an assured return and an opportunity to share in any profits. Not surprisingly the issue was a great success and opened the way for a number of other railways to come to the market. As a member of the syndicate involved in all these issues, Robert jnr. made a handsome profit.

He knew Matthew Uzielli of Devaux's through Masterman's Bank, an old and important Quaker contact of the Bensons. Devaux and Masterman's had a lasting and lucrative association that began when they backed the Paris–Rouen–Le Havre line in the early 1840s, in which Robert jnr.'s father had a stake. Masterman's leadership in railways was ubiquitous. While seeking concessions for the Nord, the Paris–Lyons and Orleans–Vierzon routes, and manœuvring for the ear of French dignatories, his group also organized the Dutch-Rhenish railway company, which for several years controlled the chief line in Holland. These were only part of his French railway undertakings, in most of which the Benson family along with the Croppers, Fosters, and Braithwaites were investors.[15]

As a result of these long-standing connections with railway finance, Robert Benson & Co. were chosen to be the Illinois Central's London agent, a position retained for over fifty years. Other shareholders included the Croppers with 12 per cent and the Wakefields with 11 per cent, while Richard Cobden, a Manchester friend of Robert jnr.'s, took $10,000, which in turn induced such prominent figures as William Gladstone, Sir Samuel Cunard, and Sir Joseph Paxton to follow suit. Cobden was a calico printer who had been co-leader with John Bright of the Anti-Corn Law League and now continued to press the cause of free trade. He backed the Illinois Central because he pictured millions of European immigrants flocking to the rich grain lands of the Mississippi through which it ran.

He enthusiastically rushed out to Illinois, reporting back to Robert jnr. that in the course of long journeys over the prairies in wagons he had gone 'twice over the greater part of the region through which our railway stretches' and was happy to say that 'we have rolling stock enough for any amount of business that can offer.' Cobden also asserted that 'although the cost of the railroad and the time required to develop it, and the consequent loss of interest have been under estimated, yet the value of the land has been undervalued to a still greater degree, and the result in my opinion will prove that the most sanguine of the shareholders have not exaggerated the ultimate value of their investment.' Robert jnr. certainly considered the Illinois Central a long-term prospect, just as he had done with domestic railways during the boom-and-bust years of the 1830s and 1840s, and it was a rewarding policy. Others such as Cobden, who despite his report expected the investment to reap immediate dividends, were disappointed. When he received calls upon his shares later in the decade he was unable to meet them and had to be assisted by a large subscription of £40,000 from family and friends including Robert jnr.[16]

The firm's railway interests encompassed lines elsewhere in America, in India, Brazil, and in Canada, where Robert jnr. was, according to Pascoe Glyn, 'prominently before the public' as 'an active member of the new Inter-Colonial Railway Co', Lord MountStephen's trans-Canadian railway. It was at home, however, that his professional standing in this field was most evident. Apart from a host of directorships in lesser railways, Robert jnr. held one of the most prestigious directorships of the day, that of the great London North Western

Railway (LNWR). Despite being a major player and almost an *éminence grise* in railway finance, he had shed none of his radical views about the management of such companies.

In *The Amalgamation of Railway Companies*, a pamphlet he published in 1872, he stated that 'millions [of pounds] had been uselessly sacrificed' by building the British network without any national co-ordination or plan. No doubt to the horror of his boardroom colleagues, he suggested that the nation's transport system should be 'controlled and managed by those who represent it rather than by small bodies of gentlemen in whose selection the public has no voice, and over whose acts they have little or no control'. He had also in 1861 turned a pamphleteering attention to India and the vast cost of introducing a railway network into the subcontinent. 'A deep study of the subject' had convinced him that India should raise the capital locally from a land tax rather than from Britain.

His interests in India had survived from his Cropper, Benson days. Indeed, in many ways his new firm's business was a continuation of that of Cropper, Benson: a general merchant house conducting trans-Atlantic, Indian, and Far Eastern trade and extending acceptance credits to firms in North America and India with a particular interest in railways and cotton. It was, however, a far smaller enterprise than Cropper, Benson or for that matter than Drake, Kleinwort & Cohen. A confidential Barings report on Bensons stated: 'The senior [Robert jnr.] is supposed to possess upwards of £100,000 [roughly £5m. today], extending their business but prudent. Alexanders [the bill brokers] have a high opinion of them and obtained this from their bankers Brown, Janson & Co. Confirmed by Bank of England, July 1857.' Their reputation and credit was first class and Glyns was pleased to note the prompt repayment of a series of loans for £15,000.

The firm extended its Indian operation to include Bombay and Karachi as well as Calcutta, sending its own representative out to develop new business, whereas in Singapore, Manila, Shanghai, and Australia it dealt with local commission agents. Bensons were quick but realistic in identifying opportunities in the new Australian wool trade; at the height of the boom Pascoe Glyn instructed their agent to be cautious in using a £30,000 credit: 'Don't go too deep with any one squatter & always get a mortgage (or something equal to it) upon the new stock' of wool for shipment to England. As for security in return for credit, real estate, stocks, or mortgages were all acceptable, Glyn explaining that 'we have some dislike to mill property—Mr B from his old Manchester experience feels this strongly'. Robert jnr. had indeed had first-hand experience of how cotton mills that had closed down fetched only a fraction of their market value as going concerns.[17]

Apart from the substantial revenue generated by the railway business, a small-sized firm such as Robert Benson & Co. struggled to earn decent profits. Trading conditions during the generally prosperous 1850s and 1860s proved unpredictable. In October 1857 the Ohio Life & Trust Co. failed, leading to a full-scale American crisis in which over 1,500 banks and 5,000 businesses collapsed. This in turn led to houses in Britain with American connections being faced with immediate demands for repayment of loans and deposits, causing numerous bank failures and an investment standstill. Yet, in the same year, the suppression of the Indian Mutiny led to a boom in the building of Indian railways and public works which was reflected in a rise of British exports to India. Thus Benson's American business was badly affected, only their policy of caution enabling them to survive intact, whilst their Indian and Far Eastern business generated easy if temporary profits.

Robert jnr.'s intuitive understanding and flair for railway business does not seem to have extended to cotton trading. Bensons' extensive American cotton business was devastated by the Civil War. They lost money in 1862 and Pascoe urged Robert jnr. to keep out of cotton until the end of the War. 'I only hope B will keep cool & not rush off to sacrifice the cotton,' he wrote in 1863 to David Hodgson. Pascoe had declined to participate in an American cotton deal on offer through Liverpool, foreseeing the difficulty of any Confederate ship breaking through the Unionist blockade. Robert jnr., however, rashly took a stake with the potential for enormous profits, only to see the ship lost along with his money. 'B has utterly dished your operations. His precipitancy about cotton is sad,' Glyn wrote a few days later. Although some cotton was imported from India it was never as profitable as American cotton could be.[18]

No sooner had the Civil War ended than 'Black Friday', 11 May 1866, took its toll on City firms. 'No single bankruptcy', declared *The Times*, 'has ever caused so great a shock to credit.' Amidst panic, the Bank Rate went to 10 per cent. The cause was the £5m. failure of Overend, Gurney & Co., the City's leading discount house with roots deep in Quakerism. The ripple-waves of shock engulfed firms world-wide, including Masterman's Bank and Henry Chapman & Co. of Montreal; the latter left Robert Benson & Co. with a 'heavy loss', which reduced their capital by at least £30,000. William Benson wrote, after Robert jnr. had been staying with him: 'I hope these few days of country air & rest may have done him good—but he has many anxieties.'[19]

A worrier by nature, Robert jnr. in these years had much to worry about in both his personal and business life. After the birth of their third child, Mary, in 1853, Eleanor had suffered so severely from post-natal depression, then diagnosed as 'nerves', that she had collapsed under the strain of a breakdown. Despite an endless succession of 'cures' taken at various Continental spas, her mental condition deteriorated. 'Illnesses like hers are very trying,' cousin Robert Dockray sympathized. 'The indefinite nature of it makes it still more so—it is so difficult to know what is best to be done. I would however encourage you to be patient, and not to be too anxious or expect any very immediate amendment'. This proved a more than realistic assessment.

Thirteen years later, in January 1867, he wrote 'I feel so very much for you in your great trial'. Robert jnr. had had to settle Eleanor in a separate establishment at Pembury near Tunbridge Wells where she could be close to her doctors and secluded during bouts of mania. To all intents and purposes he was now a widower and, like his father, left in the role of sole parent to his two sons and daughter. Although by convention Victorian women were largely kept apart from matters of business, within the confines of a good marriage a wife could none the less provide support, encouragement, and, if needed, a restraining influence. His grandmother, Sarah Rathbone Benson, was testimony to this. At a time when he was experiencing difficult conditions in business affairs, such support was effectively lost to Robert jnr., just as it had been to Alexander Friedrich Kleinwort after Sophie's death.[20]

Although trading conditions gradually improved in the late 1860s and 1870s and Bensons made substantial profits in some years, constant worry about his wife's health undoubtedly affected Robert jnr.'s own health and prematurely aged him. He died suddenly of a heart attack at the age of 60 on 12 January 1875, leaving his two sons as partners in Robert Benson & Co. and a substantial personal fortune to them and his daughter. Alexander Friedrich Kleinwort died aged 71, almost exactly eleven years later in 1886, from a throat ailment that turned to pneumonia. He, too, left his two sons as partners in the family firm, Kleinwort Sons & Co., and a substantial personal fortune to them and his two daughters. Whereas Alexander Friedrich died a contented man, Robert jnr. died a worried one; the future of Kleinworts, unlike that of Bensons, was secure.

PART TWO

Banking Brothers
1850–1961

5 The Expansion of Kleinworts

THE succeeding pairs of brothers who now directed Kleinwort, Sons & Co. and Robert Benson & Co. brought very dissimilar qualities and philosophies to the two partnerships. Their education, social position, and apprenticeships had little in common, not surprisingly, given the emphasis placed upon the German heritage of the Kleinwort sons. Considered by their fellow countrymen as Germans living in London, largely unassimilated into the national life of their father's adopted country, they moved in the circles of the cosmopolitan *haute bourgeoisie* of Europe. The Benson sons, by contrast, were not only indigenous Englishmen, but they swiftly glided from their father's world of the well-to-do professional classes, which was so stalwart a feature of the mid-Victorian years, to take their place as members of the ruling landed class.

Their respective business philosophies naturally also reflected these divergent backgrounds. As first-generation Englishmen, Herman and Alexander Kleinwort were anxious for the success which would nurture their dynastic desires and consolidate their newly acquired position in the City. Their father had inculcated in them the belief that the family firm always came first: they must concentrate upon the affairs of Kleinwort, Sons & Co. to the exclusion of all other interests. Profit generation was seen therefore as the means to make the business stronger. This was not at all what the Bensons thought. Robert, always known as Robin, and Constantine were much less single-minded when it came to managing the family firm and they were often deflected from the business of wealth creation. For them, profit generation was merely the means to an end, one which was invariably outside the business, such as the creation of one of the finest private collections of Italian art in Britain. Nor were the Bensons remotely interested in the creation of a business dynasty. Their belief that life was an adventure to be enjoyed to the full did not allow for the consideration of any ambition that would require such dogged application to a single aim. 'Never become anchored—don't start a dynasty,' was advice that Robin Benson later urged upon his children.[1]

None the less the pairs of brothers had much in common, not least the way in which their business careers developed. Each pair would be perceived by posterity to divide into the strong and the weak, the leader and the follower.

Thus Alexander Kleinwort and Robin Benson were deemed successful but Herman Kleinwort and Constantine Benson failures. Although such judgements were both simplistic and also inaccurate, in each case one brother did remain active within the firm whilst the other 'retired' early; the reasons behind these events proving markedly different. Moreover, in both cases the relations between the brothers clearly affected the partnerships' ability to develop the business and to take the right commercial decisions. In the Kleinworts' case sibling rivalry acted adversely upon one brother whilst spurring on the other to achieve success. In the Bensons' case, the absence of any rivalry enabled them to sustain a close personal and thus working relationship to the undoubted advantage of their firm. The foundations for these contrasting fraternal relations had been laid by Alexander Friedrich Kleinwort and Robert Benson jnr. They had had sole parental responsibility since in effect both the Kleinwort and Benson boys were brought up in motherless households.

Herman and Alexander were 4 and 2 years old respectively when their mother died in 1860. Despite a phalanx of nursery staff marshalled under the benign reign of Nanny, their greatly loved Barley or Barleycorn, and the presence of two of their father's sisters, later known in the family as the Ferocious Aunts, they were really brought up by their father. According to Emma Steinkoff, a Greverus cousin, 'he was everything for his children—father, mother and most trusted and best friend'. Although he was an old father and seemed the typical Victorian paterfamilias, there were large chinks of warmth and affection in the armour he wore as the strict disciplinarian ruling their lives and the household at The Glebe with a rod of iron.

'Your dear father gladly spent time with you, as seldom fathers do,' Emma Steinkoff later told the boys' eldest sister Wilhelmina. 'On a *hot* Saturday morning he would sit with you for *relaxation* in the chickenyard just because the children enjoyed it. I often used to admire his endurance.' He also gladly entered into their games when they were young and tried his best to make up for the loss of their mother. He even had little Alexander's cot moved into his own bedroom immediately after her death. Inevitably the two girls, Sophie and Wilhelmina, the latter known as Minnie in the family, received more of their father's affection than their younger brothers did; they remained at home, his expectations were lower and he demanded less in terms of scholastic prowess from them. In spite of this, they too were taught Latin which was highly unusual for the period.[2]

When young, Herman and Alexander were also educated at home, sharing drawing, gymnastic, and dancing lessons with their sisters. The children went riding every afternoon, after which they exchanged visits with friends chosen mainly from the German mercantile colony that flourished in Camberwell. This 'little Germany' boasted an array of tempting German delicatessens, toy shops and haberdashers; other suppliers, including the local undertaker, had learnt to insert notices advertising *'hier spricht man deutsch'* to attract local trade. Although usually on good terms with British neighbours, merchant families such as the Kleinworts, Donners, de Cleremonts, Brandts, Beneckes, Huths, and Schröders tended to socialize almost exclusively amongst themselves. On Sundays the Kleinwort children met their German friends at the local Lutheran church, the German Evangelical Church in Windsor Road on Denmark Hill. Their parents and grandparents had raised the money to build the church which was consecrated in December 1855. Here the pastor conducted the service in German for a congregation of up to 300 people. A third-generation Kleinwort descendant recalls how they 'clung loyally to the language of their fathers, which, often to the dismay of their British-born offspring, they spoke stentoriously and unabashed in public places'. In this, of course, they differed little from their ruling family, for Queen Victoria and her many relations spoke German freely amongst themselves.[3]

Writing in 1873 about private (as opposed to joint-stock) banks and bankers, Walter Bagehot asserted that 'The banker's calling is hereditary: the credit of the bank descends from father to son; this inherited wealth brings inherited refinement.' Alexander Friedrich's desire to create a banking dynasty and his efforts to fit his sons for their 'calling' reflected Bagehot's words. Once a week the boys were taken by their father to his City office in order to familiarize them with banking business; they often returned home with 'dear Mr Cohen', a great favourite with all the young Kleinworts. Thus from an early age Herman and Alexander were introduced to their inheritance under the tutelage of their father. He would discuss business matters with Edward Cohen in their hearing and then explain to them the reasoning involved behind any decisions. Although this was of inestimable value for their future careers, the finer points must have been somewhat lost on boys aged 9 and 7. Their father, however, held firm views on the necessity of training them almost from the cradle. He was equally undeviating about the form this training should take. They should have a command of foreign languages and clear handwriting, and undergo a thorough, testing clerkship rounded off by a period abroad visiting the bank's correspondents and agents.[4]

Thus, instead of being sent off to an English boarding-school at the age of 12, both boys were dispatched to school in Germany to perfect their German. The regime at the Real Gymnasium in Karlsruhe proved a shock. Alexander had followed Herman there in 1870 and at the end of the first year wrote to

Nanny: 'You can imagine, we have got hard work here viz: from 8–12 2–4 5–6. 5–6 are privat [*sic*] lessons, and on two days we have till 5 and then no privat lessons, but always an hour in the evenings, and sometimes two, for the next day.' And despite being considered German in London, it also required a considerable effort for him to withstand the teasing—'little man from a little place'—over his name and Englishness. 'I have now got more acostomed to scool life,' he admitted to Nanny, even if 'the boys still kick up a row about my name'; though, in the way of children, adversity soon brought acceptance and a show of solidarity, for 'they have got quieter now, because I had . . . one hour arrest for not knowing something'. Alexander was often in trouble with his masters, whereas Herman was a model pupil. The difference in their characters became more marked once Alexander joined his elder brother in 1874 at the Institut Supérieur de Commerce in Antwerp where they studied French and business studies.

Their father was a hard taskmaster when it came to passing exams, which he understandably considered essential, having himself had no formal schooling after the age of 16. Herman was a clever boy, meticulous about his work, confident, 'inclined to babble over-hastily and presumptuously' in his father's opinion but easily up to gaining honours. 'Tell Herman that I shall think of him on Wednesday—He must be *calm* and *confident*—*not arrogant*, that is no use, but also not despondent,' their father instructed Alexander on 10 October 1874. '*I myself* am absolutely calm about it, because I have the conviction that Herman will not just about pass but that he will pass well, even very well.'

Alexander, however, was less punctilious, more impulsive, and apt to leave things to the last moment. Their father had to instruct that 'From the moment of receiving this letter you must prepare yourself . . . You must read my letter at least *three* times!' And when discussing his son's exams, he complained of a '*most* hastily written' letter in which Alexander had said 'lessons are going "all right"'; this was much too slapdash for his liking. Alexander must be 'well prepared' for them, 'not merely just scrape through!'

He exerted a sustained and at times relentless pressure upon Herman and Alexander to succeed. 'The main thing is the institute, the coming examination, and you must not forget it for a moment.' A parent who feels deeply the lack of some experience can place too much importance upon it when it comes to his children's turn. Alexander Friedrich certainly fell into this category when it came to his sons' education. Having cajoled and berated them by turn, he then tried a little emotional blackmail:

These examinations are the first chance, the first chance in life you have—you and Herman—to give me really *great* pleasure—I really do not know whether anything in

> life would give me greater pleasure than if Herman, for example, came out top in the next examinations. And nothing would grieve me more if he did not pass. I would feel frightfully ashamed and depressed . . . If you do not succeed in passing the examinations honourable [*sic*] then it can only be because thoughtlessness and laziness prevent you—I really feel perturbed when the *possibility* enters my mind and I hardly know *how* I would be able to endure it—You both love me, I know! I believe, too, I deserve your love through the care which I have borne for you since you were alive—I have the best hopes of you but I do not know; from time to time a certain fear arises in me—Do you take your work seriously enough? What if Herman failed! It could drive me to despair.

Where Herman was concerned his fears proved groundless. Minnie's husband Robert Martin wrote, 'I see that Herman is mugging up enormously. What an erudite brother-in-law I shall have! I was quite worried how thin the poor youth is becoming!' And he was the first to congratulate him 'for his brilliantly concluded examinations'.

Alexander, however, continued to fuel his father's fears. He could be flippant and, worst of all, he was extremely careless over his letters, which were often illegible. Alexander Friedrich had obviously forgotten his own youthful shortcomings in that department. His 17-year-old son's handwriting remained 'very deficient, feeble and tentative', five months later it had grown 'worse and worse'—his letters 'unrecognisable'—and he had to point out the consequence of such a deficiency: 'if you come into the business in two years time and write as you do today or perhaps worse, how *can* I make use of you? You would write letters which I could not sign and fill ledgers with scribbles—Make my life at the office misery.' He added despairingly 'I have so often exhorted you in vain, that I hardly know any longer what I should say to make you pull yourself together seriously.'[5]

Alexander Friedrich's continual comparison of the two boys was even less healthy. Letter-writing and post times were then organized with the precision of a timepiece, being the chief means of commercial and personal communication. Whenever Alexander's letters arrived, as they frequently did, two days after being written, a reprimand would reach him by return post, 'you must have taken them too late to the Post Office'. This in itself was not unduly damaging to Alexander's morale. The reminder however, one of countless in a similar vein, that 'Herman's letters always arrive at the right time' proved far more so in the long term. It added salt to a wound which was then barely noticeable but inexorably began to fester under Alexander's skin—a wound that eventually burst open to reveal a depth of sibling rivalry which was almost unfathomable.

This was never their father's intention. A stickler for detail and a disciplinarian he may have been, but he truly loved his sons and had no wish to drive a wedge between them. Although a busy man, he took the time and trouble to write long letters full of advice and home news, concerning himself with every aspect of their lives. It was he who encouraged them to dance and attend balls and have fun—as long as it did not interfere with their studies. Their Nanny told them that 'he never looks so happy as when you are at home'.

He merely held up the good in one son to encourage improvement in the other; unfortunately, far from encouraging, it positively discouraged. Although in later life Alexander was known as the dashing, extrovert brother and Herman as the quiet, introverted one, in youth it had been the reverse. Herman was gregarious and basked in the easily earned approval of his father and friends. Even when he faltered—'in the evening we played some pieces on the piano to Papa, Alexander did his part very well and Papa was delighted with it, Herman did not succeed so well, he made a great many faults'—he remained unabashed, secure in his position within the family. Alexander, on the contrary, found life more difficult. 'My temperament is of a far more quiet nature than that of Herman &, consequently,' he wrote, 'I do not openly express my affections for somebody.'[6]

His quiet nature did not prevent him from expressing great anger when he was gated by his landlord in Antwerp for staying out late and made to perform doorman duties for fellow late-night revellers. 'From the beginning', his father harshly commented, 'I could very well imagine that *you* had created the "scandal" by unnecessarily provocative behaviour—I fear you have been positively impertinently rude. You were what the English call ungentlemanly and that has shocked me.' Nor would it be the last time Alexander was involved in similar escapades.

Nevertheless, in the end student follies were forgettable in the grand scheme of things, whereas anything connected with his son's training for the bank was of immense consequence. 'I do not want to blame. You are still young and inexperienced,' he wrote after one escapade. He hoped that 'your own deliberations, without my intervention, would show you *where you* had gone wrong'. It was as if he recognized an underlying strength of character in his withdrawn, somewhat rebellious, younger son. And, indeed, out of this seemingly unpromising material there would emerge a banker of the very first class.[7]

After gaining the Licencie en Sciences Commerciales from the Institut in Antwerp, first Herman in 1876 then Alexander in 1878 returned home truly trilingual in English, French, and German. 'The older you become the more it means to me to have you about me in order to be able to talk to you more,' their father told them, delighted to have them back so that he could begin the second stage of their training at Kleinwort & Cohen. They started as clerks on a monthly salary of £8 which, since they lived at The Glebe, was by no means a pittance. A sum of £10 per month was then considered sufficient for a young man to live quite comfortably. Even so, their father was keen that they should be on the same footing as any other salaried clerk in the office; he particularly did not want them 'to get used to "too much"' in the way of expenses and advised them 'not [to] create too many needs' for themselves but to lead a spartan existence with plenty of exercise and fresh air.

Although he was in his sixties and had a good stable at The Glebe, Alexander Friedrich still liked to walk from there to the office every morning, driving by carriage only when the weather was '*very* poor'. Herman and Alexander, who could afford otherwise, had to undertake a four-mile hike, joining the swarms of clerks who tramped over London Bridge into the City before 9 o'clock every morning. Far from putting them off, in later life they not only retained the habit of going for long walks but often preferred to walk back from 20 Fenchurch Street to Mayfair or Belgravia after a day in the office.[8]

By present-day standards the office they joined was tiny. The firm was run by their father and Mr Cohen, ably assisted by the senior manager, Robert Denecke, and four senior clerks. These were the correspondence clerks who also supervised particular aspects of the business. The young Kleinworts had known them from childhood since the senior clerks and Mr Cohen always dined at The Glebe on Sunday evenings. There was also a number of ledger clerks, who kept the firm's books, and junior clerks, who opened the post and made the pressed copies of letters by way of learning the business. They were sometimes joined by the apprentice bankers, mainly young Germans sent by their families to serve short apprenticeships for a very small wage before returning home to work in the family firm. They were usually relatives of the partners or sons of family or business friends. At one point Alexander Friedrich refused to take on a friend of Herman's 'as we are bursting *with beginners* I would not have been able to find him anything to do'. Most of the clerks were German and the atmosphere at Kleinwort & Cohen was very much of a family since the office was also staffed by young Drake, Cohen, and Kleinwort relations. This was quite normal: most firms then consisted almost entirely of family members, especially at management level. The emphasis on family connections had been deepened further when Herman and Alexander's brothers-in-law, John Charles Andreae and Robert Martin had been brought into the bank after their marriages, for they were already related to each other as first cousins.[9]

The Andreaes, like the Greveruses, were descended from a long line of theologians and scholars—their name evolving from one Stephen Enderis who lived in the fifteenth century in Bavaria. One of his descendants, Johann Valentine Andreae, was a famous seventeenth-century divine, mathematician, and poet, whose main work, *Christianopolis*, published in 1619, was in the same vein as Thomas More's earlier *Utopia*. Johann Andreae has been described as a father of Rosicrucianism and 'flower power' and fittingly, roses appear on the Andreae family coat of arms.

Later generations, however, left the groves of academe and divinity for the more commercial world of book printing. By the eighteenth century they had become a substantial merchanting family in Frankfurt and well known for their patronage of the arts. Philipp Bernhard Andreae sent his son John Charles, always known as Carlo, to London to gain commercial experience. Here he lodged with his cousin Robert Martin through whom he met Sophie Kleinwort. After their marriage in 1873 he joined the Kleinwort bank but left it five years later when his father-in-law advanced him £30,000 from Sophie's inheritance with which to start his own City business.

Despite possessing a more English-sounding name, his cousin Robert Martin also came from Frankfurt. The Martins were an ancient Rhenish family from the Weingarten area where successive generations bore the armorial title of Hereditary Forester to the King. At the start of the nineteenth century Robert Martin's grandfather, Philip Ludwig Martin, became a partner in his father-in-law's sizeable dry-salting business and, like John Wakefield of Kendal, dealt in gunpowder during the Napoleonic wars. His son, Robert Martin's father Gustav, gained his doctorate of law at Heidelberg and Munich before frequenting the artistic salons of Frankfurt. He knew Mendelssohn through the Bernhard Andreaes, who regularly held musical soirées and readings, and in 1836 married their musical daughter, Emma. In 1865 their son, Robert, went to gain business experience in London at Robert de Clermont's firm, the de Clermonts being cousins of his and also kinsmen of his Donner aunt, both of whom were neighbours and friends of the Kleinworts in Camberwell.

De Clermonts was a small banking business with offices in Paris and London, where Robert looked after the German accounts and correspondence. In April 1869 de Clermont told Gustav that Robert 'showed diligence and conscientiousness in the work entrusted to him' and he was sent for a spell to the Paris office, returning to London when the Franco-Prussian War broke out in 1870 and severely disrupted European trade. De Clermonts suffered considerably, and they and Drake, Kleinwort & Cohen were but two of the many firms which incurred large losses through bad debts as a consequence of the war. With an unexpected amount of time on his hands, Robert was one of the young men Minnie Kleinwort found in de Clermont's garden 'throwing apples about'. After their marriage in 1872 Alexander Friedrich offered him a partnership in Kleinwort & Cohen, as the firm had then become after Drake's retirement. To his surprise Robert declined, saying that at the age of 26 he was not yet mature enough to assume such a responsibility. The understanding, however, was that the offer would be repeated in the near future.

He had become a Manager by the time Herman entered the bank as a clerk in 1876 but remained so when Herman joined the partnership in 1881. When the partnership was restructured after Edward Cohen's retirement in 1883 it was not renamed Kleinwort, Sons & Co. with the purpose of excluding sons-in-law. Hambro, Baring, Schröder, and Rothschild sons, sons-in-law, and nephews all provided a pool from which to replenish the partnerships of their firms. In the case of Kleinworts, the pool consisted of two sons and two sons-in-law. Alexander Friedrich was extremely close to his two daughters and their families; he saw them every day on his way back from the office and they always spent Sundays at The Glebe with him. It was quite understood that when the young Andreae and Martin sons grew up there would be a ready-made training ground for them, with a place in the bank for the eldest or most suitable; the assumption being that, like their fathers before them, they would come in with a smaller capital and percentage of the profits than Herman and Alexander and their sons.

Herman and Alexander, however, did not endorse their father's aim of propagating a dynastic firm through including the Andreaes and Martins in the partnership. They interpreted Carlo's departure in 1878 to start his own business, Nestlé Andreae & Co., as removing the Andreaes from any partnership considerations. In the case of the Martins, when the partnership was reconstructed Robert did not push himself forward to claim the place previously offered to him, nor did he ever intimate that he was ready to do so—as he later remarked, 'To the great relief of the Kleinworts!' Like his father before him, Robert found more pleasure in music and art than in commercial ventures. A kindly, honourable man, he possessed the ability but not the ambition to devote himself exclusively to his father-in-law's single-minded style of banking. He remained for thirty years at Kleinworts, in the 1880s on a salary of £5,000 per annum but with a share in the profits which easily doubled his income in good years—'and with Kleinworts they were mostly good years', his son recalled.[10]

By 1886 the Kleinwort brothers had settled down in worldly terms. They had interrupted their clerkships to travel abroad for fifteen to eighteen months to meet the bank's agents and clients. The brothers had no need for the more familiar traveller's paraphernalia of visas, passports, and money, they travelled armed only with the firm's letter of credit. 'Merchants and bankers in every port of significance were familiar with the Kleinwort Letter of Credit', Cecil Elbra, later the firm's general manager, explained. 'And this ensured a friendly reception.' On their return they had been promoted to manager status before joining their father in the first partnership of Kleinwort Sons & Co. in 1883.[11]

Alexander Friedrich had continued to dominate their lives even in young adulthood and they remained firmly anchored to the family circle in Camberwell. After his marriage to Marguerite Günther in 1881, Herman moved the shortest possible distance away—to The Platanes on Grove Hill opposite the Martins at Redcourt and the Andreaes at Crestalta (both on Champion Hill) and a bare quarter of an hour's walk from his father and Alexander at The Glebe. Alexander continued to live there after their father's death on 7 January 1886 so that the Kleinwort enclave remained rooted in Camberwell, just as the two brothers initially intended to keep the bank rooted in 'the old way' under their direction. 'That is our aim in life', Herman told Mr Cohen, and to begin with so it was.

The first task that they faced was to ensure the continuance of the bank's business. Under the terms of their father's well-considered will, Minnie inherited £150,000 [£8.9m.] and Sophie £120,000, having already received £30,000 in 1878. These sums were to remain in the business and be repaid over twenty annual instalments, though repayments could be made sooner if their brothers wished. The remainder of his entire property was left in equal shares to his sons, Herman receiving part of the estate in cash (£203,400 [£12.1m.]). A week after his death they were able to inform the Bank of England that they would have a working capital of between £550,000 and £600,000 [£35.8m.]. 'We cannot state the exact figure until everything is settled and our books are closed,' Alexander told their New York agent on 16 January 1886. In the period following their father's death they were frantically busy. A letter had to be personally written to every client and agent with the sole purpose of reassuring them that the firm was unaffected by the founder's death. 'My brother and I will continue the business without making any changes', Alexander assured one client, H. Albert de Bary & Co. in Belgium, adding that, 'the active capital remains the same'.

It was imperative to retain their clients' confidence and thus their business: 'continuity' and 'capitalization' were the key, conveying above all a message of safety. As the founder of Seligmans, Joseph Seligman, said in 1867, 'The main thing in a banker is safety, with ability to reach his money at a moment's call'; whilst at the smaller firm of Frederick Huth & Co., Huth's son-in-law Daniel Meinertzhagen declared that 'it is not the greater or smaller profits that matter as much as the safety and regularity with which the concern is conducted'.

A bank's credit rating was also assessed on the basis of whether it could be considered 'safe and likely to continue so'. A large working capital was no guarantee of the coveted A1 credit rating, since it could be tied up in assets that suddenly proved illiquid, such as unsaleable bonds or property. Kleinworts' large capital of around £600,000 was less than Rothschilds', Stern Brothers', and Barings' but on a par with Lazards'. Kleinworts' credit rating was still A1, whereas an 1883 report found Lazards 'good for what they undertake, and wealthy, but speculative and wide-spread. Their acceptances would not be taken at the finest rates and their credit must therefore be considered 2nd class.' Their only sin had been to pursue an aggressive policy in competition with such larger rivals as Morgans and Seligmans. This remains the classic banking problem: how to balance safety with expansion.[12]

Alexander Friedrich's stated policy had been that Kleinworts should 'continue to do a large and increasing business, but it is more important to do a profitable safe business—to avoid reckless speculation and all parties who do not deserve and inspire confidence'. Yet Kleinworts under its founder had certainly been expansionist: aggressive, quick to identify new opportunities and willing to take large risks for increased profit—though only through people known to the partners. 'We would at all times rather increase the number of our correspondents than the transactions with a few of them', Alexander Friedrich had stated, 'large credits are desirable only when the position of the parties concerned is thoroughly known to us.' This policy of spreading the risk by keeping a large number of moderate credits running simultaneously, rather than large credits for a small number, was followed by Schröders, as well as Barings, then the leading accepting house (whose £6.7m. outstanding in 1870 would grow to £15m. by 1890). It was in direct contrast to that of Rothschilds, who preferred to lend to a few clients on a very large scale, thereby avoiding bad debts by a closer supervision of credits.

The way in which Herman and Alexander kept a close tally of their clients' standing was a continuation of their father's methods. As an *aide memoire*, they kept little black leatherbound books which at a cursory glance looked like address books. However, the word PRIVATE was stamped on the outside; and inside, the pages bore confidential details of conversations with their clients and reports on their financial position. They had been trained by their father to keep such a record as an indispensable tool of business; he himself had kept a series of such books.

Thus when, for instance, one of their Manchester cotton-spinner clients, Mr Ellinger of Ellinger & Co., wanted to arrange a further credit, Alexander knew that 'the *cash* capital of his firm is *over* £100,000', which sum did not include 'the value of his copper rollers (about £7,000) or of machinery also worth abt £7,000'. If a new client was introduced, down went the details into the little black book. Mr V. M. Seminario, who was introduced by an old client, J. R. Leseur of

Hamburg and Caracas, stated on 6 September 1889: 'We are four brothers together and our father commandites us. Our working capital is fr.2,000,000—but as we all possess private means besides, our responsible capital is fr.6,000,000. We have just arranged a credit with Frühling & Goschen & also have one at the Credit Lyonnais'. The Kleinworts also found out that the Seminario father was worth fr.15,000,000 so that arranging a credit for their Guayaquil (Ecuador) trade was a pleasure.[13]

During the previous decade Kleinworts had provided credit facilities for a number of leading American coffee importers, including one of their oldest clients W. H. Crossman & Brothers, New York coffee brokers with whom their father had first done business from Havana through Ferdinand Karck. Herman had naturally called on them while he was in New York at the end of 1886, when the firm was run by George Crossman and Henry Sielcken. The latter partner was a friend of the family and became attracted to Herman's second daughter, Helen, upon whom he wanted to press magnificent diamonds. He could certainly afford such luxurious gifts, for the growth of the firm, as recorded in Alexander's little black book, was impressive.

Sielcken told Herman in New York that their profits at the end of 1886 amounted to $400,000 on an increased capital of $900,000. Ten years later the capital, even after payouts to partners, had risen to $1.2m. But the great leap came in the early years of the twentieth century. Sielcken wrote to Kleinworts on 14 March 1901: 'On 1 Feby when closing our books we had $2,160,000 and we have made a great deal of money since, coffee working for us like a charm.' The charm clearly continued to work, for by the end of 1909 the firm, now called Crossman & Sielcken, had a net profit of $1.01m. on a capital of $7.81m. Crossmans' steadily rising capitalization and profitability brought, in turn, an increase in business for Kleinworts, who in the following year made £46,000 [£2.1m.] through them; it was exactly the sort of operation they liked to service, as indeed would any accepting house. Kleinworts' own growth in the three decades leading up to 1914 was equally strong.[14]

From 1880 to 1890 the business of the bank doubled. Acceptances outstanding in 1890 amounted to just over £5m. and, despite the large sums totalling over £500,000 paid out to Edward Cohen, Minnie Martin, and Sophie Andreae, the capital employed in the firm had increased to £817,214. The firm made a net profit of nearly £130,000 [£7.5m.], of which the partners' proportion was £32,000 [£1.8m.] each. One of the changes introduced from the mid-1880s under the Kleinwort brothers was to invest a large proportion of their capital in stock exchange securities—a sure sign of the stability of the bank's business and of the young partners' confidence in themselves and their firm. Such confidence was not misplaced. By 1900 acceptances had increased by just over £3m., while the capital had grown to over £1.6m. The firm's net profit was £154,000 [£8.4m.] with the partners receiving £45,000 [£2.4m.] each. Corresponding figures for the firm in 1913 were £14.2m. acceptances outstanding on a capital of £4.4m. Given that their father had started out in 1855 in a partnership capitalized at £200,000, such growth was remarkable. It made Kleinwort, Sons & Co. probably the fastest growing accepting house, ahead of its main competitor Schröders who had acceptances of £11.6m. and capital of £3.5m.; by 1913, apart from Rothschilds, Kleinworts was the pre-eminent accepting house in the City. To discover how Herman and Alexander steered the bank into such productive waters it is necessary to look at where they continued to fish in their father's pools and where they changed course to discover new business.[15]

Russia, then undergoing rapid industrialization, was one area where they followed their father's account-seeking course. Kleinworts worked with a variety of companies there, usually German in origin or with some German connection. They appointed a Moscow agent, Edward Stolterfoht, who was German and dealt with their mainly German client list of cotton spinners, commodity merchants, and chemical manufacturers; and to reduce the risk, many of the credits granted were reimbursement ones in which a local bank guaranteed the acceptance.

Trading with Russia, however, was never easy. Kleinworts continually had to be on their guard for political as well as economic reasons and were correspondingly severe with clients. Unfavourable reports about conditions in Moscow and the Russian chemical industry spelt the end of one client, the poor Mr Borchardt's credit line: 'Would he please cover the drafts accepted for his account at maturity and consider the credit granted to him since then as cancelled?' Although Mr Borchardt was not a client to take such treatment without a murmur and marshalled allies in the form of larger Kleinwort clients—the Disconto Bank, Messrs Wogau & Co. and the Wolga-Kama Bank—Kleinworts remained resolute.

The partners explained their policy to Stolterfoht in May 1888. 'If the standing and way of business of a customer is such that the solidity of the latter gives cause for anxiety at the first crisis, then we would rather not work with him at all. We must not lay ourselves open to the charge that we are as generous in the provision of credits as we are hasty in withdrawing them.' The firm was equally clear about the way in which a credit should be used. Carl Stucken & Co. had a credit line of £10,000 but had only used a small amount of it to date, which was clearly unprofitable for Kleinworts. 'Perhaps they can give you the assurance that they will use the facility in a more regular fashion; without such an assurance an increase would not be convenient to us,' No. 20 informed Stolterfoht. Despite using a firm hand, Kleinworts never succeeded in obtaining a huge amount of business from Russia; they had to be content with earning a steady 4–5 per cent of their total commissions from Russian accounts. As events turned out, they were no doubt glad the percentage was not higher.[16]

Herman and Alexander also followed their father's policy in other parts of the world. They maintained substantial accounts in Scandinavia—where their agent Goran Corin, a Swedish cotton broker, was notably forthcoming in producing new business, supplying their fourth largest source of commission earnings—and in Britain. In fact the United Kingdom was their second largest area of operation and produced an increasing share of revenue. The majority of clients were located in Manchester, Liverpool, and London and were mainly connected with the cotton trade; many were accounts opened by their father in the days of Drake, Kleinwort & Cohen. The largest Manchester cotton spinners E. Ashworth and Co. remained valued clients, as did the Liverpool affiliate of Alexander Sprunt and Co. of North Carolina, by 1914 the largest United States cotton exporting firm.[17]

Kleinworts also financed the import of cotton from Egypt for Stucken and Co. of Liverpool, and in February 1890 gained notoriety over another of their Egyptian imports. When their client refused to accept a shipment of fertilizer, Kleinworts were left with the cargo. This consisted not of fertilizer but the raw material for it, namely 180,000 mummified cats excavated from their ancient burial ground in Egypt. Kleinworts consigned the 19½ tons of embalmed cats to auction where they fetched £3 13*s.* 9*d.* per ton; the auctioneer knocked the lots down using one of the cats' heads as a hammer.[18]

Kleinworts continued to finance the sugar and cigar trade in Britain, specializing in companies with a Cuban connection such as C. Czarnikow Ltd. This leading firm of produce merchants and brokers, a main importer of Cuban sugar, was one of their largest United Kingdom clients. Julius Caesar Czarnikow, its founder and a former Camberwell neighbour, was frequently invited to shoot at Wierton, Herman's country property, or to dine at Curzon Street, where Alexander now lived. Czarnikow and Alexander regularly indulged in cigar-smoking competitions. On one occasion both contestants were so determined to win that they ended up flat on their backs on the floor, holding the stubs of their cigars upright. It was only after Alexander made his opponent laugh that Czarnikow's ash finally fell off, giving the victory to Alexander.[19]

Herman and Alexander adhered to their father's restrictions on the amount and number of credits for South American trade owing to the risks of operating there; long credits of six months or more before payment were quite usual. Even so, the bank had managed to earn 10.7 per cent of its commission from South America in 1871. Regardless of the profitability of operations in Brazil and the Argentine, where their clients were mainly in the coffee trade, the partners decided not to try to emulate firms such as Barings, Antony Gibbs, or Huths that traditionally specialized in that part of the world.

The temptation must have been great, for Latin America as a whole was undergoing a period of extraordinary growth, with a massive programme of railway construction stimulating the expansion of industry. Whilst Barings and Morgans fought over State bond issues, and Bensons backed Brazilian railways, Kleinworts cautiously restricted their exposure. Herman, as senior partner, propounded the safe approach to South American business, thereby avoiding 'the reckless speculation and all parties who do not deserve and inspire confidence' (his father's words) with which others in the City involved themselves at their peril. Barings, in particular, found themselves overexposed and facing bankruptcy when the Argentinian economic boom, which they had largely financed, faltered. In 1890, a year when Kleinworts' bad debts were a mere £4,300 on earnings of £149,000 and the partners' capital was £817,214, Barings had liabilities of £20.96m. and were unable to discharge them as they fell due.

The collapse of Barings, followed by its reconstruction on a smaller scale, meant that suddenly there were major opportunities for other houses. This particularly applied to North America, where Kleinworts not only continued to do the largest part of their business, with a rapid turnover of credits generating ever larger commission earnings, but also now entered into new areas of operation, such as the underwriting of American issues and a larger participation in the foreign exchange markets.[20]

When Herman and Alexander first took over the partnership in 1886, the business was fairly evenly spread geographically, with American and German firms being the most important sources of revenue. Under their direction, however, by the first decade of the twentieth century United States' acceptances generated 45 per cent of acceptance revenue and commission earned from America soared. Commission earnings were £24,000 in 1890; £51,000 ten years later, and reached a pre-1914 high of £92,000 in 1905, compared with £20,000 that year from the United Kingdom and £9,000 from Germany. The growth of their American business was not due to any remarkable efforts by Winter & Smillie, their agent in New York; the Kleinworts regularly visited the United States and became increasingly dissatisfied with their agent's conservative approach. They therefore decided to appoint regional agents, the first appointment going to J. B. Moors in Boston in 1890.[21]

The situation in New York had not been resolved when, in June 1897, a visitor to 20 Fenchurch Street changed the course of their American operation. Armed with a letter of introduction from their old friend Herman Sielcken, which naturally gave an immediate entrée, Samuel Sachs called on Herman and Alexander to try to interest them in forming a connection with his firm Goldman Sachs & Co. of New York.

The Goldmans and the Sachses had emigrated from Bavaria in 1848, the year of European revolutions, and were soon part of the New York Jewish set that included the Guggenheims, Schiffs, and Warburgs and who founded such well-known Wall Street banks as Lehman Brothers, Speyer & Co., J. S. Bache & Co., J. W. Seligman & Co., and Kuhn Loeb & Co. They made the transition from selling goods to selling money extremely quickly and were so intermarried that aunts and nieces were often sisters-in-law as well. Goldman Sachs & Co. came into being because two Goldman sisters married two Sachs brothers. Marcus Goldman had made his fortune and established himself as a merchant banker from the most unprepossessing headquarters: a cellar room next to a coal chute housed his banking operation which was largely an al fresco one.

Goldman, like the Lehmans and Seligmans, carried his business in his tall, black silk, 'chimney-pot' hat. Every morning he visited the small businesses of the lower East Side, where the wholesale jewellers and the hide and leather merchants were located. In return for cash, he purchased commercial paper or promissory notes at, say, a 9 per cent discount and tucked them inside the inner band of his hat for safe keeping until he visited the commercial banks in the afternoon. As he met his fellow bankers also making their rounds, each would bow and appraise the height of the others' hats. From the beginning, Marcus Goldman was able to sell as much as $5m. worth of commercial paper a year in this way.

By the 1880s he was carrying $30m. worth of paper a year and had decided to take on a partner, his new son-in-law Samuel Sachs. The firm had become the leading dealer in commercial paper in New York but, after Goldman's death, his son Henry and Samuel Sachs wanted to expand into other areas of operation. Henry was especially keen to take the firm into raising capital and bond dealing but, according to Walter Sachs, 'even then we apparently had some difficulty in initiating business in bonds'. A collaboration with a leading London merchant bank would be highly desirable to develop the business along the lines of commercial credits and foreign exchange.[22]

Since Kleinworts did not know them, Samuel Sachs suggested that they first check the firm's standing in the New York market whilst he took a Continental holiday. There was only one man to approach on such a matter—the Rothschilds' agent in New York, August Belmont, a legend on both Wall Street and Fifth Avenue. He had established himself as an immensely successful banker and, on the basis that conspicuous wealth creates confidence, as a leading social figure in the city, making it his business to know everyone.

In 1897 Goldman, Sachs & Co. were considered relatively small fry compared with Kuhn, Loeb & Co. or Rothschilds, and the 83-year-old Belmont took his time about replying to Kleinworts' discreet enquiry. When he did deign to respond, his note described Goldman Sachs as the 'one firm about which nobody can say anything against'. This was understood by all parties to be a praiseworthy endorsement and, on 21 July 1897, Kleinworts agreed to begin joint account operations. During the honeymoon period when both firms were becoming accustomed to one another, Kleinworts limited business to discounting bills, financing tobacco purchases, and generally providing credits for Goldman Sachs's clients in New York.[23]

At first Kleinworts were very much the senior partner in the marriage. They already had an excellent reputation in Europe and a greater capitalization. Henry Goldman told Alexander in 1898 that Goldman Sachs's responsible working capital was $1.6m. [£21.3m.] with the partners' private property worth another $400,000 [£5.3m.], at a time when Kleinworts' partners' capital was £1.4m. [£91m.]. They were also treated with deference by their American partners, in the way the New World then did towards the Old. Samuel groomed his 15-year-old son Walter for weeks in preparation for a Kleinwort dinner party at The Glebe. Walter could never forget the 'terrible humiliation' he suffered that night when he was so nervous that he bowed and shook hands with the butler.

The marriage nevertheless soon developed into one of equals. By 30 May 1901 Samuel Sachs was able to report that their capital had grown to $2.5m. as of the year's end 'and we have since been doing exceedingly well'. Goldman Sachs was an aggressive, astute house and they found a willing, equally dynamic partner in Alexander Kleinwort. At this stage Kleinworts was run by a partnership in many ways resembling the earlier one of Edward Cohen and Alexander Friedrich Kleinwort. Whereas Herman had become the cautious gentleman banker with the safety of operations uppermost in his mind, his younger brother was the bold, ambitious one willing to take risks to expand the firm. The partnership worked and Herman thoroughly supported Alexander's expansionist drive; without this agreement on policy, Alexander could not have taken the firm into the new, extremely profitable areas resulting from the association with Goldman Sachs.[24]

Their collaboration was mutually beneficial. At Kleinworts' suggestion, Goldman Sachs set up a foreign exchange department to increase their bond arbitrage business; and, with their help, Kleinworts built up a large business providing letters of credit for companies rather than for the more usual customer, the individual traveller, as J. S. Morgan and Brown Shipley did. The greatest benefit of this association undoubtedly lay in the field of new issues. Bensons were already fully immersed in such activity, having tested the waters with railway share issues, while Kleinworts by the turn of the century had yet to dip their toes in. They had always preferred to concentrate upon the accepting business, just as Brown Shipley had done.

Most of the larger merchant banks had not specialized in this way; they undertook both acceptance and issuing work. Rothschilds, Morgans, and Barings were three who successfully carried on both types of business, even though they tended to become better known for one particular operation than the other. Several factors had militated against Kleinworts' involvement in issuing. One was the lack of contacts at ministerial or royal level to bring such business their way; they were not in the same league as either Rothschilds or Barings, who had raised funds for foreign governments since the early nineteenth century, nor even Hambros and Morgans, more recent entrants into the challenging field of sovereign loans. Another factor was capital. Traditionally an issuing house had to be able to tie up large amounts of capital in buying the entire issue from the borrower before offering it to the market. Underwriting—whereby a group of banks agreed to take an issue if the public rejected it—did not become the norm until towards the end of the nineteenth century. As Kleinworts could now afford to enter this market, the association with Goldman Sachs came at an opportune moment.

The first issue that Kleinworts underwrote was a seminal one. Typically it came about through a family connection; in this instance a Sachs one. Julius Rosenwald had purchased a mail-order house in Chicago and wanted to expand it. Through his aunt's brother Samuel, he asked Goldman Sachs for a $5m. loan. Now Henry Goldman had long wanted to venture into underwriting in collaboration with his friend Philip Lehman of the New York firm Lehman Brothers. These two seized the opportunity to suggest instead a public offering of stock. Established Wall Street houses hardly recognized manufacturing—J. P. Morgan rejected as too speculative prospective clients such as the Goodyear Tyre & Rubber Co. and the Edison Car Battery Co.—let alone the retail sector. There had never been a mail-order public issue. Goldman Sachs and Lehmans were taking a risk, but one with immense rewards if successful. They asked Alexander to work with them at the London end and in 1906 floated Sears Roebuck & Co. The issue was a resounding success, with Kleinworts arranging the London underwriting and selling stock through their Continental clients. It was the beginning of a most rewarding partnership in company finance.

Although many firms turned up their noses at helping privately owned industrial and retail companies 'go public', the Goldman / Lehman / Kleinwort team knew no such qualms and successfully brought out and underwrote fourteen such issues between 1906 and 1914. The first shares to be offered in a chain store were not issued by an established market leader such as J. P. Morgan but by the new dynamic trio, which raised $6m. for F. W. Woolworth & Co. in 1911. The difficulty of marketing and placing such a large issue, and the hostility felt by Wall Street for this type of company, is illustrated by the terms. They were hugely advantageous to the bankers. Goldman Sachs, Lehmans, and Kleinworts bought the stock from Woolworths and then set up a syndicate which purchased the shares from them, marketed them, and arranged for them to be underwritten. The trio retained 20 per cent of the common *and* preferred stock, but the total price was less than the value of the preferred stock alone, so they got the common shares gratis for bringing out the issue. They had already arranged a $13.5m. issue for the Studebaker Corporation the previous year; after Woolworths they brought amongst others the Continental Can Co. to market, in issues totalling $23.75m. in 1912 and $12m. in 1913. Detailed figures are not available but Kleinworts' stock operation profits leapt during these years, actually doubling in 1912 to nearly £235,000 [£11.4m.] as a result of these company finance deals.[25]

In many of them Alexander, ably assisted by his nephew Herman Andreae, worked closely with another German banker, Saemy Japhet of S. Japhet & Co., which had opened a London office in 1896. Although well established in Frankfurt and Berlin, he found that breaking into the City was 'like trying to climb a wall; and having already placed my hands firmly on the top, someone came from the other side to beat me off'. Nevertheless, by offering a partnership to Gottfried Loewenstein, one of the most skilled arbitragists in Europe, Japhet was able to establish his firm as one of the City's leading arbitrage and foreign exchange houses. Alexander knew of Japhet through his friend Sir Ernest Cassel, the outstanding financier who was a member of Edward VII's set. Cassel had introduced Alexander to Sir Basil Zaharoff, the munitions magnate, who held a large shareholding in Japhets. As a result Japhet was invited to join Kleinworts' syndicate for American issues.

Japhet himself was so aggressive, however, that he could not wait for the shares to be issued in Europe but began selling them beforehand. This not unnaturally severely disrupted the market for the issue. Although it would have been quite in order for Alexander to remove Japhets from the issue in question and any future ones, he contained his justifiable wrath, recognizing that the strength of Japhets' placing power on the Continent was necessary to the success of the issue. In this, as in many other instances, Alexander showed how he had learnt to weigh up a situation dispassionately, not to take matters subjectively or be deflected by personalities. 'It does not matter what others think of you,' his father had told him, 'it does matter what you can achieve.' Alexander later told his youngest son that he had learnt from his father to listen 'quite dispassionately to the expressions of different people' so that he could make sound judgements and act decisively. In consequence he became a man who was respected throughout the City.[26]

It was Alexander who masterminded the next development in the trio's activities. Their placing power for the early American issues in Germany, Holland, Scandinavia, and Belgium had proved excellent but Alexander had found it difficult to operate with equal success in France. His plan was that they would join forces with Henri Hoechstaedter to set up a banking house in Paris with a capital of fr.5m. [£9.5m.]. This firm, known as Messrs Henri Hoechstaedter et Cie, would help place American securities in France. The Trefoil Syndicate's share of fr.3m. was made up by a contribution of fr.1m. from each of its members—Kleinworts, Goldman Sachs, and Lehman Brothers. Henri Hoechstaedter and his partner contributed the remaining fr.2m. The firm commenced business on 20 September 1911, and by the following June the profit and interest due to the Trefoil Syndicate amounted to fr.187,186,000 [£350,000].

Kleinworts, however, had no other company finance business and had been unable to compete with their main acceptance rivals, Schröders and Barings, for lucrative business in the issuing boom of the late 1880s. Schröders, for instance, had expanded their issuing side by finding clients in Persia and South America and had also been active in the 1850s–60s in Cuba, where Kleinworts could have won the clients if they had been interested. Herman Andreae persuaded the Kleinwort brothers to try to win some independent deals and the first issue that Alexander arranged was for £20m. Republic of Cuba's 5 per cent Treasury Bonds in 1911, which was successful. He quickly followed it with a $6m. issue of 5 per cent mortgage bonds for the Cuban Ports Co., which proved less straightforward. Whereas Charles Drake had made a great deal of money out of his eight-year franchise to dredge the mud from the port of Havana, charging each foreign vessel using the harbour and making at least $500,000 by 1846, Cubans sixty-five years later were not so acquiescent about the introduction of an extra port tax on all goods unloaded in harbour. The Cuban government's attempt to impose the tax in order to earn the interest payable on the bonds and their ultimate repayment was challenged in the Cuban courts. The firm's struggle with the issue was relished by Morgan Grenfell, a leading issuing house but one which lagged well behind Kleinworts in accepting: 'Kleinworts', wrote Teddy Grenfell, 'seem to have taken the [Cuban Ports] bonds & issued them at very little profit to themselves in order to appear as an issuing house, and no doubt they have repented at leisure.'[27]

While their diversification into the issuing business met with mixed success, the brothers' divergence from their father's course in another area helped to establish Kleinworts as the leading accepting house in the pre-1914 period. Along with Schröders, they followed a high-risk policy of maintaining a much greater ratio of acceptances to capital than other banks were prepared to do.

In the nineteenth century firms tended not to accept bills totalling more than 3–4 times their capital and reserves. By the next century this practice had become a convention among accepting houses, as Sir Robert Kindersley of Lazards explained to the Macmillan Committee on Finance and Industry in 1931. Under Alexander Friedrich's direction, as the capital had grown, so, naturally, the volume of credits granted had increased, though remaining within the 1 : 4 ratio considered prudent as an upper limit. Once Herman and Alexander were in sole charge, however, they raised the capital / acceptance ratio to 1 : 5 and consistently remained above the customary ratio until 1908, when the ratio fell to near the 1 : 4 mark where it hovered until 1914. The partners' unorthodox tactics enabled the bank to undertake a much greater volume of business with a consequent rise in profits.

Kleinworts were not the only firm to employ such tactics. In boom years the increase in trade had often tempted other firms to rise above the accepted ratio, but only for a short period. This was where Kleinworts outdistanced the other houses. They employed this strategy consistently throughout two decades. Although the evidence from other firms is fragmentary, it appears that Hambros, the fifth largest accepting house, had a ratio of 1 : 2 in 1905, while Antony Gibbs only allowed theirs to rise above this to 1 : 3 on two occasions during the period 1870–1910. Brown Shipley in contrast were much larger and much bolder. When their capital was £1.8m. they had allowed their acceptances to fluctuate between £6m. and £9m. in the mid-1870s.

Yet it was none other than Brown Shipley who in 1891 were critical of the increasing volume of Kleinworts' acceptances: 'The amount and unwieldiness of their acceptances as compared with their means is beginning to excite unfavourable comment.' Six years later Kleinworts still remained committed to a 1 : 6 ratio and were seeing their capital growth outpacing more orthodox firms. 'With no great desire to expand and even less inclination to experiment', Brown Shipley were one of the houses being left behind. They had forfeited their eminent position in the league table of Anglo-American houses through the inexpedient combination of a withdrawal of capital by the partners and a failure to keep up with trading conditions and new opportunities in America. 'It will be as well not to send for a while blank endorsed bills of Kleinwort, Sons & Co.,' they advised their New York partners in 1897.

Although Brown Shipley had to admit that Kleinworts 'are of course perfectly good', they nevertheless went on to report in 1897 that 'just now the market is very full of the name and for some time past indications have come to us from the discount houses that their lines are full'. Brown Shipley added, somewhat disingenuously, 'Of course we do not want to shut down the name altogether, but to suggest that you send us for a while more moderate accounts.' Such comments naturally coloured the way in which Kleinworts were regarded despite their good name. Consequently their reputation as risk takers grew as the quantity of their paper in the market mounted.

Their unpopularity with the principal discount houses also grew. The result was that by 1899 the rates offered for Kleinwort bills were above prime rate, thereby reflecting Lombard Street's concern. 'You will notice that Kleinworts bills do not command such good rates as those of other drawers by 1/16th of one percent,' reported Brown Shipley. Discount houses such as Union Discount and Alexanders were so 'full up' with Kleinwort paper that the manager of Union Discount's own bankers, the London and Westminster Bank, felt obliged to warn them about the City's disquiet over their unconventional policy. Others were not so charitable. The scion of one City house sniffed in November 1900, 'Personally I am glad to think that Barings' credits are not to be got as easily as Kleinworts' or Schröders' because I am vain enough to think that the goodwill represented by our name is in a different class from that represented by the above named and their like.' The brothers, however, were not prepared to abandon a strategy that had achieved signal growth just because it met with a little opposition. They knew they were trading from a position of strength; others unfortunately did not. In 1904 Seyd & Co., the credit reference agency, estimated Kleinworts' capital at £1.5m. when it was in fact well over £2m. Other City houses including Brown Shipley may also have underestimated their size and concluded they were in danger of overextending themselves.[28]

City institutions were also anxious about the large number of Kleinwort bills being drawn by American firms. 'Meanwhile the discount market has apparently lost its head as you will have seen from the Papers,' Alexander wrote to Herman Sielcken on 19 August 1907. 'Rates have jumped up, there is much wild talk about what is going to happen in America and we believe quite a number of our Banks and Discount houses decline to take any American drawn bills no matter on whom they are drawn! We have rarely seen our market in such a foolish and hysterical condition.' It appears that Schröders and Kleinworts were the houses most mentioned 'tho' what', Alexander continued, 'we poor miserable sinners are supposed to have done or in what way we are supposed to have "financed" America to too large an extent, I cannot say'. What he could and did say was that Kleinworts were doing a large and profitable business in America where, as elsewhere, their affairs were never in better shape, 'whatever may be said by senseless or ignorant fools and jealous competitors'. The only cloud on Kleinworts' financial horizon was caused by the City's scare-mongering. 'I confess that it makes me clench my teeth to hear it said that this or that Bank is full in Kleinwort, Sons and Company', Alexander admitted, adding somewhat philosophically 'however it is the penalty of success and perhaps I ought not to complain'.[29]

Unfortunately he soon had cause for further complaint over what came to be known as 'the salmon coloured bill agitation'. Rumours circulated to the effect that many of the salmon-pink bills drawn on Kleinworts by Goldman Sachs were finance bills. These bills were considered undesirable by acceptance purists, since they financed a speculation rather than a specific trade transaction. In the words of evidence Sir Felix Schuster, governor of the Union of London and Smiths Bank, gave to the US Monetary Commission in 1910, 'We do an accepting business, but when we think the bill is drawn purely for finance reasons, such as stock exchange speculation, we do not care for the business; we decline.' Finance bills could be used to increase a firm's volume of acceptance business by 'five times the amount very easily' which was why some City pundits believed Kleinworts were accepting them, given the increased volume of their bills.

In America, the National City Bank of New York was reported as saying that Goldman Sachs were drawing such bills upon Kleinworts. Alexander immediately told Herman Sielcken: 'As a matter of fact Goldman Sachs and Company have not been drawing any such bills upon us at all . . . The Bills in Question were all drawn against gold shipments precisely in the same way as those you drew, they are now maturing and of course require no renewals so that in a few weeks time there will be none left to disturb the nerves of your friends or anyone else.' Alexander decided that National City must be jealous of Kleinworts' successful foreign exchange business to have to resort to such behaviour. Nevertheless, he went on, they should not 'make statements to you that are false', even though Sielcken would disregard them since he knew that Kleinworts 'do not indulge in wild cat business'. The National City Bank should be better informed—but then what, he asked, could be expected of a bank which itself had been described by rumour mongers as 'the biggest gambling institution in the world'!?

Despite denials, suspicions remained, thereby reinforcing Kleinworts' unpopularity. Relations deteriorated to the extent that by the early autumn the discount houses were not only refusing to take more Kleinwort bills but also to rediscount Kleinwort acceptances to maturity. Kleinworts tried to ride out the storm while the discount houses tried to force them to take up some of their bills. Union Discount, the City's leading discount house, even sent someone to No. 20 to say they had sufficient Kleinwort paper on their books and ask if some could be taken up. Kleinworts' response, as uttered by Herman Andreae in his forthright way, was 'Go to hell!'

It was forty-six years before a Union Discount man dared to call again. His reception was friendlier as by then Kleinworts were 'quite prepared to bury the hatchet'. Alexander was less forthright than his nephew but no less sure of his ground when faced with a similar request from another discount house, Alexanders, in 1907. 'I want to see how many bills there are,' Mr Wagner nervously asked.

'Why?' Alexander calmly replied.

'Well, because we want to know.'

'If they're so bad, don't buy them,' Alexander retorted. 'What did you buy them for? If you have any doubts, don't buy them. It's very simple.'[30]

It was not so simple, however, to survive the autumn financial crisis. Heavy American speculation in commodities and on the Stock Exchange had led to the failure of the Knickerbocker Trust Co. and the near collapse of other firms. It was said that American institutions had borrowed in excess of $500m. in the European markets, the larger part in London. The City certainly did not escape untainted. Rumours flew about that great names would fall, gold reserves tumbled, and Bank Rate had to be raised to a crisis rate of 7 per cent. Kleinworts escaped the worst owing to their excellent intelligence network in America and to the partnership adopting Herman's more cautious approach to business which enabled them to take measures in good time. Although they had to make a bad debts provision against profits of £229,587, their largest to date, the firm's profits actually increased by nearly £14,000 in what for many was a disastrous if not fatal year.

Most of Kleinworts' American clients were also able to survive the crisis. Crossman & Sielcken actually managed to make a profit of $600,000 on the year, but others were less successful. At the outbreak of the panic the partners had made it clear that the bank would stand behind its American friends: Alexander wrote to Samuel Sachs authorizing Goldman Sachs to draw on Kleinworts for any amount necessary. Times were certainly treacherous on Wall Street but Goldman Sachs by no means buckled. 'Owing to the fall in securities, instead of being able to say that we have 4½ millions [of capital] we knock off $750,000,' was the only indication they gave of the difficulties encountered that year.[31]

The Kleinwort partners did not wish to damage their symbiotic relations with the discount houses in the long term and they, therefore, gradually reduced the acceptance to capital ratio. Acceptances, which stood at £12.1m. at the end of 1907, fell to £10.7m. two years later. Despite a reluctant dilution of policy, their reputation remained the same. In the discount market, Kleinworts were labelled risk-takers well into the 1920s. Not that this was of undue concern to them. After all, the partners' strategy of calculated risk-taking had achieved excellent profits and remarkable growth. And, of the two partners, the chief instigator was undoubtedly Alexander. From 1907, he was aided and abetted by his nephew Herman Andreae, who joined the partnership in that year.

Herman Anton Andreae, often called H.A.A. by the staff, and Herman A. to differentiate him from his uncle Herman, was 'larger than life' and lived it to the full. His childhood, passed in the bosom of the rather pedestrian 'Little Germany' colony of Camberwell, gave little indication of his celebrated, stylish adulthood. There were, however, differences in his upbringing which set him apart from his cousins. Herman A., born in 1876, was the second son of Carlo and Sophie Andreae. He had five siblings—Alexander, Edward, Frank, Maria, and Caroline—and they were brought up in the family enclave centred on The Glebe. Every Sunday a crowd of grandchildren, nursery maids, nannies, and governesses would descend upon The Glebe for tea. 'It was like an anthill,' Herman A.'s cousin, Gussie Martin, would recall. Christmas was always divided between the Andreae house, Crestalta, on Christmas Eve, and The Glebe on Christmas Day.

Thus Herman A. regularly saw his grandfather, Alexander Friedrich Kleinwort, who always called on his way back from the City. The grandchildren would roar with laughter 'when he took out his dentures and put them in again'. The Andreae home was equally merry on other occasions; it was by far the most easy-going of the Kleinwort households. This was in large part due to Carlo, from whom Herman A. inherited his zest for life. A 'jolly, exuberant, good-natured' man, Carlo exuded *bonhomie* and was immense fun. He was also a fine horseman and passed his equestrian skills on to his children. He used to take Alexander and Herman A., his two elder sons, and their cousin Bobby Martin for daily rides. The Andreaes and the Martins were inseparable and holidayed together at Worthing. Minnie Martin remembered how Carlo 'teased us with his harmless pranks and delighted us with his priceless humour' during their New Year holiday in 1888. A fortnight later he was stricken with pneumonia, which became fatal after it had infected the second lung. On 16 February 1888 the 12-year-old Herman A. was met at the local Dames School by Aunt Minnie with the news of his death. 'It is touching to see', Minnie wrote a few days later, 'how young Alexander and Herman a watch their mother & try to cheer her up and to give her pleasure.'[32]

All the Kleinworts naturally rallied round but it was Uncle Alexander who stepped into the role of surrogate father to Herman Andreae and his three brothers—at a time when the family had been rather concerned about him. From letters it appears he had been unwell and low-spirited for quite long periods. Yet again his elder brother seemed to have the easier billet. Herman was far more settled; happily married with an increasing family and holding the inherited position of senior partner at the bank. Alexander was a bachelor rattling around The Glebe, the younger partner at the bank, and unsure of his place in the world. Carlo Andreae's death seems to have given new purpose to his life and galvanized him into playing a more active role in the bank—with notable success, as the co-venture with Goldman Sachs would show. It was perhaps also just prior to Carlo's death that Alexander's romantic hopes evaporated with the death of Louise Girard, a shock that came soon after his father's death in 1886. Alexander now gladly threw himself into sustaining the Andreaes through a sad period in all their lives. 'This is a new link with life, this feeling of responsibility which is for him salvation and a consolation in misfortune', his elder sister wrote. And, in consequence, Herman A. forged an extremely close bond of friendship with his Uncle Alexander.[33]

Like his grandfather and uncle, Herman A. was an achiever, in his case sporting as much as financial. After leaving the Dames School he became the second member of the Kleinwort family to be educated at an English public school, his elder brother Alexander being the first, and thereby embraced an ethos which in later years he would be the only one of the family to have in common with City colleagues. He attended Dulwich College before being sent, like his uncles, to perfect his languages at the Real Gymnasium in Karlsruhe and then at the Institut in Antwerp. He joined Kleinwort, Sons & Co. on 2 September 1897, just over a fortnight after his cousin Bobby Martin started. As apprentice bankers, both boys were paid £5 per month at the end of December. A year later the salary ledger records, 'H. Andreae promoted to £9 p.m.' [£585].

Since no training was considered complete without a tour of the bank's correspondents, Herman A. duly set off on his travels on 6 January 1900. By this time the firm had a fair number of clients in Japan and China, so he became the first member of the family to visit these countries. He reached China in the summer, only to find himself in the middle of the Boxer Rebellion with Peking's foreign legations under siege. It was not the most opportune moment for yet another foreigner, especially an English banker, to arrive in the city. Herman A., however, was in his element. He had left London prepared for any eventuality and perhaps the security of carrying a loaded revolver in his pocket enabled him to emerge unscathed from the Chinese fracas.

Herman A. rejoined Kleinworts on 9 April 1901 on a salary of £15 a month. He quickly proved his worth. The staff ledger bears witness to his steady rise through the firm, each promotion earning an increase in salary until in December 1904 he was promoted to manager status, carrying a salary of £83 *6s. 8d.* per month. Here it seemed he would come to rest until such time as a new senior manager was required.

Despite Alexander Friedrich's desire to create a banking dynasty and his efforts to provide a stable of successors, Herman and Alexander were determined to keep the reins of partnership firmly contained in their own hands. It had been made clear to Herman A. and Bobby Martin when they first entered Kleinworts that they could never become partners; the partnership was reserved for Herman and Alexander's sons. This was the situation when in 1903/4 Bobby Martin left to join Harbleicher & Schumann, merchant bankers and discount agents, of which he would become a partner; in 1922 he would form a new firm R. P. Martin and Co., which became one of the leading foreign exchange brokers in the City and with whom Kleinworts did a substantial amount of business. Herman A. remained as the only young member of the family employed in Kleinworts. In 1907, however, he was invited to become a partner, albeit a junior one contributing only £5,000 capital. What had caused Herman and Alexander to change their minds?[34]

The tremendous growth in the bank's business ostensibly made greater demands on the partners. Despite an increase in staff from twenty-five in 1871 to nearly eighty in 1907, every document still had to be vetted by a partner. Furthermore, it was the role of the partners and not the managers, apart from Robert Martin, to travel abroad to visit clients and, in return, to receive visitors at No. 20. Kleinworts had greatly expanded its United States business during a period of rapid growth in the American economy, so that US credits accounted for 45 per cent of acceptance revenue by the 1900s. It was more important than ever that frequent trips were made across the Atlantic. As an enterprising young man Herman A. was more than willing to undertake much of the tedious travel abroad, especially to North America for which he held a great admiration. He was considered the obvious candidate to assist the two middle-aged partners, since he was also extremely personable and, as family, of the required social standing.

The underlying consideration, which worked in his favour, was undoubtedly the growing divide between Herman and Alexander. The cohesiveness provided by the 'little Germany' enclave had been eroded once they left Camberwell. Both now maintained much larger and grander establishments. Herman had moved into 45 Belgrave Square and bought a country estate, Wierton Place in Kent. Alexander had married Etiennette Girard and finally sold The Glebe in 1909. It was given to the London County Council who demolished it, and Kings College Hospital was built on the site. His new London house was at 30 Curzon Street and, in 1902, he too had purchased a country estate, Bolnore in Sussex. Although Alexander regularly shot at Wierton in the early years of the century, his name disappeared from the game book as the decade progressed.

Herman was still a gentle, charming man but with age he had become less gregarious, more introverted and painstaking. His eldest grandson Sir Godfrey Style, who was close to him, believes that 'People were frightened of Herman because he gave the impression of being very, very strict; and further, his bright blue eyes could shine out of the pure white background of his hair, moustache and beard like pointed daggers.' This was especially apparent when he disapproved of somebody or something and, increasingly, he disapproved of his younger brother.[35]

Although both were born Victorians, and Herman remained one in attitude, Alexander, who was the more forward-looking of the two, strode eagerly into the Edwardian age. Nothing is more illustrative of their different approaches to life than their choice and use of motor cars. Herman acquired several and employed two men at Wierton whose sole function was to wash them. On his daily afternoon drive, he would sit bolt upright in the small seat so he could see and wave to people on the estate as he was carefully driven round. If his wife, Marguerite, was even slightly indisposed she was driven in a separate car, usually a Daimler, to avoid passing on her germs. He became so dependent upon the motor car that not one of his daily, long, and sedate walks in Battersea Park occurred without a Rolls Royce following behind, in case of emergencies.

Alexander, however, liked fast, high-powered coupés. As a young man he had frequently driven his own carriage to the City, vying with others in fast trotters. His motoring career began with the century, but being of middle age he declined to learn to drive knowing that his competitive instinct would cause him to speed and make the long journey from Bolnore to Fenchurch Street too tiring. Instead he gave instructions to his chauffeur that he was never to be passed by another car, and he liked to overtake every car ahead. He was never deterred by weather conditions. In severe cold he simply donned two overcoats, a tweed cap and goggles; in rain he had a waterproof tarpaulin poppered onto the car all the way round and fitted round his waist. Herman thought him 'utterly mad' for driving about in an *open* De Dion Bouton or Bentley and thoroughly disapproved of his more flamboyant choice of motor.

The elder brother was becoming a great hypochondriac. In their youth, Alexander had shrugged off or ignored their father's fussing about health but Herman, a sickly child, had had to take his strictures more seriously. Herman's student holiday itineraries always included the staid spas of Baden-Baden or

Bad Godesberg to take a cure because, according to his somewhat unsympathetic brother, 'as usual he is worried about his tummy or worried about his chest'. The obsession grew with the years, Herman paying his London doctor £500 a year and his country doctor £200 a year to visit him daily regardless of his condition.

In spite of the fires blazing throughout his palatial house at 45 Belgrave Square, he would don an overcoat to walk from the drawing room across the hall to the dining room. Such was his horror of germs, especially cold germs, that grandchildren were instructed almost from birth: 'On no account must you sneeze! Grandpapa won't have it!' To prevent draughts which could lead to colds, he had double doors installed in all his houses. A junior parlourmaid was always on duty to operate them. Martin Renner, a grandson, recalled the experience of passing through them, 'it was like being in an airlock in a ship'.

Unfortunately, Herman's preventative measures elicited impatience rather than admiration from Alexander. He knew that Herman had always disliked getting up in the morning—their father had chided his laziness in the mornings—only now it was put down to his health, as was his absence from the office on the merest suspicion of a cold. As far as Alexander was concerned Herman mollycoddled himself unnecessarily, was a fusspot, and stood in his way at Kleinworts. Herman's view was naturally rather different. He believed Alexander was inclined to take unnecessary risks, was too impulsive and slapdash. In fact from the point of view of Kleinworts, the brothers made an admirable partnership, their temperamental differences complementing each other. The sadness was that although Herman was quite content to preserve the status quo, Alexander was not. His father had told him always to remember that Herman was the *elder* and it was this that he resented; he simply could not accept that this gave Herman the right to be senior partner and thereby prevent him from introducing innovative policies as he saw fit.[36]

Nor did their marriages draw them closer together. Marguerite Kleinwort came from a prosperous family with links throughout the Continent. She was the daughter of the Antwerp banker Otto Günther, a family and business connection of the Kleinworts. The Günthers moved between Antwerp and London, operating there a branch of their firm of hide merchants, Königs Günther & Co., and another company, Liebig's Extract of Meat Co. Herman had met Marguerite whilst studying at the Institut but he could just as easily have met her in Camberwell. She was an attractive, sweet-natured young lady with a private fortune of £60,000, and she returned home one day to be told by her father, 'There are seven umbrellas in the hall and they belong to seven suitors wanting to marry you. However only one is worth considering: Herman Kleinwort.' He nevertheless discouraged all seven because of Marguerite's youth. Herman, however, refused to give up; he had inherited enough of the Kleinwort genes to persist.

Through his marriage into the Günther family Herman became part of the *haute bourgeoisie* of Europe; a member of that great international community that comprised such men as Heinrich Schliemann who made a first fortune in Antwerp, a second one in St Petersburg, and then discovered Troy. As a result Kleinworts could deal for example with the chairman of I. G. Farben (the German equivalent of ICI), and the founders of Liebig's Extract of Meat Co. (who provided beef from the Argentine). This gave the bank an edge over other more British banks and undoubtedly increased their Continental business. It also meant that if Kleinworts were asked to lend money to an unknown importer in, say, South America they could easily find out about him through Herman's contacts. It was a great strength because, before the First World War, the overwhelming majority of the bank's business was with clients of German extraction, be they in Manchester, Antwerp, Manchuria, or America.

It was also important for another reason. The Kleinwort family was not established socially in Britain; they were neither related to the aristocracy and those moving in aristocratic circles, nor did they meet them at home. Herman and Alexander had not been at Eton and Oxbridge with the sons of Gibbses, Barings, or Bensons, nor had they hunted, shot, or fished with them. Unlike Jewish bankers and South African randlords, who entertained lavishly to secure their place in society, the Kleinworts did not seek to attract either royalty or the City establishment. They were rich and well known in Continental circles, and kept their money in the family firm—unlike the Hambros, Gibbses, and Barings who withdrew large sums to finance their social position and estates.

Herman Kleinwort was none the less the first of the family to follow the traditional route laid down by older City families and establish himself as a country gentleman. At Wierton, he and Marguerite entertained such old friends as Baron and Baroness Schröder, who were also Günther connections, and the Felix Schusters, as well as county neighbours through whom they became known to the Prince of Wales's set. Although Marguerite had inevitably attracted the Prince's attention, she was socially experienced enough to keep the matter under control. Of independent means she had, according to Brandts in 1892, inherited £200,000 which 'has probably not been touched' and 'must amount to nearly £300,000' [£14.5m.]. She was also a serene, gracious woman, the perfect wife for the senior partner of an international family bank. The same could not be said of her sister-in-law.[37]

In 1889 Alexander had married outside their immediate circle. His bride, Etiennette Girard, was the younger sister of his deceased fiancée. It was a marriage which was not entirely welcomed by the Kleinworts. The Girards were not part of the *haute bourgeoisie* of Europe; they were from Vendôme in France, where for over 900 years they had been prosperous mill owners before Etiennette's grandfather emigrated to Louisiana. Her father, Étienne, was sent to school in France before returning to live with an uncle in Paducah, a part of Louisiana that became Kentucky, where he opened a general store and married Louise Colinet. Her family had fled from France during the revolution of 1848. They lost everything in the Civil War as Captain Étienne Girard fought on the Confederate side and Paducah was on the frontier between North and South. Their eldest son died of croup, and 'after that tragedy, my father then at the end of his financial tether, went abroad', Etiennette wrote. Her mother's family had settled in Antwerp where her father now joined them to become a tobacco merchant. 'Then began life in Liverpool, Bremen, Hull and Antwerp,' Etiennette recalled, 'the family joining him in the first-named town, all interspersed with trips to America. I heard of 77 crossings when I was a child,' before the final return to Louisville. In the course of his business her father dealt with Alexander Friedrich and Ferdinand Karck in Liverpool. Étienne's tobacco business prospered and he was appointed Belgian Consul for Kentucky, Ohio, and Indiana.

Herman and Alexander had met the Girards during their student days at the Institut in Antwerp, Alexander being captivated by the gaiety of Louise, one of the four daughters. He had remained attached to the family after her death and in 1889 had married the next daughter Etiennette. Alexander found the Girards delightfully different from his own family: artistic, free-spirited, temperamental. They lived happily within their moderate means, lacking the ambition to improve their lot and uninterested in the trappings of wealth or status.

Herman thought Etiennette an unsuitable wife for his brother. Alexander naturally disregarded this advice, and it certainly did not improve relations between them when Herman was proved right. Whereas Marguerite assumed the role of hostess to her husband's friends and business acquaintances with consummate ease, Etiennette came from a modest background and did not know how to support her husband in society. She much preferred to go off on long painting trips to Italy and France with her only brother, Willy Girard. Alexander did not accompany them, finding Willy much 'too bohemian'. Although her marriage 'brought her into fabulous wealth' Etiennette never really adjusted to it. On one occasion she purchased a fridge or some such appliance and actually agreed to payment by instalments, to the amazement and fury of her husband.

The couple eventually drifted apart, Etiennette immersing herself in the care of her eldest daughter Louise, who had spina bifida, whilst Alexander turned to the company of mistresses. There could be no question of divorce since it was not condoned in social or banking circles. Instead of understanding his predicament, Herman was noticeably unsympathetic and disapproving. A happily married, virtuous man, he could not come to terms with his brother's behaviour. On both sides there was ample ammunition with which to stoke their disagreement over the direction of Kleinwort, Sons & Co.[38]

The success of Alexander's expansionist policy and his more forceful nature enabled him steadily to edge his brother out of the driving seat of the firm. They nevertheless remained equal partners, so that Alexander always had first to persuade Herman of the viability of any proposal. Increasingly he was unable to budge Herman who grew more suspicious as Alexander grew more enterprising and in the process more frustrated. With only the two of them in the partnership, it was impossible for Alexander to impose his views in opposition to Herman, who in the eyes of the City was the senior partner. His solution was to appoint a like-minded third partner who would be an equally forceful proponent of moving into new, untried areas of business. Herman A. was dynamic and ambitious enough to fit the role perfectly.

Why did Herman ever agree to this introduction of a third partner? He no doubt recognized the need for one as the firm rapidly expanded and the increase in American business required more frequent trans-Atlantic visits; he may by now also have regretted the absence of other family partners to support him and intercede with his strong-willed younger brother. Although not as close, young Andreae was after all *his* nephew too, so that the partnership remained a family affair. At that time the natural business affinity between his brother and his nephew was not so apparent and anyway Andreae was to be very much a junior partner. Furthermore, Herman A. had been clever enough, as he later admitted to a nephew, to make himself indispensable to his uncles. He had not been 'a son who could automatically count upon a partnership whether earned or not' and so, he added, 'I had to work for it like a black.' As he worked harder, so his Uncle Herman was less stretched—but, equally, was gradually disenfranchised in terms of running the firm.[39]

Herman remained, however, the partner who oversaw German business in the years up to 1914. The majority of Kleinworts' clients came from Germany, yet despite being the leading Anglo-German house in the City in terms of acceptances, the amount of their German business had become surprisingly small by the 1890s. In the 1860s and 1870s Germany had provided almost half of Kleinworts' business but by the 1900s it accounted for less than an eighth, with commission earnings in 1900 of only £15,100. The growth of institutions able to provide ample credit facilities in Germany and the expansion of banks such as Deutsche, Dresdner, and Disconto-Gesellschaft, all of which established branches in London, meant that German companies could now rely upon Berlin in place of London to service their needs.

Although German banks were not conducting acceptance and other business on a scale comparable with that of the leading British merchant banks, they were a strongly competitive presence in German and British markets. The 'Dresdner Bank, like the Deutsche Bank and Crédit Lyonnais, are fearful poachers & will stick at nothing in order to get business', the British banker Sir Samuel Montagu complained in 1897. Kleinworts were never especially threatened by this aggressive stance, remaining pre-eminent throughout this period as financiers of world trade; besides which they were aggressive themselves. Their business with Germany might be much less but their business with German clients had grown enormously.

Of the forty-two largest accounts listed in Alexander's black book, seven were English whilst thirty-two were German, spread throughout the world. Of course his father had built up the firm from essentially German roots, using Hamburg and Altona contacts in Cuba and North America. He had also persuaded his old friend Ferdinand Karck to leave New York and settle in Liverpool. As the Bensons had withdrawn from that port city, Drake, Kleinwort & Cohen had decided to open an office there in 1859 to deal with the growing number of German exporters and manufacturers of textiles. Ferdinand, a partner only as far as the Liverpool operation was concerned, had died in 1893. He was succeeded as partner-in-charge by his son George Karck, of the same generation as Herman and Alexander. As in Liverpool, Kleinwort customers in Manchester, Leeds, and Bradford were nearly all of German origin. Internationally, Kleinworts dealt with a global network of German clients, who provided at least one-third of their American accounts and most of their Far Eastern and Indian accounts. In South America, where German commercial activity had substantially increased, all Kleinworts' customers were of German origin.[40]

By 1913, though, Kleinworts' commission earnings from business in Germany itself had risen considerably. German trade was now the second largest in the world and Herman was happy to increase the bank's commitment to its German clients, in spite of British anxiety over Germany's enlarged fleet. Even after the roll of German drums at Agadir in 1911 provoked an international crisis, he continued to have the utmost faith in Germany as an honourable country well intentioned towards Britain. Furthermore, many of Kleinworts' German clients were either family connections or, at the very least, loyal accounts of long standing and always personally known to the partners.

Although others saw Germany's militaristic ambitions more clearly in 1913—

the talk of politicians and even schoolboys 'was all of war, would there be one; would our country be involved'—the City closed its eyes to the unthinkable: 'There's talk of war. It will never happen. The Germans haven't the credits,' declared the governor of the Bank of England. Even in July 1914 there were few in government, let alone financial circles, who foresaw greater dangers emerging from the Austro-Serbian conflict. Herman was very much of the governor's opinion. At the end of the financial year 1913/14, commission earnings from Germany had peaked to £26,000, their highest ever. Thus, when war was declared on 5 August, Kleinworts' exposure was greater than ever before.[41]

The alarm bells had finally been heard by the City the previous Friday, 31 July, as telegraphs flooded in from the Continent confirming the breakdown of the machinery of international credit. Russia and Austria had mobilized on 30 and 31 July causing a rush for gold on all the European exchanges and, as currency rates fell, the leading currencies suspended convertibility to gold, thereby rendering the Gold Standard inoperative. The London Stock Exchange closed its doors until further notice, the clearing banks started to refuse to pay out sovereigns, demand for loans and discounts swamped the Bank of England, where outside people queued to exchange notes for gold, and Bank Rate was doubled to 8 per cent: 'A bad day. Looks like panic. All business ceased,' read the terse entry in the working diary kept by the bill brokers Smith, St Aubyn & Co. On Saturday, a working day in the City despite being a Bank Holiday weekend, Bank Rate was increased to the crisis level of 10 per cent—the highest since the Overend Gurney crisis in 1866—and there was, as Lord Rothschild told Paris, 'a great deal of talk among a great many of the large Houses in favour of a "Moratorium"'. Of some £350m. of bills circulating in the London discount market, £120m. were outstanding German, Austrian, and Russian bills, of which Herman A. estimated to the Chancellor of the Exchequer 'between £60–£70m. acceptances were for German and Austrian account'.[42]

Kleinworts and Schröders were the hardest hit of the City banks. Kleinworts had acceptances of nearly £15m., of which over half were due from Germany, Austria, and Russia, while Schröders had £11m. of acceptances outstanding. They and eleven other Anglo-German houses were unable to take up all their bills at once. When the bills fell due, at the rate of £3m. or more every working day, the acceptors would be liable for their payment. Faced with the mass default of its foreign customers, even the strongest accepting house could not long continue payments.

Herman had not altered his weekend plans, so it was Alexander who joined leading bankers at the Treasury and also called at No. 11 Downing Street to urge David Lloyd George, the Chancellor of the Exchequer, to postpone for one month payment on all bills of exchange issued before 4 August. This would enable outstanding obligations for redeeming credits to be temporarily held over and give the accepting houses time to make arrangements for their liquidation when the emergency ended. It was essential for banks such as Kleinworts, which relied upon remittances from Germany in particular and the Continent in general; these would now cease, and if they failed other City houses would topple in their wake, possibly even including the great joint-stock banks as well as merchant banks and discount houses.

The proposed moratorium was also advantageous for firms whose acceptances were mainly derived from the Americas and the Far East, since the outbreak of war had interrupted their remittances also. As Montagu Norman, then a partner in Brown Shipley, told an American colleague 'all the Acceptance Banks and Houses are in greater or lesser degree insolvent: there is hardly one among them whose cash in hand would permit of Acceptances already falling due being paid'. The Chancellor quickly agreed that a partial moratorium was necessary and so the bankers' proposition was duly enacted in a Royal Proclamation issued by the King on Sunday.

Notwithstanding that Monday, 3 August was a holiday, and the City presented 'much the same appearance as on an ordinary Bank Holiday', behind the closed doors of No. 20 managers and clerks beavered away at the books to discover the exact extent of German liabilities, while Alexander joined other leading bankers at the Bank of England to determine what further steps should be taken to resolve the financial crisis. They decided to prolong the bank holiday for three days in order to gain time to formulate a strategy to meet the exigencies of wartime operations.[43]

The extension of the Bank Holiday had the desired effect of allaying the panic and, on Friday, 7 August, Bank Rate was reduced to 7 per cent. Two days earlier, on the first day of the war, Frederick Huth Jackson, senior partner of Huths and a director of the Bank of England, had convened a meeting with partners from twenty-one of the City's leading merchant banks to consider the moratorium. It was from this informal meeting, at which Herman A. represented Kleinworts, that the powerful club known as the Accepting Houses Committee was born. Over the years its unseen influence would do much to shroud the workings of the City in a mystique which, in the eyes of institutions as well as laymen, enhanced the reputation of merchant banks. There were no written rules, the only condition of membership being a sizeable business in credits which had to be available for discount at the Bank of England. In effect this meant that the acceptance credits of members could be discounted at the finest rates in the market, given their status.

On 10 August the Accepting Houses Committee was formally constituted with Frederick Jackson as chairman, its first task being to appoint an executive committee. Five members were selected from those houses with large German exposures: Frühling & Goschen, Brandts, Hambros, Schröders, and Kleinworts. Alexander felt it was more appropriate for Herman A., as the public face of the bank and less obviously linked with Germany, to become the firm's first representative. He duly attended the conference held on 12 August at the Treasury chaired by the Chancellor 'to think out some method of setting things going again'. In the company of the governor of the Bank of England, eleven Cabinet Ministers, and representatives of the clearing banks and industry, the Accepting Houses executive committee proceeded to negotiate a plan with the Treasury. First, the Bank of England would discount bills without recourse to holders; although never officially disclosed, the amount so discounted was about £120m. Secondly, by paying interest to the Bank of 2 per cent above Bank Rate, the acceptors would be able to obtain the funds to meet their obligations at maturity and postpone payment until one year after the close of hostilities. Furthermore, after intensive lobbying by Alexander amongst others, the Chancellor agreed to extend the general moratorium to 9 November.

Kleinworts immediately availed themselves of these facilities and borrowed to meet the £6–7m. of outstanding pre-moratorium acceptances. They then set about realizing their assets as and when they could in order to reduce the sum taken up as funds became available. There is no doubt that they were badly hit, and more so than many of their colleagues.[44]

A notable feature of the City in those days was the way in which firms supported each other in times of trouble. Accordingly, the Accepting Houses Committee had called for each member to take up the moratorium facility, which they did regardless of need. Teddy Grenfell, senior partner of Morgan Grenfell, later explained to a New York partner: 'You may remember, at the beginning of the war, the Bank of England, backed by the Government, agreed to take into cold storage such acceptances, and while it was not necessary for us to avail of the cold storage, we used it to a limited extent for a short time as the large houses, including Rothschilds, had agreed to do so, so as not to make invidious comparisons between the Houses.' Morgan Grenfell paid theirs off quickly, as did Barings who were also largely unscathed; they only needed to avail themselves of the moratorium for two days, since only £700,000 of acceptances were at risk, with German debts comprising only £144,000. But then their acceptances totalled only £5.35m. compared to Kleinworts' total of £15m.

This was the downside of Alexander's expansionist capital / acceptance policy. Those houses with a largely American business escaped relatively lightly. Brown Shipley, for instance, only needed to borrow 2–3 per cent of their total liability. Hambros, like Barings, also required very little from the moratorium; at the end of 1918 they had only £600,000 of moratorium bills outstanding, whereas

Kleinworts had approximately £2.4m. Schröders, the other leading Anglo-German bank with a capital in 1914 of £3.65m., were also badly affected by the war, as were Huths and Frühling & Goschen.[45]

'The war, I fear, may be long and none can foresee its results: it must make the world and all of us poorer,' wrote Montagu Norman on 7 August 1914. 'Many will be ruined.' Kleinworts were not ruined, although their business inevitably contracted. In addition, two of their issues were badly affected. In 1915 the government of Bahia in Brazil defaulted on the interest payments due on a gold loan Kleinworts had issued; the war had disrupted their coffee exports, thereby reducing the revenue from taxes. Happily, the Bahian government was able to meet its obligations in peacetime.

In the case of the second issue, £1,068,000 of 5 per cent sterling bonds for the City of Edmonton, it was Kleinworts who pressed the stop button. Their contract stipulated that in the event of war they could stop the issue, which they quickly did when Austria declared war on Serbia. Although the Canadians argued that local difficulties in the Balkans were not sufficient to justify Kleinworts withholding the outstanding instalments due to them from the proceeds of the issue, Kleinworts were relieved to be out of a slow-performing issue and glad to have ample justification, as it turned out.[46]

In one area of wartime North American business, however, Kleinworts made 'a mint' of money. They were the chief suppliers of silver in London. As agents for American silver producers such as the American International Metal Co., Kleinworts had sold several hundred thousand ounces of silver in the London market every week since the end of the nineteenth century. The silver market consisted of four bullion brokers who attended the daily price fixing. Kleinworts were not members, yet so regularly did they enter the market and such was their importance as sellers, that they became honorary fifth members of it. The disruption of Mexican silver production after the 1913 revolution meant that during the war Kleinworts were the chief source of silver. When their silver was held up on the Atlantic crossing, the market was seriously affected. Once the United States entered the war in May 1917, however, Kleinworts' supply dried up owing to the US Treasury purchase of domestic production for coinage. They had to look elsewhere, which was not easy during wartime.[47]

As the volume of world trade declined the firm's acceptances fell sharply, reaching a nadir in 1915 of around £7.5m., half their pre-war level. Although poor by Kleinworts' standards this was none the less a good deal more than Barings, Antony Gibbs, Japhets, Hambros, or their nearest rivals Schröders (at about £5m.) could achieve. Nevertheless, the disruption to their traditional business and the absence of those British staff who were fighting at the Front cast a pall of gloom over No. 20. Business, it is true, remained possible with South America and Spain, while Russian business expanded considerably as Kleinworts, like Barings and Lazards, became heavily involved in financing the Russian war effort.

Yet, to offset this, trading with the country that had previously supplied the highest profits now proved unexpectedly difficult and in some cases almost damaging. America remained neutral so Kleinworts anticipated continuing their excellent business with Goldman Sachs. In the event, although Samuel Sachs assured Herman and Alexander that, unlike some American firms who were pro-German, Goldman Sachs stood firmly behind Great Britain in the war, relations between the two firms were strained by Henry Goldman's blatant pro-German stance.

When Lord Reading, president of the Anglo-French Mission to the USA, visited New York in September 1915 to try to raise an American loan for the war effort, Jacob Schiff of Kuhn Loeb would not participate without a guarantee that none of the proceeds would go to Russia because of its Jewish pogroms; the following day's press headlines to the effect that 'Kuhn Loeb, German Bankers, Refuse To Aid Allies' severely damaged the firm's reputation in Europe. Instead the loan went to Morgans, and Goldman Sachs were eager to participate—at which point Henry Goldman announced he wanted nothing to do with it, saying he wished to support Germany, not Britain. Since the firm could not sponsor an issue without the partners' unanimous agreement, Goldman Sachs were unable to participate. This time the headlines were utterly damning: 'Goldman, Sachs back Germany'. Kleinworts had to cable New York to say Goldman Sachs were in danger of being blacklisted in England, such was the ill-feeling generated in the City by Goldman's remarks. 'It is natural that views and opinions on such matters should differ,' Herman A. wrote with remarkable tact to Arthur Sachs, 'and I for my part always treat Mr Goldman's opinions with special respect.' Yet even he had to admit that 'it was the *publicity* given to the matter which alarmed us'. And although the Sachs partners went directly to J. P. Morgan and took out personal subscriptions to the loan, their firm's reputation was sullied as far as London was concerned.[48]

First the Bank of England asked Kleinworts to refrain when Goldman Sachs enquired about 'granting a moderate amount of clean credits to customers' with a view to preserving their joint account. Then it prevented Kleinworts from participating in the Jewel Tea Co. issue, the first time they were not involved in a Goldman Sachs/Lehman deal. 'Of course we feel it very keenly, more keenly in fact than we care to admit, that we are on this occasion debarred from playing our usual role,' Kleinworts insisted to Goldmans in October 1915. 'For a break in the history of the Trio Account, even though it is of a temporary nature, is a thing to be greatly regretted. However it cannot be helped and we can only look forward to a reunion later on.'

The reunion was further off than they imagined, for steps were also taken to stop the clearing banks from accepting New York finance bills, since such facilities gave indirect assistance to enemy countries. Bills drawn in dollars from Brazil against shipments to Italy, for example, were being taken under discount by New York acceptors, who in turn reimbursed themselves for the outlay by drawing finance bills on the London clearers. To stamp out this and similar operations damaging to Britain's war effort, the Government compiled a black list of German banks working in the Americas as well as dossiers on United States suppliers and manufacturers who might be involved, however unwittingly, in trading with the enemy.

By 1916 official attention was focused upon the international exchange business. To their embarrassment, Kleinworts were called before the Ministry of Blockade, where they were shown a large number of cables exchanged between Goldman Sachs and various enemy banks from which it was evident that Goldman Sachs were participating in an active exchange business with Germany. 'We were frankly astonished at the evident importance of these operations,' Kleinworts wrote on 12 July 'and were therefore not surprised to find the Authorities sceptical as to the possibility of entirely avoiding any indirect connection between such business and your sterling account with us.' Kleinworts had no option but to close the lucrative joint account forthwith. For, however careful Goldman Sachs were, mistakes could occur whereby a mark and a sterling transaction were connected—say the purchase of marks against Swiss francs and the subsequent sale of the latter against sterling—thereby placing Kleinworts in an impossible, almost treacherous position. From then on Kleinworts had to stipulate that they could not be included in any Goldman Sachs credit arrangements between London and New York. The reason for such extreme caution lay in Kleinworts' own somewhat invidious position; for the house itself was compromised in the eyes of the authorities, if not the City.[49]

The waves of patriotic celebration which had swept London when war broke out soon drew back to unleash an unappetizing surge of xenophobia. The most public victim was the 'Germhun' First Sea Lord, Prince Louis of Battenberg, who was forced to resign; but public outcry claimed victims from all walks of life. Anyone with a German-sounding name or connection suffered; the shops servicing the Little Germany colony in Camberwell hurriedly removed notices and incriminating merchandise such as sausages, for fear of being stoned or set alight. When one member of the British Royal Family, Princess Christian, wrote 'Our only boy is with the German Army on the wrong side!!' her words could have been echoed by Minnie Martin and innumerable Kleinworts and Andreaes about their relations in Germany. As a result, the whole family in England was under suspicion of consorting with the enemy.

This was an especially harrowing experience for the younger generation. Born and bred in England, they found themselves suddenly ostracized by their peers; their daily routine disrupted, their social life destroyed. Alexander had to remove his two middle sons Henry and Ernest from school, such was their suffering. He resolved never to subject any of his children to such a fate again and had them educated at home thereafter. His youngest son Cyril, then aged 9, later much regretted not having had the chance to meet other boys his own age. Nor were matters any easier for Herman's children. Along with their friends, his elder daughters had quickly volunteered to go to a neighbour's house in Belgrave Square to roll bandages and prepare dressings for the wounded troops in France. Almost at once, however, Sophie and Alice were taken aside and told by the lady of the house, 'My dears, I'm awfully sorry to have to say this to you but I'm afraid I must ask you not to come here anymore because of the feelings of the others.'

At one point Herman and Alexander were advised to change their name to Kenilworth, the Cohen nickname for their father Alexander Friedrich, in order to avoid the invective hurled at them for bearing a German-sounding name. They refused. If the name remained the same, little else at the bank did; conditions were considerably altered by the war.[50]

Of the staff who were German, many left to enlist at home. Those who stayed behind were interned as unnaturalized aliens for the duration of the war. Application could be made to the Home Office to obtain licences for any employees who were sworn to be essential for business purposes. The partners therefore applied for twenty or so staff to remain on, from Charles Frederick Harcke, the 60-year-old manager of the German Department who had joined the firm in 1884, to a 20-year-old clerk, Carl Jungblat.

The subsequent issue of a licence to Harcke led to humiliation for Kleinworts. It was not quite a dawn raid by the Serious Fraud Squad, but an investigation by the Treasury at the height of the xenophobia of 1914 wartime London produced much the same effect. Harcke's licence had been issued on what the partners took to be the pro forma condition that 'the books and documents of the firm shall be open to inspection by the Treasury at any time if the Treasury calls for their production'. And call they did, two days later, to launch an inspection of the London and Liverpool offices on the charge that Kleinwort, Sons & Co. were 'keeping back considerable sums of money belonging to alien enemies that ought to go to the Public Trustee'.

The partners were understandably incensed that their word was doubted and a reflection made against their honour. 'We deeply regret that you should have considered it necessary to inflict upon us what we can only regard as an indignity,' Herman A. told Sir John Bradbury, Permanent Secretary at the Treasury. The pain was not lessened by the condition that Kleinworts had to foot the Treasury bill, some £179. The investigation naturally found no evidence of any wrongdoing at either office. As George Karck announced from Liverpool, 'It was an easy matter for him [the inspector] to satisfy himself that everything here was absolutely above board & correct—the same as he had found with you . . . I am indeed sorry that 20 F. Street should be exposed to such annoyances.'[51]

Luckily the partners did not need to apply for licences for themselves since, as Herman A. stated, all three of them had been born in England. This did not, however, prevent the authorities from placing the Kleinwort brothers 'under observation'. The Director of Naval Intelligence billeted a retired British admiral as a 'guest' at Wierton for the duration of the war. With two sons-in-law on active service with the Royal Navy, Herman 'was dreadfully hurt by this', though they became good friends. On meeting him in the grounds, Herman would tease him with the enquiry, 'Now Admiral, have you come to have another search in my park for hidden guns which are going to be turned on our compatriots?'

Herman was considered a more serious threat to national security than his brother owing to Marguerite's family. Her uncle Charles Gunther (the British branch of the family dropped the umlaut in 1914) was a founding director of the Forestal Land, Timber & Railway Co. that processed quebracho extract in the Argentine. Its capital, raised by Erlangers in 1906, might be British but it was run and staffed by Germans. British military demand for leather in the initially 'horse and harness' war was large, and in 1915 a group of shareholders launched a campaign to de-Germanize the company with the words 'Let us turn out the cursed Huns: that is our duty as Englishmen.' Gunther was removed forthwith and his relations in Britain placed under house arrest.

Herman himself was more or less confined to Wierton for the duration of the war but in any case it was believed to be better for business if he kept away from No. 20 as he was thought to be too associated with Germany, just as his friend Baron Schröder was, and too partial to the Germans. Alexander, however, escaped more lightly since he was married to a French / American woman and was not the official head of the firm.[52]

The strain engendered by living under such painful conditions told upon the already crumbling relations between the two brothers. Instead of drawing them together, the war drove them irrevocably apart. Alexander had become the better-known partner in the City, although neither was a director of the Bank of England. Alexander is said to have been asked to join the Court but replied that his elder brother was the senior and, if a member of the firm were to be invited to join, it should be Herman. The offer does not appear to have been repeated so that it can only be a matter of speculation whether, with the deterioration in their relations, he might have changed his mind. On balance it is doubtful, since Alexander's opinion of the Bank was never high. His retort on one occasion to the governor's comment on Kleinwort, Sons & Co.'s business was, 'You run your bank and I'll run mine!'

He had, however, received a baronetcy in Edward VII's birthday honours list for 1909. Family opinion is divided as to whether this was a reward for financial support of the Liberal Party—he had been invited by the Liberal Association to represent Hastings but declined—or for giving advice to Lloyd George in the financial crisis of 1907 and thereafter. It was probably the former. In denouncing Lloyd George's raising of funds for the Budget League by selling honours, the official party fundraiser Jack Pease told Asquith on 3 December 1909 how he 'raised cash without ever directly associating distinctions with party funds, and alluded to Kleinwort who had that morning responded by a cheque for £20,000 [£1m.] for the Election on my bare request'. Before the end of the year Alexander received a baronetcy.[53]

The underlying reality was that prior to the outbreak of war the younger brother had gradually manœuvred himself into the *de facto* position of senior partner. Unhappy with this state of affairs, Herman had passed even less time at the office. Alexander for his part resented Herman's resistance to his wish to move a larger proportion of the firm's capital into non-acceptance business, such as the Trio Account. Herman wished to retain the status quo, arguing that Kleinworts had built up an immensely profitable acceptance business so why should they change direction and take greater risks in new areas where they had little if any experience? The advent of Herman A. into the partnership had only accentuated the gulf, since Herman was frequently outmanœuvred on policy decisions by the alliance of the other two.

Thus, with Herman largely *hors de combat* at the outbreak of war, Alexander seized the opportunity to oust his elder brother from the position of executive senior partner. There was, not unnaturally, a row. Herman lost and, given his situation, had little alternative but to resign from the active management of the bank. At the age of 58, with so much in his personal life in disarray owing to the war, he now found himself cut adrift from his family firm, one he had actively directed for twenty-eight years. He remained a proprietor, however, keeping his capital intact in the partnership, which was a matter of supreme importance because it ensured the firm's survival and continuity. He remained a partner, his name continuing to appear before his brother's on the firm's letterhead, but within Kleinwort, Sons & Co. Alexander became the senior executive partner in 1915. Their father's reiterated instructions—'Remember Herman is your *elder* brother'—had been disregarded at last.[54]

6 The Rebuilding of Bensons

ROBIN and Constantine were brought up, not under the thumb of primogeniture like the Kleinwort brothers, but with an even-handedness befitting the scions of a Quaker lineage. Their father, Robert jnr., treated them as members of equal importance in the family and fraternal relations were marked by deep affection which no hint of rivalry or urge for domination ever disturbed. Indeed, each brother delighted in the successes of the other. Like their Kleinwort counterparts, barely two years separated them; yet unlike them the Benson brothers were the closest of companions, a closeness intensified by the circumstances of their family life.

When Robin was born on 24 September 1850 his parents were still living at Fairfield, outside Manchester, where they had decided to remain until the Benson & Worthington mill business could be sold advantageously. At the time of their marriage in 1847 this had seemed an imminent event. Yet it was not for another five years, after the birth of Constantine in April 1852, that Robert jnr., having established his firm in the City at the beginning of the year, was able to wind up the mill business satisfactorily and finally remove his young family to London. They settled close to the former Benson house in Sussex Square, at Hyde Park Gardens just off the Uxbridge Road (as the Bayswater Road was then called). No. 32 was a typically solid and imposing Victorian white stucco terraced house with little to differentiate it from the neighbouring rows of the newly completed terraced houses of Bayswater.

Its interest for the young Benson boys, however, lay in the proximity to the Park, where daily manœuvres were carried out by troops in preparation for their embarkation to the Crimea. Sadly for Robin and Constantine, the troubled atmosphere was not confined to national concerns for it pervaded the very rooms of their own home. A year after the birth of their sister May in 1853, a thick curtain was drawn for ever across their lives to muffle the tragic lunacy of their young mother. Mental illness was a taboo subject in Victorian England; Thackeray, whose wife was also mentally ill, found that France was well in advance of England in the treatment of madness and he was able to place her in an enlightened *maison de santé*. After the move on medical grounds to the less noisy 16 Craven Hill Gardens brought no improvement, Robert jnr. settled

Eleanor at Stanton House, Pembury, near to medical specialists in the spa town of Tunbridge Wells.

The result was that, at a time when well-born children regularly moved between family houses, the Bensons too became much-travelled children; in their case, though, the need to be away from their mother and thus their home was the compelling reason for their migratory habits. The long-term effect was that neither boy ever really developed an attachment to any one place and both passed the majority of their lives in great comfort and style in rented property.

Throughout their childhood Robin and Constantine were almost entirely in the care of nursery staff, overseen by concerned and available relations with whom they were constantly sent to stay. The links between the former Quaker cousinhood and old Benson partnerships remained a force in the boys' childhood. When they accompanied their father to his Liverpool office, they saw much of the Cropper family and would also visit the John Croppers, who lived at Tolson Hall near Kendal, and the Wakefields whose son Jack was a close contemporary of Constantine.

When they travelled north, it was more often to visit the Moorsom side of the family, in particular their Uncle Constantine Moorsom-Maude who lived both at Selaby Hall in Staindrop, Co. Durham, and in Yorkshire where he was the Lascelles's land agent at Harewood. It was said of him that 'He'd rather have 16 horses in the stable than one woman's head on the pillow'; not surprisingly, he remained a confirmed bachelor. Uncle Con was a formative influence in Robin and Constantine's boyhood. Although strictly speaking they were London children, a major part of their year was passed in the rolling wooded hills of County Durham and the spacious moors of the Dales. There they had much to occupy them: tree-climbing in the great beeches of the Park at Harewood; riding on their uncle's big horses, even though Robin 'hated it'; in the winter hunting, a Maude passion that Constantine inherited and which required great hardiness, leaving before light and spending long bleak mornings at covert side without overcoats, gloves, or hat; in the summer fishing the rivers, standing waist-deep without waders, which did little to dent Robin's lifelong enthusiasm for the sport; and then on long autumn days there was shooting grouse on the surrounding moors, the finest in the country. These days left the boys with an abiding love of the West Riding, 'the finest county in England' Robin said; and the way of life with Uncle Con was not only their salvation but almost the chief formative influence in their young lives.[1]

Nevertheless, the influence of their father was paramount. As senior proprietor of a City firm he was inevitably absorbed in business matters, and anyway they were as often as not staying elsewhere. This was not unusual at a time when the children of gentlefolk lived separate lives with only restricted access to their parents. Even so, a characteristic of Bensons through the generations, one which shines out through surviving records, is the depth of attachment to and the pleasure they took in their young. Robin and Constantine were not brought up to breathe the family business, as the Kleinwort boys were. Alexander Friedrich saw his sons as junior partners, whereas Robert jnr. saw his boys simply as children.

He worked hard to counter the effects of family dislocation. Holidays were entirely devoted to the boys, with annual trips to the Continent, albeit somewhat at a gallop since he could not be away from the City for too long, even in that more leisured age. Robin recalled his first visit at the age of 14 to Switzerland, where their father took trouble in choosing sights that would appeal to them, such as 'the spot where William Tell split the apple off the boy's head at Altdorf; the bridge at Lucerne with pictures in the wooden roof and the Baths of Leuk, where people sit in a big mud bath and play chess'. His company was by far their best treat: 'that dear unselfish father did some sketching, and I never forget how he tried to show us how'.[2]

Their father took the same trouble over their education. The Bensons had always recognized the importance of a sound education, sending their sons to the best Quaker boarding schools. Now that he was no longer a Friend, Robert jnr. sent his sons to Eton College, generally considered the finest of schools—'The education was purely classical, little maths taught and no science'—and costing £180 [£7,000] per annum, compared to, say, £90 at Rugby. In January 1864 Robin went to the Reverend F. E. Durnford's house, where he was joined by Constantine in the following Michaelmas half. It was the year that the Clarendon Commission, appointed to investigate the growing national concern about the state of public schools, recommended amongst other reforms that modern languages form part of the regular school curriculum. As a result Robin and Constantine both became fluent French speakers. Academically Robin sailed effortlessly through college. M'tutor's report for 1866 was of the kind to gratify any parent: 'I am much pleased with yr son,' Durnford wrote. 'He does his work with facility & great correctness & satisfies me on all points.'[3]

Great stress was also laid upon the non-intellectual process of character-building—the Prime Minister, Lord John Russell, declared it 'of much more importance than the acquisition of mere knowledge'. Character was built in effect by senior boys, through fagging and flogging, the monitorial system, and, in mid-Victorian vernacular, through 'manly exercises', in other words, games. The Benson boys were as eager as any to excel at athletic pursuits and an excerpt copied out by their proud father from the *Eton Chronicle* of 14 March 1864 testifies to Robin's prowess in the Mile: 'His style, pluck and above all his patience and judgment are worthy of the highest admiration: and as he has both pace and endurance, we expect to see him victor in several of our future races.' The forecast was correct. Robin made quite a name for himself as an athlete. He went on to win the Quarter Mile in 1867, and then a rare double: the Mile and Steeplechase in the following year. He also distinguished himself in *the* major Eton game, becoming Keeper of the Field in 1868.[4]

Constantine had, if anything, a more dazzling Eton career than his elder brother. Robin preferred individual sports whereas Constantine chose mainly team sports. He followed Robin into the Field XI and was a member of the Oppidan and Mixed in 1870, but his passion was the river on which he excelled as an oarsman. He was in the Eight for two years and at stroke held the most important position in the boat. He also won the sculling in 1871. Both boys ended their schooldays as popular and distinguished figures, in the Sixth Form, members of Pop (the Eton Society) and the epitome of sporting heroes.

Though increasingly weighed down by his firm's affairs, their father none the less devoted considerable thought to the next stage in their education. Robert jnr. himself had not gone to university. In his day an apprenticeship, including a European tour of correspondents, was deemed far more important for a future merchant banker than a spell at Oxbridge. In her novel *North and South* Mrs Gaskell writes of the belief prevalent in the 1840s and early 1850s that a young man must be 'acclimated to the life of the mill, or office, or warehouse'. University unsettled a youth for these commercial pursuits. The economist James Mill doubted the propriety of sending a boy to Oxbridge for the same reason, that 'it might spoil him for commerce'.[5]

By 1866, however, when Robert jnr. was considering his sons' future, it was the apprenticeship that was thought to spoil a son's commercial prospects and Oxbridge that would enhance his career. This reversal of attitude owed everything to the increasing Victorian preoccupation with being 'a gentleman'. A social gulf now separated office from mill and warehouse, the latter two being tainted by their association with trade. Unlike the Continental *haute bourgeoisie* who insisted on apprenticeships in conjunction with some form of higher education for their sons—the educational route chosen for the Kleinwort sons—the English believed that since apprenticeships were for those entering trade, they were not a suitable training ground for young gentlemen. The university alone could add the final coat of social and intellectual gloss to a gentleman's education.

His sons had had such distinguished careers at Eton that Robert jnr. particularly wished them to have the time to try life 'on a larger scale'. University 'gives a young man a position which nothing else can do' concurred cousin Robert Dockray. 'In any case *you* will have done the best that you could do—and I am not sure that it is not the very best, early in life, to bring a man's responsibilities upon himself.' After consultation with Durnford, Robert jnr. decided on the great nineteenth-century forcing-house of politicians, administrators, and men of letters, Balliol College, Oxford. There, in October 1869, Robin went up to read Classics.[6]

Although Dr Scott held the mastership, it was that most famous of Victorian Oxford figures, Benjamin Jowett, the dean, who reigned at Balliol. A year after Robin matriculated, Jowett finally achieved his ambition to reside at the Master's lodging. Robin's intellectual reverence, however, was entirely reserved for his tutor T. H. Green, an austere, reserved philosopher who introduced Kant and Hegel to Oxford and was the dominant intellectual and personal force in the University.[7]

Participation in heady Maecenic discussion groups did not, however, divert Robin from the sporting field. He retained an untiring enthusiasm for all forms of sport except hunting. He naturally joined the Oxford Athletic Club, becoming a blue and its president. Oxford also enabled him to develop his taste for music and the arts, for which he had a natural enthusiasm. He was as active in the University musical society as he had been in the Etonian one founded by the composer Hubert Parry, who was and remained one of his principal friends. When the project for the establishment of a Royal College of Music was launched in 1882, Parry immediately brought Robin in on the founding committee.

Within his own College, Robin's friends formed a well-connected group that included Rutherford Graham, through whom Robin became an intimate of the Graham family. They thought him 'loveable in character' with 'such wonderful abilities', and he joined them every autumn in Scotland, where he caught his first salmon fishing the Tay. Rutherford's father William Graham was MP for Glasgow, an East India merchant, and, above all else, a great collector of pictures, especially Italian Primitives. A dealer had only to murmur to him, 'Vergine—intatta—sulla tavola,' to lure him to any distance. Yet he also collected Pre-Raphaelite pictures, many of them almost fresh from the artist's brush. 'One could use no other word but genius for his perception and instinct for painting', Burne-Jones said of his great patron and friend. 'It was infallible; he was never wrong.' William Graham became Robin's artistic mentor. Robin's own collection of Italian paintings would later provide a significant contribution to the continuation of the family business.[8]

Oxford set Robin securely in the world of nineteenth-century cultural distinction and influence. A slim, dark-haired, 'good looking man of middle height', he was blessed with an innate charm which, if less conscientious, he could have used to slide through life without recourse to mental effort. However, his intellectual agility and Quaker genes predetermined a more serious approach, added to which the effect of his mother's illness and the example of a hard-working, devoted father had strengthened his character. He possessed the education, the confidence, and the healthy ambition to play his part in the world, leaving Oxford in 1873 with the inclination to succeed, though without any specific long-term goal; his interests were always too diverse to channel into any one overriding objective.[9]

There seems to have been no question of Robin now joining his father at Bensons, just as there was no question of Herman and Alexander doing anything except join theirs at Kleinworts. Instead he had decided to follow his barrister uncles, William Benson and James Moorsom, to the Bar. On 25 January 1873 he had been admitted to one of the Inns of Court, the Honourable Society of the Inner Temple, eating his dinners there during his last two terms at Oxford prior to a pupillage at chambers in London before his call to the Bar.[10]

Oxford had also separated Robin from his brother for the first long period in their lives. Where Robin was contemplative and artistic, Constantine was a man of action with a latent scientific bent. Taller, stronger, and burlier, Constantine had chosen to follow his barrister uncles to Trinity College, Cambridge, which he entered in the autumn of 1871. There he exhibited no great desire for learning, but a complete absorption in rowing. He naturally joined the Trinity Boat Club, competing for and winning the Colquhoun Sculls. Thereafter the river entirely claimed him: he gained his blue in 1872, rowing at no. 2 in the winning Cambridge boat, and was also in the 1873 and 1875 Boat Races.

Although he rowed for Cambridge that last year, he no longer represented Trinity College, owing to the death of his father on 12 January. An unexpected and numbing event in itself, it also disrupted the family business. Announcing his death, *The Times* wrote: 'The esteem in which his personal character was held has added to the grief with which the intelligence has been received by the mercantile community.'[11]

No one, however, was prepared for the tragedy that Robin jnr.'s death heralded in the lives of his children. Since he had made more than adequate provision for them, leaving an estate worth over £95,000 [£4.1m.], of which £30,000 was easily realizable, this was understandable. After provision for Eleanor his estate was to be divided between the children, two-fifths portions for Robin and Constantine and one-fifth for May. He had even arranged for 16 Craven Hill Gardens to remain as their home with funds for Mr Leak, the butler, and the household so that there should be no disruption to the even tenor of their family life.

The only possible delay envisaged by the executors to a swift disbursement of the estate lay in the process of differentiating between Robert jnr.'s personal estate, his majority share of the partnership with Robert Wigram and Richard Glyn in Robert Benson & Co., and his own personal account with the firm. Since none of the executors, the boys' uncles—Constantine Moorsom-Maude, James Moorsom, and William Benson—had any real knowledge of the business side of Robert jnr.'s estate, they had to rely entirely upon the two remaining partners for information.

It soon became apparent that with about £63,000 [£2.7m.] of his estate vested in the firm, of which £40,000 was to his credit in the Private Ledger and £18,000 in the General Ledger, disbursement would be a complex matter and it would be some time before these sums could be paid to the executors for the settlement of bequests. Their task was further complicated by an instruction in the will that, on their father's death, Robin and Constantine be forthwith admitted into the partnership, presumably with the intention of continuing the family interest in the firm and safeguarding their future. Far from securing their future it almost destroyed it. Had they known what was to come they would never have complied with their father's wishes.

In terms of disbursement it involved further delays in settlement of the will, while the old partnership was wound up and replaced by a new one. On 19 January 1875 Robin and Constantine, 24 and 22 years old respectively, became partners of Robert Benson & Co. A circular was to be sent out to customers stating that the firm would continue in business and its capital remained the same. All was thus in place for the continuation of the 'large mercantile and banking firm' of Robert Benson & Co.[12]

All was not in place, however, for the smooth continuation of the lives of the two new partners. While their father's will remained unsettled, there was a shortage of available cash. Constantine soon had to 'migrate' from the more expensive Trinity College to Trinity Hall until such times as matters were resolved. Robin was in a more fortunate position, in that in the previous October his father had transferred £3,050 [£123,300] to him to fund a business sojourn in America. Although Robin was reading for the Bar, increasingly his father had been persuaded that he was needed at Bensons. The international crash, which had started in May 1873 in Vienna, had spread its tentacles as far as America, causing widespread failure there, including that of the bankers Jay Cooke & Co., until not a single industry remained unaffected.

Among the most seriously affected was the railway industry, with work suspended everywhere, which in turn had an immediate effect upon the iron and steel industries. With ferocious speed, between one-third and one-half of the American workforce had become unemployed and eighty-three railway companies had suspended payments. As an iron rail financier, Bensons' business had been damaged, with US import prices falling between 20 and 60 per cent below pre-crash levels. So when Robin had returned from a Continental tour to attend his degree ceremony before starting his pupillage in the autumn of 1874, he had found that his father wished him to become a banker instead of a barrister. Since Robin knew little of either banking or America it had seemed opportune for him to learn about Bensons' large American operation and to represent the firm there. Robert jnr., therefore, had arranged for him to spend an apprentice year or two working with his business friends, Nathanial Thayer and Kidder Peabody & Co., in Boston. Robin had thus possessed funds adequate to bring himself home after his father's death and to see him through the ensuing harrowing period when, in his own words, 'troubles overtook the old house of Robert Benson & Co.'.[13]

At the end of May the great depression in the iron trade claimed its first victims: 'we regret very much to have to record in the first place a large double failure, which will probably produce results similar to those which followed the collapse of Overend, Gurney and Co.', *The Times* solemnly and correctly predicted on 1 June 1875. The failure of the Aberdare and Plymouth Iron Cos. with liabilities of £1.3m. in turn brought down the large bill brokers, Sanderson & Co. of Lombard Street, whose liabilities were £7m., and two American iron merchants, Gilead A. Smith & Co. with £600,000 and Edward Corry with £200,000. On the London and Manchester Stock Exchanges, eight or nine dealers in Erie and other American and Canadian shares also defaulted.

Within a fortnight the large Manchester and East India trading firm of Alexander Collie and Co. suspended payment with liabilities of £3.4m.; as bills under discount matured, some 200 firms previously of unquestionable worth but who had traded with Collies, suddenly found themselves in difficulties. It seemed to more than one City authority that the Black Friday collapse of Overend, Gurney & Co. had been overtaken in magnitude as the City, nine years later, resounded with the echoes of default and liquidation. It transpired that Collies' failure was due less to over-extension than to fraud. As the City awaited further revelations concerning the escape on bail of Alexander Collie himself, fresh mercantile disasters were chronicled daily.[14]

One of the firms badly affected by the Aberdare and Sanderson embarrassments was Bensons. Despite an exhaustive trawl to call in outstanding debts, the catch of remittances remained small compared with liabilities, incurred mainly through bills drawn and accepted to fund Aberdare and Plymouth. The full horror of their firm's situation was revealed to its new young partners as they discovered a litany of lapse: accounts had not been properly kept; the books only balanced up to 31 December 1874; after their father's death no statement of account had been furnished by the surviving partners, Wigram and Glyn, to customers; nor had this been done on their own introduction as new partners; and, finally, no circulars had been issued to explain that the accounts of the old and new firms had been amalgamated.

With such blinding evidence of aberrancy in accounting and company procedures before them, Robin and Constantine immediately told their Uncle William Benson and then went to their bankers, Glyn, Mills, Currie & Co. There they saw their father's former partner, Pascoe Glyn, who had been 'very sorry to leave Benson' when invited to become a partner in Glyns in 1864. Their interview led to a professional examination of the firm's books by Edwin Waterhouse—a partner in Price Waterhouse and also a family friend and another Liverpool Quaker connection—in order to determine whether it would be possible for Glyns or for Robert Benson jnr.'s executors to save the firm. The result, that Waterhouse 'could not advise one or the other to render assistance', compelled the announcement of yet another failure: that of American merchants and agents of the Illinois Central Railroad Co., Robert Benson & Co., on 16 June 1875.

'It is understood that their liabilities are heavy, being over one million [£43m.],' noted *The Times*, whilst *The Economist* commented: 'The firm has not lately been in such good credit as it once was, but its position was formerly a high one, and its late Senior partner, who died a few months ago, was a director of The London and North-Western Railway.' Barings' Character Book records the slide in the credit standing of the house. Whereas on 22 December 1871 Kleinwort, Cohen & Co. received the entry 'first rate', Robert Benson & Co. were 'fair to good credit'; by 27 August 1874 Bensons were only 'fair credit', and by October 'respectable but extended'. Just before Robert jnr.'s death, Barings wrote: 'Robert Benson & Co. respectable, in fair credit, are inclined to do rather too large a business.' There was no suggestion of scandal or dishonour in Bensons' failure five months later; it was undoubtedly a case of over-extension, as Barings (who were themselves to suffer the same trouble twenty years later) had correctly observed.[15]

Why and how had this once fine firm, descended from Rathbone & Benson and then Cropper, Benson, fallen? When Robin and Constantine's father had started Robert Benson & Co. in London, he had continued to operate mainly in those trades pursued so successfully by Cropper, Benson and within which he had experience and clients. Unlike its predecessors, Robert Benson & Co. was not flush with capital, and although this increased to £200,000 mainly through American railway issuing and stock dealing, the 1860s were a hazardous decade for the firm. Between 1864 and 1870 the firm suffered heavy losses, as Robert Wigram admitted in 1877: 'I should have no hesitation in saying they were over £60,000 but I cannot state the figures.' This display of ignorance by a partner did not augur well for Bensons' affairs.[16]

The losses derived first from the American Civil War, during which the Union blockade of the South had completely disrupted trade, in particular Bensons' profitable Liverpool cotton operation. No figures survive, but if market leaders such as Barings could see commission income on Liverpool cotton business fall in one year from £32,000 to £14,000, then some idea of the firm's losses can be gauged. American recovery after the Civil War was a slow process and in the meantime Bensons invested too much capital in financing the import of Indian cotton at inflated prices in order to fulfil contracts with its Lancashire outlets and try to recoup some of the American losses. Bensons were then badly caught out after the Civil War, when Lancashire demanded American cotton, in very short supply, in preference to the lower-quality Indian; and, in the ensuing slump, prices in Bombay cotton fell from 2*s*. a *lb*. to 6*d*. and less. They were unable to look to the China trade for recompense since tea had been oversupplied to European markets, and the trade in silk had long been unsatisfactory. Furthermore they had lost money in Overend, Gurney's spectacular failure in May 1866, and much more when Masterman's had failed later that year. These losses were further compounded by those made in the iron trade.[17]

In search of a more profitable activity Robert jnr. had expanded his American railway business by diversifying into the iron trade with the purchase, manufacture, and delivery of rails and rolling-stock. This was a well-established strategy for Anglo-American firms, the market leaders Barings and Peabodys (from 1864 J. S. Morgan & Co.) had first purchased iron for eastern and southern railroads well before the Civil War. Both houses were far more strongly capitalized than Bensons, but using his excellent north-western contacts, Robert jnr. had built up a sizeable operation from the 1850s onwards as American railroad building boomed in that part of the States.

It was an operation calling for an expertise that, in spite of his knowledge and love of railways, Robert jnr. did not possess. There was little uniformity in rails used by different American railroads, and the volatility of the iron market made it difficult to strike a good deal. In 1851/2, for example, prices for iron rails had varied from £4 15*s*. to £9 10*s*. per ton. Through his connection with the Liverpool–Manchester railway, Robert jnr. sensibly entered into an 'adventure' or partnership with its reputable rail supplier, Thompson and Fothergill, partners in the Penydarren and Plymouth, the Tredegar and, latterly, the Aberdare Iron Companies, all in South Wales.

Unfortunately, after the senior partner retired, Richard Fothergill, MP for Merthyr Tydfil, clashed with his new partner, the better-known Ebbw Vale Iron Co. and, with his remaining partner Arthur Hankey & Co., was forced to buy them out. Hankey's injection of capital did not compensate for Ebbw

Vale's withdrawal: since then 'there has been one continued struggle with respect to finance, to pay the instalments of outgoing partners and to find working capital to carry on with'.

Bensons were either failing in their intelligence gathering or, more likely, were finding the operation successful enough to disregard the declining conditions of Fothergill and Hankey's companies. This was rash, since it was generally accepted that 'for the profitable carrying on of a large ironworks probably no business of any description requires the partners therein to have a larger command of capital at all times at their disposal than this business'. To meet their voracious demand for short-term credit, Fothergill and Hankey made use of finance bills drawn, naturally, on their London merchant partner Robert Benson & Co.

Part of Bensons' heavy loss of over £60,000 occurred as a result of trading losses sustained by the Aberdare Iron Co. which then drew on an ever larger number of bills that were accepted in good faith by Bensons. Robert jnr. took the long-term view, as was later freely acknowledged, that the Aberdare and Plymouth properties were exceedingly valuable coalfields and that once the depression had lifted they could be turned to good account. Others, unfortunately, were not prepared to wait for the upturn.

In the early summer of 1875 the City decided to take a stand against the flood of Aberdare paper being placed on the market by Sanderson & Co., the Lombard Street discount brokers. Scottish and Northern joint-stock banks were the first to request some of the money lent to Sandersons at 'call' on the security of Aberdare and Plymouth paper. It was then discovered that Aberdare had been drawing accommodation bills on the Plymouth: 'How much shorter would have been the financing career of the Aberdare and Plymouth Iron Companies,' asked *The Times* on 17 June 1875, 'if the bankers who have been hit by that disastrous culmination could have had but an inkling of how much of that paper was being held by their neighbours, and of the extent to which it was ever being renewed and shifted from one to the other?' In the course of March and April 1875, Aberdare renewed ten bills with Bensons. On 16 June 1875 bills drawn by Plymouth amounted to nearly £2,000, while their New York agent, John S. Kennedy & Co. was owed over £63,000 by Bensons. *The Economist*'s post-mortem on Bensons was all too true: 'The difficulties seem to have arisen entirely from the firm going out of its usual business as an Exchange house' and 'its attempted extensions in other directions'.[18]

It must indeed have felt the longest day of the year when, on 21 June, the partners presented their petition to the London Bankruptcy Court for the liquidation of the firm. The outcome of the general creditors' meetings at the Guildhall Coffee House on 14 July, and a subsequent meeting on 4 August, was the appointment of Edwin Waterhouse as trustee (or receiver) and a resolution that Bensons would be liquidated by arrangement, not by bankruptcy. In other words, all four partners wished to honour their debts and arrange repayment while their creditors recognized their intent and had no need to serve a writ to force them to pay via bankruptcy proceedings.

Unfortunately the straightforward winding-up process was stalled and the agony of the young partners prolonged by two separate yet not unrelated developments. Both concerned their father's estate, still unsettled. The initial difficulty of differentiating between Robert jnr.'s personal and business estate was now compounded by the need to differentiate between the liabilities of his old firm and the new one. Edwin Waterhouse described the uphill task in his journal: 'an impossible endeavour was made to separate the existing liabilities for which he was responsible from those which had arisen since his death, with a corresponding division of the assets into two portions'. For instance, one of the firm's East India clients, Ker Dods & Co. of Calcutta, had shipped £4,000 worth of teas which had been sold partly before and partly on 12 January, and partly after Robert jnr.'s death, for which they had not been paid. Waterhouse had to admit that even with his long experience in such matters the 'problem proved beyond my powers, and also puzzled the astute lawyers who represented the separate interests'.

One of the astute lawyers was Andrew Kelley of Hayes, Twisden & Parker, the Benson family solicitors who represented the executors and the personal estate of Robert jnr. Astounded by the failure of Bensons, he and James Moorsom were advised by an eminent QC, Herbert Cozens-Hardy, to claim the amount of £65,002 10*s.* 3*d.* [£2.8m.] from the firm as still outstanding to the estate of Robert jnr., this they duly did at the various creditors' meetings. In addition, on 22 June, James Moorsom and his fellow executors also filed a bill of complaint in the High Court for the administration of the trusts and estate of Robert jnr., since they had no idea of Bensons' affairs and could not possibly determine whether, if proved, the creditors' claims were entitled to be met from the whole or just part of Robert jnr.'s various estates and, if the latter, which part.

There seemed no clear-cut path through the neglected undergrowth of Robert jnr.'s affairs. In 1870 he had borrowed money on private security for the use of the firm; he had also injected additional capital, yet left unaltered the original partnership articles, and he had never requested any capital sums from his partners. It was impossible to disentangle his affairs 'and at last it was agreed [in court] to merge, as I had recommended, the supposed two estates into one. Even thus I found the matter a heavy piece of business', sighed Edwin Waterhouse.[19]

It was an even heavier piece of business for the Benson family. The Chancery suit, Benson *v*. Benson, dragged on for four years, naturally at great cost to everyone concerned. It became clear that Robert jnr.'s remaining estate would not amount to more than about £20,000 [£866,000]. This was not enough to meet the provisions of his will. After a court ruling that the executors were not entitled to rank with other creditors until all debt incurred prior to Robert jnr.'s death had been fully paid—some £81,285—the executors withdrew from the action in 1876; although the order to wind up the suit and settle costs was not made until November 1879. Long before then, the holders of bills used to fund Aberdare and Plymouth had been fully paid and the main creditors had received an initial payment from the proceeds of the sale of Robert jnr.'s extensive railway holdings.

Unlike their sister May, who eventually collected some £5,000 from one of their father's trusts, Robin and Constantine received nothing. Their admittance as partners in Bensons effectively disbarred them from benefiting in any way from his estate. It was even considered risky for them to benefit from their mother's trust funds in case they were considered the property of the liquidator and it led to questions about her mental capacity. This was just one of many problematical issues confronting the Benson boys.

They were now homeless, because 16 Craven Hill Gardens and all its contents had to be sold by auction in July 1875 with the proceeds paid into court. Amongst the articles sold were some belonging to the boys, Robin's books, *Froissart's Chronicles*, Blackstone's *Commentaries*, and Taine's *Literature Anglaise* sold at Christies for £1 14*s*. 0*d*., and his grey mare sold at Tattersalls for £33. He had to claim them back from the court and put them towards meeting creditors' claims on those Benson debts incurred during their short-lived tenure as partners. Even May, not involved in the business, had her godparents' presents removed. A court order was required for their return and to allow their mother to repurchase her own furniture, plate, and effects, valued at £244 8*s*. 0*d*., from the estate of her husband. Stanton House had to be sold because it had been purchased by him, and the boys had to resettle Eleanor elsewhere. Using funds from her trust and with the help of their uncles, they purchased the comfortable Edenbridge House at Edenbridge, Kent for £2,220.[20]

Unable to stay with her for long owing to her insanity, they had to find somewhere else to live. Robin and Constantine were able to take rooms in London thanks to the old family butler, Mr Leak, who had set up a lodging house in Charles Street, just off Grosvenor Square, and was only too happy to help the sons of his former employer. While in those days it was quite usual for young men to take lodgings, it was considered impossible for a young girl, even though accompanied by her maid. May therefore had to resume the peripatetic existence of her childhood, paying extended visits to family and friends.

The friends who proved most supportive were the Croppers. They remained steadfastly loyal despite losing considerable sums through the bankruptcy. Edward Cropper's railway investments (he had financed the Narberth Road Railway and the Maenclochog Tramway Co.) had been handled by Bensons and he alone had lost some £8,553 in the Benson crash. All the Cropper family's American investments had also been transacted through Bensons. John Cropper, another of the former Cropper, Benson partners, had died in 1874—his US investments alone worth £64,000 [£2.6m.] when he died—but May visited his widow Anne in Liverpool and often stayed with their eldest son, another James Cropper, and his wife Fanny at Ellergreen outside Kendal. James had moved to Kendal in 1845 to run a papermaking business owned by the Wakefields in Burneside, a business which his descendant still directs today. Fanny was a direct descendant of the John Wakefield who had been such a formative influence on Robin's great-grandfather. Thus the Quaker ties had never loosened between these three families and, when the Bensons were in trouble, the Wakefields and Croppers rallied round.

Shortly after hearing of the Benson failure, James Cropper invited Robin and Constantine to Ellergreen to discuss their future. They pledged to meet their liabilities in full but the question was, how? Both assumed that the City provided the best solution, since they could start there straight away without further training. They would try to resuscitate their father's core American railway investment business, where Robin anyway had made business contacts of his own during his short time in Boston.

Another idea emerging from lengthy discussions with their uncles was that Constantine should, in the Moorsom tradition, become an engineer. 'At the head of all the new professions must be placed that of civil engineer,' remarked a Victorian commentator on the state of England in the 1880s, and it was beginning to feature prominently among the chosen occupations of public school boys. Besides utilizing Constantine's scientific bent and general knowledge of railways, its chief advantage was that, of all the major occupations in Victorian England, there was none 'in which a capable man without much money could more readily establish himself than engineering, if only because no one could draw a hard and fast line between any of the rungs of the ladder which ran upwards from dirty-handed fitters like the young George Stephenson to the proudest consulting engineer who ever graced the Institution'.[21]

Although both the family's well-known engineers, William Scarth Moorsom and Robert Dockray, were dead, contacts remained strong enough to ensure that a trainee place could be found for Constantine, either at a railway works (where the founders of Bentley and Rolls Royce motor cars had received their early training) or at a foundry near to the Croppers and Wakefields. Accordingly, while Robin attempted to rebuild their fortunes in the City, Constantine began engineering, with the option of joining his brother later or starting his own engineering firm.

Impressed by the young mens' integrity and ability, James Cropper had no hesitation in joining their uncles to provide them with the capital necessary to make a fresh start. In August 1875 he lent them £1,000 and gave Robin his first piece of financial business: to look after his American investments, which were mainly in railways. Robin later told his wife that 'he was a dear, dear, staunch friend to us', and he and Con remained forever grateful for his unstinting support. Robin inscribed on the front of his copy of the 'In Memoriam' booklet issued after James Cropper's death: 'For my children, that they may someday know what manner of man he was who acted like a father to my brother Con and me after our father's death in 1875, when the troubles overtook the old house of Robert Benson & Co.'[22]

As Constantine joined a works at Barrow-in-Furness—conveniently near to Fanny Wakefield's niece and ward, Emily Weston, whom he wished to marry when his financial situation improved—Robin returned south to begin a new life in the City. The £3,000 given by his father had disappeared in the Benson crash, but he had collected the capital sum of £2,500 from his uncle Con, funds advanced against an inheritance from his great-uncle William Maude, and James Cropper. This was not nearly enough, though, to launch a City business. He therefore had to cast around for a suitable partner and, once again, it was from the pool of old Liverpool connections that one emerged. On 25 September 1875 an announcement in *The Times* disclosed that 'Mr J. W. Cross and Mr Robert Benson have entered into partnership under the style of Cross, Benson & Co., for the purpose of continuing a portion of the late Mr Robert Benson's business in American securities &c.'[23]

The decision to concentrate upon this area of business was sensible. It was the successful portion of the old firm, the one which Robin's father had imprudently neglected towards the end of his life. Robin had only been in business a short if shattering time; his experience had been gained mostly in America, and anyway the Benson connection there was of long standing, dating back to his great-grandfather. Furthermore, Robin's new partner had a host of American connections of his own, having spent eight years working in New York. Cross was very much the senior partner, as the title of the firm inferred; the elder by ten years, he also contributed the larger share of capital, £5,000, to the partnership. At this stage Robin was, in his own words, delighted to 'bow to his superior wisdom' in business matters.

A tall, bearded man with 'a habitually cheerful face', Johnny Cross was exactly the right person to help Robin resuscitate the Benson business. Educated at Rugby, he was an athlete, a good conversationalist, and a successful banker. Despite his relative youth—he was only 35 in 1875—he had already acquired a considerable reputation on Wall Street as a 'sound money man'. His background complemented Robin's and, significantly, they shared the experience of surviving family commercial disasters.

His forebears were entirely Scottish and he remained intensely proud of this ancestry, although his parents moved south of the border during his childhood and he thereafter resided in England. On both sides the family fortunes had originally been made through the West Indian trade. On his paternal side from the first-known Robert Cross, Dean of Guild and Baillie of Glasgow in 1682, who formed what became the 'Company of Scotland trading to Africa and the Indies' in 1695, down to Johnny's father, William Cross. On his maternal side the Dennistouns, too, were West Indian merchants and the family firm, J. & A. Dennistoun of Glasgow, was judged by contemporaries to be 'one of the greatest Glasgow merchant houses' operating in the transatlantic cotton trade.

William Cross, a partner in Dennistouns, had moved to Liverpool to manage the Liverpool Borough Bank after Dennistouns purchased a controlling interest in 1846. When the Borough bank failed in the panic of 1857, W. G. Prescott told Lord Overstone on 4 November 1857 that it had 'met with a well merited fate' and, although by this time Johnny's father had taken over Dennistoun's new London branch, Dennistoun, Cross & Co., his were the policies that did much to bring the bank down. His training and experience were not those of a cautious banker but of an aggressive merchant financier accustomed to a lifetime of risk-taking, not risk-securing.

The Cross family were especially hard hit as, ever the optimist, William Cross had held on to his large Borough Bank shareholding when other members of the family were selling. Nor could he look to the parent company for financial salvation. Despite the basic soundness of their business (they would make a profit of £86,000 for the year), Dennistouns were badly affected by the panic in America, where some £2m. was outstanding, and with the spectre of ruin facing other Scottish banks Glasgow was in such a ferment that troops were kept under arms. As Dennistouns wobbled, fissures, in the form of slight delays in remittances from America, appeared in its foundations, bringing the whole firm crashing down with liabilities of £3m. 'None who were in business in Glasgow then will ever forget the day,' Johnny Cross's uncle William Wood lamented. 'Distrust was universal and panic reigned supreme.'

The cumulative effect was to swallow up all the Cross capital; it also put paid to Johnny Cross's further education. He had to leave Rugby early, forgo university, and start work. It was this experience of the 'shadow side' of City life, when business affairs went wrong, that he would share with Robin Benson. Both had fathers whose financial acumen disintegrated in later life in the face of adverse, more competitive trading conditions. The shrewd caution of their forebears, enabling them to survive in an age when communication was far slower and trading conditions far more hazardous, had been cast aside as their own naïve optimism and trust in colleagues blinded them to the realities of commercial survival. Their sons inherited their financial acumen—but were far more realistic.

Johnny did extremely well in the New York office of the restructured Dennistouns and became junior partner in 1861. He then flexed his muscles of independence and left Dennistouns when the Oriental Bank of London 'the greatest banking institution in The East India and China Trade', opened The British and American Exchange Banking Corporation, the first new foreign bank to be established in London under the Limited Liability Act of 1862. John Dennistoun was the first to bless the defection: 'What a grand opening too for Johnnie Cross! We are grieved very much to part with him, but we should not hesitate about advising him to accept it'. Although he subsequently returned to Dennistouns London office, disagreement over partnership matters meant that by 1872 Johnny had established himself as an agent for the purchase and sale of American securities. His old firm gradually atrophied until the younger Dennistouns sold the remaining business to the German Bank of London Ltd. in 1913. Johnny's business, in contrast, had a bright, successful future ahead of it, especially after he decided to join forces with a younger partner to form the firm of Cross, Benson & Co.[24]

Unlike Kleinworts across the way in Fenchurch Street, Cross, Benson's offices at 38 Cornhill were neither large nor imposing; they had no need to be since at first they accommodated only eight men, so small was the business. Robin brought with him Charles Fricker, his father's clerk for five years, and Beale, his father's bookkeeper, to join Johnny's clerk, two messengers, and the office boy who made up the fires, swept the floors and changed the ink-pots, water-jars, and pens. Their business was investment, principally in American securities, sold to private clients in small parcels. At first the clients were chiefly culled from the large circle of Cross and Benson family and friends. Cross's clients included various Dennistouns, Woods, and Langs, fellow Rugbeians Charles Bowen, William Bullock Hall, and Francis Otter (the latter two his brothers-in-law), and family acquaintances such as Herbert Spencer and the novelist George Eliot, whose income had risen dramatically after the publication of *Middlemarch*. Cross's nose for investment is evident from the way he increased her 1872 income of £3,000 to nearly £5,000 [£187,000] the following year.

Unlike Robin, however, Johnny Cross was not a young man in a hurry to build up a business and restore the family fortunes. He had sufficient capital and income to live comfortably, to indulge his predilection for arduous physical exercise: climbing, rowing, tennis, particularly hunting ('What lovely hunting weather it has been. I had a nice little run with the foxhounds on Friday and I generally get a day a week with the Brookside Harriers'), and later golf; and to leave most of the day-to-day management of the firm to Robin. This was an ideal arrangement, giving Robin the benefit of Johnny's experience, investment expertise, and capital without the usual accompanying subordination. Although it had been agreed that he would assume complete control of the business when Johnny retired, this was more a formality than a requirement.[25]

It was thus in large part Robin who presided over the growth of the fledgling investment firm from its earliest days. The increase in business was sufficient to warrant a move into larger premises at 4 Bishopsgate Street Within. Here Robin built up Cross, Benson portfolios in American securities. These, especially US rails, had remained low in the aftermath of the 1873 Wall Street panic and the City did not share Robin's view that American rails offered tremendous investment opportunities. At this stage the bulk of railroad development had been confined to eastern lines such as the ignominious Erie and other New York and New England railroads. Furthermore, America was in the depths of a protracted commercial depression. Yet Robin believed that the growth of grain and kindred products, then in their infancy, would make Chicago a great world market through the development of Midwestern railroads.

As he wrote in an article for *Macmillan's Magazine* in 1881, only a few years before 'they had burnt Indian corn for fuel on the Mississippi River Steamboats, and wheat had been left to rot in Californian fields' because 'it cost too much to carry it where it was needed'. Since then, freight wars between the newly developing railways at a time of falling demand had not only reduced the cost of transportation but had also led to the consolidation of rival and insolvent systems. Robin was therefore convinced that American Midwestern rails and the land surrounding them were ripe for Cross, Benson investment.[26]

There were several factors that enabled him to succeed in this specialized area of operation. The fact, as Sir John Jeans discussed in 1887, that American railway securities 'are a much greater lottery than English shares and they require to be much more closely looked into', had frightened off the major London issuing houses in the aftermath of the 1873 crisis and subsequent depression, and they rarely placed American rails directly on the market. Instead American houses took over the securities and off-loaded them for sale in smaller parcels to City firms on a commission or profit-sharing basis. This meant that Cross, Benson could compete in the market against the much larger firms of Barings, Rothschilds, and the emerging Anglo-American houses, J. S. Morgan, Seligmans, and Morton Rose.

Furthermore, compared with British railway securities which over 1870–8 had yielded an average of 9.4 per cent per annum, US railroads during these years 'would have been found a poor holding', according to a contemporary stockbroker. It was during the latter part of this period that Robin, against conventional wisdom, had bought cheaply, *before* a renewed demand set in for Yankee rails. In 1879 'a sudden rise occurred. Some have more than doubled in price.' The area which Robin and Johnny had identified as providing the best long-term gains for investment emerged far quicker than anticipated as a winner; and would remain one throughout 1875–1914 when, despite the volatility of market forces, Yankee rails remained a standard item in the portfolio of British investors.[27]

Another factor in the firm's success was that whilst the fledgling Cross, Benson focused almost exclusively upon American railroad investment, wily older birds such as the longer-established and better capitalized City competitors were involved in much more diversified and geographically dispersed businesses. This had been sound policy in the days when the risks of overseas trade were too great for any firm to concentrate its operation too narrowly but the inauguration of telegraphic communication between Europe and America, widely used from the early 1870s, obviated the need to continue along this course for safety alone. From 1872 the Exchange Telegraph Co. collected up-to-the-minute prices from the floor of the Stock Exchange to send out on tape to banks and subscribing firms, which led to a greater mobility of capital and the development of more sophisticated dealing.

Large houses were unable to adapt quickly to the changes wrought by this new technology and such firms as Antony Gibbs agonized about which area of specialization to choose. As Robin later wrote: 'The invention of the cable doubled and trebled the business of financial [investment] banking, while it destroyed the old business of the British merchant; it became necessary for him to control his merchandise from its production to its consumption, or to specialise [as an accepting house], or else to become a merchant in securities in order to live.' It was this latter path that he chose. While Kleinworts specialized in acceptances, Cross, Benson specialized in investments.[28]

The firm also had the advantage of being British at a time when the City was reluctant to assimilate the influx of American and German houses. George W.

Smalley, a distinguished American journalist working in London who knew Robin and Johnny, wrote in the *New York Tribune* about Morgans that, 'They would tell you in the City that American methods of finance were not altogether liked in London, that Mr Morgan's methods were not liked, that the commissions paid tended to demoralise the market, and that it was as well Mr Morgan should let the fact that London was not New York sink into his mind.' American houses had long been thought brash and speculative. For instance, Levi P. Morton, head of Morton, Rose & Co., was deemed 'a rash and risky speculator' in 1877. It was to Cross, Benson's advantage that most were in their infancy and relatively inexperienced at transmitting European capital to American companies. Some had barely recovered from the 1873 crash; Drexel & Co. and Morton Rose & Co. had two-thirds of their capital locked up in railroad securities that they could not sell, while Seligmans, new to London, had one-third in the same asset. Thus from the point of view of clients, Cross, Benson might have been less well capitalized but they were soon seen as part of the City establishment and, accordingly, judged safer than their Anglo-American competitors.[29]

Nor did these attributes work to their disadvantage on the other side of the Atlantic. Their excellent New York and Boston contacts ensured first-rate American financial intelligence and awareness of the latest investment opportunities. While Robin's participation in railroad investment opportunities began to restore the Benson fortune, it was in a related yet quite separate field that he was able to make the financial killings that really secured and increased it. He made well over £500,000 [£25m.] from US stock holdings through a combination of his own prescience and a friendship that Constantine had forged at Cambridge. This led to a large amount of business for Cross, Benson in Iowa and gave the firm the entrée to railroad development in Chicago and the Midwest, an area ripe for expansion and opportunity. At the height of its operation in 1884, the company that Constantine ran with his Cambridge friends, financed by Bensons, and in which Robin personally had a substantial stake, was Iowa Land, 'the largest foreign company doing business in the United States with a capitalisation of $5,000,000 and stock selling on the London Exchange at a premium of twenty-five per cent', the *Le Mars Sentinel* declared in 1882. Through their holdings in Iowa Land and Close, Benson & Co. (a development company formed by Constantine and two friends in America), and their land and stock investments, the Bensons had become rich men, each easily worth over $500,000 [£5m.] in America.[30]

It was also an undoubted advantage for Cross, Benson to have Constantine as a partner *in situ* in the Midwest from 1879. The Bensons' Iowan odyssey had started with his decision to leave engineering. Although he had found it both stimulating and varied at first—'my work at the laboratory is very interesting', he had written to Uncle William Benson, 'it teaches the manipulation of experiments and analyses if nothing else'—three years at Barrow had decided him against engineering as a career. When Edwin and Georgie Waterhouse stayed with him and May in September 1878, they were taken to see the iron- and steelworks at night 'always a marvellous sight'. Con and May were more than accustomed to the furnaces, yet May admitted that Barrow 'was a good preparation for hell, if you wanted one'.[31]

After three years in an industrial environment, Constantine craved some other means of making his fortune. The opportunity came in the form of an invitation from his old Cambridge rowing friend, William Close. 'I took the bold step,' William told his elder brother James in the late autumn of 1879, 'of saying that if he came out to us, we would take him in partnership with us, provided he could command £15,000 [£750,000] to invest with the firm.' The venture was a land development company that concentrated its purchasing power upon that area of the Great Plains between the Mississippi and the Missouri which goes to form part of Iowa, Minnesota, and Kansas. Despite being 'the garden of the Mississippi', Iowa land was much cheaper than that of states such as Virginia, Illinois, Colorado, and Wyoming, all of which were attracting settlers and investors during this period. Hard-pressed speculators wished to offload their holdings during the depression, as Indians threatened and a series of grasshopper plagues devastated the state in 1875 and 1876. The Closes took advantage of these two factors to purchase an initial 3,000 acres in western Iowa at only $3.50 an acre. They struck further good bargains with the railways who were also sellers of fertile land, in their case received as grants from the Government. Since neither the Indians nor the grasshoppers returned, Close Brothers was in business to attract British investors and settlers to what became known as the Close, or the English, Colony in Iowa.

Constantine's enthusiasm for the Close project proved contagious. His kinsman Jack Wakefield was enlisted as an investor and travelling companion for a recce to Iowa, as was his cousin, Cecil, successfully recruited during a New Year visit to the William Bensons at Alresford. 'I am very glad Cecil thinks of Iowa,' May Benson reassured her uncle on 2 January 1880. 'I am sure you would like Mr Close, he inspired all here with confidence in his sense and goodness.'

The Bensons were not alone in being inspired by William Close, who acted as the publicist for the firm: his long letter to *The Times* in November 1879 about farming prospects in Iowa had been reprinted 'in hundreds of papers' and he daily received 'many letters from farmers etc' interested either in investing in the Close land or in emigrating to Iowa. At the same time numerous Cambridge undergraduates had been enticed to emigrate to the Colony. It was only after he had overenthusiastically sent a circular to 'every clergyman in the kingdom' from the address of Trinity College and began receiving replies of forty to fifty letters a day that the Master of Trinity intervened with the air of one clearly not inspired by the Close Colony. Robin Benson, in contrast, stepped in to offer office space at 4 Bishopsgate, which became the London address of the firm, and to invest in Iowan land on his own account as well as for Cross, Benson clients.[32]

The appeal to investors such as the Bensons and Wakefields was in the first place that the project was not purely speculative. The land was not being held or offered merely on the chance of a rise in value: rather it was being improved. Houses were built and soil was ploughed so as to produce income from legitimate agricultural business. In the second place, it was a British-run project staffed by young English gentlemen seized with the idealism of creating a colony of 'like-minded men and women', as William Close wrote on 2 December 1879, a group 'so self-contained and resourceful, so sure of native abilities and talents' that they would easily surmount the problems facing all prairie pioneers. Thus 'not only would Iowa become *the* place to be, but money could also be made there, doubling the attractiveness of the venture'.[33]

The Close Colony was not the only venture to attract British gentlemen either as investors or settlers. Cattle-ranching in the 'Wild' West was already drawing quite a crowd of British gentry who went out to make money in what Moreton Frewen called 'a savage country' where the rewards could be outstanding. Moreton and his brother Dick, for instance, had brought out $39,000 to invest; at the end of their third year they had $80,000 and Moreton expected to net $1.25m. by the fifth year. Institutional interest in cattle-ranching started after the first shipment of refrigerated meat to England in 1880, stimulating British demand for cheap American beef, forever damaging the domestic industry.[34]

When it came to other forms of farming, however, the Close Colony had the field more or less to itself. It was particularly successful in attracting would-be-trainee settlers because the 1870s and 1880s were a period of severe agricultural depression in Britain. Reduced rents meant that many landowners could no longer support their offspring. Correspondence on the subject of 'What to do with our Boys?' appeared in *Harper's New Monthly Magazine* and elsewhere as fathers grappled with the problem of how to recover rents and provide for their sons. The Close Colony offered, for a fee of $500 per annum, to teach these boys about agriculture at the 1,000-acre Dromore Farm in Iowa.

When the Benson party arrived there in the spring of 1880, they emerged, the *Le Mars Sentinel* reported, 'from the recesses of the Pullman palace cars dressed in the latest London and Paris styles, with Oxford hats, bright linen shining on their bosoms, a gold repeater ticking in the depths of their fashionably cut vest pockets'—with, to the amazement of the local population, eighty-two pieces of luggage unloaded for just one of the families. The Bensons, like most of their colonizing compatriots, were bringing as much of their piece of England with them as they possibly could. Indeed, unlike other Europeans, the English in Iowa had no wish to integrate and become part of the melting-pot of America.

What Constantine and Emily found transplanted in Iowa was a little English town complete with taverns; the Prairie Club 'with English and Scottish newspapers and magazines in plentiful supply, imported wines and spirits, billiard tables and traditional British cooking'; hunting, and polo—the high-living frontier British were among the earliest polo players in America.[35]

Constantine almost immediately decided to join the Close team, the name of the company being changed to Close, Benson & Co. to reflect the new partnership, his injection of capital and the sizeable Benson land holding. He assumed responsibility for the general financial side of the firm and railway transactions. The Close company had already received requests to act as agents for several railroads, which owned most of the remaining available prairie land that Close, Benson needed to buy to meet the voracious demand of investors and settlers. To prevent the charge of collusion over the price of land, Constantine proposed to form a separate company to deal specifically with the railways. He and William Close, then in London, duly organized the creation of the Iowa Land Co. Ltd., with a capitalization of £500,000 [$2.5m.] provided by Robin and six other London investors, to act as the finance and banking arm of Close, Benson. Robin was also able to put his brother in touch with an Oxford acquaintance, E. F. 'Henry' Drake, who was land agent for the Sioux City & St Paul Railroad. This introduction culminated in an important business deal for the Iowa Land Co. With effect from April 1881, it became sole agent for the disposal of Sioux City & St Paul land at a price of between $6.50 and $12.50 an acre, a price level which easily allowed for resale at a good profit. Over the next few years, Constantine sold through the company over 96,000 acres of Sioux City & St Paul land.

This operation was halted in the autumn of 1882 after the Milwaukee Railroad disputed Iowa Land's purchase of a further 27,000 acres from Sioux City & St Paul, claiming the lands belonged to them. It seemed both railways had been awarded the same land rights, but which railroad had been granted them first? Since neither could agree, Iowa Land had to place $160,653 in escrow and stop all resale of land, so that their business was effectively frozen. The partners also started to disagree.[36]

In the spring of 1884, when the firm had 270,000 acres in hand and was expanding into neighbouring states, the partnership of Close, Benson & Co. was officially dissolved. The catalyst was Johnny Cross's retirement from Cross, Benson the previous year. In reality he had been a sleeping partner since 1877, when he had become like a 'dear nephew' to his financial client George Eliot. He had persuaded her to marry him in 1880, but her death eight months' later saw no correspondent increase in his attendance to business at Cross, Benson; on the contrary he decided to write her life, an undertaking which entirely occupied him until publication in 1885. In a position to withstand his withdrawal of capital, the firm became Robert Henry Benson & Co. in 1883, reverting in 1884 to its old title, Robert Benson & Co., with Robin as the senior and indeed the only partner. This, in turn, prompted Constantine to scrutinize his position in Close, Benson, where increasingly he was at odds with the direction of the firm yet unable to change policy, because he would always be outnumbered by Closes. With Robin's support, he decided in the autumn of 1883 to leave this partnership and start his own company.

The Benson interest in Close, Benson and Iowa Land was by this time large, the initial investment in 50,000 acres at $6 per acre having grown like Topsy with every company purchase, and it was no easy matter to arrive at a fair division. The Closes, not unnaturally, demurred at losing a large share of their companies. Constantine turned to Robin for help, and his brother interrupted a visit elsewhere in America in order to stop off at Sibley 'to try to compose [Con's] difficulties with the Closes'. Robin's solution was to separate the two main companies. Since Constantine was the power behind Iowa Land he should take it over, Close, Benson should cease and the Closes should put their interests together into Close Brothers. From the Benson point of view this meant that the two firms in which the family had an interest now became all Benson.[37]

In April 1884 Constantine took in his cousin Cecil Benson as a junior partner in C. W. Benson & Co., and the two were joined by Ker D. Dunlop, who would become the mainstay of the firm and the resident administrator of all the Benson US railway interests. Dunlop, who had joined Cross, Benson in November 1879 through the Cross / Dennistoun connection with Charles Gairdner of the Union Bank of Glasgow, formed a deep admiration for Robin. 'I never knew him to be out of temper once, or even slightly testy', he later wrote. The Iowa Land Co. continued to purchase land from its office in Sibley; but to expand their operation and be in a position to take advantage of greater railroad opportunities, Constantine and Ker Dunlop went north-eastwards to the thriving city of St Paul on the bank of the wide waterway of the Mississippi.[38]

This was a crucial decision in the development of Robert Benson & Co.'s railway interests. The firm was now even better placed to participate in North American railway issues, again the preoccupation of London and New York investment houses. Robin, through his Oxford friends, introduced all manner of people to, and became very experienced in, this area of financing—so that, whether it was for Illinois Central or Canadian Pacific, we find his name in the promotional documents. His firm's original capital of £7,500 had increased by 1888 to £157,000, reaching well over £200,000 in 1890 [£11.5m.]; profits were also a healthy £24,000 [£1.4m.] in 1888, though they fell in 1890 owing to the Baring crisis.[39]

The organization of the London market for American securities was by then well established. Transatlantic communication had become cheaper and faster since 1866, when a maximum of seven one-word telegrams a minute could be sent at a cost of £20 each; by 1908 the cost would fall to under 2*s*. and the average rate increase to thirty-two a minute. Similar developments in steamship transportation and the railway network had fostered the migration of people and of capital; and, with a decline in the cost of information, British investors were better able to take advantage of investment opportunities in the United States. The pioneering America, in which Close, Benson first invested, was becoming a land of corporate and bureaucratic organization, that attracted unprecedented amounts of both foreign portfolio and direct investments.

Much of this investment was channelled through Anglo-American houses in the City. The London market was dominated by two houses, Barings and J. S. Morgan, who between them accounted for 50 per cent of all the American issues in this period. Bensons was among the next group of firms which accounted for nearly 40 per cent of stocks issued in London between 1865 and 1890, the value of Bensons' market share being calculated at £6.07m.

During these years many of the firms listed in Table 6.1 underwent radical transformation, not least Bensons itself and certainly the once powerful Jay Cooke, which crashed in 1873 and was then transformed into Melville, Evans & Co. It would never recapture its importance. By the 1880s the other firms besides Barings and Morgans also considered of the first rank in terms of American issues were Rothschilds, Brown Shipley, Morton Rose, Seligmans, and Speyers. These formed the backbone of most of the important syndicates.

Of the smaller firms working intermittently with the main houses on particular issues but more often acting together within their own syndicates, Bensons were at the forefront. Others included Gilliats, whose senior partner John Gilliat became governor of the Bank of England in 1884; the Scottish American Investment Trust, dominated by Robert Fleming; and Rathbone Brothers in the person of William Lidderdale, who had been a partner since 1864 and was a director of the Bank of England, becoming governor in 1889. All these men had in common a first-hand knowledge of the United States and an excellent network of American contacts.[40]

TABLE 6.1. *American and Canadian Railroad stocks issued through London merchant banks, 1865–1890*

Bank	Value of issues ($m)	% of total issues
Baring Bros.	34.68	28.7
J. S. Morgan	26.09	21.6
Bischoffsheim & Goldschmidt	10.17	8.4
Morton, Rose & Co.	9.48	7.8
Speyer Bros.	9.16	7.6
Brown, Shipley & Co.	6.39	5.2
Robert Benson & Co.	**6.07**	**5.0**
Jay Cooke, McCulloch & Co.	5.12	4.2
L. Cohen & Sons	2.31	1.9
Union Bank of London	2.24	1.9
Thomson, Bonar & Co.	2.00	1.7
J. H. Schröder & Co.	1.85	1.5
R. Raphael & Sons	1.50	1.2
Seligman & Co.	1.40	1.2
N. M. Rothschild & Sons	0.80	0.7
C. de Murrieta & Co.	0.55	0.5
C. J. Hambro & Sons	0.50	0.4
Henry S. King & Co.	0.45	0.4
Jay & Co.	0.10	0.1
TOTAL	120.86	100.0

Sources: S. D. Chapman, *The Rise of Merchant Banking*, 97; D. R. Adler, *British Investment in American Railways 1834–98* (Virginia, 1970), app. l; *The Statist*, xxii (15 Dec. 1888), 685.

Thus in August 1883, when the railroad magnate Henry Villard organized the Northern Pacific's 'Driving of the Last Spike' party at Deer Lodge, Montana—to celebrate the link-up of the Pacific Northwest with the Mississippi Valley where the Northern Pacific met the Oregon Railway and Navigation Co.—Robin was on the guest list. Among the cream of governmental and financial figures who attended were the British Ambassador Sir Lionel Sackville-West, the governor of the Bank of England, a lord chief justice with a number of Members of Parliament and the former American president, Ulysses S. Grant. President Arthur himself joined the party at the Lafayette Club in St Paul where, in reply to his speech, General Terry gave the address entitled 'The Army—Holding the Savages in Check while the Shores of the Continent were United'.

Villard spared no expense as his four train-loads of guests rolled for a month in private cars across America. Robin's carriage companions were Vicary Gibbs, the son of the merchant banker Henry Hucks Gibbs, Albert Grey, the nephew and heir of Earl Grey, and Albert's brother-in-law George Holford. They got on famously together even after Robin, fooling about in the train, was shut up in a bunk that they could not open. When eventually released he emerged black in the face and barely alive.

All was not what it seemed on the junketing surface. 'Though we, his guests, did not know it,' Robin wrote, 'Villard was on the eve of a financial crash himself and must have been suffering torments while he entertained us;—until the strain became too great and he fled back to creditors in New York and the temporary ruin of his stockholders.' Villard's railroad was complete but in 'the widespread wreckage' of the Northern Pacific many suffered. Robin himself not only burnt his fingers over Northern Pacific stock but, having remained with the British Ambassador and some fifty guests, he found himself 'in a wooden hotel, only half finished but of colossal dimensions . . . all alone in the wilderness', where, Pepita Sackville-West wrote in her journal, he also 'got scalded in the Yellowstone Park sitting on an extinct geyser which woke up suddenly and burnt his Bobo badly. He could not sit down afterwards for a week!'[41]

These early years of railroad kingship were exhilarating. Travel by rail was regarded as a wonder and a pleasure; railroads were welcomed as instruments of prosperity and opportunity. There was a magic about them which enthralled the Benson brothers and many of their peers. To bring civilization and industry to acres of prairie untouched except by Indian hand was the stuff of Victorian dreams; in an age of empire-building, an age which valued self-reliance and opportunity, to build a railway through the Midwest was a worthwhile contribution. To see, as Robin and Constantine did, the effect upon some tiny isolated pioneering community of the arrival of the iron horse was unforgettable. In the words of the Iowan hymn writer, Dr W. S. Pitts, the coming of the railroad was 'like food for a starving man, like fresh fuel to a smouldering fire. The town awoke from its lethargy. It received the road with open arms, and man to man clasped hands and thanked God and took on new courage.'

The Benson brothers saw fortunes made and lost and somehow the ruthless competition and the survival of the strong at the expense of the weaker were dwarfed by the sum of national gain, the scope for honest labour and the immense rewards for the successful. Nevertheless, for those such as Robin and Constantine who understood the wreckage caused by a railroad failure such as Northern Pacific, or who suffered from the financial strain and loss in the early days of, for instance, the Canadian Pacific, the toll on their personal health was heavy. It was a brutal climate in which to operate and Constantine, who remained in the thick of it, later paid the price.[42]

Profitability from Bensons' perspective was no straightforward matter. Successful investment in American railroads had not become any easier as, besides the secret rebates and readiness to use the slightest pretext to break any understanding, booms and busts heightened by scandal continued to characterize the industry. In the 1850s Barings and Glyns had not known they were to be directors of the Grand Trunk in Canada until they read the prospectus; twenty years later one of its shareholders reported that commissions and bribes were universally sanctioned by most officials. In September 1873 Beatrice Webb accompanied her father on one of his numerous transatlantic business trips. 'Uniquely typical was the life on board a president's car on an American railway,' she observed, 'above all, the consciousness of personal prestige and power; the precedence of the president's car over all other traffic; the obsequious attention of ubiquitious officials; the contemptuous bargaining with political "bosses" for land concessions and for the passage of bills through legislatures—altogether a low moral temperature.'[43]

Not only had the Benson brothers to negotiate these minefields of obfuscation, corruption, and 'back-room dealing' without compromising their own moral standards and their firm's commercial reputation but, in common with other City colleagues, they even found themselves at times running the railroads in which they had invested. Bensons were one of a group of disgruntled investors who joined Gilliats reorganization committee to run the Denver & Rio Grande Railroad. The railroad baron, Jay Gould, had moved in on it in 1883 and driven the stock down from an inflated $113 to $18. When he had started buying the shares, the *New York Herald* had been amazed that anyone wanted a line which 'has nothing but two streaks of iron rust and the right of way through snow-filled canyons and plains whose only productions are sage-brush and Indians, a few borrowed locomotives and cars that serve to annoy the jack rabbits along the 1,000 or more miles of road.' After Gould had lost control, it was the small London group which included Robin and his colleagues, Robert Fleming and Howard Gilliat, who started to reorganize the road. In 1894 they removed the president and replaced him with an English partner in Gilliat's New York office, and Robert Fleming said 'Put the knife in deep' in terms of reorganization.[44]

'It is the function of financial [i.e. investment] banking', Robin Benson believed, 'to encourage the right men to develop the right enterprises and capitalise them into good securities for distribution'. This, in effect, was the line of approach adopted by the British houses in the 1880s, and by Constantine in St Paul. The latter introduced Bensons to the St Paul crowd of railroad men and financiers, thereby enabling it to build up a good niche business in Western railway finance. To take one example out of many, the firm was heavily involved in the activities of what became the Chicago and North Western Railway, which Constantine and Adolphus Stickney built up from St Paul. An impoverished young Maine lawyer, 'A.B.' Stickney had gone West and cut his railroad teeth on the St Paul, Minneapolis, and Manitoba; but, with a burning desire to head his own railroad, he found a dormant yet incorporated railroad, the Minnesota & Northwestern, acquired the unused franchise and, with charter in hand, set about attracting financial backing from, amongst others, the Benson brothers.

Constantine immediately joined Stickney in building up the railroad. Con used his Iowan expertise to look for profits from land sales and to develop a modest stockyard into the South St Paul Stockyards, which became the Minnesota & Northwestern's leading revenue producer after Gustavus Swift, the 'Yankee of the Stockyards' who revolutionized the Chicago meat-packing industry, was persuaded by Con and Stickney to lease the stockyard in 1885. Swift was a valuable connection for the Bensons. He loyally managed the capital of his London associates as if his own and also introduced the Bensons to leading western financiers such as Harry H. Porter, involved for almost fifty years in the construction and consolidation of railway systems based around Chicago and who also set the Union Steel Co. of Chicago on a sound financial footing. That, too, was an important contact. 'Porter's crowd', Robin wrote, 'were stronger in Western Railroad finance than Morgans' and made their mark 'before the rise of Kuhn, Loeb & Co. and the great Jewish houses'. Through Porter, Robin also made long-term investments in other railway and land development schemes.

Robin, one of Stickney's first English investors, also conceived the strategy for the development of the Minnesota & Northwestern as a future tributary line of the more important Illinois Central. The strategy, as worked out with Stickney in 1883, was to expand the Minnesota & Northwestern through taking over smaller lines, but never in such a way as to compete with the Illinois Central; and to build it up in areas which would be attractive to the Illinois Central, achieve a healthy balance sheet and then sell out to the Illinois Central for a large profit.

All went according to plan until in 1885 Stickney suddenly acquired an ailing Iowa line, the Dubuque & Dakota, known as the 'Damn Doubtful', a Butler County resident declared, because its 'time schedules were as uncertain as a political platform'. Stickney's purchase was 'a surprise to the best posted men in railway circles' and not least to the Illinois Central, which was furious at the secret sale since Stickney's line would now 'greatly injure' their Dubuque & Sioux City line. It was also a surprise to the Bensons, for it was no part of their plan to upset the Illinois Central. Robin wrote of Stickney: 'You could trust him with money uncounted and his only defect was that he had too much courage. "Be bold, be bold, (as Spenser says in the *Faerie Queen*), but not too bold".' And, 'Stickney met his fate when he collided with E. H. Harriman of the Illinois

Central. He broke our plan as originally laid out and made the road an independent road.' In consequence 'he lost his only railroad friends and when they saw him "holding a block of ice, they let him hold it". So the wolf pack got him, for every mile of his road became competitive.'

Bensons, nevertheless, continued to support him, believing that the railroad and warehouse group would win through and remain a good profit centre for them. 'To us Stickney's life and health are more important than any other single thing,' Robin reiterated to a fellow investor, Everard Hambro. 'Therefore I am the more anxious to save him all financial worries, using his brains for the practical operating, or policy, while we control the finances.' They successfully arranged the finance in April 1887, by offering 5 per cent first mortgage bonds to extend the line to Kansas City, thereby linking it with the vital gateways of Minneapolis, Chicago, and St Paul, and creating the Chicago, St Paul & Kansas City Railway, or the 'Maple Leaf' line.

Although the Illinois Central was miffed about Stickney, the Company remained on excellent terms with Bensons, still their London agents. Bensons' involvement in building the line has remained evident. 'Find a US railroad driving on the left', runs the aphorism, 'and it will almost certainly have been financed by the British.' Their relationship was renewed through a deal with the Illinois Central in 1981. This was followed by a $160m. private placement in 1991 when Robin's grandson, David Benson, delighted to see a historic relationship crystallize once more remarked, 'It's nice to have been invited to help again.'[45]

When Robin travelled out for the inauguration of the completed line in 1888, he was not allowed to devote himself entirely to railroad affairs. Nor did he want to in the company of his bride, Evelyn Holford. Their marriage was a significant factor in making the Benson family business more secure. Two developments had brought them together.

The first concerned pictures, which Robin had started to collect in earnest. On 5 December 1884 he had been taken for the first time to Christies by William Graham, who helped him buy a Burne-Jones picture, *Forge of Cupid*. Under Graham's wing Robin encountered most of the leading figures in the Victorian art world. In particular, he was given an immediate entrée to Sir Coutts Lindsay's Sunday afternoon parties at the Grosvenor Gallery, which provided some of the high points of the London season in the 1880s. The Grosvenor Gallery opened as an avant-garde shop window for those artists who refused to produce conventional pictures of highland cattle for the Royal Academy. Coutts Lindsay founded it so that his friends Whistler and the Pre-Raphaelites could exhibit their pictures somewhere, and it was an immediate success. 'To believe in it and to profess it became a stamp of artistic sensibility,' wrote E. F. Benson; it became 'a sort of religion to the highly cultured', featuring in Gilbert and Sullivan's *Patience* as the 'greenery-yallery Grosvenor Gallery'. Anyone interested in modern pictures visited this temple to aestheticism with its Whistler ceiling of a clear blue sky powdered over with stars and phases of the moon in silver. Here Robin encountered William Graham's collector friend and Coutts Lindsay's brother-in-law, Robert Stayner Holford, the father of his future wife, Evelyn.[46]

The Holfords were Gloucestershire country squires who, like their Stayner ancestors, were 'loaded with wealth' although their source was New River water rather than the Spanish Main. After much anxiety and loss, Sir Hugh Myddleton's Company of Adventurers in partnership with James I succeeded in bringing New River water to supply London. At first, in the words of a great seventeenth-century adventurer, Captain John Smith, 'the returns neither answered the general expectation nor my desire' but by the middle of the next century they far exceeded expectation. While Robert's grandfather Peter was governor of the New River Co. (from 1753 to his death in 1803), the growth in both the population and industrial requirements of London caused the company to become immensely profitable, so that returns on their large investments in it multiplied to leave the Holfords enormously rich by the early nineteenth century. On the death of Robert's uncle in 1838 his inheritance even included a cache of bullion. According to family tradition, when he went down to inspect the Niton estate, he uncovered chests of gold buried during the threat of Napoleonic invasion in 1804; they were said to be worth £1m. The following year Robert's father, also governor of the New River Co. and a former Secretary of the Board of Trade, died leaving him the Westonbirt estate in Gloucestershire and a further fortune so that, at 31, he was described as the 'richest commoner in England'.

Robert Holford was the 'ideal connoisseur', a collector 'with an eye for quality and the means to indulge it without stint'. His earliest passion was for landscape gardening. He assembled specimen trees from all over the world, many contributed by research expeditions to China and South America, to produce the gorgeous livery of a Westonbirt autumn. One of his head gardeners wistfully observed that 'no other man planted like Squire Holford' for he 'could see a perfect landscape' where others could see only flat ground; he created horticultural pictures which can still be seen today at the Westonbirt Arboretum, one of the pre-eminent arboretums in the country.

After plants and trees, his greatest enthusiasm was reserved for his picture collection and the buildings in which to house it. In 1839 he began with the purchase of four pictures including a Tintoretto; by 1853/4 he had bought over

100 pictures to form a significant collection. Dr Gustav Waagen, a contemporary art historian who examined it, praised the excellent powers of judgement and catholicity of taste of such a 'youthful proprietor', whose collection contained works by Titian, Lotto, Veronese, Reni, Rubens, Velasquez, Van Dyck, Rembrandt, Murillo, Claude, Poussin, Cuyp, and Wouvermans.

In 1849 Robert Holford had turned to his trusted Clerk of the Works at Westonbirt: 'Thomas, you must build me a house for my pictures.' This Thomas duly did, erecting the grand Italianate palazzo of Holford's dreams under the supervision of the architect Louis Vulliamy. Built as a work of art in itself, Dorchester House was distinguished for its grand central staircase hall and splendid state rooms spectacularly suited for the display of the picture collection and the entertainment of London society. In 1854, to celebrate his marriage to Mary Anne Lindsay and the opening of the house, he gave a fancy-dress ball at which all his guests were dressed to represent famous Italian portraits. A shared love of such pictures undoubtedly furthered Robin Benson's acquaintance with Holford and his suit with his daughter Evelyn, always known as Evey.[47]

The second development that brought them together was his position as the friend and financial adviser of her brother, George Holford. Although George was the heir to an immense fortune, much of his wealth was settled. Any funds over and above a most generous allowance had to come from his father. After Eton, George had received a commission in the 1st Life Guards and thereafter led the commensurately expensive life of a high-spirited young blade, much in demand as an eligible *parti* during the Season. By 1884, the year after the Villard 'Last Spike' trip, he had amassed a debt of £7,000 [£383,000]. This may have been a gaming debt or one involving the upkeep of a mistress; whichever, he wished to spare his people 'all knowledge of what must pain them'. Such a decision made it difficult to provide security for a loan without recourse to his father or the Holford financial advisers. Albert Grey first put George in touch with his mother's cousin Harvie Farquhar, a partner in Scotts Bank, but he stated that they never lent without security.

In some trepidation the 24-year-old approached the second name on his list, Robin Benson, whose only caveat was 'whatever we do we must do *thoroughly* now: with no idea of borrowing more later: that is always onerous & a position I shdn't like to be in'. It was exactly the reception George wanted. 'He was *too good natured* for words & took a lot of trouble,' he confided to Albert. '*He is a* good chap is he not; He quite staggered me by offering immediately to give his name to help me as a suretie [*sic*]; just think; & I have no claim on him whatever.' George was overwhelmed by 'the extraordinary friendship of the act' and from that moment he unreservedly placed his trust in Robin.

As for Robin, by arranging the loan—of £7,000 for seven years at 5 per cent and life insurance of £5,000–6,000, half with and half without profits at an average premium of £2 *0s. 7d.* per £100, which he perceived as of minimal risk—he had gained for Bensons an important client. George not only put some of his own capital into Bensons, but he also transferred to the firm the running of his substantial investment accounts; and this, in turn, brought new business from a wide circle of his family and acquaintances. As George's friend, chief financial and art adviser, Robin became a frequent visitor to Westonbirt for Saturdays to Mondays. 'The real and genuine love that George has had for so long a time' for Robin was in itself, Lady Crawford thought, the best recommendation the Holfords could have about him.[48]

Robin, according to Evey's elder sister Minnie, the Countess of Morley, had 'been desperately in love for a long time', and when, in May 1887, he found his feelings reciprocated, he and Evey became engaged. The Holford family were delighted, especially as they were gaining a son rather than losing a daughter. Evey's sisters Minnie Morley and Alice Grey had married young and gone to run their husbands' country houses Saltram and Howick, leaving Evey as the sole daughter at home for ten years. Although Evey's mother suffered from delicate health, far from being kept with her, Evey was encouraged to accompany her father on his frequent Continental tours to look at pictures. While 'Maysie' Lindsay lay on her sofa, painted, and wrote novels—*Strathrowan* was published in 1878—and plays, one of which was performed to acclaim at Olympia with Marian Terry, Evey presided at her father's table and, to all intents and purposes, ran Dorchester House and Westonbirt.

At the time of her engagement to Robin, she was a cultured, well-travelled 31-year-old, long used to commanding large battalions of staff. Observing her at the engagement dinner at Dorchester House, Minnie Morley wrote, 'Evey looks excessively happy. She amuses Alice and me enormously. I suppose it is natural her not being like a young girl but she has dropped quite into Robin's wife, not his fiancée at all and talks in the most matter of fact unshy way as to what they shall do in household arrangements and everything else.' Minnie also believed that though Robin was not in the least a weak man, Evey would be a wife with very much the upper hand who would continue to play a pivotal role at Westonbirt and Dorchester House.

This was easier to achieve because, as Minnie put it, Robin 'only possesses as far as I can make out two relations in the world, a sister a very nice woman married to a London clergyman a Mr Hoskyns & a brother who is married and lives in America and manages the other end of the business.' Robin's mother had died in 1883 after throwing herself in a manic fit at the fire; his Uncle William Benson, who had been so supportive throughout 'the Benson troubles' had died in the early part of the year; apart from Con and May only Uncle Con at Selaby and Uncle James Moorsom remained of his near family. This was seen as an advantage by the Holford side. 'I think it will be less of a severance than other marriages might have been,' declared Evey's Aunt Harriet, Lady Wantage, to Maysie Holford 'for I think Mr Benson will soon become one of us—& from not having an absorbing family circle of his own, will soon be a real Son to you.'

Another advantage to the match was that Robin could keep Evey in the style to which she had long been accustomed. Her sisters had married into great positions but not great wealth. Evey's Aunt Margaret, the Countess of Crawford and Balcarres, felt glad that 'Evey will not have to measure with care and anxiety her daily expenses but have the gracious gift of great wealth which no one will use better.' It was less Robin's fortune that impressed, however, than his unassuming, intelligent character. Evey's cousin Ludovic Balcarres enthusiastically described Robin as someone who 'held such a high position as an honourable and high-minded carver out of his great fortunes and one whose mind and tastes and feelings broadened and did not narrow with great success'. Moreover, Evey's knowledge of art and Italy—she was fluent in Italian—would be tremendous assets to Robin; she could join with him in acquiring 'the beautiful things that he has such a care for' and help him to create their own picture collection.[49]

Their wedding on 7 July 1887 at St George's, Hanover Square followed by a breakfast afterwards at Dorchester House was 'a most gorgeous affair', an experience, wrote Dearman Birchell, a Benson relation, 'like those imaginary ones concocted by Lord Beaconsfield in *Lothair* for the admiration of a luxurious and sumptuous age'. The church was closed to all but ticket-holders and each guest was given a white buttonhole as their passport to Dorchester House. There, related that seasoned observer, Augustus Hare, 'all London flocked through the rooms to admire the presents, which were indescribably splendid'. While Robin may have had few close relations, he had the most presents. 'The collections of old silver, Queen Anne especially, old engravings, paintings, 1st editions of costly books like Ruskin, dressing cases—three or four with superb silver mountings, old china, watches, clocks, cameo-mounted articles from Italy, in fact such a sight I never saw or imagined nor am I able to throw any light on the regal magnificence of the display, unless,' joked Dearman Birchell, 'all his clients have to a varying degree profited by his unequalled good fortune.'

Dorchester House provided an unequalled setting for the wedding breakfast. 'The scene on the beautiful white marble staircase was charming,' enthused Augustus Hare. 'Above, under the circular arches, between the pillars of coloured marble, and against a golden wall background, the overhanging galleries were filled with all the most beautiful women in London leaning over the balustrades.' It was a dazzling display of colour, fashion, wealth and, above all, joy for a love match.[50]

After a short honeymoon, Robin brought his bride home to 18 Kensington Square. He had lived there since moving out of the Charles Street lodgings in 1882, so as to provide a home for his sister May and a base for Constantine and Em when they visited England. Evey's description of a typical evening's entertainment there gives us a picture of their newly married life: 'We really had great fun: Mr Balfour came about half past six to play lawn tennis & soon after Burne-Jones turned up & Alice [Grey] & Henry James the novelist & at half past seven George & Albert & the Laurence Drummonds arrived which made us ten.' She and Robin had arranged a dining table halfway down the garden beyond the hammocks; Evey had decorated the table with glasses of sweet peas '& you can't think how pretty dining there looked', she told her mother. 'Nobody was in evening dress so we were all quite warm & they were all in tearing spirits & very amusing.' After dinner the party adjourned to the American exhibition to see Buffalo Bill before George took them to the switchback railway, 'which we were determined to try; I think Alice & I were both rather nervous at first,' admitted Evey.[51]

The delights of life in Kensington were not to contain them for long. Although their more artistic friends lived west of the Park, the Bensons' social life was centred firmly in the great houses of Mayfair. Before the marriage Robin had approached his father-in-law's friend, the Duke of Westminster, about building a house designed by Norman Shaw in Park Lane but the sale and development of the site had to be postponed for legal reasons.

Rather than wait indefinitely with no firm agreement in place, Robin took a long lease on 16 South Street. Redecoration was not completed by the time he and Evey returned from honeymoon so they based themselves at Kensington Square before leaving in August for a series of Highland visits. On their arrival back in London at the beginning of October 1887 they stayed at Dorchester House for several days before walking through the communicating gate at the bottom of the long, deep garden which led into their own smaller garden at 16 South Street. It was to be their London home for the next forty years.

An atmosphere of warmth and comfort pervaded the fine house where Robin and Evey created a haven of welcome for their extended family and a 'clearing-house' for all the family news. Harriet Wantage's nephew Thomas Loyd recalled 'How often did I go to South Street, be told to stay to dinner while [Uncle Robin] . . . vanished in search of claret and then afterwards talked over problems with him while Aunt Evey put in from time to time a most pertinent criticism over her spectacles and the inevitable needlework!'[52]

As Christmas with the Wantages at Lockinge and January with the Holfords at Westonbirt beckoned, Robin became unwell. The accumulated strain of the past twelve highly charged years, which had included, at their nadir, bereavement and bankruptcy, and, at their apex, great personal happiness and success, had finally taken its toll on his health. Evey confided to her mother that 'though he has done very little work he comes home quite exhausted sometimes & goes to sleep in the middle of dinner without eating anything'. Consultation with Sir Andrew Clarke yielded a diagnosis of nervous exhaustion with a recommendation 'to take him away as soon as possible, out of reach of his work', to the Riviera or Italy. Evey's worry that his condition might develop into a real breakdown, as had occurred in the case of her Uncle Bob Wantage, was allayed by Clarke's opinion that 'Rob has a very good constitution, but an extraordinarily nervous temperament which would probably get much stronger as he grew older.' Clarke was entirely correct. Robin's health rapidly recovered during a January holiday in Paris and thereafter remained good, apart from an attack of peritonitis, almost until the end of the 1920s, when he would die after a stroke.[53]

Although Robin could be spared for a while because Constantine was in London, Evey reported from Paris on 22 January 1888 that he had already deserted her for a business meeting in the City. It was not, in fact, the best time for him to be absent from London, for the City was then in the grips of the 'Trust Craze'. This was to be a significant development for Bensons and provides another instance of Robin's forging role in the creation of an industry in which the bank remains a force today with investment trusts of £2.0 bn. A feature of the inflationary years of 1882–90 was the establishment of combinations, 'corners', promotion companies, and trusts such as were adopted in America. English trusts were for the most part nominally investment companies which traded on the assumption that they could average investors' risks better than investors could do alone. Some trusts operated to dispose of accumulated securities, others as bona fide investment institutions conducting a respectable and responsible business. It was the development of the latter type of investment trust vehicle, one which allowed venture capitalists to spread their risk and to diminish their chances of repeating such disasters as had befallen Robin's father, that would provide the 'bread and butter' of Bensons' business for a good many years.

The first investment trust, the Foreign & Colonial, was established in 1868, though it was the success of two Scottish-based trusts formed in 1873 that led to the trust craze of the late 1880s. Robin was familiar with both: the Scottish American Investment Trust Co. Ltd., which he knew through his New York agent J. S. Kennedy who also acted for this trust; and the Scottish American Investment Trust started by Robert Fleming. Robin knew him through the Rathbones, as Fleming's first wife was a Rathbone, and Johnny Cross, whose Scottish financial connections were excellent.

Like Robin's father, Robert Fleming had lost money in the Overend Gurney crash of 1866—though considerably less, since he was only a private clerk in Dundee at the time. Fleming had to compromise with the liquidators to meet calls but, although legally discharged, he determined to pay his debts in full, which he was able to do before his first Trust was formed in 1873. Thereafter, he always remembered a friend's proposed stamp for the foreheads of ambitious financiers: 'A fortune once acquired should never be endangered.'

Fleming's skilful management of the original Scottish American Investment Trust and its three successor trust companies, for all of which he was secretary, brought them safely through the successive panics and depressions of the 1870s. This was especially remarkable since all his Trusts' early investments were made in US railroad mortgage bonds whose value subsequently tumbled. Yet all interest coupons on the company's bonds were paid, the market value of the Trusts' securities showed an overall increase and the dividend was the promised 6 per cent for 1873 despite the autumn financial crisis. Later Fleming joked that in the company's cable code, the word conveying that all coupons due had been paid was 'miraculous'. He followed a sound, conservative policy whereby there was no reliance on borrowed money and no risk beyond the subscription. To take the example of his first Scottish American Investment Trust: the original £300,000 invested in 1879 had a market value in 1883 of £464,686.

Fleming's success quickly made him the doyen of the investment trust movement in Britain and America. At the height of activity in 1888 over seventy companies were registered with an aggregate capital exceeding £70m. These trusts siphoned off British savings into United States investment and grew powerful through a combination of daring faith and careful judgement, as exhibited by principals such as Fleming. Although based in Dundee, each year Fleming's financial interests took him to America; in the crisis year of 1893 he would cross the Atlantic seven times. When in London it was Robin Benson who informally provided him with office space in Broad Street, until he opened his own London office at 2 Princes Street in 1900. Apart from his own trusts, many other investment companies used his firm as their London representative so that his influence was tremendous. He was thus an important City connection of Robin Benson, whose own influence in this field mushroomed until he came to sit on so many boards that he eventually had to shed them like leaves onto his junior partner, a policy that would become a bone of contention later on.[54]

The second important City connection Robin made during this period was also a Scotsman. Alexander Henderson, later Lord Faringdon, was the senior partner of the stockbrokers, Greenwood & Co. Railways provided the link between them; Greenwoods acted as brokers to most of the main British railway companies along with American and especially South American ones. A decisive, self-educated man, Faringdon was a respected City figure renowned for his South American interests. It was through him that Bensons first came to take a stake in the Central Argentine, the Argentine Great Western, the Central Uruguay, and the Buenos Ayres Great Southern Railway companies to name but a few. Robin's friendship with Faringdon and his younger brother Harry Henderson started in 1886 and they remained 'intimate . . . through good times and bad and,' Robin later wrote, 'never have I known them veer a hairsbreadth from the honourable course—which', he added, 'is also in the long run the money making course!'[55]

Robin had returned from Paris in the winter of 1888 to attend a board meeting of the London Electricity Supply Corporation and to make arrangements to form his own investment trust. His absence on a five-month trip to North America meant that his Merchants Trust was not registered for business until 16 February 1889. With a capital of £2m., of which half was subscribed, Merchants Trust largely concentrated upon investment in American railroads; not surprisingly the Trust was run by a group of men who were highly knowledgeable about American investments in general and railroads in particular.

As the economist Inglis Palgrave explained in 1893, the success of trusts such as the Merchants 'is based on the fact that they have been managed by boards containing men well known by name in Great Britain and men who understand the conditions of success in making investments in the United States'. When choosing his partners, Robin approached men who amply fulfilled both criteria. Under him as chairman, the board consisted of Colonel Robert Baring (brother of the senior partner at Barings), Charles Bright (a partner at Antony Gibbs), William Campbell (a director of the Bank of England), Howard Gilliat (a partner at Gilliats), Charles Hambro (brother of the senior partner at Hambros), and Lord Kinnaird (a partner in Ransome, Bouverie & Co. which merged with Barclay, Bevan, Tritton & Co. in 1888). Robin stated in 1892,

> Our business is simply that of an investment company, which was formed in 1889 in order to spread its investments carefully over the world, in securities yielding from 5 to 6 per cent, and in the belief that the principle of average would compensate the risk of seeking so high a rate of interest. Our business is not to keep shifting our securities, but rather to hold them and to change them only with a view to greater profit or greater security.

Many trust companies foundered. The *Statist* rightly warned how 'promoting syndicates and limited liability ventures, which have failed to successfully float various companies and scratch issues, find a "trust" a valuable receptacle for all sorts of indigestible rubbish'. In contrast, Merchants Trust survived the unexpectedly difficult trading years of the 1890s through combining cautious, largely non-speculative investment with a better geographical spread than some of their competitors. The *Statist*'s analysis of the 1890/1 results of thirty-six trusts revealed the Merchants Trust as among the more productive. Befitting a trust that specialized in American railway investment, over 47 per cent of its portfolio in 1891 was invested in the United States; the next largest shareholding, nearly 20 per cent, derived from the Colonial sector, with another 14 per cent from South American railways, whilst domestic and Continental sectors accounted for only about 12.5 per cent.

Although the Board stated in the 1892 report that it took 'no initiatives in the intricate modern business of creating, introducing and placing securities' and only underwrote shares 'for no larger amounts than we were able to hold till doomsday if need be', the directors found it much more difficult than they had expected to apply the principle of average and obtain good results. Expenses were kept to a minimum and the Board took 'a certain pride' in obtaining commissions from various sources for the Trust Company, some of which the Directors could easily have kept for their own firms.

Nevertheless, in common with other leaders of British investment during the 1890s, the Board found it a continuous struggle. In looking back over the period from 1888, Robin confessed in 1901 that

> . . . we none of us knew how difficult, nay, how impossible it is to apply the principle of average successfully all over the world. We now know that some countries are to be avoided entirely. Still less did we foresee the crisis of 1890 and the consequent liquidation; nor had we sufficiently appreciated that the principle of average was sound at bottom, but that if one went investing £5,000 all over the place one was bound to lose money. There is often more risk about £5,000 in one thing than about £100,000 in another. Many investments needed a great deal of looking after, and involved attendance on committees, and outside work of a special character before they came right; in short, the work was a great deal heavier and more responsible than my colleagues and I ever imagined, when in 1889 we undertook to try and look after other people's money.

The work was, none the less, worth the effort. Merchants Trust continues to flourish today under its original name with funds of some £300m.[56]

The crisis of 1890 that Robin and even his fellow board member Colonel Robert Baring had not foreseen concerned Barings, which had been over-optimistic in the Argentine. Tom Baring memorably evoked the firm's plight:

'The name and the glory and the position and everything is gone . . . Verily a great Nemesis overtook Croesus.' Fortunately for the Barings, in place of the usual attitude of *sauve qui peut*, the bank was bailed out by a damage limitation exercise organized by Robin's fellow director on the CSP & KC railroad, William Lidderdale of Rathbones, then Governor of the Bank of England. He introduced to the City the principle of a mutual guarantee to sustain liquidity, later dubbed the principle of 'commercial salvage'.

Dick Meinertzhagen recalls in his boyhood diary that the first occasion on which he met Robin was at a Baring house on 2 November 1890. Dick's father was a partner in the family bank, Frederick Huth & Co., and, 'owing to an upset in the City', Charles Goschen was staying with them. 'Apparently a firm called Baring's is going to go smash, so today they all drove over to Norman Court and they took me along with them. I never saw such a lot of long-faced bankers all looking as though it was the end of the world.' Dick recorded that 'As soon as we arrived at Norman Court all these old gentlemen shut themselves up in the smoking-room whilst I was sent out into the garden . . . After the conference everyone seemed pleased and smiling and I was introduced to a Mr Robert Benson and a Mr Nathan [*sic*] Rothschild.'

Robin was one of many in the City who subscribed for preference shares in the insolvent bank; these shares were apparently not redeemed until the 1920s. The crash itself had severe repercussions on the US market. Whereas acceptance firms such as Kleinworts would benefit through filling the void temporarily left by Barings, issuing and investment firms such as Bensons suffered from the collapse in both the price of American rails and general investor confidence. Barings had only just headed a syndicate to place £6m. of St Paul, Minneapolis, and Manitoba bonds, at that time one of the largest financings by an American railroad in Europe, and only the year before had taken over the management of the Atchison, Topeka & Santa Fe line. Now, in November 1890, it had to sell its holdings in the Atchison along with other American securities and was unable to place more than half of the St Paul, Minneapolis, and Manitoba bonds, with disastrous consequences for other US railroads looking for London financing. Revolution and financial crisis were rampant in 1890 so that, as Max Wirth wrote in 1893, 'with such a compound mixture of financial losses and dangers it is not surprising that the minds of European investors became utterly depressed'.[57]

Although the drama of the crisis receded, no revival of British interest in American securities occurred; indeed on the Stickney lines three-quarters of the shares held abroad in 1890 were, by 1891, held in the United States. There was some urgency about the CStP & KC railway. Its debt level was soaring and in 1889—with a loss of $731,358 due to the agricultural depression, slashed tariffs, and rate wars—the company had asked bondholders to forgo payment of their interest earnings for three years. The Barings crisis and subsequent depression had thwarted hopes of recovery. Unless the high fixed charges could be reduced the railway would be in danger of foreclosure. Robin moved quickly to tackle the problem.

His solution was to issue gold debenture stock, long favoured by British railway companies but little known and never used to the same extent by American carriers, owing to self-fulfilling investor resistance. The attraction for Stickney's company of a debenture instrument was that it made the railroad a mortgage-free property with only a lien on its income. Robin also appointed a London Finance Committee consisting of such old friends as Edwin Waterhouse, Howard Gilliat, Alexander Wallace (a director of the Bank of England), and Sir Charles Tennant, under the chairmanship of William Lidderdale, which made the reorganization more attractive to investors. Even in the depressed climate of 1892, the issue was well subscribed. In terms of the railway itself, the reorganization created the new Chicago Great Western Railway Co. which linked the gateways of Chicago, the Twin Cities, St Joseph, and Kansas City.

Although the issue was deemed a success, there was considerable opposition from a small yet extremely vocal group of bondholders. They publicized their stance in the *Investors' Review*, a journal that was waging a campaign against that 'paralytic bank', the Bank of England. The reorganization of the CGW provided a ready arsenal with which to bombard the Bank of England publicly about its connection with American securities.

Where Robin publicly stated that 'interest in the new 4 per cent debenture stock is obviously safe', the *Investors' Review* declared 'It is nothing of the sort.' Urging the bondholders to turn out 'the self-imposed' London Finance Committee of the CGW, 'a commonplace financial transmogrification of amateur financiers who emulous of the successful American railroad "boss", build a new line and get the British public to pay for it', and 'replace them by men they can trust', the journal censured the Bank of England. The Bank had apparently claimed that CGW's prospects were excellent and 'always touted so for the bonds of this miserable abortion of a railway' whose reorganization might otherwise have died at birth. The *Review*'s campaign finally drew blood in 1894 from an unexpected quarter when it emerged that the Bank's chief cashier had resigned after being accused of persuading a number of the Bank's old customers to invest in CGW securities with money borrowed from the Bank. Whilst this was manna to the *Investors' Review*, it had no ostensible effect upon the reputation of either the CGW or Bensons.

Although the reorganization had been a forced one, its timing proved ideal.

A panic on Wall Street in May 1893 ushered in a period of depression in America: nearly 200 roads had failed by the time prosperity returned in the late 1890s. The CGW, however, survived through reorganization and innovation. Stickney's bold management style and Bensons' financial expertise combined even in the face of sustained opposition and a poor economic climate to produce better results. Bensons' investment in the group of companies was extremely rewarding, with Robin alone receiving an income of £2,000–4,000 [£243,000] a year.[58]

Other American plans did not materialize as originally envisaged. Another development, the clearing yards in Chicago alongside the Illinois Central Railroad, proved an extremely long-term investment. The Clearing Industrial District Inc. was capitalized in 1898 at $4m. when H. H. Porter, a Chicago consortium of Marshall Field, Armour, Swift, and McCormick, and Robin, who distributed some of his share to Albert Grey and the Prince of Wales, each took a 25 per cent interest. The construction of the yards cost $2m. but they were sold for $4.4m. in 1912, the remaining assets being put into real estate. Clearing remained in the Benson portfolio until 1971 when, with Robins' grandson David on the Board, British shareholders arranged the sale of the company for $44.5m. Some $7.5m. found its way back across the Atlantic, 'a nice legacy', the *Financial Times* commented 'of the time at the end of the last century when British merchant banks helped to finance the expansion of American railways'.[59]

They had also helped to finance Southern African ones, though Robin's interest there was much less of a hands-on one than in America. This was owing partly to a greater reliance upon others—he never visited Southern Africa—and partly to the exigencies of commercial life there. Bensons' involvement in Southern African railways and mining was dominated by Rhodes and his Chartered Co. Lord Salisbury, both Prime Minister and Foreign Secretary for much of the 'imperial' period, might with fastidious detachment publicly define British policy on the partition or scramble for Africa as 'drifting lazily downstream, occasionally putting out a boat hook to prevent a collision', but he none the less positively encouraged his Consuls and High Commissioners to extend the all-red map of British influence. When Cecil Rhodes, 'an erratic young diamond magnate', pressed for permission to extend the power of the Cape Colony northwards to outflank the hostile Boers in the Transvaal and Orange Free State, the Government agreed, mainly because nothing was demanded of the British taxpayer and it made political sense.

Rhodes had made a second fortune in the gold rush on the Rand that began in 1886 and wanted to create a company of adventurers in the mould of the East India Company and Hudson's Bay Company, and the revival of a Chartered Co. incorporated by the Queen's authority appealed to the imagination of investors and public opinion because it combined business enterprise with political loyalty and an element of delectable swashbuckle.

On 29 October 1889, Queen Victoria signed a Royal Charter granting Rhodes and his syndicate concessions extending half-way up the east coast of Africa between Central Africa and the Transvaal, then called Zambezia but eventually renamed Rhodesia, which they would colonize and finance through their British South Africa Co. (the Chartered Co.). Robin's brother-in-law Albert Grey became a director and when, owing to his part in the Jameson Raid in 1896, Rhodes was forced to resign as Cape Prime Minister and chairman of the Chartered Co., Albert took his place at Chartered after being appointed the Administrator of Rhodesia.

Albert saw the British Empire not as painting the map red but as carrying light into the darkness, especially in South Africa. Adverse opinions, such as that of his brother-in-law Lord Minto, that the Chartered Co. 'was engaged in a disreputable attempt to lay hands on the wealth of the Rand under the pretence of patriotism' were inconceivable to Albert, whose integrity and sincerity about Rhodes and the work of the Chartered Co. brought investment and support from all quarters. The Benson brothers were soon involved.[60]

Although Rhodes's whole scheme was predicated upon the discovery of a new Rand to finance the Chartered Co.'s colonization—in the same way the discovery of the Rand in the Transvaal in 1886 had financed its expansion—Robin, who soon became Albert's unofficial adviser, thought the development of 'Railways, & land,—*à l'Americaine*' should come *before* gold mines. It was Constantine, however, who in 1896 went out to Southern Africa to devise the introduction of a railway system and to build the first railroad in the new colony, the Rhodesian Railway, which would be linked to the Cape Railway line. 'Do you remember several years ago the talk we had over Canadian Pacific methods & how to improve upon them in S. Africa?' Robin asked Albert. 'I am in hopes that Con will see & organize this.' Constantine's ultimate goal was to get a railway system 'into working order that is common to the whole of South Africa'.

Despite his technical knowledge and experience, Constantine quickly found that commercial conditions in Southern Africa were quite unlike those prevailing in the Midwest of America. There had been no native uprisings there; nor had the Indians provided a cheap labour force as the black Africans were expected to do in Rhodesia. British settlers at Salisbury did not do any menial or manual labour for themselves. When Albert tried by personal example to show 'what damned nonsense' this was, and invited the settlers to plant a tree without black or paid labour in honour of the Queen, the only tree planted was his own gum-tree at Government House.

Furthermore, there had been no red tape in America compared to the burgeoning bureaucracy in Southern Africa; nor did any of his American lines have to avoid hostile neighbouring states, as the Cape and Rhodesian lines had to avoid crossing the Transvaal and Orange Free State by making a detour into Bechuanaland (now Botswana). Constantine therefore had to negotiate terms which were fair to three railway companies and then receive agreement not only from the Cape Government, obtaining permission from the Colonial Secretary regarding title to any property required for operation or maintenance, but also from Cecil Rhodes, whose interests did not always coincide with those of Her Majesty's Government. It was a delicate and time-consuming role especially as he was also acting for Rhodes and two other randlords, J. B. Robinson and Alfred Beit in all their railway interests.[61]

Robin soon became concerned: first, that his brother was being badly used by those who did not possess the same gentlemanly qualities; second, and in common with many others, that the operation of the British South Africa Co. was not above board. Potential abuses were rife in a company that possessed the sole right to grant concessions and also benefited from the flotation of companies exploiting those very concessions. After peace had been signed at Pretoria in May 1902, thereby officially ending the Boer War, and Southern Africa had picked up the threads of commercial life, Robin brought two plans off the back-burner. One was to encourage the appointment of sounder men onto the boards of the main concessionary companies so that commercial practice was tightened up. The other involved the separation of the two functions of the British South Africa Co. through the creation of the Charter Trust & Agency Co., which would manage the agency and financial side of the business.[62]

There was some urgency about the implementation because Cecil Rhodes was due to depart for South Africa at the end of January 1902. Robin promised to have the prospectus cut and dried by mid-week, 'which I did & went up by the first train' he proudly reported to Evey on 23 January. 'Albert is pleased to say that I have helped him much & put it on a different & higher plane & tomorrow we meet the solicitor & settle matters a step further. I don't think there will be any difficulty in getting the £1,000,000.' After Rhodes died in March, the British South Africa Co. tried to renege on the division but by that time the Charter Trust & Agency was established with a board of directors that included Robin.

Furthermore, Albert obtained permission from Lord Milner, High Commissioner for South Africa and Governor of Cape Colony, for the Charter to finance the building of a railway to connect Johannesburg with the Cape Town–Bulawayo line, which would provide 'a natural channel to convey to Rhodesia the overflow of capital & settlers from Johannesburg'. He wanted Robin to come out next year: 'I wish he were with me now—There is so much going on which wd interest him.' Robin, however, never made the journey. This was a mistake which he had not made with the American side of his business, believing then in the advantage of seeing for himself. In part he had originally left Southern Africa to Constantine to oversee, but Constantine was in no position to act as his 'eyes and ears' by the early years of 1900. Reliance upon Albert Grey, who could be carried away by enthusiasm and was no financier, was not a good substitute. For these reasons the Benson and Merchants Trust Southern African portfolios produced a relatively smaller share of the profits than their American counterparts.[63]

The business of Bensons was by no means exclusively confined to railway finance. The finance of technological innovation continued to attract Benson interest and, as a high-risk specialization, provide either large profit or loss for the firm. Just as predecessor Benson companies had financed innovation in transport—by ship, canal, and railway—so the late nineteenth-century firm financed innovation in electrical power and machinery. The success of such pioneering projects depended upon timing and the state of the capital market. It also, as Ranald Michie has pointed out, depended upon the effects of government legislation at both the national and local level. 'Playing second fiddle in the orchestra of progress is not a very glorious proceeding; and it is well to understand that the reasons we did not play first fiddle or lead the whole orchestra are to be sought among the Blue Books and Acts of Parliament and not in the supposed degeneracy of our engineers and capitalists.' Nowhere was this more applicable than in the development of electrical enterprises.

When Sir Coutts Lindsay had opened the Grosvenor Gallery in 1878 he had been able to display his 'modern' pictures clearly by installing a modern system of lighting. London at that time was mainly lit by oil lamps, gas, and candles. In place of the usual smoky gaslights, Coutts had substituted electric light provided by his own small generating plant in Bond Street. Out of this revolutionary development sprang the first systematic attempt to light London by electricity. Coutts next formed a limited liability company under his own name and in May 1885 the first installation ran and supplied light from his 'Grosvenor' central generating station. In less than two years the supply cables stretched throughout Central London.

In 1887 Robin was consulted by Coutts about forming a new and larger company to appoint Sebastian Ziani de Ferranti, a young electrical engineer who would earn the title of the 'Edison of England', to build a huge power-station at Deptford. The London Electric Supply Corporation Ltd. was backed by a capital of £535,000 privately subscribed by twenty-eight shareholders, of which Coutts held a majority with Robin as one of the minority shareholders. The aim was to supply all London's light and power from one huge station at Deptford. Robin later recalled that 'Extravagant estimates were formed of the profits that lay before the company, and to many of the shareholders it seemed that an El Dorado had opened at their feet.'

Their illusions proved short-lived. When Ferranti's cable design was opposed by the Board of Trade, he had one of his assistants hold a chisel which was then driven through the live mains. Only the survival of the assistant convinced the Board of Trade to allow the new design! The death knell sounded when the Board refused to confirm the company's monopoly in London and encouraged competition from twelve conventional, smaller power-stations with lower operating costs whose districts overlapped. Although the London Electric Supply Corporation was on the right track and the scheme was 'a work of genius, the first embodiment of the modern system of electricity supply using large generating stations in favourable sites and high-voltage transmission to consuming areas' it was none the less a commercial fiasco. By 1895 its capital was reduced by one-third, dividends were non-existent, the quoted value of the shares was dwindling to nothing, and ruin loomed large.[64]

Only the appearance of a 'white knight' in the form of Coutts's brother Robert, Lord Wantage saved the company from liquidation. Evey's Uncle Bob was a distinguished public figure. Destined for the East India Company, he had taken instead a commission in the Scots Guards. Field Marshal Lord Wolseley said of him that 'men felt that they could not go wrong if they followed his lead' and he returned from the Crimea a national hero, being one of the first to win the Victoria Cross and having it conferred upon him for two separate acts of valour at Alma and at Inkerman. Yet his interests were by no means confined to soldiering. When urged to give up some of his public business he would answer with words dear to many a Victorian heart, 'but I must do something to justify my existence'.[65]

After Robert's marriage to Harriet Loyd, the only surviving child of Lord Overstone, the wealthy banker, the role of fairy godparents to the extended family circle was one which the childless Wantages assumed with relish—be it financially enabling the Albert Greys to accept the Governor-Generalship in Canada or supporting a wayward nephew. So when Coutts's London Electric Supply Corporation foundered, Robert Wantage, who was not an original shareholder, none the less stepped into the breach with the necessary capital. When yet more capital was demanded he increased his holding until he had practically the controlling interest in the ordinary share capital of £550,000. As the company lurched on through the 1890s he provided a further £170,795 by way of loans, refusing Robin's advice that the burden should be borne by all shareholders equally. 'I thought, as a director, I had some responsibility for driving the coach into the ditch, and I was not going to ask anybody else's help to pull it out again.' Eventually he took command of the company and appointed a receiver, not to wind up the firm as advised, but to pull it round.

This he did after three years, thereby saving the London Electric Corporation from the fate of many promising pioneering undertakings that cannot afford to hold on until their ideas bear fruit. By this time, 1904, Robin had become a director and, along with Howard Gilliat, he worked hard to forge a link between the firm and the railways. 'I have just got through my London Electric meeting this afternoon, an easy task enough for there was no heckling—only one question,' he told Evey. 'But we have lots to think about as directors of the company, namely how to find from £100,000 to £750,000 for the development of the business.' The funds must have been found for, although it only paid its first dividend in 1905, eighteen years after formation, London Electric went on to pioneer the supply of electric power to the London, Brighton and South Coast Railway for running trains.[66]

A part of Robin Benson positively enjoyed the challenge. He might blame British industry, as he publicly did in a Merchants Trust speech in 1907, for 'maintaining antiquated conditions or proscribing new ones in the imaginary interest of the community, whereby producers, capitalists and labour together, got an inadequate return for their risk and less than in other countries'; he might find it far safer and more remunerative to send capital abroad, borne out by the average return over eighteen years on home investments of 3.15 per cent compared with 5.34 per cent on American rails; but he did not hang back when faced with an opportunity to become involved in financing technological innovation, despite his personal knowledge of the considerable risk of loss. He even became a director of another London electric company, the St James & Pall Mall, and then turned his attention to American public utility companies, becoming a director of Western Union Telegraph Company and a director and chairman of the Anglo-American Telegraph Co. Ltd.[67]

At the height of the excitement generated by the London Electric's Deptford scheme, Robin had become involved in another effort to finance innovation when in 1899 Constantine was asked by George Westinghouse jnr. to join him in setting up a British operation. Robin had come in with his own funds along with a good deal of Merchants Trust money, partly from a belief in the project and partly to support his younger brother, who had returned to London in 1889. Constantine continued to oversee American business along with his resident partner, Ker Dunlop, travelling over to St Paul and Chicago several times a year.

George Westinghouse jnr. was one of the many excellent contacts he had introduced to Bensons. The Wall Street commentator, Barron, described Westinghouse, known as the inventor of the airbrake, as 'one of the two great figures of the early days of the American electrical industry'. By 1892 Westinghouse Electric and Manufacturing Co. employed 9,000 men and was capitalized at over £4m. As orders from Britain and her Empire increased substantially in the 1890s, it made sense to open an English subsidiary to manufacture the required electrical plant rather than incur the cost of shipping it from Pittsburg.[68]

The British project could almost have been tailor-made for Constantine as a vehicle for his expertise in finance, land development, and railways; even his early days with the furnaces of Barrow could be brought into play. Despite the considerable support of the American parent company, the project remained an extremely ambitious one, conceived on a much larger scale than, say, the Deptford electrical scheme.

Constantine's first act as chairman was to form a company, the British Westinghouse Electric and Manufacturing Co., with an initial capital of £1.5m., a substantial sum in those days that was raised through a successful flotation managed by Bensons in 1899. He procured a site for the proposed works at Trafford Park, Manchester, where work started in 1899 to complete the first industrial estate in Britain—an enormous factory complex that included a works railway line. The company also undertook to house its workforce; and Constantine's involvement displayed a concern for the welfare of the men and their families, and an understanding of the relation between living and working conditions and productivity, which harked back to his Quaker forebears and to Richard Reynolds at Coalbrookdale. Trafford Park Dwellings Co. Ltd. acquired 120 acres of land upon which to build 3,000 new houses, models of nineteenth-century luxury with electric light, heat, and water. As an enlightened employer, Constantine believed that his workforce should have first-hand knowledge of the by-products of their factory, while the company would attract quality people in the process.

Such benevolence was expensive. The capital of the company had to be increased to £1.75m. in order to complete the factory complex within six months. Although at the first proper AGM, held in November 1899, results showed orders worth £829,000 had been received, a net profit of £10,777 made, and a dividend of 6 per cent paid, 'various delays had occurred in the completion of the works at Manchester'.[69]

This was only one of many delays Constantine had to face as his schemes foundered on the rock of Parliamentary obfuscation. His long-term plan for a complete electric tramway system to replace the horse-drawn ones south of the Thames, for instance, was stymied by Parliamentary delay in changing the powers of operation of British Westinghouse.

As orders more than doubled, opportunities for expansion increased and the company made a net profit of £49,533 in 1900 but the cost of completing the ambitious works became harder to sustain and the strain upon Constantine greater. He was forced to seek a further injection of capital to resolve one of the greatest technical problems: how economically to turn fuel into power and recapture and utilize the gases lost or wasted from the blast furnaces. This was but one of the many technical problems added to the long list of matters over which he had overall responsibility. He came to feel helpless on the face of a mountain of work which he struggled to ascend but upon which he thought himself unable to establish even a toehold.

'We are all so anxious about Con who has a regular nervous breakdown,' Evey Benson reported to her mother on 13 June 1900. Robin had noticed a growing tendency to indecision and feeble-mindedness, unusual in his brother. 'The first signs of this were just two months ago', he told Evey on 1 July, 'when he began to worry about the Westinghouse Co.' Two days later when Robin gave him an engineering journal which contained an account of the acclaimed Westinghouse Exhibit at the Agricultural Hall Exhibition, poor Constantine 'trembled at the sight of it and did not dare to read it'.

Three weeks of 'pampering' with his wife, brother, and a nurse at South Street and Dorchester House brought little improvement. After treatment at Mr Metcalfe's hydropathic establishment near Oxford, the diagnosis was not one to reassure his family: it described Constantine at 48 as 'a man without hope, confidence or enterprise, who has felt for years his own inadequacy *vis-à-vis* the situation he was in and is now worn out by it and his vitality is greatly reduced'. His family found it difficult to relate this to the athletic, highly active Constantine they knew, a man who had made a fortune in America and was game for most things. Yet Metcalfe insisted this shrivelled, mostly silent figure they now beheld would not be strong again for at least a year. 'This is no sudden breakdown', he stated, but the slow grinding of the machinery of the brain to a halt.[70]

It transpired that, along with the Westinghouse worries, Constantine had been greatly exercised by the financial difficulties of his first cousin, Cecil Benson. As the man who had brought Cecil over to the Close Colony and subsequently taken him on as a junior partner in the Iowa Land Co., Constantine wrongly believed himself responsible for Cecil's near bankruptcy and blamed himself for it. In fact Cecil's parlous position owed nothing to American business matters and a great deal to Tattersalls. To spare Constantine further worry, and in his role as head of the Benson family, Robin in 1897 agreed to help shoulder the education of Cecil's sons, Hugh and Ralph. He was already educating another cousin, Eric Benson (the son of Sir Frank Benson, the Shakespearean actor/

producer whom he also continually bailed out). The understanding was that Cecil would reform himself for, as Robin explained, 'what troubles me most is, not the losses over Tattersalls, but that you and Connie have lived so long beyond your income.'

Robin and Constantine were especially troubled by their cousin's situation. The Cecil affair had raised the spectre of their father's bankruptcy. The lesson that Robin and Constantine had learnt early was, in Robin's own words, that 'To live within his income is part of the first duty of man. The other course makes him an adventurer, costs him all self-respect and leads to dishonour.' Although the brothers appeared to have overcome the unhappy experience of their youth, Cecil's predicament so distressed Constantine that he never recovered his peace of mind.[71]

He had to resign as Chairman of British Westinghouse, announced at the AGM on 25 November 1901, although George Westinghouse insisted he retain a seat on the board. Contrary to his own belief, Constantine was thought to have achieved a great deal at British Westinghouse. The delays over the completion of Trafford Park had been overcome and production was on course. The financial plans had also been realized. 'A very busy day', scrawled Robin on 7 March 1902, 'allotting all the afternoon applications for the 4% debenture stock of the Westinghouse Company. It has been a very successful piece of finance and Westinghouse has telegraphed his congratulations to me and Henderson [of the stockbrokers Greenwood & Co.]. And everybody is pleased.'

Although in 1903 Constantine was able to take a more active interest, that summer, while visiting the Westinghouses in Pittsburg, he again broke down. Mary Cropper noted in her journal that he 'got a little excitable today, just enough to make Em feel thankful he is under care, but nothing alarming—it would have been nothing to notice in a sane man', but Con had already slipped into a Stygian state of semi-madness. Some advance had been made since his mother's day in the treatment of mental illness. There was no need to buy a separate house this time: a nursing home at Sibford Ferris near the hydropathy would provide good care. There he died in December 1905 from general paralysis of the insane and epileptic seizure.

Thus he did not live to see his project, British Westinghouse, succumb to government interference, and be all but wrecked by the American crisis of 1907 that brought down American Westinghouse, whose gross sales had nearly doubled from £3m. to £5.7m. The concern was basically solvent and doing a profitable business, so the company discharged the receivers at year-end. According to a fellow industrialist, George Westinghouse 'lived and slept with the airbrake but when it came to other things he could not give them his attention in detail'.

The British company had clearly received even less attention in detail and only survived by raising a mortgage on Trafford Park through Bensons. After years of what the *Financial News* called 'exceedingly disappointing results', British Westinghouse would manage to claw its way into profitability and, in 1919, Bensons would act in its takeover by Metropolitan Vickers (Metrovik), which would become one of the two principal root companies of Associated Electrical Industries (AEI). The tragedy of British Westinghouse was that there was nothing wrong with the concept itself and the entrepreneurial innovation was to be lauded. It was, once again, the dead hand of unimaginative Parliamentary regulation that stymied the British company. Smarting from his 1907 loss of £20,000 [£1m.], Robin blamed John Bull and fiscal policy for the failure of such manufacturing concerns in Britain. In his annual Merchants Trust speech in 1907, reprinted as *The Knell of Laissez Faire*, he stated that 'It is also indubitable that we are behind America and Germany in the application of electrical power to suburban railways and to manufacturing generally.' One reason was the Government's attitude to these industries, another was its taxation policies whereby 'profits for many years have been so slim' that reserves could not be accumulated to scrap antiquated plant for replacement by up-to-date machinery. For him the history of British Westinghouse perfectly illustrated how difficult it was to make money under British conditions and to obtain a fair return on cost.[72]

The lack of investor confidence in 'home industrials' was manifest in the 'drain of capital' which, in the panic reaction to the Liberal Government's welfare and taxation policies, became an 'expulsion of capital'. The new Chancellor of the Exchequer, David Lloyd George, increased the flow after his People's Budget of 1909 introduced a supertax designed to fall upon the wealthy. The City rose up in horror to protest, Lord Revelstoke of Barings declaring in the House of Lords that 'The legitimate flow of capital abroad had become an exodus.'

As chairman of Merchants Trust, Robin was only too aware of the depreciation of domestic securities. In 1907 the Trust had, out of total funds of £2,240,890, only some £364,000 invested in domestic securities, since 'all our experience is in favour of sending capital abroad', he reiterated, and 'it is a very serious thing for our legislators to consider and it is one which cannot be shelved and left to work itself out on laissez faire principles.' For he knew that it was a quid pro quo: that he, like other nimble-footed investors could take advantage of gold in Transvaal or rubber in Malaya, but any windfall was largely bought at the expense of domestic portfolios.[73]

Fortunately, losses made on financing innovative industries were more than offset by the 'windfall profits' gained in the imperial investment booms of the

1890s and early 1900s. Empires were fashionable everywhere, 'the grand excitement of the day, bringing into every household almost every week, intoxicating tales of triumph and heroic disaster'. The last great field for imperial expansion was Africa where Britain was the chief, if mightily opposed, imperial Power and, as we have already seen, the Benson involvement in imperial expansion focused upon Southern Africa and came through family connections. Once again Robin acted as a catalyst for harnessing passive investment by providing the inspiration for a group of patrician families who needed a wholly trustworthy adviser, one who was moreover clever, and part of their inner circle.[74]

In his early career Robin had relied upon his own family connections in railways and in America as a source for business opportunities. After his marriage, he relied more upon the extended Lindsay family and their innumerable connections such as the Loyd banking family. The way in which the Benson–Holford–Lindsay–Loyd–Grey–Grenfell circle of family and connections relied upon each other for financial advice and business was far from unusual in Victorian and Edwardian England. Long acquaintanceship and trust were the most important criteria for investment on the part of the larger investor. Ranald Michie has found that the influence of relations or 'the web of kinship' was paramount in the nature and direction of investment. Thus an entrepreneur planning a new venture looked first to contacts of blood and marriage (as being the most trustworthy) when arranging the finance. For the Bensons this 'web of kinship' had merely replaced the Quaker kinship of their forefathers.

The same pattern emerges in their social life and choice of marriage partners, where they looked to their extended family circle to supply both. At the time of Robin's engagement, Mrs Holford had been congratulated upon gaining a son; she might equally have been congratulated upon gaining another family financial adviser and banker, since Robin was but the newest City recruit into the Lindsay clan. Evey's grandmother, Anne Lindsay, was herself at the heart of a web of banking kinship as the daughter of Sir Coutts Trotter, a banker and partner in Coutts & Co.; her cousin, Alexander Trotter, joined the broking firm of James Capel; one of her sisters married Gibbs Antrobus, whose brother Sir Edmund Antrobus was a partner in Coutts & Co. Nor were the Lindsays of Balcarres strangers to the wider world of commerce. Anne's father-in-law the Hon. Robert Lindsay had, as a younger son, left Balcarres for India, where he had made his fortune with the East India Company. On his return home he had bought the family home from his elder brother the 6th Earl of Crawford and Balcarres, who had married the heiress of Haigh Hall where he lived, believing himself too poor to support both establishments. The discovery of rich seams of coal on the Haigh estate had enriched him overnight and laid the foundations for the renowned Lindsay collections of pictures, stamps, and books. Thus finance, trade, and industry underpinned the wealth of this illustrious family.

Rather than actively seeking new investment opportunities as he had to do in his early days in the City, such opportunities now came to Robin through the web of kinship. A not inconsiderable part of the funds placed at his disposal for investment purposes and in his investment trusts were provided by family; the Benson interest in Southern Africa is one example of this type of investment opportunity where, besides railways, Robin had substantial holdings in companies such as Rand Mines and he also financed such mining developments as Mersina (Transvaal) Ltd., Matabele Gold Reefs, West Nicholson Gold Mining, and United Excelsior Mines. Most of these were made on the advice of Albert Grey or his son-in-law Arthur Grenfell, a fellow director of the Charter Trust & Agency, who both passed on information in confidence to close relations such as Robin, George Holford, and Lord Wantage. 'You ought to keep your Nicholsons and to buy some Globe and Phoenix [Rhodesian gold mining companies],' Albert urged Lord Wantage. 'Lawley writes me from Bulawayo to say the further they go with the Globe and Phoenix the richer they find her and in some parts she is fabulously rich. Lawley thinks the shares ought to go to £20, but please don't quote him. They now stand about £4.'

Albert, in turn, relied upon the advice of Robin, who acted as his personal (merchant) banker when he was Administrator of Rhodesia and, to a lesser extent, when he was Governor-General of Canada, owing to Arthur Grenfell's large Canadian interests and frequent visits to the Dominion. Robin's cautious approach is evident from his correspondence with Albert and George Holford, for whom he continued to manage investments, dispensing sound advice based upon careful appraisements, and taking time to consider an opportunity from every angle. He thus acted as a rein on Albert rushing headlong into new schemes.

Robin's dissatisfaction with Charter Trust & Agency affairs was removed by the reconstitution of the company into an investment trust in 1907. By this time, the British South African Co. had cancelled their contract with the new Charter Trust, to Robin's relief. 'I never cease to be thankful that you are out of the Chartered Co.,' he told Albert:

> We are being pressed by some large shareholders to change the name; they arge [*sic*] that but for the name our shares wd be at par—which is probably true. But I don't want to be the first to publicly cut loose—as if we were not stayers & they were a sinking ship. We are going on allright & you must have been pleased to see the declaration of an interim divd. at 5% rate free of tax . . . Our capital (£750,000) is now almost free from the risk of Rhodesia.[75]

The web of kinship also enabled Bensons, which was never in a position to take the lead in an issue for a foreign government, to participate in the underwriting system widely adopted after the Barings crisis, one which spread the risk among a larger number of banks, trusts, and brokers. In one issue for an American cotton company Barings and Kidder Peabody were the joint lead managers but the underwriting was parcelled out among thirty-eight banks, trusts, and brokers. The two participating British trusts were Robert Fleming & Co. and Merchants Trust. This is just one example of the way in which Merchants' funds gave Robin the leverage to participate in the system.

Robin's circle also encompassed the literary, the academic, the political and the artistic. Increasingly, he devoted more time to the manifold interests derived from these sources in place of those directly concerned with the expansion of Bensons. He corresponded at length with Edwin Cannan, an early and celebrated Professor of Economics at the London School of Economics, on the merits of various gold and currency theories. The sustained controversy in the mid-1890s over bimetallism occupied him for a number of years. He sat on the committee of the Gold Standard Defence Association and wrote copiously against bimetallism to persuade others, especially his old friend Arthur Balfour, who was officially First Lord of the Treasury and unofficially his uncle Lord Salisbury's deputy prime minister.

In 1896 a storm of silver sentiment blew through America. Robin wrote to Albert of 'a stampede for free silver' with the prospect of 'the people being led by the politicians for the third time to the brink of the precipice'. When Mr Wolcott, senator for Colorado, arrived in London with a United States government mission to seek British support for adopting silver, Sir Michael Hicks Beach sent him to the Bank of England where he was naturally welcomed by three bimetallist past governors, Lord Aldenham, Riversdale Grenfell, and William Lidderdale. They agreed to propose that the Bank of England could put into force an old Act to keep 25 per cent of the Bank's reserves in silver. John Gilliat, another ex-governor, became nervous and confided in Robin, who immediately asked George Peel, the secretary of the Gold Standard Defence Association, to blow the whistle in *The Times*.

'Like most other people I was incredulous when I heard of the Bank's pledge,' Robin told a colleague, 'and I came to the Court today [16 September 1897, for a semi-annual meeting of stockholders] expecting a complete and reassuring answer,' that proved unforthcoming. He believed that the Bank had no business making 'concessions to . . . the "selfish and particular interest of silver mining communities" led by the Senator from Colorado'. He felt so strongly about the Bank's willingness to tamper with its reserves that he and Lord Morley sold their Bank stock forthwith.[76]

Whereas Robin might have parted easily with his Bank stock, it would take much more than a metal controversy to part him from his fine collection of paintings, undoubtedly the overriding interest of his life. He loved fine pictures but weeded out and traded them as an analyst or portfolio manager appraises investments. Although he would doubtless have found the Kleinwort strategy of committing almost all their capital to building up Kleinwort Sons & Co. sound, his own approach was to spread his capital outside Robert Benson & Co. and, only if necessary, unlock reserves for business purposes through the sale of his pictures or porcelain.

He had started to collect pictures in the 1870s at the tail end of a period when the finest works were generally bought cheaply by either wise directors of the National Gallery, in the persons of Sir Charles Eastlake and Frederick Burton, or a few discriminating collectors. After William Graham's death his executors sent 486 pictures (320 Italian) for sale at Christies in April 1886. Yet, apart from a few expensive pictures, the sale fetched only £23,409, about £70 a picture. Robin bought twelve Italian pictures at the sale, including Piero di Cosimo's *Triumph of Chastity*, which laid the foundation for the future Benson collection, one that Lord Crawford, himself a discerning collector, called 'the finest personal collection—the finest specialised collection he had come across'.[77]

His wife's role in its creation was substantial. She had a trained eye and decisive views. 'To know what you like instead of saying Amen to what the world says you ought to like, is to have kept your soul alive.' Evey stood beside him as an equal in all matters artistic and together they built the collection. In many ways their partnership as collectors was illustrative of their partnership in marriage. Robin, swift as Perseus in his youth, had become less hasty with age and took an inordinate amount of time over everything, making sure of his opinions. 'Rob has gone to the Capitol for a first view of it,' Evey wrote from Rome to her mother in February 1893. 'It is quite hopeless my going to everything with him for he is so terribly in earnest that hours are nothing to him.'

Evey, on the contrary, flew through galleries and museums, deciding in a twinkling whether a work was worth a second microscopic appraisal by Robin. His description of her was typical: she had surpassed herself with 'two hours in the Accademia delle belle Arte in the morning and one hour in the afternoon in the Palazzo Publico—both devoted to the Siennese School alone. She is a marvel at sifting quickly the good from the bad.' Their tastes coincided, however, and though they adopted a different approach to the art of viewing, their conclusions rarely differed. While Evey travelled abroad in search of the Chinese porcelain, Persian rugs, and the smaller works of art with which they adorned their houses, Robin visited Agnew's and Spier's, devoted long hours to provenance and monographs, and catalogued the Holford and Wantage collections as well as his own. In addition, he and Evey acted as consultants to George Holford, suggested additions and purchased pictures for him. When approached to sell a Rembrandt, Robin advised George, 'Never sell anything that is first rate: but anything that is second rate let go when a fair bid comes, or clear it off at Christies. You will always be able to do better.'

Robin did not, however, follow his own sound advice when it came to other specialist areas. Approached by Rosenbach, a famous American dealer in rare books, to sell part of the Holford Library that had lain undisturbed at Dorchester House since his father's death, George asked, 'Do I need any money?' 'Well, you never look at them much', answered Robin, 'so you could realise a few if the price is really good.' Robin proceeded to tell Rosenbach he could choose any ten books for X amount of money. Apparently Rosenbach accepted with alacrity, but chose only one: a first folio of Shakespeare![78]

Such misjudgements never harmed the Benson picture collection. Distinguished for its four panels depicting scenes from the life of Christ painted for Siena Cathedral by Duccio *c.*1310, it also contained works by the great masters of three centuries with a smaller collection of fifteenth- and sixteenth-century portraits. Some idea of the quality and range can be gauged by the fact that all the masters featured in this collection, from Bellini, Giorgione, Botticelli, to Correggio, Titian, and Veronese, are also to be found in the Metropolitan Museum in New York, the Frick Collection, the Thyssen Collection in Madrid, the National Gallery of Art in Washington, and the National Gallery in London.

The Bensons enlarged their collection in a period when prices had started to rise. Many a time Robin had to redirect wonderful works of art, which were too expensive for him, to the Wantages. 'Tell George [Holford],' Robin told Albert Grey in August 1896, 'that the Wantages not content with buying 4 Corots and an Alma-Tadema have bought the 2 celebrated Pesellinos from the Torregiani Palace—the parents of all the finest cassoni of the XVth Century—very large & containing the whole story of David—things I have longed for for 20 years—but quite beyond us.' (In 1974 the Pesellinos were lent by the Loyd Trustees to the National Gallery, London.)

Things were not, however, entirely one way. The Bensons had sold their copy of Burne-Jones's *Love among the Ruins* in order to finance the purchase of an Andrea del Sarto picture. 'It is an age of Miracles!' Robin exulted to his eldest son. As he and Evey sat at South Street after tea, 'a letter was brought to me, and Liddiard [the butler] said there were two men downstairs with a big picture. Up it came and lo! It was *Love among the Ruins*—not the one we sold but the far finer original. Some good fairy bought it and has made a present of it to us. Who do you think it can be?' The good fairy was none other than Harriet Wantage.[79]

The bulk of the Benson collection had been acquired before 1900. Thereafter Robin's energies were chiefly directed towards saving works of art for the nation. The Edwardian period witnessed a steady stream of important works disappear across the Atlantic into the mansions of Frick, Isabella Stewart Gardner, Widener, J. P. Morgan, and Johnson, who were all preoccupied with assembling notable collections. The pressure from competing foreign millionaires attracted works off the walls of British country houses and into the dealers' galleries like iron to a magnet. According to Sir Charles Holmes, the Director of the National Gallery, 'Those who had anything saleable rushed to take advantage of the golden harvest' while English fortunes weighed down by social and territorial obligations had little to spare for patronage at a time when Sir Robert Witt declared 'the rich were so poor that they could not live because of the income tax [at 1*s*. 8*d*.] and dared not die for fear of the death duties'. Furthermore, any cautious connoisseurs had bolted out of the field, frightened off by the outrageous prices.

A groundswell of complaint propelled D. S. MacColl and Claude Phillips to float the idea of a Friends organization for the National Gallery, which became the National Art Collections Fund in 1903. Robin along with Roger Fry, Herbert Cook, Charles Read, Robert Witt, Sir Isidore Spielmann, and Sidney Colvin were elected onto an executive committee of eighteen under the chairmanship of Evey's cousin 'Bal', Lord Balcarres, for whom Robin had a great admiration.

With £200 in its pocket to fight off the transatlantic predators and foreign museums, the NACF set to work to muster its forces. Most of the early battles were fought to save old masters from export. In 1905 Agnews, who were sympathetic to the NACF, offered the Fund first refusal of Velasquez's *Rokeby Venus* at the then staggering price of £45,000. Robin enlisted the support of Arthur Balfour, the Prime Minister, who wanted 'big & important things secured for the nation instead of a multitude of small things & this one he regards as one of the biggest & most important chances'.

Despite such backing, the Treasury obdurately refused to help and only the intervention of the King saved the masterpiece; his delicately dropped words of regret precipitated a deluge of money with which to buy the picture for the National Gallery. 'You know what a near thing it was,' Robin exulted to Lord Balcarres in January 1906. 'We may as well trim our sails to the favouring gale, treble our subscribers & be a greater power henceforward.' In the same year Robin replaced Lord Grimthorpe as treasurer and watched over the NACF's finances 'with an experienced and zealous eye'.[80]

He brought the same enthusiastic indefatigability to his position on the

Council of the Victoria and Albert Museum (formerly the South Kensington Museum) which entailed an immense amount of detailed work. He hoped that his V. & A. colleagues would prove easier to work with than Lord Curzon whom he found impossible. In 1912 Robin was invited to become a trustee of the National Gallery, a sign of his position as an *éminence grise* in the art world. Curzon, head of the Board of Trustees, was unhelpful when Robin attempted to clarify matters of division on the Board. Across one of Robin's letters, Curzon rudely scrawled 'Read this incredible letter. The man does not even know what a "covering letter" is. Oh my God.' It seems that Robin's introduction to the National Gallery was not original in its discomfort. The Director learned from 'a most distinguished Trustee, a veteran maître d'armes of debate, a leader in every grave political contest for twenty years or more' that 'Not one of his major activities took so much out of him as a Board meeting at Trafalgar Square.'[81]

In order to contend with such stimulating activities, Robin had long had to rely upon the help of a junior partner to manage the daily business of Robert Benson & Co. This was quite a normal arrangement in private banking firms. Senior partners were usually involved in matters of policy and supervision, in maintaining a presence in the City to promote the interests of the firm which allowed for ample opportunity to pursue outside interests. In general, senior partners of firms such as Bensons were 'gentlemen capitalists' who devoted no more time to work than a landowner to the management of his estate. It was therefore more often than not junior partners and managers who ran the business.[82]

Being on the issuing side of the merchant banking wall, Bensons' business was sporadic, demanding great efforts for a short time, unlike Kleinworts' on the accepting side, which was regular, demanding sustained routine attention. The styles and characters of the partners almost reflected their respective businesses. Herman and Alexander were required to attend No. 20 with regularity whereas Robin could be absent while devoting himself to an outside interest but then return to create some new piece of business for his firm. The official office hours at Bensons were from 10 to 6, but as Frank Woolridge would explain, 'There was no such thing as office hours. If there was something on, we'd stay till midnight.'[83]

The office he entered as a junior in 1911 was at Gresham House in Old Broad Street, which had housed the first Robert Benson & Co. office in London in 1856 and to which Bensons had returned in 1888. The staff in 1911 consisted of: four clerks, C. C. Hellings, W. T. Bannister, R. C. Noakes, R. H. Graveley; Carter, who did the cables into code; an office boy and two typists, whose wages totalled £181 4*s*. 10*d*.; and Mr and Mrs Tyrell, who did the portering and housekeeping at £104 15*s*. p.a.; all of whom operated under the office manager, Thomas Rowe, who, whatever his managerial skills, undoubtedly equalled them with his financial ones. While at Bensons, he built up a fortune sufficient to allow him to retire in the 1920s to Australia, retaining investments in Bensons' Australasian funds and commercial property as a tie with the old firm. Before retirement, however, he ran Bensons in conjunction with the junior partner, H. A. Vernet.

Henry Vernet had become a partner in 1891; it is believed he worked his way up from the position of managing clerk, which he had assumed in the 1880s. In the absence of surviving personnel records this cannot be verified; and it would have been rather unusual for a man of Vernet's background to have worked for so long as a clerk in a firm in which neither he nor his family had an interest. Vernet came from an old Swiss Huguenot family, one which had long been bankers in Geneva and at one time employed Necker, the French Finance Minister, in their bank. Vernet's father, a former Swiss consul in London, had been a partner in Morris Prevost & Co.

Little is known of Henry's career until he became a junior partner in Bensons. This may have been the result of large losses that, his family has been told, he sustained in the Barings crash. He 'lost £60,000 and was virtually wiped out'. If he was only a clerk, even a managing one, this was an enormous sum to lose. Alternatively, it may be that he only came to Bensons after the 1890 crash, that Robin Benson knew his father and was prepared to help out a young, able chap who needed to make his own way in the world in much the same way as he himself had been helped by Johnny Cross and the Croppers in 1875. Such a supposition can be bolstered by one link with Barings, namely that from the very first Henry Vernet busied himself with South American affairs in general and those of the Argentine in particular.[84]

The close working relationship between Bensons and Greenwoods had led to an increase in Argentinian business, as Alexander Henderson's brother Baillie Henderson was a contracting engineer out there. At the Benson end it was dealt with by Vernet. Robin thought highly of him and, not wishing to sit on yet more City boards, he suggested Vernet in his place. In this way Vernet came to be a director of two of Robert Fleming's trusts, one of Sir Alexander Henderson's, and several South American railway companies. All of this supplemented his income since, in those days, partners in City firms were allowed to retain outside directorship fees.

Such activity certainly lent further weight to the City reputation of Bensons and attracted new business opportunities in South America and Mexico. This, combined with a boom in 1911 after the accession of George V, led to an increase in capitalization for Bensons. The original capital was £50,000, a modest figure compared to the Kleinwort fortune; but it must be remembered that, in contrast, the Benson fortune was positioned outside the business. Bensons' capital was now increased to £170,000 [£8.7m.], with Robin providing £150,000 to Henry Vernet's £20,000. The firm's balance-sheet totals had risen from £502,837 in 1910 to £588,87 by the following year. Although Robin may have hoped that the results of 1911 inaugurated a return to the profitable years of the late 1880s, he was to be disappointed. Profits, which were divided between the two partners on either a 4 : 1 or 3 : 1 ratio depending upon the source of profits, fluctuated widely between a high of £27,272 in 1911 to a loss of £3,599 in 1913, due largely to the uncertainty of world affairs.

As Robin warned in his Merchants Trust speech on 28 February 1913: 'The chief danger to credit, I venture to think, lies in politics. They are in a state of confusion on both sides of the Atlantic.' A Balkan war, a United States presidential election, which replaced years of Republican rule with a Democrat (Woodrow Wilson), and high British interest rates had combined to produce a fall in share values which wiped some £14,578 off Bensons' portfolios. David Bevan, of the stockbroking firm David A. Bevan & Co., came in with a capital injection of £40,000. Bensons survived 1913 only to find that it had been but a dry run for 1914 when 'the shadow of war crept into every heart'.[85]

With an immediate exodus of staff to join the services on the outbreak of war in August, Robin as 'an old crock' of 64 was left to run Bensons in their new offices at Old Broad Street. Henry Vernet went off to run the Paper Commission with Sir Max Aitken, leaving Robin in sole charge for the first time for years. It was the same all over the City. At Barings they were reduced to 'a very elderly party', as Gaspard Farrer noted, 'old crocks who ought by this time to have been on the shelf'. Robin could perhaps consider himself to have been put on the shelf for the amount of actual business he had to oversee was minimal.[86]

Normal share dealing was virtually suspended (the Stock Exchange itself was shut until January 1915) and the firm's large American business fell away to a trickle. In exchange for war bonds, the British Government had commandeered American securities held by the British to help finance the war, whilst the issuing business was particularly dormant. Thus, the purchase and sales of stock almost ceased and Bensons' bread-and-butter business nearly dried up. Other City firms experienced similar difficulties; only the few firms with little exposure to either the Central Powers or America remained relatively buoyant. Morgans were kept busy acting as the British Government's agent for the purchase of war materials and in raising war loans in America, while other issuing houses languished; even accepting houses without any German exposure found business very quiet.

Bensons' losses in the first two years of the war amounted to a staggering £59,485 [£2.6m.], the worst in the history of the firm. Capital fell from £170,000 to £110,000 in 1915 and the firm had to rely upon loans of £60,000 from the Bank of England and £40,000 from Barclays Bank to tide them over. By 1916, however, only £20,000 remained outstanding to the Bank of England and this was repaid at the year-end. Through the good offices of Kidder Peabody, Bensons and indeed Barings unofficially participated in a new issue for the American Telephone & Telegraph Co.; any transaction that drew money from Britain was vetoed by the Treasury so the AT&T issue was officially *verboten*—though Kidders credited its friends as if they had participated. Otherwise Bensons scrabbled for irregular business commissions and share dealings which they would normally have avoided. Nevertheless, the firm turned the corner in 1916 to return to profitability, albeit on a much smaller scale than pre-war.[87]

With his business reduced to a holding operation and his family life disrupted by the war—all three sons and one son-in-law were serving at the Front, as were innumerable relations, friends, and members of his domestic staff—Robin was nevertheless busier than ever. He was able to devote himself to his writings about economic and financial policy and to cataloguing the Holford collection of pictures. He was still regularly consulted about finance by Arthur Balfour, who had become an elder statesman to Asquith's coalition Government and succeeded Churchill as First Lord of the Admiralty in 1915.

Throughout the war, Robin continued to act as an unofficial City adviser, writing for example on 3 December 1915 about the lack of cohesive Government policy to secure subscriptions to the next big war loan. 'The patriotic public longs to lend a hand & would pledge its securities to help to take the next war loan, but is paralysed because there is no free and cheap money market. That is what I am pleading for—cheap money—one of the greatest boons and most powerful of weapons.' Robin felt it was essential to reassure the public and the City that 'we are *not* drifting and that we *have* got a plan of finance to see us through.'[88]

In May 1916 he prepared for Arthur Balfour a 'Resumé of War Finance', widely circulated and well received in the City. He also enlisted Balfour's help in winning round the Treasury to a banking scheme to foster British enterprises and investment in Italy. He also helped to create the British Italian Corporation in 1916, into which he invested some £10,000, and he remained a shareholder when it became the British Italian Banking Corporation in 1923. Sir Rennell Rodd, the British Ambassador in Italy and an old university friend, was in London for its birth and later wrote, 'after much energetic pioneer work, Benson and his friends succeeded in establishing a very strong combination between most of the leading banks of the United Kingdom'.

At this point, however, an insurmountable obstacle was placed in the way of success: some of the directors of some of the banks lost their nerve; it was the middle of a World War and they demanded a guarantee over the first few years. Robin immediately turned to his well-placed friends, Arthur Balfour, H. H. Asquith (still Prime Minister) and Walter Runciman at the Board of Trade. Their warm support induced the Treasury *mirabile dictu* to guarantee a return of 5 per cent on the capital for five years. The Corporation then set up its own fully owned banking arm, the Banca Italo-Britannica, with a head office in Milan and branches throughout Italy. This bank developed into the fourth or fifth largest commercial bank in Italy, while the commercial enterprise side of the Corporation diminished in operation until eventually in peacetime it ceased completely, leaving only the pure banking business.[89]

Robin also gave a great deal of thought during these war years to business conditions after the war. In a booklet published in 1918, he suggested the creation of a central bank which would liquefy Government securities and make them available for reconstruction by allowing their holders to borrow on them; it would 'do for the lock-up capital in Government Securities what the Bank of England does for the Bill Market'.[90]

Such theoretical musing about national policy was superseded in 1918 by the very real problems small City firms such as Bensons faced, as they sought to rekindle their old businesses from the ashes of a pre-war world that had smouldered away. Although fit and healthy, Robin was nearly 70, an age reflected in his office name, 'Old Mr B.', and correspondingly ill-suited to the role much needed at Bensons of dynamic young business-getter. He was happy to allow Henry Vernet, still a junior partner, to resume, indeed expand, his position as partner-in-charge until such times as his three sons had recovered from the war and were ready to assume control of the family business. His decision to allow the partnership at Bensons to drift in this way was one that would create enormous difficulties for his sons and Henry Vernet in the future.

Thus, at the onset of peace, Bensons and Kleinworts found themselves in similar situations. The capital of both banks was vested in men who had been extraordinarily successful in their business careers: Robin, although born into wealth, had started his business career with nothing and amassed a fortune of well over £1m.; Sir Alexander Kleinwort similarly began with inherited wealth, but retained his to increase it substantially. Yet both men were now drifting towards the twilight of their careers and, though each had sons to take up their mantle, they were as yet too inexperienced or too young to do so. The direction of the family banks was therefore vested in men—Henry Vernet at Bensons and Herman Andreae at Kleinworts—who had a lesser equity interest and to a certain extent remained in the eyes of the world the junior partners. Although this would be mitigated at Kleinworts by the fact that Herman Andreae was a member of the family, it would none the less lead to the same difficulties for the young Kleinwort sons as it did for the young Benson sons when they wished to assume control of their respective banks.

7 Reversal and Recovery

PEACE brought perils as grave as any in wartime for such City firms as Kleinwort, Sons & Co. At the end of the war in 1918 their acceptances were down to a mere £5m. from the 1913 high of £14.2m. Due to increased trading in the Americas, however, the partners' capital had grown slightly to £4.6m., which was £263,000 more than in 1913. Lloyd George's triumphant return from the Versailles peace treaty conference fed the optimistic mood of the country, a mood that was nurtured by the 'restocking' trade boom of 1919/20. At Kleinworts profits had remained undistributed throughout the war but in 1919 the partners shared £300,000 [£6.8m.]—after transferring nearly £257,000 to a contingency account to provide for moratorium interest paid to the Bank of England and retaining £29,000 undistributed—and £114,000 [£2.2m.] in 1920. When acceptances leapt to £15.5m. in 1920, and capital rose to over £5.2m. [£101.4m.], it seemed as if they had quickly re-established their pre-war business and their position as the leading accepting house in a country that would continue to dominate the finance of world trade as it had done prior to 1914.

The boom was illusory. Assuming an insatiable demand for their goods, manufacturers increased production only to be faced with a glut throughout the world. Exports became a trickle; government spending was slashed; prices tumbled and unemployment rose causing strikes. In this climate of rising bad debts and lower income Kleinworts' acceptances plunged to £10.5m. and their capital to £2.6m. in 1921, undoubtedly one of the worst years for commerce. Indeed, the whole of the 1920s proved to be volatile trading years; the boom or bust conditions severely tested the managerial skills of Alexander and Herman A. They now had to operate in an environment which bore little resemblance to that pre-war world in which Kleinworts' star had shone so brightly in the financial galaxy.

America had long provided the firm with its chief source of revenue. Before the war, the United States of America had been a debtor nation, borrowing from Britain to build its infrastructure; it had been the single most important area of British overseas investment. The war had reversed this. Britain was now the debtor nation, owing the United States of America £850m. by the end of the war. Furthermore, wartime demand had revitalized American industry, so that American imports of British goods decreased just when Britain needed to increase her exports to repay her debt. This, together with the growth of institutions able to provide ample facilities in America, meant that companies no longer required trade credits from London. Although America remained a source of revenue for Kleinworts, it was no longer their chief source. American acceptances fell away in the face of dollar credits, so that commission earnings plummeted from £78,000 in 1920 to a mere £14,600 in 1928. Kleinworts had to look elsewhere for profits.

At the height of the illusory boom it appeared that domestic business would compensate for the decline in American credits. Earnings in 1922 had soared to £208,000 as their mercantile and manufacturing clients geared up production and capital investment, and required correspondingly larger credits. The majority of these clients were in the cotton trade, an area of specialization that continued to provide Kleinworts with their customer base throughout the world. When the artificial boom quickly evaporated, Kleinworts were left with a level of UK commission revenue which, although double its pre-war level, steadily declined throughout the decade.[1]

Nor could they look to Russia, for it was another area where earnings had declined. During the war Kleinworts had made substantial profits from providing credits to finance the notably unsuccessful Russian war effort. Although Kerensky's provisional government upheld all existing credit agreements in 1917, the Treasury, unlike the Foreign Office, was sceptical of the regime's future and told Barings who, with Kleinworts and Lazards, were the houses most involved in Russian business: 'The more roubles you buy, the more orders will be placed here . . . it is a morass we have no intention of paving.' All too soon Kleinworts incurred large losses when the new Bolshevik government prevented companies from repaying their foreign debts. Thirty years later Kleinworts still had claims of some £75,000 outstanding on Russian firms. In the case of one 1917 debt for £13,591 of acceptances with L'Azoff Don Commercial Bank, the possibility of repayment only came to light inadvertently in 1954 when it emerged that Barings had long held large pre-war Russian bullion deposits in their vaults. There was great excitement in the Banking Hall at No. 20 when the news came through that the L'Azoff Don debt was being repaid with interest, thereby giving Kleinworts a substantial windfall profit.

Repudiated debts did not, however, prevent Kleinworts from doing business with the new Russian regime. They quickly established themselves as leaders in the *del credere* field, whereby they earned substantial commissions from credit insurance. In the early days of the Bolshevik Government, before it had established its credibility, Kleinworts would guarantee Russian bills against insolvency and, for taking the risk, earn a large fee. It was good business because they dealt with clients for whom they had granted reimbursement credits in pre-war days and this partly made up for the losses incurred on pre-1917 debts.[2]

Elsewhere the recovery of pre-war debts was more successful. Herman was more than vindicated for his faith in Germany honouring her debts. The whole of the sums owed by clients in Germany and Austria was repaid—and with interest. This was in large part expedited by the efficient machinery of the British Government Clearing House which had settled most claims by 1921.

The trio's (Kleinworts, Goldman Sachs, and Lehman Brothers) Trefoil syndicate partner, Henri Hoechstaedter, bemoaned the lack of similar progress in France in 1921. The situation with the Trefoil's largest claim, on the Berliner HandelsGesellschaft, was not promising: 'we have not only not obtained any payment on account of it nor can we at all ascertain or state, as little as any other French creditors, at what period or periods we shall receive the payments in reimbursement of our claims'. In these circumstances, and taking into account the changed conditions prevailing in America, the trio decided not to renew the syndicate's fr.3m. interest in Henri Hoechstaedter & Co., which was duly put into liquidation.[3]

The chief way to make money in the 1920s was in foreign exchange and stock arbitrage operations. Kleinworts already had a small foreign exchange (forex) department, which they rapidly expanded during the 1920s, a period in which they established themselves as market leaders. Henri Jacquier, later manager of this department, recalled that Kleinworts 'had in those days a tremendous reputation in the world for Foreign Exchange dealing'. From small beginnings before the war, when the department had largely concentrated upon dealing between London and New York in conjunction with Goldman Sachs, it now expanded to take account of the enormous increase in forex business resulting from the introduction of currencies in the new central European states as well as the traditional dollar and Continental currency business. Although Kleinworts, in common with all merchant banks, had always needed to convert money from one currency into another, most international transactions had been quoted in sterling so that they had never specialized in foreign exchange work as Japhets, S. Montagu & Co., and Seligmans had done. These were the leading houses in the foreign exchange arbitrage business whereby fluctuations in exchange rates were used to buy currency in one market and sell in another.[4]

Despite the introduction of the telephone, long-distance communication between most countries remained by telegraph. This worked well for acceptance transactions and correspondence; it did not for foreign exchange deals. By the time a telegram was received in New York, rates had often changed, turning a profitable transaction into a loss-making one. When Goldman Sachs cabled that they had bought 1m. florins, Kleinworts were dismayed since the Dutch currency was steadily depreciating, but this news had not yet been received in New York. 'You are, of course, quite right that we have a great advantage over you,' Herman A. admitted to Arthur Sachs on 27 October 1920, 'in that we can remain in constant telephonic communication with the principal centres.'[5]

His remedy to speed up transactions and reduce related losses was to install two telegraphists complete with the necessary equipment in the foreign exchange department to keep in constant touch with New York; this also obviated the frustrating wait for a cable opening, which could take hours. For a short while this gave them a march over other houses and did much to establish the firm as one of the leading dealers in the City.

They also expanded into forward dealing, whereby the uncertainty in exchange rate movements was reduced by purchasing currencies in advance in order to supply a client in one, two, or three months' time. Although forward exchange markets had come into existence before the war, they were not widespread; the more conservative institutions disapproved of them as unacceptably speculative. This did not deter Kleinworts, who saw the opportunity for profitable activity and entered the market with gusto. It was yet another area in which their partnership with Goldman Sachs thrived, though they also worked on joint account with a number of firms in Berlin, Amsterdam, Budapest, and Paris.

Herman A., who was now the partner who largely oversaw the Goldman Sachs account, took a particular interest in their foreign exchange business as well as that of Kleinworts in general. He strongly believed in the practice of taking profits and cutting losses, and this became the guiding policy of Kleinworts' foreign exchange department.

There was an uncomfortable moment in late 1920 when it was discovered that a loss of £50,000 for the Trio Account stemmed not from current business but from an undisclosed deal made four months previously. Even worse, the transaction was for 15.1m. marks. Given the German situation, Kleinworts had 'always been pessimistic as regards Marks, and do not hold a single Mark for our own account'. As the forex manager complained to Herman A., 'Obviously, if we wished to speculate in exchange, we should do so for our own account, and it is rather disconcerting to be faced with a notification four months after the business is done that we are committed to an important transaction without our knowledge.'

Herman A. in turn brought the matter up with Arthur Sachs, his corresponding partner in Goldman Sachs, so that the mistake would not be repeated:

> The loss is certainly a nasty one and will take a good deal of making up. Please do not think we are grumbling or criticising you, for, as you know we are good losers, but I think it would be well to bear in mind the lesson which this incident teaches, viz. that it is one of the first principles of arbitrage business *to cut a loss as soon as it arises*. If that principle is not adhered to strictly, one must sooner or later, get landed with a big position.

He and Arthur Sachs also exchanged letters about the dollar/sterling rate and Government restrictions on lending abroad which stemmed from the British authorities' concern with the weakness of sterling. In 1919 Britain had been forced off the gold standard; it was the primary goal of the Bank of England and the Treasury to return to it, and so sterling had been 'pegged'. Herman A. was invited to write a series of articles on foreign exchange and international finance for an influential periodical, *Sperlings Journal*, under the name 'Acceptor'. His first article on the dollar aroused considerable attention in the City, though he did not 'suppose it will move the "powers that be"'. In it he had advocated that the artificial pegging of sterling against the dollar should cease. This would immediately restrict British imports from America, thereby removing any need for the British Government to limit them, a policy that was seen as unfriendly in American government circles. He was surprised but naturally pleased to discover that 'the article had a much greater effect than . . . anticipated and led in fact directly to the removal of the "peg"'. This series of articles undoubtedly enhanced his already formidable reputation in the City and reflected well on Kleinworts' foreign exchange department.[6]

In those days of the early 1920s, the foreign exchange department comprised forty to fifty people. Under Charles Henderson, the manager, there were four English and two Continental dealers in the dealing room supported by about forty staff in an outer office. Every dealer then required about six to eight people behind him to do the routine bookkeeping and correspondence. The bookkeepers, who kept the Conti Nostri, as the bank's own foreign currency accounts were called, were often aspirant dealers waiting for a chance to demonstrate their money-making skills.

Henri Jacquier was one who successfully made the transition from back office to dealing room. He began by helping the Continental dealer M. Villemin when there were two simultaneous calls between London and Paris, proved indispensable, and was appointed the second Continental dealer. At that period most of the activity was in French francs and Dutch florins and there were great profits to be made. In 1925 Kleinworts made £138,000 [£3.8m.] from foreign exchange dealing and at one point in 1927 the bank stood to make a profit of £250,000. The foreign exchange markets were as volatile then as they are now (Kleinworts making a loss of £1,000 in 1926). Dealers correspondingly had to be able to stand by an instant decision and as Eric Pratt, a junior Kleinworts dealer, said: 'It isn't a business for natural worriers, there's an awful lot to worry about without even looking.' Times were certainly worrying in the Kleinworts dealing room in 1927 because, according to Jacquier, 'our propensity was to sell short of French francs and we thought things were worse in France than anywhere else', so that the £250,000 profit haemorrhaged away until 'we finished the year with about £5,000 profits only'. Jacquier nevertheless received his first bonus of £250, an enormous amount in those days and almost equivalent to his annual salary.

Despite the disadvantage posed by slow and, if by telephone, inaudible communications, it was far easier for a bank to take advantage of market conditions in the 1920s than in the present day. There was no compulsion to retain a department solely to provide clients with a fully comprehensive service; nor were staff fired as a consequence: they were merely 'exchanged' or redeployed to another department regardless of their specialization. So when the years of hectic activity in foreign exchange came to an end in the late 1920s, partly due to the stabilization of the French franc, the partners closed this department and opened a new one. This was the Stock Arbitrage department, which bought securities in one part of the world and sold them at a profit in another. André Brack, an expert in stock arbitrage who headed the department, was considered outstanding. A volatile Frenchman, he was phenomenally quick both at making a calculation and at losing his temper. 'One had to make allowances for things being swept onto the floor and huge bursts of temper,' recalled his assistant.[7]

It was not so much a matter of making allowances as of having little choice in the matter. Staff were at the mercy of their superiors. Job satisfaction was not recognized as an issue for management consideration; on the contrary, it was believed that staff were lucky to be given a berth at Kleinworts. If they chose to jump ship they would not be given a reference and would therefore be unlikely to find employment elsewhere. Herman A., for instance, 'never hesitated to refer to labour as a commodity' and, apart from the managers, he would have been hard pressed to put a name to any of his employees. As far as they were concerned he was a remote 'literally feared' being, who ignored them when he walked through the office. There was complete segregation between the partners and the ordinary staff in that the partners dealt with the managers who spoke to the submanagers who spoke to the staff. If a member of staff had to address a manager, he always called him 'Sir', and the manager called him by his surname.[8]

At Kleinworts, the 1920s ushered in the era of The Manager, that all-powerful figure who directed the business of the firm and held the lives of the workforce in thrall. In the nineteenth century the office was tiny and conducive to easy, close relations between the partners and their clerks. Alexander Friedrich had known every clerk in his employ since he had usually engaged them himself and he felt it his duty to exercise a paternalistic influence. From 1920 to 1924, however, the staff had increased from over 100 to nearly 400, and they had not been engaged by the partners but by the managers; more often than not by the staff manager, Mr Harmon. In complete contrast to Bensons but more in keeping with Schröders, the active partners, Alexander and Herman A., did not know their employees because they had no occasion to meet them. They entered the bank by a different door, had rooms off their own corridor at the back of the banking hall, and lived a separate working existence.

Their correspondence was collected and delivered in silence. If they required a letter to be written the internal telephone would buzz on the desk of a manager or, in his absence, a submanager, a light indicating which partner required assistance. On one occasion Ernest Pudney, an office character and practical joker who spoke his mind at a time when ordinary staff were seen and not heard, was passing a desk on which the telephone was buzzing, answered it and was ordered by Alexander to 'Come In'. 'Naturally I obeyed and was not given any opportunity to speak but seeing an unexpected face, he said "Are you a correspondent?" I said yes and he gave me 4 or 5 personal letters to which after a short briefing I was instructed to reply. I did what was necessary, was told to sign them and send them off. I had committed "the unpardonable sin".' Although Alexander was unaware of the *faux pas*, being only concerned that the letters were written, the manager was furious. The natural order of management had been upset; an ordinary member of staff had invaded the sanctity of a partner's room and, even worse, sent off the correspondence without the authorization of a manager. It was the custom for all correspondence written by or on behalf of the partners to be placed in a special folder and circulated for the managers to read. Pudney was reprimanded and told, 'Well, you've got a damn cheek!'

If the staff considered the partners a feudal, benevolent autocracy, they deemed the managers an outright dictatorship. The managers commanded the staff in the name of the partners. Whilst staff were never made redundant and could look upon their jobs as tenure for life in the normal course of events, if they crossed a manager they could be sacked on the spot. Arguing a point was not allowed. Although the forthright Pudney was sacked and reinstated three times, managers rarely resorted to such dramatic tactics; they preferred instead the softer approach of penalizing an employee by refusing to increase his salary. Jacquier, who fell foul of a manager over some South American accounts—'trivial really. I had three differences with him for which he castigated me pretty strongly . . . I should have known . . . that you must never put a big man in the wrong'—had no increase in salary for fourteen years. He believed that this demonstrated how entirely the partners relied upon the managers, since they never questioned why he had had no rise and if this meant his work was substandard why he had never been sacked.

Pudney, too, was left without a rise by another manager, though after seven years he boldly submitted his case directly to one of the partners. The result, which supports Jacquier's thesis, was that Alexander immediately gave him an increase of £24 a year, a rather good rise in those days; he also stipulated that anybody who had a grievance should let him know. The majority of his employees, however, would not have dared to approach him, nor would they have found it easy to do so since all communications had to be channelled through the managers.[9]

The management structure at Kleinworts was relatively simple in the 1920s. The business was divided into three areas: credits, stocks, and consignment or commodities. The senior manager, Mr Watson, was manager of the Consignment Department, which carried on the firm's traditional mercantile business. As such it was a busy department, employing some eight people in the financing of exports and inter-country trade. The export of Cuban cigars came under its remit and coffee, for instance, was purchased in Brazil and shipped to Sweden. Mr Watson was much taken up with a sugar plantation in Trinidad, the Waterloo Estates, acquired by Kleinworts in connection with a bankruptcy. He sent his son, Captain Watson, out to manage and nurse it into profitability before eventually selling it to Tate & Lyle. One of the perks of this department was that items like cigars, boxes of chocolates, and Australian cherry brandy were made available to staff at favourable prices.

The next manager in terms of seniority was James Somervell Knott, who managed the Stocks or Securities Department which included Foreign Exchange and Arbitrage. In 1923 Charles Henderson was promoted to full manager of Foreign Exchange, Knott retaining the Investments side. By the late 1920s, however, Somervell Knott was in rather a nominal position. Since the partners took a keen interest in the investment side, in effect their own investments, the leading brokers and bill brokers were allowed direct access to their rooms. Although the brokers used to see Knott and he in turn would pass on their recommendations to the partners, they increasingly bypassed him to deal directly with the partners. 'A gentle, well-mannered man', Knott was by no means a dictator to the staff, who considered him 'a real gentleman' who took a personal interest in their lives. When a member of staff's wife was stricken with severe stomach trouble, Knott arranged for her to be admitted for tests at a London teaching hospital under the care of his own surgeon daughter.[10]

Other managers, however, were less inclined to show such consideration to their staff in business hours. The hub of the bank remained the Credits or Acceptance side, divided geographically into little principalities. Their managers were highly skilled at granting credits to foreign customers and dominated the bank. One of the managers whose presence was most feared by the staff was Stirling Karck, the grandson of Alexander Friedrich's friend Ferdinand Karck, who in 1858 had left New York to open Kleinworts' office in Liverpool, where he was a partner. He had built the Liverpool business into an important profit centre for the firm, making net profits of £25,000. Years later a heavy loss was incurred on a South American account, but it was a moot point whether London should bear it as bankers or Liverpool as merchants. Despite his successful record and intimacy with the Kleinwort family, it ended in Ferdinand losing a substantial part of his capital, which had reduced him to a salaried partner with a small percentage, a position that Stirling's father, George Faber Karck had inherited. Thus Stirling had been brought up on an equal footing with the Kleinworts and the Andreaes, was well educated, fluent in French and German, and had been sent round the world to complete his banking apprenticeship with a view to succeeding his father. Yet upon his return, it was made clear that the association was not what it had been. There could be no prospect of a partnership, even at the Liverpool office.

The Cunard and White Star Line decision to make Southampton their home port had sounded the death knell for Liverpool's importance and prosperity, as all the large commodity firms moved their head offices to London. Kleinworts' Liverpool office became a branch of its London commodities department, which Karck joined in October 1904 on a monthly salary of £7. He thereafter had to be content with a prospective managerial position and he duly became manager of the French and Belgian Departments, whilst also remaining in charge of the Liverpool cotton accounts but at strictly manager level, unlike his father and grandfather. Placed in an invidious position in terms of status, he became 'a man disappointed in life' and ruled over his principality none too benignly. He was once heard to say 'You don't want to worry about your friends—stand on their neck and get a bit higher,' and even one of the partners admitted that he was a very difficult man to please.[11]

When it came to considering the manager of the Spanish and South American Departments, however, the partners could find few if any 'failings' in either character or business acumen in their manager. José Mayorga's words 'were accepted by the partners as gospel'; and, of all the managers, he was the one who, in a different age, would have been offered a partnership. He was built very much in the mould of Alexander Friedrich Kleinwort, being extremely hard-working and adept at identifying opportunities. There were relatively few career openings for a young man from a humble background in Southern Spain so in 1907, at the age of 20, he decided to seek his fortune in London, then the pivot of the commercial and financial world. Spain, then as now, exported large quantities of fruit to Britain, and Mayorga travelled to London on board a vessel carrying grapes from his native town of Almeria. He decided to enter banking, hand-delivering letters of application in order to avoid the cost of postage stamps. With the success of his application to Kleinworts, however, his pay was soon set at £5 [£273] a month, a fair wage for a correspondence clerk in 1909.

José Mayorga began his banking career under Mr Satzger of the German Department, who was then also responsible for South American business; most of the bank's Latin American clients were of German extraction, hence their grouping under Satzger, even though much of the correspondence increasingly was conducted in Spanish or English. Mr Satzger was thought to be rather withdrawn and uncommunicative by the staff but he had no trouble making a point quite clear to Mayorga. In spite of being a correspondence clerk and therefore usually engaged in writing letters, as he sat writing one day Mayorga was asked 'What are you doing?' by Satzger. 'Writing a letter to my mother,' replied Mayorga. 'Writing a letter to your Mother? The paper is not yours. The pen is not yours. The ink is not yours. The time is not yours. What do you mean? Put it away,' ordered Satzger.

Such chastisement did little to dent Mayorga's confidence. He was 'a very strong', determined man. When he found that with marriage and the birth of his eldest son, Pepe, he needed to supplement his salary, he took on translation work for the Spanish Embassy, rising early in the morning in order to complete one or two translations before leaving for a day's work at Kleinworts. He soon proved so adept and reliable that he was asked to translate directly for the ambassador, the Marqués Merry del Val, who 'became quite fond of him and gave him a lot of other chances of earning money'.

Mayorga's main objective, however, was to succeed at Kleinworts. He learnt the business and waited for an opportunity to show his mettle and earn promotion. It came with the outbreak of the First World War, when much of the bank's normal activity was disrupted and it had to try to expand its business in parts of the world outside the theatre of war, such as in Spanish-speaking countries. Kleinworts' long-standing Cuban sugar interests had been neglected, so yielded little revenue and a question mark hung over many of their accounts there. The bank was also owed money by a Cuban firm, so Mayorga believed that by making a trip to Cuba he could not only settle the matter but also look into old accounts and drum up new business.

He duly approached Mr Satzger with this proposition. It fell on deaf ears. 'Well that was something which was considered most ridiculous at the time. The Managers were the only ones who could do a thing like that. The employee had to just sit still and not speak until he was spoken to more or less.' Mayorga was not prepared to forfeit an opportunity for doing business so easily. There seemed no alternative but to approach a partner, even though he had never seen any of the partners before, let alone spoken to them. Nevertheless, he courageously knocked on the door of the youngest partner and, meeting Herman A. for the first time, he said, 'I've been working here now for 7 years and I wanted to come and see you with an idea that I've had that I think would be good.' He then went on to explain his plan. According to Mayorga's son, Pepe, Herman A. 'was so staggered by the impertinence of his suggestion' that he had to tell Alexander about it immediately. Mayorga was eventually summoned to Alexander's room for vetting purposes and was told, 'My nephew's been talking about this. I think it is a good idea and I think you should go. Do you have any clothes?' Mayorga answered, 'One suit for the summer and one for the winter.' 'Well,' commented Alexander, 'you'd better get yourself some clothes. Since you've got to go to New York first, go to Goldman Sachs and then from there you go down to Cuba.'

This trip was the turning point in Mayorga's career. It proved a resounding success; the debt was settled, he brought back new business, such as the United Railways of Havana, and he met the Sachs family, who reported back favourably about him to London. On his return Mayorga started to move up in the bank, now marked out as a business generator. After gaining responsibility for South America he further enhanced his reputation by managing to obtain much-sought-after supplies when Britain was buying meat from the Argentine during the war. Discrepancies in the credit lines were delaying matters. 'Forget the little discrepancy,' he is supposed to have ordered, 'get the credit through because we need the meat.'

By 1921 he had been given the signature to become a manager, a person of substance who had to receive clients of the bank at home. José Mayorga, however, lived in an unprepossessing house in Crouch End. 'Well, you had better move and get yourself a nice house somewhere,' was Alexander's comment. Mayorga also received a tax-free salary of £2,000 [£43,000] per annum plus bonuses, unusually large. Managers at Kleinworts and elsewhere in the City were extremely well paid as befitted those who actively ran the businesses.

Mayorga's rise through the bank was almost plain sailing because, early on, he proved himself indispensable to the partners. He 'had a very ingratiating character; he made friends very easily and he created confidence very easily'. The partners lived a life apart even from the managers, in whom they tended to inspire feelings of fear rather than respect. Mayorga, however, was the only person in the whole firm who 'was able to climb behind this barrage of protection'; and 'in the end he became their most intimate friend', one who could speak his mind to them freely, as the partners came to rely upon him for everything. Throughout the 1920s he was given further responsibilities, so that his principality came to encompass South America, Spain, Scandinavia, and Italy. Later, in the 1930s, he added foreign exchange and finally all general administration, becoming general or executive manager, the supremo of Kleinworts outside the partnership.

As far as the staff were concerned he was a tough 'stand and deliver' employer, known in the bank as the Black Panther. Despite being lame, he had boundless energy and was 'tremendously enthusiastic with an excitable temperament; if he was interested in something it sounded as if there was a row going on! If he was really angry with somebody, the whole building was almost shaking!' There were other managers. Mr Saager, one of the staff managers, who also acted as chief bookkeeper and oversaw the partners' private ledgers, and Mr Veraguth 'who looked more like an orchestra conductor' and was there by virtue of his brother, a famous Swiss doctor who had treated the Kleinworts, but what he did was not clear even to the staff. 'He really was a grand gentleman director' who was never seen to busy himself with the bank's business. It was clearly José Mayorga who loomed large before all of them as the dynamo of the bank.[12]

Through Mayorga's aggressive courtship of new business, Kleinworts were prominent in providing credits in countries whose domestic capital markets were unable to finance their rapid industrialization. During the 1920s Mayorga increased the firm's Spanish business, establishing, for example, an excellent relationship with the Banco de Barcelona, through whom reimbursement credits were arranged for Spanish companies. As a result, Spain became a significant area of operation. He had used the same tactics in the provision of credits to South America with notable success. The exception was Chile, but only because he diverged from acceptance credits to make a foray into the foreign issuing business; and Chile proved to be predatory country for a Kleinwort fledgling issue.[13]

In the first place, Rothschilds and Morgans had co-managed the last Chilean Government loan in 1909 and, with their long experience of international loans, they were formidable opponents. In the second place, given the changed environment whereby New York now had much more capital to invest than London, American banks were determined to capture markets such as Chile from the London banks. It was not, however, an easy task to defeat them in a rate-cutting contest as they were prepared to work without any profit or even make a loss in order to win future business. They also had no compunction about using local intelligence to steal a march on British competitors. And finally, Kleinworts' choice of local agent told against them and only served to emphasize their inexperience in dealing with foreign governments.

In 1922 Rothschilds, Kleinworts, and numerous American banks tendered for the $18m. 20-year loan for the Chilean Government. Within a few hours of the receipt of Rothschilds' offer at Santiago, the terms had been leaked to the agents of the American bidders, who immediately added an extra ½ per cent to their issue price offer. The Chilean Minister of Finance none the less favoured Kleinworts' offer, sending an enquiry concerning their standing to the Chilean Minister in London. His reply dashed any hope of success: 'they were a second or third rate firm'. Kleinworts were ruled out forthwith. José Mayorga immediately instructed their agent to report the matter to the British chargé d'affaires in Santiago, a Mr Bateman, who in turn sought clarification from London. The Department of Trade advised the Foreign Office that 'Messrs. Kleinwort Sons & Company are a British institution and they are, in fact, one of the two leading acceptance houses in London. The reputation of the firm is beyond question, and the statement attributed to Señor Augustin Edwards that they should be regarded as a "second or third rate firm" is devoid of justification.' Furthermore, Kleinworts' capital of £4m. and acceptances of £11m. made their standing unquestionable.

Whilst Bateman prevaricated about contradicting Edwards's report in case it ruptured diplomatic relations between Chile and Britain, a further political dimension to the matter emerged. Kleinworts' choice of a German bank to represent them in the negotiations was regarded by the British Government as unfortunate. 'Messrs Kleinworts have shown a want of tact, and given rise to a certain wounding of susceptibilities and an amount of speculation which is totally unwarranted,' complained Mr Bateman. Kleinworts' longstanding connection with the German South American Bank of Berlin was immaterial. By entrusting a small unimportant German bank with the delicate task of handling a loan, Kleinworts were, in Chilean eyes, signalling that the larger, well-established British banks—such as the Anglo-South American Bank and the London and River Plate Bank—were incapable of dealing with such international business. Since the Foreign Office was keen to encourage commercial relations with Chile, they felt that British financiers must alter their representation in order to succeed in loan operations there. Kleinworts received a diplomatic rap on the knuckles over the affair. José Mayorga was an audacious and aggressive banker, but such traits were not ones to soothe prickly foreign governments or to withstand patiently the equivocation and protocol surrounding negotiations with politicians and civil servants. His choice of agent had been damaging to the bank's interests.[14]

Despite Mayorga's aggressive expansion of the Spanish department, the largest and most important department in the bank in the 1920s remained the German Department, then the most profitable. 'Everybody was afraid' of Mr Satzger, the manager, though they admitted that 'he had a tremendous memory'. From the sum of £5,000 in 1920, commission earnings had overtaken those of the United Kingdom and United States combined to yield £160,000 [£4.4m.] by 1925, an all-time high for the decade. Extra staff had to be taken on to cope with the enormous increase in the amount of work generated by the 'terrific business with Germany'. The Berlin section alone swelled to eighty people, since the firm acted as correspondent for virtually every bank in Germany. As that country set about reconstruction, her demand for money was insatiable. Kleinworts' reputation as an Anglo-German house was of great benefit in the ensuing scramble among London and New York bankers to take advantage of the extremely high interest rates and the boom in company business.[15]

Apart from old clients in textile manufacturing and the wool-combing industry, the firm also provided credits to the cream of Germany's industrial companies, which had once again begun to dominate Europe. The Ruhr magnates Thyssen, Siemens (a Martin connection), Stinnes, I. G. Farben Industrie (a Herman Kleinwort connection), and the Essen magnate Frederick Krupp were all major Kleinwort clients. They also aggressively sought further German business, buying into the Boehmische Escompte Bank and joining the board and starting a large lending schedule with German Landesbanks, such as the Landesbank der Rheinprovins, to finance local authority construction programmes.

Satzger also turned Kleinworts' attention to Austria. Montagu Norman, governor of the Bank of England, had instigated an international loan programme to restore the economy of this crushed country, whose empire of fifty million people had been forcibly reduced to a republic of six million. Kleinworts decided to set up a commercial banking business in Vienna to take advantage of the anticipated Austrian reconstruction boom and entered into a partnership with the prestigious private German bank, Mendelssohn & Co., to create the firm of Kux, Bloch & Co. In 1922, in a move recalling the formation of the Trio Account, they invited the Bayerische Vereinsbank to participate.[16]

The spectacular growth in the German department's business did not entirely dispel doubts about Germany's economy. As a precaution against the risk of German bankruptcy, Kleinworts granted only reimbursement credits—usually denominated in sterling rather than marks, so that the borrower bore the risk of the depreciating German currency. By August 1923 one dollar was worth 100 million marks and on 4 November, 200 billion marks. As Max Warburg noted in his diary 'The mark no longer merits the name of currency; it has become an illusion, pure and simple.' By now the Allies were prepared to reconsider the issue of reparations. The Dawes Plan of April 1924 reduced the level of reparation payments and raised an international loan to rebuild the economy, so that Germany could meet her obligations. The resultant monetary stabilization and debt consolidation produced an economic revival that led to a huge increase in German business for London banking houses in the mid-1920s.

Kleinworts, in common with other Anglo-German City houses, took very much the short-term view about Germany's future. They lent heavily there throughout the 1920s and continued to extract the largest share of their commission revenue from the German department. Mr Satzger apparently became alarmed at the high level of German acceptances and warned the partners of the dangers but they took no notice. With the decrease in American business, they were determined to take full advantage of the profit-making conditions prevailing in Germany. Besides, they were much exercised about partnership matters at this time.[17]

All three partners possessed large personal fortunes, far larger than those of their Benson counterparts. Throughout the volatile trading years of the 1920s the bank's capital averaged between £3.5 and £4m. [£93.5–£107m.], well ahead of Schröders, Barings, Hambros, Gibbs, and Bensons; the partners had also benefited greatly from their stockholdings in American companies such as Woolworths and Goodyear, whose issues they had financed with Goldman Sachs and Lehman Brothers. As Alexander said on more than one occasion: 'I have made more money sitting down than working.' Since in 1920 he and Herman were now of an age (62 and 64 respectively) when they might well be sitting down more than doing anything else, they had to plan ahead to limit the impact of their death or retirement on the capital base of the firm and on the partnership, just as their father had done after the death of James Drake in order to minimize the effect of Edward Cohen's retirement on the firm's capital.[18]

One solution would have been to convert the partnership into a private limited liability company, thereby following in the footsteps of Barings and Glyns, which had been incorporated before 1914, and those that would be taken by Morgan Grenfell, Helbert Wagg, and Lazards after the war. The

Kleinworts, however, were firmly of the view that partners in a banking firm must have enough faith in their business to be entirely content with the unlimited liability of their partnership.

There was another way to safeguard their capital that was at that time largely untested by City firms. Ernest Spicer, a valued friend and partner with the bank's accountants Spicer & Pegler, suggested that by forming a Trust company with a substantial capital which could be lent as working capital the partners could use it as a corporate partner in their existing firm. Thus, on 19 October 1920, the Drake Trust Co. Ltd. was incorporated with a capital of £1,500,000 divided into 1,490,000 non-cumulative preference shares and 10,000 ordinary shares of £1 each. The preference shares were subscribed for by Herman and Alexander and 745,000 allotted to their private family trust companies. The ordinary shares were subscribed for by all three partners in the proportion of their participation, that is 40 per cent to Herman, 40 per cent to Alexander, and 20 per cent to Herman A. The Drake Trust became a partner in Kleinwort, Sons & Co. with no liability for losses, but with 50 per cent of the profits; the object being to save supertax, but more importantly to ensure the continuity of the business on the deaths of Herman and Alexander, when the shares would pass to their heirs, thereby leaving the capital undisturbed in the partnership. The Drake Trust thus advanced £1,500,000 to Kleinworts for twenty-one years ending on 31 December 1941.[19]

Whereas it had been a straightforward exercise to safeguard the capital of the firm, it proved to be anything but straightforward to safeguard the partnership by ensuring a smooth succession. In the period from the retirement of Edward Cohen in 1883 until the incorporation of the Drake Trust in 1920, there was, surprisingly, no deed of partnership. Matters were arranged informally by Herman and Alexander as equal co-proprietors. By 1920, however, partnership participations were being queried, so that arrangements started to be formalized. Although the partners signed a Management Agreement, whereby 25 per cent of the profits were first allocated to the active partners Alexander and Herman A. before dividing the balance between them and Herman, there was still no partnership deed and no agreement about the introduction of fresh partners. Herein lay the obstacle to a smooth succession. As so often in the past, Herman and Alexander were diametrically opposed to each other's proposals.

Time had not been a healer in their case and they barely spoke to each other; indeed they had little need to do so. Whenever Alexander was at No. 20, usually between Monday and Friday, Herman stayed away. This did not mean, as Alexander's family were led to believe, that Herman never did, and had no reason to, visit the bank. On the contrary, he had the best of reasons, namely that at all times, and regardless of his deteriorating relations with his brother, he was a major partner in the bank and his capital in the business was £2.64m. [£51.4m.] in 1920. If he had chosen to withdraw this sum, Kleinworts' business would have been severely reduced, if not aborted. And, even as a 'sleeping' partner, he was personally liable for 40 per cent of any losses incurred. Indeed, to the outside world he remained the senior partner, his name appearing before his brother's on the firm's letterhead. He therefore made certain that he was kept informed about every aspect of the bank's operations on a regular basis.

His first liaison officer was Mr Saager who 'remained a kind of catspaw to find out everything' to relay back to him. On retirement he was replaced by Mr Daly, known in the family as Bill Baily. He in turn was followed by Reginald Bridle. A diplomat by nature and a good organizer, he became confidant and right-hand man to all the partners and had the unique honour of being addressed by them as 'Dear Bridle'. Successive generations of young Kleinworts and Andreaes also turned to him for guidance about their affairs and, to them, he was known as Benevolent Watch Dog, signing his letters, BWD Bridle. 'A very kind person' he did his best to bring together the two branches of the warring Kleinworts. Sir Godfrey Style remembers seeing him often, for 'Dear Bridle was our much-loved link with the bank.' He used to come from the City every evening in winter to 45 Belgrave Square, and about three times a week in the summer to Wierton Place, 'to report exactly what was going on, and my grandfather never missed a trick'. Bridle told Godfrey how on one occasion at Wierton, he had been asked how some particular deal had gone off. He had answered, ' "We made just over a million, Sir" and your grandfather looked up at me and grimaced, which he did when he disapproved, and said "Only that, poor Bridle!" '

In addition to receiving these reports, Herman used to visit the bank every Saturday, then a normal working day but one when Alexander was usually absent, and remain there until 3.30 p.m. His style of management was quite different from the other partners. Although he only came in once a week he was far more accessible to the staff than either Alexander or Herman A. As Gordon Tettmar, the bank's first company secretary, recalled: 'Sir Alexander had very little to do with the staff. He relied on his Senior Managers and the rank and file only saw him arrive and go.' Herman, in contrast, would arrive and proceed to take a walk round the bank. He would sometimes be accompanied by José Mayorga, who would explain recent developments and introduce new members of staff. Although awed by the presence of a partner, a singular occurrence in their lives, they were pleased by his interest. His aversion to the cold was well known and, even though he now never set foot in the bank on other days, they always had a fire lit every day in one of the rooms at No. 20 'because that was Mr Herman's room'.

Prevented from playing a more active role, one might have expected Herman to have had his chosen successors in place to protect his interests. It was Alexander, however, who, in June 1926, first expressed a desire to bring his two sons into the partnership. Herman agreed, provided he could bring in two of his sons-in-law. Unhappily, Alexander resolutely refused and in consequence, Herman withheld his consent over the introduction of Alexander's sons. The ensuing bitter row produced the final, lasting break between them. In the normal course of events each would have passed his interest in the partnership to a son or sons, as their father had done. Herman, however, had only daughters —seven of them. He therefore quite naturally wanted to introduce sons-in-law into the partnership. Only two, both naval men, were available and willing to pursue a City career: Captain the Hon. Trevor Parker, who came from a long line of distinguished judges, and Commander Paul Bridgeman, a nephew of the 4th Earl of Bradford. Alexander was opposed to them because they were naval officers and sons-in-law, even though his father had offered partnerships to two sons-in-law, while Herman A. was after all the son of a son-in-law.

Alexander then declared they were unsuitable for the firm. Unlike other City houses, such as Bensons, Kleinworts had never taken personable, capable, but non-professional young members of the family straight into managerial positions, so that Alexander could more easily claim exceptions should not be made for Parker and Bridgeman. It was unfortunate for Herman that none of his family were the right age to start as a trainee; his eldest grandson Godfrey, for whom he cherished partnership hopes, was just entering Eton. Although his sons-in-law had already started to work in the bank, the situation *vis-à-vis* the partnership remained at an impasse.[20]

Alexander, however, was in a far stronger position because he had sons—three of them, after two others had died young. He had already ruled out the eldest, Alexander Santiago, even though at 34 he was just the right age to become a partner. Alexander Santiago was far more of a Girard than a Kleinwort and proved to be a hopeless businessman. After a couple of years at No. 20, when some of the clerks took unfair advantage of his naïvety and gentle nature to make him an easy butt for their pranks, which only served to emphasize his unsuitability as a banker, he was removed. Alexander was intolerant of his son's artistic leaning and, judging him unfit as his heir, 'simply blanked him out completely'. Although his mother kept in touch, and insisted he joined the family at Christmas, he became an unmentionable non-person to his disappointed father. Alexander Santiago trained as a silversmith, payments for his tuition going through the bank, and joined Ashbee's Arts and Crafts Guild at

Chipping Camden. There he lived for many years, cut off from his family and large cousinhood.

The death of his next two sons, Frederick aged 1 in 1896 and his favourite Henry from pneumonia in 1921, just prior to entering the Navy, meant that Alexander could only pin his hopes on his younger sons, Ernest (born in 1901) and Cyril (born in 1905). They were ideal candidates, intelligent, eager to learn about the family business and with several years bank training already behind them. It was unfair of Herman to object to them; he did so purely in response to Alexander blocking his own candidates.[21]

What is more surprising given the sensitivity of the partnership issue is that neither Herman nor Alexander objected to Herman A.'s proposal in 1925 that his two sons, Herman K., always known as Sonny, and Peter Andreae, should be able to become partners. Inevitably this threatened a dilution of the Kleinwort participation. Indeed, in 1935, Cyril spoke out against this to Spicer, receiving the reply: 'Now, as to the equity of the present Agreement, it is not for me to say that Mr Andreae should have had no rights to introduce his sons as Partners, nor is it for me to suggest that Sir Alexander acted unwisely in agreeing to Mr Andreae's having those rights.' Why, then, did Alexander and Herman agree to it? The answer lies surely in the absolute confidence Alexander had always placed in Herman A., who was, after all, his favourite nephew. And both Kleinworts admired the way in which, denied any corresponding advantage, their nephew had started at the bottom, worked very hard and earned his partnership and fortune through ability alone. He had, in the process, made them a good deal of money as well. The extent of their regard for him is evident from the fact that had they both died prior to 1 January 1927, the whole of the business of Kleinwort, Sons & Co. would have belonged to him. And neither of them had put him under any legal obligation to take their sons or sons-in-law into the partnership.[22]

Although originally a junior partner, Herman A. had become a vital cog in the bank's wheel. He and his Uncle Alexander were very close, though he maintained good relations with Uncle Herman and acted as their go-between. Moreover, he was very much the public face of the bank. The Kleinwort brothers were rich private bankers with the emphasis on private. Alexander's baronetcy and membership of his local Liberal association were his only concessions to a public persona; otherwise neither brother played any part in public life. 'We prefer to remain ⅞ submerged' was how they put it.[23]

Herman A., on the contrary, had a considerable public reputation and his exploits were reported by the newspapers. He excelled as an athlete, hunting man, and skier, but it was more for his outstanding skill as a yachtsman that he was celebrated. In the days when he built *Corona* (1925) and the 23-metre

Candida (1928), yacht owners had professional skippers to take the helm and race their yachts. Herman A. was one of the first amateur owners to take the helm in races of the Big Class.

One of his great rivals in the 1920s, the gentleman helmsman Sir Philip Hunloke was a captain in the Navy and skippered the royal yacht. Once, when racing at Cowes against the King and Hunloke on Britannia, Herman A. registered a protest which he duly won. This gave rise to a certain amount of muttering in yachting circles. Not content to let the matter drop, Herman A. compounded the ill-feeling generated by his win by writing a letter to *The Times* to explain what he thought was the interesting tactical point behind his successful protest. 'The feeling was one did not do such things especially when the King was involved,' recalled his nephew Henry. 'Herman was just not sensitive to such matters,' and as a result made enemies.

A man of very strong convictions and outstanding personality, increasingly he came to dominate the bank from without and within. He thus entered the partnership discussions from a position of strength, as evidenced by the fact that while his Kleinwort uncles squabbled about their nominations, his were nodded through. Whereas, at the start of his career, it was unthinkable that he should become a partner, now it was unthinkable that his heirs should not. Herman A. had a large role in the bank because he bridged the generations between his uncles and his much younger cousins. Within the partnership negotiations, he was quite agreeable to both sons and sons-in-law becoming partners provided his own sons had equal rights to the partnership. As the issue became more acrimonious, he maintained a watching brief, realizing that, being the youngest, he could afford to wait. By December 1925, however, he was persuaded by his uncle Alexander to break the deadlock by supporting his offer to buy out Herman's large interest in the business; an offer which was rejected without hesitation. The impasse was eventually settled by Herman withdrawing his right of veto on condition that Paul Bridgeman be given a partnership, and Alexander made a payment of £50,000 in lieu of Trevor Parker's claims to a partnership. By this time, the matter had almost resolved itself, though to the disadvantage of Herman and his descendants.[24]

Trevor Parker proved to have a greater affinity for the Navy than for Kleinworts, so that he was more than happy to accept £50,000 to put into his own business. Although he had little aptitude for City life, he went into the discount house Ryder & Co., but, according to one descendant, 'had to be bailed out many times by H.G.K.'. Paul Bridgeman had wanted to be a doctor not a banker. Nevertheless, he proved more able to adapt to Kleinworts' style of operation and for a while became manager of the Stock Department, though his interest was more in the welfare of the staff than in share prices. They had cause to be thankful that he stayed at the bank, for it was through his efforts that a pension scheme was first mooted and a sports ground with a pavilion was purchased for their use at New Malden in Surrey. He died prematurely in 1930 from streptococcus poisoning, leaving Herman with no family representative to look after his large interest at the bank. He, none the less, kept his capital in the bank, receiving 5 per cent return on it. Loath to compete against his more forceful, antagonistic brother, he rarely again asserted himself over its direction.[25]

In December 1926, Alexander was at last able to welcome his two sons Ernest and Cyril into the partnership, giving each an initial capital of £50,000 [£1.4m.], the same amount with which he and Herman had entered the partnership in the 1880s. He believed that he must quickly set his house in order to make up for lost time after the false start with his eldest son who, in the normal course of events, would have been made a partner at the end of the war and have accumulated eight years of experience at his right hand. As it was, Alexander had to introduce his heirs to the intricacies of the partnership at the relatively advanced age of 68. Although fit and healthy, he was nevertheless concerned they would lack sufficient experience in the event of his untimely death. Whereas he and Herman had worked for five years, admittedly with time off for travel, before entering the partnership, Ernest had worked for three and Cyril for only one year. Their training might be shorter than customary but, being of the right calibre, their future at the bank was now assured. Ernest later emphasized the point, if from a rather biased point of view: 'The claims of inheritance and family were only accepted where fitness to conduct the business was present. My [eldest] brother, and H.G.K.'s two sons-in-law, were given their chance and, being found unfit, were turned out.'[26]

Alexander had always assumed that his sons would enter the family firm and had decided that as second-generation Britons they would be brought up as English boys and given an English rather than German education so that the Continental influence of their heritage was weakened. This was reinforced by the lack of regular contact with their mother's family—owing to the increasing estrangement of their parents, who took holidays separately—and by the fact that Ernest and Cyril were not close to their mother. Holidays were taken with their father, and from an early age they thought of Etiennette as 'aloof and uncaring'. Consequently they ignored her and worshipped their father. It is some measure of the boys' relations with their parents that they called them 'mater' and 'pater', conveying respect rather than cosy affection, and sounding quite formal compared with the pet nicknames used by their elder sister and other relations. 'To me anyone less like a Mater than their 5′2″ excitable, artistic, voluble, affectionate very French little mother is hard to imagine,' their niece Annette wrote.

Ernest and Cyril had an exceedingly difficult time as children. Their mother suffered from migraines and was often unable to participate in family life. She had lost her second son, her first was the despair of his father, and her eldest child Louise, 'Pearly', was a paraplegic who was more or less discounted by him. Etiennette devoted herself to Pearly and always put her first, worrying about what would happen to her. She therefore had much less time for her younger sons, who were left almost entirely in the hands of 'Nanna' their loving nurse. Believing themselves rejected by their mother they turned to their father for everything.

In many ways their childhood mirrored his: he too had been brought up by a nanny and his father, though as a result of his mother's early death. It was perhaps worse for Ernest and Cyril Kleinwort, as their mother was very much alive. Alexander, however, did not repeat the mistake his father had made: he never praised one son more than the other or compared them with each other. After Henry's death, his two youngest sons were even more precious to him and 'he adored them'.[27]

Although absorbed in the world of business, he nevertheless saw much more of them and therefore was able to impart his knowledge of the City and of Kleinworts' business. This was especially so because his plans for their education had fallen through. 'Neither Cyril nor I went to school at all,' Ernest explained. 'I went to a prep school for a couple of terms with my brother Henry but he was so unhappy there that he was taken home and I came home with him.' The Germanophobia of the First World War and Alexander's consequent anxiety for his children also kept the boys away from public school. They were educated at home by a tutor, Evan McColl, and by their second sister Henrietta who taught them literature and history.[28]

Ernest loved learning and was academically very bright. He used to help Cyril who, as his father had before him, found studying more tedious. Their sister used to say that once you had their attention, their powers of concentration were tremendous; the problem was getting the attention. Not that Henrietta had much trouble for she was 'very Kleinwort', which in the family meant having a strong character and great determination. She was undoubtedly the linchpin of the family: she acted as her father's hostess and ran the household for her mother; she was pivotal in Ernest and Cyril's lives; she taught them and looked after them emotionally, yet remained close to her mother, of whom she was very supportive. Henrietta's marriage in 1920 left a great void in the Bolnore household.

The other person who was a great force in the boys' childhood was their uncle Willy Girard. Their father might have had little time for his artistic ways but they loved him. Willy Girard was important to the boys because he played with them. Together they climbed trees and went on hikes through the woods, where he taught them about birds and wildlife, instilling in both a love of animals and in Cyril a love of birds. Again, it was Uncle Willy who showed them how to make things and taught them carpentry; they even constructed and erected a tree house under his guidance.

He was, in effect, the only uncle they knew and the only relation they saw regularly since the Herman Kleinworts and the Martins had almost no part in their lives and Carlo Andreae was long dead. It was the same with their large cousinhood, most of whom they hardly knew. Herman A. they did know, but with at least twenty years between them it was from a distance, as an older, rather dazzling figure who inspired a certain amount of hero-worship for his sporting prowess. His children 'Sonny' and Peter were their age but away at school, where Peter died aged 16, so that it was not until much later that they really came to know Sonny. Thus it was Uncle Willy who provided the only fun in the strained atmosphere of Bolnore.

It was otherwise a self-contained, somewhat lonely existence. The absence of schoolfriends, indeed of any friends, and any form of peer pressure left its mark, and the concept of 'mucking in' for example, was quite alien to them. Once they had made a decision about how to do something, they expected it to be done their way; but if not, then they just blanked out the whole episode. They were later judged to have been spoilt ('they always more or less had anything they wanted—lovely horses, cars, motor bicycles') and never really had to do anything they did not want to do. Having no experience of childhood friendships they did not later form close friendships, and moved through life set apart from their peers. During the Second World War, the Admiral in charge of the Orkneys praised Cyril for doing a wonderful job but was puzzled by his lack of camaraderie. This was soon clarified. 'Do you know,' he said in amazement, 'I have discovered he never went to a school and so never had to fit in with other men.'[29]

From the point of view of their future careers in the family bank, however, there were distinct advantages to their upbringing. The absence of good friends and corresponding outside influences bound them closer to each other, and to their father. He more than anyone was their link with the outside world, their future, and, not unnaturally, his was the dominant influence. He was revered by them and everything he advised they accepted as right. In terms of their banking future, being at home meant that he could instruct them in the basic principles of the business. Mealtimes when Alexander was at Bolnore provided a regular opportunity for discussion. The family breakfasted together and, 'enormously enjoyed lively debate with forcefully expressed opinions'. As boys and young men they had, their niece recalls, 'explosive temperaments and loud voices and were very emotional'. Under their father's instruction Cyril grew more even-tempered and dispassionate; Ernest, however, always remained prone to short explosions of temper and 'fusses'.

On Alexander's return from No. 20, the boys and Henrietta would join him for tea in the morning room. 'Always the same number of cups of tea, a boiled egg, and the same number of pieces of bread and butter,' recalled a granddaughter. 'We were much intrigued by his habit of folding the bread and butter neatly and eating his jam separately with a spoon'. Ernest showed the same precision with regard to food: 'He always had the same amount of food every day—it never varied, there was never one piece of toast one day and two the next.' After tea their father was at his most expansive, and would talk at length to the boys about the bank, often as he walked through the grounds to inspect his trees. He liked to point out what he had planted, so that conversations about the firm were interspersed with a 'Remember—that's an *"Abies Pungens Glauca"*,' and so on. The boys also dined with him but, tea apart, he was impatient about meals. He always missed the first course, only joining the family for the main course which he ate at speed. He then stayed until the end of dinner, talking to the boys while he smoked a cigar. Immediately after the last puff he would be off up to bed.[30]

The boys thus saw a great deal more of their father than was usual in those days. In the course of their lengthy daily discussions, he passed on to them information about the City and the bank's clients, as well as insights into the business. He had a phenomenal, almost photographic memory. The boys were enthralled by his instant recall of, for instance, the exact details of his foreign travels in the 1880s, and the business of Kleinworts. One of the strengths of Kleinworts was the continuity of approach to the business of banking over the generations. Much of Alexander's teaching was based upon what his own father had taught him. Two dicta which the boys were exhorted to follow and which they held dear were 'Moderation in all things' and 'Never become emotionally involved in any business problem'; both dicta had been urged on the young Alexander by his father. Similarly, just as his father had done, Alexander encouraged his boys to take plenty of exercise and develop their sporting instincts as an antidote to desk work at the bank. Ernest and Cyril were mad about hunting, became good shots, and, like their cousin, good skiers.

Yet Alexander also tried to impress upon them the need for self-discipline and an understanding of the responsibilities attached to great wealth. In this he was ultimately successful. The 1920s was a decade of contrast, when the strikes and slumps affecting the majority of the population hardly ever impinged on the frenzied partying of the Bright Young Things. Ernest and Cyril were presentable rich young men, who with their blond aquiline features and smart sports cars could easily have escaped into this milieu. That they did not owed everything to their father and his precepts. He did his best to ensure they were not too spoilt; for instance, giving them motorcycles but on condition they knew how to put them together. So they had spent hours dismantling and putting them back together and, whenever a mechanical fault occurred, they were the ones to repair the machine. They shared their father's passion for fast cars, but their first cars came attached with the condition that they and not their father's chauffeur were responsible for maintenance and repairs. As a result they acquired a specialized knowledge of the workings of a motor car and would dash off letters to the managing directors of motor car companies. These were not letters of complaint but of general comment on a car's performance, with praise or suggestions for improvement.[31]

In January 1920 Ernest went up to Jesus College, Cambridge, the first of his family apart from Great-Uncle Siegmund to attend university. He achieved an upper 2nd in Part I, modern languages, and the only first in Part II, economics. Cambridge undoubtedly coloured Ernest's outlook on life and bolstered his self-esteem. He was clever and now, pitted against his peers for the first time, he knew it. He was an ideal candidate for postgraduate work followed by an academic career, though by temperament he did not have the patience and equanimity to deal with students. He was mesmerized by detail and applied himself with abandon to acquiring knowledge. However, none of this was allowed to interfere with his father's plans. Ernest's future was at Kleinworts.

He entered the bank in 1923 and Cyril, at the age of 20, joined him two years later, having studied French and German at home. Cyril was not as academically clever as Ernest. In this he took after his father, who when young had disliked studying and had to be chivvied along. Cyril preferred to get on with life and rarely read a book. Later, however, he expressed regret: 'The tragedy of my life was that I was educated privately and I never went to university.' His lack of education, as he felt it to be, lent him humility, and he was always prepared to listen to the views of other people. Indeed he welcomed them, and accepted their ideas if they were the best way forward. He had no intellectual pride. In this he was quite different from his elder brother. Yet there was a complete absence of rivalry between them. Cyril might wish that he had had a university education, but he never resented his brother having received one. In the same way that his grandfather had revered his father's further education because he had none, Cyril, too, revered Ernest's university education. Of the two, however, it was Cyril who possessed the greater qualities of leadership. At the same time his unfailing respect for Ernest's strong intellect and powers of application never dimmed throughout their long careers together and, even when Ernest was wrong, Cyril never lost respect for him.[32]

The boys always felt, quite justifiably, that they had a head start in learning about the business: 'Father talked nothing but merchant banking, so we couldn't help absorbing it.' Alexander, nevertheless, made them start as trainee clerks on the bottom rung. Both began in the English Department under Harold Heys, who would recall how he 'used to instruct them in various things because Sir Alexander was always keen the sons should start at the beginning and go right through, so they knew all that was happening in the office, you see'. After a lengthy spell with him, the boys spent a week or two with selected members in the department before moving on to every other department.[33]

Ernest and Cyril became partners unofficially in 1926 but officially, by deed of partnership, on 1 January 1927. If Herman A. was the public face of the partnership, then Ernest and Cyril quickly became the human side of it. They were the first partners that many of the staff knew as colleagues. At one time Ernest was working with Ernest Pudney, who had on his desk a book entitled *The Capital Levy* by Professor Pigou. Ernest told him Pigou had been one of his dons at Cambridge and 'We had a short chat about this book which was ended by Ernest saying "he's a silly ass" anyway.' The significance of this for Pudney was that it would have been impossible for him to have had a similar conversation, or even the opportunity for one, with the existing partners. Ernest and Cyril were much more a part of the bank than their father and cousin appeared to be. Like their Uncle Herman they walked round the office. 'You see Sir Alexander never came out to see anybody, nor would H.A. but Ernest and Cyril would come out and see somebody if they wanted to, and if they passed you they would say "All right, Judd?"' remembered a commissionaire.[34]

They showed themselves to be the human side of the partnership in an even more significant way when, at the behest of Cecil Elbra and Paul Bridgeman, they instigated a review of the firm's pension arrangements. Such arrangements had hitherto been organized on an *ad hoc* basis entirely on the whim of the partners: 'if they liked your face they treated you accordingly. If they didn't like your face it was just too bad'. There was no such thing as a statutory retirement age. If a member of staff wished to retire, the onus was on him to suggest it to a manager or, if more senior, to a partner. He would approach 'Sir Alexander as the Senior Partner, cap in hand and say, "I am nearly 70 years old and feel that the time has come for me to ask permission to retire" to which Sir Alexander might say, "You are much too young to think of giving up working. Look at me! You never hear me talk of retirement." And stroking his patriarchal beard, he might add, "Well, if that is your wish we will discuss what we can do for you."' Alternatively, he might not add the latter remark, so that the man had to continue to work until he had plucked up the courage to raise the issue again.

Moreover, if an *ex gratia* payment was awarded, it took no account of the cost of living or years of service. It was seen simply as a one-off gift from the partnership. Ernest Pudney remembers meeting a retired colleague who, in reply to his question about how he liked retirement, answered, 'Would you like to live on £17 a month?' Pudney was very shocked and mentioned it to Cecil Elbra, 'who was the most understanding of all the managers at that time and he was just as distressed as I was.' Elbra, then a new manager, and Paul Bridgeman enlisted the support of the new young partners, with the result that a pension scheme was inaugurated, in many cases doubling the original payment, although the amount awarded remained at the discretion of the partnership. Eventually in May 1937, Cyril introduced a contributory pension scheme arranged by the North British and Mercantile Insurance Co., of which he was a director.[35]

Success in improving the working conditions of their staff was not matched by improving the trading conditions of their bank. Although in 1927 Kleinworts possessed approximately £3.78m. of capital, acceptances were some £16.5m., and the firm easily maintained a leading position among accepting houses, the Kleinwort brothers' first three years in the partnership were not easy ones. Trading conditions remained volatile, not helped by Britain's ill-conceived return to the Gold Standard in 1925. Although the firm continued to focus upon Continental accepting business, the partnership was prepared to experiment with diversification. Herman A.'s fascination with American corporate finance led him to take Kleinworts into a new area, domestic company finance. Traditionally, merchant banks had confined their activities to acceptance and foreign and government work. Domestic company finance was considered beneath them, largely remaining within the sphere of the stockbroker and the often disreputable 'company promoter'. The informal post-war embargo imposed by the Bank of England on foreign issues altered this, so that even ultra-conservative Barings began to look around for British companies in which to invest.

Despite Herman A.'s efforts, Kleinworts were never prominent in this field since the houses that did succeed were all primarily issuing ones. Not only were Kleinworts still at the starting gate with regard to foreign issues but they had yet to saddle up when it came to domestic new issues and company finance work. It was, however, an area of expansion with the attraction of larger commissions than conventional accepting business produced. It was also a high-risk business—but then, Herman A. was a great risk-taker, believing that people were in business to take risks. If after hearing the story on a speculative investment he took a favourable view, he would often say, 'Put in £5,000'

[£143,000]. Although Alexander was less impulsive than his nephew, he was just as willing to take risks—indeed it was the hallmark of Kleinworts' trading success. When in 1922 it was disclosed in the City that Gerard Bevan's concerns—Ellis & Co., one of the leading firms on the Stock Exchange, and City Equitable, a reinsurance company—had failed, Alexander asked the senior manager, 'How much have we lost on Mr Bevan?' The manager proudly answered, 'We have not got a penny owing to us on his account.' 'Good Heavens!' Alexander exclaimed, 'We should have done, he was a money maker.'[36]

While Kleinworts lost nothing on Mr Bevan, they lost a great deal on Mr Hatry. A company promoter and financier with a magnetic personality, Clarence Hatry was one of the leading personalities in the City of the 1920s. He was 'a spellbinder' according to Ernest Kleinwort, while the Marquess of Winchester, chairman of the various companies comprising the Hatry group, described him as 'an example of the alert business brain having an unusually quick perception of any proposition, a marvellous gift for sifting the intricacies of a Balance Sheet, a power of putting his case with a clarity of expression rarely found apart from legal training, coupled with an apparent frankness which amounted to a charm of manner.' Many fell under the spell, including Herman A., who ought to have been less susceptible.

Hatry's meteoric rise had not been entirely without setbacks, setbacks which might have alerted the more cautious investor. He had organized the flotation of British Glass Industries, which came to a disastrous end in 1926, and of Jute Industries Ltd. which had to undergo a scheme of drastic capital reduction. Set against these there were however, notable successes. At the peak of his career, around 1927 to 1929, he mobilized an array of interdependent finance companies to promote department stores, which he brought together in the Drapery Trust and then sold on to Debenhams; to back automatic vending machinery, in his company Associated Automatic Machine Corporation (AAMC), a well-established concern with a good profit record; and to promote automatic portrait photograph booths in his company Photomaton Parent Corporation. He had also set up several successful investment trusts. In conjunction with three of the clearers (Lloyds, Barclays, and the National Provincial Bank), Kleinworts had been persuaded to lend him considerable amounts of money on a collateral of shares in his already established companies. Thus they made loans of £180,000 to his Austin Friars and Dundee Trusts on the security of shares in his Associated Automatic Machine Corporation.[37]

Herman A. had been introduced to Hatry by his younger brother Dr Edward Philip Andreae, who was a good scientific engineer and a brilliant industrialist. 'Dr E.P.', as he was known at No. 20, acted as Kleinworts' company doctor, nursing back to health ailing companies in which the bank had a substantial or major shareholding if not outright ownership, so they could be disposed of profitably. As such he played an important part in developing Kleinworts' operations in company finance and made a great deal of money for the partnership.

After being appointed managing director of the British Glauzstoff & Co., which produced artificial silk by the cupramonium process, he met Sam Courtauld and engineered the Courtaulds take-over of British Glauzstoff Silk Co. He then became a partner in the small issuing house, Sperling & Co., which also produced the financial journal for which Herman A. wrote his articles. In 1931, the Sperling partnership was dissolved when its senior partner, Sir Edward Mackay Edgar, was made bankrupt after the notorious company promoter, James B. White, organized a pool in his British Controlled Oilfields shares, which had collapsed.

Sperlings had become a major promoter and had joined up with Hatry to form the Sperling Combine, intended to gain control of a number of shipbuilding companies in order to rationalize the industry. Through them Kleinworts advanced £50,000 as a deposit on the purchase price of the Northumberland Shipbuilding Co. and also bought £325,000 of its shares. Northumberland then proceeded to take over Workman Clark, followed by W. Doxford & Sons, the leading marine engine manufacturers, and Fairfield Engineering, builder of destroyers. When, in the economic slump of 1926, the companies started to lose money, Kleinworts stepped in to buy Northumberland's assets from the Receiver (Spicer & Pegler), and ended up owning 100 per cent of the shares of Fairfields and Doxfords. The partners appointed Dr E.P. as their managing director and he kept the firms alive despite the lack of a single order for five years. He would eventually sell the failing Fairfields to Lithgows in 1935 for £50,000 and succeed in turning Doxfords round, bringing it back to prosperity, so that in the early 1950s, Kleinworts would be able to float the company on the stock market and dispose of their majority shareholding at an excellent profit.

In similar fashion the bank acquired the entire shareholding of John Bright Bros. Ltd., a textile firm that Dr E.P. Andreae turned from being a moribund money loser into a little gold-mine. It was also through Dr E.P. that Kleinworts made a valuable connection in the person of Leslie Urquhart, an outstanding mining engineer. As the mining industry expanded from the late nineteenth century, merchant banks such as Rothschilds, Erlangers, and Mathesons had financed exploration companies; Kleinworts similarly backed Urquhart's famous copper-mine at Mount Isa in Queensland, Australia, by taking equity shares. In 1929, Dr E.P. became chairman of the Mining Trust Co., formed to hold large blocks of these shares, with a capital of £918,000. Urquhart, who kept the largest holding, ended up making considerable profits as did Kleinworts.

These entrepreneurial venture capital operations were very much the contribution of the Andreae side of the partnership and had naturally brought Hatry into Herman A.'s circle. Their paths had also crossed during Hatry's attempt to rescue the City Equitable Insurance Co., in which Kleinworts were shareholders. Herman A. had been quick to support Hatry's next project, an assault on the closed market for corporation loans. In 1924 Hatry set out to undercut the three Stock Exchange firms which had dominated the market, using as his vehicle his Corporation and General Securities Ltd. This proved to be Hatry's star turn. Between 1924 and 1929 Corporation & General made 36 public issues for local authorities, many oversubscribed. His success meant that Herman A. was more than willing to back his next project.[38]

However, Montagu Norman refused to support Hatry's scheme for a gigantic merger of firms that would produce some 60 per cent of Britain's steel, saying the time was not propitious for throwing good money after bad into a stagnant market which had still to be properly surveyed. Since Kleinworts had never been influenced by the utterances of the Bank of England, Herman A. remained eager to finance Steel Industries of Great Britain Ltd., an issue which seemed to have every prospect of success and was genuinely needed by the depressed, fragmented steel industry in the summer of 1929. Hatry had registered the company in June, but the issue, already postponed several times, had yet to appear.

As a result of the delay, Hatry's Austin Friars Trust was in the market to borrow three months' money and, on 18 July 1929, Kleinworts agreed to lend £100,000 on the collateral of 25,000 7 per cent £1 AAMC preference shares, followed by a further loan of £55,000 on 7 August. The next day Hatry's Dundee Trust was in the market and Kleinworts lent it £30,000 on the collateral of 65,000 ordinary shares in AAMC. In fact, Hatry had been making the rounds of the City, desperately trying to raise money and turning to forgery to keep his companies afloat. Fraudulent scrip was printed and, together with genuine certificates, used as security for widespread borrowing. Thus some firms advanced money on good certificates whilst others, including Kleinworts, advanced on bad ones. With superb impudence Hatry even persuaded some lenders to give up perfectly good certificates in exchange for his newly printed bad paper. He was also busily engaged in a share support operation, with the number of shares purporting to change hands being inflated way beyond the number that really existed.

As rumours of bogus dealing thickened in a generally uneasy market, Hatry shares began to fall until they collapsed on 19 September. That afternoon Clarence Hatry and three of his associates met Lord Winchester in Room 80 of the Charing Cross Hotel. 'We have sent for you', said Hatry, 'to tell you we are all criminals.' On Winchester's advice they immediately gave themselves

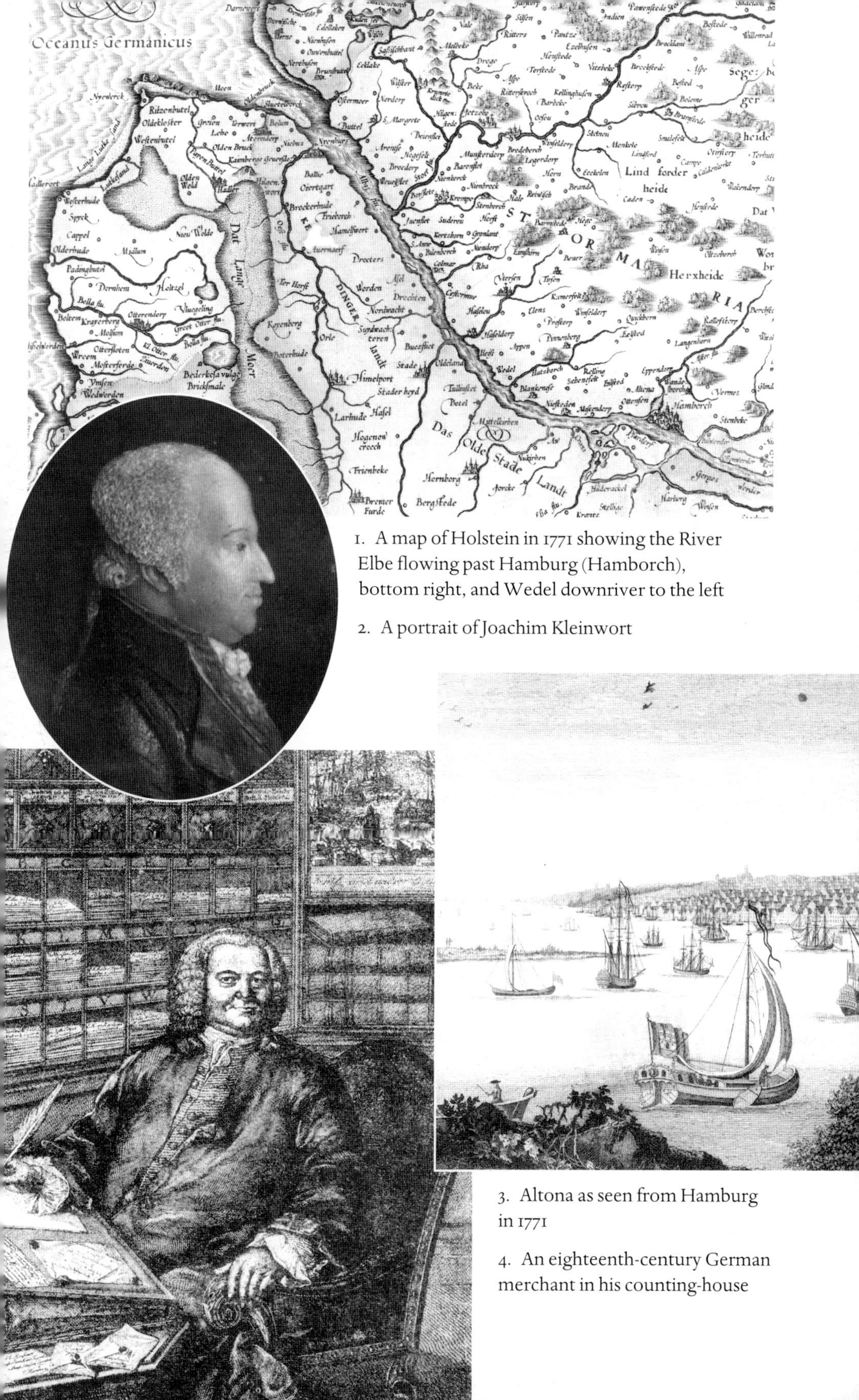

1. A map of Holstein in 1771 showing the River Elbe flowing past Hamburg (Hamborch), bottom right, and Wedel downriver to the left

2. A portrait of Joachim Kleinwort

3. Altona as seen from Hamburg in 1771

4. An eighteenth-century German merchant in his counting-house

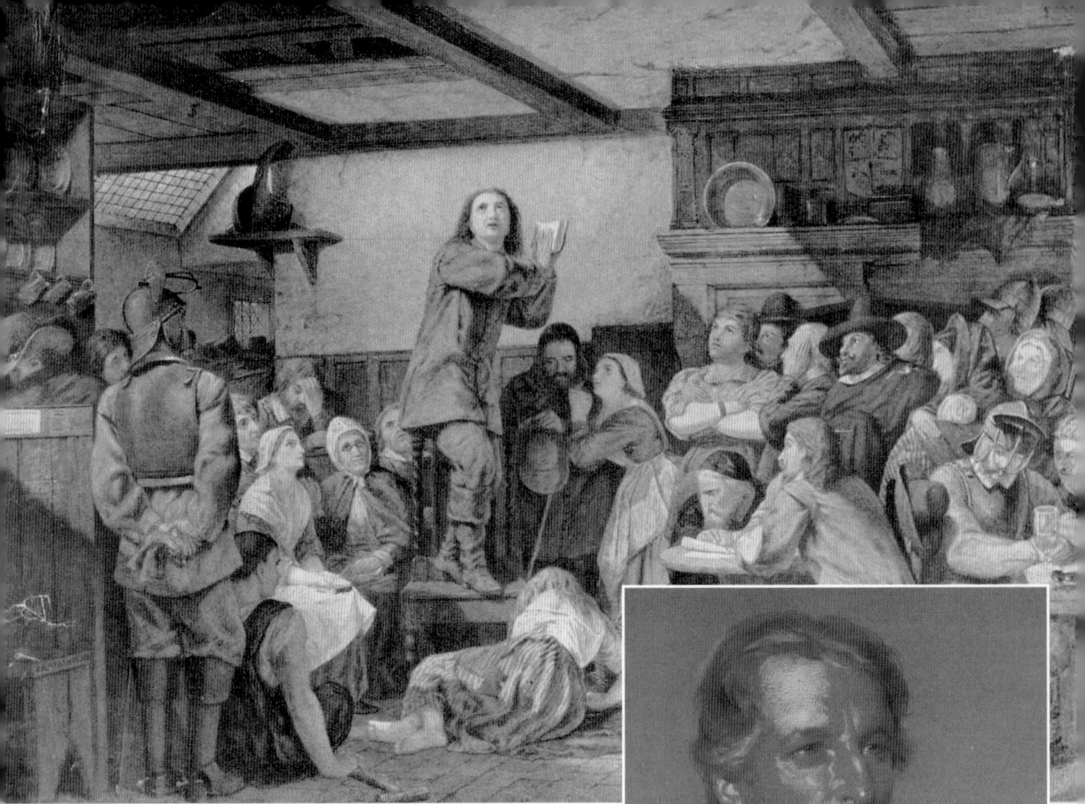

5. George Fox preaching at a Quaker meeting in 1647

6. John Wakefield, kinsman and business mentor of Robert Benson

7. Sarah Rathbone Benson, in Quaker cap

8. William Rathbone IV, partner and brother-in-law of Robert Benson, painted by J. Allen

9. 'A truly successful and honourable merchant': Robert Rathbone Benson, by George Richmond

10. James Cropper, the founding partner of Cropper, Benson

11. Cropper, Benson's the *Bengal*, by Robert Salmon. After the abolition of the East India Company's monopoly, she was the second ship to sail from Liverpool to India and, from Quaker pacifist sensibilities, carried wooden rather than real cannon to scare off enemy attack

Cropper Benson business interests

12. Incoming Black Baller passing The Battery, Liverpool in 1829. A black ball features on the ensign and on a sail of the Cropper, Benson ship in the centre of the picture

13. The Liverpool-Manchester Railway Line, 1831

Cuba as it was in Alexander Friedrich's day

14. A view of Havana, Cuba

15. Loading sugar at the dockside in Havana

16. Herman Greverus shortly before his retirement in 1855

17. Sophie Kleinwort (née Greverus) painted after her return from Cuba in 1855

18. No. 20 Fenchurch Street built for Drake, Kleinwort & Cohen by the architect Edward Ellis in 1863

Dated 22nd December 1857

Agreement
—of—
Copartnership
between
James Drake del Castillo, Alexr
Kleinwort and Edward Cohen Esqres
To commence and take place on and
after the 1st day of January 1858.

19. The Agreement of co-partnership between James Drake, Alexander Friedrich Kleinwort and Edward Cohen drawn up in 1858

20. Bills of exchange, the foundation of Kleinworts successful accepting business. These are examples of sixty-day bills drawn on Kleinwort & Cohen by Drake & Co.

The three partners
Clockwise from left:

21. Santiago Drake del Castillo

22. Alexander Friedrich Kleinwort before 1886

23. Portrait of Edward Cohen by R. E. Morrison, 1882

24. Robert Benson jnr. (1814–1875), the founder of Robert Benson & Co., chalk drawing by George Richmond in 1857

25. His wife Eleanor Benson (née Moorsom) also by George Richmond

26. Panic in the City in 1866: the Overend, Gurney Crash in which Bensons lost money

The children of Alexander Friedrich Kleinwort

27. Herman and Marguerite (neé Günther) Kleinwort shortly after their marriage in 1881

28. & 29. Alexander Kleinwort in 1894. His wife Etiennette (née Girard) as painted by Hacker in 1906

30. & 31. Robert Martin, who refused the partnership in Kleinworts offered to him after his marriage to the eldest Kleinwort daughter Wilhemina (Minnie) Martin

32. & 33. Carlo Andreae who started his own business after his marriage to Sophie, the younger Kleinwort daughter

Goldman Sachs & Co New York
Mr Goldman states personally 1898
Nov 1 The responsible capital
working in our business is
$1,600,000 — and outside of the business
the private property of the partners
is worth abt $[illegible] — making
a total of $[illegible] —
Mr Sachs states on 30 May 1901 Our
capital per last Bal sheet of 31 Dec
was $2,500,000 — and we have since
been doing exceedingly well
S. Sachs 16 June 07 We have made
$1,200,000 — that year and our
capital is now 4 1/2 millions
S. Sachs 16 April 08 Owing to the
fall in securities instead of
being able to say that we have
4 1/2 millions we [illegible]
750,000 $

34. The Andreae brothers as students, from the left: Herman, Edward (later Dr E. P.), Alexander, and Frank

35. Entries on Goldman Sachs & Co. in Alexander Kleinwort's little Black Book

36. The new junior partner. Herman A. Andreae at his desk in 1907

The First World War

37. A crowd awaiting news by the Stock Exchange, before it was closed on 31 July 1914

38. Robert (Bobbie) Martin in uniform

39. Herman Kleinwort's registration certificate, 1915

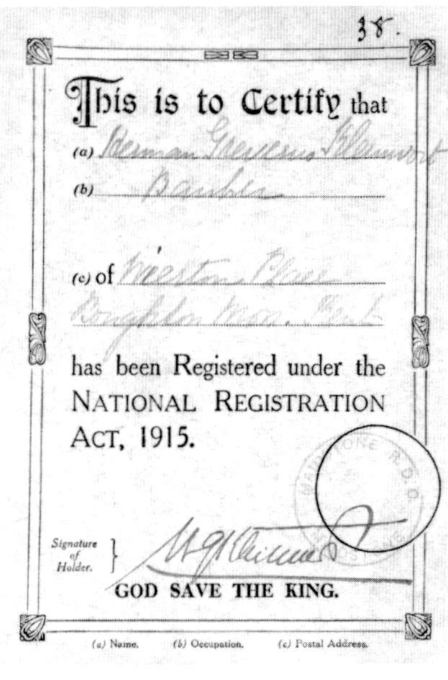

38.

This is to Certify that

(a) Herman Greverus Kleinwort

(b) Banker

(c) of Weston Place, Boughton Mon., Kent

has been Registered under the NATIONAL REGISTRATION ACT, 1915.

Signature of Holder. } H G Kleinwort

GOD SAVE THE KING.

(a) Name. (b) Occupation. (c) Postal Address.

40. The trio of Benson uncles who helped Robin and Con after the failure of Robert Benson & Co. in 1875. Clockwise from the left: Constantine Moorsom-Maude, William Benson and James Moorsom

41. Johnny Cross, before he founded Cross, Benson with Robin Benson in September 1875

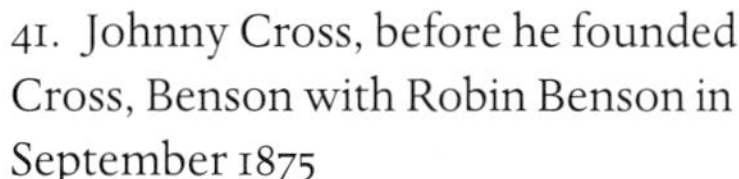

42. Robin Benson at the time of his marriage in 1887

43. An American Golden Spike Ceremony, like the Vuillard one which Robin attended with George Holford and Albert Grey in 1883

44. Evey Holford, photographed before her marriage to Robin Benson in 1887

45. George Holford in the 1880s

46. Dorchester House. The Grand Saloon, looking to the Drawing Room. Displayed in these rooms are: on the left,
The Abbé Scaglia by Van Dyke;
on the facing wall clockwise from the left,
Cosimo I. de'Medici by Bronzino
A Rehearsal by Schiavone
Eleanora da Toledo by Bronzino
Salome by Pordenone
Landscape by Richard Wilson
Tivoli by Gaspard Poussin
Martin Looten by Rembrandt;
through the doorway,
Madonna and Child after Andrea del Sarto
View of Dordrecht by Aelbert Cuyp

47. Emily Weston and Constantine Benson at the time of their marriage in 1880

48. The coming of the railway to a Mid-Western town in America in 1885

49. Herman and Marguerite Kleinwort with their seven daughters. From the left: Marieka, Sophie, Helen, Mrs Kleinwort, Marguerite, Alice; seated in front of Herman: Daisy and Lily

50. Sir Alexander and Lady Kleinwort with Ernest, on the far left, and Cyril, between them

51. Kleinwort Sons & Co. staff dinner at the Holborn Restaurant on 6 April 1923. The English and Accounts Department is seated at the first table with Cecil Elbra facing eighth from the right. The German Department takes up the whole of the second table with John Holm seated facing first on the right

52. José Mayorga, General Manager of Kleinworts

53. At the ledgers in the 1920s

54. Sir Alexander Kleinwort on the deck of a cross-channel steamer with the Prime Minister, David Lloyd George in 1921

56. Close-up of Herman Andreae at the helm of *Candida*

55. *Candida* at Cowes Week in 1930

The Bensons by John Singer Sargent

57. Robin (1850–1929) and Evey (1856–1943) and their sons, from the left: Guy (1888–1975), Rex (1889–1968) and Con (1895–1960)

58. The Benson and Holford family at Buckhurst Park. Guy Benson 'quite the young man in the City' had just entered Bensons.
The back row includes Robin Benson (3rd from left), Rex (3rd from right) and Guy (2nd from right). Seated in the middle row are from the left Lady Holford, Sir George Holford, Evey Benson and on the far right her sister Alice, Countess Grey. Seated in the front from the left are Con and Lindy Benson

59. H. A. Vernet, chairman of Bensons, at his desk in 1929

60. C. C. Hellings, the General Manager of Bensons

Bensons staff

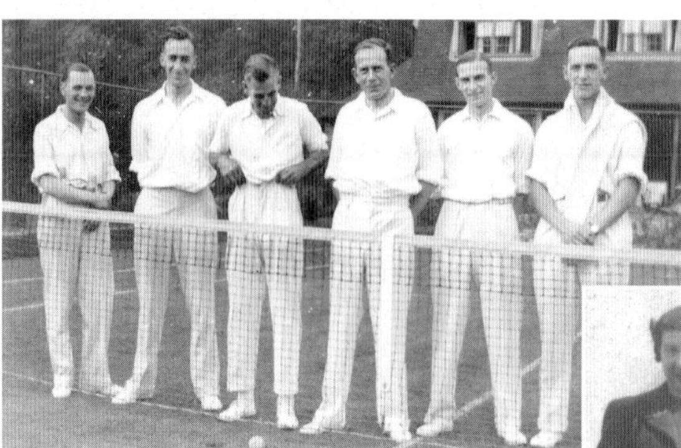

61. Tennis at Wooldridges. From the left: Robert Clifford, Joe Payne, Frank Wooldridge, Bill Hole, Victor Lewis, and Harry Purkington in 1931

62. Les Girls on the top of Gresham House in 1940. From the left: Floss Lincoln, Brownie, Elaine Jackson, and Poppy Hutchins

Kleinworts in the Second World War

63. Staff haymaking for Ernest Kleinwort at Heaselands in 1940

65. Herman K. (Sonny) Andreae in 1941

64. Staff forming a Home-Guard at Bolnore in 1940

66. Sir Rex Benson. Chairman of Bensons and Robert Benson Lonsdale 1936–1959

67. Leo Lonsdale. Chairman of Lonsdale Investment Trust 1947–1961

68. G. P. S. ('Phil') Macpherson. Chairman of Robert Benson Lonsdale 1959–1961

DATED 9th July 1947

LONSDALE INVESTMENT TRUST LIMITED

and

ROBERT BENSON AND COMPANY LIMITED

AMALGAMATION

Agreement

This Agreement is made the Ninth day of July One thousand nine hundred and forty seven BETWEEN LONSDALE INVESTMENT TRUST LIMITED (hereinafter called "the Vendor Company") of the one part and ROBERT BENSON AND COMPANY LIMITED (hereinafter called "the Transferee Company") of the other part

WHEREAS :

(A) THE Vendor Company is the beneficial owner of the whole of the issued share capital of the Transferee Company

(B) By an Extraordinary Resolution of the Transferee Company passed on the Eighth day of July One thousand nine hundred and forty seven (a copy of which Resolution is set out in the First Schedule hereto) the capital of the Transferee Company has been increased from Four hundred thousand pounds to Eight hundred thousand pounds by the creation of Four hundred thousand new Ordinary Shares of One pound each for the purpose of acquiring from the Vendor Company part of the undertaking of the Vendor Company on the terms of a draft agreement referred to in the said Extraordinary Resolution

69. The Amalgamation Agreement between Robert Benson & Co. and the Lonsdale Investment Trust in 1947

70. Staff Garden Party held at Leo Lonsdale's country house, Kingston Lisle Park. Leo Lonsdale is watching a race, with Con Benson on his right

71. The architects of the KB merger: Mark Turner and Cyril Kleinwort in 1961

Bensons & Kleinworts Merge to Form £60m. Banking Group

72. Headline announcing the KB merger in 1960

KLEINWORT, BENSON LIMITED

Consolidated Balance Sheet as at 31st December 1961

LIABILITIES	£
Share Capital—	
Authorised and Issued—	
5,000,000 Shares of £1 each, fully paid	5,000,000
Share Premium Account	500,000
General Reserve	1,500,000
	7,000,000
Current, Deposit, and other Accounts—	
Including Reserves for Future Income Tax and Contingencies and Balance of Profit and Loss Account	41,992,553
Dividend to Parent Company	336,875
Acceptances on behalf of Customers	15,964,618
	£65,294,046

ASSETS		£
Current Assets—		
Money at Call and Short Notice, Cash at Bank and in hand and Balances with Bankers Abroad		15,643,362
Bills Discounted		1,131,318
Advances to Customers and Other Accounts		22,152,118
Investments, at or under cost—		
Quoted	£8,565,811	
Unquoted	1,466,711	
		10,032,522
		48,959,320
The market value of Quoted Investments was greater than the stated Book Value. In the opinion of the Directors the Unquoted Investments had in the aggregate a value not less than the amount at which they are stated.		
Liability of Customers for Acceptances		15,964,618
Fixed Assets—		
Freehold Premises, at cost, *less* amounts written off		370,108
		£65,294,046

Consolidated Profit and Loss Account for the year ended 31st December 1961

	£	£
NET PROFIT FOR THE YEAR		600,506
After providing for Taxation, and after appropriation to reserve for contingencies.		
Add: Balance brought forward—		
Kleinwort, Benson Limited	36,010	
Subsidiaries consolidated	61,756	
		97,766
		698,272
Deduct: Transfer to General Reserve	250,000	
Provision for Dividend to Parent Company *less* Income Tax	336,875	
		586,875
BALANCES CARRIED FORWARD—		
Kleinwort, Benson Limited	41,729	
Subsidiaries consolidated	69,668	
		£111,397

73. KB Ltd.'s balance sheet as at 31 December 1961

74. The bicycling chairman: Ernest Kleinwort, the first chairman of KB Ltd., with commissionaire H. F. Stedman in 1966

75. Rex Benson with his son David in 1959, seated on a less arduous form of transport

76. Ernest Kleinwort and his son Kenneth

77. Cyril Kleinwort with his youngest daughter Susanna in 1973

78. The memory of the firm: Floss Lincoln and her portrait gallery at Aldermanbury House in 1965

79. The KBL tea ladies. Tea was wheeled to all members of staff twice a day until 1984 when machines took over

80. Chairmen of the KB Group

Robert (Bobby) Henderson, 1974–89

David Peake, 1988–93

81. Chairmen of KB Ltd

Gerald Thompson, 1971–3

Michael Hawkes, 1984–7

82. The foreign exchange dealing room in 1969

83. The dealing floor at the time of the Big Bang in 1986

84. The KB Group Board of Directors in 1994. Back row, from the left: Sir Michael Jenkins, Robert Jeens, Sir Nicholas Redmayne, Robert Harley, Colin Maltby, David Wake-Walker, Brian Manning, Bay Green; front row, from the left: Lord Rockley (chairman), Robin Fox, Simon Robertson, and David Clementi. (Tim Barker was absent)

85. The non-executive directors of the KB Group in 1994. From the left: David Peake, David Benson, Sir Kenneth Kleinwort, Ian Steers, Jaime Carvajal, Jeremy Lancaster, Takeshi Ohta, Sir Philip Haddon-Cave

86. Announcing the Dresdner acquisition of Kleinwort Benson on 26 June 1995: Lord Rockley, chairman of the KB Group 1993–6, and Jürgen Sarrazin, chairman of Dresdner Bank

up to the City of London police and were remanded for a week, bail having been refused owing to the seriousness of the crime. At their own expense they were conveyed by taxi cab from the court to Brixton Prison.

The Hatry crash quickly rebounded through the banking halls of the City. Only after three months unravelling the tangle of honest and fraudulent dealings on the Stock Exchange did Kleinworts learn the total of the losses they had incurred on their loans and holdings of Hatry Co. shares. It was in the region of £700,000 [£20.5m.]. Their association with Hatry proved even more expensive when they had to sue AAMC for damages. AAMC refused to issue Kleinworts with share certificates to honour the certified transfers of shares issued as security by their registrars, Secretarial Services Ltd., also a Hatry concern. AAMC argued that the certified transfers covered shares which either did not exist or were held by persons other than the transferors named. They could not be held responsible for the fraudulent acts of the registrars and the Hatry directors. Although Kleinworts were awarded damages of £72,000 with costs in the High Court in November 1932, the judge overturned the decision on appeal.

This was a serious case both for the law and for the City. As a matter of principle Kleinworts took the case to the House of Lords. There, in February 1934, the decision once more went against them. Apart from the original losses and the lawyers' expenses incurred during the years of litigation, the ruling left them and the City uneasy. A certified transfer had traditionally been regarded as an indisputable obligation of the company involved, either to return the old certificates if the shares were not passed for transfer or to produce in due course a new certificate. It was never conceived that a company was not entirely responsible for their employee or agent, yet this was the effect of the Lords' judgement.[39]

The Hatry failure had further serious repercussions. Within weeks the City's struggle to withstand a financial slump was defeated by events in America, where rising prices and increased business activity over seven years had culminated in a period of wild speculation earlier in 1929. On the New York Stock Exchange margin requirements dropped to only 10 per cent, thereby attracting even more gamblers. According to Cecil Elbra, 'There was however a sense of brooding unease stalking the places where men foregather and nowhere was this more apparent than in banking parlours.' The partners were sufficiently uneasy to consider selling most of their large holdings in American securities. Herman A. went off to New York in the late summer in order to liquidate their position.

This had unfortunate consequences for, as Cecil Elbra wrote, 'predictions of impending disaster were lacking; people did not want to believe that the gambling frenzy then infecting all classes of society was anything else but a healthy sign of man's progressiveness'. Herman A. was caught up in the heady 'buy, buy, buy' atmosphere, swept away by the overwhelming feeling, especially in Wall Street, of super-optimism. Instead of selling, he bought. 'His speculative side misfired' and he returned with a message of complete faith in the United States market. Alexander, always the more prudent and less speculative of the two, did not buy any more shares but, largely because of his nephew's optimism, neither did he sell. When the Wall Street crash came on 'Black Thursday', 24 October 1929, the partners' exposure was larger than ever. They were caught off-guard, Alexander even commenting, 'I see they're having a little trouble in New York. Of course, it won't affect us.'[40]

This was, of course, exactly what it did. In terms of immediate business Kleinworts were not badly wounded by the crash, for American accounts were no longer the mainstay of the bank's operation, and had not been since before the war. Commission earnings simply continued their slide, down from £13,000 in 1928 to £11,000 [£340,000] in 1930.

The partners' personal holdings, in contrast, suffered severe damage. They had very large American portfolios whose value now plummeted; the Moonhill Trust, which held the Kleinwort family's American shares, halved in value from £4.1m. to £2.1m. [£65.1m.] almost overnight. Although the extent of the damage to future business was not immediately apparent, financial paralysis inexorably crept over the City. The world had relied for too long on the readiness of America to lend unlimited money and buy their goods. American lenders now called in their debts and investment ground to a halt. As economic conditions worsened around the world, unemployment in Britain soared, as exporters watched their markets dwindle away and the economic freeze of the 1930s began to grip, and retrenchment became the order of the day. Ernest and Cyril had been in the middle of their world tour at the time of the Wall Street Crash. They returned to No. 20 in 1930 and in the following year saw all the firm's capital locked up. This unfortunate state of affairs was caused by the German Banking crisis, which almost destroyed Kleinwort, Sons & Co.[41]

The crisis began on 11 May 1931 when the Creditanstalt Bankverein, Austria's principal bank, collapsed. Amongst other debts it owed £10,587 [£350,000] to Kleinworts. The Austrian government's imposition of exchange controls trapped £300m. worth of short-term loans in Austria. The fear engendered by these events caused Hungary to follow suit. Foreign creditors started to call in their loans and the run spread to Germany, which on 5 June declared herself unable to pay reparations. Although President Hoover attempted to ease the financial pressure on Germany by declaring on 20 June a one-year moratorium upon the repayment of all First World War intergovernmental debt, this had little effect on international confidence.

The situation remained grave enough for a group of leading London bankers to appoint on 10 July a nine-member Joint Committee to represent the Accepting Houses Committee and the British Bankers Association in discussions with the Bank of England and the Treasury about the crisis. Ernest represented Kleinworts on the Committee, a function that Herman A. had performed in similar circumstances in August 1914. The Joint Committee proceeded to discuss calling in German credits with the governor of the Bank of England. He strongly advised against it, stating that British banks would be unable to liquidate German short-term debt entirely; instead, they should try to restore confidence in Germany. 'I say Germany is a good bet in the long run and needs help and comfort rather than worrying,' Norman had written in his diary just before the crisis began. Thus, while banks of other nations were scrambling to recall their loans, City banks such as Kleinworts and Schröders made no attempt to withdraw their loans and credits. Even when on 13 July one of Germany's largest commercial banks, the Darmstädter und Nationalbank, closed its doors leaving the entire German banking system near to collapse, City banks stolidly held to the agreed policy.[42]

Yet they were in a perilous state. Kleinworts was but one of the many banks which had invested heavily in German municipal and commercial undertakings. It had been a most profitable exercise, borrowing in Paris at cheap short-term rates of 2 per cent and lending to Germany at long-term rates as high as 8 per cent. Now alarmed French bankers called back their loans. Even more perilous was the declaration of a suspension of payments in Germany whereby the withdrawal of foreign deposits was also banned with short-term credits frozen. This created a furore in London where City merchant banks were owed some £64m. [£2.1bn.]. For the first time in their history Kleinworts faced insolvency. Out of their entire outstanding acceptances, one-third (£5.8m.) were German. An additional £3.5m. of funds were on loan or deposited in Germany with a further £2.7m. of municipal loans. All were now frozen.

The deliberations of the London Conference, a gathering of world leaders urgently assembled by the Foreign Office in the middle of July, produced no solution. Indeed, the statesmen proposed that the bankers in the form of the Joint Committee resolve the German problem. A German subcommittee under the chairmanship of Frank Tiarks of Schröders was entrusted with the task of negotiating an agreement between the short-term creditors and their German debtors. The outcome was the first *Stillehalter* or Standstill Agreement of 19 August 1931, whereby credits to Germany were frozen but with interest guaranteed. The agreement was designed to last six months, by which time it was hoped that the German economy would recover. In the event it had to be renewed annually until 1939; and it would not be until a further twelve years had elapsed that the Joint Committee could conclude that almost all of the Standstill debts had been repaid.

Kleinworts therefore found themselves with defaulting debtors owing them £12m. [£397m.], nearly four times the partners' capital. A Bank of England report revealed that six accepting houses—Kleinworts, Schröders, Huths, Japhets, Goschen & Cunliffe, and Arbuthnot Latham—were technically insolvent owing to their standstill debts. None could look for recovery through increased trading revenue. Kleinworts acceptance business, which had averaged £16.2m. over 1929–31 tumbled to £12.1m. by the end of 1931 and reached a low of £8.9m. in 1933. They were not alone in this sea of disaster. Schröders' acceptances fell from £12.5m. in 1929 to £3.5m. by 1932; Hambros' fell less sharply from £12.25m. to £7.25m., owing to their smaller German exposure; Barings' business almost disappeared, from £6.5m. to £1m., whilst Lazards had to be rescued by the Bank of England in July 1931, and needed another £2m. the following year. A senior Lazards partner wrote to express his regret 'that circumstances led us to request facilities at so inconvenient a time'.[43]

Kleinworts, too, had no alternative but to seek outside support. The partners asked their clearing bankers, Westminster Bank, for a substantial overdraft facility to see them through. Although Kleinworts were an old and valued client, the Westminster was also helping other accepting houses, including Schröders, whose debt was the second largest at £4.5m., Hambros, Brandts, and Goschens, as well as innumerable businesses, through the crisis. Terms were perforce severe: £1m. was allowed on the security of gilt-edged securities to be lodged with the Westminster with a further £2.5m. secured on the partners' outside assets.

The partners, however, balked at having to pledge their own assets and looked to the Bank of England to guarantee their overdraft. This it would not do. Norman did not regard the issue as one of national importance, nor did he believe that Kleinworts would, in fact, fail and bring disrepute to the good name of the City. Lazards had been in such difficulty that he had been forced to intervene to save them but Kleinworts were not in this position and therefore he deemed their difficulty a private matter between themselves and the Westminster Bank. Struggling as they were for survival, the partners were upset by this decision. That they did indeed have grounds for concern is evident from the fact that they took up the entire overdraft facility of £3.5m. on the Westminster's terms. A Bank of England report on the situation of the acceptance houses noted that, 'with the exception of Kleinworts, the position of all seems not unsatisfactory, none of them having taken exceptional facilities'.[44]

As a miasma of depression engulfed the globe, governments resorted to unorthodox measures to combat the economic uncertainties of the 1930s. Kleinworts resorted to a policy of thrift and austerity. They proceeded to reduce the level of their acceptance commitments; realize their more liquid assets in order to reduce their overdraft—which they cleared by September 1932—and the number of their Standstill Bills in the discount market; and authorize a regime of austerity at No. 20.

Spicer & Pegler, the bank's accountants, had advised the partners that Kleinworts were overstaffed and that costs must be cut by sacking staff surplus to requirements. This was the first time in the history of the firm that such an exercise had even been considered, let alone implemented. The boom of the early 1920s, combined with the large amount of German banking business, had more than doubled the staff to just under 400. Job security until retirement had been a uniformly recognized characteristic of employment in merchant banks. With evident reluctance Alexander asked José Mayorga to review the position of every member of staff, with a view to at least half leaving the bank.

The gravity of the situation had already been brought home to the staff when the half-a-crown-a-week Christmas bonus was discontinued. As people sat idling time away in the once bustling German Department and longer coffee breaks were taken in the nearby Lyons / ABC, Mayorga devised certain guidelines for his review. There should be no favouritism, last in would be first out unless someone had to be retained to do a vital job, in which case they would have to take a substantial drop in salary. Walter Michaelis, who was one of the few to survive in the German Department, had his salary cut by £100. Mayorga's son Pepe recalls that 'Father suffered terribly in trying to get rid of people who he'd been working with for years and years.'

Every Friday approximately twelve people were dismissed, until the total number of staff fell to 175. Usually either Mr Saager, who was about to retire himself, or Mr Harmon, the new staff manager, would send for one of the commissionaires. Mr Judd remembers that as he came out of Harmon's office the eyes of the staff 'used to follow me round as though everybody thought, "is it me or is it him or who?"' They knew the commissionaire's request, 'The staff manager would like to see you', was the fatal first step to being discharged. With redundancy having become a more commonplace experience today, it is difficult to imagine the absolute terror felt by the people who worked at Kleinworts, indeed at any City firm during the early 1930s. At Schröders, for instance, staff numbers fell from 276 to 157 in 1930–32. There were no pensions or redundancy compensation, nor any long-term unemployment dole to cushion the blow—only one month's salary and few if any jobs to be found elsewhere. It was a most distressing period, one that marked those who lived through it. The cautious, ultra-conservative bank worker of the 1950s more often than not had been a young out-of-work bank clerk in the 1930s. He abhorred risk-taking in case it threatened his job security.[45]

The atmosphere in the City was extremely gloomy and there was relatively limited business activity. Given the contraction in staff, Cecil Elbra's initiative to introduce mechanization into the bank was considered timely and won the full support of the younger partners. Whereas most City offices used typewriters by 1914 if not by 1890, the majority of Kleinworts' correspondence had been written by hand until 1925. Copies were made by a process of damp cloths, which were placed with the letters between two pieces of cardboard and put into a hand operated press. If the cloths were made too wet, the ink ran and smudged the letter, rendering it illegible.

Herman A.'s letters, however, had been the first to be typewritten in about 1910. Ernest Pudney could remember seeing the typing machine operated by the firm's first female typist Gracie Munroe—but her desk had to be surrounded by a screen and tucked away in a remote corner; Alexander would agree to her employment only if he neither saw nor heard her. Cecil Elbra introduced many more of these machines so that each department contained one, the only hiring of staff in the early 1930s being for typists. Dorothy Gunn, who had been made redundant from Schröders in 1931, joined Kleinworts as a typist two years later. The majority of her correspondence was in German and French, which she bashed out on the enormous old Underwood machines—'heavy as lead, and when I had finished a day's hard banging on them all the veins were standing out on the backs of my hands. Oh, it was hard going.' Accounts were also done on new costing machines, 'huge machines like locomotives which made a great noise—clank crank!' The noise of these machines echoed round the emptiness of recently vacated stools and desks in the once thriving offices of No. 20.[46]

There were changes, too, at the partnership level. It was Herman A. who dealt with the executive decisions on a daily basis, although no major policy decision was made without Alexander's knowledge and agreement. The only evidence of his 77 years was a proclivity for catnaps. He remained a man of extreme punctuality. People in the nearby village of Cuckfield could set their clocks by his departure for London, when his Bentley roared through in the early morning, while the policeman on traffic duty on London Bridge would say 'Quarter past three' as his car passed on the return journey. His passion for speed and a smooth drive continued unabated.

The precision with which he ordered his life, so at variance with his student days, remained undisturbed. On his arrival at Bolnore, his first act was to plunge his flowing white beard into a basin full of lather, 'brushing it forward all covered with foam'. In the presence of visiting grandchildren he would chant, 'There was an old man with a beard who said it is just as I feared . . .' Then, stopping only to collect a walking-stick, he went straight outside for a three- or four-mile walk on the estate and local roads. The stick was used not as a walking aid but as an indicator; he would flourish it to identify a tree or shrub of especial interest. Otherwise he carried it with one gloved hand above the other, straight up the middle of his back. His granddaughter retains a mental picture of his 'figure seen from the back as we capered along behind: trilby hat, curly white hair, long, dark coat and body braced by this vertical walking stick, held crook above the shoulder blades.' It was during one of these walks down a country lane that he was knocked into a ditch close to the entrance to Heaselands by a cyclist who did not bother to stop. Alexander developed pneumonia and, according to Ernest, was prescribed the wrong drugs. He died on 8 June 1935. It was a sad, unnecessary ending for this distinguished man whose banking career spanned fifty years.[47]

Described as the epitome of the London accepting banker and one of the great Edwardian private bankers, he was a man of impressive figure and strong character. Never part of the establishment, he was none the less a powerful force in the City. By 1935 he took a back seat but, Pepe Mayorga was told by his father, 'if he spoke anywhere to people in the City, or anywhere else, he was always treated with the greatest respect'. He moved confidently through the banking world, having acquired, through experience and intellect, a wisdom about business. He had, nevertheless, made mistakes which his father might well have avoided.

On the business side, he had ignored the warning signs in both Germany and America, allowing too large a proportion of the bank's business to be tied up in Germany, so that when disaster struck a substantial part of the bank's capital was locked up. Against that, he did not allow the firm to lend indiscriminately to German clients. Throughout the 1920s and 1930s the partners' policy was one of cautious expansion in the face of conflicting and volatile conditions. While General Renner, one of Herman's sons-in-law, 'had been predicting death and destruction for a long time', clients such as the Devisenbeschaffungsstelle GMbH were distinctly optimistic. Herman A. told Alexander in 1928, 'Anyway it is best to be on the safe side and I agree that we ought to be very chary regarding the granting of credits. As you know, so far we have only done so in cases where we have had direct application from A1 concerns.' Herman A. added that he believed that Satzger was right when he said the German banks were 'themselves much too scared after their previous experiences' to overextend.

Where Alexander might have acted differently was in his failure to rein in some of his nephew's more impulsive speculations and venture capital operations. Herman A. was remembered by José Mayorga as an extremely effective and competent banker, 'clever and able' although 'he made mistakes which cost him dearly'; as they did Alexander in the Wall Street Crash. Alexander had always believed that risk-taking was part of his business. The losses sustained in these areas in the 1920s would have been easily recoverable but for the German debt. At the time of his death Alexander had seen the end of his bank's reign as the leading accepting house, as Kleinworts' position at the top of the business league table was toppled. Hambros, Barings, and Morgan Grenfell, whose balance sheets were not hampered by German debts, were, in contrast, expanding their businesses.[48]

Alexander nevertheless left estate officially valued at £616,328 [£21m.] in his will. After bequests to Etiennette, his mistress Countess Dachkoff, and his daughter Henrietta, he left his property equally to Ernest and Cyril. Neither Louise nor his son Alexander were mentioned in his will, a basic provision having been made for them long before. The total value of his assets, including those made over in the Kleinwort, Sons & Co. balance sheet, was, however, far, far higher. In 1935 it exceeded £6m. [£204.8m.]. On the personal side, his break with his brother Herman was a sorrow to both sides of the family. Shortly before his death, Alexander had attended the funeral of his sister-in-law, Marguerite. He had tried to patch up matters. 'Look, let bygones be bygones,' he is reported to have suggested to his brother. But Herman would neither forgive nor forget and the two branches of the family continued to be estranged on Alexander's death.[49]

Alexander's death not only occurred at an unfortunate time for the firm in terms of the standstill debts, but it also had the unfortunate effect of immediately reopening the old partnership wounds: the level of participation in the firm's profits and losses, and Herman Kleinwort's position within the partnership. Herman refused to accept Spicer & Pegler's low valuation of the German debts in case it set a precedent for when his share and interest had to be ascertained. The valuation was vital to the firm, because if the German debts were taken as having a face value of £7.3m., then Alexander's proportionate share was £85,000; whereas if Spicer & Pegler's much lower valuation was accepted, then Alexander's estate would become insolvent. 'The position indeed is a most extraordinary one', declared Counsel. 'His estate is shown as indebted to the firm in a sum of over £794,000 which exceeds the whole of his estate by over £110,000. On this footing therefore his estate would get nothing from the firm but the firm would take his whole outside estate and even then leave a deficiency of over £110,000. His estate therefore would be wiped out.'

Spicer's valuation of the German losses at £3,297,945 was divisible as follows:

Herman Kleinwort	40%	£1,319,178
Alexander Kleinwort	26⅔%	879,452
Herman Andreae	20%	659,589
Ernest and Cyril Kleinwort	13⅓%	439,726

Although Ernest and Cyril bore the smallest proportion of these losses, the sudden death of their father was disastrous in terms of their interest in the bank. It remained a minority one *vis-à-vis* Uncle Herman, whose share of the profits rose from 30 per cent to – 40 10⁄11 per cent. Furthermore they received no share in the management remuneration, since their father's 12½ per cent devolved upon Herman A. The realization of their position gave them in Ernest's words 'a serious shock'. They felt, Ernest said, that a strict application of the Partnership Deed was unjust to them, their father's heirs, who would 'be providing about ½ of the firm's total responsibility and ⅔ of the active personnel'. Surely they were entitled to a far greater share.

They, therefore, pressed their senior partners for a readjustment. 'We suggest', Ernest wrote to Herman A., 'that we simply take over the Pater's participation as it was.' Whilst this would remove a significant slice of profit participation and management remuneration from the two Hermans, the Kleinwort boys dangled a large carrot before them in the form of the German losses which they would also take over. In this way, as Ernest put it, 'All difficulties in agreeing a valuation of the German and other assets would be avoided.' After considerable discussion, the two Hermans accepted this suggestion; they were, Spicer noted, not 'wholly activated by philanthropic motives' since, with 'vast' commitments in Germany, losses rather than profits 'loomed in the background'. Thus although the German debts were calamitous for the firm and the senior partners, in fact but for them, Ernest and Cyril would only have possessed a minority participation in the family bank. As it was, they consolidated their position as proprietors with the majority stake, almost at one stroke.[50]

The position of executive senior partner none the less devolved upon Herman A. as a matter of course. He was far more experienced and obviously senior to his two cousins, who were then aged 34 and 30 respectively. Although the 1930s were not much of a money-making period, when the market did experience its first rise in 1935 the partners' large private shareholdings quickly began to recover as the majority were in good companies, and they began to feel more bullish about future business.

It was in 1936, the first year of Herman A.'s reign as senior partner, that Kleinworts was enmeshed in a net of intrigue and Buchan-like exploits due to its financial involvement with the Nationalist side during the Spanish Civil War.

Kleinworts had maintained a strong presence in Spain from the days of Drake, Kleinwort & Cohen. In the 1920s and 1930s, Señor Brugada acted as their Spanish agent, although Mayorga was the force behind increasing their business, further enhanced at partner level by Herman A. as he regularly entertained King Alfonso XIII of Spain and other Spanish dignitaries at Cowes on his yacht *Candida*. After the monarchy was overthrown by a Republican–Socialist coalition in November 1931, Kleinworts' foreign exchange business had increased dramatically.

The advent of a left-wing government had put the peseta under further pressure on the foreign exchange markets. Kleinworts' reputation in Spain and their strong presence in these markets led the Spanish Government to ask the firm to act on their behalf on the European foreign exchanges. The Minister of Finance, Indalecio Prieto, personally gave Mayorga the mandate to protect the peseta and the two of them became good friends in the process.

In the course of his frequent visits to Madrid, Mayorga also acted for another client, Juan March, whose situation was somewhat unusual for a Kleinwort customer. At that time he was incarcerated in prison in Madrid as a symbol of the wicked monarchist past. Although inconvenient, it was not an uncomfortable stay; he had his own suite of rooms, his secretaries and an excellent table at which to entertain a stream of visitors. In the unstable political climate produced by the Government's radicalism, Mayorga advised March to remove his wealth abroad for safety. According to Pepe Mayorga, far from speculating against the peseta to sabotage the Republican government as was later claimed, his father had devised a scheme whereby March's funds were used with the knowledge of the Bank of Spain to support the peseta, thereby enabling March to place part of his fortune abroad.

Juan March became Kleinworts' largest Spanish client. He was a charismatic financier who had been born in 1880 on the island of Majorca, for centuries a centre of piracy and privateering, and later smuggling. The duty levied on imported tobacco was exorbitant and corruption rife, so that the monopoly-controlled tobacco trade was universally unpopular. The Spanish authorities, like their Havana counterparts in the days when Alexander Kleinwort avoided excise duty by smuggling in shirts, adopted a lax attitude towards tobacco smuggling. It was therefore 'viewed with sympathy', as a Spanish newspaper observed in 1916, 'It is a protest against an odious monopoly.'

Juan March lost little time in organizing his own highly profitable form of protest. He started out as a messenger boy in the offices of a Majorcan businessman but quickly began to trade on his own account in tobacco and land. His objective was the dominance of the tobacco trade, which should have been impregnable, given the offical monopolies.

According to Pepe Mayorga, March was 'an irresistible man if he wanted to get something. Absolutely irresistible.' His genius was to combine an outstanding mathematical ability with ferocious powers of concentration. As March later admitted to the Cortes, the Spanish Parliament, to deny that he had 'dealt more or less indirectly in contraband' would be 'puerile'. His achievement was to turn the tobacco-smuggling trade into what a Spanish Finance Minister termed, with grudging respect, a 'modern, technical operation'. After gaining a foothold in North Africa in 1906 with the purchase of an Algerian tobacco factory, his business expanded dramatically when he won the tobacco monopoly in French Morocco. In 1910, the first year under his direction, it earned him £1m.

By the following year, Spanish duty revenue had decreased so precipitously owing to March's operation that the Spanish authorities decided it would be far better to have him on their side. Accordingly they granted him the tobacco monopoly for Spanish Morocco and North Africa. By the time he and his bank, Banc March in Palma, became Kleinwort clients in the 1920s, March's personal fortune was estimated to be some 20–30m. pesetas ($4–6m.). When March needed to raise £70m. to buy the Trans-Mediterranean Co., a maritime shipping company then based in Madrid, he applied to Kleinworts for the credit. Mayorga had no hesitation in granting him the credit with which to add shipping to his empire.

March was released from prison by the 1933–6 right-wing coalition Government, under which Spain was gradually sliding into violent anarchy; a situation exacerbated by the general election of February 1936, in which the Popular Front, a coalition of left wing parties, had gained a majority. Opposing right-wing factions coalesced behind a nationalist group of plotting generals to overthrow the Government.

March was a fervent supporter of the Nationalist side led by General Francisco Franco, in their fight to overthrow the Spanish Government. He became their main source of finance during the Civil War and since March's principal financial adviser had long been José Mayorga, March naturally turned to him whenever he needed to arrange financial transactions in support of Franco. It was in keeping with his character that such business transactions were conducted, more often than not, in a somewhat unorthodox manner.

Thus, acting for their client Juan March, Kleinworts carried out a number of large transactions during 1936. In March 1936, Kleinworts contracted to supply £500,000 worth of credit to the Nationalists. They increased the credit line to £800,000 in August and raised it again in December 1936 to £942,000 [£31m.]. The guarantor was Juan March who, despite his sympathies, drove a hard bargain when it came to interest and repayment conditions, which greatly annoyed the generals.

After the outbreak of the Civil War in July 1936, March began to deposit staggering amounts of bullion in the Bank of Italy to finance Italian involvement in the war and the supply of transport to Spain, again arranged by Kleinworts. Leonard Steljes, a manager in the Foreign Exchange Department, had built up Kleinworts' bullion business to take advantage of the 'sovereign boom' after Britain abandoned the Gold Standard. India, which had previously hoarded her bullion, disgorged £173m. of gold in 3½ years to March 1935. The scale was such as to help Britain recover financially and boost the business activity of firms such as Kleinworts. Their main suppliers were a Bombay firm of bullion brokers, Premchand Roychand, with whom Steljes established joint arbitrage accounts. Herbert Heys remembered when there were 'sufficient gold ingots on the floor in the strong room to say you could walk on a path of gold'. If Kleinworts were dealing for March they were certainly moving gigantic quantities, for records show that he deposited 49½ metric tons on 3 September (in 1936 1 metric ton was $1,235,000), followed by 72 metric tons on 9 September in Italy. Such was March's financial power that he could make gold deposits greater than the gold reserves of many countries. In the depressed trading conditions of the 1930s, the March account was an important one for Kleinworts to have.

General Franco, who led the rising to seize command of the élite Spanish Army of Africa in Morocco, had, however, been banished to the Canaries by the Government. The only means of escape was by airlift, but there were no reliable civil aircraft to be had in Spain. The conspirators—in the person of Marqués Luca de Teña, proprietor of the newspaper *ABC*—turned to March for a solution. March, then in Biarritz, immediately asked Kleinworts to make funds from his sterling account available to the *ABC*.

José Mayorga had not intended to go into No. 20 that particular Saturday but his friend Luis Bolín, the well-known London correspondent of ABC, had sent a message to say that he urgently needed to collect certain funds from Kleinworts. Mayorga went to the bank and handed over £10,000 in cash to Luis Bolín and Juan de la Cierva, the inventor of the helicopter. Cierva had been asked to buy a plane capable of travelling all the way to Las Palmas, then at least a three-day trip. Cierva chose a de Havilland, but it ran out of petrol and had to make a forced landing in France. The authorities, suspicious of the pilot's lack of papers and destination, grounded the aircraft.

On the Monday morning Luis Bolín was back at No. 20 for another £10,000 plus some extra to cover the purchase of two gasoline tanks to attach to the wings of the replacement aircraft. This time Cierva chose a Dragon Rapide, a transport bomber, piloted by an Englishman, Captain Bebb, who believed he was being asked to ferry a 'Rif chieftain to a revolution'. Douglas Jerrold, the sympathetic chairman of publishers Eyre & Spottiswoode, had also procured three innocent passengers to accompany Luis Bolín and provide an air of normality to the venture.

The outcome of this journey has been immortalized on film and the aeroplane rests in a museum in Spain. Bebb reached Las Palmas safely despite losing his radio operator, dead drunk in the kasbah at Casablanca. Franco crossed from Tenerife to Las Palmas and was flown by Bebb up through Morocco to arrive at Tetuan, almost opposite Gibraltar, on 18 July. That same day rebel generals marched on Madrid, but were held at bay by armed factory workers loyal to the Republican Government, and both sides dug themselves in for a long and bloody war.

The Spanish Civil War was transformed into an international issue by the participation of Fascist Italy and Nazi Germany on the Nationalist side, and of Soviet Russia on the Republican side, despite being signatories along with neutral France and Britain to a non-intervention agreement. It was March who ensured Italian intervention. At the start of the war many of the garrisons had received the signal to rebel but had dithered, waiting for others to act. They were now held by government forces, mainly the armed populace. Franco's loyal army of Africa was unable to relieve them because it was marooned in Morocco; Government warships standing by near Gibraltar put to sea each time troop ships were spotted trying to leave Morocco. The only way troops could reach mainland Spain was by air.

The exiled King of Spain, then in Rome, was asked to approach the Italian Foreign Minister, Count Ciano, with an order for twelve combat aircraft for shipment to North Africa. Since most of Spain was still in Government hands, the Italian Government did not have great confidence in the Nationalists and insisted upon payment in advance by an irrevocable letter of credit drawn on London. The Nationalist side was so desperate for funds that General Jordana called together loyal heads of Spanish banks and Juan March, and then locked them into a room with the words, 'No one is coming out of here until I have the money.' March was the only one with the foreign assets and credit immediately available in London. He asked Kleinworts to advance about £10m. to the Nationalists. The purchase of the twelve planes went ahead, although only six arrived on schedule in Spanish Morocco, the remainder having landed in French Morocco where they were detained by the authorities. In terms of air support, March eventually simplified the further purchase of Italian planes by buying control of the manufacturers of the aircraft, the Savoia Co.

During another Nationalist cash crisis, No. 20 bore closer resemblance to an up-market pawn shop than a merchant bank. Much of the financing of the Nationalist side 'was arranged in London on the strength of international bonds belonging to members of the Spanish nobility, which were deposited with Kleinworts and the listing of which is one of my earliest recollections at the time', Gerald Thompson recalled. Members of the Spanish aristocracy who had fled to London, Spaniards resident in London, and Nationalist sympathizers donated their jewellery, coins, and gold as security for these bonds. Queues formed outside the bank and along Fenchurch Street as Spaniards brought their valuables in: 'it was astonishing—all the jewels and gold that came in—it really was amazing!' Other donations were raised by a special committee, whose members visited British firms with interests in Spain. The Nationalists had pledged these international bonds to secure the debt incurred by financing the war. These bonds were held by Kleinworts for March's account since he had provided the loans.

On the outbreak of the Second World War in 1939, Herman A. and José Mayorga asked Montagu Norman for his view of the value of the, by now, Spanish Government's warloan. Governor Norman's response—'Who knows what the value is?'—astounded them. In view of this, March told Kleinworts to call in the loan. When informed, the Spanish Ambassador, the Duke of Alba, stormed out of No. 20. As the money was not repaid, Kleinworts had to sell the bonds on the market, thereby incurring the Spanish Government's displeasure. The Duke of Alba never forgave Kleinworts as he assumed it was their decision rather than March's. 'Everybody thought it was Kleinworts' money', Pepe Mayorga explained. 'It looked that way. They were sitting on the money—but it was Juan March's money.'[51]

It was German rather than Spanish concerns that most exercised the partners throughout the late 1930s. The City, especially after Hitler's invasion of Czechoslovakia in 1938, was caught between the conflicting interests of international economic liberalism and nationalism, even those who were naturally jingoistic realizing that their economic interests were international. At Kleinworts the partners were faced with the dilemma of whether to maintain or reduce the existing level of their German business.

The firm was not in a strong position as the majority of its business originated in Germany and it still held large German debts. Moreover, the partners had had to use a large portion of their capital to clear some £5m. of this debt in line with Bank of England policy. In 1937 the Discount Office asked them to reduce their outstanding standstill bills by 30 per cent, some £3.5m.; fortunately that year the firm had made a profit of £1m. [£31m.]. A similar request to reduce their bills by £1.5m. was made in 1939 and, although the firm was on course to make 'a fairly substantial profit', the decision was made to write off £3.1m. of German debts, resulting in 'a gigantic loss'. The partners had to negotiate an overdraft facility of £1m., using their outside assets as security. They continued to value the remaining £4.5m. of *Stillehalter* debt at 10 per cent on their books in the belief that it was recoverable.

Kleinworts therefore had no wish to break off relations with old and valued German customers and, ever mindful of the importance of facilitating the repayment of the German debt, they maintained their German business. They were by no means alone. In 1939 Hambros, Schröders, Westminster Bank, and the Midland Bank, for example, counted the steel firm of Friedrich Krupp of Essen as a client. Some of Kleinworts' staff nevertheless felt that the firm should adopt a more cautious approach to German customers. One case in particular, an arrangement to supply dyestuffs from a Lancashire company to an old customer, I. G. Farben, caused discomfort in the office, even though the partners had been in the vanguard of the City when it came to voicing opposition to Nazism. During the height of appeasement Joachim von Ribbentrop had visited Britain in March 1938 to promote 'friendship' between Germany and Britain. At an important City luncheon to fête him, Herman A. had created an uproar by publicly asking, 'How come you are not servicing the interest of loans from the City but buying and investing in equipment of a non-pacifist nature?'

Whilst transactions with Germany went ahead, and in the chaotic conditions of the summer of 1939 Kleinworts entered into a credit agreement with Krupps whereby they granted further facilities of £330,000 to be guaranteed by Krupps' shareholding in a British company, Hard Metal Tool Manufacturing Ltd., those with some other clients were stopped. John Holm, the new manager of the German Department, arrested a client's ships in the Port of London, notwithstanding that they had escaped the German invasion of Denmark and had come to London to help fight the war. The arrest was invalid and the client arranged to repay the debt from Far Eastern assets. Kleinworts were never forgiven. José Mayorga also made one of his few errors of judgement when he cancelled the credit line for 'Gussies', Great Universal Stores, thinking they would go under because of their 'tally' business, which would be uncollectable during wartime. 'He didn't understand the English market and it took years for Kleinworts to live that down,' the assistant manager of the English Department would ruefully comment.[52]

The Second World War disrupted Kleinworts' business to a far greater degree than the First World War had done. Within the first year the firm lost its whole client list in Italy, France, Belgium, Luxembourg, Holland, Norway, Denmark, much of Poland, Austria, Czechoslovakia, and Germany when these countries fell under the Trading with the Enemy Act. Business was 'perforce frozen, it was a case of putting it on a "care and maintenance" basis, a task that', Ernest recalled, 'fell to my lot'. Acceptances in 1939 slumped to £2.7m., only serving to reinforce the fact that Kleinworts had slipped even further from their former position as the leading accepting house; their place was taken by Hambros with acceptances of £10m.

In terms of capitalization, however, the firm as a result of its recent reorganization remained relatively healthy, given the losses sustained in Germany. Kleinworts were at the top of the league table in terms of capital and reserves during the early war years. After Morgan Grenfell reduced their capital to £1.5m. in 1942, the Bank of England warned that they might need a larger capital later and that unfavourable comparisons could be drawn with competitors such as Barings (£3.4m.) and Kleinworts (£4.5m.). Although the partners' capital was only £1m. in the accounts, hidden reserves and total assets were £5.2m.

The firm needed such reserves, for acceptances would fall right away to £0.5m. by 1941. Moreover, with wartime restrictions and government financing replacing private trade, business in the capital markets had contracted miserably with little immediate hope of recovery. Unlike Morgan Grenfell, Kleinworts were ill-equipped to participate in the revival of private transactions, particularly of investments, since their small investment department was entirely concerned with the private fortunes of the partners. Whereas Morgan Grenfell saw their profits double with an increased income from investments and a large participation in the public issues of fixed interest debt for industrial companies, Kleinworts remained stagnant without the means or the expertise to participate effectively in such ventures.[53]

Partnership affairs, by contrast, were anything but stagnant. Ernest and Cyril had proceeded to open negotiations with Herman A. on forming a new partnership agreement that would come into effect upon Herman Kleinwort's death or retirement. These negotiations were by no means straightforward and, at times, became distinctly unfriendly.

Cyril had been told by his father just before he died that, taking into account the normal expectation of life, the existing partnership deed gave Herman A. 'the beneficial ownership of the whole firm'. While Sir Alexander seemed sanguine about this, his sons were not, and determined to equalize their position forthwith. They resented the fact that Herman A.'s capital contribution to Kleinwort, Sons & Co. was 'unduly small' compared with his participation in the profits and losses of the business. As matters stood, on the removal of Herman from the partnership, the lion's share of his direct participation would be allocated to Herman A. It was for this reason that Ernest and Cyril wanted to agree terms with him in advance.

At first the negotiations begun in 1937 progressed smoothly. Herman A., though under no legal or moral obligation to reduce his participation rights, knew the mind of Sir Alexander and was eager to uphold the spirit of the original partnership deed: that the Andreaes as junior partners should not have a greater share overall in the profits and losses than the Kleinworts as senior partners. By a gentleman's agreement the partnership term was extended from 1941 to 1946 and the division of any recovery of Herman's share of the German losses was fixed at 43 per cent for Herman A. and 28½ per cent each for Ernest and Cyril. But none of this could come into force until Herman had been forced to retire. He had to do so before 31 December 1941—the date of the termination of the existing partnership—because if he remained a partner he would be in the strongest position when it came to agreeing terms for the new partnership deed.

The active partners therefore exerted serious pressure on him. Family lore is that Herman A. took advantage of his uncle's failing health and at last managed to wring an agreement to sell out 'for a paltry amount' just prior to his death. When Godfrey Style went to see Herman at Wierton in 1940, he found his dying grandfather broken in spirit and tearful about the sacrifices he said he had been forced to make in the firm's interest. Holding up one hand, Herman said in a whisper, 'They have taken millions from me'. No written agreement of this has survived—although Spicer subsequently admitted that Herman agreed to retire on terms which were 'extremely favourable both to the firm and to the continuing partners'.

This was less surprising than might at first appear. At the age of 83, stunned by the onset of another world war, Herman was not a man who was prepared to provide yet another threat to the continuing existence of his family firm purely for reasons of personal gain. This was extremely fortunate for Kleinworts: had he insisted upon removing even his securities pledged to the Westminster Bank, the firm could not easily have continued in business. Instead he agreed to sacrifice the whole of his capital in the firm and £400,000 gilt-edged securities pledged by him with Westminster Bank; he also relinquished his £1.3m. share of German losses in return for securing £150,000 of his personal fortune and an indemnity against all further losses. Finally, he agreed that his share of the Drake Trust Co. loan to the firm should not be repaid but should remain as responsible capital; and should be invested in 5 per cent cumulative preference shares of the new company on conversion of the firm into a limited company. Herman Kleinwort continued to believe that he remained morally bound to honour the original intention of supporting the firm with substantial capital purely for the benefit of posterity.

Having brought about their uncle's long-hoped-for retirement on 31 December 1939, Ernest and Cyril continued on the offensive with regard to Herman

A.'s share in the firm. On 4 January 1940 Ernest declared that he wanted profits and losses of the firm to be allocated equally among the three partners rather than in the partnership proportions. Herman A. complied with this but was unable to agree to purchase a third share of their family trust's £750,000 interest in the business.

His refusal led to grave disagreement among the partners. The Kleinwort brothers seriously considered terminating the partnership, threatening that if Herman A. 'did not accept the proposals' they would 'smash up the business on 31 December 1946'. Although Spicer was confident that neither of the Kleinworts 'would have the nerve to risk the total destruction of the old family business merely to spite their partner', the disagreement cast a pall over relations between them.[54]

The partnership operated against a somewhat unhappy background throughout wartime, though the remaining staff at Kleinworts had no inkling of it. To escape the danger of bombing and destruction of records City firms moved their main offices out of London. Arrangements were made at Kleinworts on the weekend before the declaration of war to evacuate the bulk of the staff, together with all the booking machines, to Sir Alexander's old home, Bolnore, near Haywards Heath. Gordon Tettmar was sent down to organize this country office. The billiards room became the general office, the day nursery housed the remnants of the German Department and some of the smaller sitting-rooms and ante-rooms were turned into offices for the managers. When the Bolnore office was slack, Ernest insisted the staff were put to work outside on the estate.

With Cyril away serving in the RNVR, Ernest was also the partner-in-charge of the holding operation at No. 20. Herman A. rarely came up from Hampshire, but when in 1942 Ernest, too, joined the services, Herman A. took over supervision of 'affairs of state', as the office called it, and paid twice-weekly visits. He was nearly 70 and somewhat deaf, so Ernest Pudney was deputed to take care of his safety in the event of daylight enemy attack. He insisted on working in his own office, which was especially vulnerable to bombing because it contained a large, quite beautiful apse-shaped window. Pudney's job was to pilot Mr Andreae from his desk and shut him up in the large corner wardrobe whenever danger threatened. Herman A. was once talking to Ernest Spicer when suddenly Pudney heard the sound of a flying-bomb. 'Come on, Gentlemen, into the cupboard,' he interjected. They then began to argue who should go first. Pudney had to grab them by the arm and push them into the wardrobe. As they were getting inside, there was a shattering explosion. Herman A. turned to Ernest Spicer and asked, 'Did you hear something, Spicer?' The bomb had fallen just around the corner by Monument, too near for comfort.[55]

The remaining twenty-eight staff at No. 20 were far more safety conscious. The defence of No. 20 was orchestrated by Andrew Crew the acting cashier. The distribution of gas-masks, whistles, and torches, the sandbagging of the building, the arrangement of lectures on first aid and gas attacks, the conversion of the basement into two large air-raid shelters, complete with snooker table, dartboard, and camp-beds—were all measures to protect the staff. Their desks were moved away from the windows and clustered in the centre of the main banking hall, 'with bare spaces everywhere all the way round, and most of the offices were bare anyway'. Mr Vidoudez acted as day-watcher and would sound the air-raid warnings from his roof-perch. At a yellow warning staff had to gather their papers ready to move and at a red warning they 'had to scuttle quick' down to the basement. Dorothy Gunn and her colleague Miss Willey were, in effect, the cash department. They lived with the cash cupboard key around their necks. The minute the warning sounded one of them grabbed the small cash box—containing £1,000 for the day's work—and the other the big leather security wallet containing the securities deposited by stockbrokers in lieu of funds borrowed.

Such precautions were necessary because on several occasions the building was damaged. The large plate-glass windows along the front of the building were often blown in and staff would enter the banking hall to find it smothered in glass or covered in thick black soot if a nearby chimney had received a direct hit. Finally, the windows were boarded up leaving the staff to work by electric light for the duration of the war. Conditions of work were uncomfortable and the staff slept on camp-beds in the shelters, with women in one shelter and men in the other; but they were as warm and as safe as anyone else during the Blitz. There was also a tremendous sense of camaraderie and support. The men often played poker long into the small hours and, as Dorothy Gunn remembered, the women tried 'to lump our bits and pieces of food together and get up a party for whoever was leaving [to join the Forces] . . . and we could really put on a big spread between us . . . in one of the air-raid shelters'. Two engineers would rig up a loudspeaker system and attach it to a gramophone 'and we had dancing. We kept this up till about half past two or three in the morning.' Such frivolities helped to alleviate the relentless cacophony of bombs and guns and the grim reality of the desperate plight of family, friends, and colleagues throughout these years of war.[56]

The Second World War seemed but the apocalypse of a continuous period which had started with the First World War, one during which Britons lived surrounded by crises and explosions of political and economic instability, when war or it's spectre was ever abroad somewhere in the world. Yet many of the populace—and certainly the two Kleinwort and the three Benson brothers—had been born into an era which seemed so stable and indestructible, one when peace, not war, provided the normal and expected framework of their lives. It is this contrast which has enveloped the era before 1914 with a retrospective haze of nostalgia. It was during those pre-1914 years that the Benson brothers grew to manhood. Separated from the Kleinwort brothers by more than a decade, Guy, Rex, and Con Benson were even more the products of that era of peace, confidence, wealth, and empire; and they, like Ernest and Cyril, saw the England and Europe of their childhood shattered. Their 'souls already seared' by war, they too had to rebuild their lives and businesses in a transformed world.

8 Heirs of the Establishment

BORN in the heyday of the Victorian world, those years between the 1887 Golden and the 1897 Diamond Jubilee when the flourish of imperialist swords proclaimed Pax Britannica, Robin Benson's three sons were rocked in the cradle of Britain's ruling classes. Their first steps took them into a circle interwoven with some 1,500 privileged families who matter-of-factly bred their children to take their place at the pinnacle of the largest empire in the world.

Thus although the Bensons were, like Ernest and Cyril Kleinwort, the sons of a City merchant banker, they were brought up with quite different expectations. Whereas the Kleinworts led a self-contained, rather lonely existence, neither being sent to school nor given the opportunity to form life-long friendships when young, the Bensons had a large, warm, and fun-loving family circle, were sent as a matter of course to school and were surrounded almost from birth by numerous relations and family friends, so that they had every opportunity to forge friendships, and, indeed, did so easily. As a result the Bensons benefited from a much more rounded upbringing. Their parents' marriage was one of singular happiness and no one parent was a dominant influence over them as Sir Alexander was over his two youngest sons.

The fundamental difference, however, lay in the long-term view taken of the family business. In contrast to Ernest and Cyril, destined from birth to enter the Kleinwort bank, Guy, Rex, and Con were not brought up as future bankers. In this they were no different from their Baring, Grenfell, Gibbs, and Fleming contemporaries, most of whom followed the same path of public school and Oxbridge. Whilst Robin Benson hoped that one of his sons would succeed him, simply to oversee the family investments if nothing else, he did not consider it to be preordained. Accordingly, at Kleinworts the succession was planned, whereas it was not at Bensons.

Robin Benson was content to leave such matters to the future and to enjoy his role as a formative influence in his sons' lives. He saw no need to confine their horizons to the City. If anything, within the family he appears to have minimized his City interests in favour of his many other activities. Ernest Kleinwort's remark that 'Father talked nothing but merchant banking' found no echo in the Benson household, where it would have been a case of Father talked everything except merchant banking. When he did discuss City affairs it was to ponder currency theories and general economic policy rather than points of interest in Bensons' business. 'He liked, after dinner, when the ladies had left the room and the port was going round, to ask us: "What is a pound?"' a member of the family would recall. 'It seems that Sir Robert Peel had first asked that question, and that it had never been answered to either Sir, or Uncle, Robert's entire satisfaction.'[1]

The dissimilarities between the Kleinwort and Benson houses continued into the third generation. We see not only the same differences in the type of business, Kleinworts remaining largely an accepting firm and Bensons an investment and issuing firm, but also in their style and approach to it. For the Kleinworts banking continued to form the main interest of their lives, together with the belief that the family firm always came first. For the Bensons, however, banking continued to be but the means to an end, just as it had been for their father, with the family bank enabling them to lead the lives they wanted. The Benson lack of dedication was unfortunate; not for them—they led highly enjoyable and full lives—but because it later led to an impression that, in contrast to the Kleinworts, they were dilettantish. In fact, between them they brought to the family firm qualities of leadership, personal kindness, humour, clear-mindedness, and, above all, an excellent management of people. They knew that human beings rather than balance sheets made a business. Their sound judgement about people was invaluable in negotiations, in ironing out the wrinkles of business and in building up a good team.

The reminiscences of their staff reflect how contented they were at their work and how well they were looked after. 'We were like one big happy family,' is a sentence that frequently recurs. Even more revealing is the sense of enjoyment associated with the firm, not a quality generally associated with Kleinworts. Although this is partly explained by the difference in the nature of their businesses—Kleinworts being more routine and less varied than Bensons—nevertheless it is clear that the Benson partners valued their staff more highly than the Kleinwort ones ever did. The working environment at Bensons was epitomized by a camaraderie in which people clearly enjoyed themselves; no mean feat in those days of laborious drudgery, when accounts and letters were all done in copper-plate and a mistake meant starting from the beginning again. This sense of enjoyment in turn reflected the way in which the Bensons' own family life and attitudes had been shaped.

'I think it would be difficult to find a FAMILY to whom that word means more than it has always meant to us,' Guy Benson told his mother on the occasion of her 80th birthday. 'You & father gave us the perfect home & filled it with such love & affection.' Even allowing for the tendency to eulogize on such occasions, this was clearly a sentiment shared by all the Benson children.[2]

They were close to their mother, who unusually combined the traits of a zest for life and adventure with a great sense of calm. There was nothing frenetic or restless about her: 'she knew how to sit still' and quietly listen so that her children and family sought her out as the receptacle of their confidences and worries. 'Whatever bothers & troubles we have had we have always come to you knowing that your remarkably wise counsel could never fail us,' were the words of a son, reiterated by more than one within the family. She 'was never ruffled' and somehow, 'after a talk with her it seemed silly to fuss as one had been doing'. Of her children, Guy and Con had inherited the Benson tendency to fuss, less predominant in their father than it had been in their grandfather and great-grandfather. But when they fussed, it was always Evey who smoothed things over and arranged matters to everyone's satisfaction. Her temperament was such that her son Rex could only recall one occasion when she publicly rebuked his father and that was when he appeared one morning clean shaven. She was appalled and life did not properly return to normal until his neat fine beard was duly restored. She gave generously of her time to those in trouble; and in illness 'there was nothing more completely soothing than the advent of Aunt Evie [*sic*]'.

For her children, above all else, their mother radiated enjoyment, retaining till her death 'a lively interest in everything'. Rex, when still unmarried, continued to confide his love affairs to her when she was over 70. 'I told her all about B and though deliciously old fashioned in her views, she helped me as nobody else could. What a wonderful mother-in-law she would be,' he noted in his diary. 'She has such a glorious open mindedness coupled with her Holford puritanism.'[3]

The Benson sons had an equally ready receptacle for their confidences in their father. In an age when most of their contemporaries saw relatively little of their fathers, he was unusual in that he made himself available and was demonstrably pleased to be with them. Be it romping in his early 50s in the nursery with his youngest daughter Lindy or going stalking with his sons—'How I should have liked to have had Guy out with me stalking,' he wrote from Glen Affric. 'I wonder if 20 years hence the boys will ever feel that they would like to have me!' They did! He took a delight in their company and their *on dits*, which he enjoyed quoting: 'Con "Is that large piece of chocolate for Daisy?" Nana "No, dear, it's for you." Con "Oh Nanny, what a small piece!"' An affectionate father, he was eager to do all he could for them. His letters often end with a 'How can I help you?' and they knew that they could always turn to him regardless of the problem. 'I hope as the new experiences crowd in, whenever you feel puzzled—or indeed whether you do or not—you'll write to your mother and me about everything and be sure we'll help you all we can,' he told Guy when he left school.

Thus, as a father, he was not at all frightening or heavy-handed, in spite of his considerable powers of intellect and occasional sudden temper, which manifested itself when he sensed meanness. During a visit to Paris he bought an expensive present. When charged extra for the string tying the parcel he was furious. His erudition was neither dry nor stultifying, because he carried his learning lightly and was full of enthusiasm about ideas, books, music, and art, and he loved to share his knowledge and experiences. He was not a man to fuss but such outbursts of temper as he showed were squalls of irritation, which quickly disappeared over the horizon. He was well aware of the loss, however momentary, of control and would be endearingly contrite afterwards.

At a time when adolescents mooning over unrequited love turned to the piano rather than rock music, Guy once passed a morning repeatedly playing the same music. 'This morning I lost my temper with Guy,' his father wrote from Westonbirt. 'After breakfast he sat down to the piano to play old Boris Godounov—you know the old tune I am tired of.' His father slipped away unseen to wait upstairs for half an hour until it was over, whereupon he returned to the library to set to work on his Burlington Club catalogue when Guy promptly started playing again. 'I fairly flew out at him, saying "Guy do you want to drive me mad, eternally playing that old tune & when the day is done what is there that you can show that you've accomplished?"' Having poured it all out in a letter to Evey, he was full of apologies to Guy and probably gave him tickets to a concert; presents were usually the way he salved his conscience.

If the Benson children were brought up with any dicta, as the Kleinworts were, they would have been 'Accomplish something every day' and 'Keep accounts'. Robin freely admitted that 'Many times I have started a note book & failed—because only on rare occasions did I succeed in accomplishing anything! & the failures,—the lost days,—were too numerous & made me shamefaced.' He wanted to help, not to find fault and applied the same criteria to keeping accounts. It was a precept he had adopted and one he wanted to instil into his children, but by persuasion rather than command. He did not 'really care' what they spent their pocket-money on, as long as they kept accounts. As he wrote from Longleat to Guy, 'All I do want is for you to know where your money goes.' Unlike Alexander Friedrich, he was not bothered by poor handwriting or presentation. Rex compiled his accounts in a slapdash fashion on odd scraps of paper; nevertheless the message came, 'Tell Rex, Father will send him another pound at once now he has received the accounts.' He was also understanding about learning to live within an allowance. 'If you can't do it, tell me, & we'll go into it together, but first get in all outstanding bills,' he advised his sons.[4]

Cherished by such parents, the Benson children had an excellent start in life. The eldest child, Guy, was born in May 1888, and barely a year separated him from his next brother, christened Reginald but for ever known as Rex, yet the two were as unalike as it is possible to be. Guy, all Lindsay in appearance with his good looks and average height, none the less cut a pale, almost gaunt figure beside his darker, more heavily built brother who had inherited the buccaneering Lindsay spirit and the Holford way of following the pursuit of the moment with relish, so that he radiated energy and vibrancy.

The eldest daughter was the tiny but pretty Daisy, actually christened Winifred Margaret, who was two years younger than Rex. She was followed in 1895 by another brother, named after his Uncle and Great-Uncle Constantine and known as Con. A slim, tall boy, he resembled his father in looks and character. Both possessed considerable powers of concentration. Seated at a writing-table in the billiard-room, Robin would happily read some learned text or write up a catalogue of pictures oblivious of his family careering round the room in the throes of playing billiard fives. Con would immerse himself in lepidoptera. 'Con is still hard at work setting his butterflies and was awfully pleased when I presented him the other day with a moth which I had caught on a wall and which he said was a Tiger-Moth,' Rex informed his mother from school in 1904. While he was away at school, Con left his prized collection in the care of the youngest member of the family, Rosalind, whose name was immediately shortened to Lindy and who was born in 1899, the year in which the Bensons moved into a country house.[5]

The elder children were already accustomed to dividing their time between 16 South Street and their mother's family house, Westonbirt. Their grandmother continued to welcome them there after their grandfather's death in 1892, as their bachelor Uncle George, an equerry to the Prince of Wales, largely based himself at Dorchester House during his attendances at Court. From 1899 the Bensons passed their formative years near Withyham in Sussex, at Buckhurst Park, which they rented from the Sackville family who lived at the even larger glory of Knole.

'We were both Rob and I very much taken by Buckhurst,' Evey rushed to tell her mother, for though 'not particularly pretty and there is no very large room in it' she considered that all in all 'it might be made very comfortable and homey', not words which are automatically associated with a 50-bedroom country house. Robin was most taken by its rural location 'and hardly any neighbours which delighted him', and its proximity to a good railway station

3½ miles away from which he could reach Victoria in 'only just an hour', as well as the 4,000 acres of good shooting that came with the property. They decided to make an offer straightaway to Lord De La Warr.[6]

What is surprising is that their offer was not one to purchase Buckhurst but to rent it, at first on a three-year lease, and then on a 21-year lease with the stipulation that they could improve the property as they wished. The reasons Robin Benson expended the rough equivalent of £1.5m. in renting rather than buying a country estate was in the first place due to the agricultural depression which had started in 1873. The ownership of land offered a poor return on investment, some 2 per cent compared with the average 8 per cent on capital. Although ownership of a country estate was still deemed desirable for those seeking social acceptance, Robin had long possessed the entrée to Court and society. Not that he ever went willingly to a Court levee. He was delighted when a meeting he chaired to settle the destiny of the Manila Railway detained him sufficiently long to preclude his attendance at Court. 'I won't deny that I was relieved at not having to go through that ridiculous performance at St James's Palace', he grumbled to Evey.[7]

In the second place, he knew from his brothers-in-law all about the problems of maintaining estates during a period when, far from producing wealth, land was a drain upon it and needed to be subsidized by income from other sources. He had no wish to tie up his capital, nor could he forget the 'bankruptcy' of his youth, so liquidity was all the more precious to him. By renting Buckhurst he gained the pleasure of running the estate and occupying a country house in exchange for a rent he could well afford, keeping his capital available to support Robert Benson & Co.

Thus from Robin's point of view his decision to rent was not so remarkable; what is remarkable is the extent to which he 'improved' Buckhurst for the benefit of future Sackvilles rather than future Bensons. As even the first footman observed, 'he must have spent a considerable sum of money on alterations and improvement', carried out by the architect Edwin Lutyens. Under the Bensons' instructions, he converted the chapel at the south-west corner of the house into a music room, transferring the oak panelling to the hall; created a marvellous long library, reminiscent of the Longleat library Robin so admired, out of three small ante-rooms; and extended the north-west wing to house a billiard-room and a tea-room.

Although Lutyens complained about Evey's taste—telling his wife, 'She is one of those people who don't understand a blank wall and sees in it no difference from a mere factory wall. Nor does she understand the absence of bay windows and porches etc. But that is her fault not mine'—Evey made no complaints about his work, 'quite English in feeling, simple and reserved, derived from sixteenth-century precedent', in keeping with the original Buckhurst. Perhaps Lutyens did not enjoy working under a penalty clause. When Guy commented on how much work there still remained to be done, his father replied that 'they are under a penalty to complete by 15 April which will make them hurry up'. Robin also had electric light installed, which meant that a powerhouse had to be built to house the two generators, hardly an inexpensive undertaking.[8]

No expense was spared outside either. A nine-hole golf course was laid out, later expanded into an eighteen-hole course with a professional *in situ* to teach the boys and their friends. There was a wide array of alternative pursuits on offer since the racquet court had been redone at a cost of £280 (roughly £7,000 today) and a splendid cricket pitch was laid down in the Park complete with a matting pitch at the side. Professional cricketers, Webb of Kent and Hayes of Surrey, were engaged to coach the boys and their friends. Younger cricketing members of the household staff would be pressed into service to bowl and bat, and were able to improve their own game by watching the coaching. The Bensons were judged 'ace bats . . . Mr Rex especially so', and he soon proved too good for the Buckhurst team.

A soothing background was provided by the gardens, 'perfection beyond all dreams'. The daughter and sister of great horticulturists, their mother was now able to display her own talent. Amidst much hilarity the young members of house parties would be set to work to build bridges in the Japanese water garden. Heather was planted, summer-houses built, undergrowth hacked down to make paths through the woods and parks. The effect was 'sylvan England at its best'.

If the gardens were the perfection of Buckhurst, music was its joy. All the Benson children were musical, and their talent was fostered by their father's deep love of music and his musical parties, a feature of Buckhurst. As a patron of the Royal College of Music, their father would arrange for a College quartet to play during a Saturday to Monday and would invite those who shared his appreciation to listen, to play, and to sing, in what Hilda Grenfell called 'a real orgy of music'. As Rex grew older, he too would be asked to play and did so entirely by ear. 'A song or tune has to be whistled to him once and he immediately can play it, a very great gift,' his cousin Sybil Grey wrote in admiration. Many were the occasions at Buckhurst and at Taplow, Hatfield, and Cliveden for instance, where Rex proved the life and soul of the gathering, with the young seated in circles on the floor while he led the singing from the piano deep into the night.[9]

The children's happy existence at Buckhurst was necessarily interrupted by school. The three boys went to Ludgrove, Guy going first in 1898, and becoming

Captain of the School before passing into Eton in 1901. 'Guy has taken FIRST IN TRIALS,' his father proudly proclaimed on Christmas Eve. 'It is the first real test in his Eton career. I think he'll race, if only we can keep him outside that fatal influence that pervades Eton boys—not to sap [to work hard]'. His father remembered that after taking a first in his first trials he had consistently worked the bare minimum to scrape through. Guy, a clever boy who learnt easily, always looked as if he was not sapping. Rex, however, was different, not at all afraid of admitting how hard he had to work. 'I am awfully relieved that I have got Remove [the top form into Eton],' he told his mother, 'I have been sapping like a demon today (Sunday if you please).'

He had joined Guy at Edward Impey's house in 1902. Steeped in the traditions of the British Empire, which his family had served in India for generations, Impey had a profound admiration for the works of Kipling. He imbued his pupils with the imperial ideal of public service and prepared them to rule and command as gentlemen who, above all, deserved to rule. The growing British Empire demanded more rulers, hence the emphasis at Eton and other public schools on character, hardiness, and responsibility rather than scholarship. Rex thought Impey an almost ideal housemaster, the only beak who 'says "Damn" like you or me'.[10]

The cult of sport and the widespread admiration for the sporting hero was at its height when the Benson boys were at Eton. First-class athletes like their father, they quickly made their mark in running, hurdling, and jumping. Unlike their father, they proved to be considerable cricketers and all three were capped at Eton. Rex in particular played a superb game. 'The consistent batting success recently of Benson has given much pleasure to many supporters of the light blues,' applauded *The Times*. When he captained Eton at Lords, however, he was bowled for a duck and was, not unnaturally, dejected.[11]

The difference between the brothers was that Rex and Con turned about quickly from such incidents and sailed straight on to meet the next challenge. Guy, being more sensitive, was grounded by them and took much longer to recover. For many years their father took a deer forest in Scotland in August. The first one, in 1902, was at Benmore Lodge on Loch Ailsh in Sutherland. Here Guy and Rex shot their first stags. Although the ghillie said they would both make fine rifle shots, he thought 'Rex will be the best both at gun & rifle, because he doesn't take missing to heart like Guy'. This is not to say that Guy lacked spunk. On one occasion someone tripped him up a few days before he was going to run in the half mile, which he had a good chance of winning. The scab on his badly grazed knee made his leg much less flexible so, shortly before the race, he cut through the scab with a knife!

When the Bensons decided that their Uncle George Holford was becoming too staid and preoccupied with his health, they got him up to Glen Affric. 'There is nothing like stalking for bringing back youth and health and spirits,' their father declared. George Holford continued to play a pivotal role in Robert Benson & Co., providing capital and portfolios to be managed. He was also a much-loved and influential uncle, welcoming them and parties of their friends to Westonbirt and Dorchester House. Whenever the boys were competing in an important race or match, Uncle George would try to be there to cheer them on to victory, and his support was especially valued by Guy.

What emerges from Guy's letters to his uncle is the complete lack of any sense of rivalry, envy, or irritation with his younger brothers. His devotion and loyalty to them and the pleasure he took in their successes continued throughout all their lives. He did not have Rex's ambition and energy but he did share what Impey recognized as his 'transparently frank and truthful' character. In a letter giving Uncle George the date of the final day of sports, Guy mentions that Rex had been asked to play a trial match with Holland Hibbert to decide which of them would play racquets for Eton at Queen's Club. 'There is not the slightest doubt which is the strongest, most brilliant or least nervous or quickest player. The only point Hibbert has in his favour is a certain amount of steadiness.'[12]

As their father and uncle before them, Guy and Rex were popular boys at Eton, both being elected to Pop, the Eton Society of which Rex also became president. They were at the centre of a group of close companions who would be immortalized by those who survived them; polished in memory to efface any tarnish of reality so that their reputation shines out for ever from that almost mythical Edwardian world. 'All was friendliness and gaiety and sunburnt mirth,' Lawrence 'Jonah' Jones wrote. The 'dancing and extravagance and lashings of wine' are part of the rites of passage of the young. Yet they here refer to memories of the summer of 1913 and have taken on a legendary quality, implying that the lives of that generation must have been more wonderful than any other because so many of them were to die prematurely in the mud of Flanders.[13]

Rex followed Guy from Eton to their father's old Oxford College in the autumn of 1908. Balliol after Jowett had retained its pre-eminence, its undergraduates characterized by what Asquith described as 'a tranquil consciousness of effortless superiority'. Neither Benson succumbed to Max Beerbohm's 'the actual magic of Oxford' to the extent that their father had done. For Guy it was but an echo of Eton. All his friends there were Etonians and, far from entering into a new world, he remained rooted in the old; like the rest of his set almost too attached to their school so that everything that came after never quite matched up to their years at Eton. He remained, to a degree, so rooted all his life. Rex, in contrast, looked forward not backwards. He longed to be done with college life, to be out in the wider world and, in particular, to enter the army.[14]

'He is full of the Army as a career and has no notion of what the atmosphere of Balliol and College discipline may do for him,' his father had warned his brother-in-law Albert Grey, by now the Governor-General of Canada, before Rex arrived to stay there in August 1908. He wanted Rex to obtain his degree, which meant three years at Balliol, whereas Rex talked 'as if he will only stay there a year'. It seemed a waste for someone of whom Impey had said, 'I have never had a boy with greater gifts, of vigour of mind and body', to forgo an Oxford education. Robin hoped that Albert could persuade Rex to postpone entering the Army. 'Please use your influence to get him to submit to Balliol and get all the good out of it that it has done for Asquith, Milner, Curzon and hundreds of others,' he begged.

If anyone could change Rex's mind, it was Albert Grey, who, of all the uncles, was closest to him. Rex was 'quite wild with delight at the prospect of going out' to Government House and he was not at all disappointed with Canada, for the visit combined enjoyment with adventure. The latter occurred during a trip to British Columbia, where the headlines in the Canadian papers reported the 'Governor-General lost in a snow flurry' in the Kootenays. The party had to proceed on foot to find the nearest village and sent Rex ahead on the third day, 'to try and make contact with any human being' he could discover. Eventually he unearthed some woodcutters who helped him rescue his Uncle Bertie and Harold Lowther and they 'all got together again about midnight'.

'I wish you could have seen Rex on the march, chopping down the trees across the trail,' Albert wrote to Robin, 'I do not know how he managed to get through that tramp with a tight-fitting pair of top boots impeding circulation and compressing the muscles of his legs and feet. Anyone else would have suffered tortures, but he did not seem to mind. He did not take these top boots off from Sunday morning until Wednesday night, sleeping in them three nights; being afraid that if he took them off he would not be able to put them on again!'

By the end of Rex's visit, Albert entirely supported him in his wish to enter the Army. His only hesitation was over whether Rex was too good for it: 'The ordinary routine work of the Garrison officer, with the deadly dull daily talk of Mess would kill him.' Nevertheless, after a year at Balliol, doing the minimum of work but the maximum of any hunting and polo he could muster, Rex overcame his father's opposition, went down from Oxford in the summer of 1909 with no regrets, and entered straight into an attachment with the Life Guards.[15]

If his tutors and family had a criticism to make of him it was that he acted too impetuously and could be too self-confident: 'a little more ballast and thought before action' was how Impey had summed it up. This weakness was evinced when he sat for his Army exams blind, completely unprepared and without having given the matter a thought. His failure was a shock and thereafter he took his father's oft-repeated advice to heart: '"Genius (they say) consists in an enormous capacity for taking pains." And if you just take pains in everything you'll be all right.'[16]

After three months at Göttingen University in Germany and three months cramming in Putney, Rex took and passed the Army exams. He was immediately gazetted into the 9th Queens Royal Lancers, one of the finest British cavalry regiments. The 9th Lancers was almost a club, chiefly composed of Etonians who were the sons of old members of the regiment. Fitness, loyalty, and compatibility but, above all, a love of horsemanship characterized the regiment. As a keen foxhunter and polo player Rex was in his element. The regiment had its own stables and polo ponies, working to the adage that 'The Horse Sport is Good for the Character'. Although the regiment was due home very shortly from South Africa, Rex could not bear to wait for their arrival. The War Office understandably refused to pay for his passage out to join them. Undaunted, Rex stoked his way over in a Union Castle boat to save money and arrived in June in Potchefstroom, where manœuvres involved an endurance test of riding over 100 miles in a day and camping on a kopje with the alluring name of Stinkboomsfontein. The Army had a much more relaxed attitude in those days. When the regiment departed for England in October, Rex and a fellow officer were given leave to go on a safari to Nyasaland instead, not rejoining the regiment until the end of February 1911.

The following two years of soldiering based at Canterbury, the most sought-after cavalry station, were entirely pleasurable. It was at this time that Tommy Lascelles wrote of Rex, 'I believe him to be the perfect soldier, and about as perfect a gentleman as one could find in England', and as such he was socially much in demand. Rex also found time to hunt with the Duke of Beaufort's hounds in the company of an old schoolfriend, Stewart Menzies, whose mother, Susannah Menzies, had recently married George Holford.[17]

Although Rex competed in polo tournaments in London and Canterbury, his notable polo victories of these years were scored in Calcutta and Simla. In 1912 he had taken up his appointment as ADC to the Viceroy, Sir Charles Hardinge, later Baron Hardinge of Penshurst. Hardinge wielded through his Council an executive authority far greater than the King's. Yet he also had to exercise a personal influence and to do so required travelling throughout the vast lands of the Indian Empire to be seen by his people. As one of his ADCs, Rex saw at first hand the inner workings of Britain's most prized possession. An ADC, however, holds a junior position so that Rex could participate in the polo and pig-sticking, tiger hunts and gymkhanas, far more than his overworked Viceroy. Rex and his fellow ADC, John Astor, won the coveted Calcutta Cup against a team of Indian princes by 8 goals to 4 during Christmas 1913.

Guy, too, was far from Buckhurst for those Christmas holidays. After taking his degree in the summer of 1911, he had evinced no partiality for any particular career. A berth at Robert Benson & Co. seemed the obvious solution. 'Guy very well groomed, quite the young man in the City—very nice & very proper' was the favourable verdict as he began his City career in that pre-war era. His father decided that it was all very well for Guy to be presentable, but he must also undergo a period of training in the firm's American business.

The plan was for Guy to pass a year in America: first in Chicago with the Chicago Great Western Railway Co., where the chairman had offered 'to take him and push him through the various departments of the CGW Ry so that he may see and learn the inside of railroad management'; and then in New York where his father's friend Edward (Teddy) Grenfell, of Morgan Grenfell, had arranged a place for Guy at the Guaranty Trust. Although Guy's position would be that of a trainee clerk, his father had given him an interest to look after by way of making the drudgery worthwhile. Bensons still had a stake in Clearing Industrial in Chicago, and Guy was appointed a director so that he could look after the Benson investment. 'We saw Ogden Mills in NY and discussed the position of their investment—Guy being present,' his father wrote home.

His sojourn in America could not have come at a more opportune moment. 'Mima' Cecil, whom he wanted to marry, had become engaged to someone else in the spring of 1912. Guy's father had hurriedly finalized arrangements and booked his passage. Guy had discovered that, if he delayed his departure for a week, he could go to Aintree for the Grand National and sail from Liverpool on 12 April aboard the *Titanic*. His father, however, would not countenance it; engagements had been finalized in America to which his son must adhere. His insistence saved Guy's life: the *Titanic* struck an iceberg and sank on 15 April.

His father tended to fuss more about Guy, perhaps sensing a vulnerability absent in his younger sons or just in the hope of eliciting some response. During their previous journey back from America on board the *Lusitania*, Guy's reserve had been more noticeable than ever. It was 'quite funny how little' he responded to his father's small talk. 'You & I communicate with each other even without a word—by a look, a smile, or a movement,' Robin had written in bemusement to Evey. 'But he & I are sealed books to each other.' He did not take offence because Guy's manner was exactly the same with other people. He could not help making the comparison with Rex. The famous music-hall entertainer Harry Lauder had also been on board, and seeing him walking on deck Robin had wryly thought, 'Wouldn't Rex just have been his bosom friend by this time! But Guy won't go up & speak to him, though Dunlop charged us to!'

Although Robin kept his own counsel, he was less inclined to let Guy 'live & learn' when he proved unwilling to stick to the clerical routine of the Chicago Great Western Railway office. The workaholic attitude now often associated with American business methods seems to have been noticeably absent from the pre-First World War America. Guy's friends assured him that during the hot summer weather he would not be able to work an eight-hour day and would need to go out into the country at least one afternoon a week, which, Guy complained to his father, 'I know the CGW won't let me do'.

He found the hours at the Guaranty Trust office in New York more to his liking. 'The Guaranty Trust has now moved into its new palatial offices & during the 3 or 4 days of moving pandemonium raged. I took advantage of it & last Friday went off to Nassau, Long Island & played golf all day.' From his reports and letters home, it is impossible to realize that these were the years of Roosevelt and Taft's trust-busting, when Frank Kellogg, whom Robin considered one of the great lawyers of America, had been acting for the US Government in suits brought against Standard Oil, Union Pacific, and other conglomerates. Kellogg had been Bensons' American lawyer from St Paul days and, when he had visited Oxford University in 1910, Guy had been detailed to look after him.

Guy possessed, Impey wrote to his father, 'a refined natural taste for what is best in everything in literature and art—a very clear head, a good memory', and developed an abiding love of opera; what he did not possess *au fond* was an interest in finance and world affairs. A steady, loyal man, he remained attached to Robert Benson & Co. out of a sense of duty to his father, not from any personal satisfaction. He was largely indifferent to momentous events, remaining absorbed in his own preoccupations. Years later he confided in a nephew that his interest had never been properly stimulated. He had never been put through the mill. 'I never really had any responsibility much because my father spoilt me and I was never expected to work. He taught me to be lazy.' His father would doubtless have been saddened by the gulf in understanding revealed by Guy's admission. Guy was after all his likely heir at Robert Benson & Co.; yet even by 1913 it was apparent that his interest and attachment to its affairs lay in his head, not his heart. As it was, he gamely returned to the firm's offices at Old Broad Street in the autumn of 1913 to start his career in the City.[18]

The Prime Minister, Herbert Asquith, spent the 1914 Whitsun Saturday-to-Monday at Buckhurst, motoring down after lunch on Saturday with his wife Margot and daughter Elizabeth. Buckhurst he described as 'a really beautiful park, with fine gardens and water'. Father of six fine sons including one of the brightest of his generation, Asquith nevertheless was most impressed by Guy and Con, 'the two nicest & most desirable young men (with OC [his favourite son]) of my whole acquaintance—manly, good-looking, with charming manners & plenty of intelligence'. Within three months they and his own sons would be involved in trench warfare on the Western Front.[19]

On 6 August Rex took leave of Lord Hardinge at Simla before starting the long journey home so as to rejoin his regiment. On 25 August, armed with a hog-spear and an enormous scimitar, he found the 9th Lancers were part of the 2nd Cavalry Brigade on the retreat, just after the Battle of Mons had pushed them back to the Marne river. He was, though, in time for the Battle of the Aisne when, on 12 September, his regiment crossed the river under continual shell-fire with a heavy loss of life that included his close friend 'Rivy' Grenfell. 'I have survived up till now and am as fit as a fiddle, but have had two horses shot, and my pipe taken out of my mouth by a shrapnel bullet in the last ten days,' Rex informed Lord Hardinge on 24 September, making light as so many did of the ghastliness of the war.

By the time he was given an unexpected 72 hours' leave at the end of November, he had been mentioned in dispatches by the Commander-in-Chief, Sir John French, and awarded one of the first Military Crosses. The Germans had taken Lille and massed for an attack at Ypres, which the British managed to stem, but again only at the cost of heavy casualties. The 9th Lancers had a disastrous day at Messines. A fellow officer, Charles Norman, wrote: 'Our casualties were very heavy in officers and men. The wounded, of whom I was one, were collected in the cellar of a cottage which was the Regimental Aid Post.' Rex and three others had held this cottage for 46 hours, under continual fire with the Germans within 50 yards. There was no respite for food or sleep, nor even to remove three dead bodies which had already lain there for nine days.

> The time came when the Germans, attacking with greatly superior numbers, had broken through the British line on both flanks of the village and the Regiment, still holding its own front, had to be withdrawn to avoid encirclement. There was no means of getting the wounded away and they had to be abandoned. Rex came down the cellar stairs, told us of the situation and that anyone who could move should come out quickly. He saw me lying half naked in the straw, having had my top clothing largely cut away by our M.O. Without a second's hesitation he took off his fur-lined British Warm coat and put it over me with a 'goodbye and good luck, Charles'. In a very few minutes I was a prisoner-of-war.

Those who survived such episodes suffered torments. After meeting Rex on leave in London, Tommy Lascelles wrote in his diary: 'Rex himself, though his nerves were steady enough outwardly, looked and talked like a man of fifty, and his father told me that each night he was at home, he was continually leaping out of bed, thinking there was an alarm and that the Germans were upon him.' Rex found London 'horrid', with the war naturally dominating conversation but trivialized by topics such as Margot Asquith's children's governess being German. It was almost a relief to be back at the Front.

The Allied offensive at the second Battle of Ypres in May 1915 was frustrated by the German use of mustard gas. Rex was severely gassed and wounded by a bullet which destroyed the brachial artery and part of the nervous system of his right arm. He was eventually taken to No. 7 General Hospital, Boulogne, where two of his closest friends Edward Horner and Julian Grenfell died while he was there. A week later Francis Grenfell, Rivy's twin, was mortally wounded . . . and so the roll-call of the dead in their tens of thousands was heard in the churches of Great Britain and the Empire to the whispered refrain 'We shall remember them' as the war stretched interminably on.[20]

The miracle for the Bensons was that all three of them survived. Guy joined the Queen's Own West Kent Yeomanry and was sent to the Ottoman Front at Gallipoli. Con, who had just left Eton and was preparing to follow his elder brothers to Balliol College when war was declared, found him there after he also joined the West Kent. All too soon he had to be invalided out of reach of the machine-gun fire. After being pronounced fit, he transferred to the Grenadier Guards and was sent to the Western Front, where he passed the summer of 1916 fighting in the Battle of the Somme, as the British advanced 7 miles at a cost of over 400,000 lives. His regiment was submerged in the mud of Passchendaele during Haig's Flanders offensive of 1917, fought in incessant driving rain. 'It is too glorious about Con. I am more proud than I can say,' exulted Guy on 27 September. 'And it reads like a jolly good DSO from [his brother-in-law] Hereward's letter.' Guy and Rex clamoured to know the details since Con was very bashful about it; but when pressed he explained to his mother, 'It was a question of a patrol and a slice of ground grabbed from the Huns when they least expected it. It was not done by anyone's order but simply because I had to move or be shelled to small pieces.' Aged 22, he was at this time the youngest serving officer to receive the DSO. Yet even under fire in the trenches he would scribble a note home about his beloved lepidoptera: 'Will you remind Lindy to keep an eye on that chrysalis . . . and also ask her whether she has put camphor in all the boxes.' It is this juxtaposition of extraordinary courage and immense suffering with the daily concerns of ordinary home-life that makes so poignant the accounts from soldiers at the Front during the First World War.[21]

Con was wounded yet again, 'a grazing shot in the chest', in the Great March offensive of 1918 when the Germans drove the British line back 40 miles from St Quentin. Before being shipped back to England he managed to see both his brothers. Guy had also been serving on the Western Front as intelligence officer of the 2nd Cavalry Brigade, and Rex had endured half a dozen operations on his smashed arm at Dorchester House which, like many large houses, had become a hospital. He had been sent officially as liaison officer with the Ministère de la Marine in Paris, but unofficially as representative of the head of the Secret Service (MIIC). This had involved 'all sorts of curious work for "C" ' with the head of the French Sûreté who, it is said, 'was himself responsible for hiring Mata Hari'. The legends surrounding this famous female spy are innumerable but, at some stage, Rex was himself caught up in her web of intrigue whereupon (it is claimed) he extricated himself by arranging for her capture.

At the end of 1916 he had caught typhoid, which also claimed his mother, who was extremely ill throughout December. In order to keep their three sons and son-in-law informed of her progress, Robin 'hit on the bright idea' of reporting her condition in the personal column of *The Times*, though without mentioning her name. A few days later Military Intelligence paid calls at South Street and Printing House Square and were relieved to hear that these cryptic messages were not coded signals by German spies to their 'sleepers'![22]

On his return to France in 1917, Rex had succeeded Major Louis Spears as liaison officer between General Franchet D'Esperay, commanding the Groupe des Armées du Nord, and Sir Douglas Haig, Commander-in-Chief at GHQ. It was an independent, important post that required diplomacy and the ability to overcome the petty detail and red tape which could obstruct implementation of decisions. He did so well that he was moved over to the British Mission at Pétain's GHQ at Compiègne.

In the summer of 1918, Rex went on leave with Con and Lindy to Grogarry Lodge, South Uist. This was the first of many visits by successive generations of the Benson family and their friends to the Western Isles. However, even that remote area of the world had a share in the theatre of war. 'We had rather an exciting crossing from Oban,' Con related to Guy. Apparently their ferry boat, the *Plover*, was sighted by a German submarine and a pitched battle ensued for 40 minutes in the middle of the Minch. The Bensons put up a determined fight.

> We only had 3 boats and the R.N.V.R. men on board had panicked & went away in those 3 [boats]. So we were left with the women and children & a few rafts, firmly lashed to the deck. No patrols nearer than 150 miles and no land in sight. The submarine made very good shooting & hit us once somewhere below the waterline, a glancing shot, and also put two shrapnel in the rigging which luckily did no damage. She plugged in all about 30 shots at us. Our one Gunner who had not bolted behaved splendidly and fired about 35 shots with the 13 pdr, getting quite close, but not scoring a hit. Eventually for some reason best known to himself, the hun gave up, and we crawled into Castle Bay, Barra. Lindy behaved splendidly.[23]

The war also crawled its way unexpectedly into peace, hostilities ceasing on the Western Front at 11 o'clock on 11 November 1918. Rex's work with Pétain at the British Mission finished after the Armistice, his role being acknowledged by the French, who awarded him the Croix de Guerre and the Légion d'Honneur; and he then transferred to Sir Henry Wilson's staff at the Peace Conference, which formally began in Paris in January 1919. The Peace Treaty was signed at Versailles in June. Rex had obtained tickets to the gardens in front of the Palais de Versailles for the family to watch the celebrations. After the Germans had signed the Treaty, guns were fired and the 'Big Three'—Wilson, Clemenceau, and Lloyd George—walked down through the gardens, heralds of a new era of peace in an uncertain post-war world.

For those like the Benson brothers who had survived, it took an almost inhuman effort to keep their years of youth and war service in perspective. Some could only live on arrested in the memories of their magnified youth so that they were more easily able to evade the shock and responsibility of their survival. Others propelled themselves into the new post-war world as standard-bearers for the lost generation of their family and friends, feeling in the words of Con's fellow-Grenadier, Harold Macmillan, 'an obligation to make some decent use of the life that had been spared' to them.[24]

In common with their fellow-soldiers, the Bensons were in a state of shock. Rex had told Lord Hardinge: 'So many of my friends have been killed that one wonders if there will be any left.' His son, David, remembers on his first day at Eton being taken to tea at Rowlands, where displayed on a wall was a large photograph of Old Etonians attending a dinner at Oxford in 1910. Rex, uncharacteristically because he seldom spoke about the war, proceeded to name them. It became a roll call of the fallen: after almost every one Rex said 'He died . . . he died . . .'. In spite of being scarred physically and mentally, the Bensons were more fortunate than many in having employment waiting for them. Guy went straight back into the family banking firm and the routine of the City of London, Rex returned to the life of a soldier, rejoining the 9th Lancers in Ireland to combat the Black and Tans, and Con had been invited to join the staff of George Lloyd, who had just been appointed Governor of Bombay.[25]

The early post-war years were an interesting if dangerous time to be in India. During the first six months the Governor had to deal with serious disturbances as the Indian Home Rule Movement, led by Mahatma Gandhi, was flexing its muscles against a Raj weakened by the war. George Lloyd was Governor not only of the City of Bombay but also of the whole of Western India, a region which stretched from the borders of Baluchistan to the big jungles in the South. Con was not just his ADC but his personal assistant and generally his social eyes and ears, for as George Lloyd explained, 'I have talked freely to him of all my work in a way that I should not do to any other ADC.' George Lloyd counted upon him for everything and 'whenever there was a difficult piece of work to be arranged, Con generally had to do it simply because everyone could have absolute reliance upon its being done right'. As far as Lloyd was concerned, Con was the hub of the whole show, the 'cool-headed and quiet planner of everything'.

When the time came for Con to return home, the Governor was immensely downcast. Con's 'dog-like worship' of him reminded Rex of his own special relationship with Albert Grey. He always treasured the last letter he had received from Uncle Bertie on his deathbed in 1917: 'My beloved Rex, I am sorry I cannot see your jolly and cheery face again in this life, but I hope my influence will be always around you. I have, as you know always had a great belief in you, knowing that you only want your opportunities to enable you to do great things.' Con was in much the same position with regard to George Lloyd, who later would be of considerable help in furthering his career in the City.[26]

Rex stayed with them at Government House before Con's return home in the spring of 1921 and when George Lloyd offered him the post of military secretary, Rex accepted it. At this juncture in their lives and somewhat surprisingly, neither Rex nor Con had considered Robert Benson & Co. as a career option. This was very much in keeping with their father's philosophy that 'Everyone should lead the life they choose, make their own contribution and not be tied down.' He had never taken a dynastic approach to Bensons, nor did he believe in primogeniture. His eldest son had ended up in the family firm, but not because he had forced him to be there. Rex and Con were quite aware of this; they were equally aware of the need to settle on careers. Their Indian letters are sprinkled with requests for Guy 'to keep his eyes open for a job' and references to approaching some of the large international firms on their return home. The plan was for Con to tackle them first and, once he was fixed up, then Rex would leave India and start to look around himself.

Con arrived in London determined 'to get into some big firms such as Morgans, Shell, Lazards, Anglo-Persian Oil, any of those or their like which have world wide interests.' He would train for two or three years before moving on to a better position elsewhere. Although he and Rex kept being told how difficult it was in the post-war economic climate to obtain this sort of job, Rex for one thought otherwise. 'They themselves are always saying it is difficult to get the right sort—& Con is the right sort.' Con had already written to Sir Marcus Samuel of Shell, all he now had to do was '"tout" "tout" "tout" round until he gets himself in'.[27]

Their plan went awry through two unforeseen developments. While Rex went about his duties in Bombay, eagerly awaiting the results of Con's job strategy, Con had caught chickenpox at Buckhurst. Quarantine was strictly observed and everyone there had to remain *in situ* until the period of quarantine expired. 'I always felt pretty sure from what I knew of Con that he would get his way in the end, but he seems to have made dramatic use of his incipient chicken pox', George Lloyd wrote to Evey after the announcement of Con's engagement to Lady Morvyth 'Dickie' Ward. Her family were neighbours of the Holfords in Park Lane and her father, Lord Dudley, had taken Rex to fish the Thurso in 1917. 'What splendid news about Con,' Rex wrote. 'I know they will be as happy as larks. They are absolutely suited to each other. At last the Benson star has shone out.' It was to shine out again a bare week later when Guy became engaged to a Lindsay cousin, Violet (Letty), Lady Elcho, an imaginative, great-hearted woman who saw the best in everyone. Strength of character carried her through the blackest period of her life after her husband Ego Charteris, Lord Elcho, was killed in Egypt during the Great War.[28]

Rex missed both weddings because he remained in India to help organize the official and highly successful tour of the Prince of Wales in 1922, for which he was awarded the MVO. He returned home at the end of the year, but not for long. He had scarcely seen his family and new sisters-in-law before he rushed off to Russia on the first sales trip of his life. The Government had decided that Britain must reopen trade with post-revolutionary Russia. Rex was given a large cargo of tea, amongst other basic commodities, and was sent to Batum without possessing a word of Russian. It turned out to be a language it was much better not to know. His companion Tommy Carr, who could speak it, was promptly seized and flung into gaol. Rex worked his way across the country to Moscow dressed as a Russian but without a word of the language. None the less, undaunted, he proceeded to sell £10,000 worth of goods, hiding the Russian bank notes he had received in payment inside his boots underneath his socks. There was a sticky moment when he was searched at the Russian–Polish frontier; fortunately he was not asked to remove his boots, and the Bank of England duly honoured the bundle of notes without question, despite the fact that they were full of holes.[29]

Such adventures were no substitute for a career, however, and Robin now decided that Rex and Con should settle down and learn about the family business. Rex was sent on trips to Bolivia, Argentina, Mexico, and North America to investigate the condition of various Benson interests, while Con went to learn the rudiments of banking at the British Italian Banking Corporation's bank, Banca Italo-Britannica, in London.

Bensons' business had been more or less moribund during the war and was not showing signs of rejuvenation. In the five years from 1919, distributable profits were an average of £1,860, hardly enough to ensure the future of the firm, unless matters were taken in hand to produce new sources of profit. The trouble was that London was no longer the world's leading international financial centre. America had become the major creditor nation, so it was New York that had the capital to invest internationally: Bensons' old business of exporting capital to invest in America was largely at an end.

The cornerstone of Bensons' pre-war business, the American railways, formerly so profitable, now paid poorly and anyway were no longer a field for expansion. New industries had risen in their place but, unlike some other merchant banks, the firm had not been quick enough to identify new opportunities in, for instance, the automobile industry. Moreover, their South American and Mexican business had slumped after the war due to political instability. In 1923 Rex's father sent him on a mission to Mexico to investigate the position of an enterprise in which he had taken a major share as far back as 1889. The Mexico Cotton Estates of Tlahualilo had previously been profitable, but were now threatened with sequestration by a Government committed to breaking the power and wealth of foreign-owned companies. Nor could they look to Europe for new business, since they had never been a force on the Continent and so were not placed to participate in the 1920s recovery boom as Kleinworts were.

It is hardly surprising that Robin Benson became increasingly gloomy, if realistic, about the future. The house in South Street was let for the summer, Rex grumbling about the 'poor price' obtained. His father believed that Bensons could only compete for new business and support an enlarged partnership by reorganization and an increased capitalization. He was in his 70s and did not possess the energy to provide the dynamic leadership required to steer Bensons into new financial arenas, and he looked to his sons to drive the firm into the new post-war era under the guidance of Henry Vernet.[30]

In order to formalize this, the existing partners entered into a new partnership agreement in 1924, with Rex becoming a full partner and Con, still a trainee, a limited one. When Guy had become a full partner in 1919, the total capitalization of the firm had remained at £110,000, provided in the sums of £80,000, £20,000, and £10,000 by Robin, Henry Vernet, and Guy respectively. The profits, however, had been distributed on the basis of half to Robin and a quarter each to Henry Vernet and Guy. In the new agreement of 1924 the divisions were made as follows:

Robin Benson	£21,000	30%
Henry Vernet	£20,000	33%
Guy Benson	£23,000	25%
Rex Benson	£23,000	10%
Con Benson	£23,000	2%

Whilst Con was not liable for any losses or debts beyond the amount of his capital contribution, he could not take part in the management of the business, though provision was made to bring him in as a full partner at any time but especially in the event of his father's death or retirement.

The next move in the reorganization strategy was to consider the capitalization of the firm, which had long remained at £110,000, in keeping with Robin Benson's policy of putting capital to work outside rather than solely inside the business. Thus, in order to replenish the reserve fund and make up some of the losses sustained during the war and early 1920s 'Old Mr B.' realized some of his external assets, held to meet just such a contingency. In 1924 he consigned a major portion of his splendid collection of early Chinese porcelain and pottery for sale at Christies. Until recently the bulk of the collection had been exhibited on loan at the Victoria and Albert Museum. It was so well known that dealers sailed over from New York specially to bid for some of the 215 lots. The two-day auction in July fetched £36,934 with some record prices; for example, an exquisite pair of small Ming bottles were sold for 6,400 guineas.[31]

This did little, however, to safeguard the capital base of the firm in the long term. After a period of consultation with their legal advisers, the partners decided to convert the partnership into a limited liability company. A similar course had been followed by Barings and Glyns before the war and would be taken by Morgan Grenfell, Lazards, and Helbert Wagg, though Kleinworts had preferred to use a trust vehicle as a corporate partner within the existing unlimited company. On 31 March 1926 Robert Benson & Co. was re-formed with a capital of £400,000 of which 10,500 £1 management shares were held by the partners (now the directors), and George Holford. Much of the capital, however, was represented by shareholdings and property which could not be immediately realized.

In the event, changes in the Benson family brought about the realization of some of these assets, though in one case it removed a sizeable one. George Holford died in September 1926. To the question posed by a granddaughter, Peggy Wake, 'What did Uncle George do?', Evey Benson had replied, 'He was at Court and he attended the King.' 'And didn't he do anything else?' the girl continued. Proudly Evey answered, 'He was the best backgammon player in London!' After his death, the drawers of his writing table at Dorchester House were found to be crammed with IOUs, many presumably owed from backgammon winnings; he had never cashed them, he had no need. He also never seems to have opened a business letter. Despite such unbusiness-like habits, Evey Benson could have answered that he had done something very important in his life: a large sum had remained to be invested or used in joint ventures at Bensons for over forty-two years.

Uncle George, in life the best of uncles, remained so in death, for he left his huge fortune (some £3m. in 1927, about £82m. today) and 'unsettled' estates to them. By the terms of his father's will, if George had no children, the entailed estate was to be settled on his elder sister so that her eldest son Lord Morley inherited the Westonbirt estate and Dorchester House. Since he already possessed his own estate, Saltram, with the exception of the Arboretum and Silkwood the Holford estates were put up for sale. The remainder of his estate, including the Holford picture collection, was to be sold by George's executors and the proceeds distributed to his Morley, Benson, and Grey nieces and nephews.

It fell to his executors, Guy, Rex, and Charles Grey, to arrange the dispersal of the Holford collections after probate had been fixed in March 1927. The executors, in effect Rex who carried the others with him, decided that the highest sums would be obtained at auction. The Italian pictures were sold first in 132 lots on 15 July 1927. A week beforehand Rex had left some notes detailing their reasons for choosing to sell at this time—for in his will George Holford had made it clear that he left it entirely up to his executors to choose the time—together with his estimate of the proceeds, in a sealed envelope. 'It is rather interesting and rather remarkable,' Guy wrote to his mother after the sale, that Rex thought that the illuminations, for instance, would fetch 10,000 guineas and they fetched 10,181 guineas, 'so that his estimate was an amazingly accurate one, infinitely more so than any of the experts, professional or otherwise, whom we had talked to at intervals'.

In memory of George Holford the Bensons had agreed to contribute 10,000 guineas towards the purchase of one of the most important pictures, Lorenzo Lotto's *Portrait of a Lady as Lucretia*, for the National Gallery. This meant that with 6,000 guineas from the National Gallery, and 3,000 guineas from the National Art Collections Fund they could bid up to 19,000 guineas at the sale. A few lots before their bid, Rex positioned himself out of sight behind the rostrum with Sir Robert Witt, a trustee with his father at both the National Gallery and the National Art Collections Fund. Martin of Christies also positioned himself to bid on their behalf. Guy described the next few tense moments. 'From about 11,000 gs it became a duel between Martin and Duveen and, eventually our limit was reached. Rex quietly authorised Martin to go on for one or two bids, and ultimately said to him quietly—"You can bid another 500 and that is absolutely our last." This brought the figure to 22,000 to which mercifully Duveen made no reply.' The picture hangs in the National Gallery today.

The prices achieved at the second Holford sale in 1928 were even higher. *The Times* reported that the proceeds, £364,094 achieved for seven lots, constituted a world record for one day's auction of pictures. The five Rembrandts bought by their grandfather, Robert Holford, in the 1840s, which accounted for a great deal of this record, were considered as late as 1961 to be the most expensive that had ever been sold at auction. The two sales raised in excess of £2m., over £55m. today. It says much for Rex's judgement that he chose to sell when he did; within two years, art prices had collapsed.[32]

In terms of Robert Benson & Co. the death of George Holford meant that the firm had to return the Holford funds to his estate. In order to facilitate this a bank loan of £30,000 had been arranged. Clearly the shortfall in capital would have to be replenished to support the newly reorganized firm. The only remaining 'hidden' reserve that was an easily realizable asset was the Benson picture collection. To part with a collection that they had built up together from the earliest days of their married life, one that had brought them such joy and occupation, was a great sadness to Robin and Evey. Yet the sacrifice was one which they judged necessary to secure the future of their sons and the family firm, and for Robin this had been the underlying *raison d'être* of the collection.

Two such important collections on the market simultaneously would be a flood of *richesse*. It may have been to avoid the *embarras* that the Bensons, not wishing to depreciate the value of the Holford bequest for their cousins and themselves, decided to 'do a deal' with Duveen, who had long coveted the collection and had ready buyers for it in America. Otherwise it seems strange that they should have agreed to sell to him rather than at Christies, since it was believed that the collection would have realized far more at auction. Although Robin lost the three Giovanni Bellinis from his collection, he had gained one from the Holford collection: his children had paid £6,510 for the *Portrait of a Boy* by Giovanni Bellini at the Holford sales and presented it to him. Robin and Evey had already made the collection over to their children for taxation reasons so that, when the entire collection of 114 early Italian paintings was sold *en bloc* to the ubiquitous Joseph Duveen for $4m. (then about £620,000) in 1927, the proceeds went directly to them.

The Benson family and their possessions would contract further in 1929. Old Mr B. had begun to fail in the previous summer of 1928, to the extent that his family had even anticipated that the Christmas of 1928 would be the last one together at Buckhurst. So it proved to be and was the best Guy ever remembered. 'It is a great feat to get together all the members of a family for 3 generations, with all their dependencies, & keep them for 4 days without a suggestion of a squabble, particularly among 15 children below 16 years of age! I don't think I have ever seen so many children so happy together. Well done & yours is the credit, I think father ought to write a poem about it!'[33]

He was, however, more likely to write about 'his precious Italian paintings' than compose verse. Once in a while, he would take his musings into the office at Old Broad Street for typing. Old Mr B. would arrive during the lull of the lunch hour when it was quieter and sit down beside a secretary and dictate fluently in Italian. The poor girl would have no idea how to write the words so he would patiently spell each one out for her. She remembered him as 'Sweet, absolutely, and having done that, he and old Shaw, who was our only commissionaire, about the same age as Mr Benson, would depart down to Old Broad Street to the ABC at the bottom and have a cup of coffee and a bun and then he'd go home.' Not many chairmen would fraternize with their staff in such an open, natural manner; inconceivable at, say, Kleinworts. Yet this was very much the Benson style, earning them the loyalty, respect, and affection of the people at Robert Benson & Co. 'Incapable of malice, tolerant in his judgment of others', Robin Benson was, Sir Rennell Rodd wrote in *The Times*, 'a wise and kindly counsellor to those who sought his advice' whosoever they be; his staff were no exception.

By February 1929, Rex reported 'Father very bad. Farquhar Buzzard says no hope of his ever really getting well. Mother wonderfully brave.' He died on 8 April 1929 surrounded by his family and the pictures and *objets* he most loved. His interest in games had never abated; he had continued to go deer-stalking at an age when most men take to slippers, and could slice a ball on the Buckhurst tennis court that defeated even youthful opponents. Amongst the many tributes and obituaries, Sir Rennell Rodd's emphasized his talent for friendship, his courteous modesty, and the way in which he had 'in a remarkable manner acquired the art of being a father'. It was undoubtedly in his marriage and family that his happiness and enjoyment of life lay. 'That dull City' as his wife called it was never dull for him, nothing in life was, but in his latter years he neglected it in favour of the attractions of family life, literature, art, and philosophic debate, all of which brought him greater happiness. A clause in his will referred to a letter of instruction to his children about his financial provision for them. Yet, after careful consideration of the matter, he had concluded that he trusted their own judgement completely, deciding not to place any restrictions on the way in which they could deal with the money he left them. The only advice he tendered showed uncanny foresight: he suggested they keep their money 'really liquid as a reserve against political and financial risks'.

His death inexorably proclaimed the end of an era for his children, a parting of the ways from their youth, first signalled by the death of their Uncle George. Westonbirt was now a school, Dorchester House had been demolished to be rebuilt as a hotel, and Buckhurst, so long the centre of their home life, was also given up. All five were long settled in their own well-furnished married homes and their mother had exchanged South Street for Walpole House, Chiswick

Mall, shortly before their father's death. So there was little room for the absorption of a great deal of the Buckhurst furnishings, apart from the lovely carpets which they all wanted and one or two of the best pieces of furniture. Later generations might rue it but there was little alternative to holding yet another family sale.

On 5 May the family gathered at Buckhurst to decide what they wanted to buy at the sale. 'Mother to be the final arbiter.' They were so busy that there was little time to be sentimental and sad. A week later Rex walked round the house for the last time. 'Feel very sad now that Buckhurst is coming to an end,' he admitted, 'Every corner is full of reminiscences.' Those Buckhurst days would be remembered by so many for 'the Beauty of the gardens & the lake', Evey Jones wrote. 'The Fun of the company—The Songs we sang—the playing in the Music Room, Guy, Rex & all our host of friends who came & came again. The golf & the blue bells & the building of the Bridge in the Lake. Uncle Robin's pleased detachment & love of literary perfection—& his rose champagne. Oh great days of youth & Happiness & warmth pervading.'[34]

With the death of Robin Benson, the firm finally turned its back on the nineteenth century to face the twentieth. This was in keeping with the national, indeed international trend, albeit occurring somewhat later at Bensons. The 1920s was a decade of transition; at the management level, from the dominance of individual men to that of boards of directors and large institutions; and at the staff level, from the handwritten to the use of machines. The transition was a gradual one. The atmosphere in most City offices remained Edwardian. Dress was formal, with hard collars *de rigueur* for even the most lowly of clerks. At Bensons the chairman always wore a frockcoat and silk hat.

Changes did not occur overnight and in the case of Bensons they took years to be implemented. The move to a limited liability had been, in effect, the only major change at Bensons in the immediate post-war period, but it had not brought in its wake any changes in the way the company was run. When Robin Benson was alive, his sons were content with the status quo since the responsibility was ultimately his. By the summer of 1929, however, this was no longer the case. They not unnaturally became restive, believing changes had to be made to drag the firm from the mores of a partnership of two men, in which one was definitely the senior partner through capital ownership, into the mores of a company with four directors and an increasing staff and, hopefully, business.

At this time, unlike Kleinworts, Bensons lacked the most basic managerial organization. Under the partnership, there had been no need for departmentalization. The office was small, with fewer than twenty people, and the chain of command simple. Robin Benson had increasingly delegated everything to

Henry Vernet. He ran the business with the manager, Charles Hellings, who co-ordinated the investment and issuing business with the investment trust business. His staff did not even really work to area; if there was a lot to do in the 'private clients' sector then they downed tools and worked on that until the job was done, moving on to the bookkeeping if that was where the help was next needed. This remained the case even when more staff were taken on for specific areas in the spring of 1929. 'It was a family concern and we all mucked in. Everybody helped everybody else, and if there was a difference on the accounts we would help Payne,' Robert Clifford remembers. 'If there was a difference on the security side then Wooldridge would come and help us.'

The firm's telephonist was similarly expected to apply herself to other duties. The switchboard consisted of two lines with twelve extensions when Miss Violet 'Floss' Lincoln joined in 1927. She was paid 35*s*. a week and expected to help with the typing and, most time-consuming of all, with the copying. Office procedures were as laborious at Bensons as at Kleinworts, with all the books and accounts still done by hand. After being clamped in a copy book, the originals of all correspondence were still put out to dry, like washing on a clothes line. The arrival of Floss Lincoln increased the number of female employees to three out of a total of twenty-five staff. Apparently, 'the crusty old gentlemen' in the Merchants and Charter Trust Cos. were so suspicious of them that they at first refused to allow them in their offices!

The non-departmental approach applied equally to those beginning their careers, usually as office boys. Their duties no longer included making up fires and sweeping the floors as they would have done half a century before, though postage remained a responsibility. A 17-year-old or 19-year-old was paid £100 a year in 1927/8 and passed the first six months running round delivering securities to the brokers, taking coupons for cashing to the banks and generally familiarizing themselves with the way everyone worked. 'You were as much at home in their office as you were in your own.' There were distinct advantages to this system, as Harry Purkington recalled. 'If we had a difference on the brokers' account, for instance, I used to go along and just walk into their office and go straight to the ledgers and look things up myself.'[35]

At director level, however, there were distinct disadvantages to the old system; the main one being that the reins of executive power were held in the firm grip of the new chairman, Henry Vernet, alone. Yet he provided no effective leadership, being content with the status quo. This one fact was crucial to the direction of the firm during the 1920s and early 1930s. Instead of being welcomed onto the board, the Bensons were stonewalled by the experienced, rather brusque, shrewd Vernet, who tenaciously clung to his power. As they discovered, it was a frustrating experience to lay siege by chipping and butting rather than ramming him with a full arsenal, for they did not want to lose him, valuing his experience and record. They just wanted to budge him into agreeing to changes and taking the lead. He, however, actively discouraged their investment suggestions, regularly turned down their ideas and somehow never implemented agreed changes in policy. Some understanding of the Bensons' position emerges from Rex's diaries and from staff interviews. For instance, although they were 41, 40, and 34 respectively in 1929, Vernet openly spoke of them as 'the boys', a nomenclature adopted rather more affectionately by the staff. None the less its use added to the impression that they were not serious, that they played at business, and would much rather be elsewhere. It was also an impression that suited Vernet and one he made no effort to dispel.

There was inevitably a noticeable absence of teamwork at director level during these years of difficult trading conditions. The leadership was divided and there was deadlock—undesirable conditions for any firm but especially so for one that badly needed to improve profitability. Rex nevertheless soldiered on in his battle to improve the overall management of the firm, but it was uphill work all the way. There was, for example, no such staple in the daily office diet as a partners' meeting: a routine, if informal, event at Kleinworts. At Helbert Wagg's they were called 'Mothers' Meetings' but only took place each Thursday morning at 11 o'clock, and in most other City houses, they were usually of short duration but held on a daily basis. At Bensons, in contrast, the decision-making had long been entirely Vernet's. The advent of Guy into the partnership had not checked his authority, since as the junior of the two it was Guy who consulted Vernet rather than the other way round. Furthermore, Guy on his own was no match for the wily, experienced figure of Vernet, highly regarded and respected in the City. It was only after first Rex and then Con had entered the partnership and then become fellow directors that Henry Vernet's citadel of power was attacked.[36]

The initiative was taken by Rex. When he circulated a confidential memo amongst the board in the summer of 1929, his purpose was to introduce basic management techniques, with a view to modernizing the firm, and more importantly to dilute Vernet's powerful hold on it. He first suggested that the importance of daily private directors' meetings be recognized and instituted. Used to an effective chain of command and communication in the Army and at Government House in Bombay, Rex was dismayed by the lack of any structure of command at Bensons; on occasion the firm was almost rudderless since the man who ran the show only gave part of his time to it and made no especial effort to put Robert Benson & Co. first, which, apart from its deleterious effect, meant his availability for meetings was infrequent.

In a dig at the new chairman, Rex stated that: 'Owing to the Board Meetings of individual members of the Firm, it is, for the time being, nearly impossible to get the same fixed hour everyday.' He suggested, with masked irritation, that on the two or three days when it proved impossible, a meeting could be held at lunch in the office. There was nothing masked about his final sentence: '*It is the Chairman's duty to see that these meetings are held*, and that the staff realize that partners are not to be disturbed.' Henry Vernet made a habit of continuing to sign letters during meetings and frequent interruptions occurred when clerks came in to give him messages and correspondence. All of which, unfairly or not, led to the impression that he was not giving the matter at hand, namely Benson business, his undivided attention.

His outside directorships became a thorn in the Benson side. Not that the Bensons were against such extracurricular activities for they could provide extremely useful connections; indeed, Guy had taken his father's place on various investment trust boards and at the Court of Governors of the London Assurance Group, while Rex sat in his place on the board of the Anglo-American Telegraph & Telephone Co. Since they were relatively young they could expect to be invited onto others in the course of their careers. What they were against, however, was the large number of Vernet's boards. When Rex totted them up in 1929 they numbered twenty-four, which had earned him £17,500 in 1928, far more than their father's directorship fees. By the following year they amounted to over £20,000, more than twice his income as a partner in Bensons. 'What incentive can he have to promote the interests of R.B. & Co.?' asked Rex. The answer was very little, but that is not to accommodate Henry Vernet's view of the matter.

In many ways his situation was a direct result, on the one hand, of Robin Benson not providing him with sufficient incentive, and on the other hand, Robin's generosity in initially suggesting him for directorships on a fair number of boards. Although he was responsible for a large part of the income of the firm, he only ever received 25 per cent of the profits and 5 per cent return on his capital of £20,000. In later years he came to feel this was inadequate recompense and began to supplement his income by multiplying his outside directorships.

Although Guy, Rex, and Con liked him personally, they were intolerant of his blocking attitude because as their father's heirs they had a far larger amount at stake than he had. Thus, whenever there was a difference in policy or disagreement over an investment decision, the thorn of outside directorships and his position as their chairman with equal power of veto on decisions penetrated a little deeper.

Rex, in particular, found it increasingly irksome when his investment suggestions were turned down by Vernet. While in America to play polo, Rex had bought £25,000 worth of stocks without authority when Guy had agreed to take only £12,500 for a client. Vernet had subsequently rapped him over the knuckles: 'No partner or director has any business to commit the firm except by agreement with the other partners or directors. And every effort should be made, every time, to see that the agreement is unanimous.' Vernet had long ago adopted Robert Fleming's motto 'Learn to say No', and he believed that it was often as important to do nothing as to do something. It was vital that Rex understood that 'we are all of us risking something more than money: we are risking our reputations as business men'.

While Rex entirely accepted this, admitting that sometimes he was 'a little frightened of myself as I get led away with enthusiasm', he also believed that his father had built up Bensons by taking calculated risks; yet the company was now run by a man of 65 who had grown even more cautious with age and seemed to eschew risk-taking altogether. During the heady summer days of the 1925 rubber boom, Rex made a profit of £12,000 in sales of rubber shares before he had to leave for a trip to New York. He learnt there that at a time when people were still fighting over such stocks, Bensons had simply held on to £29,000 worth of stock and no one had tried to sell it: 'What an opportunity we have lost in rubber!!' He blamed Vernet who had sat on the fence as usual so that nothing was done. The two men remained at loggerheads over business decisions and, in consequence, there was no hope of implementing a coherent strategy and the teamwork so essential to the firm's success.

There was a further consequence of this division on the board. The cult of youth was not a feature of the inter-war City; a man under 50, if not 60, remained at a considerable disadvantage *vis-à-vis* his elders. 'No one in the City will listen to what you have to say for twenty years,' a senior partner at Cazenoves warned a junior one. As a senior man, Vernet's influence in the City was much greater than his younger partners. If they had been able to work together with less friction, there might have been a greater opportunity to bring in new business; for ideas proposed by Robert Benson & Co. would have been better received coming from the elder statesman chairman than his younger directors. Moreover, Vernet did not hand on directorships to them, so that in many cases long-standing Benson connections ended with his death.

Rex's second proposal in 1929 concerned the delegation of responsibility so that no one partner, i.e. Vernet, was responsible for the whole. Representing the difficulties as being 'more psychological' than anything else, he emphasized that 'the time has now come when duties must be decentralised' within a department. Furthermore, each director should be responsible for his own special department and report on its activities at the daily meeting. Flexibility and freedom of action between the directors and the departments would be respected so that each of them, for example, could retain his own private clients though their records would be centralized in one department, as were American dealings.[37]

All this seems perfectly straightforward if not essential for the smooth running of the firm. To a later age, the wonder is that Bensons was able to operate for so long without the benefit of such infrastructure. Yet Rex's suggestions met with little active encouragement at board level. Vernet thought it unnecessary. Guy supported the plan but took little initiative to persuade Vernet to implement it, while Con was absent from the discussions. It was all most discouraging. There the plan would have languished but for the determination of Rex and the support of three allies at the manager level. Between them they introduced departmentalization into Bensons and the managers started to concentrate upon the development of specific areas of business.

The man whose support was vital to Rex was Charles Hellings, the linchpin of Bensons as both a manager and an income generator. Rex learnt that Vernet listened to Hellings: 'HAV suddenly decided to buy Imps on pressure by Hellings,' he noted in his diary. So instead of badgering Vernet, if Hellings approved of it, Rex would get him to approach Vernet. At some stage Henry Vernet must have seen through Rex's strategy; the next time there was a disagreement with frayed tempers, he accused Rex of 'perverting' Hellings with his schemes. Hellings, however, believed that Bensons needed active rather than passive leadership and was fully behind the changes suggested by Rex.

Charlie Hellings had joined Bensons in the 1890s. His parents were the master and mistress of the Workhouse at Plympton in Devon. Plympton was the Saltram estate village and Lord Morley, probably impressed by Charlie's mathematical ability, had sent him up to Bensons. He thrived in the City, progressing from office boy to clerk and from managing clerk to the dizzy heights of manager by the time Vernet joined the partnership. A kindly, placid, heavy man he possessed the gifts of a photographic memory and instinctive market sense, and earned a well-deserved reputation for being an investment wizard. His juniors remember that he carried with him an order book bulging with loose pieces of paper but 'if you looked at his order book there was never anything written in it. He carried the whole thing in his head.' Bill Hole, his number two in the office, was devoted to him. While still a junior clerk, Hole was working late one night in order to process the dividend for one of the trust companies. It was a time-consuming business going through all the different shares to calculate the gross, tax, net, and dividend figures on each one. He had several hours' work ahead of him when Hellings reappeared after having had his evening gin with the brokers at Coates. With a 'Give those to me,' he disappeared holding the long sheets of paper, only to emerge from his office in about twenty minutes saying, 'There you are, Goodnight!' The work was done. Hole was so amazed that he went to Hellings' office to see how he had done it so quickly. 'I searched his waste paper basket, I looked everywhere, no scrap paper.'

Hellings rarely left the office so that the brokers, still wearing their top hats, used to saunter into Gresham House to have a chat with him about the market. He was consulted by many people, including Kit Hoare (who was Herman A.'s close, personal friend and Kleinworts main broker), for he assembled an extraordinary knowledge of the position and prospects of a vast range of the companies whose shares were quoted on the Stock Exchange. In charge of the private clients' accounts under Guy's direction, he also undertook all the investment dealings, which was the prime part of Bensons' business, and he made a great deal of money by being able to cut his losses; he never waited for a stock to recover. If it had not done well within a limited period, it was sold. Profits had started to rise from 1926 and, by 1929, the firm was showing a profit of £140,188, of which the largest proportion originated with C.C.H., as he was affectionately called by the staff.[38]

From 1924 to 1929 Bensons derived its profits from three sources. The half brokers' commission on the sale of securities and underwritings represented the 'bread-and-butter' business of the firm and roughly covered the overheads. The more speculative business of trading in securities provided the 'jam', which was a generous amount in 1929. As Rex pointed out, however, 'To depend for our jam entirely upon the marketing of securities is not satisfactory, nor is it sound.' For once Vernet entirely agreed with him. In order to diminish the ratio of capital and profits attributable to trading, the directors decided to concentrate the firm's efforts on the development of the American and the issuing business.

The old established investment house of Clark, Dodge & Co. had been Bensons' principal correspondent in New York since before the Great War. In 1926 they had opened an office in London in Bensons' building at 24 Old Broad Street and had appointed Colonel Eddie Coombe as their representative. He and the Bensons became close friends. Rex had apportioned responsibility for the American department to himself in his blueprint for Bensons' future development, as he was determined to maintain Bensons' traditional role as an Anglo-American house. He decided to issue a weekly research newsletter together with assorted circulars and pamphlets to the firm's American clients as a marketing tool to encourage them to give a percentage interest in their business in return for the business that Bensons gave them. On 10 May 1929 he concluded a satisfactory meeting with Ben Mosser, his Clark, Dodge colleague in New York, and Henry Vernet. Bensons would publish the first issue of their newsletter on 9 July while Mosser arranged to give Bensons a small interest in all Clark, Dodge undertakings.[39]

The development of Bensons' issuing business was nominally Con's responsibility. It proved impossible for him to direct it, largely because he was absent until 1932. When he did return to Bensons, he was a changed man. Each of the Benson brothers had inherited certain traits of character from their father: Guy his meticulous attention to detail and his precision; Rex his enthusiasm, personality, and skill at games; and Con his intellectual ability, sound judgement, and powers of concentration, all of which enabled him to dissect the most difficult financial problems. This he was called upon to do by Montagu Norman after three of the London clearing banks asked the Bank of England's help to stave off disaster at the British-Italian Banking Corporation in the winter of 1928/9.

Its subsidiary, the Banca Italo-Britannica, was in serious financial difficulties due to incompetent management, every conceivable method of faking accounts, and the bad luck of those who had speculated with the bank's resources. Liquidation seemed inevitable when the governor was asked to mount a rescue operation of some £2m. by the three largest of its eighty English shareholders, one of whom was Robert Benson & Co. Immersed in the struggle for the Gold Standard, the Bank of England feared the Banca's collapse would threaten British international credit. The governor therefore agreed to organize a team of investigators, place his nominees on a reconstituted board, and contribute £250,000 in exchange for the clearers making up the remaining £1.75m. themselves.

The governor's nominee director was Sir Rennell Rodd's son, Francis, of Morgan Grenfell. His reorganization team consisted of Patrick Ashley-Cooper, M. Terestchenko who had been Kerensky's Foreign Minister in 1917, Ralph Hamlyn of Bensons' accountants Binder Hamlyn & Co., James Henderson of J. & P. Coats, C. F. Cobbold (a future Governor), and Con Benson, who had trained with the Italian Bank. Months of relentless investigation followed in which Con's analytical skills came to the fore. He enjoyed wrestling with a problem and worked at it extremely hard until he had found the solution. Thus much of the burden of this complex, protracted exercise fell upon him. According to his nephew Peter, 'He came back having rescued far more money than anybody had ever dreamt of ever seeing again.' Norman was extremely pleased and, having been marked as an able young man, Con would doubtless be called upon again to serve the financial community. He had indeed sufficiently made his reputation for one of the shareholders, Lloyds Bank, to put him on their board, thereby becoming their youngest ever director. It seemed the start of a meteoric City career.

Unfortunately Con was unable to take his seat on any board for a considerable time. In the autumn of 1929 he had a severe nervous breakdown. The recovery was protracted and painful. After convalescing at Grogarry in South Uist, which the Bensons leased from 1918 to 1939, he and Dickie left on a long, slow journey round South America, a complete change of scenery being thought essential to recovery. 'Health—improving, but Oh Lord, it is slow and at times I have gone backwards,' he wrote to Guy from Santiago on 19 January 1930. 'In fact I never realised quite how bad it was until I started, and it will take some time.' It took several years before he was again well enough to make a full-time contribution to Bensons. Even then, in search of an elusive return to good health, Con would disappear for months at a time to take a rest cure in Switzerland or to some spa in the Alps, from which Dickie would return unable to give a good account of him. 'I like not this quack doctor in N.Y. If he needs psycho-analysing he had much better try Martin,' Rex wrote of his brother's latest cure.

Con 'was very able', Bobby Henderson, later Chairman of KB, recalls, 'and he had great charm and he was really talented' but after his breakdown he never recovered and could never resume the path to a great career in the City or public life. He suffered from bouts of depression and worried he would fall ill again if he worked too hard at anything, so that he appeared lazy and hypochondriacal when it was the fear of another breakdown, exacerbated by his bad lung, that caused him to try to avoid what would now be termed 'high stress work'. Putting together deals at Bensons fell into this category. He would use all his energies to map out a strategy, become worn out in the process, and hand everything over to a subordinate; while in meetings he would nervously but painstakingly construct a pile of tiny pyramids beautifully torn from a sheet of foolscap paper, folding and tearing throughout the proceedings.

His condition was naturally a sadness to his brothers but an especial blow to Rex. With Con away for so long, Rex had to carry the burden of opposition to what he called 'the HAV problem' more or less alone. He had been kept going by the knowledge that Con would soon join him when it would be easier to thrash matters out. 'If only the Benson team can get together in the City,' he would confide to his diary at moments of deep frustration. Con's intermittent presence also foiled Rex's plan for the development of Bensons' issuing business. When the opportunity arose for the firm to manage its first public issue, Rex had to rely upon the expertise of a new young manager rather than his much more experienced brother.[40]

George Wansbrough was the first management recruit at Bensons in the new era. Educated at Eton and Cambridge where he was a pupil of Keynes, Wansbrough decided against Barings after Sir Edward Reid, the son of a Baring, warned him 'You must realise that not being a relative of the family, you cannot look forward to a partnership.' So, without a Baring fiancée to hand,

Wansbrough walked round the corner to Bensons, where Guy assured him that the Bensons would be disappointed if he did not prove worthy of a partnership. Wansbrough started at Bensons in 1927 and was soon employed on the British Power & Light project, which was to prove a milestone, if not a millstone, in Bensons' issuing history.

The firm's long-standing interest in electricity had led to an approach from George Twiss, an enterprising electrical engineer. The establishment by the 1926 Electrical Supply Act of a Central Electricity Board to build a 'grid', so as to provide a cheap and abundant supply of electricity throughout Britain, had led him to form five companies to take out provisional orders in areas till then without a public supply of electricity. Twiss estimated that an investment of £220,000 would be needed over two years, after which each company could be sold to investors for £250,000–300,000. After confirmation of the feasibility of the scheme from their engineering friends at the London Electric Supply Corporation, where Vernet had replaced Robin Benson as a director, Bensons took a stake of £100,000 in February 1929. Rex also persuaded Edward de Stein of de Stein & Co. to do the same. 'He wants 1% clear on his share and should just about get it,' Rex noted. De Stein possessed a flair for spotting businesses worth restructuring and was one of the most successful company financiers to emerge in the 1920s. Sam Insull, who had created a large group of American utility companies out of Edison's electricity supply empire and sold many of his concerns' shares to Bensons' investment trusts, had taken the remaining £20,000.

In April, Twiss approached Bensons with the idea of forming a holding company to take over the capital of his existing group of companies together with that of two North Wales power companies. A team at Bensons spent the whole of April working on the details of the £1.6m. British Power & Light Corporation scheme. When Rex returned from America at the end of the month he found them all 'with hair standing on end reading at least the 15th British L & P prospectus. Wansbrough looks very overworked: Guy also very nervous & de Stein like a cat on hot bricks.'

It was Bensons' 'first big venture' and looked set for a fair sailing. Rex briefed *The Times* and *Daily Mirror*, who while agreeing to give it a good puff said they did not think it would go down well. The City was depressed at the prospect of a Labour Government and after talking to a lugubrious Kit Hoare, the prominent broker, Rex began to have mixed feelings about the success of the issue. The prospectuses were all out on 4 May but Kit Hoare now stated that he was unable to place the underwriting of the issue, leaving Bensons and de Stein vastly overcommitted. Insull saved the day by offering £320,000, with further amounts taken up by Clark, Dodge, Schröders, and Brown Brothers. The issue was none the less a complete flop. To make matters worse, Bensons had taken on a temporary man to run the issue, who proceeded to sell the stock of people who had not collected their share certificates and to forge transfers. Happily, to lose money on a first issue was then regarded by the City as MPs regard a maiden speech, with receptive indulgence; indeed Helbert Wagg's first public issue of Marks & Spencer stock was equally unsuccessful. Bensons in fact did not lose money, in spite of their temporary man's activities, and were judged unlucky rather than incompetent. The British Power & Light issue was an important first step in the direction of a fully fledged corporate finance division, one that in future years would often become the largest profit centre at the firm. Another seed was sown that year through Bensons' involvement with Montagu Norman's Bankers' Industrial Development Co. Ltd. (BIDC).[41]

This was never a particularly successful venture but its significance for Bensons was that it brought the firm into closer contact with small industrial companies, furthering their issuing work and enabling them to work alongside other colleagues as established members of the inter-war City tea-party. Thus, although Bensons was a much smaller-sized firm than Kleinworts, its profile in the City was much higher. Both firms were trying to increase their domestic issuing work at this time; and this proved a much easier exercise for Bensons.

In the 1920s the presence of the 'company promoter' made company finance seem a disreputable, seedy, fly-by-night operation: many promotions were fraudulent and companies unsound. Not surprisingly many private investors eschewed industrial shares, as did the big institutional investors. The law still did not insist on the disclosure of enough information to give a true picture of the state of the company involved; published accounts, even of A1 companies, did not need to reveal more than the absolute minimum of information about capital and profits. If even ICI could be formed with a higher value set on the shares of the merging companies than their assets justified (this £18m. of 'goodwill' was carried in the accounts from 1926 to 1956 and was perfectly legal), what might less scrupulous companies do? Barings had an almost inviolable rule against advancing cash against shares and were so restrictive of credit that they refused to double an existing credit and then withdrew one of £200,000 from the well-established international firm of Lever Bros.

After the post-war informal Bank of England embargo on foreign issues, however, even ultra-conservative Barings began to look around for British companies in which to invest. The gradual expansion in domestic corporate finance attracted those houses with a reputation as issuing houses, and suited their expertise. Banks such as Morgan Grenfell, Lazards, Rothschilds, and Barings formed a group to aid Montagu Norman in his attempt to reorganize British heavy industry, for an additional and significant spur was provided by the Bank of England's drive to revitalize depressed British industry through rationalization. Small industrial firms were encouraged to merge into more economic and competitive conglomerates. In doing so the need to raise the uneconomic small sums of capital from the banks was obviated and issues of over £200,000 were much more feasible.

Bensons therefore joined the seventeen leading houses including Morgans, Lazards, and Rothschilds to form the Bankers' Industrial Development Corporation (BID). Kleinworts, however, were not part of the group, although their close rivals Schröders were. In the event many of the BID's schemes proved unworkable and earned for it the sobriquet 'Brought in Dead'. Nevertheless those houses that did participate gained experience of the steel industry which bore fruit in later years for both Morgans and Bensons. But there was a greater storm on the horizon.[42]

In the autumn of 1929, just when business seemed set to progress, the Great Crash occurred. At Kleinworts the partners, whilst personally incurring losses, saw their bank remain largely unscathed; at Bensons, however, the partners incurred heavy losses on both fronts. Their exposure to American securities was large. Within the first two hours of trading on Wall Street that Black Thursday, 24 October, almost $10 billion was wiped off the market value of quoted shares and the resulting shrieks were so fearful at the New York Stock Exchange that the gallery had to be closed. There were no shrieks at Old Broad Street, just a baffled silence broken by bursts of flurried activity to liquidate where possible. But even this activity ground to a halt over the following weeks and months as America and Britain were engulfed by depression.

The City became unnaturally quiet. Investment business, the mainstay of the firm, faded to nothing and the whole office sat idle. The staff came every day but there was literally no work to do. To while away the hours between 10 and 6, the staff amused themselves by tossing a tennis ball into a wastepaper basket at six tries for sixpence; the girls would knit and sew; other chaps would play cricket in the long corridors. 'We sat idle the whole time and I think the worry at that time was whether any firms *could* succeed.' The one aspect of the Depression that did not affect any of Bensons staff was the threat of redundancy. Unlike many other City firms, including Kleinworts, Bensons kept all their staff. In all the partners' discussions about economizing it was the one option never once considered. The attitude was that Bensons was a family firm that stuck together through thick and thin, and everyone counted. Staff were rewarded by bonuses and presents of wine and silk stockings in the good years and the bad. Thus in the depths of the Depression when there was very little business, the partners gave them a bonus for having worked so well during a 'trying' year! Bensons lost £147,000 in the first year of the Depression and everyone prepared themselves for further losses to come.[43]

The years 1930–2 were dark ones. 'Con is ill at Burgh House and Guy goes north at the end of the week. HAV rather worried but who isn't at the situation?' Rex asked in 1931. 'Germany bankrupt; France unrelenting with her troops mobilised on the frontier—America in a pretty poor way with a winter of unemployment in front of her. This country already taxed out of existence with a huge deficit in its budget, a spendthrift Socialist government and the pound sterling being sold everywhere.' During those three years, the firm lost £305,508. Yet Bensons credit was high and their bread-and-butter business was better than it used to be. 'We shall pull through but how to make money back that is lost?' was the question at the forefront of the partners' minds. As they struggled to find solutions, all the old partnership problems became magnified.[44]

Whichever way the Benson brothers turned they came up against the problems of Vernet and his apparent lack of leadership. Rex felt the firm was over-invested and wanted to liquidate the 'bunged up' securities on the basis of selling everything that 'We do not think we should buy *were* it offered to us now,' but HAV rejected the advice, eliciting from Rex: 'I really believe, if left to himself, that HAV would not sell or buy anything!' It was the same story when on 20 May 1931 Hellings suggested moving funds into gilt-edged securities. They were slightly down, so HAV refused to allow a purchase in spite of the pleas of all three Bensons. 'Gilt edged in the skies,' reported Rex a week later. 'We should have made £15,000 had we bought ½ million.'

The final straw came when Vernet started to blame Rex for the firm's losses in the Wall Street Crash. Rex felt this was so unjustified that he was rendered speechless and walked out of Vernet's office. 'I could not have stood it for I do not honestly feel myself to blame and should only have started an argument and done myself no good in this present highly strung condition.' He did apologise for his behaviour but it marked the nadir in their relations. While Rex was appreciative of Vernet's 'great qualities & experience'—he was a 'wonderful Chief of Staff & a great Chairman or director of Trust Companies'—it all made him 'feel just too damned tired & dispirited, not because RB & Co has had a bad year but because the "team" will never fit in & work.' Rex's impulsive enthusiasm was anathema to Vernet and its effect was to make him even more obstructive to change. Thus, at a time when the firm badly felt the need for direction, the antlers of the partners continued to be locked over every single aspect of the business and opportunities for new business were passed over.[45]

In desperation, the Bensons thought of merging with the stockbrokers Greenwood & Co. Lord Faringdon had once intimated to their father that he would be glad if their respective sons could get together in the future. His sons Alec and Arnold were at Greenwoods but neither was especially dynamic and none of his grandsons were interested in a City career: he had made them too rich in Robin's opinion! When the Bensons' younger sister Lindy was unhappy out in the Sudan where her husband Walter 'Ben' Pollen was an Administrator, their father had fixed up for him to go to Greenwoods. The understanding with Lord Faringdon was that in time Ben Pollen would be offered a partnership there. According to a niece who loved him dearly, Ben, an extremely good-looking man with 'a wicked tongue in his head', had acquired 'some very pasha-like attitudes'. The drudgery of mastering brokering and starting at the bottom did not quite suit after ruling a large area of Sudan. He would have much preferred to be at Bensons but his brothers-in-law thought it would be a mistake and anyway there was no unissued capital with which to buy him in.[46]

The combination of Benson partnership anxieties, the sudden death of Alec Henderson on 2 November 1931 which left Greenwoods vulnerable at the top, and the feeling that it might help solve Ben Pollen's predicament persuaded the Bensons to make an overture to Lord Faringdon. Rex wondered whether they might be substituting two Vernets for one, since Faringdon was an octogenarian. On balance he thought not, for Faringdon was undoubtedly a leader, in fact just what Bensons wanted. Nothing came of the initial talk for the simple reason that Faringdon was already negotiating marriage with the stockbroking firm of Cazenoves, the two firms merging in March 1932 to form Cazenove, Akroyds & Greenwood & Co.

Before Bensons had time to make overtures to anyone else they were themselves the subject of one from Bruce Ottley of the issuing house Erlangers. The firm's large interests in South America and company finance coincided with those at Bensons and both were also members of the Bankers' Industrial Development Corporation. Although the marriage would have thrilled the City, Vernet was entirely against it. 'He is quite happy to go on as he is,' Rex gloomily pointed out. But after Vernet did some pointing out of his own, namely that the state of Bensons' balance sheet would frighten off any eligible suitor, the overture was given a cool reception at Gresham House.

In fact the Benson gloom was steadily dispelled as business began to improve towards the end of 1932. By the end of the following year the firm seemed to have turned a corner in more ways than one. Henry Vernet had fallen ill with pneumonia in October, seemed to recover but died quite suddenly from a heart attack in November. In spite of their many differences, Guy also spoke for his brothers when he wrote, 'His death will be a terrible loss here.' They had always felt like amateurs in the face of his long years of experience, but the fact that they now showed themselves quite capable of directing it without him was one of the pleasant surprises of the year ahead. An immediate and less pleasant surprise came when Mrs Vernet refused to sell back her husband's

1,100 management shares and the ensuing unseemly wrangle ended the long connection between the two families.[47]

At last the Benson brothers were free to run the firm in the way they chose. Rex's diary entry in the spring of 1934 reflected their feeling of liberation at turning yet another corner: 'This is first day of the New Year of finance for RB & Co. We have had a wonderful year & made back almost all our capital.' Their investment trust business, started in 1889 with Merchants Trust, had remained the core bread-and-butter business which saw them through the ghastly depression years. Commission earned on the purchases and sales of shares on behalf of the various trusts had produced 80 per cent of the investment advisory account earnings in 1930/1, at a time when every other part of the firm's business was showing a loss.[48]

The trusts had lost none of their popularity during the inter-war years, as the British investing public remained predominantly interested in spreading its risk. Bensons had built up a stable of investment trusts and, as the senior citizen of the group, Merchants Trust maintained its momentum and respectability under the chairmanship of Con. He was also chairman of the Traction and General Trust originally formed to specialize in railway investments at home and abroad. During the 1920s and early 1930s many of their by then unremunerative holdings were sold off. Bensons unfortunately no longer had an equivalent of Flemings' Maurice Hely-Hutchinson who, possessing an enviable grasp of American railroad finance, was able to steer Flemings safely through a period during which railway investments and assets were drastically reorganized. Neither Guy nor Con, the two who had been sent to America to familiarize themselves with railroad finance, had stayed the course, while in his latter years Henry Vernet had concentrated more upon the South American railroads. After his death, the old Benson connection with South American railroads surprisingly seems to have been allowed to fade away; Vernet had made no attempt to introduce any of the Bensons onto his boards and future business was correspondingly lost. Eventually the Traction & General was renamed the British American General and its holdings changed to reflect this.

The third trust, the Charter Trust created in 1907 with Albert Grey to specialize in Southern African investments, basically mining and railways, used to have two subsidiaries. Trust & Agency Assets was a development of Cecil Rhodes's interests in Rhodesia, which eventually wound itself up and went to the 'Unclaimed' department of the Government, while London, Foreign & Colonial Securities was very small and was easily absorbed by the Charter. During Guy's chairmanship of the Charter it also expanded its registration department to take on outside work; the first such client was a London firm of leather merchants, Barrow, Hepburn & Gale. This formed a new adjunct to the in-house registration work which, with dividend payments, comprised the work of the trust staff. The work was immensely time-consuming. Eric Innes recalls that 'The old addressograph machines and an awful lot of hand work, made it almost a perpetual thing. They paid dividends quarterly then and by the time you had finished one you started doing the envelopes for the next lot.'[49]

The expansion of registration work at the Charter Trust had occurred at the time of the British Power & Light issue. As Bensons' issuing work increased during the 1930s, so the registration department expanded and it began to act for large companies such as Morphy Richards, Aveling Barford, and later on Cadburys and Tescos. Although the department was a service rather than a profit centre, Bensons built up an excellent reputation as good registrars. There was considerable prestige to be gained from acting in this capacity for well-known companies which, at a period when domestic company finance was a source for profits, helped to promote the image of Bensons in the City. This in turn increased the new issue business, for 'management of companies wanting to go public would naturally go to people who knew what they were doing' and Robert Benson & Co. had that reputation.

The remaining two trusts in the group were new additions. Unlike his brothers, Rex had not been given a well-established investment trust to run. His father had given Rex the then moribund English & New York Trust in the belief that he had the drive and energy to revitalize it. The Trust had been registered in 1912 and lay dormant thereafter until, in 1928, Rex decided to activate it. Alistair Craig, a colleague and later director of Bensons who worked alongside Rex on the trust side, recalls that he had 'the outstanding ability to get on and do things . . . he was a devil for work' but even more admirable was his ability to select the right people. 'He did get round him a most fantastic team of people, there's no doubt about it.' This was as true of the English & New York Trust as of his other concerns and the trust team provides a good example of the Benson club in these years.

When Rex wanted to revitalize the English & New York Trust [E & NY] he naturally invited colleagues from those City houses to which Bensons were closest to join him on the board and to set about raising the capital at what was rightly perceived to be a difficult time. Bensons' closest rivals continued to be Flemings who had retained their position at the top of the investment trust league table. Robert Fleming had died in 1933 but relations between the two houses continued to be close since two of the four partners were old family- and schoolfriends: Philip Fleming, who was an Olympic gold medallist oarsman with 'an amazing flair for smelling the market, most amazing, just like his father', and Maurice Hely-Hutchinson, who masterminded their American business. The third partner, Archie Jamieson, a shrewd Wykehamist became a close friend of Rex's, with whom he shared a gift for friendship, an enjoyment of America, and a capacity to have fun while working hard. Fleming and Jamieson joined the board in 1928.

Flemings, under the direction of these gentlemen and Walter Whigham, continued to have enormous financial leverage in the City; they exerted a direct and indirect influence on the investment policies of some fifty-six investment trusts, whose collective resources totalled about £114m. in the early 1930s. Some inkling of their standing in the City can be gauged by the fact that it was common practice for City firms sponsoring new issues to consult two organizations on the terms before flotation: Flemings and the Prudential. Since Flemings and Bensons were regarded on Wall Street as the two leaders of the investment trust movement, their combination on the E & NY Trust board was an effective and successful one.

Rex further bolstered the board with two other friends—one a partner at Morgan Grenfell, the other at Helbert Waggs, and both Grey connections. The first was R. H. V. 'Rufus' Smith, a great-nephew of Albert Grey, who had joined Morgan Grenfell where his father Lord Bicester was a partner and his cousin, Teddy Grenfell, was the senior partner. Relations between Morgan Grenfell and Robert Benson & Co. were close and, although Bensons were not in the first division, they were often members of Morgan syndicates and drawn in on other Morgan business. The second was Jonah Jones, who had married Rex's cousin Lady Evelyn Grey. Jonah, an old school- and Balliol friend, was a man of wit, who regularly won *Spectator* literary competitions; he eventually became an eminent author, leaving his readers with a description of board meetings in the City of his day, doubtless in part reminiscent of the English & New York board meetings that he regularly attended in the 1930s.

> There is gossip and chaff and the latest good story before a conference or board meeting gets under way; it is all friendliness and informality; the debate saunters off into byways; the real point is sometimes not reached until we are washing our hands for lunch. The comfort of our partners' rooms, the deep leather sofas, the open fires, the pictures on the walls, all encourage a rather cosy, lounging method of discussion.

The pace was certainly more leisurely and conducive to friendly discussion, but Rex for one would certainly not have waited until lunch to reach the point. A decisive man, he despaired of the 'hesitations and long-windedness' of the City, and tended rather to rush through meetings with what Con termed his 'sergeant-major' attitude. None the less he would have been in accord with Jonah's words, 'But it was agreeable to work in an atmosphere where mutual liking played as large a part as the cash nexus. There was competition, but it was amicable, even generous.'

The E & NY Trust that these men directed began with a capital of £750,000 and was almost immediately affected by the Depression. 'With this appalling American market and the revolution in Brazil it is pretty hard to find an investment for Trust companies,' Rex grumbled after one 1930s board meeting. Following the collapse on Wall Street only one-eighth of the funds were invested in America in the early days of its existence; but by the mid-1930s this had risen to just under one-third. Rex's hard work and enthusiasm, coupled with the skills and experience of his co-directors, pushed the Trust forward to increase its capital to £1.35m. in 1935; and it was soon one of the largest of the Benson trusts. In 1986 it was renamed the Kleinwort Overseas Trust and currently manages assets worth £235m.[50]

The fifth stable-mate in the Benson Investment Trust group was one of the smallest but also one of the most successful that Bensons managed. It was formed in 1930 and George Tinn, who became the secretary, can remember 'when Sir John Brunner introduced his son Felix to Rex Benson and Hellings and they formed Brunner Investment Trust by selling Brunner Mond shares'. The trust was specifically formed to invest Felix Brunner's inheritance after his father's company was absorbed into ICI in 1926. Felix Brunner, however, was no passive investor and held clear views about the investments. His desire to stay in industrials for example, after receiving advice to the contrary, was certainly more than justified in the long term.[51]

While commissions from investment trusts, the family trusts such as Four-Name and Crosby, and private clients' accounts kept the firm going during the Depression, it was nevertheless the 'jam', the stock-dealing, that enabled Bensons to replenish lost capital, especially in 1933/4 when the firm had a particularly good year. A great many shares had collapsed in the slump, providing unprecedented scope for an experienced dealer such as Hellings to spot those due for a resurgence; he had a sixth sense about cumulative preference shares which had fallen into arrears and lost value but were about to start paying their dues and would rise accordingly. Hellings also made a major contribution to the firm's participation in new share issues through his family stockbroking contacts at George Whitehead & Chown and Rowe Swann.

The year 1934 was significant for the firm. The Benson team finally 'got together in the City' with Guy as the new chairman. He functioned much better than his younger brothers had expected and they made a happy triumvirate, with the advantage that they could blame each other when business was left undone! George Wansbrough had joined them on the board in 1932 at the young age of 28, having acquired a great knowledge of the electricity supply industry. He used to deputize for Henry Vernet, at first occasionally and then regularly, when Vernet no longer had time for the chairmanship of British Power & Light. It is interesting that no one ever expected H.A.V. to relinquish the post. Of course there was no customary retirement age from boards in those days and 'pressure of work' or 'outside interests' were unknown as reasons for standing down. Directors, too, complied with Herman A.'s injunction that 'a man works until he drops', and senility, absence, or uninterest were no obstacles to membership of a board; death or handing over to a son to ensure the continuation of a family interest were the more usual agents of change. Thus, at Bensons, Wansbrough was devoting practically all his working hours to British Power & Light for which the firm brought out two highly successful further issues. The partners therefore decided to recruit another outside executive to look after private clients' investments.

They chose Michael Colefax, the son of their former neighbours who lived at the Buckhurst dower house. Sybil Colefax was a celebrated hostess in a golden age for the party-goer. Fantastic sums were squandered on decorations and themes yet Sybil's exquisite taste did not require extravagance to succeed: 'everyone sat on the floor at Sybil Colefax's', Diana Cooper wrote of one gathering, 'while Rubinstein played Chopin and Noel Coward strummed and crooned'. It was exactly the sort of party the Bensons enjoyed and were invited to attend. When her bright young son, with Oxford and a few years at a firm of City stockbrokers under his belt, wanted to move on, it was easy to arrange a place at Bensons. At first Michael Colefax acted as a deputy to Rex, accompanying him on marketing trips to America and to the Continent.[52]

Although he had been recruited for the private clients' side, it was in the area of new issue business that Michael Colefax proved most valuable. His father Sir Arthur Colefax was an eminent lawyer and a Solicitor-General. During the Great War he had been chairman of the Patent Board when Dr Chaim Weizmann, a lecturer in Chemistry at Manchester University, had invented a product, urgently needed at the time, to coat aircraft. Colefax had defended Weizmann's interests in a post-war legal action and the two men had become close friends. Weizmann persuaded Balfour that part of Palestine should become a homeland for the Jewish people, and later became the first President of Israel. Through the Colefax–Weizmann friendship, Bensons came to know the Sieffs of Marks & Spencer and George May of the Prudential Insurance Co.

Many of Marks & Spencer's suppliers were small textile firms in need of capital, a problem then endemic to the economy as a whole. Since Marks & Spencer could not meet or guarantee the need of such suppliers they looked around for City friends who could. George May, secretary of the Prudential, was keen to direct investments into industrials and agreed to underwrite small issues for them and their connections. Through Michael Colefax, Bensons were asked to bring out two such small issues for the Full-Fashioned Hosiery Co., totalling £100,000, in 1933/4. The presence of the Prudential as underwriter meant there was little possibility of loss. Moreover Bensons now had an unrivalled opportunity to repeat the operation. It was an area in which several City firms were already doing well; in particular Erlangers and Higginsons, who were headed by friends of the Bensons.

Unfortunately, Bensons were slow to grasp the opportunities, the problem being the lack of any real strategy in the firm. Unlike their father, grandfather, and great-grandfather, the present generation of the family did not have one fixed area of specialization. Their father had identified American railroads as the business to be in at a particular time; whereas his sons juggled with various aspects of different businesses but never made an overriding commitment to any particular one. Their resources were spread far too thinly and Rex's original plan to divide the business into departments had not really worked at the partnership level, since the partners continued to dart all over the place. Nor was there any such thing as forward planning. Admittedly there were extenuating circumstances to consider; internal problems and the dire economic situation had made commercial survival difficult enough and the partners' minds were entirely focused upon that priority.

Nevertheless when the firm began to turn the corner, none of them concentrated upon the future direction of the firm; instead they reacted to events, to the marketplace, and to business suggested to them. This is easy to do in the short-term and in the middle of a bull market when it is relatively simple to make money; but in this sense none of the Benson sons were their father's heir. He had excelled at the long-term view; the pity was that after the Great War he had more or less removed himself and there was no one to replace him as a strategist.

Thus the opportunity to specialize in the supply of finance to small, relatively unknown industrial companies was not immediately identified as a way to build up the new issue side of the business. Bensons' attitude, however, was very much in tune with the City's state of mind. Company finance then meant financing well-known companies whose names were household ones, such as Horlicks. Helbert Wagg's public issue for them attracted widespread support because the company's products were so familiar and so skilfully advertised. Full-Fashioned Hosiery was not in this league although it would later become better known as Kayser Bondor. However, Michael Colefax joined the board in 1934 and was thereafter in a stronger position to urge the firm to develop business in the field of company finance.[53]

Happily, an opportunity soon presented itself, and although none of the partners realized the significance of the move at the time, it was one which would turn Bensons into a major issuing house and bring them a partner of immense talent and vision. 'Discussed with Eric formation of new finance house Tatham & Turner! Believe we could do well to finance these two bright boys. Con & Mike also bitten. Must sound Guy,' Rex jotted down in his diary on 28 September 1934.

When they had been casting around for possible sources of capital to inject into the firm in 1931/2, Adams, Pitfield & Co. had suggested Eric Tatham to them as a sleeping partner. He had inherited his father's jobbing business and had a close relationship with Adams, Pitfield & Co., an aggressive firm of Canadian brokers with whom Bensons had recently started a joint account 'placings' venture, selling Canadian securities to clients with no offer to the public. Although they rather overreached themselves on their first test case of 4,000 shares each of British Columbia Power 6 per cent Preferences and National Telephone 7 per cent Preferences, having to take up about £50,000, they remained in the market and markedly improved their performance. When Tatham's jobbing business fell, a casualty of the Depression, he contacted Bensons.

There matters might have rested but for Adams, Pitfield and an extremely bright young man at M. Samuel called Mark Turner. He had no doubts about the opportunities that existed in the field of company finance and, unable to act upon them at Samuels, recognized the Tatham–Benson–Pitfield connection as a suitable vehicle for the development of this business. He had been introduced to the Bensons by Ben Pollen, whom he knew in the City, and he already knew Eric Tatham. He therefore quickly suggested to Eric that they form a finance company with the backing of Bensons and Adams, Pitfield.

It was this proposal that Eric took into Bensons on 28 September. Michael Colefax then persuaded Rex and Con that Tatham & Turner would be a great addition on the personnel side, as Bensons could offload all their new issue business onto them. Negotiations proceeded well until Con suddenly took fright, believing that by financing them Bensons could be accused of having a partnership with Pitfields. Rex decided that the best solution was to leave Con alone with Eric and Mark for the evening; by the end of it Mark had worked his magic and Con was entirely in favour of the venture. Both he and Con understood the intricacies of banking and got on extremely well together.

Thus, on 20 November 1934, an agreement was signed. Named after Eric Tatham's house, the Kenterne Trust was a wholly owned subsidiary of Bensons that would act as Adams, Pitfield's correspondent with Eric and Mark as its managing directors. Kenterne Trust was given a little office on the sixth floor of 27 Old Broad Street adjoining Gresham House and the directors immediately set to work. Eric Tatham 'was a charming fellow', not 'very able to construct a deal'; but what he could do was to introduce people and act as the contacts man. Thus from the outset, Mark Turner proved the inspiration behind Kenterne's strategy.[54]

Kenterne was an extremely small operation but that did not deter him in the least, for its potential was large. Mark's motivation owed a great deal to the example of his father, a man who never fulfilled his potential. Christopher Turner did well at Oxford and passed out first in the Foreign Office examinations. As the youngest in his family, however, he had very little money, wanted to marry and, in consequence, took the first job offered him in spite of the fact that it required some private means; thereafter he remained a clerk in the House of Commons.

Mark was born in 1906 and at the end of the Great War he was sent to Wellington instead of Eton because he was not considered healthy enough; the reason was difficult to fathom, Mark was always an immensely fit man. At Wellington he did very well, becoming head boy, and was all set to go to Oxbridge when disaster struck. The discovery that funds set aside to cover his years at university had been depleted by a crash in Burma rubber shares put an immediate end to his university plans. In some desperation his mother, who came from a rich family, made contact with some of her father's City friends and a place was found for her son at the merchant bank, M. Samuel. Thus, at the age of 18, Mark started his City career as a messenger boy.

While he may have set forth with few of the obvious advantages, he none the less possessed many of the qualities which can determine success. He had an inquiring mind and an extraordinary way of learning more about a business than the proprietor and his directors knew themselves. Furthermore he retained the knowledge in a prodigious mental filing system so that he was never at a loss to supply people with encyclopedic details, rendering them speechless with wonder in the process. This remarkable memory, and the background information it provided, meant that he could identify the key issues in an apparently intractable problem and could see clearly how a business fitted into place and in which direction to steer it.

Yet there was nothing mechanical and unimaginative about Mark. People fascinated him and, although he was not necessarily the best judge of them, he brought out the best in them. Full of drive and energy, he was also able to concentrate and to communicate extremely well. His enthusiasm was infectious and people literally flocked to his side. He was marvellous company and enjoyed everything from unworkable deadlines to catching the evening rise on his favourite loch, from an unyielding client to making golfballs run down sandcastles on the beach. Relaxing over lunch after a gruelling morning of negotiations he would say 'Isn't this all such fun!' and, as one of his brothers-in-law confirmed, it truly all was because he made it so.

His advancement during his ten years at M. Samuel was connected with his ability to analyse a firm's balance sheet so as to identify a promising company in need of financial aid to achieve growth; thus at Kenterne he concentrated upon searching out capital-starved businesses with good potential and competent management. The idea was to build them up so they could become absorbed into Bensons' clientele. Everybody's bible in those days was a set of Exchange Telegraph (Extel) cards produced on subscription, which listed by individual card every single quoted company together with the latest results and pertinent commercial details. Mark would study them, as he had done at M. Samuel, and spot when a company would be in the market for money. Contact would be made by Eric Tatham or Ben Pollen, who had left Cazenove, Ackroyds & Greenwood & Co. to join them at Kenterne. Turner and Pollen then went to visit prospective clients together.[55]

One of their earliest pet projects was christened 'No-nail boxes' by the family. A British steel manufacturing company in Dutch ownership had invented an elephantine machine that could produce flat plywood sheets bonded by strips of steel which had only to be pulled into shape to form a box. 'The No-nail gang lunched. Mr Bogaert etc all say we must order 2 machines. This means £10,000 more. Is this going to be Benson's fortune maker?' Rex wondered on 16 June 1935. Everyone was optimistic, and in no time the whole Benson tribe owned shares in the company and were rooting for its success. This was achieved but not without a certain amount of risk. Mark and Ben once set off round the whisky distillers to sell them No-nail boxes in which to export their whisky, 'and they staggered from one whisky party to another' feeling the effects but 'still supporting each other with a solemn sadness'.

Then the machines proved unreliable, so that orders remained uncompleted and by the winter of 1936/7 it was clear that in its present state No-nails was not going to be Bensons' fortune-maker. New machines and new management were essential to meet the large potential demand. Kenterne's scheme was to put Ben Pollen in as chairman of the restructured company and inject a further £60,000 to produce a minimum output of 1.2m. boxes. This naturally required skilful negotiation since the Dutch owners held an exaggerated idea of the value of their company and would not willingly relinquish control. Bensons, however, were not sanguine about the outcome although as yet they had no first-hand experience of Mark Turner as a negotiator.

The No-nails situation was but a trifling one out of the many deals cemented by Bensons, but it is illustrative of their approach, and the type of business that they developed during the inter-war and pre-merger years. Mark was a brilliant negotiator and he negotiated this and all future agreements on the principle that 'no deal would endure, no business prosper unless all concerned were happy with the arrangements'. An old American friend recalled seeing him in action early in his career. Mark had negotiated a deal and received everything he wanted. The two sides prepared to leave when Mark suddenly said to his own colleagues, 'This is no way to conclude a negotiation. They're left broken and defeated!' He immediately brought the other side back to the table, renounced some of the advantages he had gained—and made friends for life. The next time they and their colleagues needed help, they asked for Mark Turner.

When it came to No-nails, the result exceeded Bensons' expectations: 'much to my surprise succeeded in coming to an agreement with the No-nail Proprietary Co.,' Rex noted in his diary on 5 March 1937. Mark had achieved a much better agreement than the owners were originally prepared to accept. The new basis was 75 per cent to Kenterne and 20 per cent to the company, royalties reduced from ⅝ to 5/16 with a minimum of £3,000 per annum provided 1.6m. boxes were sold. No-nails was not out of the woods but the company finance was in place and Ben Pollen was 'reasonably optimistic' that the company would succeed. The No-nails saga would continue over many years but in the mid-1930s provided Kenterne Trust with its first though not its most profitable business. A variety of industrial companies followed, mostly in textiles but also in steel, paper, and catering, for which Bensons' then sponsored issues.[56]

By no means all of Bensons' new issue work originated with Kenterne during this period. In April 1936 a £300,000 Anglo-Palestine Bank issue came to Bensons as joint lead managers with the Jewish Colonial Trust, who had approached Con through George May of the Prudential. 'Our Anglo Palestine Bank issue was oversubscribed 36 times,' Rex crowed. It was the second Benson issue in a fortnight to be oversubscribed; the first, forty-seven times oversubscribed, being the Mitchell Shackleton & Co. Ltd. share issue they did with Cohen, Laming & Hoare. As Rex said, 'The old firm is looking up.' Con for his part brought in a Round Oaks Steel Works issue of £100,000 through his brother-in-law, the Earl of Dudley, who had recently been elected president of the British Iron and Steel Federation. Con also initiated a small issuing business in South Africa with the Charterhouse Investment Group; on this occasion Rex was the partner to urge caution, feeling that the firm should take time to consider all the options first. 'A great amount of thought and chewing the rag is necessary over all these moves.'[57]

Bensons also made two joint issues in London with the Charterhouse Investment Trust, a firm which specialized in small industrial issues, and altogether Bensons were responsible for seven issues of less than £200,000 during the mid-1930s. This compares well with the performance of other small issuing houses. In 1937, for example, Helbert Wagg, which was a much better-known issuer, sponsored six issues, only one of which was for over £300,000, while Charterhouse sponsored over ten issues though for even smaller amounts. In contrast a first-division house such as Barings sponsored only six issues—but five were over £1m. All Bensons' issues were undertaken to establish their name in the area of industrial company finance rather than to make much profit, for issues below £200,000 were regarded as uneconomic loss leaders. New issue work was a high-cost exercise, as Bensons and Kenterne knew. Apart from the brokers' fees, the legal fees, postage, and other small charges incurred, there were the advertising costs which could easily reach £5,000 for minimum coverage in the national press, and the most expensive components of all, the underwriting and overriding costs, usually 2.5 per cent. These costs were standard, regardless of the size of the issue, which was why the City regarded smaller issues as uneconomic.[58]

It was certainly not easy for a second-division issuing house such as Bensons to break into the large issue league. By definition these were usually blue chip issues which were invariably the prerogative of the first-division houses. The only way for Bensons to increase the size of their issues was to look outside the blue chip, first-class companies to those companies whose shares would be less secure and the demand for them correspondingly unpredictable. In February 1938 Bensons took this path with their largest issue after British Power & Light.

'Mossy' Myers, a stockbroker, owned two chains of furniture shops, British & Colonial Furniture Co. and Cavendish Furniture Co., which were a feature of every High Street. Started in 1899, they were successfully managed businesses and Myers had come to the market in the past, although as Rex observed, 'He does not put his issues out well on the market always and many have gone to discounts'. On this occasion, however, he asked Bensons to sponsor an issue of £1m. Rex immediately asked 'Teddy' Grenfell, now Lord St Just, at Morgan Grenfell, Sir Guy Granet at Higginsons, and G. F. Abell, a chief general manager at Lloyds Bank, to come in; none of them had any objection—if the issue was a good one. Sam Hamburger, the able new-issue manager at Bensons, did his best to ensure that it was. He came up with the idea of issuing a joint debenture for the two separate companies, apparently the first time such a financial vehicle had been used.

So, on 7 February, Rex decided to sponsor the issue of £1m. 5½ per cent debenture stock, his reasons being that Myers was an honourable man, the issue was a good one with excellent security and 'if we make it a real success it will be a great feather in our caps and should bring us good business'. The firm then set about getting the issue underwritten by lining up Scottish trust and insurance companies, de Steins, Erlangers, and Pearl Insurance and going the rounds of the City. It was discouraging work at first, only £600,000 was in sight on 2 March after trying their own friends, with many refusals coming from the English insurance companies. Rex started to weigh up whether to withdraw from the issue or not, but decided on balance it would do more harm than good. He persuaded Myers to do the issue at 5.5 per cent but then discovered that Myers' bank, the National Provincial, would not lend him £100,000 for the preparation of the issue, only £75,000, even after Rex and Guy had been to see the bank's general manager. That evening Bensons sent out about £900,000 of underwriting letters with Myers providing the remaining £100,000. However at the eleventh hour, Bensons had to turn to their friendly bankers, Lloyds, who agreed to lend £200,000 after the National Provincial refused to help.

Unfortunately, even a friendly banker could not save the issue. The success of Bensons' last issue of £400,000 for which they had received applications for £7m. led Hellings to issue an order for the whole of the staff of Bensons to be at Gresham House at 8 a.m. to meet the expected rush. When the door opened an hour later, however, far from being overwhelmed, not a soul appeared. 'Our issue was the completest possible failure as far as the public was concerned,' Rex mournfully recorded, 'only just over £6,000 subscribed out of £1 million.' It was with justified relief that he wrote, 'To think that we might have had to take up all the slack, had we not been fully underwritten.'[59]

The issue had undoubtedly been affected by the uncertain political situation and threat of war which overshadowed the City during those years of 1937–9. Sino-Japanese fighting had disturbed the markets in 1937, in particular the American market which 'went up in smoke' in September. Rex had only returned from America a month before, feeling optimistic about its prosperity and about the value of Bensons' large US stockholdings, which looked ready to improve in value. Since then stocks had depreciated by 30 per cent to leave Bensons with a paper loss of some £180,000. The slide had continued throughout October 1937 due to rumours of European war as Germany and Italy sharpened their teeth in the Mediterranean, Spain, and Austria. 'Another bad break in USA market. Values fallen out of all recognition—sent £40,000 to Chase to refreshen our account. These are trying times,' Rex observed. Bensons' paper loss by now amounted to some £300,000 and Gresham House was full of gloom.

The atmosphere had been no better at Blenheim Palace where Rex was staying over the New Year. Winston Churchill had been so gloomy over Japan and Britain's air force policy that Rex had doubted whether 1938 would be a better year after all. At the time of the British & Colonial Furniture issue in March the City was reeling from the grave news that Germany had bitten off

Austria. For Rex and the more prescient, such as Churchill, this was the beginning of a long European march into war. 'If the Germans can do this', he reasoned, 'then they will find some equally drastic method of "freeing Germans in Czecko Slovakia". That will mean war if we are to stand by France.' Then the markets began to topple with 'much fear around' at 'all the usual Nazi methods going on in Austria'. City talk everywhere was of war. It was thus a most unpropitious time to be bringing out an issue and it made business throughout the remainder of the year utterly unpredictable.[60]

Bensons, in common with the rest of the City, persevered. There were a large number of syndicated deals, a class of business which flourished in the inter-war years. Syndicates were formed to protect a company issuing additional capital or releasing a large holding; in order not to disturb the market, the syndicate would gradually absorb the shares. Although Rex was concerned that Bensons' book was far too heavy and their commitments too great, he had to admit that business was 'humming and every day we are asked to take on 3 or 4 new placings or underwritings'. He nevertheless believed it was more important than ever to have funds liquid, as his father had advised in 1929, to meet the difficult times ahead; too many underwritings were unwise. Happily Rex was in a position to take the initiative in this and other areas of policy because he had replaced Guy as chairman of Robert Benson & Co. in 1936.

Guy had risen to the challenge of the chairmanship and impressed both his brothers by 'being much more on the job'. Two factors, however, militated against his enjoying a peaceful chairmanship. The first was that he disliked taking difficult decisions. Hellings was deeply critical of George Wansbrough and spoke to Rex about it after having already told Guy. Rex in turn noticed that George seemed to be distancing himself from the daily business of the firm; he flitted in and out and nobody knew what he did with himself. Rex made a mental note to have a word with him though Guy should really have done so—'what a lot of things Guy should have done!!' It became apparent that George's fervent brand of socialism was unpopular, that he had had several upsets in the office, presumably with Hellings, as he had bought and sold 20,000 British Power & Light shares, which was treading on Hellings's toes. 'It is the old story—no guiding hand—hence no discipline,' Rex reiterated. George Wansbrough subsequently resigned and went on to a distinguished career in the electrical supply industry, but his departure did little to lighten Guy's load.

The second factor which disabled Guy was that he fell neatly between his more dominant brothers, who often disagreed about the direction of the firm and policy matters. Each in turn would try to persuade Guy to take his own side against the other. It was a terrible strain for Guy as he endeavoured to act as peacemaker between the two. Rex rather resented the fact that for no apparent reason he was often the only one in the office. 'Con never turned up in the office at all and GHB [Guy] only for a little. Had to take all decisions over two big loans,' he complained; while Con resented the fact that Rex, who had received no professional banking training, should always assume that he was the better leadership material and tended to pull 'older brother' rank on him.

This should, however, be seen in proportion. On personal issues Rex and Con were absolutely loyal and unstinting in their support. They and their families were part of an extremely close cousinhood which extended through the generations and they saw a great deal of each other. On partnership issues they could and did often disagree and did not disguise it behind the closed doors of their rooms. A good 'blow-up', as Rex called it, often cleared the air and they all got back down to business again.

With Guy, however, evidently feeling the strain of his responsibilities, the issue of leadership came to a head with the entrance of a new partner to ease Rex's workload. Rex desperately needed help with the American investment side: 'I feel very tired with the eternal American business & nobody to handle it but myself and Sam Hamburger,' he wrote after a very busy day in the office. Usually he thrived on good American business, finding it the most enjoyable side of Bensons. Rex was at home with the country and visited it twice a year, sailing across to New York and travelling on to Chicago with social breaks in Palm Beach and Long Island where he always played polo. He thus came to know many people there and formed many lifelong friendships. His unquenchable high spirits, zest for life, and great style struck a chord in the hearts of many Americans and the goodwill he created was of incalculable value to Bensons.[61]

His long love affair with America had been further consolidated by his marriage in 1932 to an attractive, fair-haired American. Leslie Foster came from an old Chicago family and had first been married to Condé Nast, the proprietor of the *Vogue* empire of magazines. 'Her taste was impeccable', Luke Asquith, a young friend of the family, recalled; and she was greatly admired, sharing with Rex a capacity for friendship and enjoyment that inspired devotion from others.[62]

As American business surged after the New Deal took effect, Bensons decided they needed another partner who would have experience of the technical problems of company law and finance and could take on the investment side of the business to free Rex for more company finance work. This was the second key appointment for the future development of Bensons and, like that of Mark Turner, it introduced professionalism into the partnership where it could be most effective.

The appointment came about through Michael Colefax, who was invited by George, now Lord May, to join the board of the Great Northern Investment

Trust in which the Prudential had a major stake. Board meetings were held in Glasgow and there Colefax was introduced to many of the Scottish firms of solicitors and accountants who managed investment trust companies in Glasgow and Edinburgh. In the course of building a Scottish connection for Bensons he came to know the partner concerned with investment trusts at Layton-Bennett, Chiene & Tait. This was G.P. (Phil) S. Macpherson, who so impressed Michael Colefax that he suggested to the Benson partners that Phil Macpherson take George Wansbrough's recently vacated place on the board. Con and Michael opened discussions in September 1935 and Rex met him three months later, writing after their meeting, 'Think he will join our team, but he is very Scotch & hard headed.' But join he did in the spring of 1936 to the delight of the partners. They had no doubts that Phil was the right man for the investment side, then the main side of their business.

Phil Macpherson was a chartered accountant, but that could be considered the least interesting of his many attributes. He was a Highlander, born in 1903 in Inverness-shire, and this determined much of his life and character, for he possessed the self-reliance and uprightness so endemic to Highlanders. He won a scholarship to Fettes where his athletic prowess was but a springboard to an outstanding career at Oxford from where he went as a Davison Scholar to Yale University. He was only 17 when he went to Oriel College on an open classical scholarship, yet he possessed the self-discipline to combine excellence at his studies with excellence on the playing-fields. 'Not many men would get a first in Mods and a first in Greats and captain Oxford at Rugby!' David Kenyon-Jones, a fellow rugby player, declared.

Phil Macpherson went on to become one of the 'greats' of rugby. He first played for Scotland in 1922 and three years later he led Scotland to victory against England to win the Triple Crown at Murrayfield. As a player he has been called the 'greatest attacking centre of his era'. He ran beautifully, 'swayed this way and that, changed pace' and 'would slip past defenders in a twinkling of an eye—indeed before you could say Phil Macpherson!' and leave 'everybody standing for a wonderful try'.

He did not retire from active rugby until 1932, so that it was interwoven into his years training as a chartered accountant in Edinburgh. He was still playing when he first became a partner at Chiene & Tait but had retired by the time he became a director of the Standard Life Assurance Co. However the aura of his legendary rugby days clung to him at Bensons. A colleague can recall the visit to a small company in Wales when the negotiations became 'distinctly sticky'. During a break, one of the directors of the company tentatively asked if Phil could possibly be 'The G.P.S.M.'. Upon confirmation, the atmosphere changed dramatically and negotiations proceeded apace.

Phil's arrival at Bensons was a major step forward and immediately led to a considerable reorganization of some of the older investment trusts. The Charter, for example, had become a semi-moribund concern full of old mining shares which earned little profit. Phil took it to pieces and reconstructed it to make it more successful. His arrival had also underscored the fact that Guy was not a full-time chairman. 'With Macpherson coming in & our many outsiders, how are we to run efficiently without a head-piece?' Rex had worried. One solution suggested by their cousin Charles Grey was for Rex to become managing director. Guy had agreed to consider the idea while Rex was away in America unscrambling the utility colossus, Automatic Electric, a casualty of the 1929 collapse.[63]

Rex had returned from a whirlwind tour of New York with Phil Macpherson where they were 'on the run from dawn to dark' to find that neither projects nor his managing director idea had gone any 'for'arder'. 'They had done nothing about Beachnut except write a circular letter which was so ill-worded that it was misunderstood by several readers. A few telephone talks would have done the trick in ½ hour—instead of 12 days,' he complained. As for the leadership issue, 'They talk of wanting more help which is indeed necessary; but every new man we take in will show more and more the need of "direction" from the top and more efficient office management,' he had concluded. Something had to be done, but as usual nothing would be done unless he pushed his brothers into action. Con, however, did not want Guy to relinquish the chair to Rex even though Guy agreed 'he did not feel equal to taking it on' full-time.

Eventually Rex forced the issue, and while Con did not oppose the change he shared Vernet's view that Rex concentrated too much on the stock-market side and was too 'speculative minded'. This did not make it especially easy for Rex, who none the less agreed not to 'dragoon' as Con feared. Guy remained a partner and continued much as before but for Rex it was a major change. He was at last able to become the chairman of Robert Benson & Co. and took over in 1936. His first steps were to try to introduce a team spirit at the top, 'at present everybody works as individuals too much', and to reintroduce partnership meetings, which had lapsed again.[64]

Thus the years leading up to 1939 saw a revitalized firm, one which had its management team in place, the directors on salaries of £3,000 [£95,000] with profit-sharing in 1937 providing another £6,400 [£200,000] each, the firm's reserve fund having been rebuilt after the Depression to over £100,000, and the business improving every day. Both Mark Turner and Rex were in the throes of developing new schemes. Mark's was a trading company, the Hungarian Export Co., which was a trade-credit business encompassing Turkish and Greek tobacco, an area in which Rex was involved through the British Near-Eastern Co., which dealt with Turkey and in which he had invested his own money. Rex was also in the process of launching a Canadian project with Pitfields, Robert Benson & Co. (Canada), which would be a merchant banking and investment business.

These ambitious projects required considerable financial backing. But Bensons were already stretched. In 1937 their investments totalled about £580,000 in England and about $1m. in the United States, on a capital of only £400,000 with £100,000 reserves. The partners were in complete accord that this was far too small a capital for the amount of business done and the search for a way to increase their capitalization would preoccupy the partners until the events of 1939 overtook them.

Although they would have preferred the solution of a sleeping partner who would put 'some senior capital into the firm', they were increasingly attracted to the idea of a merger with another City firm. This was a highly unusual move in the inter-war period, for the City was then dominated by proprietorial houses. Lord Faringdon, for example, had only considered merging his firm with Cazenoves because none of his grandsons or extended family wished to enter the business and he could not otherwise secure its future in the long term.[65]

Bensons did not need to take the initiative down this somewhat uncharted course because they already had a suitor. They had long been ardently wooed by Higginson & Co., an American firm which had opened in London in 1907. The senior partner in England was Rudolph de Trafford, who had suggested the idea to Rex over a drink at Buck's in September 1936. While Rex thought it 'tantalising & we should be a very strong house both banking & investment', he hesitated over the main disadvantage that 'the family nature of the Benson house would disappear'. By October, G. L. Abell of Lloyds Bank had dissuaded Con who had originally been in favour. Con did not like the banking and acceptance end, which Rex thought curious. The reason was that Higginsons had lost a great deal of money in the German banking crisis and in common with Kleinworts held a large standstill debt on their books.

On balance, therefore, the odds crystallized against the marriage in 1936. Bensons' rejection, however, did not deter Rudolph de Trafford, who persistently kept the door open for a renewal of talks. With the threat of war and a loss on their balance sheet, however, the Benson partners agreed to reopen discussions about a marriage in the autumn of 1938. Preliminary discussions ended on 5 October with the conclusion that the merger was viable, although the Benson brothers were only reluctantly prepared to relinquish their independence. While Higginsons did not supply much manpower they had a good clientele, especially in the field of industrial company finance. Bensons would also be able to liquidate the 5.5 per cent preferred Robert Benson & Co. shares and the Holford interest.

An insurmountable impediment to the merger suddenly appeared. 'Guy returned from his holiday in S. Uist and has immediately, poor man, got embroiled in a Con–Rex controversy.' His two brothers could not agree over the leadership of the merged firm. Rex proposed to remain chairman of the new board whereas Con insisted that Higginsons' Tom McKettrick, who was a trained banker, would be the better choice. Con reasoned that it would take Rex longer to learn banking than McKettrick to learn investment, about which he already knew a good deal.

Guy offered to talk to Con to try to find out what was behind his surprising choice of chairman. 'Dear Guy has no fun ever and tries to act as peace-maker,' Rex wrote rather sadly. Con then admitted he had not really considered the implications, not least that the City might view the idea of a Benson–Higginson merger with McKettrick at the head as a rather a strange one, given that Higginsons were only bringing in £200,000 of capital and little entrepreneurial talent.

In the event the merger foundered on the ratio of control and price. Higginsons wanted 60 : 40 in Bensons' favour whereas Bensons wanted 75 : 25, on the grounds that Higginsons did not really add much to their profits and the capital remained fairly small, though they gained the prestige of a banking house. Rex wrote in his diary after telling Rudolph of their decision, 'I am much relieved that this most difficult decision had been taken. I think on the whole we were right, though I cannot help thinking that we were actuated more by the fact that we should, so to speak, lose our independence if we merged and became a bank, than by the lack of a suitably sized capital.' These words about the importance of retaining independence would epitomize his feelings when Bensons were next on the brink of merging with an accepting house.[66]

Relief at the end of the Higginson affair was short-lived. The merger discussions had taken place against an international build-up to war. Con had even appeared at one of the Higginson meetings in his RAF uniform, being a reserve officer in that service. Rex was in very low spirits. 'Is it possible,' he asked, 'to be bright and cheerful when the world has gone crazy again and all that we fought for and our friends died for in 1914 appears to have gone into the air?' Instead of the anticipated major thrust of expansion they were faced with the disruption of the firm's business.

Even so, disruption in the firm's offices was kept to a minimum because Bensons had long been 'on alert' for their own mobilization. As early as January 1939 Rex had left the Pollens at Norton and motored over to Cheltenham to look over three houses and arrange for Hellings to inspect them during the week. By March the firm had purchased Elms Court, outside the centre of town near the race course, and installed Dick Silvester and his wife as housekeepers there to await the arrival of staff in the event of the outbreak of war. Rex also went through the arrangements for the evacuation of Bensons with Hellings and Bill Hole, the office manager. Hole had already got out mobilization orders for the office in terms of what the staff would be doing or wanted to do in the war. Most of the young men had joined the Territorials, the Fire Brigade, or the Balloon Barrage and had received adequate training by the time war was actually declared.

The week before the declaration, Frank Wooldridge, the company secretary, together with two men and two women, was sent off to Cheltenham. 'Take your typewriter and enough stuff for a week,' they were told. They were to remain there for the duration of the war, fully five years. All the registration work was moved to Cheltenham and duplicates of all the London work were sent down and kept at Cheltenham. A special safe room was built in the house to store all the firm's records as a precaution against the anticipated bombing of London. Cheltenham also housed a secret cache of Rex's collection of old silver (mostly acquired in lieu of a debt owed by How's of Edinburgh), though not, as expected, in the safe room. He preferred to bury it in a concreted hole in the garden and, with the help of Floss Lincoln, chose a spot. The secret was rather a formality, however, since the spot was neatly pinpointed under a square of grass of completely different appearance. In the event it was not dug up until after the war when, to his dismay, Rex discovered that the sulphuric spa water had seeped in with disastrous results.

The evacuation to Cheltenham left the London office with a skeleton staff under 'C.C.H.' [Hellings], by now somewhat aged but still resplendent in black morning coat with a black ribbon from his eye-glasses, John Read, a new junior clerk who remained as he suffered from heart trouble and was indefinitely deferred from joining up, and the indomitable Floss, who kept everyone's spirits up through blackout and Blitz. Twice during the Blitz Gresham House was wrecked, first when a land-mine flattened neighbouring Palmerston House and second when the Dutch Church in nearby Austin Friars was destroyed. The staff had long been advised to make their wills but, as they surveyed the wreckage that morning, they realized they had not been very wise in appointing each other as executors. There and then they sat down amidst the rubble to make out new ones, this time appointing their Cheltenham colleagues as executors.[67]

When the war ceased, scarred and moulded by their wartime experiences, the Benson and Kleinwort partners and staff returned to their respective City offices changed men and women. The onset of peace naturally brought relief but it also brought the challenge of starting all over again to rebuild their lives and the moribund business of their firms. Both sets of partners would be met by old, unresolved problems of operation. The Benson partners were in a more fortunate position in that they had been about to embark upon a major programme of expansion and were confident of being able to recapture the momentum again. The Kleinwort partners, however, returned to a bank that had never recovered from the German moratorium and the damage inflicted by the Standstill debts. The challenge they faced was a daunting one; it was, none the less, one which had to be met if their firm was to survive in the post-war era.

9 Kleinworts and the Urge to Merge

WHEN the war ended, the curtain of the post-war era opened onto a scene of economic disintegration. Physically shattered by German bombs, the City lay exhausted amidst the rubble of her former power as a financial centre of the world. Britain, now a debtor nation, could no longer lend money to the rest of the world, and foreign investment had largely been expended in the war effort. The pound was only worth half its 1914 value and quickly had to cede its place as a reserve currency to the American dollar. Attlee's newly elected Labour Government was committed to fulfilling an election promise to nationalize steel, coal, transport, and the Bank of England. This policy did little to instil confidence in the City and over the next few years sterling lurched from crisis to crisis.[1]

The abrupt end of Lend-Lease; the mushrooming balance of payments deficit estimated at £750m. in 1946; and the pound's convertibility into dollars from July 1947, which fuelled the purchase of American nylons, petrol, and cigarettes; all combined to lead to a run on gold and a flight from sterling. The ensuing crisis ushered in the first of many post-war austerity plans, though austerity was hardly an unfamiliar concept to the British. Coal supplies had run out in the 'big freeze' winter of 1947 and two million men were thrown out of work. By 1948 rations had fallen below the wartime average. Then recession struck America and, with Marshall Aid euphoria ebbing away, Cripps devalued sterling from $4.03 to $2.80 in September 1949. The cost of living soared, a loaf of bread costing 25 per cent more.

In many ways the post-war experience of Kleinworts and Bensons replicated that of the nation. Like other City houses, they stumbled along among the detritus of their war-devastated businesses trying to find a way to recover their pre-war level of operation. Both firms diversified by looking outside their traditional businesses for profits, though with mixed results. Following the national example, both houses also looked to America for their future prosperity.

Ernest, aged 44, and Cyril, aged 40, returned from their war service to a business that was a pale shadow of its pre-war self. They were determined, however, to revive it, and whilst Herman Andreae remained the senior partner, they provided the dynamo that led to recovery. But recovery proved no easy task. Many ventures were to prove abortive, others close to disastrous, but the skill and nerve of the brothers held and in the end ensured that their patrimony prospered.

The going was initially heavy, the economic backdrop hardly being conducive to Kleinworts' acceptance credit and foreign exchange business. Many of the wartime controls remained in place, the most restrictive of which were the Exchange Control regulations introduced on 4 September 1939, and the majority of Kleinworts' business had been in parts of the world which fell outside the Sterling Area. This area had been so designated as a wartime measure in 1939 and covered the Commonwealth countries excluding Canada and a small number of other countries which kept their currency reserves in London. It meant, in effect, that Kleinworts was unable to trade with most of their customers. Furthermore, other restrictions turned the simplest everyday transaction into an irksome, time-consuming process. 'The despatch of a small shipment of six drums of lubricating oil involves the filling in of forty-six forms, requiring forty-two signatures, not including the customer's invoice or delivery notes,' was but one example of the bureaucracy of control regulations. The effect of these controls on a firm struggling to resurrect itself was paralysing.[2]

Conditions at No. 20 were equally stultifying for the staff. The office was old-fashioned and the atmosphere deadening to those returning from the services. The nucleus of people who kept the firm going during wartime had been the older members, whose overriding concern was to maintain their jobs and the status quo. Most of the younger ex-servicemen found it difficult to adjust to this regime, their problems exacerbated by the lack of business.

Gerald Thompson returned to No. 20 to resume his place in the fast lane as an assistant manager in the Banking Department. He remembers the immediate post-war years as 'a period of locking the safes' and of carrying out 'the endless administrative chores which kept the enterprise in being'. Junior members of staff welcomed the opportunity to leave the bank in order to deliver four or five bars of gold in a taxi to Johnson Matthey or Rothschilds: 'It was an escape from the mundane clerical work for a day.'

While some of their more senior colleagues believed that this treading-water operation would eventually lead to a surge of new business activity, others were less optimistic. 'I must say that I was one of the pessimists,' Gordon Tettmar would record. 'I thought that all that Kleinworts had to look forward to was nursing the Partners' investments.' E. C. Fitzsimmons, who had joined the firm in 1937 as a foreign exchange clerk, was transferred to the English Department as a junior correspondent owing to the dearth of foreign exchange business after the war. The dealers were hampered by exchange controls which entailed applying to the Bank of England, sending round an E form, obtaining permission, and then, finally, doing the deal. 'Rumour had it', Fitzsimmons would recall, 'that in those first years after the war, profits were so low that it was considered quite likely that we might shut down and become just an investment trust and that would be the end of Kleinwort, Sons & Co. as it had been.'[3]

Those with ambition could not see any great future to strive towards and became increasingly frustrated; yet with other City firms also still feeling their way, there was little hope of better prospects elsewhere. Consequently, competition for promotion was keen within Kleinworts, even to the first rung of the managerial ladder, the half-managership, when the coveted 'signature' was made jointly with someone else. Opportunities, however, were few with the business reduced to what was, effectively, a holding operation.

There was, none the less, a significant intake of new blood at a more junior level. Many of the foreign staff, formerly the backbone of the firm, did not return after the war. Replacements were found amongst the ranks of young ex-servicemen, some of whom, such as Steven Stephens, Leslie Stanforth, and Bill Mundy had worked previously in the City; others such as Bill Baldock and F. A. James entered through a Government training scheme run for ex-servicemen. Finally, in place of the nineteenth-century apprentice banker came a twentieth-century graduate trainee from New College, Oxford, Michael Hawkes.

For all these young men, entry into Kleinwort, Sons & Co. took them into an unfamiliar pre-war world. The clerks still perched on high, leather-seated stools at high desks and recorded the accounts by hand on large, long sheets. Only the customers' accounts were compiled on the Burroughs machines. Smoking was forbidden while the partners were on the premises. Thus staff had half an hour in which to smoke until just before 10 o'clock when the managers arrived. Just as in pre-war days, smoking was allowed after 3.30 by which time the partners had usually left the building. 'Who can forget', Ernest Pudney has asked, 'Commissionaire Darby announcing in military fashion, "Gentlemen, the Partners have gone. You may smoke. Got a cigarette old boy?"'[4]

The most peculiar aspect of the new entry's working day was the absence of any work. Every department formed its own coffee syndicates to go out to one of the numerous Lyons or ABC coffee houses dotted about Fenchurch Street, all of which seemed to be peopled entirely by fellow City clerks, 'all drinking coffee at 4d a cup and smoking like chimneys'. After his three-month tour round all the banking departments, Michael Hawkes was given a clerkship in the English Department which included Scandinavia. There was so little business being generated that he had ample time to investigate an ongoing credit of £37 which showed up in the accounts of a UK subsidiary of United Dominion Trust and had arisen from an error a clerk had made in 1932. Although the accounts had been compiled every quarter since then, no one had bothered before to query this unusual and paltry sum. In addition, Hawkes's colleague Stanforth 'used to get very neurotic if he had no work to do', so, though clerking in one of the supposedly most active departments covering Great Britain, Scandinavia, South Africa, and Australia, lack of business enabled the three clerks to give Stanforth all the available work to do while they followed their respective pursuits: 'I used to get on reading for the Bar—under the desk with my text books from the Rapid Results College,' Michael Hawkes remembers, 'and one by one I ticked off the five exams while I was working.'[5]

The partners were now faced with the novel situation of 'getting business'. Not since the early days of Drake, Kleinwort & Cohen had the firm actively had to seek business, least of all on the banking side of its operations. Unlike their grandfather, Ernest and Cyril had no experience of looking for clients; Herman A. had—he had started the firm's Canadian business—but he now considered himself 'an old horse' who 'has done his job and deserves to be pensioned off'. José Mayorga, another dynamic business-getter, was so disenchanted with the post-war City environment and Kleinwort, Sons & Co.'s chances that he emigrated to the Argentine in 1946, acting as the firm's correspondent in Buenos Aires. While not exactly disenchanted, Herman A. was less sanguine than Ernest and Cyril about the firm's chances in securing 'all the business they wanted', believing that 'We shall have to search for it and that is where vision and initiative will be required to overcome the very great difficulties which we shall encounter in the "brave new world" of business.'[6]

It was, indeed, to the brave new world of post-war America that the Kleinworts looked for new business. They had long wanted a new American connection and had always remained optimistic that one day market conditions would enable them to recapture their large American business. After their world tour in 1929, Ernest and, in particular, Cyril had returned captivated by the vibrancy of the United States and keen to foster business there.

They held substantial dollar assets in their Moonhill portfolio and when, in 1940, the Treasury had sequestered them they had asked if £500,000 could be retained in order to form a New York branch, which would be in the national interest since it would secure a flow of dollars into Britain. Although the Treasury had acceded, Herman A. had not hesitated to express his doubts, telling Ernest 'Frankly, if we decide to call the whole American scheme off, I should not cry over it. I am not enthusiastic about results; hope I am wrong.' He believed that 'the business looks rotten' from the firm's, as distinct from the partners', point of view, on the grounds that Kleinworts would be locking up funds without much hope of any return for an indefinite period. Then Spicer had stated that their chances of success would be much greater if they amalgamated with an established New York business and had suggested their old colleagues, Goldman Sachs & Co. When John Holm, the highly capable if autocratic Kleinwort, Sons & Co. manager, wanted Kleinworts to become partners and take a direct interest in Goldman Sachs, however, Spicer had vetoed the idea: because of unlimited liability the partners would be risking their entire fortunes, besides which Goldman Sachs were only offering a 'measly' 6 per cent per annum return whereas Kleinworts wanted a minimum 10 per cent. The Kleinwort / Goldman marriage never materialized and the American scheme lay dormant until 1945 when the Bank of England agreed to the use of dollar assets for the establishment of a New York subsidiary—but only on condition that they were used in support of a national export drive to 'earn dollars' for Britain. In the gloomy post-war period, this was Governor Catto's all but invariable response to pressure on the City for action.[7]

Kleinworts were now impaled on the horns of a dilemma. On the one hand they wanted to build up their American acceptance business. Yet after the war there was less scope due to the fiercely competitive American banks, who were not only financing US corporations, but were also competing with City merchant banks for London-based business. Kleinworts would have first-hand experience of this when a client, Dansk Esso, ran down their £2m. revolving acceptance credit facility in 1960 because American banks offered them cheaper finance. Nevertheless, prepared to accept the challenge on the strength of their good acceptance name, Kleinworts found themselves stymied by the Bank of England. On the other hand, they now had permission to establish an import / export agency in America.

Although at first glance this seemed far removed from a banking business, it was of course an area in which Kleinworts had built up considerable expertise through its Commodities and Merchanting Department, the one field of operation which had maintained the firm's traditional nineteenth-century mercantile function. In the days of Drake, Kleinwort & Cohen, Ferdinand Karck had managed the Liverpool branch specifically to trade in commodities. Both the London and Liverpool branches had also supervised the shipment, warehousing, and sale of those cargoes which formed the security upon which the firm granted acceptance credits. Thus by the 1880s the firm had begun to act as importers rather than merely as agents for acceptance credit clients. This importing business had remained significant during the inter-war period. It was, for example, as an importer of gum arabic for the confectionery trade that the indomitable Frank Vines of the Liverpool office travelled to the deserts of the Sudan and formed an important and long-lasting link with the Bittars, an entrepreneurial Khartoum family with interests in cotton, sugar refining, and general merchandise.

After the Second World War, the old Commodities and Consignments Department was hived off into a separate limited company, Fendrake, under the direction of Colonel Christopher Hudson, a friend of Cyril's. A former executive of the cotton firm, J. & P. Coats, he was 'a highly entertaining' and most persuasive man. Sir Norman Biggs, a former director of Kleinworts, recalls that the only bad debt he felt personally responsible for was incurred on a 120-day bill against toys that Hudson had implored him to accept in order to secure an agency for a Fendrake outlet. Biggs forgot how Maynard Keynes had once said to him: 'Oh you bankers! You always think a situation will hold till a 120 day bill matures!' The toy manufacturer, however, went under, and only after much hard work was the eventual loss minimized. But the experience was not without value. Biggs learnt two lessons, first never to start a fire to roast Fendrake's chestnuts and secondly that when faced with selling a mountain of toys not to let buyers pick out only the dolls and the train sets![8]

In spite of these and other hiccups, Fendrake quickly became the epicentre of a global trading empire, in concept if not in practice. Urged on by José Mayorga and John Holm, Cyril was keen to grasp the opportunity to establish a trading company in America and—as enthusiasm mounted—why not a series of companies located in Canada, Brazil, Argentina, South Africa, and the Far East as well? Each of these offices would represent UK manufacturers in the overseas markets and thus drum up exports. Fendrake would be the link in this international chain by placing orders with UK manufacturers and arranging the shipment of finished goods abroad. Kleinworts itself would benefit in the event of related requests for trade credits. Ernest, ever the more cautious banker, expressed reservations. The firm, he later wrote, 'had no knowledge or experience of the export business in finished goods, particularly not to the most difficult of all markets, the USA'. It was only 'after considerable hesitation' that he was won over and the project received the green light.[9]

An expansionist mood quickly swept through No. 20 as a spirit of pioneering and patriotism took hold. In 1946 the new chain of companies was formed under the name Drake, with Drake America Corporation as the jewel in the chain's crown. John Holm moved to New York but the first check came when he died suddenly of cancer before he had time to establish even the office. This was unfortunate, for Drake America represented what was then a very large investment in hard currency, £3m. [£55m.]. Cyril had to spend several weeks in New York before he had established a replacement team. George Artamanoff and a colleague, former Sears Roebuck executives, were appointed US managing directors and they recruited a seasoned merchandiser, Joe Givner from Macy's, to manage it.

The operation quickly went into orbit. The original aim was to organize and finance the export of quality British textiles and leather goods. The most successful item in terms of turnover was, however, the entire export output of grey cloth from the Czechoslovakian state-owned woollen mills. This deal originated from a German wool client of Stirling Karck, one Alex Berglas who, among many other assets, owned a mill in Yorkshire and large shareholdings in the largest woollen mills in Alsace—a shareholding he increased using the sizeable commission on the Czech deal. He had also put A. Kiener & Co., a big Alsatian mill on which Kleinworts had substantial outstanding claims, into reasonable condition by increasing output enormously. He was known as 'Kilometre Berglas' because he never considered it worth producing material for an order unless it was at least a kilometre long.

Unfortunately the Czech deal was not enough on its own to sustain Drake America. Attempts were made first, to import thick, woollen socks which (like the Kleinwort ostrich feathers of the early 1900s that suddenly went out of fashion) were unseasonal, surplus to requirements, and cost the firm large sums of money; second, and more successfully, to act as agents for Rowntree's chocolate; and thirdly, to sell a revolutionary form of snow-plough for runway clearance, a product in which Drake America had purchased the US marketing rights, but which had to be sold off for next to nothing after several snowless winters. Expensive English leather goods were also traded through the purchase of the New York retailer, Mark Cross Inc.

Drake America's interest in Mark Cross stemmed from a Kleinwort bad debt with the English Mark Cross, which supplied and shipped leather goods to the New York retailer. 'Mark Cross was fun' but, as a director of the time recalls, 'we never made any money from it.' Cyril eventually brought in a friend, Maybelle Jones, to put it into order before it was sold. The problems of stock control, shoplifting, and other retail hazards were somewhat beyond the ordinary experience of the partners and managers of Kleinworts. Yet increasingly they were called upon to deal with them. After the original team was lured elsewhere, the staff at Drake America were out of their depth and accordingly had to be replaced time and again. One new manager was almost immediately discovered to be 'as straight as a corkscrew' whilst a massive warehouse robbery was suspected to be 'in-house'. At No. 20 the memory of that period is of Cyril and Christopher Hudson struggling hard to promote the business and to conserve liquidity and capital in Drake America, while stories of tremendous losses were percolating through the office.

Difficulty in finding suitable management abroad was clearly a problem, but the cause of the ultimate failure of Drake America by 1957 was, in the subsequent words of a director, that to comply with the Bank of England's terms 'Cyril committed us to a piece of business we knew nothing about,' and which called for a degree of professionalism and commercial experience that was not easily drawn from acceptance credit work or stock exchange operations. It had been hoped that Drake America would win customers by being able to provide prompt supplies to American retailers more quickly than American suppliers. This entailed bulk buying and holding large warehouse stocks in New York which not only needed financing but carried the trade risks of fashion and seasonal demand. Kleinworts were simply not equipped to provide such expertise, nor were they successful in hiring it.

After lengthy visits throughout 1948 and 1949 Cyril and Hudson decided to appoint an English director, Adam Johnstone, a qualified merchandiser from Littlewoods. Before going to New York he tried to introduce modern management techniques into No. 20, in the course of which he drew up a Management Succession Replacement Chart to identify who should take over when someone was away or retired. He showed it to Herman A., who snorted 'When a man's broken to his knees, we lend him a man for half a day to pull him up again.' Johnstone's suggestions ruffled the partners and he left within a relatively short time. Drake America Corporation staggered on with the partners lowering their expectations in tune with the shrinking business and in 1957 they eventually took the decision to off-load it, although a buyer was not found until 1965. In Ernest's words, it was 'our most unfortunate failure'.[10]

Kleinworts were not alone in having difficulty metamorphosing into an import/export agency. Hambros, too, leapt with gusto into America when they started the Hambro Trading Co. of America Inc. in Louisiana, which in turn set up the Hambro House of Design to sell British and Scandinavian goods in New York. This was not a successful venture. Thousands of pots of fine English honey fermented in the heat of summer to explode in a Chicago warehouse. A consignment of Scottish kippers had to be dumped in the North River when it was discovered that the fish were the wrong size for the American market. It took six years of disasters before Hambros wisely decided to close down the House of Design and write the episode off to experience, having learnt that a modern merchant bank should stick to banking.[11]

Kleinworts also learnt this lesson from the other links in the Drake chain which proved equally problematic and irksome, if less costly in resources than Drake America. Hudson opened an office in Kuala Lumpur, but it was never profitable and closed in 1950, as did its Canadian counterpart, although there the firm did manage a liquidation dividend. Other merchant banks had similar experiences in Canada. Antony Gibbs, who had been persuaded by the Bank of England to open an office there to promote British exports, also had to liquidate its operation in 1955.

In São Paulo, Charles Gray formed Drake Brazil with Kleinworts as his majority shareholder. Remembered as 'an honest, loyal, hard-working and very likeable man, anxious to build up a successful future for all concerned', it was through no lack of competence or effort on his part that the venture did not flourish. The problems lay not with Brazil, but with London where Fendrake failed to supply the necessary back-up and Kleinworts the necessary credit; the bankers at No. 20 were finally too cautious—but with the wrong Drake venture.

Elsewhere in Latin America, the partners considered the possibility of a Drake Chile and Ernest duly embarked on an inspection tour with his wife Joan. They had a hair-raising flight over the Andes during which the pilot was forced to make two attempts to cross the highest peaks, just scraping over them at the second attempt. On landing in Chile, they discovered it was the inaugural flight. This experience did little to inspire Ernest with the confidence necessary to start a Drake Chile and the idea rapidly subsided. Even Drake Argentina, a far more promising venture since José Mayorga provided the third leg to the main Drake America–Fendrake axis within the Drake chain, proved problematical. Ernest and Cyril had taken its success for granted without a full understanding of the trading environment. Eventually, after purchasing 50 per cent of Arnott & Co., whose proprietor, Frank Arnott, was an English engineer long established in Buenos Aires, and withstanding an alarming deterioration in business in the Argentine, the partners saw the writing on the Buenos Aires wall—but too late to avoid liquidation in 1955, from which the firm recouped very little.

The Drake diversification experiment was undoubtedly a failure for Kleinworts. All the Drake companies were either closed down or sold off at varying losses. Kleinworts had little expertise in either long-distance management or the patient constructive efforts needed to create a continuing overseas market for British goods. Of all the partners, Ernest was the one capable of such application—but to issues, rather than to people and their marketing difficulties. Cecil Elbra summed up the thinking at No. 20 when he wrote: 'As one who had a good deal to do with the business, I thought then as I still think now that we were right in the context of the times but, as events developed, too much of our time, energy and money were being expended in enterprises which were getting us nowhere rather fast.' There was, none the less, one positive aspect to the Drake episode, namely the experience derived from it by the partners which proved invaluable later on during the overseas expansion of the firm's core banking business.[12]

In the immediate post-war period, however, it was more a case of survival than expansionism. When the partners decided to renew old contacts in order to resuscitate the banking business, Spain was at the head of the list owing to their strong pre-war presence. Ernest was by now very much the dominant partner, so it was he who went out there in early 1947. Far from courting business, however, he almost discouraged it. The firm was then undertaking a large amount of documentary credit business with, amongst others, the Banco Exterior de España. The Spanish economy had recovered well from the Civil War and several of Kleinworts banking clients were doing so well that they wanted to increase their credit lines.

Unfortunately, without José Mayorga to guide him, Ernest was nervous about allowing such substantial increases in spite of the evidence before his eyes of a relatively sound economic base. He was concerned that Franco's Government would not last; a misjudgement certainly, but one made without the benefit of hindsight. By agreeing to only temporary increases, he demonstrated a lack of faith in the firm's Spanish clients. And his excessive caution was a mistake which in the long-term cost the firm valuable business. Ernest, however, did not want to put too many of the bank's eggs, which were in short supply, in one country's basket after his experience of the German moratorium. José Mayorga's financial acumen and knowledge of the banking business were sorely missed at a crucial time in the firm's history.[13]

It was through Mayorga that Norman Biggs was persuaded to leave the Exchange Control section of the Bank of England for a managerial position at Kleinworts. Biggs was a man of outstanding ability whose prestige and experience, it was hoped, would revitalize the banking activities of Kleinworts. The firm's need to seek help from the Westminster Bank had led to the view, supported by Lord Catto at the Bank, that expertise should be recruited to bolster the management. Thus, in 1946, Norman Biggs was in place to tour South America in order to drum up more business with old and new clients.[14]

The opinion that Alexander Friedrich had formed in the 1880s—namely, that the risk was too great for a successful Latin American operation—remained as true as ever. As Mayorga found in Argentina, business communities were bedevilled by racketeers and corruption which only exacerbated the volatile political climate. In spite of this unpromising environment, Biggs managed to win Bahia's Institute of Cocoa agency to sell their cocoa in Europe. This not only provided the Liverpool office with much-needed work but also enabled the firm's otherwise unemployed foreign exchange dealers to keep their hands in by trading in cocoa. Although the firm continued to work with numerous South American banks, particularly on the documentary credit side, little other new business emerged.[15]

It was much the same story in Scandinavia, though for very different reasons. When Herman A.'s only surviving son, Sonny, visited Denmark he quickly discovered that Danish banks were determined to eliminate foreign competition in the finance of exports, while government restrictions meant that there was little hope of finding import business. The rest of Scandinavia proved to be equally stony ground for Kleinworts.

A charming, mild-mannered man, Sonny Andreae was, of all the partners, the only one to have undergone what would today be regarded as a classic City education: Eton, Oxford, and, highly unusual in the 1930s, Harvard Business School. Although the eldest son of a very rich man, he was kept on a shoe-string allowance. 'What's the use of going to Harvard on a million dollar name with a five cent income?' he was heard to mutter.

Somewhat surprisingly, his education and social attributes were in no way allowed to further his career at Kleinworts. This was entirely due to his father. Old Herman A. remained a dominating person. Sonny, according to his second son Mark, undoubtedly suffered from being the son of 'such a dynamo'. It was Mayorga rather than his father who had looked after him when he joined the firm in 1936, even to the extent of providing him with the money to buy a new shirt to wear to work. At the firm he was underrated because he was under the dominance of his father; and his epilepsy, triggered either by a fall from a horse or an aeroplane crash, and delicate health contributed to his being overshadowed by his tough father.

Where the old man remained very remote, however, Sonny was easily accessible to the staff; there was little of the proprietor and much more of the present-day director in his approach. A great cricket fan, he was often to be seen by the ticker, enquiring 'What's the cricket score?'; and whereas his cousins Ernest and Cyril did not often greet the staff as they passed by, Sonny always did. When on his first Christmas Eve at the bank, he came past the Exchange Department and stopped, waved his hand, and called out 'Merry Christmas to you all', everybody was speechless.

Sonny had become a partner when the partnership agreement had been renewed in 1946. Although his father and the Kleinwort brothers did not always see eye to eye, Sonny got along very well with them. In 1947, at a difficult point during the protracted negotiations over the company conversion scheme, Ernest reassured Herman A. that he 'need not have the slightest fear for Sonny's position in the firm'. Whilst Sonny was a valued and indispensable partner, it was even more important to the Kleinworts that 'we have built up between the three of us, on a basis of mutual confidence, a very friendly and happy spirit of collaboration.' This did not prevent Ernest from opposing the Andreae right of veto as enshrined in the partnership deed while simultaneously insisting that the equal Kleinwort right was transferred to the new company in the form of voting shares. Sonny trusted his cousins and gave way gracefully—something his father would not have done.[16]

Ernest at this time was equally absorbed in attempts to revive the firm's German business. It soon became evident that it would be neither a straightforward nor a speedy process. First, the German economy and most of the banks were in default. Secondly, after the end of the Second World War in 1945 Germany remained a country under Allied military occupation, with each of the four Allies administering its own occupation zone and a sector of Berlin until the early 1950s. The occupying forces had drastically reduced Germany's industrial power through the dismantling of equipment, and the future level of production was restricted to half its 1938 volume. Thus one of the firm's largest and oldest pre-war clients, I. G. Farben, was dismantled into several smaller companies. Such limitations hampered German recovery and were only relaxed in order to meet the German demand for greater economic freedom shortly before the creation of the Federal Republic of Germany in 1949. Nevertheless, it was not until 1950 that limits on steel and iron production, for instance, were lifted, largely as a result of the Korean war and the advent of the 'Cold War'.

Kleinworts' attempts to take advantage of improved economic conditions to revive German business were also impeded by the fact that, willingly or not, many of their clients had provided economic support to the Nazis. I. G. Farben for one was implicated in the monstrous economy of the concentration camps. Given such war legacies, it was a delicate business to reopen lines of communication, let alone do business, especially since, unlike the more tolerant and economically realistic British, the Americans were at first determined to limit German reconstruction. But German recovery was imperative if British firms such as Kleinworts were to be repaid their pre-war debts and find new business.

Kleinworts therefore embarked upon a course of 'recce' visits. The largest pre-war German producer had been Krupp's, the great armaments firm whose 1940 debt to Kleinworts of £289,728 had been reduced to £123,601 under Standstill debt arrangements. Ernest now sent Walter Michaelis, manager of the German Department, to investigate the position of the firm with a view to negotiating repayment of this old debt. Michaelis found the Krupp's works completely devastated. 'Halfway between Duisburg and Essen,' he reported on 26 October 1947, 'one passes through a vast complex of twisted steel girders and on asking what it was I was told, to put it colloquially, "That is Krupps, that was."' The once mighty firm was in the hands of a British controller who interrogated him about why Kleinworts had lent money to Krupp's as late as 1939. The ramifications of the Standstill Agreement proved too esoteric for the controller, who made his disapproval clear; and given the stigma attached to the Krupp name, Michaelis advised the partners to proceed with caution when dealing with German companies.[17]

His advice was easy to take because there was little immediate business in Germany. 'I have been striving these last months to commence trading with Germany but despite plenty of goodwill all round so far the obstacles, both economic and bureaucratic, have proved insuperable,' another Kleinwort manager, Albert Haynes, wrote to his old German friend Hermann Abs in the summer of 1947. Abs had been a managing director of Deutsche Bank during the war and as such held for interrogation by the Allies afterwards. As soon as he was cleared by the denazification panel, the Allies courted him but could not agree for which of them he should work. With 'a world-wide reputation as being one of Germany's cleverest bankers', Haynes wrote in a memo to the partners, 'he is extremely ambitious and will undoubtedly become a force again'. It was in fact not long before Abs was actively involved in the financial affairs of his country. His position as chairman of the Standstill Committee in pre-war Germany rendered him even more eligible later to lead the German delegation to the International Conference held in London in 1951 to settle German pre-war and post-war debts. Germany's assumption of responsibility for these debts, made in the form of a declaration by Dr Adenauer, was one of the conditions laid down by the Allies for the revision of the Occupation Statute. Adenauer's declaration set in train the recovery of both Germany as a political and economic entity and the repayment of her debts to City institutions such as Kleinworts.[18]

This was of crucial importance to the firm and no one realized it more than Ernest. The total amount of German debt remained at £3.9m. excluding interest. Its recovery was vital to the security of the firm; and Ernest, like his Uncle Herman before him, continued to have faith in German honour, even coining the phrase 'the courageous banker' for someone who continued to believe that the German claims would be validated. He thus embarked upon what was to be his most important contribution to Kleinworts, namely the settlement of the German debts. In his work as a leading member of the British Banking Committee for German Affairs and on the Creditors Committee appointed by the Tripartite Commission on German Debts, he was able to bring a power of concentration and mastery of detail to bear on the negotiation of a settlement between Britain, France, America, and Germany. In doing so, he served his bank and his country well.

The International Conference on German Debts, held at Lancaster House and known as the Lancaster House talks, began in London on 25 June 1951. As a representative of the British Banking Committee, Ernest attended the preliminary talks between the three Western Allies and various creditor groups. On 5 July they were joined by the delegation from Germany led by Kleinworts' old friend Hermann Abs. He had already reassured Haynes in 1947 that 'any German company engaged in exporting or importing needed to keep its credit unmarred and would strain every nerve to repay the old debts, if not in 1950 then in 1960'. At the closing session of the preparatory talks he reiterated the message, this time on a national scale.

The object of these talks was to establish the views of the various parties on a range of questions prior to the main debt conference due to assemble towards the end of September. In Ernest's opinion, scribbled on 19 September 1951: 'Practically nothing was clarified, let alone decided, at the June conference. Unless a vast amount is decided in October, the November conference will be a complete washout!' In the event the conference was postponed by a British Government unwilling to take decisions on German debts prior to a general election. This allowed more time for preparatory work. On the British side this was done by an internal committee of the British Banking Committee for German Affairs (BBCGA) that had been formed from the old German Standstill Committee set up by the Accepting Houses Committee in the 1930s, in which Kleinworts had played an important role.

At the time of the formation of the smaller internal working committee under Sir Edward Reid of Barings, Kleinworts had queried the appointment, as 'Barings interest in Germany is comparatively small but now they will get the contacts & business!' In the event Reid remained the chairman as everyone else hoped he would. According to Hermann Abs, 'He was wonderful. He had a way of summarising: stammering, stuttering but to the point.' Ernest in effect became his deputy; and, as Reid later said, he proved 'absolutely brilliant at the debt negotiations'. Abs, from the opposite side of the negotiating table, 'greatly admired' him.[19]

Ernest and Sir Edward Reid worked well together to protect the Standstill corner, but there were many problems to solve. The British were unable to persuade the Americans that it would be both unjust and impracticable to accord the same treatment to the Standstill debt and the German Government's bonded debt. The Americans argued that if repayments on bonded indebtedness were to be scaled down, then the sacrifices should be shared by other classes of creditor; whereas the British could not see why the German Government's position should have any bearing on the Standstill debtors' as private institutions with extremely strong finances capable of repayment.

'Recommercialization', whereby the present freeze on the Standstill credits was removed so that they could be put to use to finance German foreign trade, proved another obstacle. According to Ernest writing on 9 November 1951, it was 'characterised by them [the Americans] as a "transparent device" on the part of the Standstill Creditors to get out ahead of everybody else'; but the Standstill creditors maintained that they were at a distinct disadvantage since they owned assets that were completely frozen and useless. Recommercialization was essential to unfreeze them, otherwise there was no hope of Germany obtaining the foreign finance she badly needed to support her growing external trade and to repay her debts.

Behind the scenes, the working party of the British Banking Committee enlisted the support of Hermann Abs to achieve American capitulation. At a meeting held on 4 December 1951, Ernest's suggestion that German debtors 'speak out and state that they cannot do without the credits for recommercialisation' was adopted by Abs. He agreed to publish a statement in favour, though he wished to avoid the impression of asking for credit; at the subsequent meetings of the Lancaster House talks, which began at the end of February 1952, the Americans took a far more sympathetic view and accepted the need for recommercialization. After each meeting Ernest summarized the day's discussions together with his own proposals, so as to elicit comments from his colleagues at No. 20. In this way his own input into the international proceedings was an accurate reflection of the firm's view.

The conference lumbered on throughout the spring with the press devoting innumerable columns of newsprint to predictions of the outcome and the supposed negotiating stances of the ultimately thirty-odd nations involved. After reading one such article on 17 May 1952 Ernest scrawled wearily over it: 'The *Financial Times* evidently knows far more about what we are doing than we ourselves!!' He believed the talks would soon break up, as indeed they did after the German delegation presented 'a miserable offer' as a settlement.[20]

The Germans proposed to cancel arrears of interest and write off up to half the capital amount of debts. Although the Creditors Committee rejected the proposals, the talks did not completely collapse. Ernest, in particular, had long maintained that the best way to secure repayment of the Standstill debts was by negotiating separate settlements of pre- and post-war debts directly, so he was relieved that the Tripartite Debt Commission at last was persuaded that this was the right course. In June 1952 the separate negotiations policy bore its first fruit when, on behalf of their constituents, Sir Edward Reid, Ernest, and Hermann Abs reached an agreement on the repayment of Standstill debts largely through recommercialization of credits. This agreement acted as a spur to other debtor–creditor groups, so that on 8 August the International Conference adopted settlement terms for all pre-war German external debts. It was a great achievement and, after ratification, enabled British banks to recover a substantial proportion of their debts.

At the opening session of the conference Britain had £65m. of Standstill debts; by April 1954 only £9.5m. remained. Germany's export and industrial recovery had far surpassed Allied expectations and she was able to release increasing amounts of Standstill debt for recommercialization. This was warmly welcomed by the City, especially as Germany was awash with sterling funds. Since she now had little need for the facility of recommercialized British credits, a substantial proportion of them were repaid; and, at long last, Kleinworts were able to make good their German losses.

The way was now open to resurrect the company scheme. The conversion of the partnership into a limited company had been *en tapis* since Alexander's death in 1935 and reflected a City trend for incorporation. Robert Benson, Antony Gibbs, and Brown Shipley were but three houses to take this road after the First World War. Other firms had placed the holdings of their principal partners in trusts. Thus Rothschilds was effectively controlled by Rothschilds Continuation Trust and Barings introduced a similar arrangement. Kleinworts, who had kept to their original structure, were now also forced to change. Spicer had submitted numerous memoranda to the partners to the effect that it was necessary to protect the firm from the inroads into capital incurred by the lethal combination of heavy taxation and death duties then at the high rate of 75 per cent. Limited liability had also become an attractive proposition after the losses incurred by the partners in the 1930s. Hugh Dalton, the Labour Chancellor, was pressing companies to 'plough back' their profits into the business, rather than distribute them by dividend, so any consequent build-up of reserves would be immune from surtax, which at one point Ernest and Cyril paid at 110 per cent. Tax issues were thus of paramount importance when it came to making any commercial or management decision.

They decided to form an exempt private company, whereby the partners-turned-directors had the privilege of limited liability without the requirement to make public their accounts. On 13 January 1948, Kleinwort, Sons & Co. Ltd. came into being with an authorized capital of £4m. in the form of ordinary and A and B preference shares. The former partners owned all the ordinary voting shares and the B preference shares, whilst the A preference shares were held by 'The Cousins', Herman Kleinwort's family.[21]

These A and B preference shares were, of course, the old Kleinwort family trust shares that had capitalized the former partnership. Their *pari passu* status had been an essential ingredient of the partnership. By now differentiating between them, Ernest and Cyril were abandoning their father's agreement and effectively dispossessing their uncle's family—and removing any obligation except a moral one to return any of the Standstill debt to him or to his heirs.[22]

The conversion into a limited company also changed the Andreae family's equity in Kleinwort, Sons & Co. Many months of attack and counter-attack went into the negotiations. The Andreaes wished to maintain the status quo by preserving the blocking rights they had all enjoyed under the partnership deed. The Kleinworts insisted that the business was the rightful property of the Kleinworts and not of the Andreaes. They therefore refused to incorporate the rights of the partnership into the new company articles. With deadlock and threats about the firm's future flying around, Sonny decided that, since the battle was over him, he must break the impasse. He had to convince his father and Spicer that he was not, as he reiterated on 13 November 1947, 'going to sell his birthright for a mess of potage'. They feared that without keeping an equal vote, Ernest and Cyril would use their majority 75 per cent interest to alter the partner participations and vote the Andreaes off the new board. Sonny, however, concluded that a moral right was better than any legal one obtained at the expense of Kleinwort goodwill: 'After all these discussions, of which I can always remind them, they would have to have hides of leather to do the dirty on me now.'[23]

The company scheme therefore went forward, placing control of the bank firmly in the hands of Ernest and Cyril Kleinwort. When it was discovered in 1954 that there remained a way in which the voting control of Kleinworts could still pass into Sonny's hands it was hurriedly arranged that the Kleinwort brothers would pay £50,000 each in consideration or the surrender of his rights. Sonny suggested on 23 December 'that it might be simpler all round if we scrapped the existing Pre-Emption agreement and entered into a new one more in keeping with the circumstances of today', and this was duly done as part of a further capital reorganization exercise, which came into effect in June 1955.[24]

The partners, as they were still called, were concerned about the effect of succession duty on the capitalization of the firm. Cyril felt that in the coming years the bank would have 'very much more capital than would be required for a Bank with the business which we now have'. By 1954 a gross profit of £1m. was expected, due mainly to the speedy recovery of German debts and their greater than anticipated value; though investment holdings, like Fennington/Bright and the general savings on surtax, were contributory factors. Since none of these resulted from trading activity, the pessimists, who held that the firm would function solely as a vehicle for the partners' investments, seemed confirmed in their view. The partners themselves felt that, faced with sluggish business activity, it was vital to minimize tax liabilities and utilize the surplus capital of the firm.[25]

The way in which Ernest and Cyril resolved the problem illustrates the very different qualities they brought to a fraternal partnership in many ways outstanding for its complementarity and tolerance. Cyril was the strategist. He would sit back in his chair and contemplate. Then he would summon a member of staff. 'I have been thinking,' he would say, and it might be about a new direction he wished the firm to take, or 'that there might be something interesting if we took a major investment in a small insurance company. Here are some names. Would you look at them and see which would be the best one?' When the answer was brought in, he would accept it.

Lord Limerick, who joined the firm as a fresh young accountant in 1958, felt that Cyril 'always paid you the compliment that you had made a professional assessment . . . and so you could deal with Cyril very much more quickly' than with Ernest. Cyril did not want 'to dig around and ask how on earth did you come to that extraordinary idea'. He relied upon the judgement of his staff, 'was very calm and would make a decision quickly'. By so obviously placing trust in his staff, he made them feel responsible; and they had to, and wanted to, get it right. F. A. James was in the Trustee Department and worked closely with both men. He expressed the difference between the brothers as 'Ernest would call me a B.F. one minute and forget it the next. If I ever got to the stage where Cyril called me a B.F. I would know my days were up because he didn't lightly take that view, and if he did you were damned forever.'

Ernest had a very different *modus operandi*. He was the tactician. When he summoned one of the staff, 'his ideas were so frothing that nothing would wait . . . and woe betide you if you weren't at your desk at the moment he wanted you. "Where have you been? Must talk to you about . . ." and off he would launch into a ream of instructions to look into a scheme to reorganise the Banking department or develop one of Cyril's ideas about a new form of business.' When the requested documentation and report were brought in, he would immediately subject it to a microscopic examination, so that the first ten minutes would be devoted to editing the punctuation. Unfortunately this obsession with minutiae had the effect of entirely obscuring Ernest's other qualities. It acted as a smoke-screen so that many of his staff only saw a fussy, mercurial man who was preoccupied with trifling details; they did not appreciate his innovative role in policy making.

Cyril may have had the broad brush but Ernest provided the canvas and the paints, and they jointly created the picture. Many of Ernest's ideas, however, never reached the canvas even though days might have been spent in preparation. Senior staff learnt to walk the delicate tightrope of discouraging schemes which had no future, without causing offence. They would either say, 'there may be some problems but let's see if they are insuperable' or else, with great daring, 'well, fascinating but actually it won't work'. As Pat Limerick recalls, if there was one good reason why it was unworkable then 'the beatific smile would come and he would say at once "Oh well, never mind. We will have to do something else." '[26]

Thus, in July 1954, Cyril suggested several possible schemes to make a large proportion of surplus capital available to the partner-directors to meet death duties, one of which was to expand one of their investment trusts to act as a holding company. It was then over to Ernest to examine the possibilities in detail. 'Ernest could never delegate anything to anybody—he must do it himself,' recalled one of his staff. So only after twelve days' work with the general manager, Cecil Elbra, did Ernest decide that the best solution was to pass over the investment business and surplus funds to a trust company and form a holding company to hold it and the ordinary shares. By the summer of 1955 the capital reconstruction was completed. At the close of business on 30 June 1955 Kleinwort, Sons & Co. changed its name to Kleinworts Ltd. and transferred all its banking activities to a new wholly owned subsidiary called Kleinwort, Sons & Co. Ltd. The partners, though continuing to hold shares in the subsidiary company of Kleinwort, Sons & Co. Ltd., retained control yet were in a position to meet death duties through offering shares to the public through the holding company, Kleinworts Ltd., which had a share capital of £4m.[27]

Although initially the brothers each had different plans for the capital reconstruction of the firm, Ernest willingly allowed his to be dropped in favour of Cyril's better ones. The brothers were, above all, a team. There was an absence of any rivalry between them and they understood one another perfectly. Ernest was excitable and always interfering; his temper would flare at the slightest provocation and immediately fizzle out like a damp squib. He constantly bombarded his brother with ideas but took no offence when they were deflated. A 'great woofly bear', he was all bark and no bite. Cyril was quite different. According to one colleague, he was a strange mixture, 'very, very charming but hard as nails when he wanted to be'. He, generally speaking, 'never interfered in what his brother was doing unless there was a strong feeling [against it], when Cyril would come in with a view. If he ever did that Ernest would almost always follow it.'[28]

After their broadening wartime experiences they had returned to No. 20 intent upon implementing reconstruction and change as part of their strategy to ensure the survival of the firm. In 1945 they were considered unfashionably young to be running an accepting house. Ernest was 44 and Cyril 40 when, apart from Helmut Schröder who was Ernest's age, most proprietors and partner/directors were at least 60 and belonged to Herman A.'s generation. Lord Bicester of Morgan Grenfell was 78, Lord Kindersley 74, Alfred Wagg of Helbert Wagg was 68, Arthur Villiers of Barings was 64 while his deputy was

74. By and large the chief personalities in the City were distinctly aged, but so were many of their opposite numbers in industry and politics.[29]

Since Herman A. no longer came into No. 20 on a daily basis, although he was kept informed of all developments and consulted by his young partners, one of Ernest and Cyril's first priorities was to bolster the partnership through the injection of new blood. Recurrent bouts of ill-health meant that Sonny was not always at the office. So when the firm became a limited liability company in 1948, they took the momentous step of looking outside the family for fellow-directors. This was still worthy of comment in the City of that period. Merchant banks had long divided their people into gentlemen and players, with the gentlemen being family proprietors. Banks such as Hambros, Barings, Bensons, Samuels, Morgan Grenfell, Schröders, and Rothschilds were largely run by the families and associates of the founders; even Bensons, more of a meritocracy than most of these firms, numbered three full members of the family and one nephew-in-law among its six partners. Of Kleinworts' fellow Accepting Houses Committee members, only Lazards had moved away from hereditary leadership when the French proprietors had stepped down in 1905. Yet their replacements were hardly a revolutionary, meritocratic new broom; both Kindersley and Brand were part of the City establishment, moved in the highest political and social circles and, in turn, formed their own banking dynasty.

The Kleinwort brothers' decision to appoint non-family directors did not herald a strictly meritocratic new broom at No. 20 whereby suddenly players could become gentlemen. To use the Kleinwort vernacular, within the three-tier structure of generals (partner-directors), lieutenant-colonels (managers), and NCOs (staff), the lieutenant-colonels were not about to become generals. Managers had never become partners unless they were family, as in the case of Herman A.—and that had been fortuitous, to bridge the generations of Kleinworts. None of the graduate or servicemen intake of the 1950s arrived with expectations of reaching the board. The highest level to which they could aspire was to be a manager. And even those demi-gods, general managers such as Cecil Elbra and Leonard Steljes, who had risen in the war and taken over from José Mayorga, did not aspire to becoming partners or directors: 'partnerships for those who weren't family were not thought about', Cecil Elbra has confirmed. 'The senior managers were professionals hired to run the business, they hadn't got any hope of becoming directors. The presumption was that the family would continue to provide directors.'[30]

Ernest and Cyril, however, produced only one Kleinwort director between them. While it was still considered only natural that Ernest's son, Kenneth, would ultimately become a partner-director as the heir to his large family shareholding, the brothers did not cast about in other family waters for new directors. Despite assurances given to Uncle Herman, they had made it clear to Godfrey Style when he called after the war that 'they were very sorry but no, they had no place for him at No. 20. He had better get a Name at Lloyds' if he wanted a City career. In 1948, however, the Kleinwort brothers decided that the firm needed professional directors. This significant innovation in the firm's history was part of their strategy to haul Kleinworts into the more competitive environment of the post-war world. It was a necessary step for the firm was in danger of being left behind in new business developments, especially on the company finance and investment side. It had become evident to Cyril, in particular, that the firm had to diversify into these areas, in order to compete with banks such as Morgan Grenfell, Hambros, and Lazards, and it needed professional directors to head the operation.

Kleinworts' first professional directors were, surprisingly, already members of staff, though neither Norman Biggs nor Ivo Forde had been regarded as ordinary managers. Ivo Forde was a connection by marriage in that his first cousin Betty was married to Cyril, so that he naturally had a much closer entrée to the partners. A colleague describes him as 'a large man with great spirit, both physically and mentally powerful' and he was 'very well liked' in the office and in the City in general. He was a Forde of Seaforde in Northern Ireland but he also had strong German connections as his mother was Lady-in-Waiting to Queen Victoria's eldest granddaughter, Princess Charlotte of Prussia. His father died when he was young, and after taking a First at Cambridge he decided to seek his fortune in America. It was an inauspicious time to do so for he had barely completed his training at the Guaranty Trust Co. of New York before Wall Street crashed. 'I could afford to be completely philosophical', he later explained, 'because I personally had been wiped out during the first day'. This was not that serious, for he had started with only a little money in the market and the lessons he learnt during those turbulent years in New York proved valuable.

He returned home just as Kleinworts recognized that the firm needed someone on the investment side. Herman A. had wanted to build up this area in the early 1930s but Sir Alexander had turned down the idea: 'Quite impossible to take on any more people when we've just sacked 250!' By 1935, however, the firm's business with Germany was booming and America was emerging from the Depression. It was essentially Cyril's concept that the firm should enter the investment management business, and he had therefore asked Ivo to do what he could on the investment side.

Ivo Forde could certainly do something, for prior to his arrival there was no investment side. 'There was a securities side,' he would recall, 'but there was nobody there apart from the partners, to a small degree, who really knew anything about investments.' It was a one-man department until 1937 when he brought in his old Guaranty colleague Arthur Stilwell, who invariably responded to greetings with 'oh, SB, SB!' (Still Breathing, Still Breathing). The two of them worked very closely with Cyril who was fascinated by the investment side of the business and made it an especial interest. Stilwell worshipped Cyril: 'I would have let him walk all over me.' At the time that Edward Halliday completed portraits of the three partners, which still hang at No. 20 today, he said that Cyril had the face of a pope. Stilwell entirely agreed. Cyril 'understood so quickly and you could talk to him and he never took offence, at least not with me, and I used to be quite frank with him at times'.

Cyril learnt a great deal from Forde and Stilwell, both of whom were astute professional investment men. When he joined the firm, Ivo Forde's first task had been to look after the family's American portfolio which held the bulk of their money and required updating after the 1929 crash and the Depression. After the Second World War, he realized the 'firm was starting again from scratch' and that he had a wonderful opportunity to build up the Investment Department into a sound profit centre. Through family contacts and word of mouth, new private clients came in with a minimum account of £250,000, considered high in those days, at a charge of a ¼ per cent. He also continued to run The Book, that is the investment portfolio of the bank itself, its holdings in equity and fixed-interest securities. Ivo did not confine his activities solely to the Investment Department. He had taken over the chairmanship of John Bright & Sons and Doxford & Sunderland Shipbuilders from Dr E. P. Andreae. Ivo's reconstruction and successful sale of these two industrial enterprises showed that, in his obituarist's words, 'his was a practical, rather than purely theoretical investment bent'.[31]

Whereas the Investment Department had been started as a strategic move to diversify business, the Trustee Department was started purely through force of circumstance. There had been no Trustee Department formerly because the firm was a partnership and in effect Spicer & Pegler provided trustee services for all the family. Shortly after Kleinworts' incorporation in 1948, Frederick Smith, the new manager of the Securities Department under Ivo, was approached by two nominee trustees of an old Klondyke Gold Mining family trust with the request that Kleinworts assume the trusteeship. In the belief that the firm would lose the account otherwise Smith sent F. A. James off to sit the Institute of Bankers Trustee examination so that he could return to start the Trustee Department with Alma Timlett as the bookkeeper. Since, as James admitted, 'one didn't have a Trustee Department for one client', he set himself the delicate task of weaning away all the substantial family trusts from Spicer & Pegler, who remained advisers but were replaced as trustees by Kleinworts Trust Department. It became a busy department; 'there was always movement, planning exercises, swapping one Trust, forming new Trusts'.

Gradually throughout the 1950s the firm's trustee and investment business expanded. Ivo Forde evidently had tremendous flair, an instinct about investing. Brian Rowntree joined Kleinworts in 1949 as a trainee investment analyst reporting to Arthur Stilwell who by that time had become the manager. One morning Ivo Forde came in to tell Stilwell that he was to sell every French share owned by every client. 'He was within 2 days of the then absolute all time peak of the French market,' Rowntree recalls, 'That was just investment feeling. I had a tremendous admiration for him.' Ivo in turn relied upon Stilwell who was equally respected by Hoare & Co. and Rowe & Pitman, the brokers with whom he mainly dealt. Although men such as Kit Hoare and Julian Martin-Smith had direct access to the partners, as they had always had before the war, they soon realized that whatever was agreed in the partners' rooms had to pass muster with Stilwell. He was, James observed, 'the ultimate sieve through which any investment had to go.'[32]

American investments had long formed the major holding in the partners' portfolios, largely due to the firm's triangular underwriting syndicate with Goldman Sachs and Lehman Brothers. Kleinworts had resigned with reluctance from the syndicate when the US tax authorities decided to expand their sphere of taxation from income generated in the United States to income world-wide. Relations with both houses continued none the less and, on the investment side, were cemented by Ivo Forde's American experience. Kleinworts also maintained strong connections with Brown Brothers Harriman, Kuhn Loeb, Dean Witter, Smith Barney, and Alexander Brown of Baltimore.

The firm was also successful where it chose to expand its international banking business. Norman Biggs, who would leave Kleinworts to take up another appointment in 1952, was busy rebuilding the international syndicated acceptance credit business and negotiated the Anglo-French Wool Credit as well as a large syndicated credit to Poland, the first City credit of substance to a communist state. Overseas, chiefly through the efforts of Stirling Karck and then Norman Biggs, the firm built up a presence in Southern Africa. Karck's specialized interest in the French wool industry naturally extended to French offshoots in the South African wool business; Clothier & Poole became Kleinworts' agents there and laid the foundation for the substantial business developed by Norman Biggs.

Then in 1958 the Industrial Development Corporation of South Africa (IDC), a South African government-sponsored organization handling £80m. worth of Government funds, invited Kleinworts to form a partnership with them and other local mining and insurance houses to establish the Accepting Bank for

Industry Ltd. (ABI). With no real money market and only one other accepting house, part of the Anglo American Corporation operating with an associated discount company, the ABI was obliged to perform both accepting and discounting functions. The ABI was immediately profitable for the firm and prospered to the extent that the Standard Bank sought to wrest control of it from Kleinworts. 'I would fight to the last ditch to retain it—whether it is the Standard Bank or any other bloody bank' the old warrior, Herman A., declared. 'After all it *is* our baby—now others see that it is a lusty one they want to join in—by all means as long as the control remains in our hands.'[33]

It is evident that where the firm chose to expand or diversify its traditional business overseas it was immeasurably more successful, even when operating under unfamiliar market conditions, than when it chose to experiment with an entirely new line of business. The obvious advantage of experience gleaned over many years in following the traditional route of business carried more weight in the post-war years owing to the marked increase in competition. It was far more difficult for a bank suddenly to diversify its operation. A team of key personnel could not be lured away to form the nucleus of a new department as they often are today.

The bedrock of Kleinworts' operations remained the acceptance credits with a dash of fortuitous foreign exchange business. To use the historic barometer of the merchant banker, the acceptance figure of £700,000 at the end of the war had climbed to £3,562,812 by 1947 which, together with deposits etc., produced a balance sheet figure of £11,036,527. At the start of the 1950s acceptances stood at £4,858,469, the balance sheet total was nearly £13m. and declared reserves were £500,000. As the 1950s progressed so did the expansion of the firm's acceptance business and their balance sheet. By the end of the decade its acceptances had soared to £12,158,207 with a balance sheet total of £39m. Capital and reserves had reached over £5m. with profits running at over £1m.

The growth in acceptances was largely due to the growth in business generated by the Scandinavian department. This became a major profit centre for the bank in the late 1950s and throughout the 1960s. The firm had an old association with Scandinavia, reaching as far back as the Kleinwort, Cohen era. It had provided the firm with a steady but unspectacular business, mainly because the area had long been the preserve of the Anglo-Danish bank Hambros, which was very strong there. Hambros, however, did not deal directly with clients; they lent money on a documentary basis through the banks. When Kleinworts cut out the banks and went directly to the clients they uncovered an untapped reservoir of business for which there was no competition. In the words of one member of the department, it was as if every company had the Union Jack flying in anticipation of a visit from Kleinworts.

Herman A. had looked after the area as a junior partner and was succeeded by Sonny, who still took an interest in it, but it was managed by Cecil Elbra with the help of various young men, including Michael Hawkes. In addition to his Scandinavian responsibilities, Elbra was also, in effect, general manager of the firm; so after taking the two junior members of the department, Kenneth Kleinwort and Michael Hawkes, on a probationary tour of Scandinavia, he left the main work to them. Kenneth, as a future proprietor, soon moved on to gain experience in the German Department, leaving Michael Hawkes in day-to-day charge.

It was not all plain sailing for Michael Hawkes, for the work was gruelling. On his first trip in April 1960 he visited thirty to forty firms of which ten or twelve were already borrowing money from Kleinworts by means of the bill of exchange, which in the 1950s and 1960s was the only way in which money could be lent abroad. Long evenings of schnapps drinking were a prerequisite to drumming up business, and a strong constitution was a great asset. The Corin family, who had been the firm's agents since 1904 and were marvellous business-getters, provided riotous dinners 'with everybody drinking everything under the sun' except the young men from Kleinworts who had learnt to nurse their drinks. The Corins would find the client companies and Hawkes would go along to talk to them as a sales representative. The companies were chiefly importers, preferably from the UK although Kleinworts were allowed to finance non-UK imports in sterling. The Corins and Hawkes approached any importer, be it of fertilizer, cotton, or even chocolate. They also tapped the farmers' co-ops which were a marvellous source since they had a monopoly on feed and grain. The business started rolling in and by 1965, with the Corin agency making £50,000 per annum, the Scandinavian Department would account for £400,000 with very low overheads, which was a large slice of the £1m. the Banking Division would contribute to overall profits.

Looking back, Michael Hawkes attributes his success to the unsophisticated market and his ability to elucidate matters of foreign exchange to his clients. A great many of the clients needed accommodation and finance in dollars and, at that time, Kleinworts had no available dollars. Elbra and Hawkes therefore arranged for the exporter of goods to a Scandinavian client to draw a bill of exchange on Brown Brothers Harriman. They could accept US dollars at 1 per cent per annum and Kleinworts, on receipt of the documents, would add 1¼ per cent commission, thereby giving the Scandinavian client dollar accommodation at 2¼ per cent over the New York discount rate. This became an even more profitable operation when Kleinworts could obtain dollars through the Eurodollar market; they could then lend the money directly from their own dollar deposits at the same rate.[34]

The creation of the Euromarkets heralded a new era in the firm's fortunes as well as in the City at large. The credit for the development of the Eurobond market has traditionally gone to Siegmund Warburg, but it would be more accurate to say that several people developed the idea of a Euromarket more or less simultaneously. The Russians are said to have been the first to deposit their dollars in Paris with Banque Commerciale pour l'Europe du Nord, whose telex address was Eurobank, rather than in New York. At Kleinworts the belief is that they themselves were one of the founders of the Eurocurrency market in conjunction with the Bank of London and South America led after 1957 by Sir George Bolton.

The Kleinwort Foreign Exchange Department had been moribund after the war, so much so that for a time it even relinquished its office space to J. March & Co. Ltd., Juan March's London import/export subsidiary. Conditions changed when, in 1957, the Bank of England imposed restrictions on the way in which sterling could be used to finance international trade outside the Sterling Area, at a time when there was an ample supply of dollars in foreign hands owing to the American trade deficit. The dollar, anyway, was regarded as the major currency and by 1958 most of the Western European currencies were almost freely convertible into dollars. Fortunately one of Kleinworts' largest international accounts had deposited some £2–3m. worth of dollars at No. 20, and so with the benefit of these non-US owned dollar deposits Kleinworts' Foreign Exchange Department was again in business.

Henri Jacquier put these dollars to use in an imaginative way which enhanced the firm's City reputation. All the banks dealt in New York in clearing-house funds, but certain transactions required the use of federal funds which could be created by leaving clearing house funds on the US account overnight thereby creating 'Feds' that could be used the next day. Jacquier and his new manager Herbert Cherrill, who had taken over after Leonard Steljes joined the March Corporation, started arbitraging between the two types of funds in 1958/9. They were able to exploit an anomaly in the value dates being the first to free-ride on 'the Thursday/Friday technicality', as it came to be called. This gave Kleinworts three days' receipts when lending 'Feds' over the weekend at the cost of one night's interest on Thursday/Friday clearing house funds, a simple, effective, and highly profitable use of the firm's deposits. Michael Hawkes remembers a dealer being told about Jacquier's deposits, which at first remained secret even from Cherrill. He was told 'with bated breath that Jacquier's deposits had reached $16m.'. This $16m. grew until Cherrill was told and Sonny Andreae was let in on the secret. Eventually other banks realized the significance of the Thursday/Friday Eurodollar deposits and also entered the market so that it became more difficult for Jacquier to make such large profits.[35]

It was at this stage that people in departments such as Scandinavia began to look for commercial outlets for Eurodollars amongst their client lists. A further development to emerge from the early Eurocurrency market was in the Deutschmark trade. Kleinworts actually started the business of lending funds in Deutschmarks by borrowing dollars or using their dollar deposits to switch into Deutschmarks. The Bank of London and South America also started to trade in Deutschmarks, but Kleinworts were particularly strong in this field owing to their access to large amounts of dollar deposits and also their traditional strength in German business. After the war, they had kept their hand in by doing a 'terrific business' in 'Blocked' Deutschmarks and under Michaelis running the German money market with Schroders in London.

Although the partners had been sceptical about the success of the Euromarket —Ernest for one always said it would come to an untimely end and wrote that Cherrill's money business had got to be reduced at some time and should be watched—they at least allowed the firm to participate in the market, unlike the Hambros partners who kept their bank out of it for at least three years, because to them the market seemed too volatile and unreliable. As the Eurocurrency market mushroomed it became a major source of Kleinworts' business and in the early years contributed some 50 per cent in terms of profits.

The Eurodollar market, in turn, led to the development of the Eurobond market. In 1956 Siegmund Warburg of S. G. Warburg was asked by the president of the ECSC to place a $40m. loan on their behalf. This was the first long-term dollar loan for a European institution subscribed largely from European sources. It would lead to substantial further business for Warburgs, in particular the first medium-term dollar loan of $15m. worth of bonds on behalf of Autostrade Italiane in 1963. The loan was issued in Luxembourg in US dollars for an Italian company who signed the contract in Holland, a deal that has been seen as the real start of the Eurobond market. Other merchant bankers were also wondering how to use the huge offshore holdings of dollars as the basis of a new capital market. Although a force in the Eurodollar market, Kleinworts had no base from which to compete in the bond market. In the first place they had no Company Finance (hereafter known by its later title, Corporate Finance) Department and in the second they had few of the right contacts with which to start doing this business.

Unlike other Anglo-German houses, notably Schroders, Kleinworts had never done more than dabble their toes in the pool of new issuing business. There is no evidence that this was a set policy and it may have been simply a case of personal proclivity on the part of the Kleinworts. In 1953 Ivo Forde had managed the John Bright issue, but although successful it had not led to much further business; and he regarded corporate finance business 'as a sort of, what you might call, side-kick to the investment side'. But as the corporate finance opportunities soon became more evident, Cyril became keen to enter the field and continue the policy of diversification away from accepting business. Corporate finance was attractive since it was largely confined to domestic activity, and would reduce the firm's exposure to sovereign risk. Cyril persuaded the other partners that Kleinworts must have an in-house department and the search was on for the right man to head it.

It so happened that Ernest knew a Sussex neighbour David Robertson who, as a managing director of Charterhouse Japhet, was an experienced corporate practitioner. Kleinworts asked him to start a Corporate Finance Department. He came into the bank, Ivo Forde recalled, 'as a sort of manager without a title' and became the third non-family director in 1955. It quickly became clear that although Kleinworts had a name as international bankers, they had none as corporate financiers in a field led by Morgan Grenfell, Lazards, Hambros, and Barings. Kleinworts were known to the Bicesters and Kindersleys of that world but, unlike Bensons, from a distance. When the seminal Aluminium War broke out in 1958, with Warburgs taking on the City establishment over a hostile bid for British Aluminium, Kleinworts were not courted by either side: 'they were not in the inner councils', David Robertson stated. Only very late on, as the establishment defenders grew more desperate, did Charles Hambro call at No. 20—only to be told by Cyril that, for what it was worth, he thought Warburgs were right.

'It was very, very difficult', Ivo Forde remembered, and uphill work for David Robertson to start a Corporate Finance Department. In those days corporate clients remained utterly loyal to their issuing houses; they could not be lured away by the bait of better terms. There were a few small deals such as Kraft and Drake & Gorham but none that put Kleinworts on the map. The denouement of the Aluminium War signalled, in the words of Warburg banker Henry Grunfeld, that 'merchant banks had to be more on their toes. The comfortable unenergetic life was coming to an end. Merchant banks began to realise the importance of specialist departments to deal with these special situations.' This confirmed Cyril's view that Kleinworts must become a corporate player, especially since the Old Guard 'clubbiness' of the City, the idea, David Robertson explained, that 'there was a code of behaviour that was adhered to, and that people could be expected to overcome possible conflicts of interest, was beginning to break down'. Since Kleinworts had always been something of an outsider and an unknown quantity, they had nothing to lose and everything to gain in this new climate.

It was essential therefore that they were not left behind in what promised to be an area of great expansion in the 1960s, namely the new issue business.

David Robertson's struggle to secure corporate finance business had deepened the partners' awareness that Kleinworts were the only leading accepting house that did not possess an active stake in this area. Furthermore, the position of all the other leading firms was so well entrenched that, as David Robertson pointed out, 'it would be extremely difficult to equal them'.[36]

Their desire to compete in this area was further increased by the knowledge that corporate finance work was less capital intensive than wholesale banking. Demand was rising for much larger credit facilities from the giant units that were emerging as industry continued to rationalize through a process of absorption and merger. The partners recognized that they needed to broaden the capital base of the firm so as to be able to meet this demand as well as reduce their exposure to sovereign risk. All these factors combined to build up a strong momentum within the firm towards the acquisition of a new issue business in order to become less dependent upon pure banking and to be able to contend on an equal footing with their competitors.

More impetus was given by the announcement on 7 August 1959 of the proposed Philip Hill, Higginson merger with Erlangers. Philip Hill had already merged with Higginson & Co. to form Philip Hill, Higginson. Its subsequent rapid growth with assets increasing from £5m. in 1952 to £20.5m. in 1959 and profits jumping from £282,000 to £1,340,000 came largely from its very active new issue business. Under the dynamic team of its chairman Rudolph de Trafford and managing director Kenneth Keith, Philip Hill, Higginson had dramatically increased its market share of corporate finance business; and by merging with Erlangers, the new group would gain a useful acceptance credit and important foreign exchange business as well as enlarge its capital base by £8m.

In an article about this 'powerful new group', the *Economist* commented that:

> Few people would be surprised if other mergers follow. At a time when some of the traditional business of merchant bankers is being done by the clearing banks with their long-term advances, and other business is being hit by the discount houses, quoting fine rates direct to certain finance houses and industrial companies, merchant bankers find important advantages in bigger groupings and a stronger capital base.

After reading of the proposed Philip Hill/Erlanger merger, David Robertson had no doubt about which direction the winds of change were going to blow through the City. 'I have come to the conclusion,' he wrote in a confidential memorandum to his fellow-partners on 12 August 1959, 'that we must take another careful look at the possibilities open to us for a merger.' He thus prepared a short list of possible marriage partners. It included Flemings, Helbert Wagg, and Bensons.[37]

10 Bensons and a Complementary Union

THE Benson firm of the late 1950s was very different from the one that perforce had gone into semi-hibernation on the outbreak of war in 1939. In the first instance, Bensons were no longer just Robert Benson & Co. They had merged with the Lonsdale Investment Trust in July 1947 and altered their name to Robert Benson Lonsdale & Co. in order to reflect the change in the ownership of the firm. In the second instance, they were a much more professionally managed organization than they had been in 1939. Rex's long-standing plea for a team at the top had been achieved, though the team under his chairmanship was a meritocratic rather than wholly proprietorial one. These two developments had provided Bensons with a broader capital base and stronger management, which in turn gave rise to a substantial growth in new issue business. Here, Bensons moved away from their traditional interest in public utilities to concentrate upon issues for domestic industrial and commercial companies, matching the larger City trend.

It was through Michael Colefax's efforts to drum up business in industrial company finance that Bensons met their first partner, the Lonsdale Investment Trust. Dr Chaim Weizmann, an old Colefax friend, had sold his patents for the production of gases and hydrocarbons by the Catarole process to two enterprising, if eccentric, refugees, Franz Kind and Georg Tugendhat. These gentlemen were in the oil refinery business, Kind on the construction side, having already erected plants in Trieste and Antwerp, and Tugendhat on the scientific side. They had arrived in Britain in 1936 and chosen to establish an oil refinery, which they hoped would be the first in a chain producing high-grade lubricants. Having raised the sum of £250,000 they built an oil refinery plant at Trafford Park, where the Bensons' uncle, Constantine Benson, had started the British Westinghouse operation in the late 1890s. Unfortunately for Bensons, these two unconnected enterprises shared a similar pattern of development—and eventual failure.

In 1940, Kind and Tugendhat, or K. & T. as they were known at Bensons, were still riding high and formed a company called Petrocarbon Ltd. to buy Dr Weizmann's patents and to produce certain strategic raw materials for the first time in Britain. Petrocarbon appeared an attractive investment first because Montagu Norman and the Ministry of Fuel and Power provided indispensable support, and secondly because the Government were shortly expected to take over the whole project. Although Bensons were not one of the original investors, the firm came in with an initial interest of £3,000 in 1945. Then, simultaneously, the Government decided not to take on the project, and the concept, together with its costs, grew in size like Topsy.

In order to capitalize on what was seen as a future industry, namely the development of materials from oil, the company needed to build a new and larger plant to take the manufacturing process up to its final stage of conversion to produce petrochemicals. Having already increased their initial investment on a piecemeal basis, Bensons had to decide whether to take a loss or a midwife's role in the development of a new-born industry. Michael Colefax, foreseeing great opportunities, had become a director of Manchester Oil Refinery. He swayed Bensons to stay in the game and to raise the initial £1.8m. required for the new plant, to be built by Sir Lindsay Parkinson & Co., a Benson client.

This was to be a tripartite venture. After a great deal of consideration the Finance Corporation for Industry, established in 1945 through the efforts of the Bank of England to increase the provision of finance to industry, agreed to provide half of this sum, to be contingent 'not only on the other half being guaranteed but also on its being made clear that it should be on that second half that the risks of the enterprise were to fall'. It was this second half that was divided between Bensons and the third partner, the Lonsdale Investment Trust, the largest of the original sponsors of the Manchester Oil Refinery and Petrocarbon companies.

Bensons were introduced to them by their accountant Ralph Hamlyn, another early investor, and they came to know Lonsdales well over the next year. Michael Colefax devoted most of his time to this project and was in close contact with the refinery chairman, Stuart Ebben, a South African director of Lonsdales with considerable industrial experience. Meetings between Bensons and Lonsdales were even more frequent after it became apparent that £1.8m. was but the proverbial tip of the iceberg of spiralling costs and debts of the petrochemicals projects. In the course of planning a reorganization scheme in 1947, Michael Colefax calculated that the cost of a holding company for the whole operation, to include the Manchester Oil Refinery debts, could reach £9.425m. and that the company should start with an issued capital of £6m.[1]

Thrown together to try to unravel this high-risk piece of business, one which could inflict great damage on both firms, Bensons and Lonsdales became mutually attracted by the idea of marriage as a solution to their shared problems.

From their recent experience with the petrochemicals project both firms were aware of the need to be able to finance larger-scale projects, which individually they could only meet by broadening their capital bases. This was not a new position for Bensons to be in, as they had known themselves to be undercapitalized before the war, but the signs of expansion in their post-war business had served to emphasize the fact. It therefore made sense for them to merge in order to increase their capitalization. Discussions were held throughout the early summer of 1946 and, after lunch on 17 September, Rex and Leo Lonsdale, the proprietorial chairman of Lonsdales, went so far as to discuss office accommodation with Bill Hole, Bensons' manager.

Although matters were clearly advanced, permission still had to be obtained from the Capital Issues Committee and the Treasury for such a merger, and they did not approve the proposal until the spring of 1947. The only outstanding issue to be negotiated was the value of goodwill to be placed on Bensons—as an investment trust Lonsdales had none. Bensons had been advised to compute their value by reference to the profit record for the eleven years ending in February 1946. Calculations based on an eleven-year average, including the dormant war years, provided a goodwill figure of £1 per share on the issued capital of £400,000. But if weight was given to the firm's recent performance there was a supportable case for a higher goodwill value of another £350,000. Lonsdales, however, suggested that more weight should be given to Bensons' wartime performance and came up with a goodwill figure of £200,000. The issue was amicably resolved at a meeting on 27 March 1947 when the figure of £300,000 was agreed.

On 18 April 1947 the *Financial Times* reported on the merger as 'the first instance of a merchant banking house being wholly absorbed by an investment trust'. In the days before leaks were more usual, this was considered extraordinary. Leo Lonsdale immediately called the whole of the staff in front of him to discover who had been talking about the merger. 'Not one of us had an inkling that anybody was talking to anybody, so we really knew nothing about that merger,' George Howard recalls, 'until it was . . . in the press.' The announcement was somewhat premature since the family concern only became a public limited company, the Lonsdale Investment Trust Ltd. (LIT), on 8 July 1947. LIT, capitalized at £2.25m., acquired the old Lonsdale Investment Trust Co. and Robert Benson & Co. It created a wholly owned subsidiary Robert Benson Lonsdale, known as RBL or Bensons, to carry on the old business of Robert Benson & Co. with capital doubled to £800,000. Leo Lonsdale became chairman of the new Lonsdale Investment Trust while Rex became chairman of Robert Benson Lonsdale. Rex, Con, and Phil joined the LIT board and Stuart Ebben joined the Benson board.[2]

Although this merger freed Bensons from the constraints of under-capitalization, why had the Benson brothers relinquished the valued independence of a family firm on this occasion when they had refused to do so on a previous one? The answer lay in the nature of the Lonsdale business and the role of its proprietor, Leo Lonsdale.

J. & J. Lonsdale & Co. had been a family firm of food importers which traded in the Midlands and Ireland in the nineteenth century. James Lonsdale built it into a profitable and expanding business with the help of his two elder sons, John and Leo's father Thomas. It was incorporated in 1898 with a capital of £350,000, when James retired and his son by a second marriage, James Roston Lonsdale, became a director. He was considerably younger than Thomas, who considered him and Leo's elder brother, Raymond, as the heirs apparent to Lonsdales. Consequently Leo had little to do with the business. After Eton, where he stroked the Eton Eight and was a member of Pop, he was destined for Oxford and the diplomatic service. The Great War, however, was in its last year so Leo went to Sandhurst and was commissioned into the Grenadier Guards in 1918 before going up to Oxford in 1921. The subsequent deaths of both his brother and his uncle James caused his father Thomas to insist that he leave Oxford and straightway enter the family firm.

The firm continued as wholesale and retail provision merchants until the death of Leo's father in 1931 when Leo decided to pass the provisioning business to the managing partners and to employ the family's capital in an investment trust. In May 1931 the name of J. & J. Lonsdale was changed to Lonsdale Investment Trust and it was incorporated in December with a capital of £500,000, the initial investment funds being provided by the run-down of stocks and the disposal of constituent parts of the old family business. Subsequently, in 1934, Leo sold the Midlands chain of stores, George J. Mason Ltd., to the International Tea Co. for some £1m., which provided additional investment capital. Leo had been introduced to Alfred Wagg of Helbert, Wagg through Lyulph Abel Smith, who worked there and was a connection of his wife, and the Smith banking family. Leo, in turn, introduced Waggs to International Tea. In 1935 Waggs issued a 4¼ per cent preference share for International Tea Co.'s stores in conjunction with Lonsdales, which Lionel Fraser judged 'an overwhelming success'. Leo's City career gathered momentum and he decided to link himself with a merchant bank. He chose Waggs as the ideal partner, taking a 33⅓ per cent equity interest and becoming a non-executive director of Helbert Wagg Holdings, formed in 1935 for the express purpose of holding the capital of Helbert, Wagg & Co. Ltd.

Then, through his association with Waggs, Leo decided to devote a small part, perhaps one-sixth, of Lonsdales to investment in more speculative long-term project finance. Waggs took a serious interest in financing industrial business so that Leo was able to gain some knowledge of it and, as Lonsdales expanded, he drew in more experienced men to help him direct its affairs. Robert, Lord Rockley, an Eton friend who had trained as an engineer with GEC, became a non-executive director of Lonsdales while Stuart Ebben became a director with the brief to look after the project finance side. During the 1930s Lonsdales backed a variety of industrial enterprises with mixed success. The introduction of Tampax into Europe and the Empire from America was a winner, as was a new Austrian technique for tanning chrome leather, but Dr Heyl's 'Fantastix', a plant hormone solution calculated to make the desert bloom, was not. After the war the largest venture of this kind was the Manchester Oil Refinery during which Leo realized that Lonsdales' capital was not rising fast enough to take advantage of such larger-scale opportunities and that his association with Waggs did not provide him with as active a role as he wanted, whereas one with Bensons might.[3]

From Bensons' point of view the merger with Lonsdales was ideal in that it provided a larger capital base, thereby making their business safer but without causing them to relinquish executive control. The designation, Robert Benson Lonsdale & Co. Ltd., confirmed this control and allowed Bensons to retain their identity in the eyes of the public. The Benson family interest was 27 per cent and that of the Lonsdale family 63 per cent. Leo Lonsdale was largely a passive partner in the bank and the actual Lonsdale Investment Trust was kept quite separate. It was, as the press eventually reported, a reverse takeover.

The City of the early 1950s has often been described as a somnolent place for bankers. A place where partners hardly needed to differentiate between the comfortable armchairs and roaring fires in their clubs and those in their offices; where people rushed to lunch rather than to drum up new business; and where weekends were often extended, as at Morgan Grenfell: 'By Thursday afternoon at four, one of the senior partners would come across to the juniors and say, "Why are we still here? It's almost the weekend." '[4]

Constricted by exchange controls, a weak pound and an unfamiliar Socialist Government, the City could hardly summon up the energy to earn its living—a far cry from the days of Empire and bustling glory. Nevertheless, while this applied particularly to those merchant banks with ageing partnerships such as Morgan Grenfell, and those weighed down by the tribulations of the Standstill debts such as Kleinworts, it was much less applicable to the issuing houses Helbert Wagg, Warburgs, Higginsons, and Bensons, for whom the 1950s was a decade of change and challenge when expansion and progress beckoned. Bensons, newly capitalized through merger, was well placed to participate in an increasing volume of business and to build a more professional management team at Gresham House. The staff themselves felt that the firm was ambitious and ready to expand, and were prepared to put in the hours and effort to achieve greater success.

At the time of the Lonsdale merger, Bensons was still best known as an investment house specializing in North America, and this area of operation remained very much Rex's department after the war. Following his appointment in 1941 as Military Attaché to the British Embassy in Washington, an appointment that owed much to his excellent high-level connections in America, he had travelled throughout the country on speaking tours in order to persuade America to enter the war on the Allied side. Wherever he went he knew people but he always knew more by the time he left. He had a most delightful way of getting on with everybody; 'from the liftman', as a colleague Alastair Craig described it, 'to the chairman or the prime minister, including Churchill', so he was constantly increasing his already wide circle of American friends.

After the war, when most of the firm's American investment holdings had been requisitioned, Rex set about rebuilding the business with Phil Macpherson, and he continued to travel there twice a year in order to keep in touch with brokers and directors of firms in which Bensons had an interest. In this way he followed his father's advice 'to *keep on the inside track with the management*' and 'to pick the right people to back with your money'. According to his colleagues Ronny Medlicott, who joined Bensons as a director in 1955, and Denys Oppé, who had joined Bensons at director level in 1953 via Schröders and the Industrial & Commercial Finance Corporation, Rex 'was extremely good at picking the right people, industrialists and others . . . he had that faculty of knowing who was going to be successful and who wasn't'. Professional bankers might mutter that he had no technical understanding of the business and dismiss him as an amateur but, as Peter Wake later remarked, 'You mustn't underestimate Rex.' He 'had this extraordinary flair . . . and he nurtured our American business'. In the course of his biannual visits Rex built up a fine network of broking contacts for Bensons and developed a special relationship with a New York firm, G. L. Ohrstrom.[5]

The founder, George Ohrstrom, had had an innovative career on Wall Street. He had built up a successful stockbroking business and then specialized in developing water holding and small public utility operating companies which he placed in highly leveraged holding companies. Both Bensons and Flemings invested in these companies but in the crash of 1929 Ohrstrom went bankrupt. He none the less secured their loyalty by travelling to London to see them and discuss the fall in the value of their holdings. Rex and the Fleming partner, Archie Jamieson, were impressed by his frankness and the fact that he was the only American correspondent who had bothered to come to London after the crash. They were therefore more predisposed to back his future schemes than they might otherwise have been. Ohrstrom's subsequent company specialized in industrials but fell foul of the Securities Act. It was not until 1943 that he was relicensed, forming after the war the third and most successful G. L. Ohrstrom & Co., which specialized in leveraged buy-outs.

The Ohrstrom connection, which continues today, made a 'heap of money' in the early years for Bensons, Flemings, and the investment trusts they managed. The way it worked was for George to identify a likely small industrial company with a simple approach to making products for niche markets, usually one that concentrated on metal manufactured goods or some other highly specialized product and was a leading supplier in its own field. He employed 'finders', that is brokers working on commission who would spot likely enterprises; and, when identified, Ohrstrom and his staff would scrutinize them and perhaps find one out of fifty that fitted his definition of quality, 'the Tiffany of the industry' as he used to say. There were no hostile takeovers, since Ohrstrom only pursued small family or closely held concerns in which the owners were happy to liquidate their holdings and in which there was a good management who would stay on. Ohrstrom would then report his recommendation to Bensons and Flemings, his principal British investors.

In 1948 he visited their London offices accompanied by Clint Murchison, a successful Texas oil millionaire who caused quite a sensation in his cowboy boots, brown dungarees, and stetson. Ohrstrom's first acquisition, Peerless Manufacturing, had been financed by a secured loan from an insurance company controlled by his old Texan friend, who in time also became a friend of the Bensons and Archie Jamieson. Bensons and Flemings seem always to have approved of Ohrstrom recommendations, although on occasion they would send their own men to America to scrutinize the details. The acquisition would then be financed through a mechanism rediscovered in the 1980s and termed the leveraged buy-out (LBO). Thus the LBOs associated with Kohlberg, Kravis Roberts & Co. were not original but had been used by Ohrstroms in the 1950s for finance by a combination of preference capital shares, debentures, and subordinated debt. Bensons and Flemings initially provided a relatively small amount of money, some £2–3m. for the purchase of companies in this way.

It was also a relatively simple operation. Ohrstrom raised the money through these British connections and gave the investors 60 per cent of the equity, taking the other 40 per cent for themselves. 'It was a very good deal for him but it was also a very good deal for us,' one investor would reflect. As the debt was repaid from the company's cash flow the investors were left holding the equity at very little cost and by that time it was normally of great value.

The first Ohrstrom deals with Bensons and Flemings were Dart Truck, a company which made huge 'off-the-road' trucks in a small garage in Kansas City; W. C. Norris, a small manufacturer of oil-well equipment in Tulsa; and Leach Relay Corp., a manufacturer of electrical relays and other devices. All proved immensely successful, but none more so than Dover Corporation, which was formed in 1956 to consolidate a number of industrial businesses: its share price has increased three hundredfold since that time.

As a matter of policy Rex gave his managing directors Phil Macpherson, Mark Turner, Denys Oppé, and Ronny Medlicott the opportunity to share directly through allocations of free penny stock that would otherwise have gone to the firm as commission. He believed that they were 'the works in RBL' and that, as such, were 'second to none and should be fittingly rewarded!' 'Rex', Oppé remarked, 'was a marvellous Chairman because he really looked after his subordinates. When there was a good thing he brought them in on it.' The managing directors' private account summaries reveal the rewards provided by Ohrstrom participations. Norris, for example, provided Mark Turner and Phil Macpherson with over £13,000 each in 1954, while Leach proved a winner for all of them when a tranche of shares was sold by the British to a Californian unit trust fund in 1968. Although it sounded very exciting to the young managers, Peter Wake recalled that 'Old Phil used to get worried and say it seemed rather speculative'. Phil Macpherson was none the less the first to express his gratitude for the Benson generosity shown so often to the managing directors in appreciation of their work.[6]

Rex did not confine Benson activities solely to the Ohrstrom connection in North America. He had always loved Canada, ever since he had first visited his Uncle Bertie there in 1908. 'It really is a great country: tell Father that I am sure it is a greater country to invest his money in than the States' he had then written from Ottawa; and he had tried to launch a Canadian business in 1938 to which the outbreak of war had put an end. But as soon as possible after the war and before any rivals, Rex and Mark Turner started a finance company in Canada. United North Atlantic Securities made slow progress, partly because Eric Tatham fell ill and was unable to run the office as planned. It nevertheless became profitable, before being sold for a good price to the Toronto Dominion Bank.[7]

Phil Macpherson, who as Brigadier Director of the Finance Branch of the Allied Control Commission in Vienna had 'a gruelling experience with the Russians and Americans' in 1945, had also regularly crossed the Atlantic to keep in touch with investment opinion and contacts. Under his reign the Investment Department had become much better organized. It noticeably expanded during the 1950s with the move into research, when two analysts joined Bensons to improve performance. To those used to the decisive methods of Mark Turner or Rex, he could appear indecisive because his approach was a more consensual one. A fine strategist, he liked to deliberate the pros and cons with junior colleagues at the morning investment meeting. Alastair Craig likened his rugby strategy to his investment one. In rugby he would 'jink' and elude the opposition so that players never knew exactly where he was going, and in investments he was highly successful but 'you never quite knew where he was going to shoot'.

Unfortunately, the introduction of heavy taxation and death duties after the war had squeezed the small investor to such a degree that investment trusts were no longer such profitable businesses as they had been in the inter-war period. Bensons did not make much money running them and they required a comparatively large staff, besides which the existence of Capital Issues Control had stultified them. They became less attractive to the small investor than the latest investment idea, the unit trust. Flemings forged a link with Save & Prosper, and Bensons were approached by Municipal & General, known colloquially as M. & G. Esmé Fairbairn, who had started the unit trust movement in 1935 with M. & G., was a personal friend of Phil Macpherson's so the financial connection was easily made once he decided to put 40 per cent of his share into a charitable trust and sell 35 per cent of the balance to Bensons. In 1955 Bensons invested £100,000 in M. & G., which thirty-odd years later it sold for some £80m., although by then the nature of the M. & G./Bensons connection had undergone radical alteration.[8]

The area of business that witnessed the most radical alteration at Bensons during the 1950s was the New Issues Department (now known as Corporate Finance). For the first few years after the war much of the initiative had continued to be taken by Michael Colefax, but as his outside directorships and the petrochemicals project took up more of his time, he had less to devote to Bensons; in consequence, after the merger with Lonsdales, he relinquished daily executive responsibilities although remaining on the board of RBL until 1961. The man who propelled the expansion of the new issue business at Bensons was Sir Mark Turner.

During the war Ben Pollen had warned Rex that Mark Turner was being wooed by several City firms in addition to the many oil companies which were then working with him and had already offered him positions. In replying on 14 October 1943 to a letter from Rex, Mark had expressed his satisfaction that the capital of Kenterne was intact, adding 'I should like to leave the Kenterne feeling that R.B. & Co had not lost any money there'. His reason was that 'from a personal point of view my main interest is in building up the name of the organisation I am working for. To do that efficiently and economically that name must have a good will value to start with. RB & Co has a magnificent name. Kenterne has no good will value except perhaps a little reflected glory from RB & Co.' As Mark reminded Rex, even before the war, he was more interested in bringing business to Bensons than to Kenterne!

During the war he had been drafted into the newly created Ministry of Economic Warfare where he was surrounded by Oxbridge dons and City high-flyers. From there he had served as adviser to the Foreign Office on the economic clauses of the peace treaty after which the Foreign Secretary, Ernest Bevin, asked him to act as Under-Secretary for Economic Affairs at the Control Office for Germany and Austria, a demanding position for which he had been knighted in 1946. Thus, with his reputation considerably enhanced, Mark understandably would only consider returning to Bensons as a director but, before this could be arranged, he was temporarily seconded through Thomas Robbins and Lord Bessborough to the Rio Tinto Co., then a relatively small mining house. Mark became the architect of its emergence as a major world-wide group. As the managing director he immediately set about reorganizing the company and choosing a team to run it, his most significant appointment being that of Val Duncan to take his place. Even after Mark returned to the City in 1947 he remained the Finance Director of Rio Tinto, an active position since the company was expanding rapidly and large new projects had to be financed.

Albeit in tandem with his RTZ responsibilities, Mark was back at Bensons as a director by the time of the Lonsdale merger and he was to prove the real architect of Bensons' emergence as a corporate finance house. The new issue business was on an upward trend throughout the 1950s. In the early years the average size of an issue remained small, under £500,000, which was viable by City standards but only just. Profits rose continuously, though, swelled by special 'one-off' situations such as the holding in Solartron Ltd. which Bensons sold for a large profit when electronics suddenly became the magical industry. From 1954, moreover, the issue size increased as Bensons started to attract larger clients, their biggest client at that time being Montague Burton, the High Street tailoring chain.[9]

Burtons had come to Bensons through the Marks & Spencer connection and had been a customer since the 1930s. Con sat on their board and, after old Montague Burton's death on 21 September 1952, the Burton heirs asked Con to take the chair. Simultaneously it was discovered that the stock valuation had been incorrectly compiled and overvalued for several years; thus although Burtons was a high profit business, it was making a loss. This was most unfortunate for Con, who now had to set the company to rights. 'I thought I had just accepted the chairmanship of Burtons, but look what's happened, I can't manage this alone,' he confided to Mark.

Con could easily have sorted out Burtons but he suddenly felt unable to take it on. Yet he had risen to meet far greater challenges during the war. Although a soldier, he had joined the Auxiliary Air Force before the outbreak of the war, commanding a squadron at Stanmore. In 1943 he had been transferred to Allied Military Government (AMG) which took him abroad, attached to the Eighth Army, and in July 1943 he and his group of British and American officers of disparate backgrounds—policemen from Bradford and Brooklyn, barristers from Inner Temple, roadmakers and refugees—were smuggled into Sicily for the invasion. Con performed supremely well in the war, his 'leadership, enthusiasm, humour and quite outstanding tact quickly and triumphantly put theory into practice'. Yet, when it came to a City problem such as Burtons, he was unable to fire on all four cylinders. He thus asked Mark to find somebody to help him as 'a right-hand deviller' who would really do all the work for him.

It so happened that two of Mark's corporate finance devillers, Peter Wake and Patrick Dean, had an available friend with City experience, namely Bobby Henderson. His cousin Florrie St Just was an old friend of all the Bensons, indeed her son Peter had married Rex's stepdaughter in 1948, so that Bobby Henderson and Peter Wake had known each other since childhood. He had done a stint in the family business, the Borneo Co., but did not want to remain in the Far East. He returned home and went to Jessel Toynbee, a discount house, and was looking for something more challenging when Mark Turner offered him an entrée to Bensons via a spell as Con's personal assistant at Burtons. Mark realized quite early on that Burtons needed a management team, and the way to supply one was to find a going concern that Burtons could buy to run them. An approach was made to the Jacobson brothers who owned a small Northumbrian business, Jacksons, and they agreed to the sale but then refused to sign. Mark had to persuade them by telephone. It was a breakthrough deal in terms of size for Bensons, and the Jacobsons ran Burtons most successfully.[10]

Unfortunately for Bensons there was not a queue of Burton-sized customers outside the doors of Gresham House. Mark Turner, however, was determined to attract one. He worked extremely hard but customers, as Kleinworts found, remained completely loyal to their existing banks; the system of chopping and changing advisory banks prevalent nowadays was not then customary. Bensons therefore continued to concentrate upon the small companies, working to build them up until they became big.

Mark had a client from Kenterne days, a very small company in the electrical appliance business that produced electric and then steam irons. When the market expanded the company was not generating enough money for expansion. Thus when the owners, Donal Morphy and Charles Richards, produced a brand new product, the first toaster, they naturally asked Mark to arrange the finance for them to build a factory. However, the toaster was not quite such a straightforward piece of machinery as Bensons envisaged. At the meeting held to discuss finance at Gresham House in 1949, one of the gentlemen arranged a demonstration of the product. A loaf of bread was brought from the kitchen, a bread knife produced from a dining room. With a flourish, two slices of bread were pushed into the toaster and Bensons were assured that they could proceed with the meeting because the toast when made 'will pop up and the toaster switch itself off'. Soon, however, there was a pungency about the room which began inexorably to fill with smoke as flames leapt out of the toaster. Mark hurriedly advised Morphy and Richards thereafter to eschew demonstrations of their products; Bensons nevertheless went ahead with the financing and Morphy Richards went on to become a household name which eventually ended up in the EMI group.

Not all new ventures proved so successful. There was the case of Mr Firth who acquired the rights to manufacture a prototype four-seater helicopter. It was all very hush-hush, with a secret hangar and security guards as a precaution against industrial espionage. The venture absorbed an enormous amount of money, some £80,000, with interminable progress reports from Mr Firth, who talked a technical language Bensons could hardly understand. Finally came the day of the maiden flight. Dressed with bunting, the helicopter was rolled out of the hanger with all due ceremony and launched in the manner of a ship. Amid great excitement the engines were started, the pilot waved out of the cockpit and the helicopter shuddered . . . but it never moved, not even a centimetre. Eventually Mr Firth muttered disconsolately, 'I must have got my weights wrong somewhere.'

Mark told his junior colleagues that Bensons had departed from a principle, namely that one did not back an inventor without a professional partner. It was a spectacular failure but, as Alastair Craig recalls, in those days 'Lots of things went wrong! But that was part of the joy, we were just more right than more wrong. That's the way it is, I'm afraid. If you make two mistakes and three correct decisions, you make money.' Thus Bensons had no hesitation about backing another aerial concern which initially bore the name of Manitoba and North West Land Corporation, a shell company that Bensons put to use to set up Sir Allan Cobham's business of in-flight refuelling in 1949. Sir Allan had gone all the way round the world in 'flying boats' to pioneer the Empire Air routes and had developed an airborne refuelling system. The name of the company was soon changed to the more apposite Flight Refuelling Ltd. and it was, and remains to this day, a highly successful enterprise.[11]

Bensons also made the correct decisions when they backed clients in two new growth areas, television and property. At a period when radio was still considered the superior medium Norman Collins, a BBC man, believed passionately in the future of television. In 1952 he set up the Popular Television Association to campaign for the passage of the first Television Bill by which the monopoly of the BBC would be broken with the establishment of commercial television by licence. Mark Turner met Collins through Lord Bessborough's son and backed Collins's Associated Broadcasting Development Co. Ltd.

Although it had secured its original backing on the basis of providing a seven-day service in London, it was only granted a franchise to provide a service in the Midlands and a weekend one in London—so to satisfy the Independent Television Authority Collins's group joined up with the Littler Group and the Birmingham Mail group. The company was renamed Associated Television Ltd (ATV), with Bensons and Warburgs jointly raising £5m. in 1955. At first the enterprise looked distinctly wobbly, as the cost of starting two separate stations far exceeded Collins's estimates. Mark Turner and James Drummond from Warburgs had to inform the ITA in January 1956 that the initial £5m. had almost all been swallowed up and that the company was losing money at the rate of just under £1m. a year. They agreed to raise an extra £1.5m. and on 29 May the existing shareholders raised half this capital with the other half being subscribed for by the Daily Mirror Group, then led by Cecil King, which became 25 per cent owners of ATV. In the event, as King himself said, ATV did not need his money. Revenue mounted so fast that the company could have managed without it and the original investors did extremely well, particularly Bensons with their large holding of founder shares. The office joke was: 'Well, that honeypot will keep Bensons afloat for the next five years!'[12]

Bensons' first foray into property was through a client that remains one today. Hammersons came to Bensons in 1953 when they wanted to buy the Associated City Investment Trust, a small, publicly quoted company with net assets of £60,000. Hammersons had no City experience in those days and John Read, a manager of the New Issue Department, introduced them to a stockbroker and a solicitor. The deal was that Bensons put up the money without charging a fee in return for 10 per cent of the capital. The association continued when in 1957 Hammersons wanted to purchase the Duke of Bedford's Holborn estate for £1m. Phil Macpherson got Standard Life to put up the money in return for 25 per cent of the equity in the Holborn estate and they bought £1m. of Hammerson shares for 25*s*. each. According to a later Hammerson chairman, 'That really set us off on the road' and by 1990 the Holborn estate was valued at some £125m.[13]

Although by City standards Bensons' staff of seventy was small, it was too many for the offices at Gresham House to accommodate in any great comfort.

Gresham House had always been something of a rabbit warren and in 1956 the board decided that they would have to move. In 1957 Hammersons were developing a site in Aldermanbury Square where they were offering 40,000 square feet at £1 a square foot on a 99-year lease. The partners and directors decided that £40,000 a year was too expensive and moved on to the next item on the agenda of the board meeting. Mark Turner then reappeared, having been called out to talk to a client, and asked Rex, 'What about Aldermanbury House?' to which Rex replied, 'We're not having it, Mark.' 'Oh we must have it, we must have our own front door!' responded Mark. And Rex said, 'Yes I know, but it is £40,000 a year. Where is it coming from?' Archie Andrews, the assistant company secretary, remembers that 'Mark turned the decision round, and he was absolutely right.' At first, Bensons let part of it to Barclays Bank who opened a branch on the ground floor, but then Bensons expanded so fast that within a couple of years they took over the whole building until they sold the lease for some £2m. in the late 1960s.

The move was not without drama. Gresham House itself was owned by the Gresham House Estate Co. Ltd., in which Bensons and the Rowe family had the largest holdings. Thomas Rowe the manager at Bensons had been put on the board purely as a caretaker director during the First World War and had then taken up Estate Co. shares, issued at very low prices, for 'peanuts', before leaving Bensons for Australia. By 1956, when the Benson shareholders wanted the company to expand and develop, the Rowes insisted on the status quo and were ousted at an extraordinary general meeting. When Rex later met them in the Gresham Co. office to discuss purchasing the company, 90-year-old Thomas Rowe turned red in the face, went to the door, locked it and put the key in his pocket. He then said he would not let Rex out of the room until he agreed to his terms. Rex had to sit impassively for half an hour while old Rowe poured invective on him and his father. He then unlocked the door and Rex walked out.[14]

The move in 1957 out of Gresham House signalled the end of an epoch for the staff. The atmosphere engendered there had been that of a large and happy family, one which took business seriously but never too seriously. Nearly everyone was located on one large floor and it was, above all, fun for everyone from Rex Benson, the chairman, to Maurice Green, the most junior commissionaire. The atmosphere was more redolent of a country house than a counting-house. In the shooting season, the long corridors looked more like a game larder than part of an office: venison, pheasants, and grouse all over the place as the staff were always given a brace to take home. In the summer, the windows would be wide open in the offices along the corridor and there was no secret about not having any work to do, so the boys would roll up paper into a ball from the wastepaper basket and play cricket there. 'You boys got nothing to do?' one of the partners would enquire, to which the response was 'No, sir!'[15]

It was a relaxed working environment and the partners openly followed their own pursuits at Gresham House. When Mark Turner was being recruited into the Kenterne Trust he was taken to meet Guy. Mark was somewhat disconcerted to find him absorbed in drawing a still life composition which he was reproducing with impressive skill. An American client underwent a similar experience when taken to the office to meet the Benson partners. He was first ushered into Rex's room where he found Rex in his country clothes, having come straight back from playing polo at Hurlingham. Then he proceeded to Con's room and found him doing some tapestry work to soothe his nerves. Finally he went into Guy's office where he discovered him pondering the architectural merits of a large model of a country house he wanted to build at Compton Bassett. The American declared the whole office 'absolutely nuts!'

When there was a new issue on, however, everyone downed tools to help. In the inter-war years staff were paid overtime at the double rate of 5*s*. an hour with a free Sunday lunch at the Great Eastern Hotel. The secretaries remembered the panic after the war when they used to work late and were allowed to buy some shares if there was an issue. The managing directors' secretaries had a communicating door with the dealing room. One of the dealers used to open the door and say 'Girls, do you want to buy some Rank rights?' and they would ask, 'Do we?' And he would reply 'Yes, you do', so they would buy them. Then a few days later he would open the door with the question, 'Do you want to sell your Rank rights, girls?' 'Do we?' 'Yes, you do!' And sure enough they would have gone from 7*d*. to 1*s*. 6*d*.[16]

All the doors of the office on each side of the corridor were kept open unless there was a meeting being held with a client. The staff could walk in to have a chat with Phil or Rex as with any of the staff, for everyone was approachable. The hub of Gresham House was undoubtedly 'Piccadilly Circus', Floss Lincoln's office, which everyone passed as the lift was just outside it. It was a landmark for visitors and friends who stopped to chat and look at her rogue's gallery of photographs of everyone at Bensons.

Floss was not simply the telephonist, she was the 'memory' of the firm. Luke Asquith, grandson of the prime minister and brought into Bensons by Con in 1946, recalled that a contact in America, who had not been in touch since before the war, telephoned. Before he could announce himself, Floss said, 'Oh yes, Mr so-and-so, how are you now and what's your daughter so-and-so doing now?' She had recognized his voice as she recognized so many others. Bensons did not need a reception area and receptionists when they had Floss to chat to visitors and clients. She was for 45 years, from 1927–72, a unique and loved member of the Benson team.

Aldermanbury House was quite different. It was the first new building on a bomb-site, and surrounded by wartime rubble. Before it was completed some of the staff went to look at it and returned somewhat disenchanted. 'The difference between Old Broad Street and there was . . . ghastly because there were concrete stairs and things like that,' a secretary recalls. The telephone switchboard was fitted into the basement but 'the bosses wouldn't have anything to do with that. Miss Lincoln had to be on the fourth floor!' Even so, 'Piccadilly Circus' was never quite the same after the move to Aldermanbury House in 1957. The secretaries were told to go and see Floss 'because she doesn't see anyone now'. The office was spread over several floors rather than just on the one floor, so that the former cosy intimacy disappeared and a little more formality crept in as the business became less of 'a high-class amateur game' and more of a professional one. There was a proper reception area with a front desk where at Old Broad Street there had been a counter with commissionaires from the 9th Lancers.[17]

The move to Aldermanbury Square marked a turning-point in the bank's culture on another front. The appointment of John Read as a managing director had signified a change in boardroom thinking that really became part of the ethos of the firm at Aldermanbury. He was not the first player to progress to the board because Charlie Hellings had already done so; though he had been a senior figure for so long as the all-powerful general manager that in his case the change from manager to director, from player to gentleman as it was then termed, was not at all dramatic. C.C.H. was already a director of various companies and was considered to be the Father of the Firm. His retirement in 1953 had in no way severed his connection with Bensons and he was still consulted by the partners. On his death in 1957, his widow Marion told Rex 'You don't need to be told that he loved you and wouldn't mind my saying so now.' His had been a special relationship with the partners and his elevation to the Benson board had been in recognition of that rather than heralding a cultural trend.[18]

John Read was in his early thirties when he became a director. A bright, grammar-school boy whose parents could not afford to send him to university, he had joined Bensons at the age of 17 in the 1930s, working his way up so that after the war he wrote all the prospectuses, 'almost unaided with whomever he could get to sweep up the commas', his junior colleague Frank Hislop remembers. He was swiftly promoted to manager and then began to build up his own corporate client list. Despite his friendly nature and popularity in the office, he was very much a loner when it came to business, as many corporate financiers are. He had good judgement and was an excellent deals man.

His most important deal was undoubtedly for Rank whom he brought to Bensons. At that time Rank was making no money and its bankers Philip Hill, Higginson were not especially supportive. John Read moved in to supplant them and profits did increase. Read then helped to bring Rank a major position in Xerox, which proved to be the making of its business, and managed big issues for it over the next four or five years. This was important for Bensons, because it gave the firm credibility and consolidated its reputation in the larger issue area. From the City's point of view their inclusion on the list of firms involved in the Conservative Government's denationalization of steel had marked the start of the process.[19]

This was very much Morgan Grenfell's party but Bensons had worked with them a few years earlier on the Labour Government's nationalization of the industry. They were thus invited by Cameron Cobbold, Governor of the Bank of England, to become one of the eight issuing houses which comprised the consortium that would begin to market the steel shares back to the public in 1953. The other houses were Morgan Grenfell, Barings, Rothschilds, Schroders, Lazards, Helbert Wagg, and Hambros. The unscrambling of the steel industry was a very complex and difficult operation. The first steel denationalization issue, an offer for sale of 14m. £1 ordinary shares of United Steel Companies at 25*s*. per share, was heavily oversubscribed and a triumph for the consortium. Expenses had been kept to a minimum so the consortium received a commission of 6*d*. per share and, after expenses, Bensons' share came to £6,369.

This 1953 issue was only the first of many, so that steel issues absorbed a great deal of attention throughout the decade. In 1957 the consortium organized the denationalization of the Steel Co. of Wales, at the time the largest equity issue ever made in the City, consisting of 40m. £1 ordinary shares at par, and this brought to an end the operation. As Kathleen Burk, the historian of Morgan Grenfell, has pointed out, it could be considered as the first great privatization exercise. Bensons' experience was not wasted. It would be put to use at a later date when privatization once again dominated the political and financial landscape, and then it would be Kleinwort Benson rather than Morgan Grenfell leading.[20]

Although by the late 1950s John Read's career as a company finance man had blossomed, he remained a manager just as his immediate senior, Sam Hamburger, did. Hamburger ran the New Issue Department, which had grown to include a clutch of bright young men on the fast track to directorships. There was Peter Wake who, having been wooed from Hambros, was the only executive, apart from his brother-in-law Mark Turner, to have been trained as a banker and to possess any knowledge of merchant banking in the sense of acceptance credits. He had, too, 'a marvellously analytical mind' and acted as

Mark's junior on deals, to the envy and admiration of his peers. As a Benson nephew in the City, it had always been assumed that he would eventually gravitate to the family firm, where he was viewed as future leadership material. With him was his contemporary Patrick Dean, a Lincolnshire farmer who had trained as a chartered accountant in order to follow a City career. The other young devillers could not fathom why, in Peter Wake's words, 'a chap well placed to go shooting every day would want to slave for a living' like them. The third young man was Bobby Henderson, who shared their experience of serving in the war as brother officers in the 60th.

So had two other young colleagues, Barnaby Benson and Luke Asquith. Barnaby was Guy's middle son and the only one to go into the family firm. He was full of charm and a bright, tolerant man, but he was not a dedicated banker. Where his father might have complained without justification that he was never pushed, Barnaby would have had every justification for such a complaint, and he was never really seen as being in the mainstream of the New Issues Department. Luke Asquith's Benson career, as a member of the new issues committee and secretary to the management committee, took an unusual turn when, at Rex's request, he was seconded to General William Donovan, Chief of the American Secret Service, who needed a ghost writer. Luke Asquith later returned to Bensons to specialize in small company finance under Sam Hamburger and John Read.[21]

Sam Hamburger, a small, clever man who excelled at economics, had a long innings as 'the brains' of the New Issue Department. He was also a respected joint general manager with Bill Hole. But he was never offered promotion onto the board despite his experience, astuteness, and seniority. Eventually he announced to the partners that he was leaving the firm to go to Warburgs in January 1957. This was a thunderbolt; they had simply never considered appointing him to the board, not because they doubted his ability but rather because it suited them to have him where he was. Rex was at his country house, Drovers, and immediately asked him down in order to persuade him to reconsider. Sam Hamburger nevertheless remained resolute in the face of Rex at his most persuasive. The partners were distressed and believed that the New Issue Department would collapse. It was also highly unusual in those days for a senior executive to move away to a competitor. Loyalty was taken for granted; be they clients, partners, or staff, people stayed put and it was unheard of to poach senior staff.

Warburgs, however, had no compunction about changing the rules on this count or on any other. The two houses knew each other well, having worked together since 1940 on a joint venture backing Mercantile Overseas Trading Co. (MOT) in the finance of exports. During the war, with Ben Pollen and Sam

Hamburger representing Bensons' interests, MOT started to trade with South America and China. Moreover, when Siegmund Warburg had started his New Trading Co. (precursor of S. G. Warburg & Co.) in pre-war London, he had been grateful for Bensons' interest and recognition. The City houses which had most impressed him were Bensons, Flemings, and Helbert Wagg, for he recognized them as rare animals: members of the City establishment who were none the less entrepreneurs, unlike most of the others, whom he considered stodgy. He also knew of Rex through American contacts and always said, as he did in a letter to Rex's son, that Rex was 'one of the few to welcome me when I arrived in the City'. At one time there was a possibility of a joint venture between Bensons and Warburgs in Canada but Helbert Wagg got in first so the idea was stillborn. Notwithstanding all this, Siegmund Warburg did not sound Rex out about Hamburger, as other City friends would have done at a time when, for instance, Bensons, Morgan Grenfell, and Flemings openly discussed salaries.

Hamburger, for his part, tried to allay Bensons' panic by pointing out that John Read was fully competent to take on additional responsibilities. 'In 6 months', he told Rex, 'you will probably be wondering what all the fuss was about. The RBL organisation has its deficiencies but it is certainly strong enough to take the departure of one senior executive in its stride.'

This happily proved to be true and Hamburger's departure led ultimately to John Read's appointment to the board. As Alastair Craig, who would follow Read onto the board two years later, explains: 'the Benson brothers took a little bit of a fright and decided that they had been keeping all the best staff at managerial level, when they really ought to be directors'. Thus at the time of the move to Aldermanbury House in 1957, the board consisted of the three Benson brothers, Leo Lonsdale, and Robert Rockley with Phil Macpherson, Mark Turner, Denys Oppé, Ronny Medlicott, and John Read as managing directors. In the event, the move to Aldermanbury heralded two further changes of deep significance in the future development of Bensons.[22]

The first concerned the chairmanship of Bensons. Rex would be 70 in 1959 and he decided to retire in March of that year. There was no need to hunt for a successor because the obvious candidates were already at hand. The soundings that Rex took concentrated upon two eminently suitable men, Phil Macpherson and Mark Turner. At the junior director and managerial level, the more vocal were in no doubt. Their choice was Mark, and it is not difficult to see why. He possessed a glamour for them; and even decades later, when some had become senior figures themselves, they, along with many other respected City figures, bracketed him with Siegmund Warburg as the two most exciting and outstanding personalities in post-war merchant banking. Whereas Warburg was single-minded in terms of banking, Mark spread himself in many different directions so that his input was less concentrated in terms of reputation. A brilliant negotiator, he was a great business-getter and inspired all the young people working with him, even though he could be fierce with amateurs or the slipshod. Yet, unlike some leading lights in corporate finance, he never pushed others into the background. Quite the reverse: he wanted to bring them on and include them, so that he could move on to something else—there being so many other matters competing for his attention. He was in great demand by other outside companies and sat on many boards, including Commercial Union, Mercantile Credit, British Home Stores, and RTZ. Whilst this added weight to Bensons' business it also meant that he was often absent. One textile magnate even called him Peter Pan on the grounds that when he thought that he had pinned Mark down to a long business conversation he was suddenly gone—out of the window for all he knew! His young devillers used to have to chase him to the lavatory and take a taxi with him to the other side of London, just to get his ear.[23]

It was for this reason, above all, that Rex, Con, and, more reluctantly, Leo decided to appoint Phil Macpherson to the chair. He was a very successful long-term investor and had built up that side of the business, the side on which the firm's reputation still largely rested; for, despite the great strides made by Mark, the new issue business had yet to blossom into a secure first-rank one. Phil was also pre-eminent in the investment trust world, a respected figure in the City and in Scotland, where he had built up a large Benson business, he retained the reputation of a national figure. Scottish firms were constantly trying to woo him away but he had remained loyal. This, and the fact that he was largely in rather than out of the office, decided the partners in his favour. Besides, Rex had always thought of Phil as his eventual successor from the day he joined the firm in 1937 as a director. Mark, in contrast, had come in through Kenterne and was not at first a director of Bensons itself so that somehow he always seemed slightly less qualified for the role.

It was unfortunate for Mark that his situation struck a chord in the Benson memory of the days of Henry Vernet's chairmanship and their struggles to obtain his attention and decisions amidst his many outside directorships. Thus Con believed firmly that Bensons 'had to have somebody who was planted to his desk'; while Rex told his colleagues 'it will be no good having Mark as chairman, Mark is never in the office'. So the decision was for Phil.[24]

When Phil Macpherson took up the reins in March 1959, Rex and Con remained on the board of both Bensons and the holding company. Although the natural successor to the chairmanship, Con had ruled himself out because his health would not allow him to take on such an onerous full-time position. This was to the disadvantage of Bensons in one important respect. Bensons would have carried more weight into negotiations with prospective marriage partners if either Con or Leo had been chairman of Robert Benson Lonsdale. Although the City was beginning to change and to become more professional by the end of the 1950s, merchant banks were by no means meritocratic when it came to the partners' room. Most firms were still headed by proprietors, and in those firms which had not remained proprietary the partnerships were often peopled by second and third generations of the same families. Con would also have met the requirement of being a professional, which was felt by Macpherson and Turner to be essential. However, with neither Con nor Rex at the forefront of Bensons' leadership, the proprietary, family link that had acted as a foundation for the independence of the firm was weakened and the interests of the firm were never guarded in quite the same way again.

Rex's retirement from the chair meant that for the first time in over 170 years a Benson was neither the senior partner nor a joint leader of the family firm. Rex was much missed by his staff, who adored him. Jim Deacon, one of the commissionaires, said 'I don't work for Sir Rex, he works for me.' He had always made it his business to know everybody who worked for him and this was an immense asset when it came to office management.

Rex possessed an instinct about staff problems. He would get wind of office clashes and immediately sort them out so that no grievance, whether imaginary or not, was left to fester. He was never a technical banking man but then he felt there were others to fulfil that requirement. Where he excelled was with man management and as an eponymous ambassador for Bensons. He shared with his banking ancestors the ability to pick the right people for the job and he was an excellent communicator. Under his chairmanship Bensons achieved growth and greater profitability, and moved up the league table of issuing houses.[25]

His continuing presence on the board in the capacity of elder statesman was reassuring, especially as Phil Macpherson's chairmanship proved short-lived. His first year in the chair coincided with a spate of mergers, which eventually swept Bensons along in its wake.

'Merger mania', in the parlance of the press, broke out in August 1959 when Philip Hill, Higginson & Co. attracted Kleinworts' attention by announcing its merger with Erlangers, who themselves had suffered pangs of largely unrequited love for Bensons. The firm had been the subject of Erlangers' attentions back in 1931 but the state of the Robert Benson & Co. balance sheet had precluded reciprocation. Rex, however, had continued to bear them in mind as a possible future marriage partner, should the need ever arise. Leo d'Erlanger was a good friend and the match would give Bensons not only a firm capital base but also an acceptance and foreign exchange business together with some good new issue business. Leo d'Erlanger himself intermittently reiterated that Erlangers continued to be interested in Bensons. It is somewhat surprising therefore that a Benson/Erlanger merger never materialized in the late 1950s, given that both houses were considering marriage of some sort; Mark Turner was especially keen for Bensons to extend their business into acceptance credits. But by the time Bensons might have been ready to commit themselves, Erlangers were already spoken for. Others who were less bashful during these hectic months included Edward de Stein, which flowed smoothly into the embrace of Lazards in February 1960, and Helbert Waggs, which were bought by Schroders in May 1960 while being eyed by another potential suitor, Kleinworts. In both cases an old-established, strong banking house acquired a smaller, highly active investment banking business. Thus, neither of these mergers achieved a true complementarity.

The overall effect of this outbreak of mergers was that other merchant banks started to consider whether they wanted to remain wallflowers or look around for prospective partners. The City was in a courtship mood, marriage-brokers weaving their way in and out of parlours, demure first meetings between directors and partners, trips to Companies House to discover shareholdings and annual reports, and above all, secrecy. The financial press did not stake out banking premises in those days, so it was left to the odd stockbroker who, *en passant*, might wonder why X was seen leaving Y's office on several occasions.

At the daily morning coffee meeting in Cyril's room, the largest of the partners' rooms at Kleinworts, the talk of marriage had concentrated by August 1959 upon three possibilities drawn from the list of eight houses, compiled by David Robertson at Cyril's request. Helbert Wagg were already pledged to Schroders, so Flemings and Bensons remained on the list and the partners decided that Cyril was best placed to make the first move. He was a neighbour of Richard Fleming's in Gloucestershire and they regularly hunted together, so this was not difficult. David Robertson recalls that Cyril 'cast a fly over Richard but at that stage they weren't ready'. This was not too grave a disappointment because they were aware that Flemings were pre-eminent in investment trust but not in corporate finance business. Thus fairly early on in their search for a partner, Kleinworts fixed upon Bensons, a close second to Flemings in investment trusts but well ahead in corporate finance.[26]

It had generally been assumed that if Bensons were to merge with anyone, it would be with Flemings. The two houses had worked together since Robin Benson had provided Robert Fleming with office space in the 1880s; Rex and Con had known Philip Fleming from childhood and Archie Jamieson had long been a constant companion on business ventures. Indeed, Flemings had turned down Sir Edward de Stein's firm not simply from a wish to remain independent but also because Bensons was in the background. Rex and Archie Jamieson had often discussed the future, concluding that Flemings would continue to specialize in investment and wholesale placing but might start to use Bensons as an issuing house, which would pave the way to closer collaboration. As Rex's son David points out, it was 'probably not a sensible thing, in retrospect, because the two firms were so very alike'.[27]

Mark Turner certainly took this view and had long urged the board to look at an accepting house. In the immediate post-war period, he suggested Brown, Shipley & Co. This bank was no stranger to Bensons, having been an old Liverpool house specializing in the America trade in the early nineteenth century, in rivalry with Cropper, Benson. By 1944 Brown, Shipley possessed a capital of £750,000 and had about £3m. of good acceptance credits. Rex, however, was neither committed to the idea of Brown, Shipley nor to marriage with an accepting house. He always remembered talking to Montagu Norman about Bensons' options for merging with another firm. The Governor had strongly deprecated Bensons' joining up with a merchant banking firm. 'You will find eventually that the business of the Bank will need all your money and there will be nothing left for the many initiatives in which your firm has been outstanding —And there are not many of you.'[28]

As a merchant bank, Kleinworts would no doubt have deprecated Norman's view. They had become increasingly keen on a merger with Bensons, one of the attractions being that the shares of Lonsdale Investment Trust were quoted and Kleinworts had long toyed with the idea of going 'public'. In a memo to the partners dated 12 August 1959, David Robertson admitted that he had no idea how Bensons would react to suggestions of a merger; but with the Benson brothers taking a less active part than previously, he thought they might view a merger more favourably than before. It was again Cyril who was to cast the first fly over the prospective catch, for the simple reason that he was in regular contact with Mark Turner, who was a fellow director of Commercial Union.

The Kleinwort partners had very few outside directorships, but their relations with a constituent part of Commercial Union dated from Edward Cohen's directorship of the North British Insurance Co. in the 1870s. Commercial Union thus unwittingly acted as a trysting place for a City merger. Its importance in promoting the Kleinwort suit can be seen from David Robertson's pertinent observation in his August 1959 memo that 'one of our problems in the very early stages is that, because of the fact that we are such a very private company, nobody outside Fenchurch Street has any real idea of our size so that the attraction of merging with us may not become really apparent until we get to the stage of discussing figures'.[29]

Under the aegis of Commercial Union board meetings, Cyril was able to hold some off-the-record discussions with Mark in which he was able to convey an idea of the size and strengths of Kleinworts, whose overture was music to Mark's ears. He believed that Bensons had to merge to achieve growth and was constantly telling the board and his managers that the time had come. Bensons 'were at a crossroads where if we are to continue to grow we are going to have to find an Acceptance House to join us' in order to became a fully fledged merchant bank which could provide all the services under one roof for the larger clients. Mark thought this was vital because not only were new companies entering the market-place without the baggage of old loyalties to a particular merchant bank, but takeover bids had also started to become fashionable, so that existing clients were in danger of being lost to other banks who were acting for the predators. Bensons were at a further disadvantage in that, of the three-legged stool of a complete merchant bank, they possessed only the one full, solid leg of investment management, with a second three-quarter-sized leg of corporate finance. They needed to have the third leg of banking facilities for the edifice to balance.[30]

Mark therefore took up the idea of a Benson–Kleinwort merger with all his usual alacrity and enthusiasm, and set about persuading Bensons that not only must they merge but that they must do so with Kleinworts. Although 'a very private' bank, the senior partner Herman Andreae was already known to the Bensons through Kit Hoare, who now acted as the second marriage-broker. In 1943 Ben Pollen had written to Rex about a proposal of Kit Hoare's:

> Herman A, head of Kleinworts, fearing that Acceptance Business will be very much reduced after the war, is seeking an investment for some of his money. He has formed a very high opinion of R.B. & Co., about whom his principal informant appears to be Kit. No particular sum of money was mentioned, but in reply to a direct question by me, Kit said that Herman A would never think in terms of less than £100,000 or some greater sum which would form what he described as a reasonable proportion of the capital of R.B. & Co. I then asked whether he would expect to put someone into Bensons to look after his money, to which Kit replied that he thought not.

Rex was then based in Washington, but after his return he had expressed an interest to Kit Hoare. A lunch was then arranged at Kleinworts but nothing came of Herman A.'s sleeping-partner idea, though Kit Hoare's views were sought by both houses. He had a close relationship with Herman A. and Rex and Con and flitted in and out of both firms, 'puckering his bushy eyebrows and talking like the oracle'. Thus Rex and Con naturally consulted him about the business of merging with Kleinworts, telling him, 'You mustn't say anything about this,' which he never did. Subsequently, they learnt that Herman

A. and Cyril had also asked his advice in the utmost secrecy. Kit Hoare gave both sides the go-ahead and once the initial proposals were accepted, his firm was officially brought in as stockbrokers.[31]

Once Mark and Cyril had agreed they liked the colour of each others' eyes enough to proceed, a meeting was arranged in November 1959 between Phil Macpherson and Mark Turner on the Benson side and Cyril and David Robertson on the Kleinwort side. The outcome was that both parties were in favour of marriage. The next step was for Phil Macpherson to discuss the idea in principle with Leo, Rex, and Con. This step had already been taken on the Kleinwort side, owing to the nature of their partnership whereby if Cyril and Ernest were in favour of a scheme the other partners generally fell in behind. Since Kleinworts were the wooers, they were ready to proceed to the detail. Bensons, however, still had some way to go, and it took a good deal of hard work by Mark Turner before they decided to advance to the next stage in the spring of 1960.

This round of talks concerned the breakdown of figures, and the most interesting aspect of the two balance sheets was their similarity. The ratio of profits between Bensons and Kleinworts was about 1.05 : 1 while the ratio of net tangible assets was again 1.05 : 1. In terms of earnings Bensons' figure was in the region of £1.2m., of which LIT provided £400,000, for the year ended February 1960, with future earnings estimated at £1m. as opposed to a Kleinwort figure of £850,000. The earnings ratio was thus about 10 : 8.5. Having seen the initial figures, the points under discussion focused upon staff members, 214 at Kleinworts compared with 189 at Bensons and LIT, and on the important issues of new name, location, and remuneration.

It was at this stage that Bensons began to appear lukewarm. Phil Macpherson had appointed to the board three new directors, Peter Wake, Bobby Henderson, and Alastair Craig, who were naturally looking forward to their increased remuneration. The practice of allowing director participation in certain deals had continued and a great deal of money was being earned by board members from this source. It was clear, however, that one of the conditions imposed by a merger would be the introduction of a uniform remuneration package which would have the effect of sweeping away such perks. There was thus considerable opposition from some of the directors.

There was even resistance to the Kleinwort suggestion that the merged group be housed at No. 20. The building was not sufficiently large to accommodate over 400 people, so Read and Oppé argued that if Barclays vacated the lower-floor offices, then Aldermanbury House could easily accommodate Kleinworts and Bensons. Kleinworts, however, would not relinquish their freehold site. Eventually it was agreed that both businesses would remain in separate buildings and the merger would initially be a purely financial one.

At a meeting with Phil Macpherson on 20 May, Ivo Forde raised the question of a name for the holding company. The agreed structure of the proposed joint company was to establish a new holding company which, in exchange for its own share capital, would acquire the whole issued share capital of the two old holding companies, Kleinworts Ltd. and Lonsdale Investment Trust Ltd. This new holding company would have two subsidiaries. The first would combine the banking business of Kleinwort, Sons & Co. with the issuing business of Robert Benson Lonsdale & Co.; the second would combine the investment trust business of the Lonsdale Investment Trust with the various small Kleinwort investment trusts. In the case of both the new holding company and the first banking subsidiary, Forde said that Kleinworts' name must come first. In reply Macpherson said that he had not given much thought to the matter.

Yet, when he raised the issue back at Bensons, there was considerable dismay at Kleinworts' non-negotiable stance. The two teams who hammered out the details of the merger were David Robertson and Pat Limerick for Kleinworts and Denys Oppé and John Read for Bensons. When the name issue came up, Oppé said that this could prove a difficulty. Furthermore, he felt that it touched upon the whole question of personalities at the top. How they would work together was, in his view, going to be the main problem and sticking point in the merger.

Kleinworts, however, were adamant on both points. The Kleinwort name had to come first because as an accepting house they had to predominate, 'otherwise', Ivo Forde reiterated, 'their bills would not stand up as they had done'. While Bensons were reluctantly prepared to swallow this, chiefly because it would not really affect their issuing business, they were concerned that the fact that the merger was of *equals* would be lost if the Kleinwort name took precedence in both companies, with Bensons appearing to be the junior partner. In both the Lazard and Schröder mergers, these houses were the larger purchasers of the two parties, so it was natural that their names should precede those of de Stein and Helbert Wagg; but this was not the case here.[32]

Moreover, the name question was but a preamble to the Kleinwort insistence on the precedence of Ernest (their senior partner elect awaiting the retirement of Herman A.) over both the LIT senior partner, Leo Lonsdale, and the Benson chairman, Phil Macpherson. As a Kleinwort man explained: 'It was an article of faith of the Kleinwort family, that banking was the core activity', one which they regarded as a superior activity, so that the business could not have anyone but a Kleinwort as its chairman. The primacy of the Kleinwort side reflected their ownership of the single biggest block of family shares in the combined firm. The second largest block was owned by the Lonsdale family but Leo maintained an advisory rather than executive role and his only son

Norman pursued other interests besides banking. When Gordon Tettmar and Arthur Stilwell told Ernest how pleased they were about the merger and they hoped he was going to be chairman, his answer flashed out 'Well there's nobody else, is there?'—and there really was nobody else as far as he was concerned.[33]

Bensons, not unnaturally, were dismayed by the Kleinwort implication that once again they were the junior partner in the merger. With rebellion threatening in the managers' offices and rumblings in the managing directors' rooms, Mark and Cyril got together, and Mark then set about reassuring everyone that the future would be secure. Ernest as chairman of the holding company, Kleinwort Benson Lonsdale, and the subsidiary Kleinwort Benson, would be an interim appointment. Ernest would be succeeded at Kleinwort Benson Ltd. by Cyril just as Phil Macpherson as the deputy chairman of these companies would be succeeded by Mark. In turn, Cyril would eventually be succeeded by Mark, so that it was definitely not going to be Kleinworts for all time at the helm. 'Mark in his enthusiasm to do the merger', two of his younger colleagues would recall, 'persuaded everyone that this really must happen,' in order to ensure the future growth of Bensons and the successful outcome of their careers; and it was his personality that pushed it through.[34]

Thus, during the summer and early autumn of 1960, the winds blew hot and cold but mostly the former. Leo, Rex, and Con had been kept informed at all stages and during early September Rex and Con had discussed many aspects of the marriage while at Bussento, Rex's house in Italy. As elder statesmen, they were particularly concerned about two aspects of the merger. The first concerned the continuity of Bensons' methods, which had built up a remarkable degree of friendliness and goodwill in the City. Kleinworts had two very charming owner-partners but their business by its nature gave less scope to the personal touch and was much more inflexible. The second aspect concerned the leadership of both operations and raised the question whether a banker could lead an issuing and trading operation, which is much more speculative than wholesale banking, and whether a corporate finance man could lead a more orthodox and 'rule of thumb' banking operation. Leaving Rex at Bussento after their discussions, Con motored to visit his daughter in France, where he died suddenly on the evening of his arrival, thus not living to see the consummation of the merger.[35]

Rex and Leo eventually gave it their blessing once all the managing directors decided that the marriage was a good one from the business point of view. The resulting engagement was short, since the terms were fairly easy to arrange on a willing buyer/willing seller basis. The shareholders of Bensons ended up with 54 per cent of the equity, the Kleinwort ones with 46 per cent. The major difference between the two lay in the fact that the Kleinwort shareholdings were concentrated amongst a very small family group whereas Robert Benson Lonsdale, which had long been a public company, embraced a widespread shareholding.

The announcement of the merger was made public on 18 November 1960, attracting such favourable headlines as 'Strength through Size' and 'Merchant Bankers à la Mode'. Two elements of the proposed merger in particular caught the City's interest. First, the size of the merger, which would create a £60m. group, was a surprise to many City pundits who had no idea of the capitalization of Kleinworts. 'The new company will rank as one of the largest and best diversified groups in the City,' asserted the *Daily Telegraph*. Secondly, it was a merger of complete complementarity because each firm's weakness was the other firm's strength. Kleinworts had a very strong banking business, a small investment management business, and almost no corporate finance business; whereas Bensons had an active corporate business, a good investment business, and almost no banking business. On 17 March 1961 all these businesses were merged when the Kleinwort Benson Lonsdale marriage took place. The new house could now look to the future confident that it was fully equipped to meet the challenges ahead, that the stool of their business was now a solid three-legged one.[36]

PART THREE

Kleinwort Benson 1961–1994

11 A Modern Merchant Bank 1961–1971

THE decade following the merger constituted a dynamic era in the City, reflecting the optimistic mood of a nation again enjoying the heady wine of full employment and improved living conditions. Under Wilson's Labour government a new age seemed to beckon with the cult of youth, consumerism, and the 'white heat of technology', as the country experienced an acute bout of neophilia. The evolution and rapid growth of the Eurodollar market led to the resurgence of London as a leading international financial centre. This in turn stimulated other international banking activities, thereby increasing opportunities for merchant banks. Domestically, with the restructuring of British industry, there was an increase in mergers, acquisitions, and capital raising; while the rapid growth in the funds of institutional investors generated an equally strong demand for investment management services. It was also during the 1960s that merchant banks began to enlarge the range of services they could offer their clients, as they diversified into leasing, project finance, hire purchase and insurance broking. The City, in short, was on course to resume a level of activity not seen since its pre-1914 heyday.

As a result of the merger, the newly formed firm of Kleinwort Benson Ltd., known as KB and a subsidiary of the holding company Kleinwort Benson Lonsdale Ltd. (KBL), was well placed to participate in all these developments. At the time of the merger Rex, who continued as the Benson elder statesman on the board of KBL, believed that it would 'take at least 5 years before the wisdom of this move can be properly judged'. Change was a natural concomitant as the new management tried to integrate two very different businesses, altering their culture and structure in the process. It was by no means easy. From the Benson point of view, 'nothing seemed to change for Kleinworts whereas everything did for Bensons'; they found the aftermath of the merger a traumatic period.[1]

The fact that their union was complementary meant they had been very differently organized. Kleinworts had maintained the strict hierarchical structure that reflected both its banking business and private, family-dominated shareholding. Bensons, in contrast, was run along collegiate lines reflecting its more advisory investment banking operations, public shareholding, and more modern style. The corporate finance demands of clients required people of senior status within the firm, and the need to attract and retain them had created a much more meritocratic environment at Bensons.

The difference in approach was manifested in the composition of their former boards of directors. At Kleinworts the board had consisted solely of the five partners, whereas at Bensons it had comprised twelve directors that included a number appointed on merit alone. The new KB board consisted of seventeen directors, nine from the Kleinwort side and eight from the Benson side. In order to make up their representation, the five Kleinwort partners promoted to the KB board their four most senior managers, Gerald Thompson, Walter Michaelis, A. J. Haynes, and F. W. Smith. Bensons' representatives were composed entirely of the former firm's directors. Rex Benson, Leo Lonsdale, and Robert Rockley joined the KBL board along with Ernest and Cyril Kleinwort, Sonny Andreae, Ivo Forde, Phil Macpherson, and Mark Turner.

At the management level, too, Kleinworts' wish to retain a more hierarchical structure created problems on the Benson side. 'Bensons was a very flat organisation, they hadn't really distinguished people by rank', Pat Limerick recalls. 'To fit in with the structure, so that they knew where they stood, those in Bensons who were of equivalent status and experience were made Managers' of KB. Management decisions at Kleinworts had been made by the five partners during what they called their tea-break, which was in fact a cup of coffee in Cyril's room, but Ernest and Cyril were always particularly influential. Bensons, however, had had a more consensual Board and though it inevitably helped if Rex, Phil, or Mark favoured a proposal, the outcome was by no means a foregone conclusion.[2]

The divide between the two methods of executive decision-making was apparent at the very first KB board meeting. After opening the meeting, Ernest said, 'We have decided XYZ . . .' at which there was a deathly silence before three Bensons voices simultaneously enquired, 'Who's we?' In order to accommodate a more consultative, consensual approach, Ernest and his deputy chairman, Phil Macpherson, appointed a management committee comprised of three members from each side with a revolving chairman; under Cyril it would become the Chairman's Committee, responsible for the management of KB. In contrast to the KB board, the KBL board was only supervisory and, as the years passed, it came to consist mainly of former KB board members supported by some non-executive directors drawn from outside.[3]

Friction was also engendered over other issues. In terms of remuneration, for instance, the Benson staff had earned salaries plus an annual bonus, whereas their Kleinwort counterparts had earned comparatively small salaries but were paid commission on the profits produced by their departments. Schroder Wagg had faced a similar problem, with Schroders' pay having been more in line with Kleinworts' whereas Helbert Wagg had rewarded with a more generous guaranteed income. There, the new firm decided to increase the Schroder salaries. Joe Payne, the ex-Bensons general manager of KB, introduced a new system whereby staff earned a proper salary without bonus or commission. Not surprisingly, 'he had a very difficult time, very difficult indeed', as Robert Clifford, manager of the Securities Department recalls. 'And I give him every credit, he managed so well without either suffering a breakdown or somebody batting him over the head!'[4]

Many of the Bensons staff were dismayed by the autocratic atmosphere at Kleinworts. Directors' secretaries sent over from Aldermanbury House found that their counterparts stood in awe of the directors, in a way they would never have done at Bensons. But then Kleinworts' style of communication had always been to the point: 'Take it away,' or 'Do it again,' a manager would scrawl over work submitted. Staff continued to be called by their surname, even long-serving secretaries. The Kleinwort staff naturally welcomed the more friendly Benson style that gradually permeated through to them. A significant moment had undoubtedly been Rex's first post-merger visit to No. 20 when he had gone round shaking hands with everybody and saying, 'Hello, how are you? I'm Rex Benson. What do you do?' In the words of one member of staff 'it transformed the firm'. Cyril would also be approachable when he became chairman later on.[5]

All of these local differences should be kept in the perspective of the immense amount of goodwill and the momentum that had built up on both sides to make the merger work. The problems at KB were those of a growing baby and were in no way comparable to those at, for example, the merged Hill Samuel, whose problems seemed to be more those of a rebellious adolescent. David Robertson remembers hearing about the 'terrible, terrible upheavals and eruptions going on at Hill Samuel where people were said to be very unhappy'. In the end all but two of the old M. Samuel directors left, with Michael Devas joining KB where the architects of the merger, Cyril and Mark, continued to carry their colleagues with them, so that differences were resolved rather than forcing resignation. 'Them and Us' attitudes, which only the passage of time, the process of close collaboration and strong leadership could eradicate, persisted in some merged firms for several generations. Three years after the KB merger, David Robertson was asked by Kleinworts' old solicitors how the merger was going. In answering 'quite successfully', he elicited the laughing comment, 'You can still walk round Linklater & Paines—and we merged somewhere round about 1914—and say that's a Paines' man and that's a Linklaters' man.'[6]

The teething problems and the instinctive suspicion of the other unknown half of the staff were exacerbated at KB by the impossibility of integrating the two firms physically into one building. The decision had been taken during the merger negotiations to rebuild No. 20 as a modern office block capable of housing the entire staff apart from the registration department at Newbury. In the meantime the two sides continued to operate out of separate premises; the former Kleinworts operation mainly moving to St Albans House in Goldsmith Street while the former Bensons largely continued at Aldermanbury House. There they remained until the spring of 1969, due to unforeseen delays—that fortuitously proved very profitable—in the erection of the new building at No. 20. In the meantime, Victor Lewis and his tiny banking team from Bensons simply walked from Aldermanbury House over to St Albans where they joined the much larger Kleinwort banking division, while David Robertson liaised with the Benson corporate finance division at Aldermanbury. When it came to the investment management people, however, matters were not quite so easy to arrange.

Both constituent firms had contained an investment department but their contributions as profit centres were very different. Kleinworts investment department looked after family funds and some private clients, which was never perceived as a core business, and the firm's capital, which undoubtedly contributed a major part to the bank's profits. At Bensons, in contrast, it had long been *the* core business, managing funds for both institutional and private clients, possessing a publicly quoted stable of investment trusts and the first in-house research department of any investment management house. Phil Macpherson's fiefdom was a larger, more professional department, so at the time of the merger it was naturally assumed that Kleinworts' investment side should merge into the larger Benson one.

When in due course Ivo Forde took his people over to Aldermanbury House it became clear that the former Kleinwort partners, who had traditionally overseen their own investments and the management of the firm's capital, would not part with direct control of their people. Thus, although the two operations were nominally under Phil Macpherson, KB in effect had two separate Investment Management Departments. Inevitably this caused investment misunderstandings and policy differences. In the private clients area, for example, the Kleinwort and Benson lists were kept separate and their respective managers disagreed over the Bensons policy of not charging fees. Phil Macpherson and Ivo Forde worked well together as did Rex and Ivo, who eventually took over Rex's chairmanship of the English and New York Investment Trust. They no doubt assumed that their staff would do the same, allowing the division to continue on a 'wait and see how it works' basis. As Pat

Limerick would observe 'that, with all the power of hindsight, is not a good way to run a merger. It must be made quite clear who is in charge and what the lines of responsibility might be.' The result was that the combined investment division did not fire on all cylinders; it continued to manage KB's capital very successfully and, remaining profitable, there was little encouragement to attract new outside funds. The attitude to this division may seem surprising, given that part of the attraction of a merger for Kleinworts must have been Bensons' larger and more public presence in investment management.

This, however, is to ignore the Kleinwort belief that banking was the dominant leg of the three-legged stool. The Kleinwort brothers controlled the banking business and therefore assumed they would control the new firm despite the actual equality of the merger. They had primarily wanted Bensons for its public quotation and its corporate finance capability; in their eyes its investment management capability was, and remained, a secondary benefit. As the very different cultures of the two firms were brought together, the commercial banking ethos was the one to predominate. Two factors dictated that the balance of power in Kleinwort Benson lay with the Kleinwort bankers.[7]

The first was the lack of substantial proprietorial interest at an executive level to balance the Kleinwort interest and promote the Benson view. City firms in the early 1960s were still run for the most part by men who, if not of the original proprietorial families, none the less held significant shareholdings in their firms and ruled them paternalistically. Neither of the two most senior Benson men, Phil Macpherson and Mark Turner, could be considered proprietors with a dominant interest. Whilst the merger gave 54 per cent of the enlarged equity of the new firm to the shareholders of RBL, their shareholdings were fragmented; the 46 per cent owned by the Kleinworts remained firmly in 'family' hands.

The second factor was the expansion of banking business in the City. The banking division at KB generated the largest proportion of total revenues over 1961–71, which considerably strengthened its position *vis-à-vis* the other divisions. This reinforced the banking side's view that they could dictate to the other divisions, widening the cultural gap and prolonging the 'Them and Us' attitude in the process. The two Securities Departments had also been integrated, Kleinworts sending theirs over to Aldermanbury House, and Bill Mundy, a Kleinwort manager, remembers that after about two days he walked back to No. 20 to see his boss F. W. Smith who said, 'Right, have you told them how they're going to run their work in future?' Another story that wound its way round the new firm was that of the head of banking who apparently said, 'I don't know why we bother about divisionalising the Bank. We are a Bank, I am head of Banking, and therefore I am head of everything!'[8]

The growth in the banking division stemmed firstly from the development of the wholesale money market accompanying the rise of the Eurodollar and interbank markets in London. The introduction of the sterling certificate of deposit in 1966 added further impetus to the growth of the sterling wholesale market. In the years immediately after the merger, the banking directors shared the view of many of their City counterparts in continuing to see the Eurodollar and Eurocurrency markets as 'an interesting development' within the foreign exchange dealing operation—until these markets expanded dramatically. This occurred after the US Government, faced by balance of payments difficulties, decided in 1963 effectively to close the New York market to overseas borrowers by levying an Interest Equalization Tax on foreign securities. This triggered off the Eurobond market and syndicated Euroloan business, turning the Eurodollar into a vehicle for longer-term borrowing where it had first been almost exclusively used for short-term needs. Then the British Government's 'credit squeeze' on sterling transactions in 1966 ensured that short-term foreign banking business was mainly conducted in currencies other than sterling.

These were important developments and, as a result, the Foreign Exchange Department became more significant in its own right as a profit centre rather than only as an adjunct to foreign lending. Its main purpose continued to be to service the banking division through the provision of funding and liquidity. The department remained by present-day standards remarkably small under Herbert Cherrill (who joined the board in 1965) and Henri Jacquier (who retired as chief dealer in 1966), with only 3 dealers and 14 back office staff. The subsequent leap in the dealing operation was largely orchestrated by Michael Hawkes and Clive Crook, the new chief dealer.

The expansion of the Euromarkets in the 1960s coincided with the development of the interbank market, which did not exist until 1964 because banks tended not to lend money to each other but rather through the discount houses as the market for short-term money. The impetus to change this arrangement came from the local authorities who, having been deprived of funds from the Public Works Loan Board by the Government, had to look for money in the open market, thereby offering City banks a short-term, low credit risk outlet. KB, accordingly, began to purchase wholesale deposits from other banks, with the result that, in common with other non-clearing banks, such as Schroders and Morgan Grenfell, it experienced a substantial increase in balance sheet size.

At the time, apart from its capital and a certain amount of clients' funds, the bank had virtually no natural sterling deposit base. This meant that if Foreign Exchange wanted to borrow sterling to trade dollars or create dollar deposits, they had to go cap in hand down to the basement to argue the case with the

Cash Department, often unsuccessfully. The Foreign Exchange dealers found, however, that they could themselves produce sterling fairly cheaply from the exchange market but, without a natural outlet in the Cash Department, they took the opportunity of lending it to the local authorities. The chief cashier was not pleased to discover that the dealers were using the Cash Department as a support system but retaining ownership of the assets. When his deputy asked why Foreign Exchange instead of the Cash Department was lending to local authorities, Cherrill replied 'Well you could do it but they discovered it before you did!'[9]

As the foreign exchange operation became more important, the board, in keeping with its policy of increasing the range of services KB could offer clients, decided to link gold bullion to Foreign Exchange trading through the acquisition in 1966 of a bullion broker, Sharps Pixley. The product of several mergers of old family bullion firms—the earliest, Sharp & Kirkup, dating from 1740—Sharps Pixley was one of the five original bullion companies that 'fixed' the gold price. The impetus behind the acquisition came, however, not from a strategic decision by the board, but from the Bank of England, which was looking for a strong parent for a vulnerable member of the gold market and knew of Kleinworts' pre-war interest in silver. KB drove a hard bargain whereby, unable to use the normal yardstick of ten years' profits owing to the volatile nature of the bullion market, it agreed to pay a modest part of the £250,000 purchase price up front with the balance to come after three years, if performance warranted it.

KB was not best pleased with the new subsidiary when, in the first year of operation, the US Government suddenly decided to stop selling silver and caught out the three London silver brokers rather than the intended speculators, leaving Sharps Pixley facing a £600,000 loss. Stewart Pixley, the last member of that family at the firm, recalls some rather steely board meetings and instructing his men 'to work like beavers' to try to recover the loss. 'I don't think I slept for weeks' he remembers 'until I got a handwritten note from Cyril Kleinwort saying "I know you are doing your very best, jolly good luck to you." It did us a power of good and boosted our morale no end.' Four months later, in November 1967, the Labour Government devalued the pound: Sharps Pixley, having taken the right position, made profits that amply covered the loss.[10]

The growth in the banking division stemmed secondly from an increase in acceptances, which more than doubled between 1961 and 1971, demonstrating the strength of the division's client list in Scandinavia and Germany, followed by France and Belgium, all areas in which Kleinworts had traditionally been very active, if not dominant. KB won clients away from their native banks by giving them a first-class service at a competitive rate. The new firm continued to focus upon financing the wool and leather trades in France and Belgium, for example, and the import of tractors and steel equipment into Scandinavia. One of the strengths of the division was its efficiency in document processing and back-up. Its expertise was such that it was able to identify mistakes and sort out invoice problems without even having to consult the manufacturer.[11]

The growth in KB's acceptance business during the first post-merger decade was against a trend of slower growth elsewhere in the City. This was largely due to the influx of overseas banks attracted by the Euromarkets, who discovered that they could undercut the accepting houses' traditional commission rate of 1.5 per cent. As the recognized leading 'banking' merchant bank, however, KB's business in the 1960s was large enough to withstand such a disadvantage. There was, however, a further reason for expansion that had much to do with the calibre of the men who were starting to become decision-makers and, in the process, to influence the culture of the banking division.

Although KB was a public company it continued to reflect the values of a family business. It was still dominated by family and those who had passed most of their working lives under family direction. Kleinwort men of the old school—such as two of the new directors, A. J. Haynes and Walter Michaelis—were largely products of an old-fashioned approach to banking, and the division in the main still comprised men of this ilk who processed the bulk of the work. Although another new banking director, Gerald Thompson, had also joined Kleinworts before the war, he was a man with a powerful intellect and a degree in Classics from Cambridge who combined the qualities of the articulate professional and the gentlemanly banker. A traditionalist, he was shocked to discover a junior member of staff going round the City without a bowler hat and could not countenance a banker giving lunch to a money broker: 'Brokers give us lunch, we do not ask brokers to lunch.' He none the less supported the new business initiatives suggested by more junior management, such as Michael Hawkes and Pat Limerick, and by the younger generation of recruits such as David Peake (who had joined the French desk from Schröders in 1963 and was Cyril's son-in-law), Robin Fox (a Kleinwort family friend), Tom Troubridge (the grandson of Herman Kleinwort), and Ernest's son Kenneth, who was on Michaelis's German desk.

These men approached banking from the 'technique' rather than the 'processing' school; they concentrated upon thinking of new ways of providing finance and of exploiting anomalies in the market place to give KB the competitive edge. According to Robin Fox, 'It was really only at Kleinworts that we began to get this group of people who . . . were prepared to think about new types of banking', and not move into corporate finance or investment management as so many of their peers did elsewhere. In consequence, KB's banking division was often ahead of the competition then provided by Lazards (still stronger on the export credit side), Hill Samuel, Schröders, and Samuel Montagu.[12]

KB's banking division surged ahead in several areas that were notably profitable. 'We really knew our Exchange Control backwards. There were very few people in the City who did,' Michael Hawkes explains. The Scandinavian desk started exploiting anomalies created by exchange control and by movements in the various official and unofficial exchange rates of Eurocurrencies, so that customers could borrow more cheaply from KB than from the clearing banks. Hawkes worked closely with the foreign exchange people and the techniques that they developed were then passed on to the other desks, in particular the German one where Michaelis's excellent German contacts enabled the department to lend short marks in large quantities, a welcome follow-on to the previous 'nice earner', the Thursday / Friday dollar business.[13]

Another profitable area was the Export Finance Department managed by E. C. Fitzsimmons. Although Lazards had long held a dominant position in the field, other merchant banks were seeking to capture this business which benefited from incentives offered by the British Government as part of its export drive. In 1968 KB negotiated a £14m. Export Credits Guarantee Department (ECGD) credit for the Russian Fiat–Togliatti car plant construction project, and then began to develop Comecon (as the Eastern bloc was then termed) business. This included the first British participation in the Leipzig Fair in March 1971 and, further afield, the department arranged large financings in Canada, Iran, and Algeria.

As their profit graphs displayed an upward trend during the mid-1960s, merchant banks were seeking out new ways to employ their money. Some went into film finance, others into property, and KB's banking division went into leasing, which was just another financial technique to provide secured long-term credit. KB's first large leasing—three Boeing 707s on a long-term lease to British Eagle—was publicized in the press in 1968 as 'Merchant Bank Joins the Jet Set'. As the first British bank to enter directly into the field of leasing large commercial aircraft, KB had the business to itself; but in August 1969 KB, in its role as the largest shareholder, and the insurance brokers Price, Forbes formed Airlease International Management Ltd. in a consortium with other merchant and clearing banks and Commercial Union. This company provided financial support for the ever-increasing investment that international airlines required in a period of rapid growth in terms of capacity and frequency of service.[14]

While the overall growth in business undoubtedly consolidated the dominance of the banking division, the corporate finance division also developed and expanded. Mirroring the intake on the banking side, there was an influx of new young blood in the corporate finance division that reflected the continuing family influence upon the business. Recruits included Lord Rockley's son James Cecil (later Lord Rockley and a future chairman) who joined from Wood Gundy; Rex's son David Benson who came from Shell; David Robertson's son Simon (also a future chairman), who trained with several firms including Goldman Sachs; and Ivo Forde's godson Timothy Barker, who arrived from Cambridge as a graduate trainee. All joined in the early 1960s and would assume positions of leadership by the 1980s.

The Corporate Finance division, however, had found the early post-merger years an exciting but trying time. Corporate financiers, regarded by some in the banking division as glorified stockbrokers, were insufficiently understood. However alien this sounds today, such attitudes had become entrenched because there was little interdivisional liaison at the top. Mark Turner, who could have moved swiftly to disabuse the bankers, was much in demand as a major industrial figure, and was often elsewhere in the immediate post-merger period, and Phil Macpherson, increasingly crippled with arthritis, had left such matters to others to sort out. Two corporate financiers, Read and Oppé, had become particularly perturbed, and matters came to a head over the Rank Organization, a key customer.

Bensons had believed in backing their clients, not infrequently, by taking semi-strategic shareholding positions in them. At the time of the merger its largest holding was in Rank, whose shares had increased in value from 1*s.* 6*d.* to 21*s.* 6*d.* and continued to appreciate after the merger, so that they were heading towards £5. The Kleinworts, however, took the view that acceptance credits, which were what made most of the money, must be backed by a wide spread of securities, not simply large stakes in a few companies. Accordingly they insisted that the Rank shares be sold. Corporate finance argued that the client's interpretation would be that KB had lost interest in it. The Kleinworts nevertheless prevailed, and Bobby Henderson can remember 'an extremely difficult dinner' when John Davis, the Chairman of Rank, was 'very very curt to everyone and insulted that we should be selling the shares'. Read persuaded Rank to remain a client but thereafter he was never happy, eventually leaving in 1967 and joining the Rank board. Rank was not the only large holding ordered to be sold, with the result that relations between the corporate finance and banking divisions were somewhat strained.[15]

This, in turn, meant that there was even less communication between the divisions, which affected KB's business in a more serious way. To take but one example from the 1960s, the Corporate Finance division had a successful office furniture and design client (Dexion) that it believed was overborrowed with too many subsidiaries, and which it had advised to raise funds by an issue of equity. The company did not want to dilute the family shareholding and was reluctant. The banking division, however, having been introduced to the client by corporate finance, had lent it money secured on the assets of one of the subsidiaries without any consultation with the corporate finance director responsible for the account. Although the banking division believed it to be a safe borrowing, corporate finance looked at it from the overall picture of the whole company and judged otherwise. As it happened, the company did fail. Lack of liaison and friction between the two divisions led to several similar instances and reinforced the corporate financiers' belief that theirs was an unhappy lot.

They were not made any happier by the knowledge that their division's contribution to profits was small in comparison with banking, mainly because fees charged by merchant banks were then minuscule. When, for example, KB successfully defended Greenall Whitley and Co. against a hostile Canadian bidder in 1962, the fee was a mere £15,000. What sometimes escaped the banking side, however, was the vital advantage corporate finance possessed as a shop window. This was, after all, part of the rationale behind the merger, and a good amount of business did come to the bankers through corporate finance activity, though the reverse rarely occurred. The bankers divined a certain arrogance amongst the corporate finance practitioners, and the corporate financiers found it difficult to accommodate the bankers' view that they alone drove the business whereas corporate finance, though useful, was peripheral. In corporate finance they often worked late into the night, while the bankers tended to leave at 5 o'clock on the basis that a bank made more money asleep than it did awake. A directive that corporate finance assistant managers should also do safe duty on a Saturday morning was not well received.[16]

There was, however, no avoiding the fundamental facts: the bankers made most of the money; and, unlike the banking division in its field, the corporate finance division was not then in the first rank in terms of client list and size of business. The blue-chip companies remained largely the preserve of Lazards, Morgan Grenfell, and Schröders. Nevertheless, the new KB corporate finance division, under Mark Turner's overall leadership, possessed the potential to join the top tier.

This was of necessity a slow process, since in the early 1960s client allegiances remained virtually sacrosanct. 'We didn't steal each other's clients,' Peter Wake would recall, 'there was an underlying moral code about it.' Two events altered this situation. The development of the Euromarkets, which added an entirely new international dimension to corporate finance, and the Aluminium take-over battle, after which Siegmund Warburg and Kenneth Keith started expanding their client lists at the expense of other merchant banks. As a result, what Henry Grunfeld of Warburgs termed the 'comfortable unenergetic' corporate finance world changed forever. John Gillum, who joined Bensons in 1956, remembers that 'take-overs were down in our books as "Sundry fees"' and 'those were the days when directors of merchant banks did not get involved in the small print'. As the 1960s progressed, however, they were increasingly compelled to do so, for mergers, take-overs, and acquisitions became the main business of corporate finance divisions and placed merchant banks increasingly in the public eye.[17]

The corporate finance division at KB was led by Mark Turner, the old Benson team of directors, David Robertson and two able young practitioners Charles Ball and John Gillum, who joined the board in 1963. The atmosphere remained as it had been at Bensons, extremely congenial. Martin Jacomb, a Chancery barrister who joined in 1968, found the values 'very easy ones to live with, there was a very high concentration on excellence and fair dealing. Nobody wanted to cut corners and there was no question of a sharp deal'.

The objective was to bring the division into the top rank, and the take-over boom meant that there were many deals from the mid-1960s in addition to money-raising debenture issues for clients such as Viyella. As top of the second division, KB was now in the position of being considered by large clients but in the early 1960s they were often still pipped at the post. This happened with P. & O., who went to Schröders whom they regarded as safer and more experienced. Gradually, though, with the help of Phil Macpherson's good contacts, Mark Turner worked his magic and opened doors to companies that were either household names or were soon to become them. A breakthrough came in 1965 when KB acted for United Molasses, the subject of a bid by Tate & Lyle—for whom KB now act. KB had also acted for Gilbeys who merged with a Hambros client, United Wine Traders, to form in 1962 International Distillers and Vintners, for whom KB then acted. Client loyalties at Rio Tinto, where Mark Turner was finance director, meant that Rothschilds remained their principal merchant bankers although KB started to act jointly. Other members of the team also began to bring in clients as when Bobby Henderson won Plessey in 1968 after Warburgs decided not to act for them in a take-over of English Electric. Thus, throughout the first post-merger decade, KB was slowly rising in the estimation of corporate Britain and entering the first division. 'It was very rewarding because you kept seeing the number of businesses we acted for improving in quality and size,' Bobby Henderson recalls.

Younger members of the division also found it an exhilarating experience to be part of the team effort to try to take KB upwards in the then unofficial, word-of-mouth league tables. Every piece of business was significant and, as the era of take-over battles seriously got underway, it was exciting work that involved long hours. Martin Jacomb recalls the many deals: 'Some were thrilling and some were victories and some were losses and you learned to live with those, but the feeling of elation when there were victories was great.' Charles Ball through his specialist defensive work presented KB with some of these victories and, in their wake, new accounts. His high profile and successful defence of Telephone Rentals against a hostile GEC bid in 1965, which included the dispatch of a record to all shareholders with the defence document, generated a good deal of publicity and general admiration. KB gained a reputation for defensive skills, and this did much to take it up to the first tier.[18]

The division was also technically innovative and pioneered the issue by tender, a system the *New York Times* explained 'which produces order out of chaos and reduces abuses of the fixed price system.' Peter Wake brought his constructive mind and capacity to master technical details to bear on the 'hot issue' boom by inventing the tender method of offering shares. The procedure he used for the 250,000 Parway Land and Investments Ltd. offer in 1961 was subsequently adopted by Morgan Grenfell and Warburgs and used by KB in issues for clients such as Hugh Fraser's Scottish & Universal Investments. KB also broke new ground in 1968 with the inauguration of a sterling/dollar convertible loan stock issue for NCR.[19]

By this time the City was undergoing one of its periodic bouts of 'merger mania'. This was fuelled partly by the stock market boom and partly by a government belief that size was the solution to Britain's industrial problems, a belief that in 1966 led to the formation of an agency, the Industrial Reorganization Corporation (IRC), to encourage companies to compete more effectively. KB gained a certain amount of business through the IRC, for instance when it tried to merge a trio of boilermaking companies, Clark Chapman, John Thompson, and International Combustion, and its defence of Pollard Roller Bearing Co. in the 'Great Ball-Bearing Affair' of 1968/9. The overall result was an increase in take-over activity which, not unnaturally, was welcomed by the City which started to collect larger fees, and KB was by now well placed to benefit.[20]

'Almost every day over the past few months', the house magazine commented in the winter edition of 1968/9, 'the financial press has covered at least one and frequently more situations in which KB has been involved.' As the flow of mergers and take-overs continued unabated, KB was active in more than twenty-five bid situations including three of the largest battles: Rank's bid for De La Rue in November 1968, EMI's bid for Associated British Picture Corporation in December 1968, and Trafalgar House's bid for City of London Real Property (CLRP) in January 1969.[21]

At the height of this frenzy of activity when, according to Anthony Sampson, the City looked less like a Pall Mall club than a Western saloon bar with bodies all over the place, concern began to be expressed at the disregard for the interests of shareholders and the rate at which ownership of the country's corporate assets was changing hands in a mainly unregulated marketplace; by 1968 seventy of Britain's one hundred largest companies had been involved in take-overs in a two-year period. Unlike America, the City had remained largely self-regulating: 'The point about City institutions', Christopher Marley, financial editor of *The Times*, wrote in 1970, 'is that their members' professional conduct is subject to the rules of their own professional clubs—in essence the City answers to itself for its own behaviour.' A collective integrity and honesty encouraged by the Governor of the Bank of England had long been the City's hallmark. Now, in the heat of numerous take-overs when even the best-behaved of merchant banks could become mischievous and clients, attracted by success, did not question the means by which that success was achieved, it was becoming eroded; and already the Bank was instigating the drawing-up of the first voluntary guidelines on behaviour, following take-over battles that were waged in 1966 and 1967.[22]

KB was involved in one of the last of these battles involving an electrical company, Metal Industries, which was the subject of a take-over bid by Aberdare Holdings. Metal Industries rejected an increased offer and then produced a defence in the shape of a higher offer from Thorn Electrical. A friendly Morgan Grenfell then went on a buying spree to back up the Aberdare bid and by the middle of July 1967 Aberdare had acquired 53 per cent of the capital of Metal Industries. Many a City eyebrow was raised at Morgan Grenfell's involvement—it was alleged that much of their buying had been done outside the market—but the Stock Exchange Council was not prepared to start an inquiry. Thorn had been willing to pay more, believed that the spirit of the City's own good conduct rules had been broken, and, with Metal Industries, resorted to an ingenious piece of tit-for-tat.

On the weekend of 15 July KB had devised 'a solution that set the City ablaze'. The plan was for Metal Industries to issue new shares to Thorn in exchange for part of Thorn's business, thereby diluting Aberdare's holding. This was the British Aluminium technique, but used for the first time after control had already been lost. 'It was rather like going to a tailor,' Gillum relates, 'you have a subsidiary that will roughly fit the number of shares available for evaluating it, they [Thorn] produce Glover & Main, which makes gas cookers, and say we've got this in stock which is about the right size.' Metal Industries then issued about 5m. new shares in exchange for Thorn's Glover & Main, which immediately reduced Aberdare's 53 per cent ownership to 23 per cent. Thorn then put in a higher offer for the rest of the equity.

The *Illustrated London News* might conclude 'It was a deal that gained much admiration for its brilliance'; but Bobby Brooks, who worked with Gillum, believes that 'arguably it was because of this [deal] that the Panel was brought into being. It was considered not quite cricket'. *The Times*, critical of the inactive Stock Exchange, called for government regulation on 18 July. 'City headlines in these past days have been dominated by a power struggle which has reached spectacular proportions', the Prime Minister responded at a City dinner that evening. 'It is for the City to ensure that these processes are, and are seen to be, carried through in accordance with clearly formulated rules.'[23]

Shortly thereafter, the Stock Exchange with the backing of Governor O'Brien asked the merchant banks to reconvene the working party to draw up a Code on Amalgamations and Mergers and to set up a Panel to supervise its operation. However, the Take-over Panel, which came into being in April 1968, was virtually powerless in the face of a new breed of unscrupulous City operators; and its censure was even rejected by the established City houses of Morgan Grenfell and Cazenoves following the American Tobacco / Gallaher battle in July, in which KB was not involved. Then came the indignity in October of the Pergamon Press / *News of the World* battle, conducted in blatant breach of the Code. It prompted O'Brien to revamp the Panel with Lord Shawcross becoming the first full-time Chairman, and to introduce sanctions. This was a significant moment in the history of the City. The fact that it had to resort to policing by regulatory agency was evidence of the strong winds of cultural change. Merchant banks could no longer confine their business to those personally known to them, owing to the increase in the number of companies seeking their services and the international spread of business; client allegiance was proving fragile in the face of competition that had sharpened considerably. The days of Alexander Kleinwort keeping his client records in a little black book and Robin Benson finding all the business he needed through family connections were in such contrast to those of the late 1960s that they seemed to belong to folklore rather than the same century.

Further developments reinforcing the changes occurring in the City had included an increased Government involvement through the establishment of the Monopolies Commission. This agency had foiled Ranks' bid for De La Rue on the grounds of the threat of a walk-out by the De La Rue management if the offer succeeded. 'A dangerous precedent for future contested bids', commented the KB house magazine. The new Take-over Panel was better prepared to meet such situations, especially after it cut its teeth on the Pergamon / Leasco fiasco in the summer of 1969. Cyril Kleinwort wrote in the 1969 Annual Report, 'It is satisfactory to note that the "Panel" has established itself speedily as the accepted arbiter in the more intricate questions involving shareholder protection and proper procedures.'

The Panel introduced clearer rules that required the provision of information, thereby ushering procedure manuals into corporate finance divisions, which now had to become very knowledgeable about the rules; this, in turn, would lead to the inauguration of compliance departments in the 1980s, an important change in the merchant banking arena. In the beginning there were many grey areas, in one of which KB itself recognized the Panel's powers during the Trafalgar House bid for Cementation in 1970. It was a complicated story because at one stage there were three bids for Cementation: by Trafalgar, Tarmac, and then Bovis. KB, acting for Trafalgar, had offered Trafalgar shares and 'paper' but in the course of the bid had bought a key Cementation shareholding from rival bidders, Bovis, for cash. KB was suddenly summoned by the Panel and interrogated by the Director-General, Ian Fraser. 'I had two or three days of absolute nightmare,' John Gillum recalls, 'but the support of Mark and Cyril was unbelievable.' The Panel insisted KB make cash available to all shareholders. Gillum remembers Mark Turner saying from Australia, 'Right, we won't put Trafalgar House to any expense on this, we will show (a) we support this Panel and (b) that we have got the capability for doing this.' KB had to underwrite the whole deal, with Messels arranging for it to be offloaded with the institutions. It was, according to the *Financial Times*, 'an act of generosity heralded as a triumph for the Panel'.[24]

By the end of the 1960s the Corporate Finance division was able to compete for first-rate corporate business. The elation in the division over a good deal was more frequently felt as, for example, when they acted for an old client Schweppes in their merger with Cadburys in 1969 to form a world-wide food and drink empire, for whom KB continues to act. Not all KB's deals were so successful but when it failed or lost the business, the most important factor was to protect its customers and retain its good name, an incomparable asset even today and one that had traditionally been valued above all others by the old trading and merchant houses.

In the 1960s and early 1970s merchant banks were treated with respect by the country and the media. Pejorative headlines were not then the daily fodder of the press so when in 1968, for instance, Rolls Razor, a cut-price washing machine company that KB had offered for sale four years earlier, went bust, the attendant publicity focused almost entirely upon John Bloom, the proprietor, and very little upon his merchant bank. In the case of another failure of the period, Miles Roman, a computer software company, the speed of its demise could have affected KB's reputation more seriously. When Bobby Henderson was asked why KB had put up more money when they knew they might lose it, he answered, 'It would be much worse to lose our name.' In his opinion the bank should be prepared to lose money in such situations to try to protect its customers.[25]

It is the value attached to the continuation of a good name which links the merchant banks with their predecessors and founders. It is also what separates them from some of the newer, more fleeting financial services operators; responsibility is not a concept that the latter always readily acknowledge. The long-established merchant banks, however, did and generally do. When a company (Home Counties Newspapers) in which Barings had offered shares to the public in 1969 halved its profits forecast three months later, Barings bought back the shares at the price they had offered them. 'We are not obliged to do this,' they declared, 'but we lent our name to a financial assessment which has not stood the test of time.' This was an attitude that still prevailed in the City by the end of Kleinwort Benson's first decade. It would come under increasing threat in the two following decades as the institutions in the Square Mile expanded at an extraordinary rate, entered new fields of business, and saw the 'internationalization' of financial services and the encroachment of an American culture.[26]

Merchant banks were also busy opening regional offices during this period. Increased activity and competition in corporate finance work fuelled the belief that they could capture more clients if they took their specialist services to the industrial heartland. When KB established an operational office in Sheffield in 1965 under the direction of Roger Wake, an investment banker with a fund of entertaining stories, Rothschilds and Hill Samuel had already embarked upon a similar exercise. One of the 'building bricks' that enabled KB's commercial banking operation to expand quite dramatically was provided by the building societies, many of whom were based in the North. Building society deposits became the largest contributor to KB's sterling deposit base and this was undoubtedly facilitated by the existence of a regional office.

As the bank's mainstream business expanded, Cyril and Mark Turner recognized that KB must also develop the capability to operate on a world-wide basis. In spite of the determination to internationalize, there were no formal strategic planning exercises or studies commissioned from management consultants to define the programme, as would occur today. Strategic thinking was not in the 1960s a customary feature of City management. Much as their late-Victorian forefathers had done, merchant banks still largely endorsed the cult of gifted amateurs with versatility a key ingredient in their continuing success. Although such attitudes were changing—largely through the growing presence of lawyers and accountants within corporate finance divisions to master the intricacies of more complex deals, the more aggressive newcomers in the banking arena, and burgeoning foreign competition—the cultural shift would become more apparent later, in the 1970s and 1980s.

Bobby Henderson is dismissive of the idea that KB had any grand design. An *ad hoc*, 'test the waters' approach was the preferred *modus operandi*. A question about the firm's grand strategy was likely to elicit the reply, 'We haven't got one, we live by our wits; we go where we think there is business and one thing leads to another.' Whilst there was no global drawing-board at KB in the 1960s, there was plenty of informal discussion as to the right timing and the amount of capital to deploy: 'We discussed these issues all over the place, in the lavatories, in taxis with Mark, and everywhere else,' and gradually a consensus emerged in a way that had typified the Benson approach and, under Cyril and Mark Turner's stewardship, came to be the KB style of reaching policy decisions. KB's directors were opportunistic: they believed there was business overseas and so they opened representative offices abroad.[27]

The bank's offices in the Channel Islands had come into being purely on the basis of what David Peake terms 'inspired serendipity' rather than strategic planning. In the case of the Jersey office a chance meeting in Barbados between Bobby Henderson and a future client seeking offshore banking services resulted in KB becoming the second merchant bank to establish a subsidiary in the Channel Islands, M. Samuel having already been incorporated there; although F. A. James points out that technically KB were the first, 'in the sense that we were the first to man an office there—they were administrated through a local accountant firm'. Russell Tilbrook, who had been involved in Kleinworts' South African venture, started the operation in a one-room office in St Helier in September 1962. KB proved less prescient when it decided that there would be no requirement for permanent staff initially, for accommodation quickly became so cramped that Tilbrook's wife had to vacate the office when clients arrived.

On 1 June 1963, just one year later, Kleinwort Benson (Guernsey) Ltd. was born, also starting with two staff, in modest premises on Berthelot Street. It was a pioneer in the days when it had not yet become fashionable to start a bank on the Island and neither the legal nor the business community knew what a merchant bank was; they soon discovered as the business expanded. In their first years of operation there was no Banking Act, no control on the taking of deposits, and no investor protection. Their main business was to provide services to private clients on a one-product, one-client basis, which focused upon offering deposits and loans, trustee services, and private investment management.

By the mid-1960s they were pioneers in the development of mass investment vehicles, for example forming the Kleinwort Benson Guernsey Fund, an open-ended unit trust, and continuing to administer the first one ever formed in the Islands, the M. & G. Island Fund in Guernsey and its Jersey feeder fund. The Guernsey office also set up an associated insurance company, probably the first in the Islands to offer equity-linked assurance contracts, and also built up a flourishing business in 'captive' insurance companies. First-year balance sheet totals for Jersey of £500,000 and Guernsey of £1m. would grow to £300m. and £215m. in twenty-five years, producing a substantial contribution of quality profits for KB. According to the Islands' KB chief executive, David Hinshaw, the success of this operation is due to 'the quality of our people' and KB's investment in them. From the outset great emphasis was placed upon the recruitment, training, and promotion of local staff. Thus, although the entry was not planned, its development undoubtedly was.[28]

In contrast to the Channel Islands, KB's entry into Europe had little to do with 'inspired serendipity'. As part of a somewhat cautious approach to international growth and to place assets outside the UK, KB opened a subsidiary in Brussels in 1966 (which closed in 1994), and two years later created a foothold in Switzerland, Geneva being preferred to Zurich by its Arab and Iranian clients. In 1968, KB bought control of Banque Intra, the solvent Swiss subsidiary of the Lebanese Intrabank that had recently collapsed but which the Swiss authorities none the less regarded as a clean commercial bank. Herbert Cherrill, the new managing director, arrived to find a staff of nine still working in the bank, 'its activities virtually at a standstill because nobody was prepared to deposit money with them knowing the state of the parent company.'

This proved to be a considerable disadvantage even after the name was changed to KB (Geneva). Whilst its reputation remained strong, its public profile and profitability were not. Gradually, KB (Geneva) extended its operating base to investment portfolios and trustee management. Cherrill, however, was a foreign exchange specialist rather than an investment man. Given the clear investment potential in this new Swiss-based subsidiary, KB was shortsighted in not setting up an investment department in Geneva, especially after building up business with the Middle East. This was doubtless due to perceptions in No. 20 as much as to the lack of any definite policy in the merged investment management division. In a misguided attempt to uphold the Swiss tradition of banking secrecy, the subsidiary was not integrated into the KB Group so that 'its life blood was cut-off and it jolly nearly withered'. It only began to grow after Michael Devas, an investment management director, went out in 1975 and KB (Geneva), or Banque KB as it is now called, became a modest but profitable private bank and a fully effective part of the Group.[29]

Given the importance rightly placed by Kleinwort Benson today upon their international business, it is surprising that prior to 1970 they had no investment banking representation in either the United States or Japan. This is especially striking in the case of America, with which Kleinworts and Bensons had maintained strong trading links since the eighteenth century. Two world wars, excessive volatility in market conditions, and the turn-around in the flow of capital had made City firms more domestically orientated. Those such as Morgan Grenfell and Schröders who continued to effect a large US business were endowed with the stability of well-established American partners. Although KB did not have the benefit of such a commercial advantage, it had inherited a large amount of American goodwill from both its constituent parts. Mark Turner wanted KB to do business there again and it was his idea to open an American office.

He recruited as president an RTZ colleague, Pat Robinson, and as his vice-president, David Benson, who, being Rex's son, had a marvellous entrée into America. Mark Turner's directive, 'It will be just the two of you and you will recruit people out there and get the business going,' was how KB Inc., a wholly owned American subsidiary, was born in 1970 in a dingy suite of two rooms in a Manhattan hotel on 42nd Street, known more for its seedy shops than its foreign investment banks.

They started an underwriting business in American domestic securities to increase the volume that the bank distributed. A medium-sized underwriting bracket then involved $1m. or more while a major underwriting contract could involve $3m., which was sizeable compared with European business. To do this KB Inc. recruited a first-class accountant, who was so good at producing the figures that New York's were sent to London on the 2nd of each month at a time when London itself could never produce figures by the first week of the following month; and a good syndicate head, who knew and was liked by the people in the other originating houses, so that KB Inc. began to be cut into their deals.

Although KB Inc. was a modest participator, along with Flemings and Hill Samuel, in what was known as the submajor bracket, it was able to increase its business. David Benson, who in 1971 became president after Pat Robinson's return to London, explains: 'Occasionally, if you happened to know the company which was doing the issue very well, you would be given a special position because of your close connection; and we had very good contacts.' KB America could not have developed without the help of old friends, such as Goldman Sachs. It was then considered difficult for British firms to make money in the States but KB Inc. surprised its colleagues at home by getting into deals and distributing them in a period when there was a good spread and a favourable dollar/pound exchange rate. In 1971 it was involved in 140 issues for major US names. The amounts might be thought modest by present-day standards, but in 1971/2 a genuine net profit of $200,000–300,000 was certainly respectable on a modest capital base. The nucleus of what was to become a large operation was built upon the basis of an efficiently run small business with low costs, good client relations, and enthusiastic people.[30]

Another development of this period that increased KB's international standing was the venture with the Bank of America. Mark Turner wanted to position KB for a share of the Eurobond business that he perceived as a growth area. In 1968 he had negotiated the Bougainville financing for RTZ with Tom Clausen of Bank of America, 'the biggest deal they had ever done', and believed that a venture with such a powerful bank would enable KB to win Eurobond business. In 1971 the Bank of America Ltd. was formed in which it had 50 per cent, and KB and Paribas each had 25 per cent, with Mark Turner as chairman (in addition to being chairman of RTZ and other companies).

There was a good deal of scepticism about the operation within certain areas of KB and it was not profitable in the way originally envisaged. Nevertheless, as Bobby Henderson points out, it was extremely important in other ways. The relationship 'broadcast our name all over the world', gave KB a greater international credibility, and brought it into much larger deals. In the process it also 'taught us about how American banks worked and how they shouldn't work actually!' More importantly, Bank of America persuaded KB to join it in a series of merchant banking ventures throughout the Pacific Basin, all of which strengthened KB's name in the area and reinforced its newly opened representative office in Japan.[31]

KB's presence in Tokyo was earlier than other British merchant banks, most of whom had preferred to concentrate upon Hong Kong. It stemmed first from Kleinwort, Sons & Co.'s long-standing friendships with Japanese banks such as Mitsui, Mitsubishi, Bank of Tokyo (formerly Yokohama Specie), and Sumitomo; second from the banking division being asked to visit Japan by Cyril, whose interest in the Japanese stock market in 1961 had resulted in KB substantially buying Japanese shares; and third from a KB Board meeting at which Mark Turner suddenly said, 'We really ought to take more interest in Japan,' reeling off the names of various Japanese companies that should be contacted. Struck by the potential for business the Board decided to develop a separate Japanese desk and asked Robin Fox to build up KB's Japanese banking business as part of the International Department.

Fox found an ally on the corporate finance side in Andrew Caldecott, a solicitor in his mid-forties recruited onto the board, who knew and enthused about the Japanese and their culture and actively sought business opportunities there. The opening of the KB office in the middle of the financial district of Tokyo in October 1970 brought on board Mrs Watanabe, 'whose wise counsel and loyalty' would serve no less than six leaders of an office that 'soon expanded to double and then triple figures'. Although the initial business was seen as bond and equity issues, the Japanese authorities deemed otherwise. KB Tokyo therefore became a banking office and initially arranged impact loans, short-term foreign currency loans to Japanese companies guaranteed by a Japanese bank, from which margins of 2–2.5 per cent were common though up to 4 per cent were achieved. There was also business from offshore subsidiaries of Japanese companies and from branches in London.

The development of Japanese business was due to the quality of service KB could offer and the speed of that service, the time difference enabling KB to provide funds within a day. According to Robin Fox, Japanese banks took several days and American banks were even slower. The business was a very personal one and the strength of relations with clients soon meant that KB had no compunction about lending to good Japanese companies without the security of a bank guarantee; the first instance of this being an unguaranteed loan to Nippon Steel. This business laid a foundation of friendship which was to serve KB in good stead over the ensuing decades with regular visits by senior management to broaden and cement the relationships that were being nurtured at the local level by a first-class team of resident representatives.

In the meantime, following on from the wish of Japanese banks to establish themselves in the City, Fuji Bank entered into a joint venture with KB to form KB-Fuji Ltd. The partnership was a particularly friendly and successful one, owing in large part to its managing director Tom Hashimoto, a delightful man and skilful banker who immediately established a rapport with Andrew Caldecott, David Benson, and others at KB. This resulted in a stream of issues in the international capital markets for companies within the Fuji sphere of influence (*zaibatsu*) under KB's leadership. As Fuji became more experienced in the City, however, KB's participation in the venture would drop from 50 per cent to 25 per cent before Fuji eventually bought out KB in the early 1980s.[32]

KB also hatched a fledgling Eurofinance team to tap into an emerging market that had become attractive to the firm's corporate finance clients as an alternative source of funding. In its first year of operation in 1971 the Eurofinance Department—under the dynamic leadership of Andrew Caldecott—managed public issues in the Eurodollar bond market for Plessey, Airlease, Rank Organization, Barclays Bank International, and Commercial Union totalling $180m. KB suddenly and unexpectedly found itself second in the league tables after Morgan et Cie and the future looked bright.[33]

The Eurofinance Department was effectively a microcosm of the merged firm, combining the activities of all three divisions, particularly banking and corporate finance. These two divisions worked very closely together in bringing

Eurobond issues to market and their co-operation helped to encourage integration. This had already been furthered when, after the retirement of Ernest and Phil Macpherson from the leadership of KB Ltd. in 1966, the architects of the merger Cyril and Mark had become chairman and deputy chairman.

The retirement from the KB board in 1967 of Ronny Medlicott and Frederick Smith, and the departures of Sonny Andreae and Peter Wake due to ill-health and John Read to start his own business, had allowed a transfusion of new blood, and Michael Hawkes, Frank Hislop, Pat Limerick, Arthur Stilwell, Bill Baldock, and Bobby Brooks had joined the board. Cyril and Mark Turner recognized the need to recruit men of calibre and experience who would not be perceived as either Kleinworts' or Bensons' men and who would strengthen the leadership of the firm as it expanded. Over the next few years men such as Martin Jacomb, Andrew Caldecott, and Martin Mays-Smith had been brought onto the board to satisfy this need. Integration had been additionally cemented by the move from Aldermanbury House and St Albans House into the new No. 20 in the spring of 1969 so that less of the 'them and us' attitude remained by the end of the decade.

A change of leadership occurred at the end of the first post-merger decade that marked a break with the past and reflected the goal of building KB into a modern merchant bank. In 1971, for the first time, the banking subsidiary, Kleinwort Benson Ltd., was led by a chairman who was not a proprietor. The significance of this event lies in the cultural adjustments that followed and the precedent it set in terms of the way in which KB thereafter chose its leaders.

Although Schröders, Lazards, Hill Samuel, and Samuel Montagu had all chosen to appoint non-bankers (of whom three were career lawyers) to their respective chairmanships, KB, and in particular the old Kleinwort side, considered it essential to have a banker in charge—and a home-grown one at that. Cyril had been the heir-designate to his brother from the outset of the merger and had assumed the chairmanship of the holding company in 1968, having been chairman of the bank since 1966. He proved to be a good chairman, 'influencing in his very quiet, unobtrusive but nevertheless firm way, the direction in which the firm should go'. He actively encouraged a cultural metamorphosis at No. 20: from a hierarchical structure, to a flatter, more meritocratic one. He saw this not only as the way to achieve better integration of the constituent firms, but also as consistent with changes taking place in the world at large. People who had always called him 'Sir' or 'Mr Cyril' started to call him 'Cyril' and put their head round the door of his office. He had always displayed a lack of affectation or pomposity so that the change in atmosphere at KB was in keeping with his, and, indeed, Mark Turner's, personal predilections.[34]

Cyril had become a more public figure than was usual for a Kleinwort through his chairmanship of the Invisible Exports Committee, whose task it was to emphasize the importance of earnings from non-industrial sources to the British balance of payments. He was, none the less, able to retain what Sir Kenneth Kleinwort called 'a very low profile', compared with present-day City chairmen. Cyril's chairmanship did not just marry the name and presence of a Kleinwort with the leadership of KB. As important as his encouragement of a cultural change was his propensity for taking a long-term view. David Peake, his son-in-law and future chairman of the Group, found that 'he had a great deal of objectivity, [was] very detached and wasn't fussed by little details . . . he really saw the big picture.' Cyril perceived his own role as involving the contemplation of the future rather than dealing with particular day-to-day matters and he was remembered as saying, 'the trouble with the bank as it is at the present is, you are all very busy, all rushing around, you never get time to think, you have got to have time to think'.[35]

His belief that strategic thinking was important for KB was shared by Mark Turner. In some ways reminiscent of Herman Andreae's role, it was Turner, 'that marvellous business-getter', whom the City considered the dynamo of KB. His name was widely known and well respected in boardrooms at home and abroad and in Whitehall; in consequence he had enough experience to know that a medium-sized, growing, and rapidly changing organization such as KB could not continue to assume that the business would somehow manage itself. He was more specific than Cyril, believing that 'a modern merchant bank' must develop the skills 'to think strategically' and that a management structure and systems to provide the formulation of strategy and planning should be introduced. In the climate of the late 1960s and early 1970s his approach was judged quite novel by many bankers.

As an example, he arranged for Professor Roland Smith of Manchester Business School to conduct a seminar on management planning and marketing for KB's directors in Manchester in 1970. The venture met with mixed success. Some directors found the process 'an enormously interesting exercise'. A decision was subsequently made to create the senior post of comptroller, responsible for ensuring that proper systems and people were in place for the growth of KB, with David Robertson as the first to fill the position. Others, however, were scornful of the need to improve the firm's decision-making process at a senior level.[36]

Although Mark Turner was clearly not solely responsible for this policy, certain colleagues identified him with it. This only mattered for two reasons. The first was timing, in that Cyril had announced his intention to retire as chairman of KB Ltd. in the following year. The second was because it introduced an element of corporate political manœuvring into KB that had been largely absent from its constituent firms and tempered in the merged firm at board level by a proprietorial and preordained leadership, agreed at the time of the merger and confirmed at intervals thereafter.

At the height of the dissension between the Kleinwort and Benson directors in the summer of 1963, Mark Turner, with the help of Rex Benson and Robert Rockley, had set in train an agreed reorganization of the internal management committee structure and defused a dangerous wobble in the merger integration process. 'All this has been wearisome & depressing,' he had confided to Rex, but 'everything is back on track again.' In the event, the agreement to appoint Cyril and Mark as joint deputy chairmen had been postponed until Ernest and Phil Macpherson reached retirement age in 1966.

Although some directors wanted Mark to become the next chairman, he had insisted upon upholding the merger agreement whereby Cyril was appointed and he became his deputy. When Ernest and his banking directors tried to block Turner's appointment and ensuing succession to the chairmanship, the Benson 'seniors', as Ernest termed Rex, Leo, and Robert Rockley, immediately reiterated that 'the perfection in K.B. is to have a banker chairman and an investment and issuing expert as his deputy or vice-versa'. In a memo dated 1 October 1965 Ernest stated that the seniors (the former Kleinwort leadership) at St Albans House would back 'Mark as Cyril's successor after he had served a three-year term', i.e. until March 1969. When the time came for Cyril to step down in 1969, however, Mark insisted that Cyril remain as chairman because 'he was doing so well'. The new arrangement was that he would continue as chairman of KB until 1971 when Mark would succeed him. Gerald Thompson and Bobby Henderson were appointed vice-chairmen as the heirs designate to Mark and not, as was later believed by the younger directors, to Cyril.[37]

When the time came in 1970 to appoint Cyril's successor, whilst it was assumed amongst the older hands that Mark Turner's name would be announced, this option was not presented as straightforwardly as expected. Thompson and Henderson were told by Cyril that they were the people to succeed him—but Henderson disagreed, saying that Mark Turner ought to do so. Cyril then decided to consult the other directors about Turner and Thompson as the two candidates. Many directors, however, were told by Cyril and Ivo Forde that though Mark Turner's candidature had 'great merit', a new rule on the retirement age precluded him, and were persuaded that the choice was between Gerald Thompson or someone outside. As one director pointed out, 'You have disqualified Mark, nobody can seriously say I'll vote for Mr X without knowing him, therefore by definition it's Gerald Thompson.' If the intention was to provide a consensual approach to choosing a new chairman at KB, it was resolved in a curious way.

Mark Turner's qualities of leadership, his outstanding ability, energy, and business acumen were not in doubt. It was, however, precisely because of these that a few people wondered whether he would have time to devote to the job, whether he might occasionally let his enthusiasm outweigh his judgement and not be as 'safe a pair of hands' as a banker. Whilst none of these concerns was at all soundly based—he had trained as a banker, was finance director and then chairman of RTZ and considered extremely safe and shrewd—the very fact that a few persuasive people came to share them was enough to weigh the scales in favour of Thompson. It is also clear that in certain quarters the choice was made from reasons of self-interest rather than from a judgement that Thompson was the best man to lead KB.[38]

It is equally clear that, in the 1970s, the connection between the business that a chairman with a strong external presence, 'good' outside directorships, and experience of international contacts could bring to the bank was not really taken on board at KB as being of immense consequence. A man such as Mark Turner, who was ambassadorial, enthusiastic, and who won business, would have been regarded far more highly by some of KB's more outward-looking competitors, such as Lazards or Warburgs. Siegmund Warburg's understanding that the key to good business is knowing people and the relative importance of their businesses in an international as much as domestic context enabled his firm to steal a march on its City competitors. In this sense, KB at the beginning of the 1970s was still 'woefully introverted'.

Against a background of international and domestic expansion—fired at home by the policy of the new Conservative Chancellor, Anthony Barber, of liberalizing sterling lending from official restraints that set in train a credit boom—Cyril declared 1971 'a notable year in our history'. The Group celebrated its first decade with record results: KBL's capital and disclosed reserves had grown from £13.4m. to £36.7m. and the Group's net profits from £942,000 to £3.7m. This increase was due to the bank's improved capability to react and reap the benefit of favourable trading conditions, higher margins and lower interest rates. Cyril and Mark could look back with satisfaction on the development of the merged firm, assured that within its first decade KB was in the mainstream of merchant banking and that its shareholders' expectations were being met. Under their leadership the bank had become much more integrated and the early frictions largely eradicated. As Cyril had stated on the occasion of the London staff moving into the new building at No. 20, 'Our confidence that the merger of the two Houses would lead to a considerable expansion of our mutual operations has been amply fulfilled, with the company offering the comprehensive range of services which we believe to be the essential characteristic of a modern merchant bank.'[39]

12 A Changed Landscape 1972–1994

KLEINWORT BENSON has operated in a climate of political vulnerability and economic and financial volatility throughout the two decades leading up to the present day and yet has managed to show a sustained growth in profits and balance sheet size for most, though not all, of the period. The ability to adapt to changing conditions, always of the utmost importance to merchant banks, once again enabled KB to survive and grow. In common with other firms, KB increased its market share in some areas and lost it in others. The very nature of merchant banks has always been that as one source of profit dissolves another springs up, so that in this respect little has changed throughout their history; fundamentally, therefore, the broad canvas of the risks and rewards has remained similar—but the brush strokes have altered and become harsher. The growth in the range of services and geographical spread of the business during the last twenty years has provided KB with a greater flexibility in meeting the requirements of its world-wide customers. According to its longest-serving chairman, Bobby Henderson, 'it is this flexibility, together with the importance we attach to service [to clients], that goes far to explain the continued success' of the KB group.[1]

Against the perspective of 200 years, however, the framework supporting the broad canvas is unrecognizable today. The world's horizons have continued to recede through the redrawing of its economic map. The old European industries, family-owned and managed and usually based on raw materials such as wool, cotton, and leather, faded into the background as more competitive producers emerged in Japan and the Pacific Basin. The resultant shift in wealth was a significant factor in the internationalization of financial activities which, after the adoption of a system of flexible exchange rates and of advances in information technology enabling the markets to operate throughout a 24-hour day, led to an unprecedented expansion in the world-wide operations of City financial services companies including KB.

In 1977 the first international system of interbank electronic links was inaugurated, and such new technologies resulted in the proliferation of dealing rooms in which skilled staff sit in cockpits of push-button switches and manage huge flows of capital on computer screens. The competitive environment, the speed of communication, the complexity of financial instruments, and the sheer size of the amounts of money dealt in today would be beyond the imagination of Sir Alexander Kleinwort and Robin Benson, let alone their grandfathers. While the principles of business have not changed—bankers still have to make judgements about people, credits, and risk—nearly everything else has since their time. Foreign banks, for example, used to transact London business through British banks in their day and so were not the competitive threat they are today, such is the proliferation of branches or subsidiaries of large overseas banks in the City. The Bank of America's 1974 balance sheet size of $50 billion—with $20 billion abroad, probably mostly in London—would have been an inconceivable amount to any of the old merchant banks, even allowing for the depreciation of money. The largest change of the previous two centuries has been wrought in the City by a combination of these developments and the removal of regulatory barriers, which ensured that the City remained a major financial centre.

In the competitive and testing climate of the 1970s and 1980s, when organizations and their traditional means of carrying out business were evolving beyond all recognition in reaction to 'globalization' and Government-led initiatives, merchant banks did not escape the effects of what Tom Wolfe termed the 'Me Too' syndrome of self-interest that prevailed throughout the whole of this period but was most marked in the 1980s. It became acceptable, and indeed fashionable, for staff to move between firms, where before this would have been like cutting an umbilical cord, and people more rarely made a long-term commitment to their place of employment. The widespread influence of American transaction mores has led to one of the biggest changes to have occurred in the working habits of the nation as much as the City. In David Benson's words, before 1975 'there was no doubt that everybody coming into the firm came into what they regarded as a home. Nowadays many feel they are checking into an hotel . . . looking over their shoulders to see what's better elsewhere.' This change in attitude was both influenced and promoted by the advent of a new and potent weapon in the corporate world, the predatory head-hunter, whose persuasive skills were harnessed as much by employers as by employees keen to establish their real, albeit transitory, value in the ever-expanding market-place.[2]

A corresponding change has also occurred in the commitment and loyalty of firms to their employees. 'Jobs for life' was not, until relatively recently, merely an unrealistic slogan on a placard waved by a demonstrator at a union rally; it was the customary pattern of employment upheld in Britain and elsewhere for the greater part of this century. Although there were exceptions—

such as during the deep Depression of the 1930s when, for instance, Kleinworts and Schroders made staff redundant—by and large firms expected to employ staff throughout their working lives and would even lower management salaries and lose profits to do so when times were hard, as Bensons did. In the event that a member of staff did not make the grade for promotion, he or she would have been found something useful to do elsewhere within the firm; they would not have been forced to resign or take early retirement. Whereas in the early 1970s the largest bank in the world could pride itself on never firing anyone, by the end of the decade the policy had to be changed for financial reasons. Against a background of ever-rising costs, the customary paternalistic approach to staff has long since been overtaken by the exigencies of 'the bottom line' of the profit and loss account; added to which is the need for top management to deliver to demanding shareholders—and the even more demanding media. The much larger numbers of staff also inevitably made working conditions more impersonal and more expensive.

The generous remuneration and benefits packages, together with the employee share schemes that are taken for granted in the City today, only became common in the 1980s. Young men starting out in the City before 1970, for example, were paid relatively little, remuneration expectations were lower, and the benefits were skeletal. It was in many ways competition for the bright graduates by foreign banks that led to starting salaries far exceeding the previous norm of a low wage during apprenticeship. The subsequent upward pressure on staff salaries necessitated a review of those of the younger directors. When one of them returned to London from the New York office in 1973, the chairman Gerald Thompson wrote that 'like railway cars in a shunting yard this will mean that your salary is to be increased to £10,000 p.a.'. The chairman himself only earned £35,000 per annum and the salary was all there was except for a pension and the traditional free turkey at Christmas; there were no options, bonuses, incentive shares, or even company cars then, although some of these benefits started to be introduced soon afterwards.[3]

In order to attract and retain staff in a more competitive environment, City firms added to their remuneration packages in some extraordinary ways. By the mid-1980s the City was paying itself an enormous amount of money. This was naturally exacerbated by the much-publicized 'golden hellos and handshakes' associated with Big Bang—the application of the Government's policy of deregulation to the City of London so that from October 1986 banks as well as brokers could deal in equities and government securities—and fuelled by the head-hunters; but before that the increase in job mobility, enabling staff to improve their positions and achieve promotion faster, had led to substantial incremental leaps in the scale of salaries. Although it is an exaggeration to say that money is the main driver in the business today, the culture is much more linked to immediate reward rather than building for the future.[4]

Alongside remuneration, expectations about promotion and status in the financial services industry have also become much higher. The idea of personnel departments encouraging staff to set objectives in defining their career aspirations would once have been met with bemusement if not ridicule. At Kleinworts, as late as 1960, promotion was slow and it was deemed an honour and a significant achievement to be promoted; until the merger very few had been able to work their way up to a directorship. In the 1970s and 1980s, however, the size of boards of directors throughout the Square Mile mushroomed. As one former KB director Peter Wake commented, 'Everybody has to be put on a board, you have to be able to say you're a director!'

In 1971 the board of Kleinwort Benson Ltd., the main operating company of the Group, consisted of twenty-nine directors, but by 1980 it had grown to forty. Its chairman explained KB's policy in 1972: 'We try to bring within the collegium of directors all those who are exercising prime executive duties. A director's responsibilities today are of an importance reaching beyond the Company and, like all responsibilities, are best learned by being exercised.' The expansion in the number of people exercising responsibility was seen as a consequence of running a 'modern merchant bank'.[5]

While Gerald Thompson and Bobby Henderson ran KB Ltd., Cyril remained as chairman of the holding company board, KBL, and Mark Turner continued as its deputy chairman. The separation of ownership from management not only reduced the proprietorial influence but also removed the main long-term strategists from KB Ltd. as well as ineluctably linking the chairmanship of the bank with performance and results. The constant pressure of peer-group and institutional perceptions increased the influence of the short-term view within merchant banks throughout the 1970s and 1980s. An increasingly emulative milieu and developments in faster communications encouraged a more transaction-oriented mentality throughout the City. Furthermore, the pressures of expanding businesses employing ever-larger numbers meant that boards of directors were less able to take the long-term view and to stand aloof from market-driven forces in terms of policy-making. Whilst Cyril did not necessarily need to be seen to earn his keep in terms of corporate results, his successors have had to do so. It is thus far more difficult for them to embark upon a long-term course that initially may involve losses or be slow to show profitability.

A change at the very top of an organization is, for better or worse, a major event in any firm. The way in which a particular appointee exercises power will affect the harmony of internal working relations as well as the external perceptions of the firm's performance and image. Gerald Thompson took the helm at a time when KB had to navigate some excessively choppy waters. The optimism reflected at the time he became chairman in 1971 was somewhat diminished by the subsequent grave political conditions of war in the Middle East, an unprecedented rise in oil prices, and the Conservative Government's implementation of the three-day week. Taken together with what Cyril described in that year as a 'continuously growing disorder in the international monetary system', reflecting the break-up of the Bretton Woods system in 1971, these factors allowed the KB Group to be satisfied with merely maintaining its overall market share in 1973.[6]

The directors would have been more than satisfied to have produced the same results in 1974. Cyril referred to it in KBL's Annual Report as this 'year of confusion with two general elections, three budgets, a series of three-day weeks, numerous stoppages and accelerating inflation' when property share prices plummeted and banks were locked in. The secondary banking crisis had come to a head shortly before Christmas 1973, prompting the Bank of England's 'Lifeboat' operation that eventually supported some twenty-six secondary banking institutions to the tune of about £3,000m. By the time Lex of the *Financial Times* wrote a year later that 'although we could foresee the general pattern of 1974, we had no real inkling of the scale of the crisis', sixty-five stockbroking firms had failed, the National Westminster Bank was rumoured to be in trouble and Burmah Oil had to be rescued by the Government on New Year's Eve. KB felt relieved to have escaped with only a 7½ per cent dip in profits to £4.6m. after tax.[7]

The results demonstrated the firm's commendable caution in its scale of lending to property companies during the boom. KB had only stepped up its lending after being chided for being too cautious by the Bank of England. Happily, it had not ventured in too far when a secondary bank, London & County Securities, collapsed in December 1973. KB had a then large exposure, £10m., to one company that in the event survived, but, as an assistant manager in the banking division would later point out, it was thought to be important to have some exposure. Whereas Barings might be relieved about having none to the property market in 1973, they had also clearly missed the earlier opportunity to make money, a consideration that harked back to Sir Alexander Kleinwort's approach to the risks of banking business. He would, for example, have preferred KB to be a member of the Lazards syndicate providing a revolving acceptance credit of £20m. for Rolls Royce to build the RB211 engine, even though Rolls Royce went bankrupt in 1971, than not to be included in the deal in the first place.[8]

There were still, however, deals that turned out to be not so much high-risk as plain dangerous, usually ill-conceived or involving a client who did not play straight, and in such cases all a bank could do was to mount a salvage operation to contain the damage, just as Kleinworts did in Sir Alexander's day over Bevan and Hatry. In 1973/4 KB had a much larger exposure to shipping than property when the sharp rise in oil prices pushed the shipping industry, as well as the world's economy, into severe recession. A newly signed agreement to finance the building of two tankers for lease to a Japanese company, for instance, was placed in jeopardy. It called for some fraught dealing given the amount at risk, some £50m. Unlike a later, highly publicized bought deal, Premier Consolidated Oil, that did not go according to plan, this one remained out of the public eye so that KB was able to agonize in private, bide its time for a year, and then quietly negotiate a settlement at the right time. KB eventually made a good profit but it was one deal it would rather have avoided, 'the risk was a damn sight too great'.[9]

The unsatisfactory trading climate of plunging stock markets and rising interest rates also adversely affected KB's corporate finance division where the take-over and merger boom of the late 1960s suddenly fizzled out and business became unusually quiet in 1973 as confidence evaporated from the corporate sector. Not surprisingly, there was in compensation a good deal of rescue work, advising companies such as First National Finance and others on capital reconstruction. However in 1974, in the autumn of yet another barren year, the signal that the capital markets could still operate was given by KB when it put 'some new heart' into the market with the first capital-raising exercise of any significance since the crash. KB acted as lead manager of one of the largest equity issues ever mounted in the City, one that comprised almost 40 per cent of the entire capital raised that year for British companies.

The timing appeared inauspicious and the announcement of the Commercial Union rights issue for £62m. underwritten by KB, Barings, Schroders, and Lazards, with Cazenoves acting as brokers, 'astonished' the financial community as it was made barely a fortnight before a neck-and-neck General Election. If the issue had failed it would have been, in the *Financial Times*'s opinion, the end of the line for the primary market. KB, however, was quietly confident while Cazenoves believed the issue would 'go'—which, indeed, it did, and proved to be a great success, heralding a turn in the market as the domestic capital market revived with a spate of rights issues appearing early in 1975. KB had emerged from this period relatively unscathed and, according to Martin Jacomb, the 'CU rights issue provided an enormously good spring-board to the equal top position in the first division'.[10]

A similar revival in the Eurobond markets occurred with the return of Japanese companies as major borrowers. In 1975 KB led a $20m. international bond issue for a leading Japanese trading company. The issue proved a highly successful debut but it was not without contention for political reasons. Following the OPEC rise in the price of oil, surplus petrodollars were lapping against the financial shores of the West at a time when Arab firms were precluded by the Arab Office for the Boycott of Israel from co-operating with certain foreign firms. A few days before the launch of the $20m. issue, two of the Arab co-managers suddenly informed KB that they could only participate if two 'blacklisted' banks were removed from the list of underwriters. KB and its client happened to enjoy close ties with the Arab world and wished to preplace a good portion of the issue there. The bank, however, had no wish to exclude old City friends from the underwriting, and worked strenuously though quietly behind the scenes to persuade the Arabs to withdraw their objections, but the Arabs remained adamant. The situation was further exacerbated by the American press which, noting a similar trend amongst US investment banks in two recent French issues, switched on the floodlights and brought the political and moral propriety of such behaviour into the wider public domain; even President Ford made a statement. Faced with a major dilemma, the bank ultimately held to the belief that its duty was first and foremost to its client and the issue went ahead notwithstanding such public pressures; it was a success in itself, although it left scars that took some time to heal.

Within KB it underlined the extent to which business could have unforeseen political ramifications and, in consequence, the desirability of being represented at the most senior level by someone known in Paris, New York, and Tokyo, who could bring an international experience to bear in such situations. From this point of view, Gerald Thompson was an old-style chairman in a new-style commercial world; the advance in global communications and the rising prominence of financial news in the press demanded an immediate response at the highest level and correspondingly a more public role for a chairman. By the mid-1970s too, with a number of high-powered executives on the board, there were many who thought they, too, knew how to run the bank thereby making top management more difficult for someone who did not possess the antennae for people management that some chairmen had possessed. The truism that an excellent head of division does not necessarily thrive as a chairman was later recognized by Gerald Thompson. Looking back over his chairmanship he commented, somewhat sadly, that it was not the culmination of a long and successful career that it should have been.[11]

There was in 1974 only one candidate to succeed Thompson as chairman of the bank, his deputy chairman R. A. Henderson. Whereas Thompson had not really grasped the corporate finance side, Henderson had no such difficulty as KB's first chairman with a corporate finance background; but he also made it his business to understand the banking side although he relied heavily upon Michael Hawkes to run this part of the business. Bobby Henderson's style and approach differed considerably from his predecessors, in that he was very much a 'hands-on' operator who excelled in dealing with day-to-day challenges. His junior colleagues considered him a good client man and outstanding in the fundamental task of dealing with people. As a chairman he was very accessible and inquisitive. He liked to stroll around No. 20 and talk to people, saying, 'What's going on? Tell me, I'd like to know,' and his perambulations were made not merely to boost morale but also to keep his finger on the pulse of the bank. 'You have to keep an eye on it yourself,' he would explain, especially since 'any thing that makes money quickly loses money quickly'. His direct leadership of all the operations of the firm was very strong. 'He made people want to work for him and want to work very hard,' Martin Jacomb recalls. 'He knew what business you had won and questioned why you hadn't won other business. And that's what you want out of a chairman to make progress.'[12]

Under Henderson's chairmanship in the decade 1974–83, KB enjoyed a period of great growth and success. Although volatile trading conditions continued to characterize the latter years of the 1970s—with Britain being bailed out by the IMF in 1976 after the sterling crisis—until the 1979 election returned the Conservatives to power, KB underwent a metamorphosis in size and strength. The corporate finance division had entered the top league and the quality of the banking business had improved. The balanced nature and international spread of its business allowed KB to record a 33 per cent increase in profits after tax to £20m. in 1979. KB 'are the first merchant bank to sport a £2 billion balance sheet—£2338m. in fact', announced one newspaper, while on 28 December 1979 the *Evening Standard* trumpeted, 'Kleinwort are the 1979 Kings' of City takeovers. The Thatcher Government's abolition of exchange controls in that year marked the first move in the process of market liberalization through deregulation that eventually brought about revolutionary changes to the City. Perceptions about the business climate were transformed and the corporate sector in general was more willing to take risks for the first time since the mid-1970s, so that the momentum picked up.[13]

The core business of the banking division under the continued leadership of Michael Hawkes altered considerably from 1974–83. The international banking department led by him and Robin Fox was the traditional dynamo of the business—accepting houses had always financed foreign trade and KB's business remained predominantly overseas. The English Department included English-speaking countries such as South Africa and Australia. Martin

Mays-Smith, who would later head the banking division, had found it 'incredibly old-fashioned and hierarchical' even in 1972.

It became important to focus upon specialized forms of banking activity because developments within the banking industry resulted in the traditional mainstay of international lending proving more unremunerative. Banks in the mid-1970s were already suffering from reduced lending margins caused by the surfeit of petrodollar deposits and a more competitive environment; British clearing banks were forming or acquiring merchant banking subsidiaries and the London subsidiaries and branches of foreign banks were growing from 267 in 1973 to 449 in 1982. The Bank of England's intervention was also crucial; in 1978 it decided to restrain bank lending, which led to a rise in funding by acceptance credits—at KB from £250m. in 1978 to £500m. in 1982, and Schroders' figures for the corresponding years were £152m. to £347m. In 1981 the Bank of England's decision to extend the list of banks whose bills were automatically eligible for rediscount intensified the decline in profitability of acceptance business by further increasing competition.

With its traditional accepting and lending business waning, KB was able to move away from balance-sheet-based lending and towards more innovative financing mechanisms. This trend of increased securitization of lending became more pronounced during the 1980s, merchant banks thereby strengthening their balance sheets and earning sizeable fees from servicing their clients' financing requirements. The division also continued to apply its collective intellect to creative products and remained more adventurous in banking than most competitors. A North American banking operation was revived in 1971 and generated profitable business that stemmed in part from arbitrage opportunities, after which KB moved into leveraged financing—so reminiscent of the old Benson / Fleming / Ohrstrom pre-merger operation. KB's first such deal was in 1980/1 with GE Capital, which earned returns of from 40 per cent on the equity and 3–5 per cent on the debt at a time when acceptance commissions had fallen from 1¼ per cent in pre-1972 cartel days to ⅛ per cent.

Elsewhere, Martin Mays-Smith and Simon Parker had started rebuilding the export credit operation. Out of a small, moribund banking operation in South Africa, which originated from Kleinworts' wool financing business in the 1950s, they had established a thriving export financing business for KB by the late 1970s. As the 1980s progressed KB developed a large loan syndication business in Tokyo, putting £2 billion through Japanese institutions in the first year of operation. By 1985 the division bore little resemblance to its 1960s self, though it remained profitable. Within KB it continued to bear the reputation of an excellent business, whereas within the banking division itself concern over sovereign lending exposure and disagreement over direction created unease about its future.[14]

During the second decade after the KB merger, the investment management division (known by the acronym KBIM), in contrast, remained relatively undisturbed. It continued to manage the bank's capital and, supported by a growing private client and pension fund business and a leading investment trust base, it entered the 1970s as one of the top fund-managers alongside Flemings, Morgan Grenfell, Schroders, and the up-and-coming Warburgs; in 1972 some 40 per cent of the bank's profits came from this division. Early in the following year, however, it recorded a loss of some $20m. on American investments, and thereafter it seemed to falter. It had long been more cost- than revenue-conscious, retaining a style of management that never encouraged a marketing culture amongst its staff. Elsewhere, however, thrusting extroverts began to take to the road selling products for rivals who were more proactive in promoting their services. Although KBIM held significant local authority and pension fund accounts, it failed to address the issue of tapping into the explosive growth in the market for institutional funds which other firms were exploiting much more effectively by the late 1970s.

Another factor which affected the development of KBIM was the firm's prescient and profitable investment in the M. & G. Group, which ran the largest stable of unit trusts in the country, and would manage some £4.2 billion by 1986. KB's investment induced a continuous ambivalence between itself and M. & G., where a determination to maintain management and investment policy independence—despite the presence of KB directors on its board—remained very strong. After helping M. & G. overcome short-term difficulties in 1980, KB increased its stake to 42.5 per cent. The investment management division thereupon wanted KB to acquire M. & G. but on the grounds that M. & G. would never agree to be part of the bank, KB subsequently renounced its right to acquire further shares which would have given it control, saying 'We believe that the independence of M & G has been a vital factor in its outstandingly successful record.' The decision was eventually taken to sell the firm's stake in M. & G. in two tranches, the first and major part in 1986 for some £74m., and the investment management division began to focus upon a strategy for the future that would include developing its own unit trust business.[15]

The division that benefited most from the changed climate of the late 1970s and 1980s was undoubtedly corporate finance. KB demonstrated a capacity for winning first-class corporate business throughout the period of the first two Thatcher Governments and it exploited better than any of its competitors the marvellous new seam of business that suddenly opened up and transformed the scale of the capital markets. In July 1979, the Department of Industry (DI) asked KB and Morgan Grenfell each to submit their proposals for floating part of British Aerospace, a company that had been nationalized by the Labour Government only in 1977.

When KB was selected in conjunction with the Bank of England to manage the proposed offer for sale to the public and to act as merchant banking adviser to the DI, it was the beginning of a process where, in Tim Barker's words, 'we were pushing boulders up hills which people just didn't think could be pushed'. It is easy to forget that in 1980 this was more or less uncharted territory—the steel denationalizations of the 1950s were not in the working memory of those involved—since it was not so much the flotation of a single company but of an entire industry, in this case the British aircraft and missile defence industry. As it was in the public sector, neither the Stock Exchange nor any of the merchant banks knew much about it. 'There was nothing you could compare it with so the whole financial community started with a knowledge base of absolutely zero,' Tim Barker would explain. Many people both inside and outside KB had grave doubts about the feasibility of the project, and at one stage the whole privatization programme seemed likely to be consigned to a footnote in history when the Bank of England decided British Aerospace was unfloatable and contemplated withdrawing. Neither KB nor the DI lost their nerve and the flotation proceeded.

It looked vulnerable, however, when, having announced in the House of Commons that the Ministry of Defence was allocating extra funds to British Aerospace's Sea Eagle, John Nott decided to cancel the project in a defence review. (A similar situation has since arisen in the electricity industry where, on the eve of the flotation but after all the shares had been allocated, the electricity industry regulator issued a pricing policy statement that severely affected prices of Powergen shares.) In the case of British Aerospace, Bobby Henderson had to obtain Government assurances about upholding the Sea Eagle contract before KB could proceed with the flotation. At that time the Government and Whitehall rarely met KB on a daily working basis, so that it was a novelty for the bank to be dealing with three Ministries—the DI, the MOD, and the Treasury—and it proved to be a highly complex exercise.

KB had got to know British Aerospace's business, which it believed possessed great strengths, and was not to be deterred by doubters or reluctant partners; at that time even KB's co-underwriters, such as Schroders and Morgans, came in somewhat reluctantly, and Barker recalls 'did not believe that it was necessarily going to be a thing for the future'. Notwithstanding this, in February 1981, the largest primary equity offer for sale in the UK was brought to the market: 100m. ordinary shares of 50p, representing about half the issued share capital of British Aerospace, were offered to the public at 150p per share. The issue was 3½ times oversubscribed and the shares opened at a sizeable 15 per cent premium of 21p. The flotation of British Aerospace was a landmark deal: a breakthrough for the Government in establishing its privatization programme, as well as for KB in underpinning its reputation as a top-division merchant bank. Bobby Henderson considers that though other issues in this programme were much larger, British Aerospace 'was the key because it was the first and we did it and nobody thought it would happen'.[16]

Having been judged successful the first time, KB was approached by Cable & Wireless to act for them in their flotation. The KB team comprised Tim Barker and David Clementi with Andrew Caldecott at the vice-chairman level. This was an easier project, being the second one, and took only eight months to process. It was nevertheless the largest and most publicized transaction undertaken by KB to date. In the autumn of 1981 it raised £224m., a sum never exceeded before on the London market by a previously unlisted company.

While KB was not involved in every part of the Government's privatization programme—Warburgs and Rothschilds acting in the Britoil offer—it had more than its fair share, and confirmed its reputation as the leading privatization house with the British Telecom offer that once again broke new ground in 1984. The sale of 50.2 per cent of British Telecom was the largest flotation ever contemplated and Nigel Lawson recalls that the consensus of a private dinner party given by the chairman of Standard Telephones and Cables, and comprising captains of industry and pillars of leading City merchant banks, was that the BT privatization was impossible since 'the capital market simply was not large enough to absorb it'. Somewhat naturally, the only dissenter among the guests was Martin Jacomb.[17]

KB had been invited to pitch for British Telecom and Caldecott, Barker, and Clementi prepared a 60-page memorandum. Along with teams from four other merchant banks, they were cross-examined by officials from the Treasury and the Bank of England in a beauty contest—which KB won. The original team consisting of Tim Barker, David Clementi, and Richard Murley changed after Barker left to head the Take-over Panel in the autumn of 1983, when Martin Jacomb and Lord Rockley picked up the leadership role. The team expanded gradually during 1984 to include a large number within the Corporate Finance Division as well as many others at No. 20 and in overseas offices. Their primary role was to give advice to the Government on the development of a regulatory system under which British Telecom was to operate and on the required legislation for the flotation that was enacted in April 1984.

By this time, arrangements for the flotation itself were already underway. Initially the attitude of many institutional funds was that such a large issue represented a major burden, some fund managers privately expressing the view that the size of the proposed transaction made it impossible. KB combated this by deciding to place the shares into three markets, the UK institutional, retail, and the international markets, creating tension between them through a highly innovative marketing campaign, by the end of which the BT Share Information Office telephone number had become one of the best known in the country. As views shifted and public enthusiasm grew, the idea of a shortage of shares for institutional investors took root; moreover, this was one issue for which they were unable to dictate price as the monopoly buyer.

Thus, on Impact day, 16 November 1984, when part of the issue was placed with major UK institutions with the balance of the UK offer being made available to the general public, the overall world-wide response was excellent. Some 8 million prospectuses had been printed in five countries, and the sale held centre-stage in every major financial market in the world. By tilting the allocation of shares in favour of the small investor, the issue doubled overnight the small number of people who owned shares and saw the birth of 'popular capitalism'. It attracted over 2 million applications from the general public so that, together with employees who bought shares, the company started with over 2.3 million private shareholders. The sale was the largest issue of shares the world had ever known, raising just under £4,000m. for the Government. It was judged a resounding success. The best memory for those at KB who worked on the flotation is of the final words of the *Financial Times* Lex column (not often given to outright praise) on the morning after dealings in the new shares had started: 'BT was a monumental corporate finance exercise and, in almost every respect, a monumental achievement.'[18]

Subsequently KB acted in the offerings of Enterprise Oil, Associated British Ports, British Gas, and the two parts of the UK electricity supply industry, so that privatization has provided a major element of the corporate finance division's business throughout the 1980s and the 1990s. The BT issue raised the profile of the bank to make KB almost a household name, attracting new and reciprocal business for the bank. Although this type of business absorbed a great deal of resources and was staff intensive, it has unquestionably been of benefit in terms of future business both in the United Kingdom and overseas. KB before privatization was not regarded as *primus inter pares* in the top league, as were Morgan Grenfell and Lazards; nor had it demonstrated the capability to build new relationships in the way Warburgs had been doing since the 1970s. What the privatization process did, in Simon Robertson's words, was to put KB 'on the map as a really major player . . . it was very very worthwhile business.'

The firm has subsequently been asked to advise governments across the world from Argentina to Malaysia, leading from the front in the way that

Barings and Rothschilds had done in different fields in the late eighteenth and nineteenth centuries. KB's experience resulted in, for example, its retention by the French Treasury to advise on the first of the French privatizations, the Compagnie de Saint Gobain, in 1986. The following year KB advised Credit Commercial de France on its privatization. This in turn enabled it to develop a wide range of other corporate finance business, such as lead-managing five sterling Eurobond issues for French banks to establish market leadership in this sector, arranging the first sterling commercial paper programme for a French corporation and advising another company in a successful take-over bid; all of which made of 1987 'L'annèe de succès pour Kleinwort Benson', in the words of its house magazine. In consequence of privatization, throughout the 1980s KB remained among the first six merchant banks in the flotation league, a position that would undoubtedly have delighted the former Benson new issue partners and directors.[19]

Throughout the mid-1980s the financial newspapers bulged with details of the latest round in the increasingly aggressive contested acquisition fights, in many of which KB featured. Thus in 1986, for example, the tally kept by *Acquisitions Monthly* revealed that KB headed the list in the volume of public mergers and acquisitions with over forty-three deals and their combined total value placed the firm in second place behind Morgan Grenfell. Unlike the latter, however, the KB culture did not depend upon a 'Star System', such as emerged from Morgans in the 1980s. If anything, an anti-star syndrome prevails at KB where people are given the credit for a good deal as members of a team. Michael Hawkes was quoted as describing the personality cult as 'a bore' and reiterating that KB tried to play it down as 'there are plenty of young people at Kleinworts who've got the ability to handle take overs'. Clients, however, often prefer to work closely with an individual. KB lost a starring role in the major battle between Thomas Tilling and BTR in 1983 when Tilling asked for James Rockley to head the defence team. He was not available: 'we should probably have sent a helicopter for him, but we didn't,' Michael Hawkes said. 'Tilling abandoned us and went over to Warburgs.'[20]

The continuing Americanization of the City during this period had introduced another change in the financial environment, one that corporate finance divisions in British merchant banks found difficult to assimilate. The traditional relationship approach to clients was under siege from the American transactional culture. British merchant banks still perceived it as their job to give objective advice to clients, even when by so doing they forfeited a fee. Partly to wean away clients from their existing merchant banks and partly because they did not believe they should be giving free advice, American houses in London followed the line that they were in the City to give corporate

Britain ideas; they therefore adopted the role of instigators of business with clients, pushing them into raising money or making acquisitions.

A further by-product of the American invasion of the City had been the change in fee structures since American banks charged very high fees for corporate engineering work in comparison with British banks. These fees are based upon both results and advice; a corollary can be found in the American legal profession's No Win/No Fee cases that are beginning to appear in British courts. If transactions do not take place, however, the corporate finance division forfeits a substantial part of its fees. This shift in the source of fees has produced a conflict of interest, with which merchant banks continue to wrestle. 'Do you tell your client not to do a £3 billion deal when you have a fee of £6 million riding on it, and if the deal doesn't take place, then only a fee of £100,000?' poses Simon Robertson. 'It takes a lot of moral courage to say you shouldn't do the deal.' KB none the less retains a reputation for being prepared to tell clients just that: 'we give independent advice and are very solicitous of relationships'.[21]

KB had entered the 1980s with an enhanced reputation. A retired chairman of Commercial Union considered it 'the best bank in the City, one that attracted good people and quality business'. It was against this background that the Board prepared for another change of leadership and set in train a policy review to determine the future direction of the bank in the wake of the proposed abolition of restrictive practices in the Stock Exchange. The ranks of the former seniors of Kleinworts and Bensons had been severely depleted by a succession of deaths. Rex had been the first in 1968 and it was only through the plethora of lengthy obituaries that many of the newer KB staff discovered the extent of the world-wide array of friends and contacts that he had often involved in the interests of the bank. Leo, Ernest, Sonny, and Robert Rockley had died during the 1970s, and Phil Macpherson in 1981. Both Cyril and Mark, the most influential elder statesmen, had died in 1980, within three months of each other. As Bobby Henderson wrote, it was in great part due to their combined efforts and leadership qualities that the Kleinwort/Benson union endured and that the new firm was positioned to achieve a record of growth throughout the following decades.[22]

During the fifteen years following the merger KB's profits gradually crept up to the £5m. level. From the mid-1970s there followed twelve years of exponential growth with profits doubling and redoubling to £20m. by 1983—assisted by large contributions from bullion trading. By the end of 1985 profits would double again to £40.5m. and in the last six months before Big Bang would reach £38.8m. after tax and allocation of hidden reserves. This was achieved by the traditional merchant banking business, subsumed after it reported its highest-ever performance by the switch into investment banking.

Bobby Henderson retired as chairman of KB in 1983 and the three candidates for the succession were his vice-chairmen, Michael Hawkes, Martin Jacomb, and Andrew Caldecott. After Denys Oppé decided to retire from running the investment management division, Martin Jacomb had moved there from corporate finance. Andrew Caldecott had been appointed head of corporate finance after Charles Ball unexpectedly left to become chairman of Barclays Merchant Bank in 1976. Although Bobby Henderson felt that Martin Jacomb would be better in a corporate finance than an investment management role, he could not bring him back under Caldecott. Michael Hawkes meanwhile had continued to head the banking division most successfully and in 1978 had also established KB's representative office in Hong Kong as a fully fledged branch, which was profitable a year later.

It was, therefore, not an easy choice. Caldecott led from the front, was decisive, witty, well liked by clients, and sat on a number of important outside boards; he had not, however, grown up within the mainstream, doing basic corporate finance work—and this continued to matter at KB, in a way it might not have done at Schröders or Warburgs. He was not perceived as being steeped in KB culture. Jacomb was thought by many to be the obvious choice, a wonderful adviser with a great presence outside No. 20 and wide experience, 'the sort of chap anyone would like to have on a board'; however, by his own admission, he ought to have been more decisive in running the investment management division in order to increase the profitability of what was becoming an insufficiently dynamic part of KB. In comparison, Michael Hawkes, a homegrown KB man, had been instrumental in making money for the firm throughout his long career at KB; he was not a broad client man, however, and had little outside experience.

Bobby Henderson remembers it was a most difficult decision. He finally convened a dinner at the Connaught Hotel at which the KBL board, together with the senior KB directors, chose a new chairman for the bank. A decisive intervention in Hawkes's favour was made by one of the non-executive directors who asked whom they could least afford to lose, for whilst 'you can teach a really able expert how to get on with clients, you can't very often do it the other way round'; and, as in 1971, a banker was chosen to run the bank.[23]

It was under Michael Hawkes's leadership that KB had to assimilate a new culture, one that was largely transactionary. The City had been served notice of the forthcoming changes in the regulatory framework of the financial services industry. These were the result of the July 1983 Parkinson/Goodison accord whereby Cecil Parkinson, the new Secretary of Trade and Industry, called off the Office of Fair Trading investigation into restrictive practices at the Stock Exchange in return for an undertaking that it would reform itself. This would involve dismantling the minimum commission structure that prevented price competition between stockbrokers, allowing outsiders such as foreign banks to take a maximum stake of 29.9 per cent in member firms, and removing the insistence upon single capacity and the separation between brokers and jobbers. The Government and the Bank of England believed that these 'reforms' would correct what Nigel Lawson has described as one fatal practical defect of the old restrictive system, namely that 'it was woefully undercapitalised' and was in danger of making London a backwater in terms of the global, highly competitive securities market.[24]

The Bank of England had been concerned about the haemorrhage of Stock Exchange business to other international markets, particularly Wall Street. It therefore now actively promoted the idea of large financial groups with a firm capital base that could offer a wide spread of financial services. The easiest way to achieve this was to promote multiple shot-gun marriages between stockbrokers and banking institutions. Whilst the 'reforms' meant that stockbrokers could take on the jobbers' role of making markets in equities and gilts as well as continuing their traditional business of acting for institutional and private clients, such a dual role would require substantial capital resources which stockbrokers by and large did not possess—but the merchant and commercial banks did. Furthermore, although this was not so apparent at the time, the banks were more familiar with the rudiments of trading, taking positions, and risk management than the brokers were. As one KB director later said, 'How can an agency broker know anything about trading? He never takes a principal's risk!'[25]

Against this background of unremitting pressure for change, with the Bank of England pushing hard for it, KB was faced with having to take some of the most difficult decisions about its future in an untested environment. It was therefore fitting for KB to have as chairman at this time someone who understood the grammar of trading, and the complex new instruments employed to develop the derivative products business in which the bank was becoming active. Junior directors saw Michael Hawkes's appointment as crucial in that he was one of the very rare product-oriented people at a senior level within KB. Hawkes, like Herman Andreae and Sir Alexander, was not averse to risk. They had believed in making money by taking risk—by controlling it and limiting it but none the less by being at risk—just as he did. Under his leadership KB had to formulate a strategy in preparation for the day in October 1986 when deregulation would occur 'with a bang'. At KB, as at other City merchant banks, the forecast had to be made about the way in which their competitive position would alter and which, if any, potential acquisitions should be made.

The options under consideration were to enter the securities market through the acquisition of one or more existing stock-market firms or to take the route of selective entry into particularly promising areas. Shortly after Hawkes became chairman the board commissioned an internal policy study, codenamed 'Hermes', to evaluate the issues. This was the first formalized strategic review to emerge from KB and while Hermes did not produce a plan of action, it did serve to focus peoples' minds upon the need to evaluate and structure the business in the long-term. Before consultation papers could even be produced, however, a junior director in the corporate finance division put forward a proposal for KB to purchase a well-respected firm of Far Eastern stockbrokers. The decision-making process proved so lengthy that the day that KB decided to tell the vendors that it might consider buying it was the day the vendors sold it to someone else.

The delay was no doubt caused by the fact that an overall strategy had yet to be agreed—although Martin Jacomb, who was at the leading edge of the Big Bang preparatory studies, together with the chairman of KBL Bobby Henderson (albeit somewhat apprehensively) and the corporate finance division had all concluded early on that KB must enter the securities market. The key consideration was that if KB did not possess a distribution capability in equities its corporate finance business would be eaten away by those who did possess one. The benefits of such a capability were understood as, first, that corporate finance advisers would be able to provide a higher standard of advice and service to clients than hitherto since broking and market-making activities would be supported by extensive in house research facilities; secondly, corporate finance would be able to originate and distribute securities rather than remain reliant for distribution upon a third party; and thirdly, direct access to a wider range of instruments in the international markets would increase the opportunities available to clients.[26]

The corporate financiers maintained that such a capability was essential to protect their underwriting business. They pressed so strongly for the acquisition of a UK broker and jobber that some even put their future on the line. Their view was reinforced by the importance of maintaining a leading position. KB was then one of the largest of the merchant banks with an excellent and innovative spread of business. The momentum was such that it would be difficult to turn its back on the bright lights of quality business, opt out and shrink to end up as a dull little bank. Perhaps KB's misfortune was to have been in such a dominant position just before Big Bang, confidence and optimism colouring and, in certain areas, clouding the decision-making process.

Not all directors, however, were convinced that this was the right strategy. A minority preferred the route that would avoid the stock-market altogether, would focus upon the expansion of existing strengths, and retain the capital base and flexibility to enter areas in the marketplace that were neglected. It is interesting that at the end of the discussion stage which culminated in the Hermes report about KB's strategic response to Big Bang, opposition to entry into the securities market also came from those who possessed hands-on experience of trading, albeit non-equity trading.

Michael Hawkes, however, had recognized that the lending business—historically the staple of the bank's profitability—was in decline through dramatically narrowed margins and higher risks, so that the banking profits needed to be bolstered from elsewhere. He came to believe that the securities business could replace these profits; that other dealing businesses would provide similar rewards to those that the bank's treasury operation provided. The consensus that emerged, therefore, was for KB to become an integrated bank with entry into the securities market through acquisition. This was a strategy initally adopted by Warburgs, Morgan Grenfell, and Hill Samuel and by the clearing banks. Barings and Flemings did not choose this route, preferring to grow their own securities arms, Schröders cautiously put a toe in the stockbroking pool, while Rothschilds took a 50 per cent stake in Smith, New Court, and Lazards focused upon its strong international network.

The number of eligible suitors meant that the announcement of deregulation led to an unseemly rush by a great number, though by no means all, of the City's jobbers, brokers, and bankers headlong into courtship. Thus on 15 November 1983, the very day on which a dinner was to be held for KB's Management Committee to discuss the implications of the final Hermes report, Warburgs announced the purchase of a 29.9 per cent interest in the prime jobbing firm, Akroyd & Smithers. The discussion at the dinner therefore concentrated largely upon the possibility of KB entering into negotiations to purchase another major City jobber, Wedd Durlacher Mordaunt, which was ranked equally highly. As the intensity of bidding for the limited number of stockbrokers and stockjobbers increased, the acquisition price for many of the well-known firms skyrocketed. Although Martin Jacomb was in favour of buying Wedd, the holding company board reached the conclusion, largely on the advice of the non-executive directors, that 'they were too big a bite' of capital. Wedd announced its capture by Barclays Bank on 12 March 1984, but shortly after their final embrace in June 1986 (to create Barclays de Zoete Wedd (BZW), of which house Martin Jacomb subsequently became chairman), one of Wedd's senior partners, Charles Hue-Williams, and a team of seven senior market-makers, unhappy with the prospect of being part of the large Barclays empire, approached KB. They would provide the foundation of KB's market-making capacity in equities.[27]

The next development in KB's strategy was the acquisition of a broker. After looking at five possible candidates, Hawkes and Jacomb selected the long-established firm of Grieveson, Grant. Michael Hawkes's quixotic, off-the-cuff remark to the partnership that 'We would love to have had Capels but are content with Grievesons', has been taken out of context to imply that KB considered Grieveson Grant a second-rank firm. KB had thought about other firms, for example in 1980 KB had been approached by Hoare, Govett & Co. about a four-way international merger with a jobber and an American investment bank; but Hoares quickly fell out, believing a merger would harm its corporate brokerage business, though it eventually turned to the embrace of Security Pacific. It was, however, the firm of James Capel & Co. that Hawkes really wanted—but they were so profitable that he knew such an acquisition would be turned down on price grounds by the KBL board, just as Wedd had been.[28]

Although KB was stymied in the purchase of a top corporate or institutional broker, Grieveson Grant (known as GG) were one of London's largest stockbrokers. They were one of the top three gilt brokers with a good institutional fund management business and a large, low-cost, non-fee paying private client business. Their activity both in Japanese equities and in services to Japanese institutions in the London bond and equity markets was complementary to KB's own strengths in Japan. They also possessed a considerable business in US securities and an office in Boston. The firm had originated with Thomas Grieveson who was listed as a partner in Shepherd & Grieveson in 1869, and John Miller Grant with whom he formed Grieveson & Grant, a reputable but relatively small firm that only emerged from obscurity after the First World War when the foundations of its present business were laid.

Grieveson Grant were, in fact, no strangers to KB for when they had themselves decided to look for the protection of a rich marriage partner after it became clear that dual capacity would be introduced, they asked KB's corporate finance division to advise them. One of the GG partners recalls that 'we had a lot of suitors and must have talked to 12, 15 people, before KB said "Let's take this further", and so our advisors became our predators'. Whereupon negotiations proceeded quite smoothly over the next four months. GG's chief executive, John Brew, remembers 'there wasn't much disagreement except about money though the technicalities were quite difficult to arrange'. At the time of the announcement in June 1984 that KB had acquired an initial 5 per cent interest in GG, the press speculated that the agreed purchase price for 100 per cent would be around £60m., whereas it turned out to be £44m.

Financial terms were not so readily accepted on an individual basis. The agreement to share a common pay-scale could take little account of the soaring salaries or compensation packages then being offered to traders and analysts in the City during the period surrounding Big Bang. Shortly before the merger in April 1986, when KB exercised its option to acquire Grieveson Grant, a dozen GG equity analysts left, lured by better terms elsewhere. This was an unfortunate beginning to what proved to be rocky early years of marriage.

While GG's strengths were a good fit, its very different culture was not easily assimilated. Grieveson Grant remained essentially a personal firm, despite having grown very rapidly to 800 people in the previous year. It suddenly found itself submerged in an organization that seemed much larger (KB then employed some 1,190 staff) and rather bureaucratic. Since the merger of KB's constituent firms twenty-five years before, KB's balance sheet total had grown from £60m. to just short of £6,000m., and group pre-tax profits, with no calls for new capital, had correspondingly grown by a factor of approximately thirty-five times. In cultural terms, therefore, the divide was as wide as that evinced by the Kleinwort and Benson merger that had brought together two very different and differently managed businesses. In 1961 Kleinworts had circulated their internal memos folded with comments scrawled on the back, Bensons had enclosed theirs in an envelope, and neither side had wished to change their habits. In 1985 GG's partners were amazed to receive office memos in 'beautifully inscribed' pristine envelopes: 'We never used a new envelope inside the office. Anyway, we hardly ever wrote to each other—we talked!' they asserted. In the cultural struggles that follow mergers, acquisitions, and marriages, such issues assume a relevance out of all proportion to their importance in the operation of the actual business.[29]

KB's acquisitions were not confined to the United Kingdom since its strategic response to deregulation had also focused upon the establishment of a world-wide chain of operations to provide international securities dealing and distribution. The bank was already trading in new financial instruments such as futures, options, and interest rate and currency swaps. The international capability in this area was greatly enhanced by the recruitment, in 1984, of a team of interest swap specialists, based in Los Angeles, who operated under the corporate title of Kleinwort Benson Cross Financing; Cross being the name of the saviour of Bensons in 1875 as well as indicative of the nature of the financing. It swiftly grew to become a major force in the market, thereby benefiting the firm's other international capital market operations. By 1990 KB would have outstanding over $25 billion of swaps; but, as so often happens with good ideas, the high margins would be arbitraged out by those happy to work on thinner spreads and the operation would thereafter be quietly scaled down.

The firm also positioned itself to exploit the large US market through the acquisition of a US Government Securities broker and a team of interest rate futures brokers, both based in Chicago. *The Economist*, in a major article published in May 1987, prophesied that KB was thereby 'seriously in the running to join the super league of global investment banks centred on London, New York and Tokyo', as 'the great white hope of British merchant banking'. The US investment banks were, however, bigger and much more profitable, and proved far more effective bodyguards of their domestic business than did their UK counterparts; they continued to outdistance this 'great white hope' by protecting their huge US domestic business wherein the volume of transactions was ten times as great as in Europe and the scale of fees was often larger by tenfold than European firms could charge in their own markets.[30]

The Japanese, with their tradition of remembering relationships forged at a time when only the bold would run risks of lending to their institutions, had not forgotten that KB was the first of the major British merchant banks to take this step and also to establish an office in Tokyo. The firm was handsomely rewarded when the Japanese started to tap the international markets from the late 1970s and KB featured amongst the top in the league tables of overseas houses raising money for Japanese financial and commercial companies. The late Sir Fred Warner, British Ambassador in Japan, considered that KB's 'early start and energetic conduct . . . gave it a leading position which it has managed to maintain in various activities ever since'. In 1986 the head of the Tokyo office, Hugh Trenchard, became the first foreign member ever appointed to the General Affairs Committee of the Japanese Securities Dealers Association.

The expansion in the US and Japan, reinforced by the continuing growth of the firm's domestic business, also attracted major companies in these countries as well as Europe to seek KB as a sponsor for their listings on the London Stock Exchange, and this trend was evident in the introductions that the firm handled for household names such as Exxon, Bank of America, Honda, Fuji Bank, Schlumberger, and BASF.

KB's attitude to new acquisitions both at home and abroad remained one of a slack rein in terms of initial control and direction. Grieveson Grant's name was changed to Kleinwort Grieveson and Co. but otherwise it was told that it could run the operation on its own—only if something went wrong would KB tighten the rein. GG's broking arm had moved into No. 20, where premises were available. During the rebuilding of No. 20 after the 1961 merger, there was felt to be no need for a large banking hall but Ernest had insisted KB retain one, reportedly saying 'We are a bank and we *must* have a banking hall.' This 21,000 sq. ft. hall was transformed into a massive trading floor resplendent with 350 dealing positions and the commensurate telecommunication and information systems for the new Kleinwort Grieveson Securities Department. GG's investment management arm, meanwhile, had moved into new premises at the adjacent No. 10, where KB had taken a long lease on a 56,000 sq. ft. building in which their investment management division was housed to accommodate the need for more space and the separation of this business by the Chinese Walls required by deregulation. Yet otherwise, on the surface, everything was much as it had always been as GG continued to trade normally during the six months prior to Big Bang. According to Andrew Rutherford, GG's senior partner, and John Brew, 'it was like a phoney war because you were supposed to deal with other firms as if nothing was going to happen, but running a business and getting ready for a totally different world was not easy'.[31]

After KB purchased the remaining 95 per cent of Grieveson Grant in April 1986, the enlarged group was restructured in preparation for Big Bang in October. The investment management components of KB and GG were combined to form KGIM. The stockbroking and market-making operations created Kleinwort Grieveson Securities (KGS). David Clementi moved over from corporate finance to become managing director of KGS and, recognizing that top quality research was the key to a successful brokerage business, he set about building a capability in this field. The other two arms of the new division were commanded by Charles Hue-Williams, head of market-making, and Sir Nicholas Redmayne from GG, head of sales. KGS by now included a gilt jobber, Charlesworth & Co. Ltd., that GG had suggested KB acquire.

Having made substantial investments in acquiring brokers and jobbers as well as the necessary technology, the roaring bull market in global equities quickly overwhelmed many of the arcane back-office settlement systems in the City. GG had enjoyed a reputation amongst members of the Stock Exchange for possessing an extremely efficient back office, following computerization earlier than most. This led KB to assume that GG knew exactly how to organize the back office of a much larger and quite different operation following Big Bang—an operation dealing for three subsidiaries, one of which paid commission as well as receiving it, and the others acting as principals, not just agents. KB therefore centralized its back offices under GG management in London (cash) and Tunbridge Wells, and closed KBIM's settlements office at Newbury.

As the business volume increased from 2,000 to 8,000 deals a day after 27 October 1986, the back office fell behind in the settlement of contracts to the extent that both KGS and KGIM had to draw heavily on working capital. GG's ageing computer system could not cope with the KGS market-making volume and complexity—hardly surprising since it was not designed for a jobbing back office. This problem occurred in other City back-office operations at Big Bang, and created the build-on effect of increasing everyone's problems. The two back offices which emerged largely unscathed were at Warburgs and BZW, both of whom had bought mature jobbing back-office operations rather than just a team of jobbers without an infrastructure.

The introduction of a new no-frills share-dealing exercise, Sharecall, whereby the public could buy and sell shares quickly and cheaply, was the final straw. Sharecall was not an exercise with which the GG people felt entirely comfortable. As one of their retired partners said, 'it was a cheap business and not something that was appropriate to either merchant banks or a broker like GG'. In the heady days of 1986, however, such a service was felt to be in keeping with Thatcherism's popular capitalism, an encouragement to the small investor to share in the bull market. The back-office fiasco was further fuelled by the lack of a comprehensive accounting system. Again, while GG had possessed a perfectly good system for a broker, it was not an accounting system designed for a broker plus market-maker.[32]

An efficient back-office operation is in fact the real engine of the business. When it breaks down it can bring the whole business literally to a standstill. Once the enormity of the 'gumming up' of trades within the system was realized in 1987, KB moved swiftly to resolve the settlements crisis. Hue-Williams seconded a number of front-office people into the back office to help and in February 1987 David Clementi called in Touche Ross. Subsequently Michael Hawkes hired Rab Harley, Wood Mackenzie's back-office number two, to devise new systems. The board also asked Jonathan Agnew, who amongst other roles had headed Morgan Stanley's London office and had experience of KB as an outside consultant, to join as chairman of the now-named Kleinwort Benson Securities. By August 1987 the problems were easing.

The settlement crisis and the rapid termination of Sharecall were grist to the mill to those who opposed KB's global strategy and entry into the securities market. It was not so much the strategy as its execution that was flawed. In a very short period KB had expanded into a gamut of businesses of which it had very little previous experience. Furthermore, it discovered that it could not rely solely upon acquisitions for this expansion: too many changes were occurring in the market place. KB's resources were thus fully stretched in the period immediately after Big Bang.[33]

1987, however, was made even more memorable when the buoyant bull market of the 1980s came to a sudden halt. The stock market crash on Black Monday, 19 October, occurred almost one year after Big Bang and heralded the beginning of an industry-wide shakeout. While many of their competitors suffered large losses, KB emerged from the crash unscathed and even profitable, due to Hue-Williams and his team of market-makers, who were very swift in turning the books round. Of potentially greater significance was the fact that KB had launched its first, and so far only, rights issue over the same weekend that the stock market crashed. This coupled with the great storm which then devastated large parts of Southern England did not prevent the raising of some £148m. of new capital—by the issue of 1 new share at 450p for every 3 shares then held—to increase the capital resources available for the Group's wider range of businesses (including, of course, the capital required to support the significant sums still locked up in the congested back offices).

The view among financial industry observers was that the sharp decline in equity values would have serious long-term consequences for those investment banks which were either unprepared or unwilling to tolerate loss-making positions. Following the crash, many UK as well as foreign investment banks announced dramatic lay-offs of personnel to cut costs and correct structural overcapacity that had arisen from the overambitious and optimistic expansion of the 1980s. What was clear even then was that it would take several years to realize the real profits arising from integration.

This was as true of the investment management division (which once again operated under the corporate acronym of KBIM) as of the securities division. The investment management area of the firm's business had been physically separated from the merchant banking business for regulatory and other reasons arising from the Financial Services Act of 1987. It, too, experienced difficulties during the initial period of the integration of KBIM and Grieveson Grant, largely owing to their different investment management businesses, described as oil and water by one KB fund manager. KBIM's business was based upon fees whereas GG's was based upon turnover; KBIM had 500 fee-paying accounts of a minimum of £0.5m. compared with GG's 26,000 non-fee-paying, mostly very small, accounts. Initially, 'there was just a dumping down of people together under two managing directors', an eerie echo of the state of the investment division after the 1961 Kleinwort/Benson merger. As in 1961 there was 'a great deal of mutual apprehension' about which side would emerge on top but more than a quarter of a century later tougher decisions were taken under the leadership of Colin Maltby, who was brought from the Geneva office to rationalize the entire operation of over 800 people and to improve the flow of quality earnings.

The Channel Islands subsidiaries had enjoyed an uninterrupted run of rising profits and reputation for over twenty-five years and they and the Swiss subsidiary were now formally brought into the fold of the KBIM management group. In order to maximize the boundaries of the client base to provide clients with more than just the basic stockbroking and portfolio management services, KBIM assembled all these services under the wing of a newly formed

Private Bank which could draw on the authorized banking licence that KBIM also secured. In this manner it could lend directly rather than continue to act merely as an intermediary.

The division also extended the system of charging fees on the value of portfolios to include GG's clients, as GG had always generated income through the commission earned on executing transactions. At first there was internal resistance from the GG people and concern whether this change would be understood and supported by its former private clients, who were an important part of the business. Although there were some GG defections, by and large, the change was accepted and the stability of earnings was enhanced.[34]

The winds of seemingly constant change also blew through the corridors of the 21st floor at No. 20 when a further important restructuring of senior management was announced in November 1987. As Michael Hawkes explained to the staff: 'Both the size and complexity of our operations have increased considerably over the past two years and it now makes sense to manage the Group from the top company.' The separation of ownership from management in 1971 and the changed relationship between the boards of the holding company (KBL) and of the bank (KB Ltd.) were also reflected in this decision. For the first ten years after the merger, basically the same people—a combination of Kleinwort and Benson seniors—had been responsible for guiding the affairs of the whole group, sitting in the main on both the KBL and the KB Ltd. boards. By 1971, there were twelve directors of KBL, a number which rose in 1975 to fourteen with the appointment for the first time of non-executive directors from outside the business. The first of these were Sir Francis Sandilands, chairman of the Commercial Union, and Sir Eric Drake, chairman of BP.

This worked while numbers were small and there was easy communication, but by the 1980s KBL—although the top company—had become very much like a 'House of Lords' and its chairman increasingly had little knowledge of the immediate concerns of KB. This was a system increasingly found at other merchant banks, but one that came to concern the Bank of England. At the time of Morgan Grenfell's involvement in the Guinness affair, the Governor had put a certain amount of pressure on merchant banks to ensure that the chairmen of their respective holding companies were kept both better informed about the health of their subsidiaries and more involved in the daily business for which they were publicly accountable to their shareholders. In the case of KB, ex-chairmen had traditionally moved off the executive management floor but, in consequence of the Governor's suggestion, the chairman of KBL Bobby Henderson moved back onto the 21st floor.

Furthermore, at the time of Big Bang in 1986 the board of KB had grown to an unwieldy forty-nine. The addition of directors from the newly acquired businesses made it so large as to be effective only as an information-spreading and reporting forum. In consequence it was decided to alter the whole structure so as to make the KBL board an operational one. This would provide a Group board that met frequently, knew what was going on, took decisions about budgets and systems and generally acted as 'the Board'. As part of the reorganization package, the KBL board would be strengthened by the addition of nine executive directors, who were responsible for divisional areas of activity, and the chairmanship of KBL would be made a full-time appointment with a retirement age of 60, in line with the KB chairmanship.[35]

Bobby Henderson was asked to defer his retirement from the group chairmanship for an extra year, and Michael Hawkes agreed to step down from the chairmanship of KB at the end of December 1987. His successor David Peake, a tall, determined man, was a good administrator who brought wide experience of different aspects of the firm to the chairmanship. A banker by training, he had headed the Middle East Department in 1974 followed by Project Finance before assuming charge of Group Personnel in 1984, where he oversaw the initial integration of Grieveson Grant in preparation for Big Bang. Outside directorships and a fascination with history, which he read at Oxford, provided further perspective on the rapid mutations the firm would undergo during his chairmanship. David Peake became full-time chairman of the renamed Kleinwort Benson Group PLC on 1 January 1989. At the same time the new post of Group chief executive was filled by Jonathan Agnew, a man of fine intellect and wide City experience who would chair the one executive committee that would effectively run the whole business, reporting to the KB Group board.

In this way greater emphasis was placed upon the management structure of the business, which was timely. At many of the older merchant banks, businesses that had evolved over decades were managed as loose federations mostly trading under the same name. KB's businesses formed a group of separate entities that could duplicate operations and, being in the same line of business but with different reporting lines, could often disagree with each other. This situation was exacerbated by further expansion during the booming markets of the 1980s into too many new businesses without the extra capacity to manage them. In 1989, therefore, Jonathan Agnew set about reorganizing the KB group. He cleared away the undergrowth of peripheral or loss-making businesses, so that the bank could focus upon its core ones and those areas where it could be expected to become very profitable and/or establish itself as a market leader. He also reorganized the divisions, introducing a more effective management structure with clearer divisional reporting lines. All these measures were supported by new budgetary and financial accounting systems, inculcating a cost-consciousness that had risked being overwhelmed by the previous expansion of the business. Risk-management processes had also been put into place, KB installing an executive Assets and Liabilities Committee as early as June 1988.

The management reorganization and efficiency drive did not, however, immediately produce a consistent growth in profitability. The period of the late 1980s and early 1990s witnessed a substantial deterioration in the economic and financial conditions of the main markets as recession bit deeper into the commercial and industrial fabric of Britain and other European countries. Merchant and integrated investment banks had to contend with a greater volatility in profits that seemed to be a new feature of the financial services sector. The volatility was dramatic with the KB Group announcing pre-tax profits of only £18m. in 1988, rising to £83m. in 1989 and then dropping to a significant loss of £68m. in the following year.

By this time Warburgs and KB were the only two independent integrated British merchant banks offering the full range of financial services, but it had proved more testing for KB to make the radical change in its business in the years after Big Bang than for Warburgs. KB possessed a large banking business, long considered by many to be the best in the City. Banking, however, had become unfashionable in the 1980s: it remained very competitive, operating on extremely small margins, and was increasingly seen by some in the City—despite the large foreign exchange profits made by firms such as Goldman Sachs—as yesterday's business in comparison with the more lucrative securities markets. This was reflected externally in Bankers Trust's early-1980s announcement that its future business lay in structuring deals rather than holding banking assets on its balance sheet, and internally by the lack of graduate interest in the division. Against a background of rising bad debts—many originating from lending to more speculative businesses in the United States and to medium-sized United Kingdom companies—and changing perceptions, KB's loan book of £2.3bn. in 1989 was halved and its lending business was reduced and refocused.[36]

As the recession deepened KB's confidence was further undermined by the events of 1990, its *annus horribilis*. On 6 August, in an oil market rising after Iraq's invasion of Kuwait, KBS executed a block trade of 139.9m. Premier Consolidated Oilfields shares bought at 99p with the intention of selling them swiftly on at 103p. The market deemed otherwise. As the shares slipped to 96p KBS was unable to find any buyers, ending up as an enforced holder of 29.7 per cent of Premier, an independent oil company and KB client, until finally placing the tranche at 78p on 17 October.

Premier was an expensive misjudgement, but what made KB's misery worse was that it was not left alone to lick its wounds in private as it had been when nursing previous mistakes; the transaction unleashed the media hounds in a frenzy of publicity so that KB underwent what the *Financial Times* described as 'an experience every company dreads: a profound and very public agony'. The disparaging world-wide coverage (that also included references to KB's lack of judgement in its involvement in the Fayeds' 1984 take-over of Harrods) was as damaging to KB as was the extensive extrapolation about its future by relatively recent media stars, the merchant banking analysts—those financial gurus who are extremely influential but essentially in competition with each other and indeed with the banks upon whom they report, and whose views are invaluable fodder for the financial press.[37]

While the world was being told to write KB off as an effective investment bank, KB was absorbing an important lesson which would eventually enable it to start outperforming such low market expectations: it could only achieve its optimum performance with fully integrated staff and decision-making systems. Looked at in another light, Premier was a catalytic element in fusing closer working relations between the divisions as KB had to broaden its approval procedures across divisional lines. In this way the securities and corporate finance divisions were brought closer together in a new decision-making group that, by encouraging closer co-operation, would start to lay the ghosts of interdepartmental antagonism which had haunted No. 20 since the 1961 merger, but whose presence was especially strongly felt after Big Bang.

In the meantime though, KB's reputation and morale was further undermined when the results for 1990 revealed the Group's first-ever loss which totalled £68m. before tax. This was caused by the loss of £34m. on Premier, substantial losses on Japanese warrants in Tokyo, and an increase in large bad debt charges including nearly £13.6m. lent to an associated Californian venture capital and real estate partnership. Such losses could not be completely absorbed by profits generated elsewhere as they occurred at a time when four of the bank's five divisions experienced a drop in the volume of their business.

Inevitably, KB's status was adversely affected and morale remained low throughout 1991 as it experienced a sharp downturn in winning new business and a loss in market share. All the core activities of the Group continued to undergo difficulties, which gave rise to the *Financial Times*'s widely quoted comment of 19 February 1992 that 'slipping on banana skins has become almost a way of life at Kleinwort Benson' where the cry of 'whoops' was a familiar one. The slow route to realizing the potential released first by the 1961 merger and then by Big Bang has at times been painfully traversed but it is at the low points that firms demonstrate their calibre. As before in its long history, KB's resilience in the face of adversity enabled it to start the climb back to regain quality business and its position as a leading investment bank. It reported pre-tax profits of £26.8m. for 1991 and beat market expectations in 1992 with a further 66 per cent increase in profits to £45.1m.[38]

Having undertaken a complete overhaul of its business over the previous three years, cutting costs and refocusing it, KB was probably better positioned to compete for new business in 1993 than at any time since Big Bang. An indication that it had emerged considerably strengthened from the last challenging, if sometimes harrowing, five years and was starting to recapture market share came when the Group announced pre-tax profits of £111.7m. for 1993. It was able to take advantage of the favourable financial markets to increase fee and commission income, having participated in more than 200 international equity issues and placings and worked on forty-five privatizations in sixteen countries. Furthermore, against a trend of muted take-over activity elsewhere KB became the league leader in 1993, advising on eight deals including Carlton Communication's £723m. purchase of Central Television, the largest one of 1993. 'There is a very good feeling of confidence running through the organisation,' Lord Rockley reported on 17 February 1994. 'We have had a dose of adrenalin.'[39]

After having seen the bank begin to turn the corner of recovery, David Peake had retired as chairman on 28 April 1993, though he remained on the board as a non-executive director. His successor Lord Rockley was no newcomer to the corridors of No. 20, having been one of the young contingent of corporate financiers in the post-1961 merger years. His subsequent achievements had led to his promotion as head of corporate finance in 1983 and he had been a vice-chairman of the Group since 1989. A fair-minded, self-effacing man whose firm, conciliatory approach did much to unite the Group, James Rockley brought efficacy and long business experience to the chairmanship. His outside directorships including Abbey National, Foreign and Colonial Investment Trust, Equity and Law Assurance, and Christie's International, reflected his position as a respected City figure. As he set about improving KB's performance, he confirmed that the integrated and focused approach would remain at the core of the Group's development.

At the same time pressure for a further change in leadership led to the resignation of Jonathan Agnew in August 1993 which paved the way for a new senior management structure. Bearing in mind KB's traditional preference for the home-grown, James Rockley decided to use internal talent of proven ability to run the bank, despite the desire of the non-executive directors to look outside for a replacement chief executive. Whilst the management structure that David Peake had introduced in 1989 was the right one to digest the huge changes that occurred at KB following Big Bang, and was also in accord with the Cadbury Report's emphasis upon the separation of chairman and chief executive roles—it no longer met the needs of the bank's business.

On 1 January 1994 KB returned to a collegiate management structure, the same that had characterized Bensons and numerous City partnerships. The leadership was vested in a chairman's group led by Lord Rockley and his deputy chairman Simon Robertson, a dynamic corporate financier with a formidable reputation as a mergers and acquisition specialist. The other members were Colin Maltby, chief executive of investment management; Sir Nicholas Redmayne, head of securities, and David Clementi, head of corporate finance, who became joint chief executives of investment banking; and Robert Jeens, finance director; in addition Tim Barker became head of Alco, which monitors the important risk-management function.

The KB Group now consisted of two businesses, investment management, and investment banking whose management committees would report to the chairman's group. Lord Rockley said at the time that much progress had been made in developing the integrated approach, which he believed had greatly contributed to the success the Group had had in winning new business, and the new structure formalized this development. In terms of the bank's evolution, while the collegiate approach harks back to the 1961 merger, the existence of only two core businesses is a complete departure from those days. The three-legged stool of core business has been replaced by a two-legged one and it is the previously strongest leg, the banking one, that has disappeared as a separate entity. The Kleinwort bankers would be dumbfounded to learn that Kleinwort, Sons & Co.'s great banking business now forms but a small part of the financing and advisory division within investment banking—but such are the organic changes that have transformed the City since their day, and will continue to do so.

A year later, in the face of more unsettled markets and exceptionally difficult trading conditions resulting from an upward turn in interest rate cycles in the United States and Britain, when other merchant banks were having to cut back and struggle for profits, KB's strategy enabled it to achieve respectable pre-tax profits of £97m. for 1994. Although income from dealing fell by half, income from fees and commissions rose by 14 per cent to nearly £311m., reflecting its emphasis upon client service and relationships. Unlike the large US banks, KB with its more limited capital remained cautious about proprietary trading, preferring to expand its securities and corporate advisory activities, especially in the international arena where it achieved significant growth. As Lord Rockley reiterated 'We are focusing on building businesses that play to our strengths, with a view to steady, measured expansion across the board.'[40]

KB built itself into a leading merchant bank in the 1980s, fell back in the late 1980s and early 1990s, but has survived to become one of the better performing houses. The ability to embrace new ideas and structures and the characteristics of flexibility and resilience in the face of adversity have been strengths displayed by all the constituent parts of what is today the KB Group, and they are the ones that have ensured its survival. The business no longer remains a family fiefdom—indeed family representation was reduced by the death in 1995 of Sir Kenneth Kleinwort, the last Kleinwort on the board. Despite the highs and lows of business cycles and the periodic evolutionary changes that have been imposed by war or Government, the name of the firm and the quality of its people are as valued today as in the founding proprietors' day. Throughout its history, the business of Kleinwort Benson has continued to be undertaken in the same spirit of integrity that epitomized the business of the two firms established over two centuries ago by Hinrich Kleinwort and Robert Benson.

Postscript: A European Union 1995

KLEINWORT BENSON had lived with intermittent though ill-founded take-over rumours since the 1980s and was resigned to living with yet more. These abounded in 1990 when Banque Nationale de Paris (BNP) took a 4.8 per cent supportive stake with a view to forging closer ties and, as BNP was in talks with Dresdner Bank AG of Frankfurt, there was a possibility that Dresdner might also buy into KB. In the event nothing materialized, BNP selling its KB holding in September 1993 but retaining its co-operation agreement with Dresdner.

Given the uncertain nature of the financial services industry, however, the board realized that despite, or even because of, its stronger performance and more stable profitability over the last few years, KB's continued independence might, in fact, not be in the best interests of shareholders or, indeed, staff. When touching upon the subject at a planning meeting in the summer of 1994, the chairman's group members were realistic enough to accept that it might well prove sensible to link up one day with a partner who possessed a bigger capitalization and market penetration and was the right cultural fit—but for the moment, being more than satisfied with the improved progress and profitability, they were keen to retain independence. Not having to find such a partner through necessity, KB would be able to choose its future course, should an approach ever be made, and to negotiate, should it wish, from a position of strength.

Throughout the autumn, however, it seemed as if courtship was in the air among the investment banking fraternity and 'everyone was talking to everyone'. KB, like other merchant banks, received a number of tentative approaches from possible suitors keen to increase their provision of products that span the global markets, in which size and strength are paramount. The better capitalized American investment banks, possessing a large and profitable domestic market, are looking at ways to expand their business outside the United States, especially in the event of the likely repeal of the Glass-Steagall Act of 1933 which would allow commercial banks to enter the investment banking business.

The pace of change within the banking industry undoubtedly accelerated in late 1994 and 1995. The City's self-confidence was shaken by the fate of both its newest and oldest traditional merchant banks. The fate of Britain's premier investment banking group S. G. Warburg only became an issue after its sensible plan to merge with the American investment bank Morgan Stanley fell through in December, which would leave it in a vulnerable position until Swiss Bank Corporation launched an agreed bid of £860m. in May 1995. Warburgs' decision to forgo its independence, despite being the leading British contender in the arena of global investment banks, unleashed intense media speculation about the future of other British investment banks, in particular that of Kleinwort Benson.

In early 1995 the effect of volatile markets and poor global risk control was shown macro-economically by the financial collapse of Mexico and micro-economically by that of Barings Bank. Seemingly overnight Barings was forced into receivership on 26 February, brought down by inadequate management leading to trading losses of £760m. incurred in Singapore. Several billion pounds were subsequently withdrawn from City merchant banks as corporate treasurers and overseas clients switched deposits to what were perceived as 'safer' homes at the larger banks. (Bank of England statistics reveal that deposits held at merchant banks fell from £51.7bn. at the end of February to £46.8bn. at the end of April). Barings was, however, rescued for the sum of its losses by the Dutch group ING. These events served to fuel the media speculation about further banking mergers, in which KB remained at the epicentre.

Then, in the spring, James Rockley told the chairman's group that he had received a telephone call from the chairman of the board of managing directors of Dresdner. 'I'd like to come and see you to talk about how we can develop our business together,' Jürgen Sarrazin had said, 'would you be interested?' After considerable discussion with his group, James Rockley responded 'Yes, we could be—though it depends on certain things and what you have in mind.'

Throughout the next two months KB (codenamed Carat) and Dresdner (codenamed Diamond) held a series of secret exploratory meetings, at which KB was represented by Simon Robertson with either Robert Jeens or David Clementi and Nicholas Redmayne, and Dresdner by Hansgeorg Hofmann with either Horst Müller or Gerhardt Eberstadt; both sides reporting to their respective chairmen, who in turn talked to each other. The talks were a process of working through KB's concerns, finding out about Dresdner's concerns, seeing how KB could fit into Dresdner's structure and gaining sufficient confidence in each other before taking the momentous decision to go ahead and start negotiating the deal—or back out, in which case it was unlikely Dresdner would pursue the matter further since a hostile take-over was not practicable.

Dresdner, like the constituent parts of KB, was an old-established firm. Tracing its origins back to 1772, Dresdner Bank AG has long been one of the great German universal banks, those institutions that came of age in the latter part of the nineteenth century and combined deposit banks, credit banks, and financing companies. Dresdner was one of the four largest German banks in 1905 when it formed a close alliance with J. P. Morgan & Co. in London, New York, and Paris to extend the German market for American securities and play an active role in international finance and issuing. In 1895 it opened its first branch in the City at 65 Old Broad Street, a few doors down from Robert Benson & Co., and it provided serious competition for the British accepting houses—by 1913 its total acceptances were £14.4m. compared with those of the leading British accepting house Kleinwort, Sons & Co. at £13.6m. At the time it was courting KB in 1995, Dresdner was the second largest German bank with a market capitalization of £7.77bn., ranked number 25 world-wide in terms of assets, and had reported net profits for 1994 of over £760m. with a balance sheet figure of about £100bn.

The advantages of having a parent such as Dresdner were easily discernible. As part of the Dresdner group, KB would be better placed to fulfil its ambitions with the support of its parent's capital base and strong credit rating, and with minimum overlap on the investment banking side there would be no need for redundancies or radical restructuring. Dresdner's strengths in asset management, where it ranks comfortably among the top ten asset managers in Europe, in the fixed income sector as a leading Deutsche Mark underwriter, and in the derivatives business would nicely balance KB's recognized expertise in corporate advisory and international equities and research business.

What was less easily discernible at the initial stage was their compatibility: the depth of the cultural differences and what impact Dresdner would have or want to make upon the people at KB in terms of management. It is, as Simon Robertson confirms, 'very important for our people that we can keep our own culture'. It was therefore imperative that KB remained autonomous in the daily operation of its business and reporting structure. There is a huge difference between the styles of a merchant and universal bank. As a medium-size investment bank KB's style of operation is therefore unlike that of a much larger commercial bank such as Dresdner. KB also considered the retention of its staff, their continued loyalty and satisfaction paramount to the success of any change in ownership; it is not so long ago that teams of unhappy people moved elsewhere at the height of Big Bang. It was therefore not until Dresdner could satisfy KB that it recognized and wished to uphold these cultural differences that the negotiations could move forward.

Dresdner quickly provided assurances over autonomy and declared its intention to retain the separate cultures and keep the KB team together, making the sensible decision to manage KB through its existing structure rather than try to adapt it to Dresdner's structure. Finding Dresdner people straightforward, confident of their agenda, but flexible and sensitive to KB's needs, and wanting to make the acquisition work, the directors were increasingly convinced that now was, after all, the time to join hands with another firm, and Dresdner was the right partner.

By Wednesday 14 June widespread speculation about KB's future had pushed its shares to a peak of 724p and on the following morning James Rockley announced that Dresdner had proposed the possibility of a recommended cash offer for KB at around its current market price. On 26 June Jürgen Sarrazin declared Dresdner's formal recommended final cash offer to acquire 100 per cent of the KB Group, saying 'two proud banking houses are combining forces'. Dresdner had considered a strong presence in London essential and rather than build organically, it had decided to acquire an existing successful business: 'KB is the best and most excellent fit.' In recommending the offer to KB's shareholders, James Rockley explained at the press conference that KB would be able to realize its ambitions more quickly and with greater certainty than if it had remained independent. It was, he said, a case of controlled expansion for KB.

On 7 August 1995 KB was acquired by Dresdner Bank for £1 billion. Although the firm is in a sense returning to German ownership—the first Kleinwort business was founded in Altona (now part of Hamburg) in 1786—it retains its name and its autonomous business, and remains a British firm rooted in London. Dresdner, however, in the company of other Continental banks, is following in the footsteps of those eighteenth- and nineteenth-century banking houses such as Rothschilds, Barings, Hambros, Schröders, and Kleinworts whose arrival in London built the City into the undisputed financial centre. In the Bank of England's opinion, 'the City has always thrived in the presence of foreign institutions. It is the competition between them that drives innovation.' Through its union with a Continental European bank of the stature of Dresdner, Kleinwort Benson is now even better placed to secure its future and meet the challenges which lie ahead over the next 210 years.

SOURCE NOTES

The main sources for the corporate history of Kleinwort Benson are the firm's own records, which have been divided into two collections. The first was deposited in the Guildhall Library in 1980 and consists of the accounts ledgers and information books of Kleinwort, Sons & Co., and its constituent firms, dating from 1862–1965. The second collection (KB Archives) remains at Fenchurch Street and comprises correspondence, letter books, deeds, and departmental papers dating from the early nineteenth century. Although much of this archive was lost or destroyed in the years leading up to the closure of the firm's Newbury office in 1989 when the remaining papers were transferred to Fenchurch Street, what survives provides a more personal, if random, view of the Kleinwort and Benson firms.

Three unpublished studies of the history of the firm have been deposited in the KB Archives: Cecil Elbra, 'Age of Endeavour' (n.d.), Nicholas Fitzherbert, 'Sir Alexander Kleinwort, Herman Kleinwort and their Bank' (1988), and S. Chapman and S. Diaper, 'The History of Kleinwort Benson Ltd.' (1984), all of which considerably illuminate aspects of KB's history.

Other relevant papers are to be found in the archives of banks such as Rothschilds, Barings, Morgan Grenfell, Schroders, Glyns, and Hambros. The literature on the financial services industry is a burgeoning one and it would be inappropriate to list all the printed works I have consulted, many of which are referred to in the notes. Among the works which I found most helpful are Stanley Chapman's seminal study, *The Rise of Merchant Banking in the Nineteenth Century* (London, 1972); Philip Ziegler, *The Sixth Great Power of Europe: Barings 1762–1929* (London, 1988); Kathleen Burk, *Morgan Grenfell 1838–1988* (Oxford, 1988); Richard Roberts, *Schroders* (London, 1993); Ron Chernow, *The House of Morgan* (London, 1990); and David Kynaston's splendid trilogy, *The City of London* (London, 1994; 1995), i and ii—vol. iii is forthcoming.

As for the family history, of especial value for the Bensons are the letters exchanged between members of the family dating from the eighteenth century, and the unpublished diaries of Rex Benson; other relevant manuscripts are the early Benson documents in the Armitt Library, Ambleside; the Grey family papers at the University of Durham Library; the Cropper papers in the Merseyside Maritime Museum Library; and the Rathbone papers in the University Library, Liverpool. On the Kleinwort side, the most significant papers are the unpublished journal and correspondence of Alexander Friedrich Kleinwort at Mainz; the unpublished diary of Wilhelmina Martin; Herman Andreae's papers; and Sir Alexander Kleinwort's letters and Black Book. It would again be unnecessarily prolix to list all the relevant secondary literature since reference is made to the most important in the source notes. The most pleasing works, however, are undoubtedly Robert Benson's illustrated catalogues of *The Holford Collection at Westonbirt* (London, 1924), *The Holford Collection, Dorchester House* (Oxford, 1927), 2 vols., and *The Catalogue of Italian Pictures Collected by Robert and Evelyn Benson* (London, 1914).

ABBREVIATIONS USED IN SOURCES

ADK	Sir Alexander Drake Kleinwort
AFK	Alexander Friedrich Kleinwort
Andreae MSS	Andreae family papers, Fenchurch Street
Armitt MSS	Armitt Library, Ambleside
BBA	Baring Brothers Archives, Bishopsgate
BL	British Library
Blackwood MSS	National Library, Edinburgh
Bus. Hist. Rev.	*Business History Review*
Bute MSS	Marquis of Bute papers, Cardiff
CEB	'Con', Constantine Benson
CHK	Cyril Kleinwort
Cropper MSS	Maritime Museum Archives, Liverpool
CUL	Cambridge University Library
CWB	Constantine Benson, brother of Robin
DHB MSS	Benson family papers, private collection
Drake MSS	Moorsom family papers, private collection
EB	'Evey', Evelyn Benson
EES	Ernest Evan Spicer
EGK	Ernest Kleinwort
Elbra MSS	Cecil Elbra papers, KB Archives
GHB	Guy Benson
Girtin MSS	Girtin family papers, private collection
GL	Guildhall Library
GPSM	'Phil' Macpherson
Grey MSS	Earl Grey papers, University of Durham
GS & Co.	Goldman Sachs & Co.
HAA	Herman Andreae
Hambro MSS	Hambro Bank papers, Guildhall Library
HGK	Herman Kleinwort
HKA	'Sonny', Herman K. Andreae
Int(s).	Interview(s)
KB	Kleinwort Benson & Co.
KBA	Kleinwort Benson Archives, Fenchurch Street
KBL	Kleinwort Benson Lonsdale & Co.
KDK	Kenneth Kleinwort
KS & Co.	Kleinwort, Sons & Co.
Lace MSS	Lace Mawer papers, Liverpool

LIT	Lonsdale Investment Trust
Mainz MSS	Kleinwort family papers, private collection
MB MSS	Benson family papers, private collection
Morse MSS	Grey family papers, private collection
NB MSS	Benson family papers, private collection
NJF	Nicholas Fitzherbert
Peake MSS	Kleinwort family papers, private collection
Pollen MSS	Benson family papers, private collection
PRO	Public Record Office
Rathbone MSS	Rathbone papers, Liverpool University Library
RB & Co.	Robert Benson & Co.
RB jnr.	Robert Benson junior
RB	Robert Benson
RBL	Robert Benson Lonsdale & Co.
RFP	'Lindy', Rosalind Pollen
RHB	'Robin', Robert Benson
RLB Diary	Rex Benson's diary, unpublished, private collection
RLB	Rex Benson
RRB	Robert R. Benson
SRB	Sarah Benson
SSA	Schwerin State Archives
Tolson MSS	Cropper family papers, private collection
Tomkins MSS	Benson family papers, private collection
ULH	University Library, Hamburg
White MSS	Kleinwort family papers, private collection
WSK	Wilhelmina Kleinwort

SOURCES

CHAPTER I

1. 1786 Commercial Almanack, University Library, Hamburg; int.: with Dr Ladiges, Oct. 1990; T. Sadler (ed.), *H. Crabb Robinson, Diary, Reminiscences & Correspondence* (London, 1869), i. 69, 19–20.
2. Dr McEwan int. with Dr K. Schikorski, 6 July 1990; Anon., *Stadt an der Elbe Marsch und Geest* (Holstein, 1962), 88; Adolf Ladiges, *Die 500 jahrige Geschichte des Fahrhofes zu Wedel* (privately printed, Wedel, 1980), 29–33; *Jahrbuch für den Kreis Pinneberg 1980* (Pinneberg, 1980); ints.: Dr Ladiges, Joachim Kleinwort, Oct. 1990; Hamburg notes on Kleinwort family history, trans. Dr McEwan; Johannes von Schröder and Herm. Biernatzki (eds.), *Topographie der Herzogtümer Holstein und Launenburg*, i (Oldenburg, 1855).
3. *Encyclopedia Britannica* (London, 1970), i. 691; Robert Gittings and Jo Manton, *Dorothy Wordsworth*, pb. (Oxford, 1988), 89; E. G. Griggs (ed.), *Collected Letters of Samuel Taylor Coleridge*, 6 vols. (Oxford, 1956–71), i. 435.
4. Griggs (ed.), *Letters of S.T.C.*; misc. records, ULH.

5. Walter H. Bruford, *Germany in the 18th Century* (London, 1935), 179–81; Eduard Rosenbaum and A. J. Sherman, *Das Bankhaus M. M. Warburg & Co. 1798–1938* (Hamburg, 1976), 10–11.
6. Petition, 15 Jan. 1790, 3. I. 352, Rigsarkhivet, Copenhagen, Denmark.
7. Misc. records, ULH; Gerdeshagen Estate papers, SSA; G. Freytag, *Bilder ans der Deutschen Vergaugenheit* (Hamburg, n.d.), iii. 9; Bruford, *Germany in 18th Cent.*, 127–8.
8. Gittings and Manton, *Dorothy Wordsworth*, 89; Bruford, *Germany in 18th Cent.*, 164.
9. Commercial Almanacks, 1786–9, 1792, 1796, 1799, 1805, ULH.
10. Sir Alexander Duff Gordon (ed.), *Varnhagen von Ense's Memorabilia, Travels in Europe & Germany* (London, 1847), 23; E. H. Fehling, *Veroffentlichungen zur Geschichte der Freien und Hansestadt Lübeck* (Heftl, 1925), vii. 104, 109; A. G. Martin, unpubl. typescript, History of the Lübeck Members of the Family, n.d., Mainz MSS.
11. Emil Frithjoff Kullberg, *Hinrich Dultz & Söhne* (Hamburg, 1920–39), 1–229.
12. Int.: Dr Ladiges; TKIA Vorstellungen, I. 274, 24 Mar. 1786, Rigsarkhivet Copenhagen, Denmark; Brüchregister: 5 Jan. 1786, fo. 186, 3 Jan. 1787, fo. 7, 27 July 1789, fo. 34, 4 Aug. 1790, fo. 47, 6 Aug. 1804, fo. 101, 4 Jan. 1808, fo. 145, 2 Sadtbücher Altona V61, Staatsarchiv Hamburg.
13. Gerdeshagen estate papers, SSA; Misc. records, ULH; 'Publikprotokolle', 2 Stadtbücher Altona IVa, vols. V–IX, Staatsarchiv Hamburg; int.: Joachim Kleinwort; 1214 Archiv des Patronats d. St. Johannisstifts, Altona 1821, Staatsarchiv Hamburg.
14. William Rathbone IV to RB, 17 Nov. 1786, Rathbone MSS, II. 1. 3.
15. Id. to id., 23 Sept. 1786, Rathbone MSS, II. 1. 2.
16. Paul H. Emden, *Quakers in Commerce and Industry* (London, 1939), 34–5.
17. William Rathbone IV to RB, 17 Nov. 1786, Rathbone MSS, II. 1. 3.
18. John Rutter to Abigail Dockray, 18 Mar. 1835, Rathbone MSS, I. 1. 4.; Emily A. Rathbone (ed.), *Records of the Rathbone Family* (London, 1913), 15; 'Proceedings of the Committee for the Abolition', 7 June 1787, BL Add. MSS 21254, vol. I, and Thomas Clarkson, *History of the Abolition of the Slave Trade by Parliament* (London, 1808), i. 143; F. E. Sanderson, 'Liverpool Abolitionists', in R. Anstey and P. Hair (eds.), *Liverpool, The African Slave Trade & Abolition*, Historical Society of Lancashire and Cheshire, Occasional Series, 2 (1976), 222 n. 23; Eleanor Rathbone, *William Rathbone: A Memoir* (London, 1905), 28; Sanderson, 'Liverpool Abolitionists', 199.
19. Alms 105, fos. 118, 132, Armitt MSS; Dr John Benson, Historical Notes, MB MSS; M. Armitt, *Fullers & Freeholders of Grasmere* (Kendal, 1908), 160, 141; D. W. Jones, *The Bensons of Cote How*, Cumbria Lakeland and Borders Magazine (Dec. 1968), 445–6.
20. Alms 130, fo. 7, Armitt MSS.
21. Christopher Hill, *A Turbulent, Seditious and Factious People* (Oxford, 1988), 16; R. H. Tawney, *The Agrarian Problem of the Sixteenth Century* (London, 1912), 383; Hill, *Turbulent People*, 16.
22. Alms 106, fo. 66, Armitt MSS; P. Bowden, 'Agricultural Prices, Farm Profits and Rents', in J. Thirsk (ed.), *The Agrarian History of England and Wales*, iv. 1500–1600 (Cambridge, 1967), 620–1; G. H. Sabine (ed.), *The Works of Gerrard Winstanley* (Ithaca, NY, 1941), 252.
23. E. Burrough, *A Word of Reproof* (London, 1659), 71–7; Hill, *Turbulent People*, 98.
24. Armitt, *Fullers and Freeholders*, 169–70.
25. *Piety Promoted*, 1 (1812), 565; Elizabeth J. Satterthwaite, *Records of the Friends' Burial Ground* (Ambleside, 1914), 28.
26. J. Besse, *Collections of the Sufferings . . . of the Quakers* (London, 1753), i. 674.
27. John Somervell, *Isaac and Rachel Wilson, Quakers of Kendal* (London, 1924), 11.
28. Alms 106, fo. 74, Armitt MSS.
29. Satterthwaite, *Records*, 28.

30. Daniel Defoe, *A Tour Through the Whole Island of Great Britain*, pb. (London, 1971), 549–50; Alms 106, fo. 74, Armitt MSS.
31. J. O. Lindsay (ed.), *The New Cambridge Modern History*, vii (Cambridge, 1957), 243, 59.
32. Thomas Clarkson, *A Portraiture of Quakerism* (New York, 1806), ii. 42; J. D. Marshall, *The Rise and Transformation of the Cumbrian Market Town* (Lancaster, 1970), 141.
33. Alms 106, fo. 74, Armitt MSS.
34. Ibid. 122, fos. 8, 9, 13.
35. Ibid. 106.
36. Sir G. Chandler, *Four Centuries of Banking* (London, 1964), ii. 31; Benson family notes, NB MSS; Partnership Agreement, MB MSS.
37. Somervell, *Isaac and Rachel Wilson*, 89.
38. John Satchell & Olive Wilson, *Christopher Wilson of Kendal* (Kendal, 1988), 45.
39. RB to SRB, 27 Jan. 1782, DHB MSS.
40. W. J. Reader, *A House in the City* (London, 1979), 22.
41. William Rathbone IV to RB, 15 Feb. 1787, Rathbone MSS, II. 1. 5.
42. RB to SRB, 27 Jan. 1782, DHB MSS.
43. Sanderson, 'Liverpool Abolitionists', 200; Mrs Eustace Greg, *Reynolds/Rathbone Diaries and Letters* (London, 1905), 4; Eleanor Rathbone, *William Rathbone*, 27–8.
44. Gomer Williams, *History of the Liverpool Privateers* (London, 1897), 187–9; S. G. Checkland, *The Gladstones: A Family Biography 1764–1851* (Cambridge, 1971), 27.
45. Thomas Fletcher, *Autobiographical Memoirs* (privately printed, Liverpool, 1893), 37; Eleanor Rathbone, *William Rathbone*, 55.
46. Eleanor Rathbone, *William Rathbone*, 11.
47. G. Williams, *Liverpool Privateers*, 300–1; Fletcher, *Memoirs*, 25.
48. Chandler, *Four Centuries*, 48; S. G. Checkland, *Gladstones*, 32.
49. G. Williams, *Liverpool Privateers*, 304, 315; John Hughes, *Liverpool Banks and Bankers 1760–1837* (Liverpool, 1906), 14–15.
50. The Book of Discipline as Revised by the Yearly Meeting for Pennsylvania and New Jersey in the Year 1719, Swarthmore MSS, pp. 15, 76; George Fox, *Journal of George Fox* (London, 1891), ii. 186.
51. Alsop & Hicks, Letter Book 1791–6, pp. 74, 192, New York Historical Society.
52. G. Williams, *Liverpool Privateers*, 324–5.
53. SRB to RRB, 22 Feb. 1800, DHB MSS.
54. Greg, *Reynolds/Rathbone*, 81; SRB to RRB, 4 Jan. 1801, DHB MSS; Greg, ibid. 82; SRB to RRB, 23 May 1801, DHB MSS; Greg, ibid. 88.

CHAPTER 2

1. RB to Matthias Maris, 27 Jan. 1802, DHB MSS.
2. RB to James Cropper, 22 May 1795, Cropper MSS, D/CR/10/26; Anne Cropper (ed.), 'Extracts from Letters of the late James Cropper' (privately printed, n.d.), Tolson MSS.
3. Partnership Agreement, 1 Sept. 1799, Cropper MSS, D/CR/2/2; RB to Maris, 27 Jan. 1802, DHB MSS; RB Will and Codicils, Cropper MSS, D/CR/1/30.
4. SRB to RRB, 20 Mar. 1800, and 4 Jan. 1801, DHB MSS.
5. William Rathbone IV to his father & Richard Rathbone, 22 Sept. 1803, Rathbone MSS, II. 1. 10.
6. M. R. and J. R. Audubon and Elliot Coules, *Audubon and His Journals* (London, 1898), i. 114.

7. H. F. Chorley, *Autobiography*, ed. H. G. Hewlett (London, 1873), ii. 270–1.
8. William Rathbone IV to his father and Richard Rathbone, 7 Dec. 1806, Rathbone MSS II. 1. 12.; G. Williams, *Liverpool Privateers*, 407.
9. Thomas Cropper to RRB, 23 July 1807, DHB MSS; A. Cropper (ed.), 'Extracts'.
10. Greg, *Reynolds/Rathbone*, 137; Eleanor Rathbone, *William Rathbone*, 34; Greg, ibid. 142.
11. G. Williams, *Liverpool Privateers*, 433; Thomas Cropper to RRB, 22 July 1813, DHB MSS.
12. Thomas Cropper to RRB, 25 July 1813, and John Cropper to RRB, 2 Aug. 1813, DHB MSS.
13. B. Nightingale, *Early Stages of the Quaker Movement in Lancashire* (London, 1921), 34; David Steel, *Laurence Binyon and Lancaster* (Lancaster, 1979), 4; David Dockray Will, 1807, Lace MSS.
14. Emden, *Quakers in Commerce*, 64; Cropper MSS misc., Tolson MSS.
15. Hughes, *Liverpool Banks*, 22–3; Thomas Cropper to RRB, 30 Dec. 1818, DHB MSS.
16. Eleanor Rathbone, *William Rathbone*, 63.
17. Robert G. Albion, 'Planning the Black Ball', in *Mystic Seaport Magazine*, 21–4; Cropper, Benson Circulars, n.d. Press Clippings, DHB MSS; Eleanor Rathbone, *William Rathbone*, 64.
18. Cropper, Benson & Co. Cotton Circular, cited in T. P. Martin, 'Some International Aspects of the Anti-Slavery Movement', in *Journal of Economic and Business History*, 1/1 (Nov. 1928), 137–48; Thomas Cropper to RRB, n.d. March 1819, DHB MSS; Checkland, *Gladstones*, 122.
19. James Cropper to William Wilberforce, n.d. 1821, Press Clippings, and to Joseph Sturge, 14 July 1827, Letter Book, ed. Anne Cropper, Tolson MSS.
20. Vincent Nolte, *Fifty Years in Both Hemispheres* (London, 1854), 314–18, 299–302, 325–30; Edward Cropper to James Cropper, 26 Nov. 1824, Cropper MSS, D/CR/10/43.
21. John Cropper & David Hodgson to RRB, 7 Sept. 1821, DHB MSS; Sir William Colebrooke to RRB, 18 May 1823, DHB MSS; William Cobbett, *Rural Rides*, ed. G. D. H. and M. Cole (London, 1930), i. 193, iii. 964, 990; David Hodgson to RRB, 7 Sept. 1821, DHB MSS.
22. Edward Cropper to James Cropper, 26 Nov. 1824, Cropper MSS, D/CR/10/43.
23. Hughes, *Liverpool Banks*, 27–8; Chandler, *Four Centuries*, 81, 85; John Gladstone to William Huskisson, 1 Aug. 1826, Gladstone MSS, cited in Checkland, *Gladstones*, 155.
24. John Dockray to RRB, 4 Mar. 1827, DHB MSS; Hannah Dockray to Margaret Benson, 29 Apr. 1828, Bundle E, Pollen MSS; RRB to Elizabeth Fry, 5 Nov. 1827, DHB MSS.
25. Checkland, *Gladstones*, 173–4; S. Brasier to RRB, 3 Mar. 1825, DHB MSS; Sir Herbert Maxwell, *The Creevey Papers* (London, 1905), 429; James Cropper to Eliza Cropper, 10 Aug. 1831, Cropper MSS, D/CR/10/58.
26. H. Menzies to Gisbournes, 5 Jan. 1831, and 24 Dec. 1830, 10 Aug. 1834, BBA, HC 6. 3. 1.
27. RRB to Jardine Matheson & Co., 28 June, 21 Nov. 1834, Jardine Matheson Archives, microfiche, CUL; Checkland, *Gladstones*, 317.
28. 'The Cropper Family of Dingle Bank', Tolson MSS.
29. RB jnr. to RRB, 20 Apr. 1836, DHB MSS.
30. RB jnr. to William Benson, 9 June 1836, DHB MSS.
31. RB jnr. to RRB, 8 July 1836, to Margaret Benson, 27 Aug. 1836, and to RRB, 20 Apr. 1836, DHB MSS; Messrs. Cropper, Benson & Co., List of Ships 1752–1840, Cropper MSS, D/CR/16/5; E. A. Woods, Liverpool Fleet Lists, v. 1 (Typescript *c.*1939), Liverpool City Library.
32. Eliza Isichei, *Victorian Quakers* (London, 1970), 9, 55; James Foster to RRB, 26 May 1837, DHB MSS; Isichei, ibid. 46.
33. Overseers of the Liverpool meeting to RRB, 25 Oct. 1836, DHB MSS; Isichei, *Victorian Quakers*, 47; Thomas and Anna Braithwaite, *J. Bevan Braithwaite: A Friend of the Nineteenth Century* (London, 1909), 65, 88; R. L. Brett (ed.), *Barclay Fox's Journal* (London, 1979), 15.

34. Dissolution of Partnership Circular, 30 Jan. 1838, Cropper MSS, D/CR/2/6.
35. Margaret Benson to RRB, 9 May 1844, DHB MSS.
36. Anon. (Sarah Green), *Quakerism: or the Story of My Life* (Dublin, 1851), 285.
37. Mary Benson to John Dockray, 28 June 1817, Pollen MSS.
38. RRB to Mary Benson, 27 Apr. 1819, and Margaret Benson to Rachel Foster, 25 Jan. 1822, DHB MSS.
39. William Rathbone V to William Rathbone IV, 18 Sept. 1840, 28 Dec. 1838, Rathbone MSS.
40. R. Speake and F. R. Whitty, *A History of Droylesden* (Manchester, 1953), 91; RB jnr. to RRB, 21 Nov. 1844, DHB MSS.
41. Margaret Benson to RRB, 23 May 1840, DHB MSS.
42. Id. to id., 9 May 1844, and Henry Worthington to RB jnr., 2 Apr. 1841, DHB MSS.
43. Worthington to RB jnr., ibid.
44. Margaret Benson to RRB, 23 May 1842, DHB MSS.
45. Donald Read, *Cobden and Bright* (London, 1967), 49; *Manchester Times*, 9 July 1842; RRB to RB jnr., 9 Nov. 1843, DHB MSS.
46. Harold Pollins, *Britain's Railways* (Devon, 1971), 35–40; *Companion to the Almanack 1846*, ed. Knight (London, 1846), 72, 86.
47. D. Morier Evans, *The Commercial Crisis 1847–1848* (London, 1849), 3; Emily Rathbone (ed.), *Records*, 117.
48. RB jnr. to RRB, 31 Oct. 1844, DHB MSS.
49. Eleanor Rathbone, *William Rathbone*, 120; RB jnr. to RRB, n.d., DHB MSS.
50. RB jnr. to RRB, 21 Nov. 1844, DHB MSS; A. Redford, *Manchester Merchants and Foreign Trade 1794–1858* (Manchester, 1934), 84.
51. RRB Will and Codicils, Cropper MSS, D/CR/1/30.

CHAPTER 3

1. Nicholas Fitzherbert, 'Sir Alexander Kleinwort, Herman Kleinwort and their Bank', unpublished typescript, p. 4, KBA.
2. Bruford, *Germany in 18th Cent.*, 195, 261; *Lexikon der Hamburgischen Schriftstelle bis zur Gegenwart* (Hamburg, 1857), 617.
3. Int.: Joachim Kleinwort.
4. WSK to AFK, 13 Apr. 1834, KBA; AFK Journal and Letter Book, KBA.
5. Mack Walker, *Germany and the Emigration 1816–1885* (Cambridge, Mass., 1964), 64–5, 39, 60.
6. Curt Schmack, *J. C. Godeffroy & Sohn* (Hamburg, 1938), trans. Dr McEwan; information from Dr McEwan, July 1990.
7. AFK to Herr Höber, 8 July 1838, AFK Letter Book, Mainz MSS.
8. Cecil Elbra, 'Age of Endeavour', unpublished typescript, p. 14, KBA.
9. AFK to Herr Höber, 8 July 1838, Letter Book, Mainz MSS; WSK to AFK, 2 Oct. 1838, KBA; AFK to Herr Höber, ibid.; William C. Bryant, 'Letters from Cuba', 1 Apr. 1849, in *Littell's Living Age*, 22 (July 1849), 13; Madame Calderon de la Barca, *Life in Mexico* (repr. in pb., London, 1987), 14.
10. AFK to Siegmund Kleinwort, 10–11 May 1839, and AFK to Hermann Kleinwort, n.d., Letter Book, Mainz MSS.
11. AFK to Herr Höber, 18 Mar. 1842, Letter Book, Mainz MSS.
12. AFK to Adolph Höber, 30 July 1838, to Herr Höber, 18 Mar. 1842, and to Adolph, ibid.

13. AFK to Ferdinand Karck, 21 June 1839, KBA; AFK to Adolph Höber, 30 July 1838, 4 May 1839, ibid.
14. Arthur Behrend, *Portrait of a Family Firm* (Liverpool, 1970), 199.
15. AFK to Siegmund Kleinwort, 10 Aug. 1838, and to Herr Höber, 8 July 1838, Letter Book, Mainz MSS.
16. AFK to Herr Mohring, 30 Sept. 1839, ibid.
17. AFK to Theodor Karck, 17 Aug. 1839, ibid.
18. AFK to Herr Höber, 19 Jan. 1839, and to Ferdinand Karck, 21 June 1839, ibid.
19. Samuel Byerley to Baring Brothers & Co., 30 Mar. 1837, BBA, HC 161. 1.; AFK to Herr Höber, 4 May 1839, Letter Book, Mainz MSS.
20. Richard H. Dana, *To Cuba and Back* (London, 1859), 32–3; Sir James Alexander, *Transatlantic Sketches* (London, 1833), i. 320.
21. AFK to Theodore Karck, 14 Jan. 1840, Letter Book, Mainz MSS.
22. Elbra, 'Age of Endeavour', 3–5, and information collected by him about the Drake family, Elbra History File, KBA.
23. Roland T. Ely, *From Counting House to Cane Field* (Harvard Ph.D. thesis, 1958), 441, 448; AFK to Theodor Karck, 14 Jan. 1840, Letter Book, Mainz MSS; Sir Charles Murray, *Travels in North America during the Years 1834, 1835 and 1836* (London, 1839), ii. 246–7, 252.
24. AFK to Ferdinand Karck, 4 July 1840, KBA.
25. AFK to WSK, 27 May 1840, and to Ferdinand Karck, 4 July 1840, KBA; J. Morales to H. Coit, 14 Feb. 1852, quoted in Ely, *Counting House*, 483; AFK to Herr Höber, 14 May 1841, Letter Book, Mainz MSS.
26. AFK to Herr Höber, 18 Nov., 26 Mar., 16 July 1842, ibid.
27. Morales to Coit, 13 May 1842, 17 July 1845, Ely, *Counting House*, 452, 1012.
28. AFK to Herr Höber, 17 Sept. 1842, Letter Book, Mainz MSS.
29. AFK to Herr Höber, 4, 6, 15 May, 6 June 1843, ibid.
30. AFK to Drake & Co., 25 Sept. 1843, ibid.
31. Morales to Coit, 19 Oct. 1849, Ely, *Counting House*, 481.
32. AFK Journal, Letter Book, KBA.
33. Morales to Coit, 6 June, 5 Aug. 1843, 1 Apr. 1847, 17 Oct. 1850, 19 Jan. 1851, Ely, *Counting House*, 478.
34. Morales to Coit, 18, 1 Oct. 1851, ibid., and Circular Drake Bros. & Co. (Havana) sent to Moses Taylor & Co. (New York), 31 Dec. 1851, ibid. 471, 478–9, 472.
35. Morales to Coit, 7 Mar. 1853, 14 May 1857, 25 Jan. 1845, ibid. 478–9.
36. id. to id., 26 Sept. 1855, 25 May 1857, Phil. S. Shelton to M. Taylor, 28 Dec. 1850, Shelton File, Moses Taylor Collection, New York Public Library; Circular Kleinwort & Cohen (London) to Moses Taylor & Co. (New York), 1 Jan. 1855, Drake Circular Files, Moses Taylor Collection, all quoted ibid. 472.

CHAPTER 4

1. Emma Steinkoff to Minnie Martin, 16 Nov. 1886, Greverus Family History, Mainz MSS; Elbra, 'Age of Endeavour', 11.
2. Sophie Greverus to Mathilda, 13 Jan. 1852, White MSS; Frederika Greverus notes, 12 Feb. 1831, Peake MSS.
3. Lt.-Col. A. G. Martin, 'The Captain Remembers', n.d., 24, Mainz MSS.

4. D. Morier Evans, *The City* (London, 1845), pp. v, 163; Charlotte Brontë, *Villette* (London, 1967), 48; Roger Fulford, *Glyn's 1753–1953* (London, 1953), 11.
5. Eleanor Benson to Constantine Moorsom, 7 Sept. 1843, Drake MSS; ints.: with Elaine Drake, Christopher Moorsom; notes on Moorsom family history, Drake MSS; *DNB*, 388.
6. Fulford, *Glyn's*, 124, 121, 133; B. W. Currie, *Recollections, Letters and Journals 1827–1896* (London, 1901), i. 95–6.
7. Partnership Deed, 1858, KBA.
8. Int.: Tom Girtin; Girtin Family History, fos. 55–8, Girtin MSS.
9. Elbra, 'Age of Endeavour', 25; Development of No. 20 file, KBA; Minnie Martin's Diary, 21 Aug. 1866, Mainz MSS.
10. KS & Co. Ledgers 1860–70, KBA.
11. Minnie Martin's Diary, excerpt, 1866, White MSS.
12. Elbra, 'Age of Endeavour', 27.
13. Partnership Papers, KBA; AFK to Edward Cohen, 31 Dec. 1883, KBA.
14. Elbra, 'Age of Endeavour', 31.
15. Reader, *House in the City*, 40, 47–9; M. Wilkins, *The History of Foreign Investment* (Cambridge, Mass., 1989), 110.
16. Read, *Cobden & Bright*, 40.
17. Robert Benson, *The Amalgamation of Railway Companies* (London, 1872), 1–30; Robert Benson, *Indian Resources applied to the Development of India* (London, 1861), 3; Barings Report, July 1857, BBA; Barings Customer Reference Books, 'Europe', I no. 369, BA; P. C. Glyn's Letter Book, fos. 46–7, 202, Glyn's Archives.
18. P. C. Glyn, ibid.
19. *The Times*, 11 May 1866; William Benson to Robert Dockray, 12 Apr. 1865, Pollen MSS.
20. Robert Dockray to RB jnr., 2 Dec. 1854, 17 Jan. 1867, Pollen MSS.

CHAPTER 5

1. Int.: Peter Wake.
2. ADK to Mr Engels, 15 Jan. 1886, Peake MSS; H. Wedemayer to Minnie Martin, 15 May 1886, notes on the Greverus family, fo. 5, Peake MSS.
3. Lt.-Col. A. G. Martin, *Mother Country Fatherland* (London, 1936), 5.
4. Walter Bagehot, *Lombard Street* (London, 1931), 253.
5. ADK to Charley Brown, 5 Oct. 1871; AFK to ADK, 10 Oct. 1874, 20 Jan., 28 Feb. 1875; Robert Martin to ADK, 27 July 1875; AFK to ADK, 14 Jan., 12 Feb., 4 May 1875, Peake MSS.
6. AFK to ADK, 2 Dec. 1874, Peake MSS; Charley Brown to ADK, 22 Nov. 1874, Peake MSS; Annette Donger's memo no. 2; Minnie Martin's Diary, 30 Apr. 1866, Mainz MSS; ADK to Charley Brown, 21 Oct. 1875, Peake MSS.
7. AFK to ADK, 23 Apr. 1875, Peake MSS.
8. AFK to ADK, 2 Dec. 1874, 23 June, 15 July 1875, ibid.
9. AFK to ADK, 4 May 1875, ibid.
10. A. Dietz, *Frankfurter Handelsgeschichte* (Frankfurt, 1925), ii. 580; Heinrich Hoffmann, *Lebenserinnerungen* (Frankfurt, 1926); Robert De Cleremont to G. Martin, 13 Apr. 1869, Mainz MSS; Minnie Martin's Diary, Mainz MSS; int.: Col. Alexander Martin; Martin, *Captain Remembers*, 24.
11. EGK to Cecil Elbra, notes on ADK, 18 Sept. 1964, KBA.

12. HGK to Edward Cohen, 15 Jan. 1886, KBA; ADK to H. P. Winter, 16 Jan. 1886, and H. Albert de Bary, 15 Jan. 1886, KBA; Linton Wells, The House of Seligman, typescript, i. 88–9, New York Historical Society Library, cited in S. D. Chapman, *The Rise of Merchant Banking in the Nineteenth Century* (Oxford, 1972), 72–3; Georgina Meinertzhagen, *A Bremen Family* (London, 1912), 253–4.
13. AFK's Letter Book, n.d., KBA; ADK's Black Book, Peake MSS.
14. Sir Godfrey Style to author, 23 July 1989, KBA; ADK's Black Book, Peake MSS.
15. Elbra, 'Age of Endeavour', 31; Chapman, *Rise of Merchant Banking*, 43.
16. KS & Co. to Edvard Stolterfoht, 27 Sept. 1886, 4, 24 May 1888, 25 June 1889, KBA.
17. ADK's Black Book, Peake MSS.
18. *Punch* and *Daily Graphic*, 15 Feb. 1890, Press Clippings file, KBA.
19. Ints.: Sir Kenneth Kleinwort, David Peake.
20. AFK's Letter Book, KBA.
21. Commission Book, and Winter & Smillie Correspondence Book, KBA.
22. Stephen Birmingham, *Our Crowd*, pb. (New York, 1968), 98–9; Walter Sachs to Cecil Elbra, 8 Dec. 1959, KBA.
23. Birmingham, *Our Crowd*, 153; Cecil Elbra to Stanley Miller, 17 Dec. 1959, KBA.
24. ADK's Black Book, Peake MSS; Birmingham, *Our Crowd*, 154.
25. Ints.: Walter E. Sachs, 1956, 1964, Columbia Aural History Collection, Columbia Univ. Library, NY., and US *v.* Henry S. Morgan *et al.*, Corrected Opinion, pp. 19–21, and Transcript of Trial, pp. 6652–5; Barry E. Supple, 'A Business Élite', in *Bus. Hist. Rev.*, 31 (Summer 1951), 172–4; Vincent P. Carosso, *The Morgans* (Cambridge, Mass., 1987), 498; Prospectuses, KBA; Joseph Wechsberg, *The Merchant Bankers* (London, 1967), 304.
26. Leslie Dennett, *The Charterhouse Group 1925–1979* (London, 1979), 73; AFK to ADK, 26 Jan. 1875, Peake MSS; Ivo Forde memo, 14 May 1985, KBA.
27. HAA to Henri Hoechstaedter, 15 June 1911, KS & Co. Correspondence File 1911, & KS & Co. to Henri Hoechstaedter et Cie, 2 Aug. 1912, KS & Co. Correspondence File 1912, KBA; Ely, *Counting House*, 454–5; Edward Grenfell to Willard Straight, 1 Jan. 1914, Private Letters Book 10, fos. 806–7, Morgan Grenfell Papers, cited in K. Burk, *Morgan Grenfell* (Oxford, 1989), 71.
28. Chapman, *Rise of Merchant Banking*, 74; A. Ellis, *Heirs of Adventure* (London, 1960), 121; Brown Shipley Private Letters, 24 Sept. 1897, and 3, 17 May 1899, Brown Shipley Archives, Guildhall Library; Cecil Baring to Lord Revelstoke, 3 Nov. 1900, (B) PF3, BBA; EES to EGK, 7 Oct. 1940, KBA.
29. ADK to Herman Sielcken, 19 Aug. 1907, Crossman & Sielcken Letter Book, KBA.
30. National Monetary Commission, USA, p. 38, cited by Chapman, *Rise of Merchant Banking*, 124; Ivo Forde memo, 14 May 1985, KBA; Chapman, ibid. 124; ADK to Herman Sielcken, Crossman and Sielcken Letter Book, KBA; Mr Arnold to R. Bridle, 27 Nov. 1959 and HAA's note, KBA; KS & Co., Union Discount notes, 30 Nov. 1953, p. 5, KBA; ints.: Pepe Mayorga; EGK's note re Union Discount Co., n.d., KBA; KS & Co., Profit and Loss Accts., KBA.
31. Elbra, 'Age of Endeavour', 36; KS & Co., Profit & Loss Accts., KBA; ADK's Black Book, 30 Mar. 1908, Peake MSS; Elbra to Stanley Miller, KBA; ADK's Black Book, 16 Apr. 1908, ibid.
32. Int.: Mark Andreae; Martin, *Captain Remembers*, 24; Minnie Martin's Diary, n.d. 1888, Mainz MSS.
33. Ints.: Annette Donger, Joan Kleinwort; Minnie Martin's Diary, n.d. 1888, Mainz MSS.
34. Elbra, 'Age of Endeavour', 35; KS & Co. Salary Ledger, KBA; ints.: Henry and Mark Andreae; KS & Co. Salary Ledger; int. Henry Andreae.
35. Ivo Forde memo, 14 May 1985, KBA; ints. Sir Godfrey Style.

36. Ints. Henry Andreae, Sir Godfrey Style, Joan Kleinwort, Sir Kenneth Kleinwort, Marguerite White; NJF, 'Sir Alexander Kleinwort', fo. 33, KBA; int.: with Martin Renner.
37. Ints. Marguerite White, Tom Troubridge; Alexander's Discount Co. report, 25 Mar. 1897, p. 2, KBA.
38. Etiennette Kleinwort to EGK, *c.* Apr. 1942, KBA; int. Annette Donger; Martin, *Captain Remembers*, 25; int.: NJF with Herbert Heys.
39. HKA to HAA, 3 Sept. 1947, and HAA to EGK, 11 Nov. 1960, Andreae MSS.
40. KS & Co. Commission Books, KBA; N. & S. Wales Bank Ltd., 12–14 May 1897, Midland Bank Archives, M 153/47/3; Stirling Karck to Cecil Elbra, 30 Sept. 1949, KBA.
41. Paul Vansittart, *Voices from The Great War* (London, 1981), 251–2.
42. Smith, St Aubyn & Co.'s Diary, 31 July 1914, MS 14,894 vol. 24, Guildhall Library; N. M. Rothschild & Sons Archives, X/130A/8, 31 July 1914; Elbra, 'Age of Endeavour', 38; Conference between the Chancellor of the Exchequer, Members of the Cabinet and Representatives of the Accepting Houses, 12 Aug. 1914, PRO T 172/134.
43. E. V. Morgan, *Studies in British Financial Policy 1914–25* (London, 1952), 7–8; Sir Henry Clay, *Lord Norman* (London, 1957), 76–7; *The Times*, 3 Aug. 1914, press clippings, KBA.
44. Richard Spiegelberg, *The City* (London, 1973), 72; Conference, 12 Aug. 1914, PRO T 172/134; Elbra, 'Age of Endeavour', 38; HAA to the governor, 9 Oct. 1914, KS & Co. Correspondence Files 1914, KBA.
45. Edward Grenfell to W. Porter, 7 Jan. 1916, cited in Burk, *Morgan Grenfell*, 79; Philip Ziegler, *The Sixth Great Power of Europe: Barings 1762–1929* (London, 1988), 321.
46. Montagu Norman to Caroline Brown, 7 Aug. 1914, cited by Andrew Boyle, *Montagu Norman: A Biography* (London, 1967), 98; City of Edmonton misc. papers, KBA.
47. Ints.: with Pepe Mayorga.
48. Birmingham, *Our Crowd*, 382; *The Times*, Sept. 1915; HAA to Arthur Sachs, 24 Nov. 1915, KS & Co. Correspondence Files 1915, KBA.
49. KS & Co. to GS & Co., 18 Oct. and 1 Jan. 1915, 12 July 1916, KS & Co. Correspondence Files, 1915 and 1916, KBA.
50. M. V. Brett (ed.), *Journals and Letters of Reginald, Lord Esher* (London, 1934), iii. 180; Princess Christian to Lady Agneta Montagu, 20 Aug. 1914, Sandwich MSS, fo. 234B; ints.: Annette Donger, Martin Renner, Sir Godfrey Style.
51. F. Crisp to Sir William Plender, 19 Dec. 1914, KBA; HAA to Sir John Bradbury, 14 Dec. 1914, KBA; George Karck to HAA, 27 Jan. 1915, KBA.
52. Ints.: Sir Godfrey Style; *The Times*, 16, 17 June 1916; Michael Cowan, 'Capital, Nation and Commodities', in *Capitalism in a Mature Economy*, ed. J. J. van Helten and Y. Cassis (London, 1990), 199; int.: Martin Renner.
53. Ints.: Sir Kenneth Kleinwort, David Peake, Sir Godfrey Style; Jack Pease's Diary, 3 Dec. 1909, Gainford Papers, vol. 38 F10.
54. Ints.: Pepe Mayorga; Ivo Forde memo, 14 May 1985, KBA.

CHAPTER 6

1. Ints.: Elaine Drake; misc. Drake family papers; RHB to RFP, 4 Aug. 1922, Pollen MSS.
2. RHB to RFP, 16 Oct. 1924, Pollen MSS.
3. H. E. Wortham, *Victorian Eton and Cambridge* (London, 1956), 54; RB jnr. notes on envelope, n.d., Pollen MSS.

4. W. Johnstone, *England as it is . . . in the Middle of the Nineteenth Century* (London, 1851), ii. 99–100; *Eton Chronicle*, press clipping, 14 Mar. 1864, DHB MSS.
5. Elizabeth Gaskell, *North and South* (London, 1897), 64; Richard Gatty, *Portrait of a Merchant Prince: James Morrison 1789–1857* (York, 1976), 171.
6. Robert Dockray to RB jnr., 4 Oct. 1866, Pollen MSS.
7. A. M. S. Methuen, *Oxford: Life and Schools* (London, 1887), 132.
8. Frances Horner, *Time Remembered* (London, 1933), 2; H. J. L. Graham to RLB, 13 Apr. 1929, DHB MSS.
9. Minnie Morley to Dow. Ct. of Morley, 3 May 1887, Morley Papers, BL Add. MSS 48257 vol. XL.
10. Information from The Honourable Society of the Inner Temple.
11. G. G. T. Treherne and J. H. D. Goldie, *Record of the University Boat Race* (London, 1884), 133–6, 139–40; *The Times*, 13 Jan. 1875, p. 6.
12. Benson *v.* Benson affidavit, 7 Feb. 1876, ref. J4/13, PRO; Edgar Jones (ed.), *The Memoirs of Edwin Waterhouse* (London, 1988), 102.
13. H. M. Hyndman, *Commercial Crises of the Nineteenth Century* (London, 1892), 89; In Memoriam, n.d., p. 2, DHB MSS.
14. *The Times*, 1 June 1875, p. 9; *The Economist*, 5 June 1875, p. 676.
15. Benson *v.* Benson affidavit of Charles Fricker, 12 Dec. 1877, ref. J4/270, PRO; Fulford, *Glyn's*, 178; Benson *v.* Benson, E. Waterhouse statement, 22 Mar. 1877, C/16/989/213B, PRO; *The Times*, 17 June 1875, p. 6; *The Economist*, 19 June 1875, p. 732; Character Book 12, pp. 21, 66, 69, BBA.
16. Benson *v.* Benson, Deposition of Robert Wigram, 22 Mar. 1877, C/16/989/213B, PRO.
17. Ziegler, *Sixth Great Power*, 187; Cecil Roth, *The Sassoon Dynasty* (London, 1941), 52.
18. R. W. and M. E. Hidy, 'Anglo-American Merchant Bankers and the Railroads of the Old Northwest 1848–1860', in *Bus. Hist. Rev.*, 35 (1960), 160; W. S. Clarke to Marq. of Bute, 30 May 1846, Misc. Papers, Bute MSS; C. Wilkins, *History of the Iron and Tinplate Trade* (Merthyr Tydfil, 1903), 154, *The Times*, 17 June 1875, p. 6; *The Economist*, 19 June 1875, p. 732.
19. Edwin Waterhouse's Diary, 1875, p. 169, Price Waterhouse Archives.
20. Benson *v.* Benson, depositions of James Moorsom and Andrew Kelley, ref. J4/13, PRO; James Moorsom to William Benson, 23 July 1883, and Opinion of Counsel, 20 Mar. 1878, Bundle C., Pollen MSS.
21. T. H. S. Escott, *England: Its People, Polity and Pursuits* (Oxford, 1885), 554.
22. RHB to EB, 18 Oct. n.d., DHB MSS; In Memoriam, n.d., DHB MSS.
23. *The Times*, 25 Sept. 1875, p. 6.
24. RHB to EB, n.d. [*c*.1904], DHB MSS; Edith Simcox, Simcox Autobiography MSS, 6 Jan. 1879, cited in Gordon Haight, *George Eliot* (London, 1985), 6, 518–19, 543; Acts of Parliament of Scotland, ix. 378; Norio Tamaki, *The Life Cycle of the Union Bank of Scotland 1830–1854* (Aberdeen, 1983), 4; D. P. O'Brien (ed.), *The Correspondence of Lord Overstone*, 3 vols. (Cambridge, 1971), ii. 762; S. G. Checkland, *Scottish Banking* (London, 1975), 466–9; *Memoirs and Portraits of 100 Glasgow Men* (Glasgow, 1886), i. 101; Elizabeth D. Kane (ed.), *The Autobiography of William Wood* (New York, 1895), i. 318, ii. 352.
25. Cross Benson accounts, 1878–82, microfilm, KBA; Haight, *George Eliot*, 459; Johnny Cross to William Blackwood, 15 Feb. 1885, Blackwood Papers, FF. 224–5.
26. R. H. Benson, 'The English Community in Iowa', in *Macmillan's Magazine*, 44 (May 1881), 65.
27. Sir J. Jeans, *Railway Problems* (London, 1887), 49; R. L. Nash, *A Short Inquiry into the Profitable Nature of Our Investments* (London, 1881), 47; Wilkins, *History*, 190, 115.

28. R. H. Benson, *State Credit and Banking*, privately printed (London, 1918).
29. G. W. Smalley, *Anglo-American Memories* (New York, 1911), ii. 223; R. G. Dun (now Dun and Bradstreet) credit registers, Baker Library, Harvard University, vol. 146 p. 100, vol. 200 p. 396.
30. *Le Mars Sentinel*, 13 Apr. 1882, p. 2; Jacob van der Zee, *The British in Iowa* (Iowa, 1922), 108.
31. CWB to William Benson, 17 July 1886, Pollen MSS; Edwin Waterhouse's Diary, 1875 fo. 196–7, Price Waterhouse Archives.
32. W. B. Close, *Farming in North-Western Iowa* (London, 1880), 15–24; William Close to James Close, n.d. Nov. 1879, Close Papers, cited by Curtis Harnack, *Gentlemen on the Prairie* (De Kalb, Ill., 1984), 66–7; May Benson to William Benson, 2 Jan. 1880, Pollen MSS; Harnack, ibid. 64.
33. William B. Close, *The Prairie Journal* (Iowa, 1878), cited in Harnack, ibid. 4, and *The Times*, 1, 2 Dec. 1879 (letters).
34. Laurence M. Woods, *British Gentlemen in the Wild West* (London, 1990), 3, 46–7, 53–4.
35. van der Zee, *British in Iowa*, 75, 145; Harnack, *Gentlemen*, 5; *Harper's New Monthly Magazine*, 62 (Apr. 1881), 764; R. H. Benson, 'English Community', 67.
36. van der Zee, *British in Iowa*, 102, 101.
37. RHB to Ker Dunlop, n.d. (*c*.1928), DHB MSS.
38. Ker Dunlop to RLB, 20 June 1929, DHB MSS.
39. RBL Capital and Profits memo, App. I, KBA.
40. R. Michie, *The London & New York Stock Exchange* (London, 1987), 45–6; D. R. Adler, *British Investment in American Railways, 1834–98* (Charlottesville, Va., 1970), 146, 148–9; Chapman, *Rise of Merchant Banking*, 95–8.
41. Susan M. Alsop, *Lady Sackville* (London, 1978), 59–61; Lady Evey Jones, Facts and Add. Memo, 1883, Morse MSS; RHB, Memorabilia, fo. 5, DHB MSS; Alsop, ibid. 64.
42. *Dubuque Daily Times*, 31 Aug. 1886, and *Historical Atlas of Chicksaw County, Iowa* (Chicago, 1915), 6; H. Roger Grant, *The Corn Belt Route* (Illinois, 1984), 10; RHB, Memorabilia, fo. 6, DHB MSS.
43. A. W. Currie, 'British Attitudes Toward Investment in North American Railroads', *Bus. Hist. Rev.*, 34 (1960), 207; Herapath's *Railway and Commercial Journal*, 1 May 1875; Beatrice Webb, *My Apprenticeship* (Cambridge, 1979), 7–8.
44. W. T. Jackson, *The Enterprising Scot* (Edinburgh, 1968), 48; *New York Herald* quoted in *Edinburgh Courant*, 22 January 1883; *Investor's Review*, 4 July 1894, pp. 21–4; Herbert O. Brayer, *William Blackmore* (Denver, 1949), ii. 274.
45. R. H. Benson, *State Credit*, 45; Grant, *Corn Belt*, 4, 12; RHB to RLB, 12 Aug. 1927, DHB MSS; *Dubuque Daily Times*, 24 Sept. 1879, and George M. Craig, 'The Dubuque & Dakota Railroad', in *Great Western Magazine* (May 1922), 8–9; RHB to RLB, 12 Aug. 1927, DHB MSS; RHB to Everard Hambro, 23 Oct. 1888, 19,063/28, Hambro MSS; *Investment Dealers' Digest*, 7 Oct. 1991, and *Financial Times*, 23 Aug. 1991, press clippings, KBA.
46. RHB note on J. S. Cotman picture, Pollen MSS; E. F. Benson, *As We Were* (London, 1930), 250–1.
47. R. H. Benson (ed.), *The Holford Collection, Westonbirt* (privately printed, 1924), 27; Lady Evey Jones, Holford notes, Morse MSS; A. N. L. Munby, *Connoisseurs and Medieval Miniatures* (Oxford, 1972), 147–56; Lady Evey Jones, ibid.; Dr Gustav Waagen, *Treasures of Art in Great Britain* (Switzerland, 1912), ii. 193–222; Lady Evey Jones, ibid.; Christopher Hussey, 'Dorchester House', *Country Life*, 63 (5 May 1928), 652–3.

48. RHB to Albert Grey, 2 Sept., 20 Aug. 1884; George Holford to Albert Grey, n.d. [14–20 Aug. 1884], Grey MSS; Margaret Crawford to Maysie Holford, 9 May 1887, Pollen MSS.
49. Margaret Morley to Dow. Ct. of Morley, 3 May 1887, Morley Papers, BL Add. MSS 48257, vol. XL; Lady Evey Jones, Holford notes, Morse MSS; Minnie Morley to Dow. Ct. of Morley, 23, 7 May 1887, ibid.; Harriet Wantage to Maysie Holford, 14 May 1887, DHB MSS; Margaret Crawford to Maysie Holford, 9 May 1887, ibid.
50. Dearman and Emily Birchell, *A Victorian Squire* (London, 1983), ed. David Verey, 197; Augustus Hare, *Story of My Life* (London, 1900), i. 448.
51. EB to Maysie Holford, 5 Aug. 1887, DHB MSS.
52. The Survey of London, *The Grosvenor Estate in Mayfair* (London, 1980), pt. II, vol. xl, p. 266; Jonah Jones to GHB, 8 Sept. 1943, NB MSS; Thomas Loyd to GHB, 12 Sept. 1943, NB MSS.
53. EB to Maysie Holford, 3 Dec. 1887, DHB MSS.
54. Robert Fleming to Mr Phelps, 24 Jan. 1881, cited by NJF in 'Robert Fleming Holdings' (1983), 241; Jackson, *Enterprising Scot*, 22–3; Wilkins, *History*, 494; RHB notes, n.d., DHB MSS.
55. RHB to RFP, n.d., Pollen MSS.
56. R. H. Inglis Palgrave, 'An English View of Investments in the United States', in *Forum*, 15 (Apr. 1893), 199; Merchants Trust Report, 1892, KBA; *Statist* (1894), 313, ibid. (1889), 432, ibid. (1890), 519, 565, ibid. (1891), 351; Merchants Trust Reports, 1892, 1901, KBA.
57. Thomas to Evelyn Baring, 14 Nov. 1890, Baring MSS (B) DEP 84; S. G. Checkland, 'The Mind of the City 1870–1914', *Oxford Economic Papers*, 9/3 (Oct. 1957), 274; Richard Meinertzhagen, *Diary of a Black Sheep* (London, 1964), 267; R. Medlicott memo, 17 Oct. 1983, KBA; Wilkins, *History*, 470; Max Wirth, 'The Crisis of 1890', *Journal of Political Economy*, 1 (1893), 234.
58. Grant, *Corn Belt*, 32; 'The Story of the "Maple Leaf"', *Investors' Review*, 2 (Nov. 1893), 637–46; Sir John Clapham, *Bank of England* (London, 1944), ii. 359; *The Economist*, 15 Sept. 1894, p. 1140.
59. H. P. Isham, Report on Clearing Industrial District, Aug. 1949, and letter to RLB, 7 Jan. 1952, KBA; press clippings, 20 July 1971, KBA.
60. James Morris, *Heaven's Command* (London, 1980), 521–2; John Buchan, *Lord Minto* (London, 1924), 105.
61. RHB to Albert Grey, 6 June 1896, Earl Grey MSS; James Morris, *Pax Britannica*, pb. (London, 1979), 96; CWB to Albert Grey, 19, 29 Sept. 1896, Earl Grey MSS.
62. RHB to Albert Grey, 30 June, 9 Nov. 1899, Earl Grey MSS.
63. RHB to EB, 23 Jan. 1902, DHB MSS; Albert Grey to Elsie Grey, 30 Dec. 1902, Morse MSS.
64. Ranald Michie, 'The Finance of Innovation in Late Victorian and Edwardian Britain: Possibilities and Restraints', *Journal of European Economic History*, 3/17 (Winter 1988), 493; A. G. Whyte, *The Electrical Industry* (London, 1904), 73; L. Hannah, *Electricity Before Nationalisation* (London, 1979), 10; R. H. Benson, 'Episodes of Business and Finance', in Lady Wantage, *Lord Wantage: A Memoir* (London, 1907), 304–5; I. C. R. Byatt, *The British Electrical Industry 1875–1914* (Oxford, 1974), 102–3.
65. Hon. James Lindsay, *More Lives of the Lindsays* (privately printed, n.p., 1970), 255–6, 265.
66. Lady Wantage, *Lord Wantage*, 307; RHB to EB, 25 Feb. 1904, DHB MSS.
67. Merchants Trust Report, 26 Feb. 1907, KBA.
68. Arthur Pound and Samuel Taylor Moore (eds.), *More They Told Barron* (New York, 1931), 36.
69. *The Times*, 23 Nov. 1900, p. 12, and 25 Nov. 1900, p. 5.
70. EB to Maysie Holford, 13 June 1900, DHB MSS; RHB to EB, 1, 3, 17 July 1900, DHB MSS.
71. RHB to Cecil Benson, 29 July 1897, NB MSS.

72. *The Times*, 20, 26 Nov. 1901, pp. 4, 3; RHB to EB, 7 Mar. 1902, DHB MSS; Mary Cropper, On an American Tour, n.d., Tolson MSS; Pound and Moore, *They Told Barron* (New York, 1930), i. 85; P. L. Cottrell, *Industrial Finance 1830–1914* (London, 1980), 232–3; Robert Jones and Oliver Marriott, *Anatomy of a Merger* (London, 1970), 43, 60–2, 50; C. F. Adams to RHB, 2 Mar. 1907, DHB MSS; R. H. Benson, *The Knell of Laissez Faire* (East Grinstead, 1907), 11.
73. *The Times*, 23 Nov. 1909, p. 8; R. H. Benson, *The Knell*, 8; Avner Offer, 'Empire and Social Reform', *Historical Journal*, 261 (1983), 129.
74. Morris, *Heaven's Command*, 517.
75. Ranald Michie, 'The Social Web of Investment in the Nineteenth Century', *Revue Internationale d'Histoire de la Banque*, 18 (1979), 166; Albert Grey to Lord Wantage, 10 Apr. 1899, and RHB to Albert Grey, 16 Aug. 1908, Earl Grey MSS.
76. RHB to Albert Grey, 6 June 1896, Earl Grey MSS; RHB to unidentified correspondent [Charlie], 16 Sept. 1897, DHB MSS; RHB notes for Arthur Balfour, 14 Sept. 1897, NB MSS.
77. Gerald Reitlinger, *The Economics of Taste* (London, 1961), 199; Lord Crawford to GHB, n.d., NB MSS.
78. Robert and Evelyn Benson, *The Benson Collection of Italian Pictures* (privately printed, London, 1914), p. vii; EB to Maysie Holford, 7 Feb. 1893, DHB MSS; RHB to RFP, 20 Apr. 192? (n.d.), Pollen MSS; RHB to George Holford, 24 Feb. 1893, DHB MSS; ints.: David Benson.
79. RHB to Albert Grey, 6 Aug. 1896, Earl Grey MSS; RHB to GHB, 10 Mar. 1908, NB MSS.
80. D. S. MacColl (ed.), *Twenty-Five Years of the National Art Collections Fund* (Glasgow, 1928), 5; Sir Charles Holmes, *Self and Partners* (London, 1936), 221; RHB to Lord Balcarres, 27 Nov. 1905, 26 Jan. 1906, DHB MSS; MacColl (ed.), *National Art Collections Fund*, 2.
81. Lord Curzon to RHB, 20 Jan. 1912, d'Abernon Papers, BL Add. MSS 48930, fo. 14; Holmes, *Self and Partners*, 320 n.
82. Y. Cassis, 'Bankers in English Society in the Late Nineteenth Century', *Economic History Review*, 38/2R (May 1985), 225.
83. *KB Magazine* (Spring 1982), 23.
84. Int.: David Glynne, and information from John Glynne.
85. RB & Co. Ledgers, KBA; *Statist*, 8 Mar. 1913, p. 501; Countess of Wemyss, *A Family Record* (London, 1932), 239.
86. Ziegler, *Sixth Great Power*, 322.
87. RB & Co. Ledgers, KBA.
88. RHB to Arthur Balfour, 3 Dec. 1915, DHB MSS.
89. Sir Rennell Rodd, *Social and Diplomatic Memories* (London, 1922–5), 276.
90. R. H. Benson, *State Credit*, 47.

CHAPTER 7

1. KS & Co. Ledgers 1920–8, KBA.
2. Russian Accounts, 1914–35, 24 Apr. 1917, fos. 67–8, BBA; int.: Michael Hawkes; l'Azoff Don file, KBA; NJF int. with Harold Heys.
3. Henri Hoechstaedter to KS & Co., 24 Feb. 1921, and to J. R. Shortis, 7 Aug. 1918, Trefoil Syndicate file, KBA.
4. NJF int. with Henri Jacquier.
5. HAA to Arthur Sachs, 27 Oct. 1920, GS & Co. file, KBA.
6. Charles Henderson memo, 28 Oct. 1920, KBA; HAA to Arthur Sachs, 27 Oct. 1920, GS & Co. file, KBA; *The Times*, 10 Sept. 1965, p. 12; HAA to Arthur Sachs, 24 Apr. 1919, KBA.

7. NJF int. with Eric Pratt; Brian Widlake, *In The City* (London, 1986), 146; int.: Henri Jacquier; ints.: Gerald Thompson, NJF with Eric Pratt.
8. NJF int. with Harold Heys; Ernest Pudney's reminiscences, KBA.
9. Pudney, ibid.; int.: Henri Jacquier.
10. Ints.: Gerald Thompson; NJF with Eric Pratt.
11. Stirling Karck to Cecil Elbra, 30 Sept. 1949, KBA; Int.: Gerald Thompson; Pudney's reminiscences, KBA.
12. Ints.: Pepe Mayorga, Gerald Thompson; NJF with Ivo Forde; Mayorga; Henri Jacquier; Mayorga; Sir Norman Biggs; Biggs's notes on KS & Co.
13. KS & Co., Barcelona Ledger, 1920–3, KBA.
14. Paul Einzig, *The Fight for Financial Supremacy* (London, 1931), 52; G. H. Bateman to Lord Curzon, 20 Nov. 1922, no. 276 FO/371/8440, PRO; D.o.T. to FO, 24 Jan. 1923, A480/19/9FO/371/8440; Bateman to Lord Curzon.
15. Ints.: Pepe Mayorga; Pudney's reminiscences, KBA.
16. German Ledgers 1920–30, KBA; Kux, Bloch & Co. file, KBA.
17. Max Warburg, 'Aus meinen Aufzeichsungen' (unpubl.), cited by J. Atali, *A Man of Influence* (London, 1986), 85, 91; NJF int. with Harold Heys.
18. Ints.: Mayorga.
19. EES to KS & Co., 27 May 1920, KBA; D.o.T. memo, 25 Jan. 1923, FO 371/8440 PRO.
20. Ints.: Henri Jacquier, Gordon Tettmar; Marigold Bridgeman, Mrs Grenyer; Sir Godfrey Style; Tettmar; Pepe Mayorga; Tettmar.
21. Ints.: Henry Andreae, Annette Donger; NJF with Gerald Thompson.
22. EES to HAA, 10 July 1935, KS/HAA/6, Andreae MSS.
23. Ints.: NJF with Cecil Elbra; Henry Andreae.
24. Ivo Forde memo, 28 May 1985, KBA; ints.: Mark, Henry, and Peter Andreae; NJF with Walter Michaelis; Tom Troubridge.
25. Ints.: Sir Godfrey Style, Marigold Bridgeman.
26. EGK to Cecil Elbra, 5 Oct. 1967, Points and Queries of Substance, Elbra MSS, KBA.
27. Int.: Annette Donger, and her memo no. 3; int.: Joan Kleinwort.
28. EGK to Cecil Elbra, 30 Jan. 1963, Elbra MSS KBA.
29. Ints.: Joan Kleinwort, Annette Donger; NJF with Ivo Forde; Sir Godfrey Style.
30. Ints.: Annette Donger, Joan Kleinwort.
31. EGK to Cecil Elbra, 30 Jan. 1963, Elbra MSS KBA; ints.: Joan Kleinwort; Harold Heys; with Mrs Milroy.
32. Int.: Henry Andreae.
33. EGK to Cecil Elbra, 30 Jan 1963, Elbra MSS KBA; Ivo Forde's notes; S. Diaper int. with CHK, cited in S. Chapman and S. Diaper, 'The History of Kleinwort Benson Ltd.', unpublished typescript, 1984, KBA; int.: Harold Heys.
34. Pudney's reminiscences, KBA; NJF int. with Leonard Judd.
35. Int.: Henri Jacquier; Pudney's reminiscences, KBA.
36. Ivo Forde memo, 28 May 1985, KBA.
37. J. Kinross, *Fifty Years in the City* (London, 1982), 56; Michael Hawkes to Lord Tenby, 1 Sept. 1983, KBA; Marquis of Winchester, *Statesmen, Financiers and Felons* (London, 1934), 250; Associated Automatic Machine Co. Ltd. file, KBA.
38. NJF int. with Ivo Forde; *The Times*, 9 Oct. 1934, p. 19; Ivo Forde memo, 2 Aug. 1984, KBA; ints.: John Andreae, Mark Andreae; KS & Co. to R. A. Workman, 11 July 1918, EES to HAA, 31 July 1918, KBA; Northumberland Shipping Co. files, KBA; Ivo Forde memo, 28 May 1985, KBA.

39. Andrew Boyle, *Montagu Norman* (London, 1967), 212; Statement of Claim, KS & Co. *v.* AAM Co. Ltd., 19 July 1930, KBA; Reader, *House in City*, 152.
40. Cecil Elbra, 'Age of Endeavour', 45–6; NJF int. with Ivo Forde; int.: Henry Andreae.
41. Sir Alexander Kleinwort's accounts, 1929–31, and Moonhill Trust accounts 1929–30; Ivo Forde memo, 28 May 1985; Sir Mark Turner's memorial address, 21 Oct. 1980, all KBA.
42. Boyle, *Montagu Norman*, 261.
43. EGK's German Reparations files, KBA; Spicer & Pegler memo, 23 Jan. 1942, Andreae MSS; A. C. Bull to governor, 11 June 1936, Bank of Eng. Archives, C48/396, cited in R. Roberts, *Schroders* (London, 1993), 265; Boyle, *Montagu Norman*, 264.
44. HAA and EES notes, n.d. 1940, KBA.
45. Ints.: Leonard Judd, Harold Heys, and Walter Michaelis; Pepe Mayorga; Henri Jacquier, Leonard Judd, and Gordon Tettmar.
46. Ints.: Ernest Pudney, Gordon Tettmar; NJF with Dorothy Gunn; Pepe Mayorga.
47. Ints.: Sir Kenneth Kleinwort, Joan Kleinwort, Annette Donger; KDK to Lord Tenby, 7 Oct. 1983, KBA; int.: Annette Donger.
48. Ints.: Pepe Mayorga; HAA to ADK, 3 Sept. 1928, KBA; NJF int. with Ivo Forde; Mayorga's notes, KBA.
49. Will of Sir ADK, n.d., KBA; int.: Marguerite White.
50. EES to HAA, 12 Sept. 1935, KS/HAA/6/037, Andreae MSS; EES to HAA, Opinion of Counsel, 13 Feb. 1936, Andreae MSS; EES memo, 27 May 1936, Andreae MSS; EGK to HAA, 22 June n.d.; EES, 'A Brief History of the Firm of KS & Co.', 11 June 1940, p. 9, KBA.
51. Ints.: Pepe Mayorga; John Brooks, 'The Annals of Finance, Part I', *New Yorker*, 21 May 1979, pp. 44–85; ints.: Mayorga; Gerald Thompson, Herbert Cherrill; H. V. Hodson, *Slump and Recovery* (London, 1938), 276; Joseph S. Davis, *The World Between the Wars* (London, 1975), 275; int.: Harold Heys; Brooks, 'Annals of Finance, I'; int.: Mayorga; Hugh Thomas, *The Spanish Civil War* (London, 1968), 204; int.: Mayorga; Brooks, 'Annals of Finance, I'; NJF and author's ints. with Gerald Thompson; int.: Mayorga.
52. Spicer & Pegler to KS & Co., 13 Aug. 1952, KBA; EES memo on Carry Forward Losses, 23 Jan. 1942, Andreae MSS, KBA; KS & Co. to Friedrich Krupp & Co., 26 July 1939, KBA; ints.: Gerald Thompson; Harold Heys.
53. EGK memo, 30 Apr. 1968, KBA.
54. CHK to HAA, 3 Apr. n.d. [1940]; Spicer & Pegler memo, 19 Mar. 1940, Andreae MSS, KBA; ints.: Sir Godfrey Style; EES, Reflections, 8 July 1940, Andreae MSS, KBA.
55. Pudney's reminiscences, KBA.
56. Int.: Dorothy Gunn.

CHAPTER 8

1. Lawrence E. Jones, *A Georgian Afternoon* (London, 1958), 112.
2. GHB birthday speech, 23 Sept. 1937, NB MSS.
3. Lady Evey Jones to GHB, n.d. Sept. 1943, NB MSS; GHB birthday speech, 23 Sept. 1937, ibid.; Thomas Loyd to GHB, 12 Sept. 1943, ibid.; Jonah Jones to GHB, 8 Sept. 1943, ibid.; Lord Crawford to GHB, 14 Sept. 1943, ibid.; RLB diary, 10 Mar. 1930, DHB MSS.
4. RHB to EB, 28 Sept. n.d.; RHB to GHB, 10 Oct. 1907, NB MSS; RHB to EB, 14 Feb. 1914, DHB MSS; RHB to RFP, 9 Mar. 1922, ibid.; RHB to GHB, 22 Nov. 1907, NB MSS; EB to GHB, 7 Apr. 1905, ibid.; RHB to GHB, 11 Aug. 1910, ibid.

5. Information from Lady Elizabeth Benson; RLB to EB, 24 July 1904, DHB MSS.
6. EB to Maysie Holford, 27 July 1898, DHB MSS.
7. Lord Derby, 'Ireland and the Land Act', in *Nineteenth Century* (Oct. 1881), 474; RHB to EB, 2 Feb. n.d., DHB MSS.
8. C. W. Cooper, *Town and County* (London, 1937), 87; C. Percy and J. Ridley (eds.) *The Letters of Edwin Lutyens* (London, 1985), 99; GHB to RLB, n.d., NB MSS.
9. Cooper, *Town and County*; Hilda Grenfell to Lady Evey Grey, 21 July 1902, Morse MSS; *Country Life* (11 and 18 May 1912), 686–95, 722–9; Hilda Grenfell to Lady Grey, 21 July 1902; Lady Sybil Grey to Countess Grey, 2 Jan. 1910, Morse MSS; ints.: Peter Wake.
10. RHB to EB, 23 Dec. 1901, and RLB to EB, n.d. [1902], DHB MSS; Bernard Darwin, *The World that Fred Made* (London, 1955), 117.
11. *The Times*, n.d., press clipping, DHB MSS; Cooper, *Town and County*, 87.
12. RHB to EB, 28 Sept. 1902, DHB MSS; RHB to EB, n.d. Oct. 1900, 2 Oct. 1904, ibid.; E. Impey to RHB, 28 July 1908, DHB MSS; GHB to George Holford, 13 Mar. 1907, NB MSS.
13. L. E. Jones, *An Edwardian Youth* (London, 1956), 239; Lady Diana Cooper, *The Rainbow Comes and Goes* (London, 1958), 105.
14. Lord Oxford and Asquith, *Memories and Reflections* (London, 1928), cited in Alastair Horne, *Macmillan* (London, 1988), i. 21; James Morris, *Oxford* (London, 1965), 332.
15. RHB to Albert Grey, 16 Aug. 1908, Earl Grey MSS; E. Impey to RHB, 28 July 1908, DHB MSS; RHB to Grey, 16 Aug. 1908; Lady Evey Grey to Albert Grey, 10 June 1908, Morse MSS; Albert Grey to RHB, 20 Oct. 1908, DHB MSS; RLB note to Lady Evey Jones, My Walk Across the Mountains with Earl Grey, 13 Dec. 1967, ibid.; Albert Grey to RHB, 20 Oct. 1908.
16. E. Impey to RHB, 28 July 1908, DHB MSS; RHB to GHB, 23 May 1904, NB MSS.
17. James Morris, 'Take That Smile off Your Face', *Guardian*, 25 July 1960, p. 5; RLB notes, n.d., DHB MSS; D. Hart-Davis (ed.), *The End of an Era* (London, 1986), 110.
18. Lady Evey Grey to her parents, 22 Mar. 1908, Morse MSS; RHB to EB, 4 Dec. 1911, DHB MSS; GHB to RHB, 7 May 1912, to EB, 9 Apr. 1913, and to RHB, 24 Mar. 1913, NB MSS; E. Impey to RHB, 29 July 1907, DHB MSS; ints.: Peter Wake.
19. M. and E. Brock (eds.), H. H. Asquith, *Letters to Venetia Stanley* (Oxford, 1982), 74.
20. RLB to Lord Hardinge, 24 Sept. 1914, DHB MSS; Col. Charles Norman, 'Sir Rex Benson', *The 9/12th Royal Lancers Regimental Journal* (1968), 73; Hart-Davis (ed.), *End of an Era*, 166.
21. GHB to RLB, 27 Sept. 1917, NB MSS; CEB to EB, 2 Oct. 1917, 31 July 1917, DHB MSS.
22. *KB Magazine* (Winter 1965/6), 16; RLB notes, n.d., DHB MSS.
23. CEB to GHB, 3 Aug. 1918, NB MSS.
24. Horne, *Macmillan*, i. 49.
25. RLB to Lord Hardinge, 30 Nov. 1914, DHB MSS; ints.: David Benson.
26. George Lloyd to EB, 28 May 1920, Tomkins MSS; Albert Grey to RLB, 22 Aug. 1917, DHB MSS.
27. Ints.: Peter Wake; RLB to EB, 17 Dec. n.d., DHB MSS.
28. George Lloyd to EB, 14 June 1921, Tomkins MSS; RLB to EB, 30 May 1921, DHB MSS; GHB's notes on the Lindsay family, July 1973, NB MSS.
29. RLB to EB, 11 Jan. 1921, DHB MSS.
30. Ibid. 10 June 1921, DHB MSS.
31. Articles of Partnership, 31 May 1924, DHB MSS; *The Times*, 2 July 1924, p. 5.
32. Ints.: Lady Turner; GHB to EB, 20–1 July 1927, DHB MSS; *The Times*, 18, 19 May 1928, p. 17, p. 20.

33. GHB to RHB and EB, n.d. [1928], NB MSS.
34. NJF int. with Audrey Richardson; Sir Rennell Rodd, *The Times*, 12 Apr. 1929, p. 12; RLB diary, 27 Feb. 1929; RHB memo to his children, 7 Sept. 1928, DHB MSS; RLB diary, 12 May 1929; Lady Evey Jones to GHB, 9 Sept. 1943, NB MSS.
35. NJF int. with R. L. Clifford; *KB Magazine* (Summer 1966), 28; NJF ints.: George Tinn, Harry Purkington.
36. Lionel Fraser, *All to the Good* (London, 1963), 110.
37. RLB confidential memo, 24 May 1929, DHB MSS; RLB diary, 7 May 1930; HAV to RLB, 21 Mar. 1926, DHB MSS; RLB diary, 4 Dec. 1925, 1 Mar. 1926; David Kynaston, *Cazenove & Co.* (London, 1991), 106; RLB memo, 24 May 1929.
38. RLB diary, 15 Jan. 1931, 4 July 1932; ints.: Frank Hislop.
39. RLB memo, 24 May 1929; RLB diary, 10 May 1929.
40. Ints.: Peter Wake; CEB to GHB, 19 Jan. 1930, Tomkins MSS; RLB diary, 19 June 1930; ints.: Bobby Henderson; RLB diary, 26 Oct. 1930.
41. G. Wansborough, unpublished typescript notes, private collection; RLB diary, 26 Feb., 30 Apr. 1929.
42. Ziegler, *Sixth Great Power*, 340; Burk, *Morgan Grenfell*, 96–7.
43. Int.: R. L. Clifford; RLB diaries 1929 and 1930 *passim.*
44. RLB diaries, n.d. 1931, 3 June 1932.
45. RLB diaries, 10 Mar. 1930, 20 May 1931; RLB to HAV, 10 Mar. 1930, DHB MSS.
46. Ints.: Lady Turner.
47. RLB diary, Sept. 1931; GHB to Sir Edwin Hoskyns, 13 Nov. 1933, KBA; RLB diary, 2 Nov. 1934.
48. RLB diary, 1 Mar. 1934.
49. NJF int. with Eric Innes.
50. Int.: Alastair Craig; NJF, 'Fleming Holdings', 67; Jones, *Georgian Afternoon*, 143–4; RLB diaries, 1930–1, *passim*.
51. NJF int. with George Tinn.
52. P. Ziegler, *Diana Cooper* (London, 1981), 166.
53. Ints.: Peter Wake.
54. RLB diary, 28 Sept. 1934; NJF and author ints. with Alastair Craig.
55. Ints.: Lady Turner, Roger Turner, Peter Wake.
56. RLB diary, 17 June 1935; ints.: Lady Turner; information from William Wake; Peter Wake's memorial window address, Jan. 1990; RLB diary, 6 Mar. 1937.
57. RLB diary, 24 Apr., 22 Sept. 1936.
58. Kynaston, *Cazenove & Co.*, 158.
59. RLB diary, 2 Apr., 7 Feb., 24 Mar. 1938.
60. Ibid. 3 Dec. 1938.
61. Ibid. 15 Jan. 1937, 18 Dec. 1934, 18 Apr. 1935, 27 June 1935, 20, 25 Nov. 1935.
62. NJF int. with Luke Asquith.
63. RLB diary, 9 Dec. 1935; ints.: Betty Macpherson, D. Kenyon-Jones; J. B. G. Thomas, *Great Rugger Players, 1900–1954* (London, 1955), 89; tribute to G.P.S.M., *KB Magazine* (Autumn 1981), 1; RLB diary, 3 Apr. 1936.
64. RBL diary, 3, 14, 15 Apr., 1 Oct. 1936.
65. Ibid. 25 Jan. 1937.
66. Ibid. 22 Sept., 15 Oct. 1936, 24 Oct., 13 Nov. 1938; misc. notes, DHB MSS.
67. RLB diary, 18 June 1938; NJF int. with Audrey Richardson; *KB Magazine* (Summer 1966), 28, and (Spring 1982), 23–4.

CHAPTER 9

1. Frank Welsh, *Uneasy City* (London, 1986), 15.
2. J. Jewkes, 'Ordeal by Planning, 1948', in T. W. Hutchinson, *Economics and Economic Policy in Britain* (London, 1968), 56.
3. Ints.: Gerald Thompson, Michael Hawkes; NJF ints. with Gordon Tettmar, E. Fitzsimmons.
4. *KB Magazine* (Spring 1983), 6.
5. Ints.: Michael Hawkes.
6. HAA to José Mayorga, 8 Feb. 1945, KS/HAA/6/267, Andreae MSS.
7. EGK memo, 5 Oct. 1967, KBA; HAA to EGK, 21 Aug. 1940, EES to EGK, 7 Oct. 1940, Andreae MSS.
8. Int.: Sir Norman Biggs, and his notes.
9. EGK memo, 5 Oct. 1967.
10. Ints.: Gerald Thompson, Sir Kenneth Kleinwort, David Robertson, Sir Norman Biggs; EGK to Cecil Elbra, 18 Sept. 1964, Elbra MSS, KBA.
11. Wechsberg, *Merchant Bankers*, 39.
12. Int.: Sir Norman Biggs; KDK to Lord Tenby, 7 Oct. 1983, KBA; Cecil Elbra to EGK, 20 Sept. 1964, KBA.
13. EGK memo, 22 May 1947, and letter to Señor Brugada, 17 May 1947, KBA.
14. NJF int. with Gerald Thompson.
15. Ints.: Michael Hawkes.
16. Ints.: Mark, Henry, and Peter Andreae; Pepe Mayorga; NJF ints. with Arthur Stilwell, E. Fitzsimmons, Gordon Tettmar; EGK to HAA, 22 Aug. 1947, KS/HAA/6/298, Andreae MSS.
17. Walter Michaelis memo on Krupps, 20 Oct. 1947, KBA.
18. A. J. Haynes to Hermann Abs, 6 June 1947, and A. J. Haynes memo, 12 Aug. 1948, KBA.
19. Cecil Elbra's note on the German debt recovery, 16 Aug. 1943, KBA; ints.: Gerald Thompson; Haynes memo, 31 Oct. 1947, KBA; EGK's note attached to *Financial Times*, 19 Sept. 1951, KBA; int.: Hermann Abs; Michaelis memo, 25 Oct. 1948, KBA; ints.: Abs, David Robertson.
20. EGK's notes, 9 Nov. 1951, 27 Feb. 1952, KBA; Minutes of meeting, 4 Dec. 1951, KBA; Michaelis's notes on British Banking Committee meeting, 27 Feb. 1952; *Financial Times*, 17 May 1952, in press clippings re German debts 1952–3, KBA.
21. EES memos on conversion of the firm into limited liability, 24 Oct. 1946, 20 June 1947, KBA.
22. Ints.: Sir Godfrey Style, Tom Troubridge.
23. HKA to EES, 13 Nov. 1947, Andreae MSS.
24. EGK to HKA, 23 Dec. 1954; HKA to EGK, 28 Dec. 1954; W. Sandars memo of intent, 26 Jan. 1956, KBA.
25. CHK memo on capitalization of KS & Co., 14 July 1954, and EGK memo, 30 Sept. 1954, KBA.
26. Ints.: Lord Limerick, David Robertson, F. A. James; NJF int. with F. A. James.
27. CHK memo, 14 July 1954; NJF int. with Harold Heys; EGK memos, 21 Sept. 1954, 7 Mar. 1955; David Robertson memo, 22 Mar. 1955; EES notes on a meeting, 26 Aug. 1947; EGK memo, 22 Mar. 1955; David Robertson memo, 9 July 1955.
28. Ints.: David Peake, David Robertson; NJF ints. with Harold Heys, F. A. James.
29. Richard Kellett, *The Merchant Banking Arena* (London, 1967), 94.
30. NJF int. with Cecil Elbra; ints.: Michael Hawkes.
31. NJF ints. with Ivo Forde, Bill Mundy; ints.: Gerald Thompson, Brian Rowntree, Sir Kenneth Kleinwort; NJF int. with Arthur Stilwell; *The Times*, 21 June 1989, p. 18.
32. Ints.: F. A. James, Brian Rowntree.

33. HAA to R. Bridle, n.d., KS/HAA/6/259 Andreae MSS.
34. NJF int. with Cecil Elbra; ints.: Michael Hawkes, Sir Kenneth Kleinwort; Scandinavia ledgers, KBA.
35. Ints. with Clive Crook, Brian Manning, Michael Hawkes, Herbert Cherrill; NJF int. with Henri Jacquier.
36. NJF int. with Ivo Forde; int.: David Robertson; Spiegelberg, *The City*, 70; David Robertson memo, 12 Aug. 1959, KBA.
37. *The Economist*, 15 Aug. 1959, press clipping, KBA; David Robertson memo, 12 Aug. 1959.

CHAPTER 10

1. Draft memo, 3 Oct. 1946, LIT Merger file, DHB MSS; RLB diary, Summer 1946.
2. RLB diary, 17 Sept. 1946; memo on a meeting at the Treasury, 30 Sept. 1946, LIT Merger file; *Financial Times*, 18 Apr. 1947; NJF int. with George Howard; proof of prospectus for LIT/Benson Merger, July 1947, KBA.
3. Information from James Lonsdale; int.: Norman Lonsdale; Blanche Lonsdale to Lord Tenby, 24 July 1983, KBA; notes by George Howard; W. L. Fraser, *All to the Good* (London, 1965), p. iii.
4. Ron Chernow, *The House of Morgan* (London, 1990), 519–20.
5. Int.: Alastair Craig; RHB to RLB, 12 Aug. 1927, DHB MSS; NJF int. with Ronny Medlicott; ints.: Frank Hislop, Bobby Henderson, Peter Wake.
6. Ints.: Ric Ohrstrom, David Benson, Jerry Jamieson; G. D. Smith and R. Sobel, *Dover Corporation* (Cambridge, Mass., 1991), 10; int.: Denys Oppé; RLB to Phil Macpherson, 14 Apr. n.d., DHB MSS; int.: Peter Wake.
7. RLB to EB, 7 Sept. 1908, DHB MSS.
8. NJF and author ints. with Denys Oppé; ints.: with Basil Irwin, Alastair Craig.
9. Ben Pollen to RLB, 16 Apr. 1943, and Mark Turner to RLB, 14 Oct. 1943, DHB MSS; ints.: Peter Wake, Bobby Henderson.
10. Ints.: Peter Wake, Bobby Henderson; *The Times*, 22 Sept. 1960, p. 19, 27 Sept. 1960, p. 16.
11. Ints.: Bobby Henderson, Frank Hislop, Peter Wake, Alastair Craig, James Rockley; RBL New Issues Ledger 1950–60, KBA.
12. Information from William Wake; Bernard Sendall, *Independent Television in Britain* (London, 1982), i. 20, 75, 191; Bobby Henderson, Alastair Craig.
13. Interview with Sidney Mason.
14. Int.: Archie Andrews; RLB's notes, A Little Bit of History, n.d. 1964, DHB MSS.
15. Ints.: R. L. Clifford, Alastair Craig, Luke Asquith.
16. Ints.: Lady Turner, Ronny Medlicott; NJF int. with Medlicott; ints.: Betty Whyman, Ann Meikle.
17. NJF ints. with Luke Asquith, Audrey Richardson; ints.: Betty Whyman, Ann Meikle.
18. Marion Hellings to RLB, 28 Sept. 1957, DHB MSS.
19. Ints.: Frank Hislop, Bobby Henderson, Bobby Brooks.
20. Burk, *Morgan Grenfell*, 186.
21. Ints.: Bobby Henderson, Peter Wake, David Benson, Luke Asquith.
22. Ints.: Basil Irwin; Siegmund Warburg to David Benson, n.d. [*c.*1968], DHB MSS; Sam Hamburger to RLB, 10 Nov. n.d. [*c.*1957], DHB MSS; NJF int. with Alastair Craig.
23. Int.: Ronny Medlicott; Medlicott to Lord Tenby, 17 Oct. 1983, KBA.
24. Ints.: Peter Wake, David Benson, Bobby Henderson; misc. notes, RLB file, DHB MSS.

25. Ints.: Peter Wake, Luke Asquith; Eric Tatham to RLB, 27 Jan. 1959, DHB MSS.
26. Ints.: David Robertson.
27. RLB diary, 28 Feb. 1944, DHB MSS; ints.: David Benson.
28. RLB note about governor Norman's letter, n.d., DHB MSS; Mark Turner to RLB, 10 May 1967, DHB MSS.
29. David Robertson's memo, 12 Aug. 1959, KBA.
30. Ints.: Peter Wake.
31. Ben Pollen to RLB, 16 Apr. 1943, DHB MSS; RLB diary, 22 Mar. 1944; ints. with Peter Wake; NJF int. with Alastair Craig.
32. Ivo Forde memo on record of points, 20 May 1960, KBA; ints.: Bobby Henderson, Peter Wake, Denys Oppé.
33. Ints.: Lord Limerick; NJF int. with Gordon Tettmar.
34. Ints.: Bobby Henderson, Peter Wake.
35. RLB's Bussento note, n.d. Sept. 1961, DHB MSS.
36. *Daily Telegraph, Daily Mail, Financial Times*, 18 Nov. 1960; *The Times*, 4 Mar. 1961, p. 11, 13 Mar. 1961, pp. 22, 23, 22 Mar. 1961, p. 19, press clippings, KBA.

CHAPTER 11

1. RLB Bussento notes, n.d. Sept. 1961, DHB MSS.
2. Int.: Lord Limerick.
3. Ints.: Alastair Craig, Bobby Henderson.
4. Roberts, *Schroders*, 420; NJF and author ints. with R. L. Clifford.
5. Int.: Betty Whyman, Audrey Mackenzie-Smith; NJF ints. with Eric Pratt, Henri Jacquier.
6. Ints.: David Robertson, Peter Wake.
7. Int.: Lord Limerick.
8. Int.: Bill Mundy; misc. draft notes, fo. 22, KBA.
9. Ints.: Clive Crook.
10. Ints.: Bill Mundy, Bobby Henderson, Stuart Pixley; CHK to Stuart Pixley, n.d. July 1967, Pixley Papers.
11. Ints.: Robin Fox.
12. Ints.: Robin Fox, Sir Kenneth Kleinwort.
13. Ints.: Michael Hawkes, Clive Crook.
14. *KB Magazine* (Summer 1968), 12; information from E. Fitzsimmons; ints.: Robin Fox.
15. Ints.: Bobby Henderson, Bobby Brooks.
16. Ibid.
17. Ints.: Peter Wake, John Gillum; Spiegelberg, *The City*, 71.
18. Ints.: Sir Martin Jacomb, Bobby Henderson; *The Times*, 8, 9, 14, 20, 21, 30 Dec. 1965.
19. *New York Times*, 31 Jan. 1964; int.: Ronny Medlicott; *KB Magazine* (Winter 1968/9), 3.
20. *Financial Times*, 31 Jan. 1969.
21. *KB Magazine* (Winter 1968/9), 3.
22. Anthony Sampson, *The New Anatomy of Britain* (London, 1971), cited in Spiegelberg, *The City*, 170–1; E. Stamp and C. Marley, *Accounting Principles and the City Code* (London, 1970), 4.
23. Stamp and Marley, *Accounting*, 16–18; *Illustrated London News*, 29 July 1967, p. 36; *The Times*, 15, 18 July 1967; ints.: John Gillum, Bobby Brooks.
24. *KB Magazine* (Winter 1968/9), 3; *KBL Directors' Report and Accounts* (1969), 7; Spiegelberg, *The*

City, 189; ints.: John Gillum, Bobby Henderson; CHK to John Gillum, Tuesday n.d., Gillum Papers.

25. Press clippings, KBA; ints. with Bobby Henderson.
26. Spiegelberg, *The City*, 74–5.
27. Ints.: Bobby Henderson, David Robertson, Andrew Caldecott.
28. *KB Magazine* (Winter 1988), 40 (Winter 1987), 12; int.: F. A. James; conversation with David Hinshaw.
29. Author and NJF int. with Herbert Cherrill; David Peake's notes.
30. Ints.: David Benson.
31. Gary Hector, *Breaking the Bank* (Boston, 1988), 76; ints.: Bobby Henderson, Michael Hawkes, David Benson.
32. Ints.: John Gillum, Robin Fox, Andrew Caldecott, David Benson; Sir Fred Warner, *Anglo-Japanese Financial Relations* (Oxford, 1991), 163; *KBL Annual Report and Accounts* (1982), 27.
33. *KB Magazine* (Winter 1971/2), 1.
34. Ints.: Sir Martin Jacomb.
35. Ints.: Sir Kenneth Kleinwort, David Peake, Sir William Clarke, Andrew Caldecott.
36. Ints.: Michael Hawkes, Sir Martin Jacomb.
37. Sir Mark Turner to RLB, 28 July 1963, RLB to Sir Mark Turner, 25 June 1965, RLB to EGK, 30 Apr. 1965, EGK to Sir Mark Turner, 29 July 1963, EGK memo, 1 Oct. 1965, DHB MSS; ints.: Bobby Henderson.
38. Ints.: members of the old KB Board.
39. *KBL Directors' Report and Accounts* (1968), 7; *KBL Annual Report* (1971), 6.

CHAPTER 12

1. *KBL Annual Report* (1975), 7.
2. Ints.: David Benson.
3. Gerald Thompson to David Benson, n.d. 1973, DHB MSS; information from Bobby Henderson.
4. Ints.: Chris Palmer, Simon Robertson.
5. Ints.: Peter Wake; *KBL Annual Report* (1972), 8.
6. Eric Bussiere, *Paribas 1872–1992* (Antwerp, 1992), 185; *KBL Annual Report* (1973), 6.
7. *KBL Annual Report* (1974), 6; *Financial Times*, 2 Dec. 1974, 40.
8. Ints.: Bobby Henderson, Michael Hawkes, David Wake-Walker.
9. Ints.: Michael Hawkes, Robin Fox, Bobby Henderson.
10. Kynaston, *Cazenove & Co.*, 289; int.: Sir Martin Jacomb.
11. Ints.: Gerald Thompson.
12. Ints.: Andrew Caldecott, Bobby Henderson, Sir Martin Jacomb.
13. *KBL Annual Report* (1979), 1.
14. Ints.: Martin Mays-Smith, Michael Hawkes; Roberts, *Schroders*, 488; int.: Stephen Unwin.
15. *KBL Annual Report and Accounts* (1980), 7.
16. Ints.: Tim Barker, Bobby Henderson; British Aerospace issue files, KBA.
17. Nigel Lawson, *View from No. 11*, pb. (London, 1992), 222.
18. *KB Magazine* (Spring 1985), 24–5; int.: David Clementi, James Rockley, Sir Martin Jacomb; *Financial Times*, 17 Nov. 1984.
19. Int.: Simon Robertson; *KB Report and Accounts* (1987), 17.

20. *Acquisitions Monthly* (January 1987); Spiegelberg, *The City*, 112; ints.: Sir Martin Jacomb, Michael Hawkes.
21. Ints.: Simon Robertson, David Benson.
22. Ints.: Sir Francis Sandilands; *KBL Annual Report and Accounts* (1980), 7.
23. Ints.: Bobby Henderson, Andrew Caldecott, David Peake, Bobby Brooks.
24. Lawson, *No. 11*, 399.
25. Ints.: Clive Crook, Brian Manning.
26. Information from Lord Chandos; Hermes papers, KBA.
27. Ints.: Michael Hawkes, David Peake, Sir Martin Jacomb.
28. Ints.: Michael Hawkes, Tim Barker.
29. Peter Green's notes, and ints.: Peter Green, John Brew, Bill Legge-Bourke, David Peake.
30. Ints.: David Benson, Michael Hawkes, Clive Crook; *The Economist*, 16 Aug. 1987, 49–50.
31. Information from David Peake; int.: John Brew.
32. Int.: Peter Green.
33. Ints.: Jonathan Agnew, and others at KB.
34. Int.: Colin Maltby.
35. KB Group Information: Senior Appointments / Top Management Structure: Message from Mr Michael Hawkes, 25 Nov. 1987, p. 1, KBA; ints.: Bobby Henderson, David Peake.
36. *The Economist*, Suppl., 10 Apr. 1993, pp. 16–20.
37. *Financial Times*, 25 Sept. 1990.
38. *KB Group Annual Report and Accounts* (1991); *Financial Times*, 19 Feb. 1992; *KB Group Annual Report and Accounts* (1991, 1992).
39. *The Times* and *The Independent*, 18 Feb. 1994.
40. *KB Group Annual Report and Accounts* (1994).

APPENDIX I

Partners and Directors

PARTNERS OF THE CONSTITUENT FIRMS OF KLEINWORT BENSON

Partner	*Firm*	*Dates*
Hermann Greverus	H. Greverus & Co.	1829–51
	Greverus & Cohen	1851–5
Edward Cohen	Greverus & Cohen	1851–5
	Kleinwort & Cohen	1855–8
	Drake Kleinwort & Cohen	1858–70
	Kleinwort Cohen & Co.	1871–83
James Drake	Drake Kleinwort & Cohen	1858–71
Alexander F. Kleinwort	Kleinwort & Cohen	1855–8
	Drake Kleinwort & Cohen	1858–70
	Kleinwort Cohen & Co.	1871–83
	Kleinwort, Sons & Co.	1884–6
Herman Kleinwort	Kleinwort Cohen & Co.	1881–3
	Kleinwort, Sons & Co.	1884–1939
Alexander Kleinwort	Kleinwort, Sons & Co.	1884–1935
Herman Andreae	Kleinwort, Sons & Co.	1907–47
Ernest Kleinwort	Kleinwort, Sons & Co.	1926–47
Cyril Kleinwort	Kleinwort, Sons & Co.	1926–47
Herman K. Andreae	Kleinwort, Sons & Co.	1946–7
Robert Benson	George & Robert Benson	1772–86
	Rathbone & Benson	1786–1800
	Benson, Cropper Benson	1801–2
William Rathbone	Rathbone & Benson	1786–1800
James Cropper	Rathbone & Benson	1796–9
	Cropper, Benson	1799–1801
	Benson, Cropper Benson	1801–5
	Cropper, Benson	1806–35
Thomas Benson	Benson, Cropper Benson	1799–1801
William Benson	Benson, Cropper Benson	1801–5
Thomas Cropper	Cropper, Benson	1807–19
Robert R. Benson	Cropper, Benson	1806–38
John Cropper	Cropper, Benson	1818–38
Edward Cropper	Cropper, Benson	1820–38
David Hodgson	Cropper, Benson	1806–38

App. 1. Partners and Directors

Partner	Firm	Dates
Hugh Mure	Cropper, Benson	180?–38
Robert Benson jun.	Cropper, Benson	1836–8
	Worthington Benson & Co.	1837–50
	Robert Benson & Co.	1852–75
Henry Worthington	Worthington Benson & Co.	1837–50
Pascoe Glyn	Robert Benson & Co.	1852–64
Richard Glyn	Robert Benson & Co.	1865–75
Robert Wigram	Robert Benson & Co.	1865–75
Robin Benson	Robert Benson & Co.	1875
	Cross, Benson & Co.	1875–83
	Robert Henry Benson & Co.	1883–4
	Robert Benson & Co.	1884–1925
	Robert Benson & Co. Ltd.	1926–9
Constantine Benson	Robert Benson & Co.	1875
	Close, Benson & Co.	1879–84
	C. W. Benson & Co.	1884–1905
Henry Vernet	Robert Benson & Co.	1891–1925
	Robert Benson & Co. Ltd.	1926–33
Guy Benson	Robert Benson & Co.	1919–25
	Robert Benson & Co. Ltd.	1926–47
Rex Benson	Robert Benson & Co.	1924–5
	Robert Benson & Co. Ltd.	1926–47
Con Benson	Robert Benson & Co.	1924–5
	Robert Benson & Co. Ltd.	1926–47

DIRECTORS OF THE CONSTITUENT FIRMS OF KLEINWORT BENSON

Director	Firm	Dates
Herman Andreae	Kleinwort, Sons & Co. Ltd.	1948–61
Ernest Kleinwort	Kleinwort, Sons & Co. Ltd.	1948–61
Cyril Kleinwort	Kleinwort, Sons & Co. Ltd.	1948–61
Herman K. Andreae	Kleinwort, Sons & Co. Ltd.	1948–61
Norman Biggs	Kleinwort, Sons & Co. Ltd.	1948–52
Ivo Forde	Kleinwort, Sons & Co. Ltd.	1948–61
David Robertson	Kleinwort, Sons & Co. Ltd.	1955–61
Guy Benson	Robert Benson Lonsdale	1947–61
Rex Benson	Robert Benson Lonsdale	1947–61
Con Benson	Robert Benson Lonsdale	1947–60
Leo Lonsdale	Robert Benson Lonsdale	1947–61
C. C. Hellings	Robert Benson & Co. Ltd.	1933–47

Director	*Firm*	*Dates*
George Wansbrough	Robert Benson & Co. Ltd.	1932–6
Michael Colefax	Robert Benson & Co. Ltd.	1933–47
	Robert Benson Lonsdale	1947–61
Philip Macpherson	Robert Benson & Co. Ltd.	1936–47
	Robert Benson Lonsdale	1947–61
Mark Turner	Robert Benson Lonsdale	1947–61
The Lord Rockley	Robert Benson Lonsdale	1947–61
Stuart Ebben	Robert Benson Lonsdale	1947–61
Denys Oppée	Robert Benson Lonsdale	1947–61
John Read	Robert Benson Lonsdale	1957–61
Ronald Medlicott	Robert Benson Lonsdale	1955–61
Peter Wake	Robert Benson Lonsdale	1959–61
Robert Henderson	Robert Benson Lonsdale	1959–61
Alastair Craig	Robert Benson Lonsdale	1959–61

DIRECTORS OF KLEINWORT BENSON GROUP PLC IN AUGUST 1995
(formerly Kleinwort Benson Lonsdale Ltd.)

The Lord Rockley
S. M. Robertson
T. G. Barker
D. H. Benson*
J. Carvajal Urquijo*
D. C. Clementi
R. T. Fox
C. J. M. R. Giacomotto*
M. J. B. Green
R. D. N. Harley
R. D. C. Henderson
M. C. J. Jackaman*
R. C. H. Jeens
Sir Michael Jenkins, KCMG
J. Lancaster*
B. W. J. Manning
T. Ohta*
D. A. E. R. Peake*
The Hon. Sir Nicholas Redmayne Bt.
L. M. Urquhart*
A. C. D. Yarrow

*Non-executive

APPENDIX 2

Financial Tables

(Compiled by Fiona Calnan and Martin McMyler)

LIST OF TABLES

TABLE 1. *Kleinwort, Sons & Co.: Capital, distributed profits and losses 1866–1960*

Year	Partners' Capital (£)	Distributed Profits/(Losses) (£)
1866	736,059	65,000
1867	721,449	n/d
1868	728,960	n/d
1869	819,194	57,000
1870	913,273	57,000
1871	1,073,736	133,000
1872	758,085	94,000
1873	769,738	n/d
1874	827,129	37,600
1875	844,932	n/d
1876	817,279	n/d
1877	839,491	n/d
1878	739,502	n/d
1879	752,435	n/d
1880	708,597	10,000
1881	774,380	15,000
1882	833,237	35,000
1883	896,086	82,000
1884	773,856	n/d
1885	731,716	22,500
1886	551,754	n/d
1887	613,326	40,000
1888	677,116	40,000
1889	743,891	40,000
1890	817,214	64,000
1891	848,169	n/d
1892	883,011	n/d
1893	924,869	n/d
1894	972,135	15,000
1895	1,074,460	60,000
1896	1,187,047	70,000
1897	1,318,294	80,000
1898	1,426,391	90,000
1899	1,505,789	70,000
1900	1,617,733	90,000
1901	1,661,041	15,000
1902	1,800,804	90,000
1903	1,869,896	n/d
1904	2,030,051	90,000
1905	2,180,414	100,000
1906	2,354,399	100,000
1907	2,377,804	n/d
1908	2,933,308	150,000
1909	3,207,595	100,000
1910	3,419,195	100,000
1911	3,730,525	200,000
1912	4,117,292	300,000
1913	4,406,160	150,000
1914	4,423,149	n/d
1915	4,399,534	n/d
1916	4,332,986	n/d
1917	4,507,339	n/d
1918	4,669,483	n/d

TABLE I. (*cont.*)

Year	Partners' Capital (£)	Distributed Profits/(Losses)(£)
1919	5,087,416	300,000
1920	5,232,954	n/d
1921	2,637,408	n/d
1922	4,058,157	114,022
1923	3,451,963	168,212
1924	3,465,789	473,044
1925	3,898,953	651,585
1926	4,122,983	646,025
1927	3,785,098	658,561
1928	3,977,873	874,884
1929	2,723,799	(527,473)
1930	3,069,127	(171,775)
1931	2,929,866	(144,507)
1932	3,096,916	160,224
1933	3,304,793	307,575
1934	3,366,614	325,337
1935	3,219,019	83,919
1936	3,065,192	219,866
1937	3,113,222	196,461
1938	3,274,960	137,163
1939	2,365,545	(2,514,678)
1940	1,000,000	(60,632)
1941	1,000,000	104,719
1942	1,000,000	307,765
1943	1,000,000	268,152
1944	1,000,000	252,484
1945	1,000,000	152,596
1946	1,000,000	182,813
1947	1,000,000	35,160
Year	**Share Capital (£)**	**Profits/(Losses)(£)**
1948	2,500,000	309,481
1949	2,500,000	375,753
1950	2,500,000	503,679
1951	2,500,000	509,145
1952	2,500,000	425,398
1953	2,500,000	410,829
1954	2,500,000	679,157
1955	3,000,000	542,902
1956	3,000,000	520,011
1957	3,000,000	524,069
1958	3,000,000	570,143
1959	3,000,000	1,048,406
1960	3,000,000	1,076,460

Notes: n/d = no distribution
Profits are stated without regard to taxation.
Kleinwort, Sons & Co. was incorporated 14 January 1948.
Figures are based on accounts prepared by Spicer & Pegler but do not exclude any assets which were deemed frozen from 1931 onwards.

Source: Kleinwort Benson Archives.

TABLE 2. *Kleinwort, Sons & Co.: Analysis of partners' capital 1866–1947*

Year	J. Drake del Castillo (£)	A. F. H. Kleinwort (£)	E. Cohen (£)	H. G. Kleinwort (£)	Sir A. D. Kleinwort (£)	H. A. Andreae (£)	C. H. Kleinwort (£)	E. G. Kleinwort (£)	Drake Trust (£)	H. K. Andreae (£)
1866	339,686	256,240	140,133							
1867	339,075	271,489	110,885							
1868	316,188	283,548	129,224							
1869	365,377	320,282	133,535							
1870	420,435	353,238	139,600							
1871	487,394	383,846	202,496							
1872		531,417	226,668							
1873		545,098	224,640							
1874		594,203	232,926							
1875		614,698	230,234							
1876		614,516	202,763							
1877		632,136	207,355							
1878		539,402	200,100							
1879		559,987	192,448							
1880		530,281	178,316							
1881		553,646	168,413	52,321						
1882		600,810	177,074	55,353						
1883		630,883	204,198	61,005						
1884		656,025		62,831	55,000					
1885		606,541		66,433	58,742					
1886				280,612	271,142					
1887				311,611	301,715					
1888				344,695	332,421					
1889				379,414	364,477					
1890				409,066	408,148					
1891				424,470	423,699					
1892				443,023	439,988					
1893				466,805	458,064					
1894				489,340	482,795					
1895				542,885	531,575					
1896				602,774	584,273					
1897				671,480	646,814					
1898				725,381	701,010					
1899				753,228	752,561					
1900				816,602	801,131					
1901				831,153	829,888					
1902				896,886	903,918					
1903				933,984	935,912					
1904				1,018,723	1,011,328					
1905				1,080,302	1,100,112					
1906				1,162,067	1,192,332					
1907				1,172,844	1,204,960					
1908				1,453,990	1,479,318					
1909				1,590,843	1,587,510	29,242				
1910				1,700,069	1,680,216	38,910				
1911				1,852,751	1,822,125	55,649				
1912				2,056,037	1,969,311	91,944				
1913				2,200,918	2,096,809	108,433				
1914				2,229,699	2,087,630	105,820				
1915				2,212,095	2,087,123	100,316				
1916				2,198,667	2,043,147	91,172				
1917				2,287,145	2,128,082	92,112				

TABLE 2. (*cont.*)

Year	J. Drake del Castillo (£)	A. F. H. Kleinwort (£)	E. Cohen (£)	H. G. Kleinwort (£)	Sir A. D. Kleinwort (£)	H. A. Andreae (£)	C. H. Kleinwort (£)	E. G. Kleinwort (£)	Drake Trust (£)	H. K. Andreae (£)
1918				2,383,840	2,192,662	92,981				
1919				2,584,533	2,350,386	152,497				
1920				2,642,129	2,442,017	148,808				
1921				1,314,937	1,187,234	135,237				
1922				1,276,678	1,125,437	116,449			1,539,593	
1923				976,612	806,142	109,849			1,559,360	
1924				1,033,706	781,077	96,248			1,554,758	
1925				1,195,927	773,374	112,459			1,817,193	
1926				1,284,262	696,686	270,513			1,871,522	
1927				1,272,559	168,801	351,696	64,333	64,263	1,863,446	
1928				1,375,649	116,787	328,437	82,213	82,243	1,992,544	
1929				1,088,972	(52,367)	112,025	10,056	9,653	1,555,460	
1930				995,982	(238,016)	230,566	309,059	309,546	1,461,990	
1931				960,078	(310,461)	161,967	319,928	319,190	1,479,164	
1932				1,006,121	(237,904)	154,968	335,353	341,058	1,497,320	
1933				1,114,634	(210,597)	180,601	344,952	359,290	1,515,913	
1934				1,168,904	92,308	170,039	208,414	210,398	1,516,551	
1935				1,171,131		118,802	203,405	208,134	1,517,547	
1936				1,005,786		121,060	206,912	212,225	1,519,209	
1937				1,010,672		127,954	214,035	221,338	1,539,223	
1938				1,034,036		191,331	250,611	258,496	1,540,486	
1939						247,691	281,918	288,366	1,547,570	
1940						333,333	333,334	333,333		
1941						333,333	333,334	333,333		
1942						333,333	333,334	333,333		
1943						333,333	333,334	333,333		
1944						333,333	333,334	333,333		
1945						333,333	333,334	333,333		
1946						213,334	318,333	318,334		150,000
1947						123,334	318,333	318,334		240,000

Notes: J. Drake del Castillo died in 1872 and the partnership known as Drake, Kleinwort & Cohen was dissolved.
The partnership of Kleinwort & Cohen commenced in 1872 and operated until 1883 when E. Cohen retired.
The partnership known as Kleinwort, Sons & Co. commenced in 1883.
Kleinwort, Sons & Co. was incorporated 14 January 1948.
Profits are stated without regard to taxation.
From 1929 Sir A. D. Kleinwort started to hand over his share of the firm to his sons E. G. Kleinwort and C. H. Kleinwort.
Figures are based on accounts prepared by Spicer & Pegler but do not exclude any assets which were deemed frozen from 1931 onwards.

Source: Kleinwort Benson Archives.

TABLE 3. *Kleinwort, Sons & Co.: Acceptances 1858–1960*

Year	£000's	Year	£000's
1858	500	1910	10,500
1859	600	1911	13,200
1860	800	1912	13,100
1861	500	1913	14,200
1862	800	1914	8,500
1863	1,000	1915	0
1864	1,200	1916	7,750
1865	1,500	1917	8,250
1866	1,800	1918	7,800
1867	1,500	1919	1,500
1868	1,600	1920	15,750
1869	2,000	1921	12,000
1870	2,100	1922	11,000
1871	2,600	1923	14,000
1872	3,100	1924	16,700
1873	2,500	1925	18,600
1874	2,300	1926	12,700
1875	2,000	1927	16,000
1876	2,000	1928	20,300
1877	1,500	1929	18,330
1878	1,500	1930	18,000
1879	2,200	1931	12,100
1880	2,100	1932	10,400
1881	2,200	1933	8,900
1882	2,300	1934	9,100
1883	3,000	1935	9,300
1884	2,800	1936	8,700
1885	2,900	1937	8,400
1886	2,900	1938	8,000
1887	4,000	1939	2,700
1888	4,300	1940	800
1889	4,500	1941	500
1890	4,600	1942	500
1891	4,500	1943	700
1892	5,400	1944	700
1893	5,500	1945	800
1894	5,300	1946	1,900
1895	6,600	1947	3,600
1896	6,600	1948	4,000
1897	6,600	1949	4,900
1898	7,800	1950	5,600
1899	7,700	1951	8,200
1900	8,200	1952	6,700
1901	8,800	1953	8,000
1902	9,000	1954	8,000
1903	8,400	1955	8,700
1904	10,000	1956	8,700
1905	11,500	1957	13,500
1906	11,700	1958	12,400
1907	11,900	1959	12,200
1908	10,700	1960	13,400
1909	10,600		

TABLE 4. *Robert Benson & Co.: Partners' capital and distributed profits and losses 1891–1926*

Year	Partners' capital (£)	Distributed profits/(losses) (£)
1891	50,000	10,771
1892	50,000	3,927
1893	50,000	5,714
1894	50,000	n/d
1895	50,000	n/d
1896	50,000	7,969
1897	50,000	11,210
1898	50,000	14,771
1899	50,000	3,319
1900	50,000	9,442
1901	50,000	12,183
1902	50,000	9,471
1903	50,000	11,048
1904	50,000	(16,987)
1905	50,000	14,815
1906	50,000	23,574
1907	50,000	(1,332)
1908	50,000	(71,128)
1909	50,000	27,046
1910	50,000	14,806
1911	170,000	27,272
1912	170,000	10,549
1913	170,000	(3,599)
1914	170,000	(23,545)
1915	110,000	(35,940)
1916	110,000	2,160
1917	110,000	6,186
1918	110,000	7,087
1919	110,000	4,626
1920	110,000	3,166
1921	110,000	n/d
1922	110,000	n/d
1923	110,000	1,504
1924	110,000	18,486
1925	110,000	36,365
1926	110,000	64,605

Notes: n/d = no distribution.

Distributable profits are stated after accounting for interest on partners' capital and current-account balances.

Figures do not include R. H. Benson's considerable American interests.

TABLE 5. *Robert Benson & Co. Ltd. and Robert Benson Lonsdale & Co.: Profits and Losses 1927–1960*

Year	Share capital £	Acceptances £	Advances £	Profits/(Losses) £
Robert Benson & Co. Ltd. 1927–1947				
1927	400,000	n/a	n/a	76,937
1928	400,000	n/a	n/a	65,925
1929	400,000	n/a	n/a	140,188
1930	400,000	n/a	n/a	(130,781)
1931	400,000	n/a	n/a	(86,140)
1932	400,000	n/a	n/a	(88,587)
1933	400,000	n/a	n/a	36,084
1934	400,000	n/a	n/a	176,389
1935	400,000	n/a	n/a	62,647
1936	400,000	131,957	921,841	184,773
1937	400,000	260,124	688,826	136,995
1938	400,000	104,916	435,313	(141,064)
1939	400,000	194,572	400,393	27,393
1940	400,000	60,345	346,799	(35,399)
1941	400,000	79,324	257,807	(49,578)
1942	400,000	67,405	218,621	22,414
1943	400,000	92,326	342,000	64,698
1944	400,000	71,909	364,336	28,750
1945	400,000	58,533	210,421	43,103
1946	400,000	59,983	283,258	53,769
1947	400,000	97,975	474,786	113,659
Robert Benson Lonsdale & Co. 1948–1960				
1948	800,000	205,975	448,443	121,770
1949	800,000	125,553	551,452	128,825
1950	800,000	146,436	360,165	120,343
1951	800,000	125,200	492,855	124,983
1952	800,000	175,200	519,755	131,890
1953	800,000	75,200	420,919	121,105
1954	800,000	65,200	548,949	167,772
1955	800,000	62,000	1,911,690	458,976
1956	800,000	62,000	1,269,041	330,659
1957	800,000	212,000	948,014	360,946
1958	800,000	182,281	1,535,502	429,431
1959	800,000	130,000	1,259,187	499,947
1960	800,000	139,598	1,861,527	817,025

Notes: n/a = not available.
Accounting year end was 28 February.
Profits are stated before tax.
Robert Benson & Co. Ltd. acquired the whole of the share capital of T. L. Lonsdale & Co. Ltd. on 9 July 1947.
Robert Benson Lonsdale & Co. Ltd. was a wholly owned subsidiary of The Lonsdale Investment Trust Ltd.

Source: Kleinwort Benson Archives.

TABLE 6. *Kleinwort Benson Group: Shareholders' funds and profits and losses 1961–1994*

Year	Shareholders' funds (£000's)	Disclosed profits and losses after tax (£000's)
1961	13,100	900
1962	13,500	1,000
1963	13,900	1,000
1964	14,700	1,100
1965	15,400	1,500
1966	16,000	1,400
1967	16,400	1,900
1968	17,400	2,500
1969	22,100	2,500
1970	24,800	2,600
1971	36,700	3,800
1972	43,200	5,000
1973	56,100	5,000
1974	59,400	4,600
1975	64,000	5,900
1976	68,900	6,500
1977	76,500	7,500
1978	83,800	9,100
1979	110,400	12,100
1980	154,900	22,900
1981	171,100	21,600
1982	196,800	20,000
1983	215,300	21,700
1984	247,500	30,300
1985	276,300	35,700
1986	348,100	44,300
1987	499,700	38,300
1988	483,900	8,800
1989	505,300	59,400
1990	402,900	(55,300)
1991	414,100	17,600
1992	394,300	20,300
1993	463,300	83,100
1994	481,500	71,700

Note: Amounts are after restatement of group results and include extraordinary items.
Up to and including 1987 profits were stated after transfers to inner reserves.

Source: Kleinwort Benson Group, *Annual Report and Accounts* (1961–94).

APPENDIX 3

R. H. Benson as a Collector

(By Charles Sebag-Montefiore)

ONE aspect of Benson's career which has received less notice than it deserves is his achievement as a connoisseur and collector: his collection of Italian pictures was of outstanding importance. This lack of recognition may be due to the fact that this entire collection was sold *en bloc* in 1927 to the dealer Joseph Duveen for $4m. and dispersed, mostly among Duveen's clients in America. Benson also bought early Chinese porcelain and pottery, seventeenth-century English portraits, landscapes by Gainsborough and Cotman, and works by Watts, Burne-Jones, and Sargent.

Every collector has to solve the problem of collecting wisely and well. Many are the contradictory rules put forward: buy only what you like; take the best expert advice you can obtain; back only your own judgement; never bargain over a really fine picture; refuse to pay fancy prices. Ultimately, it is the collector who has to determine the scope and extent of his collecting, limits which must inevitably depend on his object in forming it and the means at his command.

The Benson Italian collection is distinct from its contemporaries (for example those of William Graham, Charles Butler, or Frederick Leyland) in the comprehensiveness, almost academic in scale, of its chosen field. Benson justly wrote in 1914: 'The opportunities of the last thirty years are not comparable to those of the preceding fifty. Still, the present collection succeeds in illustrating historically the six principal Italian schools in a way that would be difficult for a collector beginning today.'

From the 1880s onwards, a major trend in private collecting was to form a collection representative of all schools, periods, and subjects, rather like a miniature national collection. The principal British collector along these lines was Sir Francis Cook of Doughty House, Richmond: in America there were many such collectors among whom John G. Johnson of Philadelphia and Henry C. Frick of New York may serve as examples. Benson stands at the opposite end, choosing out of the whole those schools with which he had the most sympathy. The fact that the names of the artists of the fourteenth- and fifteenth-century pictures were less certain than, say, seventeenth-century Dutch pictures, or not known at all, testifies to his connoisseurship and signifies that he was a discriminating collector.

Benson had ample opportunity to study the great Holford collection at Dorchester House and Westonbirt. This had been formed chiefly between 1840 and 1860 by Robert Stayner Holford with superbly high standards in the eighteenth-century tradition, which was continued well into the nineteenth century by Lord Hertford, the Rothschilds, and Demidoffs. Holford bought, for example, Florentine works by Perugino, Rosso

Fiorentino, and Bronzino; Venetian works by Titian, Veronese, and Tintoretto; Bolognese pictures by Domenichino, Guercino, and Guido Reni; portraits by Rubens, Velasquez, Van Dyck, Rembrandt, and Murillo; landscapes by Claude and Salvator Rosa; and Dutch pictures by Cuyp, Jacob van Ruysdael, and Wouvermans.

Benson was not, however, a pioneer collector of Italian 'primitives', that is, of the works by Giotto and his followers of the trecento and quattrocento. British collectors began to buy them towards the end of the eighteenth century: in the nineteenth century, it had become a clear feature of British connoisseurship. The Earl-Bishop of Bristol (1730–1803) was one of the first British collectors to own Tuscan pictures, and the other pioneer collectors included William Roscoe (1753–1831), a friend of Benson's grandfather, and William Young Ottley (1771–1836). By the 1820s the taste was well established among a band of collectors which included the Hon. W. H. T. Fox Strangways, the Revd John Sanford, the Revd Walter Bromley Davenport, Thomas Gambier Parry, and the Prince Consort.

By the 1880s, when Benson began to collect, the enthusiasm for early Italian pictures had taken a firm hold. Sir Charles Eastlake, the Italophile director of the National Gallery between 1855 and 1866, had bought an altarpiece by Mantegna in 1855 for £1,125 12*s*., and then achieved a coup in 1857 with the purchase of 30 pictures from the Lombardi–Baldi collection in Florence for £7,035 (an average of £235 each) which gave the National Gallery, at a stroke, pictures by or attributed to Duccio, Orcagna, Margaritone d'Arezzo, Nardo di Cione, Botticelli, Lorenzo di Credi, and, most famous of them all, *The Battle of San Romano*, painted in the 1450s by Paolo Uccello.

Private collectors continued to buy early Italian pictures: frequently the gold-backed pictures were hung alongside contemporary works by Burne-Jones and Rossetti, while Chinese porcelain stood on brackets or shelves below the pictures. An example of this style could be seen at Buckhurst, Benson's country house; William Graham, Charles Butler, and Frederick Leyland also collected in this manner, which continued into the present century with Benson's kinsman Lord Wantage.

Benson's earliest recorded Italian acquisition took place in 1884, with the purchase from the dealer Martin Colnaghi of *Portrait of a Collector* by Marco Basaiti, *Madonna and Child* attributed to Mainardi, and a panel depicting a *Triumphal Procession with Prisoners* by Andrea Schiavone. From this modest beginning, the collection grew splendidly, year by year. In 1885, he bought seven pictures, including a small gold-backed panel, *The Marriage of the Virgin* attributed to Agnolo Gaddi, a Florentine artist who was active between 1369 and 1396 and *Madonna and Child and two Angels* attributed to Bartolommeo Veneto, a Venetian artist, as his name implies, active between 1502 and 1531.

The direction and focus of the collection were set even more firmly in 1886 with the purchase at Christie's of fifteen pictures at the sale of the collection belonging to his old friend William Graham, which brought to South Street an outstanding portrait by Domenico Ghirlandaio of *The banker Francesco Sassetti and his son Teodoro*, and pictures by Piero di Cosimo, Cosimo Tura, Lorenzo Costa, Dosso Dossi, Carlo Crivelli, and Giovanni Bellini. At the sale in the same year at Christie's of pictures belonging to the Duke of Marlborough, he bought (for £86 12*s*.) a large picture by Veronese, *The Rape* *of Europa*, which had been recorded as being at Blenheim in 1766. In 1888 he acquired a second Giovanni Bellini, *St Jerome Reading*, at Lord Monson's sale and a fine panel by Vittore Carpaccio, *Lady Reading*, at the Marquess of Exeter's sale.

During the 1890s, Benson continued to add to the historical depth of his collection. This trend was helped by the purchase from his friend Charles Butler in 1891 of fourteen pictures: three extended his Sienese collection with two works by Ambrogio Lorenzetti (1319–47) and one by Domenico Beccafumi (1486–1551), and five were Milanese, including four by Luini (active 1512–32). Frederick Leyland's sale at Christie's in 1892 yielded a superb panel, *Portrait of a Lady*, also by Luini, and *The Infant Bacchus* by Giovanni Bellini.

It is not known precisely when Benson acquired his four panels by the Sienese master Duccio di Buoninsegna (active 1278–1319). They are recorded in Tuscany in 1879 and for a period belonged to Charles Fairfax Murray before passing into Benson's possession: he owned them by 1893 when he lent them to an exhibition at the New Gallery. The four panels formed part of the great altarpiece painted for Siena Cathedral by Duccio in 1308–11.

He acquired a painting by the very rare Venetian artist Giorgione by exchange in 1894. The panel, a small full-length group of the *Virgin and Child and St Joseph* seated outside a building with a landscape stretching into the distance, was possibly in the collection of King James II. It was discovered in a Brighton curiosity shop in about 1887 and bought for £5. Later it was bought for about £20 by the Brighton collector Henry Willett, who exchanged it with Benson for *Madonna and Child* by Le Maître de Moulins, which is now in the Brussels Gallery. Benson's Giorgione has belonged to the National Gallery of Art, Washington since 1951.

Acquisitions after 1900, though not as numerous as in earlier years, continued nevertheless. In 1902, when the collections of Sir Thomas Gibson Carmichael were sold at auction, Benson bought the tantalizing *Judgement of Paris*, a Florentine panel of *c.*1450, long considered a work by Pesellino, but now exhibited as the work of Domenico Veneziano (Glasgow, Burrell Collection). In 1905, the collections of Edward Cheney of Badger Hall were sold at auction: Benson bought an anonymous Umbrian work for £183 15*s*., *The Madonna of Casa Verita*, which he attributed to the school of Fiorenzo di Lorenzo, a Perugian artist who lived from *c.*1440–1522/5. The canvas depicting *The Judgement of Paris* attributed to Girolamo da Santa Croce followed at the Erle Drax sale of 1910.

In May 1911, Christie's sold the pictures belonging to the late Sir William Neville Abdy: Benson bought two pictures, *The Last Sacrament of St Jerome*, sold as the school of Botticelli for £588, and a panel, *A Pair of Lovers and a Pilgrim in a Landscape*, sold as the work of Giorgione which cost £2,572 10*s*. This last work has not stood the test of critical opinion over time and is now attributed to Domenico Caprioli, but the overall impression from the acquisitions of this decade is that Benson added fine pictures which interested him and the fact that they lacked undoubted authorship probably engaged his interest the more. It is relevant to compare the prices that Benson paid with the top prices fetched at the Abdy sale: these were £12,915 for a *Pietà* by Carpaccio and £11,340 for *Scene from the Life of St Zenobius* by Botticelli.

Benson left a permanent record of his Italian collection, 'Catalogue of Italian Pictures at 16 South Street, Park Lane, London, and Buckhurst in Sussex'. It was privately printed in 1914 in a limited edition of 125 copies for distribution to his friends and family: an unillustrated edition was also printed. The catalogue describes 114 pictures and may be said to mark the culmination of his thirty years as a collector.

In public life, Benson served as a trustee of the National Gallery from 1912 and as a trustee of the Tate Gallery. He was a member of the Council of the Victoria and Albert Museum. He joined the Executive Committee of the National Art-Collections Fund in 1903, the year it was founded, and thus became associated with the acquisition of many works of art for the national collections. He was, according to his obituary in *The Times*, 'one of the pillars' of the Burlington Fine Arts Club, contributing largely to its periodical exhibitions, and he wrote the introduction to the 1893 exhibition, 'Luca Signorelli and his School'. He lent pictures frequently from his own collection to exhibitions not only at the Burlington Fine Arts Club, but also at the Royal Academy, the New Gallery, and the Grafton Gallery, It is a tribute to the quality of his eye as a collector that of the seventy-seven pictures shown at the Burlington Fine Arts Club 1912 exhibition, 'Early Venetian Pictures', he lent no fewer that seventeen works, most of which embellish museum collections today.

Principal Italian Paintings from the Collection of R. H. Benson

The inventory below lists sixty of the principal pictures (out of the 114 which are included in the 1914 catalogue) and groups them in their schools. The year of acquisition by Benson is given and the name of the immediate previous owner together with the name of the owner in 1995, where known.

SIENESE SCHOOL

1. Duccio (fl. 1278, d. 1319): *The Temptation*
   One of four panels from the Siena Cathedral Altarpiece, in RHB's possession by 1893, when he lent them to the New Gallery exhibition, 'Early Italian Art from 1300 to 1500'. Now in Frick Collection, New York.
2. Duccio: *The Calling of Peter and Andrew*
   One of four panels as above. Now in Kress Collection, National Gallery of Art, Washington.
3. Duccio: *Christ and the Woman of Samaria*
   One of four panels as above. Now in Thyssen Collection, Madrid.
4. Duccio: *The Raising of Lazarus*
   One of four panels as above. Now in Kimbell Art Museum, Fort Worth, Texas.
5. Lippo Memmi (?1290–1357): *Madonna and Child*
   Bought in Paris *c.*1896. Now in Andrew Mellon Collection, National Gallery of Art, Washington.
6. Attributed to Ambrogio Lorenzetti (fl. 1319–47): *The Crucifixion*

Charles Butler sale, 1891. Now in New York, The Cloisters Collection, John D. Rockefeller bequest.

7. Attributed to Ambrogio Lorenzetti, as above: *The Entombment*
   Details as no. 6.
8. Barna da Siena (fl. *c*.1350): *Christ Bearing the Cross*
   Lord Leighton sale, 1896. Now in Frick Collection, New York.
9. Giovanni di Paolo (fl. 1420, d. 1482): *The Annunciation*
   Bought soon after 1902. Now in Kress Collection, National Gallery of Art, Washington.
10. Girolamo di Benvenuto (1470–1524): *Portrait of a Lady*
   Arthur Sanderson sale, Edinburgh, 1911. Now in Kress Collection, National Gallery of Art, Washington.
11. Beccafumi (?1486–1551): *The Flight of Cloelia*
   Charles Butler sale, 1891. Last recorded with Duveen (dealer).

FLORENTINE SCHOOL

12. Unknown artist, Florentine School, around 1350–75: *Pietà*
   William Graham sale, 1886. Last recorded Marczell von Nemes sale, Munich, 16 June 1931, lot 3 as by Jacopo di Cione.
13. Jacopo di Cione (fl. 1365–98): *The Trinity Enthroned with the Virgin*, panel on gold ground with Gothic arched top
   William Graham sale, 1886 (ascribed to Taddeo Gaddi). Last recorded with Duveen (dealer).
14. Attributed to Agnolo Gaddi (fl. 1369–96): *The Marriage of the Virgin*
   H. G. Bohn sale, 1885. Now in Fogg Art Museum, Cambridge, Mass.
15. Domenico Veneziano (?) (fl. before 1438, d. 1461): *The Judgement of Paris*
   Sir Thomas Gibson Carmichael sale, 1902. Now in Burrell Collection, Glasgow.
16. Botticini (*c*.1446–97): *Madonna and Child*
   Palazzo Panciatichi, Florence before 1910. Now in Cincinnati Art Museum.
17. Attributed to Botticelli (*c*.1445–1510): *Madonna and Child*
   Sir Thomas Gibson Carmichael sale, 1902. Last recorded with Duveen (dealer).
18. Attributed to Botticelli: *The Last Communion of St Jerome*
   Sir William Abdy sale, 1911. Last recorded with Duveen (dealer).
19. Domenico Ghirlandaio (*c*.1448–94): *Portraits of Francesco Sassetti and his son Teodoro*
   William Graham sale, 1886. Now Bache Collection to Metropolitan Museum, New York.
20. Piero di Cosimo (fl. 1462–after 1515): *Hylas and the Nymphs*
   William Graham sale, 1886. Now in Wadsworth Athenaeum, Hartford, Conn.
21. Filippino Lippi (?1457–1504): *Pietà*
   Bought by RHB at the railway station, Bologna, before 1902. Now in Kress Collection, National Gallery of Art, Washington.
22. Filippino Lippi: *Tobias and the Angel*

Owned by RHB by 1914 (provenance unknown). Now in Kress Collection, National Gallery of Art, Washington.

23. Raffaellino del Garbo (fl. 1479?–*c*.1527): *The Mass of St Gregory*
Owned by Sir John Ramsden, Bt., owned by RHB by 1893. Now in Ringling Museum of Art, Sarasota, Fla.
24. Raffaellino del Garbo: *Madonna and Child with the Infant St John and two Angels*
William Graham sale, 1886. Sold by Duveen to William Randolph Hearst, San Simeon, Calif.; last recorded at Christie's (anon. sale) 23 June 1967, lot 70, bought by Antiquitas for 3,500 guineas.
25. Andrea del Sarto (1486–1530): *Madonna and Child and the Infant St John*
Bought by RHB from the Villa Woronzow, Montughi, near Florence in 1900. Now in Lowe Art Gallery, Coral Gables, Fla. (as follower of del Sarto).
26. Jacopo del Conte (*c*.1515–98): *Portrait of a Papal Notary*
Sir William Drake sale, 1891. Now in Fitzwilliam Museum, Cambridge.

UMBRIAN SCHOOL

27. Antoniazzo Romano (fl. 1460, d. 1508): *Madonna and Child*
Charles Butler sale in 1891. Now in Norton Simon Museum of Art, Pasadena, Calif.
28. Luca Signorelli (1441–1523): *Madonna and Child*
Bought by RHB from the Casa Tommasi, Cortona. Now Bache Collection, Metropolitan Museum, New York.
29. Luca Signorelli: *The Journey to Emmaus* (as 30 below)
30. Luca Signorelli: *The Supper at Emmaus*
Bought by RHB from the Casa Tommasi, Cortona. Last recorded with Duveen (dealer).

SCHOOL OF FERRARA-BOLOGNA

31. Cosimo Tura (*c*.1430–95): *The Flight into Egypt*
William Graham sale, 1886. Now Bache Collection, Metropolitan Museum, New York.
32. Ercole di Roberti (fl. 1479, d. 1496): *SS Catherine and Jerome*
Condover Hall, Reginald Cholmondeley sale, 1897. Last recorded with Duveen (dealer).
33. Francesco Francia (*c*.1450–1517/8): *Madonna and Child with St Francis*
Sir Thomas Gibson Carmichael sale, 1902. Last recorded with Duveen (dealer).
34. Lorenzo Costa (1459/60–1535): *Pietà* (as 35 below)
35. Lorenzo Costa: *The Baptism of Christ*
William Graham sale, 1886. Last recorded with Duveen (dealer).
36. Dosso Dossi (fl. 1512, d. 1542): *Circe*
William Graham sale, 1886. Now in Kress Collection, National Gallery of Art, Washington.

37. Correggio (1494–1534): *Christ's Farewell to his Mother*
Acquired by RHB from the Parlatore Collection, Florence, before 1894. Now in National Gallery, London, gift of Joseph Duveen.

MILANESE SCHOOL

38. Bernardino Luini (fl. 1512, d. 1532): *The Nativity*
Charles Butler sale in 1891. Now in Isaac Delgado Museum of Art, New Orleans, La.
39. Bernardo Luini: Three panels containing scenes from the lives of *SS Sisinnius Deacon, Martyrius Lector, and Alexander Ostiarius*
Charles Butler sale in 1891. Last recorded with Duveen (dealer).
40. Bernardino Luini: *Portrait of a Lady*
Frederick Leyland sale 1892. Now in Andrew Mellon Collection, National Gallery of Art, Washington.
41. Attributed to Giampetrino (fl. first half 16th c.): *Madonna and Child*
Charles Butler sale in 1891. Now in Seattle Art Museum.

VENETIAN SCHOOLS

42. Carlo Crivelli (fl. 1457–93): *Madonna and Child*
William Graham sale, 1886. Now in Linsky Collection, Metropolitan Museum, New York.
43. Antonello da Messina (fl. 1456, d. 1479): *Madonna and Child*
Owned by RHB by 1914 (provenance unknown). Now in Andrew Mellon Collection, National Gallery of Art, Washington.
44. Vittore Crivelli (fl. by 1465, d. 1501/2): *Madonna and Child with Two Angels*
Bought in Rome before 1908. Now in Linsky Collection, Metropolitan Museum, New York.
45. Giovanni Bellini (fl. 1459, d. 1516): *St Jerome Reading*
Charles Butler sale in 1891. Now in Kress Collection, National Gallery of Art, Washington.
46. Giovanni Bellini: Altarpiece, *The Virgin and Child with SS Catherine and Lucy, Peter, and John the Baptist*
William Graham sale, 1886. Now Bache Collection, Metropolitan Museum, New York.
47. Giovanni Bellini: *The Infant Bacchus*
Frederick Leyland sale, 1892. Now in Kress Collection, National Gallery of Art, Washington.
48. Vittore Carpaccio (fl. 1490, d. 1523/6): *A Lady Reading*
Marquis of Exeter sale, 1888 (as Cima). Now in Kress Collection, National Gallery of Art, Washington.
49. Francesco Bissolo (fl. 1492, d. 1554): *The Annunciation*
Bought from the Manfrin Gallery, Venice, before 1894. Now in Norton Simon Museum, Pasadena, Calif.
50. Giorgione (fl. 1506, d. 1510): *Holy Family*
Possibly in the collection of King James II; bought soon after 1887 by Henry Willett

of Brighton who exchanged it with RHB in 1894 for *The Madonna and Child* by the Master of Moulins, now in the Brussels Gallery. Now in Kress Collection, National Gallery of Art, Washington.

51. Marco Basaiti (fl. 1496, d. 1530): *Portrait of a Collector*
    Bought by RHB from Martin Colnaghi (dealer) in 1884. Last recorded with Duveen (dealer).
52. Domenico Caprioli (1494–1528): *Lovers and the Pilgrim*
    Sir William Abdy sale, 1911, as Giorgione. Last recorded at British Rail Pension Fund sale, Christie's, 7 Dec 1994, lot 31, as Caprioli.
53. Pseudo-Boccaccino (datable *c*.1515): *Pan and a Nymph* (as 54 below)
54. Pseudo-Boccaccino: *Pan and Syrinx*
    Bought from Foster's Auction Rooms before 1894. Now in Thyssen Collection, Madrid.
55. Ascribed to Titian (fl. before 1511, d. 1576): *Virgin and Child*
    Marquess of Exeter sale, 1888. Now Bache Collection, Metropolitan Museum, New York.
56. Palma Vecchio (fl. 1510, d. 1528): Altarpiece
    Owned by John Holmes of Brook Hall, Norfolk; bought by RHB before 1894. Last recorded with Duveen (dealer).
57. Cariani (fl. 1509, d. after 1547): *Portrait of a Gentleman*
    Owned by RHB by 1894. Was in J. Paul Getty Museum, Malibu, from 1967; last recorded at Getty Museum sale, Christie's, New York, 21 May 1992, lot 23 ($63,800).
58. Sebastiano del Piombo (*c*.1485–1547): *Portrait of a Senator*
    Lord Monson sale from Gatton Park, 1888. Now in Museum of Fine Arts, Houston, Tex.
59. Bonifazio de' Pitati (1487–1553): Three panels, *Allegory of Dawn, Allegory of Night*, and *Allegory of Harvest*
    Owned by RHB by 1914 (provenance unknown). Now in Ringling Museum of Art, Sarasota, Fla.
60. Polidoro da Lanciano (1514/15–1565): *The Virgin and Child with Saints Catherine and Michael*
    Earl of Hardwicke sale, 1881. Now in Boymans-van Beuningen Museum, Rotterdam.

INDEX

Index

Index

Index

Index

Index

Index

Index

Index

Benson Family Tree

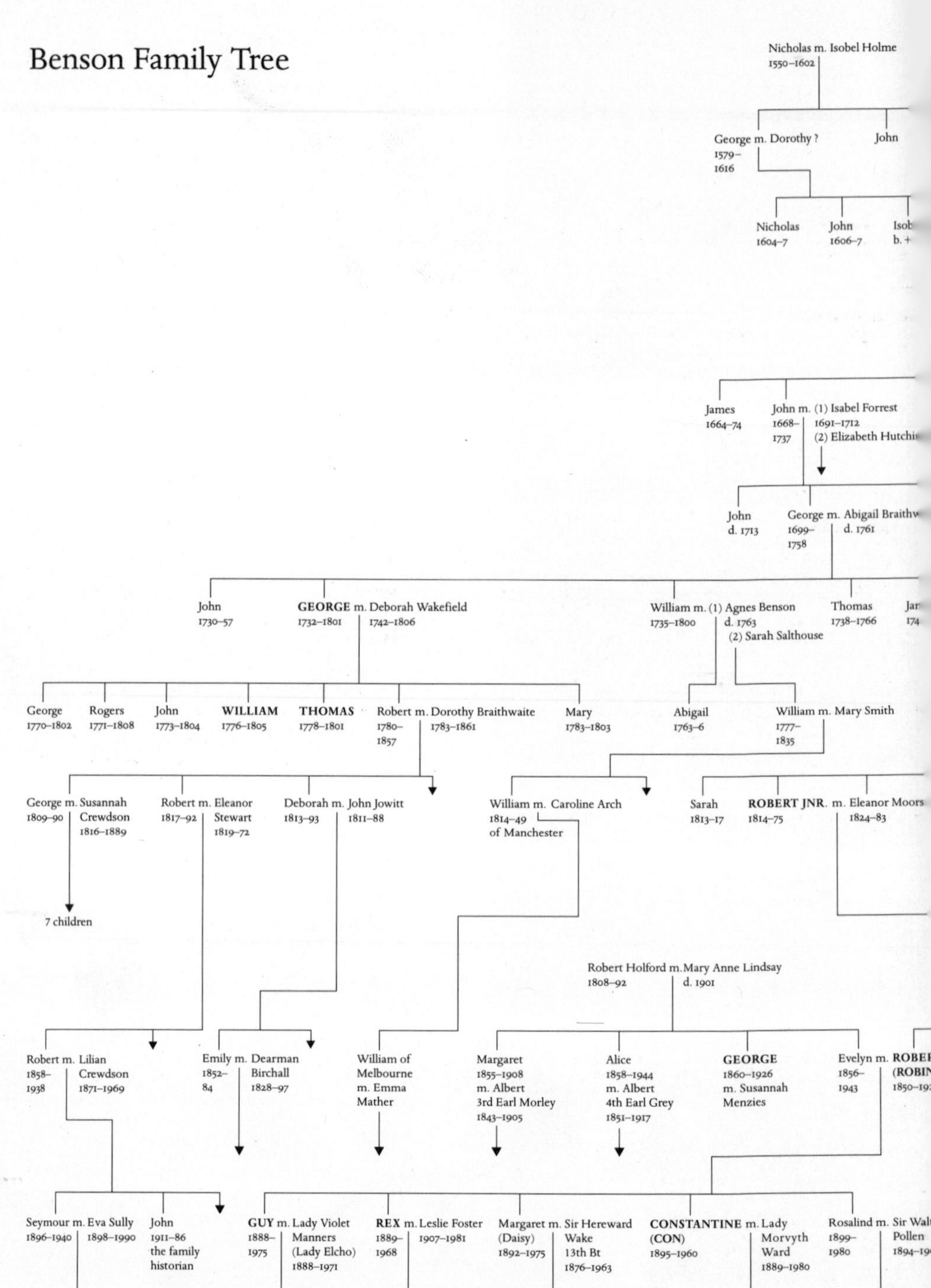